STANDARD LESSON COMMENTARY
1991-92

International Sunday School Lessons

published by

STANDARD PUBLISHING

Eugene H. Wigginton, *Publisher*

Richard C. McKinley, *Director of Curriculum Development*

James I. Fehl, *Editor*   Hela M. Campbell, *Office Editor*

Thirty-ninth Annual Volume

©1991
The STANDARD PUBLISHING Company
division of STANDEX INTERNATIONAL Corporation
8121 Hamilton Avenue, Cincinnati, Ohio 45231
Printed in U.S.A.

In This Volume

Autumn Quarter, 1991 (page 1)
Theme: From the Damascus Road to Rome

Writers

ORRIN ROOT, Lesson Development
CHARLES R. BOATMAN, Verbal Illustrations

MIKE MCCANN, Learning by Doing
JOE SUTHERLAND, Let's Talk It Over

Winter Quarter, 1991-92 (page 113)
Theme: Songs and Prayers of the Bible

Writers

JOHN W. WADE, Lesson Development
WOODROW PHILLIPS, Verbal Illustrations

MARK A. TAYLOR, Learning by Doing
KENTON K. SMITH, Let's Talk It Over

Spring Quarter, 1992 (page 225)
Themes: The Strong Son of God
God's People in the World

Writers

Lesson Development:
EDWIN V. HAYDEN (1-4), BRANT LEE DOTY (5-8),
LLOYD M. PELFREY (9, 10), J. LEE MAGNESS (11, 12),
JOHNNY G. PRESSLEY (13, 14)

THOMAS D. THURMAN, Verbal Illustrations
JONATHAN UNDERWOOD, Learning by Doing
RICK SHONKWILER, Let's Talk It Over (1-8)
DEBORAH SUE BRUNSMAN (9-14)

Summer Quarter, 1992 (page 337)
Themes: God's Judgment and Mercy
Guidelines for Ministry

Writers

KNOFEL STATON, Lesson Development

RICHARD W. BAYNES, Verbal Illustrations

ELEANOR DANIEL, Learning by Doing (1-7)
THOMAS G. MAY (8-13)
KENTON K. SMITH, Let's Talk It Over

Artists

JAMES E. SEWARD, Title Pages; NED OSTENDORF, Lesson Illustrations; ROBERT E. HUFFMAN, Maps

Cover design by Gottry Advertising & Marketing, Inc.

Lessons based on International Sunday School Lessons © 1988 by the Lesson Committee.

Index of Printed Texts, 1991-92

The printed texts for 1991-92 are arranged here in the order in which they appear in the Bible. Opposite each reference is the number of the page on which it appears in this volume.

Cumulative Index

A cumulative index for the Scripture passages used in the *Standard Lesson Commentary* for the years September, 1986—August, 1992, is set forth below.

V

VI

1

Sep
1

Sep
8

Sep
15

Sep
22

Sep
29

Oct
6

Oct
13

Oct
20

Oct
27

Nov
3

Nov
10

Nov
17

Nov
24

Autumn Quarter, 1991

Theme: From the Damascus Road to Rome

Special Features

Lessons

Unit 1. Chosen by God

Unit 2. Emerging Leader

Unit 3. Traveling Preacher

Unit 4. Destination: Rome

Related Resources

The following publications give additional help for the lessons in the Autumn Quarter. They may be purchased from your supplier. Prices are subject to change.

Acts (Standard Bible Studies), by John W. Wade. This study of the book of Acts leads readers to apply Biblical principles directly to their lives. Order #11-40105, $9.95.

Acts Map and Chart. Various maps show routes of Paul's journeys. A chart organizes the events of Acts. Order #14-02668, $6.95.

Bible Time Line. A colorful wall chart that presents major Biblical characters and events in chronological sequence and correlates them with people and events in secular history. Order #14-02628, $5.95.

Dear Theophilus, by John W. Wade. Two letters of Luke (Luke and Acts) were written to the same person and relate a unified account of the life of Christ and the early history of the church, which is considered in this book. Order # 11-41036 $4.95.

Balanced Bible Studies

THE CURRENT six-year cycle of lessons in the International Sunday-school Lesson Series concludes with the lessons of the September, 1991—August, 1992, year. The chart below shows all of the quarters of study in this lesson cycle. The first six months were spent in a survey of the Old and New Testaments, which provided a basic understanding of the Biblical account. From that point, quarters of study emphasized various Biblical books, outstanding persons of the Bible, and a number of timeless topics.

Several features of the International lessons may be noted. First, all of the major divisions of the Bible receive consideration, namely the books of law, history, poetry, and prophecy in the Old Testament, and biography, history, epistles, and Revelation in the New. More than half of the lessons are based on the New Testament, and the life of Christ is studied each year.

This year's lessons are highlighted by the color bar below. Paul's commitment to Christ will be seen in our study of Acts; comfort and challenge will be directed to us through selected songs and prayers of the Bible. God's dealings with the people of Israel through the minor prophets and later through His Son will focus on His judgment and mercy. The studies conclude by emphasizing our commission to take the message of God's mercy to the world.

International Sunday School Lesson Topics
September, 1986 — August, 1992

	AUTUMN QUARTER (Sept., Oct., Nov.)	WINTER QUARTER (Dec., Jan., Feb.)	SPRING QUARTER (Mar., Apr., May)	SUMMER QUARTER (June, July, Aug.)
1986-1987	Beginning of the Covenant People (Old Testament Survey)	The Arrival of a New Age (New Testament Survey)	God's Constant Love (Luke and Hosea)	The Righteousness of God (Romans)
1987-1988	Genesis: Book of Beginnings	The Call to Discipleship (The Gospel of Matthew)	Facing the Future With Confidence (Matthew, Hebrews)	Moses and His Mission (Exodus, Numbers, Deuteronomy)
1988-1989	Through Suffering to Hope (Job, Isaiah, Jeremiah)	Scenes of Love and Compassion (Luke)	Letters From Prison (Philemon, Colossians, Philippians, Ephesians)	Conquest and Challenge (Joshua, Judges, Ruth)
1989-1990	Visions of God's Rule (Ezekiel, Daniel, 1 and 2 Thessalonians, Revelation)	John: The Gospel of Life and Light	The Gospel of John (cont'd) Abiding in Love (1, 2, 3 John)	Wisdom As a Way of Life (Ecclesiastes, Proverbs, Psalms, James)
1990-1991	Prophets, Priests, and Kings (Conflicts and Concerns)	Stories Jesus Told (Parables)	Counsel for a Church in Crisis (1 and 2 Corinthians)	After the Exile (Ezra, Nehemiah, and Prophets)
1991-1992	From the Damascus Road to Rome (Life of Paul—Acts)	Songs and Prayers of the Bible (Song of Solomon, Psalms, others)	The Strong Son of God (Mark) God's People in the World (1 and 2 Peter)	God's Judgment and Mercy (Minor Prophets) Guidelines for Ministry (Pastoral Epistles)

Paul the Apostle

by Orrin Root

SAUL, KNOWN ALSO AS PAUL, appears suddenly in the record of the early church. At first we see him as an unimportant bystander (Acts 7:58), but he was not a bystander nor unimportant for long. Swiftly he became prominent (Acts 8:3); and from chapter 9 to the end, most of the book of Acts is devoted to his doings.

Mystery Man

Perhaps we have more information about Paul than we have about any other New Testament character except Jesus, but still many aspects of his life remain a mystery. We know that he was a Hebrew of the tribe of Benjamin (Philippians 3:5), but we cannot name his father or mother. We know that he was born in Tarsus and brought up in Jerusalem (Acts 22:3), but how long did he live in Tarsus? Did his family move to Jerusalem, or did he leave home to go to school? Did his family disown him when he became a Christian, or did they become Christians too? It is cheering to read that a nephew uncovered a plot and saved Paul's life (Acts 23:12-24), but that is about all we know about his relationship with his family.

We know Paul was a Roman citizen by birth (Acts 22:27, 28), but how did his father or grandfather get that distinction? It could be purchased with money (Acts 22:28), or it could be granted for some special service to the empire. Sometimes Paul's citizenship proved useful, (Acts 22:24-26), but sometimes it was disregarded (Acts 16:19-24).

We first read of Saul as a young man, but how young is young? Not too young to be a vigorous persecutor of the church (Acts 7:58; 8:3). About thirty years later he called himself "Paul the aged" (Philemon 9), but how old is aged? Not too old to be an energetic Christian even when he was a prisoner (Acts 28:30, 31). The young man was called Saul and the old man was called Paul. Why? We can only guess. Paul was troubled by some physical ailment that he called "a thorn in the flesh" (2 Corinthians 12:7). How would a doctor diagnose his condition?

Some students think young Saul was a married man and a member of the ruling council at Jerusalem. Others see no reason to think he was either of these. But certainly he was an influential man among the Jews till he became a Christian. Then he had a powerful influence among the Christians.

In the book of Acts we read of Paul's change from a persecutor to a promoter of the church. We can trace his three missionary journeys and his eventful trip to Rome. But how many details are left untold? Second Corinthians 11:24-27 lists some startling facts. Paul was three times beaten with rods by Roman authorities. Acts records only one time (Acts 16:19-24). Five times he was whipped in the Jewish manner, and none of them are mentioned in Acts. Three times he was shipwrecked, and all of them were before the wreck recorded in Acts. It seems that Paul was adrift for a night and a day after one of the disasters at sea. What stirring stories could be told of these and other "perils" that he mentions so briefly!

The book of Acts, then, contains little more than an outline of the work of Paul; and the thirteen lessons of this series contain much less. The printed texts of these lessons will be more meaningful if every student will read the whole book in connection with this lesson series.

Missionary Man

Paul and Barnabas are sometimes called the first Christian missionaries. Scattered Christians had long been preaching the word (Acts 8:4), but these two were specially called by the Holy Spirit and sent by the church as well as the Spirit (Acts 13:1-4). In these lessons we shall see much of Paul's work as a missionary. Several points are to be noted.

First, Paul preached the gospel, the good news that Christ died to save us and that anyone in the world can find salvation in Him (Romans 1:16; 10:12, 13; 1 Corinthians 2:2; 15:3, 4; Acts 13: 38, 39). The salvation of souls is the first aim of every Christian missionary.

Second, Paul was concerned about physical welfare as well as spiritual. Earnestly he raised money to help the poor Christians in Judea (Romans 15:25-27; 1 Corinthians 16:1-4). It may be well for a missionary to build a hospital or school, to teach good farming methods or manual skills, or otherwise to help people live more comfortably. But concern for physical welfare must not displace concern for spiritual welfare.

Third, Paul had only one message, but he changed his approach to fit different audiences (1 Corinthians 9:20-23). The first part of his speech to the philosophers of Athens was not like his opening words to the Jews in the synagogue (Acts 13:16-41; 17:22-31). Missionaries know they must meet people where they are in order to lead them to where they need to be.

Fourth, Paul was a team worker. Barnabas was his partner on his first journey, Silas on his second. He names other fellow workers in Romans 16:9; 2 Corinthians 8:23; Philippians 2:25; 4:3; Philemon 24. He mentions others who certainly were fellow workers, though not specifically so called. Many missionaries find that a team of two or ten is better than the same number working separately.

Fifth, it is interesting to see how Paul was supported. The Lord ordained that preachers of the gospel should have their living from that work (1 Corinthians 9:14), but Paul did not ask money from those he sought to win (Acts 20:33). It seems reasonable to suppose that the church that sent him (Acts 13:1-3) paid his expenses, at least for his first journey. If that church supported him in his later work, perhaps he went so far and so fast that the support could not catch up with him. Sometimes he was helped by the Philippians (Philippians 4:15-18), and perhaps by other churches (2 Corinthians 11:8, 9). At times he supported himself by secular work. His tentmaking at Corinth is well known (Acts 18:1-3). He worked also at Thessalonica (2 Thessalonians 3:7, 8), Ephesus (Acts 20:34), and perhaps other places. Still he was hungry and cold at times (2 Corinthians 11:27). At other times he had no financial problems. At Jerusalem he paid for costly sacrifices (Acts 21:24); at Rome he rented a house even while he was a prisoner (Acts 28:30). Did the church there contribute before gifts came from Philippi? Was his companion Luke a wealthy helper? We do not know. But Paul the missionary learned to be content in plenty or in want (Philippians 4:11, 12). What was most important was to keep on preaching the gospel.

Our Lessons About Paul

In thirteen lessons we are to consider some high points in the life of Paul. Our first lesson is drawn from the ninth chapter of Acts, but we need to read the first eight chapters to refresh our memory of the beginning of the church. Then it will be helpful each week to read the part of Acts that leads up to the short printed text.

The thirteen lessons are arranged in four parts, called units, with two, three, or four lessons in each part. Here is a preview.

Unit I. Chosen by God

Lesson 1. Saul was trying to destroy the church when Jesus stopped him on the highway and called him to build the church instead.

Lesson 2. Saul began to build, but his work was opposed and not very effective till Barnabas helped him find a field of service in Antioch. There he served diligently and well.

Unit II. Emerging Leader

Lesson 3. The Holy Spirit called Barnabas and Saul to leave Antioch and become traveling missionaries. Saul, now called Paul, soon emerged as leader of the team. In this lesson we see a sample of his preaching.

Lesson 4. Perils of a preacher are seen in this lesson. At Lystra the people first wanted to worship Paul, then wanted to kill him.

Lesson 5. Back from the mission field, Paul was one of the messengers that was sent to confer with the apostles and the elders of the first church.

Unit III. Traveling Preacher

Lesson 6. On his second journey Paul found a demon-possessed fortune-teller and set her free. Men who profited from her fortune-telling were furious, and soon Paul was in jail.

Lesson 7. An earthquake opened prison doors, and a heathen jailer heard the gospel and became a Christian.

Lesson 8. In cultured Athens Paul spoke to heathen philosophers instead of Jewish worshipers. The gospel was the same, but the approach was different.

Lesson 9. On his third journey Paul found a need for added teaching to some people who already had been taught about Christ.

Unit IV. Destination: Rome

Lesson 10. At the end of his third journey Paul headed for Jerusalem. We look in on his meeting with elders of the church at Ephesus, whom he did not expect to see again.

Lesson 11. In Jerusalem some Asian Jews charged that Paul taught against the law and profaned the temple by taking Gentiles into it. A mob tried to kill Paul, but he was rescued by Roman troops stationed there.

Lesson 12. Imprisoned by Roman authorities and sought by Jewish assassins, Paul saw no hope of justice in Judea. He appealed to the emperor in Rome. Our lesson text records what he said to Agrippa, king of the Jews, before he went to Rome.

Lesson 13. We close our studies with a glimpse of what Paul was doing in Rome as he waited for a hearing in the emperor's court. As we might expect, he was doing what he had been doing ever since becoming a Christian. He was preaching the gospel, winning people to Christ, and teaching them to live as Christians.

The Man Who Said, "I Must"

by David H. Ray

D O YOU REMEMBER that old Datsun commercial with the recurring line, "We are driven"? The phrase aptly describes many people, too. For some, "drive" can mean unhealthy obsession, but for others it is the key to focused and goal-centered living. Healthily driven people know where they are headed, don't get detoured, and tend to be achievers.

The apostle Paul was such a man. This was true both during his early years as a persecutor of the church and then later as one of its most ardent defenders.

Much of Paul's resolve was rooted in the basic nature of his personality. He was not the type to avoid conflict, sidestep responsibility, or be satisfied with doing things halfway. God surely recognized this personality trait when He called Paul to serve. Far more than Paul's basic nature, however, compelled his witnessing for Christ.

Vision of Christ

Paul's passion to share the faith was awakened by a dramatic vision of Christ (Acts 9:1-19; 22:3-16; 26:9-23). This event provided the focus for all of Paul's future ministry. A sacred retreat into the Arabian wilderness immediately following his conversion bound him all the more intimately to the Savior (Galatians 1:15-18).

Not a few people who call themselves Christians know *about* Christ, but have no real intimate acquaintance *with* Him. When believers lack passion to share the gospel it is often because they have neglected the vital preparation that communion with Christ provides. Paul's drive was a product of this personal spiritual discovery.

A family was returning home after attending church for the first time since moving to their new home. The mother asked her son, "Who was your Sunday-school teacher?" The little boy scratched his head for a moment and said, "I don't remember her name. But she must have been Jesus' grandmother, because she didn't talk about anyone else." A person who truly knows Christ will not be mistaken as His casual acquaintance.

After Paul saw Christ, nothing else compared. In essence Paul wrote to the Philippians, "Everything I once highly valued I now have come to regard as being totally worthless compared to the surpassing greatness of knowing Christ Jesus as Lord" (3:7, 8).

Response to Grace

Paul once lived his life harshly by the book. As a devout Pharisee, he was a strict keeper of the law, priding himself in his passion for righteous performance. He labored to keep every rule, to satisfy every requirement. After meeting Christ, however, he saw how far he had fallen short. To Timothy he wrote, "I was shown mercy so that in me, the worst of sinners, Christ Jesus might display his unlimited patience" (1 Timothy 1:15, 16*).

The Danish theologian, Soren Kierkegaard, warns of the danger of the church losing its passion for the gospel, coming to treat it instead like a piece of information—passion replaced by a description of passion. Paul was no detached messenger. Painfully aware of his personal sin, he was overwhelmed by the discovery of God's grace. In fact, Paul was so moved by the good news of grace that when those closest to him would not share his joy, he offered it to those who had once been his detested enemies—the Gentiles.

Don McKenzie writes about being called to the hospital on an emergency late one night. Walking down a darkened hallway, suddenly he was met by a man rushing out of a patient's room. The man's face was radiant as he spoke: "She's going to make it. She's better. She's going to make it." With that, the man made his way down the hall.

McKenzie knew neither the man nor the person he was talking about. He could only assume that the man had received news about someone very near and dear, and that having received the positive word he was compelled to share his joy—even with a stranger.

The apostle Paul's spirit was filled to overflowing. His discovery of grace drove him to share it with any who would listen.

Will to Obey

On the Damascus road, Paul experienced not only a vision, but he also received a commission. Late in his ministry as he stood before King Agrippa, Paul spoke of his service to Christ: "I was not disobedient to the vision from heaven. First to those in Damascus, then to those in Jerusalem and in all Judea, and to the Gentiles also, I preached" (Acts 26:19, 20).

The responsibility of sharing God's word comes to Christians not as an option, but as a divine command. We have not received the "Great Suggestion" but the "Great Commission."

Paul understood his responsibility. Again and again, he prefaced His letters by first mentioning his divine commission. He was compelled to speak because he had been called to do so. He knew his place, his responsibility, and his Master. His highest desire was to obey.

Children have a beautiful way of making statements that are both simple and profound. I once came across this powerful gem in a collection of kid's letters to God: "Dear God, Please count me in! Love, Herbie." Surrender is the prelude to service.

Compassion for People

Paul was no mere soldier, callously taking orders. He carried out Christ's commands in a spirit of obedience but he also cared deeply about people.

William Booth was a noble example of Christian compassion in the darkened world of nineteenth century England. What prompts such a life of service? Booth once wrote, "When I got the poor of London on my heart and caught a vision of what Jesus Christ, the reigning Lord, could do with those people . . . I was determined that the living Christ would have all of William Booth that there was."

Someone has said, "People will not care what we know until they know that we care." Paul revealed that he hurt so much for his fellow Jews that he would have willingly accepted being cursed and cut off from Christ if it could have meant their salvation (Romans 9:3). What compassion! Bound in prison chains, Paul wrote to Timothy, "I endure everything for the sake of the elect, that they too may obtain the salvation that is in Christ Jesus, with eternal glory" (2 Timothy 2:10). In his farewell address to the Ephesian elders he said, "I consider my life worth nothing to me, if only I may finish the race and complete the task the Lord Jesus has given me—the task of testifying to the gospel of God's grace" (Acts 20:24).

Confidence in God

After being beaten and thrown in a Philippian jail, confronted by an angry mob in Thessalonica, sneered at by Athenian philosophers, and abusively rejected by his fellow Jews, Paul might have considered quitting. But Christ met him with reassuring words: "Do not be afraid; keep on speaking, do not be silent. For I am with you" (Acts 18:9, 10). When the Sanhedrin, late in Paul's ministry, plotted to kill him, Jesus again offered assurance: "Take courage!" (Acts 23:11).

Before the angry crowds, in the hands of the Roman soldiers, or in the courts of those who held his fate in their hands, Paul never compromised his message or tempered his boldness. Listen to his confident words spoken late in his life while in a Roman court: "The Jews seized me in the temple courts and tried to kill me. But I have had God's help to this very day, and so I stand here and testify to small and great alike" (Acts 26:21, 22).

Paul would not be intimidated. God was greater than any of his foes. Riots, shipwrecks, imprisonment, beatings—none could defeat him.

It is fitting that as the account of Acts draws to a close, though being held prisoner in Rome, Paul remained a driven man. Luke's account concludes with this final tribute: "Boldly and without hindrance he preached the kingdom of God and taught about the Lord Jesus Christ" (Acts 28:31).

The gospel held God's power for the salvation of the world (Romans 1:14-17). Paul was neither ashamed nor afraid to preach it. Rather, he was constantly eager to share his faith. Nothing would hold him back. He was a man who said, "I must!"

When any Christian comes to possess a consuming drive like that of Paul, the world is certain to take notice. John Wesley once said, "When a man sets himself on fire, people will come to watch."

---

*All Scripture quotations are from the *New International Version.*

Appeal to the Highest Court

by Douglas Redford

"**W**ITH LIBERTY AND JUSTICE FOR ALL." These words of the pledge of allegiance to the United States indicate that one of the noblest ideals to which this nation is committed is justice.

In reality, however, it is hard to make the "scales of justice" balance. In a world soured by sin, the judgment of even those who are well educated in the principles of jurisprudence can become clouded and warped. Certain applications of such concepts as "not guilty by reason of insanity" and "plea bargaining" leave the average citizen confused, frustrated, and angry.

Christians have never been immune from such frustrations and miscarriages of justice. The apostle Paul found himself entangled in a judicial system filled with self-serving politicians rather than genuine advocates of justice. Yet even while appealing to Rome and waiting for the "system" to work properly, Paul was still God's man and was greatly used by Him.

A Constant Trust

How does a Christian function in a world that views who he is and what he stands for with skepticism and may treat him unjustly? Writing of Jesus' unfair treatment at the hands of His enemies, Peter states, "When they hurled their insults at him, he did not retaliate; when he suffered, he made no threats. Instead, he entrusted himself to him who judges justly" (1 Peter 2:23).

Paul was traveling to Jerusalem as he concluded his third missionary journey. He admitted to his friends that he did not know what would happen to him there (Acts 20:22). He did, however, know whom he had believed (2 Timothy 1:12). In this high-tech age of the nineties, such trust in God may appear to some totally inadequate for handling the "real world." Yet, like the seed that sprouts and quietly but effectively produces fruit, the Christian must faithfully cultivate his relationship of trust in the Lord. He can be certain that someone somewhere is going to need the fruit of that relationship.

A Compelling Testimony

Paul's journey to Rome as a prisoner provided an unusual but impressive setting in which the meaning of faith in God was powerfully demonstrated. At Crete Paul suggested to those in charge that they spend the winter in the harbor of Fair Havens because of the approaching winter season, but his advice was rejected (Acts 27:11). The pilot and the owner of the ship were seasoned veterans of sailing, and the centurion listened to them instead.

Soon a storm hit, and the situation became desperate. Luke wrote candidly, "We finally gave up all hope of being saved" (Acts 27:20).

This was just the moment when a Christian's perspective was needed, and Paul was equal to the task. He told all on board that an angel of God had assured him all would arrive safely at their destination. This time the Christian's word was welcomed, for he alone possessed a security that no one else knew.

Even amidst injustice or rejection, the believer must not lose the perspective of faith. Those among whom we live and work each day may appear calm and under control. The last person they may want to talk to is a Christian. To such persons the time may come when the terrible uncertainties of life are thrust upon them to such an extent that their world will fly out of control. Like passengers on a sinking ship, they will be tempted to give up all hope. That moment of desperation can be the Christian's opportunity to bear witness for God and the Lord Jesus. We can be certain that someone somewhere at some time will need the perspective only a *Christian* can offer.

A Completed Task

Paul eventually reached Rome, where his testimony continued to ring strong and true through personal contacts (Acts 28:30, 31) and writing (the Prison Epistles). Ultimately he would embark on another journey to a far greater City, one ruled by a Sovereign immeasurably more powerful than any emperor. There the injustices of this life would be rectified by the only Judge whose every decision is flawless (see 2 Timothy 4:8).

Every person is destined to have his "day in court." What distinguishes the Christian's outlook is that he "longs" for this day to come. Although our Judge knows all there is to know about us, in Christ He has forgiven all there is to forgive. To Him, our case has been dismissed!

May this certainty of our future give fulfillment to our present.

---

*Scripture quotations are from the *New International Version.*

Quarterly Quiz

The questions on this page may be used in several ways: as a pretest at the beginning of the quarter; as a review at the end of the quarter; or as a review after each lesson. The questions are based on the Scripture text of each lesson (King James Version). **The answers are on page 6.**

Lesson 1

1. Saul was on his way to what city when Jesus appeared to him? *Acts 9:2*
2. After Jesus appeared to him, Saul was blind for how long a time? *Acts 9:9*
3. Whom did the Lord send to Saul in order that Saul might receive his sight? *Acts 9:17*

Lesson 2

1. When Saul tried to join himself to the disciples in Jerusalem, what was their reaction? *Acts 9:26*
2. Who convinced the apostles that Saul's conversion to Christ was genuine? *Acts 9:27*
3. In what city were the disciples of Jesus first called Christians? *Acts 11:26*

Lesson 3

1. Jesus' followers from Galilee saw Him for how long after His resurrection? *Acts 13:31*
2. Paul quoted Psalm 16:10, a prophecy of Jesus' resurrection, that said God would not suffer his Holy One to see _____. *Acts 13:35*

Lesson 4

1. In what city did Paul heal a man who had been crippled from birth? *Acts 14:8*
2. Thinking that Paul and Barnabas were gods who had come to earth, the people called Barnabas _____ and Paul _____. *Acts 14:12*

Lesson 5

1. Some men from Judea taught that one could not be saved without being _____ according to the law of Moses. *Acts 15:1*
2. In Antioch what two leaders vigorously disputed this teaching? *Acts 15:2*

Lesson 6

1. When Paul and Silas went to Macedonia, they preached first in what city? *Acts 16:12*
2. What kind of spirit did Paul cast out of a girl by Christ's power? *Acts 16:16*
3. The girl's masters rejoiced because she was finally free of the spirit. T/F *Acts 16:19, 20*

Lesson 7

1. In prison, Paul and Silas were praying and singing praises to God at midnight when what occurred? *Acts 16:26*

2. The jailer, awaking from sleep and thinking that his prisoners had escaped, immediately planned to do what? *Acts 16:27*

Lesson 8

1. Speaking to the men of Athens, Paul commented on seeing in their city an altar with what inscription? *Acts 17:23*
2. Paul said that God who created the world and everything in it does not live in temples made with what? *Acts 17:24*

Lesson 9

1. Apollos, "an eloquent man, and mighty in the Scriptures," was born where? *Acts 18:24*
2. Who taught Apollos "the way of God more perfectly"? *Acts 18:26*
3. Where did Paul find some disciples who had not heard of the Holy Ghost? *Acts 19:1, 2*

Lesson 10

1. Who witnessed to Paul in every city that he would be afflicted and imprisoned when he returned to Jerusalem? *Acts 20:23*
2. Paul knew that _____ _____ would enter the church at Ephesus after his departure and bring harm to God's flock. *Acts 20:29*

Lesson 11

1. Jews from what place incited a riot against Paul in the temple at Jerusalem? *Acts 21:27*
2. Paul was accused of polluting the temple by bringing whom into it? *Acts 21:28*
3. The Jews' attempt to kill Paul was stopped by the high priest. T/F *Acts 21:31, 32*

Lesson 12

1. The Jews who knew Paul in his younger days could testify that he had lived the strict life of a _____. *Acts 26:5*
2. (Felix, Festus, Agrippa) said to Paul, "Almost thou persuadest me to be a Christian." *Acts 26:28*

Lesson 13

1. How long did Paul dwell in his own hired house while a prisoner in Rome? *Acts 28:30*
2. Even though Paul was a prisoner, he was permitted visitors and was not forbidden to preach and teach the gospel. T/F *Acts 28:30, 31*

A Chosen Instrument of God

September 1
Lesson 1

LESSON SCRIPTURE: Acts 7:54—8:3; 9:1-22.

PRINTED TEXT: Acts 9:1-16.

Acts 9:1-16

1 And Saul, yet breathing out threatenings and slaughter against the disciples of the Lord, went unto the high priest,

2 And desired of him letters to Damascus to the synagogues, that if he found any of this way, whether they were men or women, he might bring them bound unto Jerusalem.

3 And as he journeyed, he came near Damascus: and suddenly there shined round about him a light from heaven:

4 And he fell to the earth, and heard a voice saying unto him, Saul, Saul, why persecutest thou me?

5 And he said, Who art thou, Lord? And the Lord said, I am Jesus whom thou persecutest: it is hard for thee to kick against the pricks.

6 And he trembling and astonished said, Lord, what wilt thou have me to do? And the Lord said unto him, Arise, and go into the city, and it shall be told thee what thou must do.

7 And the men which journeyed with him stood speechless, hearing a voice, but seeing no man.

8 And Saul arose from the earth; and when his eyes were opened, he saw no man: but they led him by the hand, and brought him into Damascus.

9 And he was three days without sight, and neither did eat nor drink.

10 And there was a certain disciple at Damascus, named Ananias; and to him said the Lord in a vision, Ananias. And he said, Behold, I am here, Lord.

11 And the Lord said unto him, Arise, and go into the street which is called Straight, and inquire in the house of Judas for one called Saul, of Tarsus: for, behold, he prayeth,

12 And hath seen in a vision a man named Ananias coming in, and putting his hand on him, that he might receive his sight.

13 Then Ananias answered, Lord, I have heard by many of this man, how much evil he hath done to thy saints at Jerusalem:

14 And here he hath authority from the chief priests to bind all that call on thy name.

15 But the Lord said unto him, Go thy way: for he is a chosen vessel unto me, to bear my name before the Gentiles, and kings, and the children of Israel:

16 For I will show him how great things he must suffer for my name's sake.

GOLDEN TEXT: He is a chosen vessel unto me, to bear my name before the Gentiles, and kings, and the children of Israel.—Acts 9:15.

*From the Damascus Road
to Rome*

Unit 1. Chosen by God
(Lessons 1, 2)

Lesson Aims

After this lesson students should be able to:

1. Tell how Saul was called and to what work he was called.

2. Tell one or more ways in which they will help with that work this week.

Lesson Outline

INTRODUCTION
  A. Rising Conflict
  B. Lesson Background
I. ANGRY JOURNEY (Acts 9:1, 2)
  A. Controlled Fury (v. 1)
  B. Far-reaching Authority (v. 2)
    Suicide and Murder
II. SUDDEN STOP (Acts 9:3-9)
  A. Awesome Interruption (vv. 3, 4)
  B. Changed Attitude (vv. 5-7)
  C. Anxious Waiting (vv. 8, 9)
III. CHOSEN INSTRUMENTS (Acts 9:10-16)
  A. Commission (vv. 10-12)
  B. Objection (vv. 13, 14)
  C. Objection Overruled (vv. 15, 16)
    In Spite of the Cost
CONCLUSION
  A. The Rest of the Story
  B. Our High Calling
  C. Prayer
  D. Thought to Remember

Display visual 1 in the visuals packet and refer to it when appropriate. This map will be of help in lessons 1-5. The map is shown on page 11.

Introduction

The church at Jerusalem was born in power, but it was born into battle. Passionately devoted to Jesus, it met passionate opposition from the men who had killed Him—the nations leaders. Followers of Jesus had no weapon but the word of the Lord. They shed no blood but their own, but they were brave and indomitable.

A. Rising Conflict

Soon the outstanding leaders of the church were jailed and beaten, but they were not silenced (Acts 4:1-31; 5:17-42).

Stephen was an eager preacher of the gospel, and eager unbelievers tried to outtalk him. Failing in that, they brought false accusations and tried to convict him with perjured testimony. They failed again, and the court of justice dissolved in riot and pelted him with stones till he was dead (Acts 6:8—7:60).

At that point a new name appears in the record: Saul of Tarsus. He hurled no stones at Stephen; he was only an approving bystander. (Acts 7:58; 8:1). But it was not in his nature to be a bystander for long. Saul was an activist. Gamaliel the teacher advised moderation (Acts 5:34-39), but Saul the student would have none of that. Convinced that Jesus' people were bent on destroying the faith of their fathers, he was bent on destroying them.

B. Lesson Background

Was Saul himself a member of the ruling council in Jerusalem? Scholars debate that question, but certainly he had the backing of the council's majority as he led the police in a sweep of Jerusalem, searching out the followers of Jesus and committing them to jail (Acts 8:1-3).

This assault succeeded only in spreading the teaching of Jesus. The persecuted people scattered all over Judea and Samaria, and they carried the gospel wherever they went (Acts 8:1, 4). Soon they were going far beyond Judea and Samaria (Acts 11:19). Seething with frustration, Saul could see that his effort had fallen flat. The only way to stop this new religion was to follow its followers as far as they could flee.

I. Angry Journey
(Acts 9:1, 2)

As already noted, Saul was an activist. His action in Jerusalem had failed: its result was exactly the opposite of what he had intended. But Saul saw no reason to give up. He saw only a call to more extended action.

A. Controlled Fury (v. 1)

1. And Saul, yet breathing out threatenings and slaughter against the disciples of the Lord, went unto the high priest.

VISUALS FOR THESE LESSONS

The *Adult Visuals/Learning Resources* packet contains classroom-size visuals designed for use with the lessons in the Autumn Quarter. The packet is available from your supplier. Order no. 192

visual 1

Saul was furious, *breathing out threatenings and slaughter,* but he was not going to plunge into any unauthorized terrorism. Seeking proper authority for drastic action, he went straight to the top. *The high priest* was the highest official among the Jews.

B. Far-reaching Authority (v. 2)

2. And desired of him letters to Damascus to the synagogues, that if he found any of this way, whether they were men or women, he might bring them bound unto Jerusalem.

There were so many disciples in Damascus that Saul thought action was needed there. That was 150 miles from Jerusalem. In the organization of the Roman Empire it was in the domain of Aretas, king of Arabia (2 Corinthians 11:32). Apparently the governor in Damascus gave the synagogues considerable freedom to discipline their own people, and the synagogues recognized the authority of the high priest in Jerusalem. We know the high priest gave Saul the letters he asked, for the next verse shows that Saul was on the way to Damascus. Probably he took a strong detachment of police with him.

SUICIDE AND MURDER

"Wilma" had been married to "Mike" for forty-three years when she wrote to the advice columnist. Her complaint was that Mike, a smoker, had burned holes in all of his suits, ruined all the furniture, set fire to the bed, and had a heart attack, but wouldn't stop smoking. When Wilma got lung cancer (even though she didn't smoke) Mike still wouldn't stop.

Wilma's biggest complaint, however, was this: Mike read about a veterinarian who said that a dog's chances of getting lung cancer were increased by thirty percent if its owner smoked. And at that, Mike stopped smoking! He wouldn't stop to save his wife's life, but he would for the sake of his dog!

When consumed with a passion or a habit, we have an amazing ability to overlook the truth.

Saul of Tarsus, a proud Jew, perhaps had more compassion for Gentiles than for members of the family of Israel—his own people—who had turned to follow Christ. He was hurting—literally murdering—others whom he should have loved. He was even killing his own soul with his refusal to acknowledge Jesus as the Messiah. There are "none so blind as those that will not see." Let it not be said of us!   —C. R. B.

II. Sudden Stop
(Acts 9:3-9)

We have three accounts of the startling way Saul's trip was halted. Luke tells the story here in our text. Then in chapter 22 he records how Saul himself later told it to a crowd in Jerusalem, and in chapter 26 he records how Saul told it to King Agrippa. In the other accounts we find some details that are not recorded in our text.

A. Awesome Interruption (vv. 3, 4)

3, 4. And as he journeyed, he came near Damascus: and suddenly there shined round about him a light from heaven: and he fell to the earth, and heard a voice saying unto him, Saul, Saul, why persecutest thou me?

The noonday sun was brilliant, but this light was brighter still (Acts 26:13). No natural light could be so strong; it had to be supernatural. Saul dropped to the ground in reverent fear, and so did his companions (Acts 26:14). To add to Saul's terror, a voice called him by name and demanded, "Why are you persecuting me?"

B. Changed Attitude (vv. 5-7)

5. And he said, Who art thou, Lord? And the Lord said, I am Jesus whom thou persecutest: it is hard for thee to kick against the pricks.

Paul thought he was persecuting heretics and traitors, opposers of the true religion. But surely no such scoundrel would be accompanied by that marvelous and terrifying light. This speaker certainly was some great one, one entitled to be called Lord. But who could he be?

The answer was swift, sure, and crushing: *I am Jesus.* Saul had thought Jesus was a dead imposter. Now suddenly he knew Jesus was alive. Peter and Stephen and the other disciples had been telling the truth, and for that Saul had been putting them in jail. He had been trying to destroy the church, and now he knew the church was right and he was wrong. What a blow!

It is hard for thee to kick against the pricks. Saul was like an ox being driven with a goad. To escape the pricking, the ox must go as the driver wishes. If he refuses to go, he feels a sharp jab. If he kicks at it, he is only hurt the more. Just what does that mean? There are two possibilities. (1) It may mean that Jesus now was driving Saul to accept the truth. It would be hard for him to resist. (2) It may mean that something within Saul had been goading him away from his persecution and toward a friendly attitude, an acceptance of the disciples. Saul at heart was a good man. It must have been hard to keep up such a bitter persecution of people who were doing nothing but good. But Saul had been resisting the kindly inclination of his heart and plunging on in the furious persecution because he thought it was his duty.

6. And he trembling and astonished said, Lord, what wilt thou have me to do? And the Lord said unto him, Arise, and go into the city, and it shall be told thee what thou must do.

Saul was *astonished* to find that he was wrong, and *trembling* with fear. The one he opposed so bitterly was now confronting him in dazzling light. The disciples had been saying Jesus was at God's right hand (Acts 2:33; 7:56). What was this light if not the very glory of Heaven? No wonder Saul was trembling. If he had been resisting an urge to change his ways, he would resist no more. Humbly he asked, "What do You want me to do?"

It is notable that Jesus did not answer that humble question. Saul must go to Damascus and wait for someone else to tell him what to do. The preaching of the gospel has been entrusted to God's people. It is our duty to tell the whole world the way of salvation, and Jesus will not relieve us of our duty.

7. And the men which journeyed with him stood speechless, hearing a voice, but seeing no man.

The men traveling with Saul heard the sound of *a voice,* but did not hear what it said (Acts 22:9). They saw the light, but they saw *no man.* In Acts 26:16, "I have appeared unto thee" suggests that Saul saw Jesus.

C. Anxious Waiting (vv. 8, 9)

8. And Saul arose from the earth; and when his eyes were opened, he saw no man: but they led him by the hand, and brought him into Damascus.

Saul now was blind. Instead of leading a vengeful expedition to round up the disciples of Jesus, he had to be led by the hand into Damascus. Probably a lodging place had been reserved for him there.

9. And he was three days without sight, and neither did eat nor drink.

Three days! The promised instruction did not come, and Saul could not see to go looking for it. Three days of darkness, with nothing to do but think—think how wrong he had been, think how he had been fighting against God, as his teacher Gamaliel had warned (Acts 5:38, 39). Three days of remorse. Three days of fasting and prayer (v. 11). Those three days must have brought the helpless man close to despair. Surely he was ready to accept instruction when it came.

III. Chosen Instruments
(Acts 9:10-16)

This lesson is titled "A Chosen Instrument of God," but it could be called "Two Chosen Instruments." Saul was chosen for a mighty work, but Ananias was chosen to guide Saul. How often does a great man owe his greatness in part to some obscure person who helped him get started!

A. Commission (vv. 10-12)

10. And there was a certain disciple at Damascus, named Ananias; and to him said the Lord in a vision, Ananias. And he said, Behold, I am here, Lord.

Like a true disciple, Ananias responded to the Lord's call, ready to do the Lord's bidding.

11. And the Lord said unto him, Arise, and go into the street which is called Straight, and inquire in the house of Judas for one called Saul, of Tarsus: for, behold, he prayeth.

Apparently the houses on Straight Street were not numbered as houses are in a modern city. Ananias would have to inquire which house belonged to Judas. Upon finding it, he would ask to speak with Saul. *He prayeth.* Overwhelmed by guilt and remorse, Saul probably was praying earnestly that someone would come quickly and tell him what to do. Jesus had promised that he would be told (v. 6).

12. And hath seen in a vision a man named Ananias coming in, and putting his hand on him, that he might receive his sight.

Saul, waiting in darkness for the promised instruction, had been prepared for it. When a man appeared exactly as he had seen him in a vision, Saul would feel sure that man was the messenger God had sent to tell him what to do.

B. Objection (vv. 13, 14)

13. Then Ananias answered, Lord, I have heard by many of this man, how much evil he hath done to thy saints at Jerusalem.

Saul's persecution of the church was well known. People had fled from Jerusalem to escape it (Acts 8:1). No doubt some of them had gone to Damascus and carried the gospel there.

14. And here he hath authority from the chief priests to bind all that call on thy name.

Saul's purpose in Damascus was known to the people he had come to seize. Perhaps the disciples in Jerusalem had sent a swift messenger to warn those in Damascus. It would seem prudent to keep out of Saul's sight if possible, but now the Lord told Ananias to seek him instead of hiding from him.

C. Objection Overruled (vv. 15, 16)

15. But the Lord said unto him, Go thy way: for he is a chosen vessel unto me, to bear my name before the Gentiles, and kings, and the children of Israel.

The Lord insisted that Ananias must go to Saul, disregarding the danger. Of course the Lord knew there was no longer any danger from Saul. That grieving man would never again lift a hand against the true disciples of Jesus. But Ananias did not know that. It would take courage for him to go to Saul. However, the Lord did tell him the former enemy was to be an outstanding friend and advocate. The word *vessel* suggests a dish or jar in which the gospel would be carried far and wide, but the Greek word can be used of an instrument, a tool, a useful thing of any kind. The Lord had chosen Saul as an instrument that He would use in spreading His *name*, His fame, His nature, His cause, His salvation. Saul already had been told this. Jesus had stopped him on the road, not just to make him a believer, but to make him "a minister and a witness" (Acts 26:16-18). Saul was chosen to be an apostle along with the twelve chosen earlier, and not at all inferior to them (2 Corinthians 11:5). Like the other apostles, he would be specially authorized and inspired to speak for the Lord (1 Corinthians 14:37). He would be sent especially to *Gentiles* (Acts 26:17). He had been educated in Jerusalem and was as ardently Jewish as anyone (Acts 22:3; Galatians 1:13, 14), but his hometown was Tarsus, a Gentile city. For that reason he may have been better able to communicate with Gentiles. His mission was not to be limited to Gentiles, however. He would appear as a prisoner before *kings,* and would testify to them. He would preach to *the children of Israel* in Jerusalem and in many other places.

16. For I will show him how great things he must suffer for my name's sake.

Saul had brought suffering to many followers of Jesus. Now as a follower of Jesus he would learn to bear his share of such suffering. See 2 Corinthians 11:24-28 for a partial list of the things he would suffer.

In Spite of the Cost

Korczak and Casimir Ziolkowski may not be widely known, but they exemplify what it means to be consumed by passion for an idea and to follow it without distraction.

From 1948 until his death in 1982, Korczak Ziolkowski pursued his dream of carving the world's largest statue from a six-hundred-foot mountain in South Dakota. At the age of seven, Casimir began helping his father on the statue of Chief Crazy Horse (who led the charge against General Custer at Little Big Horn).

The statue still is years—perhaps decades—from completion. As of this writing Casimir is thirty-five years old, but he isn't sure he will see it completed in his lifetime. Nevertheless, facing such a herculean task, the expense, the cost in time, and the risk to life and limb are all worth it: he (or his descendants) will see the dream realized!

When Ananias heard the Lord's call to go to Saul, he voiced the normal objections about the risk involved. Then he obeyed the call, in spite of whatever the cost might be, so the cause of Christ could be advanced. Do we share that passion for the gospel? Will we obey the Lord, in spite of the cost, so that through us or our descendants the world will hear the gospel?
—C. R. B.

Conclusion

This lesson is designed to focus attention on Saul's calling to be a chosen instrument in the Lord's hand, a vessel to take the Lord's message far and wide. The printed text therefore ends with the description of Saul's future work (vv. 15, 16). At that point, however, Saul was not yet ready to start the work assigned to him.

A. The Rest of the Story

Along the road Jesus made a promise. In Damascus Saul would be told what he must do (v. 6). We cannot conclude the lesson without a look at what he was told. For that we turn to the record of his own words in Acts 22:12-16. "And one Ananias, a devout man according to the law, having a good report of all the Jews which dwelt there, came unto me, and stood, and said unto me, Brother Saul, receive thy sight. At the same hour I looked up upon him. And he said, The God of our fathers hath chosen thee, that thou shouldest know his will, and see that Just One, and shouldest hear the voice of his mouth. For thou shalt be his witness unto all men of what thou hast seen and heard. *And now why tarriest thou? arise, and be baptized, and wash away thy sins, calling on the name of the Lord.*"

Saul did as he was told (Acts 9:18). Like three thousand people on an earlier day, he was baptized in the name of Jesus Christ for the remission of sins (Acts 2:38). Saul the sinner was dead and buried; Saul the redeemed rose to walk in newness of life (Romans 6:1-4). The sins that he regretted so terribly were taken away, removed as far as the east is from the west (Psalm 103:12). He was a new creature (2 Corinthians 5:17), ready to begin the great work to which Jesus had called him. This he did promptly, right there in the synagogues of Damascus (Acts 9:20). Yet with all that, he may have seen a need for further preparation, as we shall see in next week's lesson (Galatians 1:15-17).

B. Our High Calling

Not all of us are called to be apostles like Saul. Our eyes are not blinded by a supernatural light on the highway; our ears do not hear the voice of Jesus rebuking our sins and assigning our task. Still all of us who are Christians are called with a high calling, a "heavenly calling" (Philippians 3:14; Hebrews 3:1). Among other things, we are called to the unfinished task that was assigned to Saul. We are to bear the name of Jesus before Gentiles and kings and the children of Israel.

To the apostles Jesus said, "Go ye therefore, and teach all nations" (Matthew 28:19). To the apostles He said, "Go ye into all the world, and preach the gospel to every creature" (Mark 16:15). The apostles spent their lives in this work, and probably most of them lost their lives because of it. They did not finish the job, however, and certainly Jesus knew they would not. The work had to be passed on to others (2 Timothy 2:2). Nearly all Christians agree that the unfinished work is now the work of all of us. What can you personally do about it this week? You can do several things:

1. You can try diligently to make your own calling and election sure, to assure for yourself an entrance into our Lord's eternal kingdom. Read 2 Peter 1:5-11 and check one or more things in which you will improve yourself this week:

Virtue
Knowledge
Temperance
Patience
Godliness
Brotherly kindness
Charity

2. You can speak a good word for Jesus, praise Him, tell what He has done for you, explain His way. Check one or more persons before whom you will bear His name this week:

Someone in your home
Someone in your block
Someone who works near you
Someone in your club
Someone you correspond with

3. You can give a special offering to some institution or person who is bearing the name of Jesus in a good way. Check one or more to which you will make a special offering, or better still, a regular weekly or monthly offering:

Your church
A missionary
A Christian college
A Christian home for children
A Christian home for the handicapped
A Christian home for senior citizens

4. You can pray for all who are bearing the name of Jesus where it is needed. List those for whom you will pray this week.

C. Prayer

Father, what an honor it is to be called with a Heavenly calling! Each of us who are Christians have been called to help in Jesus' work. Give us wisdom and courage and strength to be worthy of the honor You have given us. In Jesus' name, amen.

D. Thought to Remember

"Live a life worthy of the calling you have received" (Ephesians 4:1 *New International Version*).

Home Daily Bible Readings

Monday, Aug. 26—Saul's Conversion on the Damascus Road (Acts 9:1-9)

Tuesday, Aug. 27—Saul Regains His Sight (Acts 9:10-19

Wednesday, Aug. 28—Saul Preaches Jesus as the Christ (Acts 9:20-22)

Thursday, Aug. 29—Paul Begins His Testimony (Acts 22:1-5)

Friday, Aug. 30—Paul Tells of His Conversion (Acts 22:6-11)

Saturday, Aug. 31—Called to Witness to All (Acts 22:12-16)

Sunday, Sept. 1—Commissioned to Preach to the Gentiles (Acts 22:17-21)

Learning by Doing

This page contains an alternate lesson plan emphasizing learning activities. Classes desiring such student involvement will find these suggestions helpful.

Learning Goals

As a result of this lesson, your students will:

1. Explore God's appointment of Saul as an instrument to lead Gentiles to Christ.

2. Consider how viewing themselves as God's instruments will enable them to serve God more effectively.

3. Express to God a desire to be a more effective instrument for Him.

Into the Lesson

Lead your students in discussing these questions, which are included in the student book:

1. When you hear the phrase *Christian leader*, what qualities come to your mind?

2. When you hear the phrase *effective Christian leader*, what qualities come to your mind?

3. What determines if a Christian leader is truly effective?

Jot down on the chalkboard your class members' suggestions for each question. Allow up to eight minutes for discussion.

Introduce this new series of lessons by saying, "Today we begin a three-month study of the life of Paul the apostle. Paul was one of the most effective leaders in the early church. Studying his life will provide insights to help us become more effective in serving Christ.

We began today's lesson by looking at qualities of effective Christian leadership. God is concerned that we are both faithful and effective. In these studies we will focus on principles of effective Christian leadership. In one sense, every Christian is a leader in some way. If we view leadership as primarily influencing people to draw closer to Christ, all Christians have opportunities to be leaders—whether in their families, on their jobs, or with their friends and acquaintances.

Today we will concentrate on how we must view ourselves if we are to serve our Lord effectively.

Into the Word

Have your class members form groups of six to eight. Give each group a copy of the questions below and appoint a discussion leader. (The questions are included in the student book.) Allow twenty-five minutes for discussion.

1. Read Acts 9:1-19. As you read, try to imagine yourself as Saul. (Note: Paul was first known as Saul.) What is your view of yourself during the events described in each of the following sections?

—verses 1, 2
—verses 3-6
—verses 7-9
—verses 17-19

2. Compare Acts 9:15 with Acts 26:15-18. To what mission did God call Saul?

3. In Acts 9:15 the Lord called Saul His "chosen instrument" (*New International Version*); "chosen vessel" (*King James Version*). What does this phrase mean?

4. If you belong to Jesus, you are a chosen instrument of God. What are you called to do? Check out these verses: 1 Peter 2:9; Matthew 28:18, 19; Ephesians 2:10.

When the groups have completed their discussions, have them form one large group. Ask, "What was the most significant idea you heard in your discussion?" Allow class members to respond.

Into Life

Before class, prepare a poster and mount it on the wall. Entitle it, *Principles for Effective Leadership*. Each week throughout this quarter, write one principle on the poster. For today's lesson, write this principle:

Effective Christian leaders view themselves as God's instruments to be used for His purposes.

Then lead the class in discussing these questions:

1. How can viewing yourself as God's instrument enable you to serve Him more consistently and effectively?

2. What tends to keep you from seeing yourself as God's instrument? What can you do to overcome this hindrance?

3. Read 2 Timothy 2:20-22. How can we be more useful to God as His instruments, according to this passage?

Give each class member a pen and piece of paper. Ask members to write a prayer to God. In their prayer they are to ask God to help them view themselves more consistently as His instruments and to ask Him to cleanse them from anything that interferes with their usefulness to Him. Close with a time of prayer. Encourage class members to read their prayers aloud.

Let's Talk It Over

The questions on this page are designed to encourage review of the lesson Scriptures and to promote discussion of the lesson by the class. The answers provided are only discussion starters. Let your class talk it over from there.

1. What was the Lord's purpose in appearing to Saul on the road to Damascus?

The risen Lord appeared to Saul to call him to be His apostle to the Gentiles. In Acts 26:16, 17 Paul testifies that the Lord said to him, "I have appeared unto thee for this purpose, to make thee a minister and a witness both of these things which thou hast seen, and of those things in the which I will appear unto thee; delivering thee from the people, and from the Gentiles, unto whom now I send thee." One of the qualifications of apostleship in the New Testament was that a person must have seen the resurrected Lord (Acts 1:21-26). Note that Saul's conversion occurred when Ananias came to him and told him what he must do. After Saul received his sight Ananias instructed, "Get up, be baptized and wash your sins away, calling on his name" (Acts 22:16 *New International Version*). God always uses human instrumentality to proclaim the gospel, to instruct people regarding the way of salvation. It was so, even in the case of Saul.

2. Even though both Saul and Ananias were chosen by God, how were their roles different in the work of the Lord's kingdom?

Essentially, Saul's role was to evangelize masses of people: Gentiles and Jews (Acts 9:15). This he did, in a faithful, lifelong ministry that significantly impacted the entire Mediterranean world of his day. Ananias, on the other hand, was sent to witness to one man: Saul. This he did faithfully, and he significantly impacted the one person who would become history's greatest missionary.

3. Describe some feelings that would have been very natural for Ananias to have experienced when he was chosen to teach Saul.

Ananias knew of Saul's reputation as a fierce persecutor of Christ's followers, so it seems reasonable to assume that his most dominant feelings would have been apprehension and fear (see Acts 9:13, 14). Certainly Ananias had doubts about his assignment. However, we can learn from him. Even though his assumptions had been challenged and he had doubts, Ananias still obeyed Christ. To whom do you need to be an Ananias?

4. In what manner did Saul approach the tasks he was given?

Saul was an activist. Whatever he did, he did it "full-bore, pedal to the floor." His pattern of behavior never seems to have been "laid back," easy going, passive. He persecuted the Christians in Jerusalem, but that did not suffice. He pressed on to Damascus, 150 miles away, determined to destroy those who followed Jesus Christ. When he himself was converted and called to witness to the world of his day, he evangelized with equal vigor. Saul's personality was perfectly suited for the task the Lord gave him.

5. What effect may dramatic events in life have on a person's willingness to open himself to God's leading?

Dramatic events cause a person to think deeply and to be more open to options (some of which previously may not have been considered). Such events often involve significant loss: the loss of health, a loved one, a job, valued possessions, peace (for example, in a national sense). Thus illness, injury, death, and war may lead one to think seriously about the temporary nature of this life. Such contemplation may lead to an awareness and acceptance of the gift of eternal life, which God offers through Christ. Saul suffered the loss of his sight for three days, but in that loss he began truly to see.

6. Why is uninformed zeal a dangerous dynamic in behavior?

Saul, who came to be known as Paul, wrote later of the Jews, "For I can testify about them that they are zealous for God, but their zeal is not based on knowledge" (Romans 10:2 *New International Version*). So too, Saul was zealous as a persecutor of Christians. His actions were done in good conscience, but his conscience was not properly informed—he lacked knowledge of God's full truth. Once Saul was adequately informed, his zeal served God's ultimate purpose of evangelizing the world. Church history records many examples of uninformed zeal that brought suffering and death to Christians, even from fellow Christians! Our zeal pleases God only when it expresses His truth, spirit, and purpose. Imitate Paul, the missionary, not Saul, the persecutor.

Barnabas and Saul

September 8
Lesson 2

LESSON SCRIPTURE: Acts 9:26-30; 11:19-30; 12:25.

PRINTED TEXT: Acts 9:26-30; 11:19-26, 29, 30.

Acts 9:26-30

26 And when Saul was come to Jerusalem, he assayed to join himself to the disciples: but they were all afraid of him, and believed not that he was a disciple.

27 But Barnabas took him, and brought him to the apostles, and declared unto them how he had seen the Lord in the way, and that he had spoken to him, and how he had preached boldly at Damascus in the name of Jesus.

28 And he was with them coming in and going out at Jerusalem.

29 And he spake boldly in the name of the Lord Jesus, and disputed against the Grecians: but they went about to slay him.

30 Which when the brethren knew, they brought him down to Caesarea, and sent him forth to Tarsus.

Acts 11:19-26, 29, 30

19 Now they which were scattered abroad upon the persecution that arose about Stephen traveled as far as Phoenicia, and Cyprus, and Antioch, preaching the word to none but unto the Jews only.

20 And some of them were men of Cyprus and Cyrene, which, when they were come to Antioch, spake unto the Grecians, preaching the Lord Jesus.

21 And the hand of the Lord was with them: and a great number believed, and turned unto the Lord.

22 Then tidings of these things came unto the ears of the church which was in Jerusalem: and they sent forth Barnabas, that he should go as far as Antioch.

23 Who, when he came, and had seen the grace of God, was glad, and exhorted them all, that with purpose of heart they would cleave unto the Lord.

24 For he was a good man, and full of the Holy Ghost and of faith: and much people was added unto the Lord.

25 Then departed Barnabas to Tarsus, for to seek Saul:

26 And when he had found him, he brought him unto Antioch. And it came to pass, that a whole year they assembled themselves with the church, and taught much people. And the disciples were called Christians first in Antioch.

. . . .

29 Then the disciples, every man according to his ability, determined to send relief unto the brethren which dwelt in Judea:

30 Which also they did, and sent it to the elders by the hands of Barnabas and Saul.

GOLDEN TEXT: Then departed Barnabas to Tarsus, for to seek Saul: and when he had found him, he brought him unto Antioch. And it came to pass, that a whole year they assembled themselves with the church, and taught much people.—Acts 11:25, 26.

From the Damascus Road
to Rome
Unit 1. Chosen by God
(Lessons 1, 2)

Lesson Aims

After studying this lesson students should be able to:

1. Explain the meaning of the name *Barnabas.*
2. Tell how Barnabas helped Saul.
3. Tell how they will give help to someone this week.

Lesson Outline

INTRODUCTION
  A. Conflict
  B. Lesson Background
I. SAUL IN JERUSALEM (Acts 9:26-30)
  A. Rejected (v. 26)
  B. Accepted (vv. 27, 28)
  C. Threatened (vv. 29, 30)
II. THE CHURCH IN ANTIOCH (Acts 11:19-26)
  A. A Church Open to Gentiles (vv. 19-21)
  B. A Church Approved (vv. 22-24)
  C. Another Helper for the Church (vv. 25, 26)
     A Very Important "First"
III. A CHURCH HELPING (Acts 11:29, 30)
  A. Help for the Needy (v. 29)
  B. Chosen Messengers (v. 30)
     Meeting a Need
CONCLUSION
  A. Our Hero
  B. What Are You Fitted For?
  C. Prayer
  D. Thought to Remember

Display visual 2 from the visuals packet. It illustrates the thoughts in the section entitled "Our Hero" in the conclusion of the lesson. The visual is shown on page 20.

Introduction

Last week in our lesson we saw that Saul of Tarsus was an activist. When he thought falsehood was being taught by Jesus' followers, he acted vigorously to stamp it out. When he learned that the teaching was true, he acted no less vigorously to proclaim it. This he did in Damascus without delay: *"Straightway* he preached Christ in the synagogues, that he is the Son of God" (Acts 9:20).

A. Conflict

The unbelieving Jews were amazed at Saul's new activity (Acts 9:21). Saul had been their strong defender against the teaching they called heresy. To his former friends he seemed to be a traitor. They hated him more than they hated the other followers of Jesus.

Saul was thoroughly trained in the Jewish religion (Acts 22:3). He may have felt a need to restudy the Scriptures in the light of his new assurance that their prophecies were fulfilled in Jesus. Whatever his reason was, he went away into Arabia. (*Refer to the map—visual 1—from the visuals packet.*) We have no record of what he did there, but Galatians 1:18 suggests that he stayed there for about three years. Then he went back to Damascus (Galatians 1:17).

No doubt the unbelievers spoke out in the synagogue, disputing with Saul. But Saul had facts and Scripture on his side. The Scriptures foretold what the Christ would do. Jesus did what the Scriptures foretold. (See Acts 2.) With such reasoning "Saul increased the more in strength, and confounded the Jews which dwelt at Damascus, proving that this is very Christ" (Acts 9:22).

B. Lesson Background

The unbelievers did not give up because the Scriptures and facts and reason were against them. There was another way to silence the man who beat them in debate. They would kill him. Word of this was leaked to Saul and other believers, and they took steps to keep Saul alive.

Among the plotters were men of influence in Damascus. They enlisted the governor of the city to help them. He set guards at the gates so Saul could not escape. Still the believers outwitted the plotters. Under cover of night they put Saul in a big basket and lowered him from the window of a house built on the city wall (Acts 9:23-25; 2 Corinthians 11:32, 33).

I. Saul in Jerusalem
(Acts 9:26-30)

Saul had done much evil to the followers of Jesus in Jerusalem (Acts 9:13). Probably he thought the honorable thing to do was to go back there and make amends by doing good to them. So he went to Jerusalem.

A. Rejected (v. 26)

26. And when Saul was come to Jerusalem, he assayed to join himself to the disciples: but they were all afraid of him, and believed not that he was a disciple.

Well the disciples remembered how Saul had swept Jerusalem, dragging them away to jail (Acts 8:3). Now he was back, claiming to be one of them. What could that mean except that he was trying to infiltrate their ranks to learn who the disciples were and put them all in prison? No wonder they feared Saul and wanted nothing to do with him.

B. Accepted (vv. 27, 28)

27. But Barnabas took him, and brought him to the apostles, and declared unto them how he had seen the Lord in the way, and that he had spoken to him, and how he had preached boldly at Damascus in the name of Jesus.

We are not told why Barnabas believed Saul when the other disciples did not. Perhaps his generous nature made him better able to recognize sincerity. Perhaps he was the first one who cared enough to investigate. Perhaps he had confirmation from Damascus. Possibly he talked with someone who had been with Saul when his journey was interrupted by the Heavenly light (Acts 26:13). Whatever his reasons were, Barnabas was convinced that Saul was now a true disciple, and together Barnabas and Saul convinced the apostles.

28. And he was with them coming in and going out at Jerusalem.

With the apostles as well as Barnabas to speak for him, Saul was accepted by the rest of the disciples. *With them coming in and going out* means that he joined in all their activities.

C. Threatened (vv. 29, 30)

29. And he spake boldly in the name of the Lord Jesus, and disputed against the Grecians: but they went about to slay him.

Saul quickly began to proclaim the message of Jesus in Jerusalem, and he quickly aroused opposition as he had done in Damascus.

The *Grecians* mentioned here were not Greeks by race; they were Jews who had come from foreign countries where Greek was the prevailing language. Eager to prove that they were as ardently Jewish as those born in Israel's homeland, they took the lead in opposing Saul. They too found their arguments useless against Saul's Scripture quotations, actual facts, and sound reasoning. So they also looked for another way to silence Saul: *they went about to slay him.* That means they planned to kill him.

30. Which when the brethren knew, they brought him down to Caesarea, and sent him forth to Tarsus.

Learning of this threat to Saul's life, some of the brethren escorted him, probably enough of them to provide a strong bodyguard and keep

---

How to Say It

ANTIOCH. *An*-tee-ock.
CAESAREA. Sess-uh-*ree*-uh.
CYPRUS. *Sye*-prus.
CYRENE. Sye-*ree*-nee.
PARAKLESIS (Greek). par-*ahh*-clay-siss.
PHOENICIA. Fih-*nish*-uh.
TARSUS. *Tar*-sus.

---

him safe, till he reached Caesarea on the seacoast. There they probably saw him aboard a ship for Tarsus, and checked to be sure none of the would-be killers were on the same vessel.

Tarsus was Saul's hometown. Probably he stayed there a little longer than he had stayed in Arabia, but we have no record of what he did there.

At this time all the disciples of Jesus were Jews. It seems that they were content with the idea that the blessings of the Messiah were for Jews only. Jesus had told them to teach all nations (Matthew 28:19), but apparently they thought that meant Jews in all nations.

Chapter 10 of Acts tells how God put an end to that misunderstanding. In unmistakable ways He sent Peter to take the gospel to a Roman officer in Caesarea, and indicated that the officer and his family were to be accepted as disciples of Christ. Peter was sharply questioned when he went back to Jerusalem; but when the facts were known, the disciples agreed that Jesus' salvation was for Gentiles as well as Jews. Understanding this at last, the disciples rejoiced in the greatness of God's mercy (Acts 11:1-18).

II. The Church in Antioch
(Acts 11:19-26)

Meanwhile the gospel was being taken farther and farther from the starting point in Jerusalem. This is seen in the latter part of Acts 11.

A. A Church Open to Gentiles
(vv. 19-21)

19. Now they which were scattered abroad upon the persecution that arose about Stephen traveled as far as Phoenicia, and Cyprus, and Antioch, preaching the word to none but unto the Jews only.

The persecution that arose about Stephen was the one in which Saul had been violently active.

It had driven many disciples out of Jerusalem (Acts 8:1). Now the persecution was over, but some of the scattered disciples were going farther instead of returning to Jerusalem. They had taken the gospel with them from the beginning (Acts 8:4) and were still preaching it wherever they went, but *to none but unto the Jews only.* Jesus' people in Judea had learned that the gospel was for all people, but probably these scattered disciples had not learned about that.

20. And some of them were men of Cyprus and Cyrene, which, when they were come to Antioch, spake unto the Grecians, preaching the Lord Jesus.

In Acts 9:29 the word *Grecians* means Jews from Gentile countries, but here in Acts 11:20 it obviously means Gentiles in contrast with the Jews mentioned in verse 19. Some ancient manuscripts and some modern versions read *Greeks* instead of *Grecians.*

Why did these traveling disciples now begin to share the gospel with Gentiles? We are not told. Three possibilities are easily seen:

1. Perhaps some Gentiles heard them talking with Jews and asked for more information about their message.

2. Perhaps they decided that Jesus' commission was to be taken literally and the gospel was to be shared with "every creature."

3. Perhaps they now heard that the churches in Judea were sharing the gospel with Gentiles.

21. And the hand of the Lord was with them: and a great number believed, and turned unto the Lord.

A great number of the Gentiles not only *believed* the message in their minds, but also *turned unto the Lord* in their way of living, obeying His commands. This result made it evident that *the hand of the Lord* was working with those disciples who shared the gospel with the Gentiles.

B. A Church Approved (vv. 22-24)

22. Then tidings of these things came unto the ears of the church which was in Jerusalem: and they sent forth Barnabas, that he should go as far as Antioch.

We are not told why the disciples that were in Jerusalem sent Barnabas to Antioch. Perhaps they merely wanted to send greetings and good wishes to fellow believers. Perhaps they wanted to see if the fast-growing church needed more teachers to help the new disciples know and follow Christ's teaching (Matthew 28:20). At Antioch some of the new disciples may have been heathen before they heard the gospel. The believers in Jerusalem may have feared that heathen ideas and customs might be introduced into the church. Whatever the reason, big-hearted Barnabas was a good man to send. No one doubted his understanding of the gospel or his devotion to it, and everyone knew he was eager to be helpful.

visual 2

23. Who, when he came, and had seen the grace of God, was glad, and exhorted them all, that with purpose of heart they would cleave unto the Lord.

It was easy to see that *the grace of God* was at work in Antioch. People in great numbers were becoming God's people. Barnabas *was glad* with what he learned. He saw no need to urge the new disciples to change their ways; he only exhorted them to keep on with what they were doing, to *cleave unto the Lord,* to stay with Him, to be faithful.

24. For he was a good man, and full of the Holy Ghost and of faith: and much people was added unto the Lord.

Barnabas was *a good man.* Such a man would not be unhappy if the new church in Antioch was dominated by Gentiles instead of Jews. He would rejoice in the salvation of men and women and with the growth of the church.

All who become sincere followers of Jesus receive the gift of the Holy Ghost, who then lives in them (Acts 2:38; 1 Corinthians 6:19). But some give themselves up to His leadership more fully than others do. Barnabas was *full of the Holy Ghost,* eager to be led by Him. He was also full of *faith,* completely trusting the Lord and the Spirit. His enthusiasm gave new vigor to the church in Antioch, and *much people was added unto the Lord.*

C. Another Helper for the Church (vv. 25, 26)

25. Then departed Barnabas to Tarsus, for to seek Saul.

Again the wisdom and helpfulness of Barnabas are seen. He saw an eager, enthusiastic young church needing another teacher. He thought of Saul, an eager, enthusiastic, and capable teacher. He went to bring the teacher to the place where he was needed.

26. And when he had found him, he brought him unto Antioch. And it came to pass, that a whole year they assembled themselves with the

church, and taught much people. And the disciples were called Christians first in Antioch.

What a busy and happy and productive year that must have been! Bighearted Barnabas and vigorous Saul were working together at the job Jesus had given His disciples (Matthew 28:19, 20). Acts 13:1 names other prophets and teachers who were working there too. Altogether they *taught much people.*

The disciples were called Christians first in Antioch. Before this they had called themselves saints (Acts 9:13), disciples (v. 26), and brethren (v. 30). These names continued to be used. The name *Christian* appears in only two other places in the New Testament (Acts 26:28; 1 Peter 4:16), but ancient and modern followers of Jesus have accepted it as a fitting and honorable name. We are not told who first called the disciples Christians, or why. Various possibilities are seen:

1. Some students think followers of Christ first called themselves Christians, as followers of Luther call themselves Lutherans.

2. Some think outsiders first called Christ's disciples Christians, perhaps in scorn or ridicule.

3. Some think God gave the name to Christ's people. They point to the Greek word that is translated *called.* Elsewhere in the New Testament it is used of God's calling or warning or telling. For example, it is translated *warned of God* in Matthew 2:12 and *admonished of God* in Hebrews 8:5.

A Very Important "First"

Who among us can resist being interested in "firsts"? Is there a city of any size anywhere in the country that does not have a "First National Bank"? We like to be first in line or the first on our block to have a new product. Failing in that endeavor, we still like to hear about the "firsts" that others have achieved.

A rather dubious "first" was visited upon Jacob German, who was put in jail in New York in 1899. He was reputedly the first motorist to be arrested for speeding. His offense was doing twelve miles an hour, and he was arrested by a patrolman on a bicycle!

The church in Antioch in New Testament times experienced a "first." These followers of Christ were the first to be given the name, *Christian.* It was in Antioch also that, for the first time, the followers of Jesus joined together in a fellowship of Jews and Gentiles. These disciples were eager to be taught of the Lord and were willing to accept one another in spite of cultural differences. In these they are still an example to all of us as to what it means to be "Christian."
—C. R. B.

III. A Church Helping
(Acts 11:29, 30)

Possibly Barnabas reported to the church in Jerusalem that more teachers were needed in Antioch. Whether he did or not, some prophets came. One of them foretold a severe famine, which came very soon (Acts 11:27, 28).

A. Help for the Needy (v. 29)

29. Then the disciples, every man according to his ability, determined to send relief unto the brethren which dwelt in Judea.

The famine was most difficult for the disciples in Jerusalem, for two reasons:

1. Those who had money or property had used it for the support of those who had none. This was necessary in the beginning of the church. The disciples left their jobs to gather daily and hear the apostles' teaching (Acts 2:42-47). Some were soon out of funds, but the surplus of others cared for them. Thus all of the disciples could be taught intensively day after day. The wisdom of this was shown when many of the disciples were driven from Jerusalem. They were so well taught by the apostles that they were able to teach others wherever they went (Acts 8:1, 4). Thus the church spread swiftly through Judea and Samaria and then to places farther away.

2. In the persecution when disciples were jailed or driven from Jerusalem, probably much of their remaining property was confiscated.

For these two reasons the Christians in Judea were poorer than those in Antioch and elsewhere. When food was scarce and costly, the suffering was greater where the people were poorer.

Men of Cyprus and Cyrene first gave the gospel to the Gentiles in Antioch, but those men had been taught in Jerusalem. The good news of salvation came from Judea to Antioch, and the saved in Antioch thought it was only fair to send help back to Judea in time of need.

B. Chosen Messengers (v. 30)

30. Which also they did, and sent it to the elders by the hands of Barnabas and Saul.

These two were outstanding preachers in Antioch, and they were fully trusted. Both of them were well known in Jerusalem, having friends and relatives there. They were ideal messengers to carry the offering for the brethren in Judea.

Acts 12:25 records that Barnabas and Saul completed their mission and then went back to Antioch, this time taking John Mark with them. That young man was a relative of Barnabas (Colossians 4:10).

MEETING A NEED

The Great Saint Bernard Pass in the Alps mountains leads from southwestern Switzerland to northwestern Italy. At eighty-one hundred feet in elevation, the pass is snow-covered for nine months of the year. Sixty-five feet is an average year's snowfall.

Bernard of Menthon was sent to the pass in A. D. 1048 to free the area of robbers who preyed upon travelers. While there, he saw another need, this one caused by the severe alpine climate, and he stayed to found a hospice. Aided by the dogs that came to bear his name—"Saint Bernard"—Bernard and his successors saved the lives of more than two thousand travelers. The need for hospice and rescue teams had long existed, but Bernard saw the need and responded to it.

The Christians in the church in Antioch saw the need of the saints in Jerusalem and gladly did what they could to meet it. God has often used ordinary people who have recognized a need and have responded appropriately to it. The church needs people to respond compassionately in the love of Christ. The world needs to know we care.   —C. R. B.

Conclusion

This is the second of thirteen lessons dealing with Saul or Paul, a magnificent servant of Christ. For this one lesson, however, our hero is Barnabas, a magnificent helper who twice gave Saul a start in Christian service.

A. Our Hero

In a Hebrew figure of speech, a man is called a son of something he is fitted for. A son of peace is one whose thoughts and motives and talk and action make him fit for peace (Luke 10:6). A son of perdition is one whose thoughts and motives and speech and actions make him fit for destruction (John 17:12).

The apostles called a man Barnabas (Acts 4:36), and Luke translates that as son of *paraklesis,* which means help or consolation or encouragement or exhortation or counsel. Barnabas showed himself fitted to give all of those things.

He gave help, consolation, and encouragement to many when he sold his property to provide for their needs (Acts 4:37).

He gave help, counsel, and encouragement to Saul when he brought him to the apostles (Acts 9:27), and again to Antioch (Acts 11:25, 26).

He gave help, counsel, exhortation, and encouragement to the brethren in Antioch (Acts 11:23-26).

He brought help, consolation, and encouragement from Antioch to Jerusalem, and probably gave exhortation and counsel too (vv. 29, 30).

Often quoted is Jesus' word of commendation to Mary of Bethany: "She hath done what she could" (Mark 14:8). That same word may well be spoken of Barnabas. He did what he could with his talents. He did not bury a talent in the ground (Matthew 25:25); he did not hide his light (5:15). He used every talent he had and gave light to many.

"She hath done what she could." Do all of us merit that accolade?

B. What Are You Fitted For?

The editor of this book hopes I am a son of writing, fitted to write these lessons.

Perhaps you are a son of teaching, fitted to teach these lessons in a class.

Or what is your field of service?

Are you fitted to encourage someone who is sick, read to someone whose eyesight is failing, give companionship to someone who is shut in, tell a neighbor what Jesus had done for you?

Here are some questions to be answered now:

1. What are you fitted to do to help someone?
2. Who needs it?
3. What day of this week will you do it?

C. Prayer

Our Father and our Creator, You have given us minds to think and muscles to move and hearts to love. We know they are not given for our selfish pleasure. So guide our thinking and moving and loving that we will help others and bring glory to You. In Jesus' name, amen.

D. Thought to Remember

Help somebody today.

Home Daily Bible Readings

Monday, Sept. 2—Barnabas Takes Saul to the Apostles (Acts 9:23-31)
Tuesday, Sept. 3—Barnabas is Sent to Antioch (Acts 11:19-24)
Wednesday, Sept. 4—Barnabas Takes Saul to Antioch (Acts 11:25-30)
Thursday, Sept. 5—Saul and Barnabas Sent as Missionaries (Acts 12:25-13:3)
Friday, Sept. 6—Taught by Christ, Not Men (Galatians 1:11-17)
Saturday, Sept. 7—From Persecutor to Preacher (Galatians 1:18-24)
Sunday, Sept. 8—Standing Fast for the Gospel (Galatians 2:1-5)

Learning by Doing

This page contains an alternate lesson plan emphasizing learning activities. Classes desiring such student involvement will find these suggestions helpful.

Learning Goals

This lesson will help students:

1. Trace the development of Saul from his conversion to the time when he became a leader in the church.

2. Identify factors in Saul's development.

3. Cooperate with God in His development of their lives for service in His behalf.

Into the Lesson

Write this statement on the chalkboard before class: *Leaders are made, not born.* Begin the session by asking those who agree with the statement to raise their hands. Then ask those who disagree to raise their hands. Ask for volunteers to defend their position, and allow several minutes for discussion.

Then say, "Today we continue our study of the apostle Paul. We will focus on his early years as a follower of Christ, when his name was Saul. Without doubt, this energetic man had many traits of a born leader. He needed more training, however, before God was ready to 'turn him loose' as a leader. Let's explore how God prepared Saul to become an effective leader."

Into the Word

Briefly summarize last week's lesson (Acts 9:1-19). Then mention the points of the outline below. It provides an overview of Saul's early years as a Christian, as recorded in Acts 9-13 and Galatians 1:15-21. It will help if you write this outline on a poster before class and refer to it as you talk:

A. Post-conversion Experiences in Damascus (Acts 9:20-22)

B. Travel to Arabia (Galatians 1:15-17)

C. Return to Damascus (Galatians 1:17)

D. Journey to Jerusalem (Acts 9:23-29; Galatians 1:18)

E. Move to Syria and Cilicia, including Tarsus (Acts 9:30; Galatians 1:21)

F. Move to Antioch to help Barnabas in teaching the church (Acts 11:25, 26)

G. Travel with Barnabas to Judea to deliver aid to the church (Acts 11:29, 30)

H. Return to Antioch (Acts 12:25)

I. Saul and Barnabas are sent out as missionaries (Acts 13:1-3)

Although there is not agreement as to the exact dates of these events, at least ten years passed from the time of Saul's conversion until God directed that Barnabas and Saul be sent out as missionaries.

After presenting the information above, have your class form two groups. Appoint a discussion leader for each group and give the following assignments:

Group One: Read Acts 9:20-30 and discuss:

1. How was Saul initially received by the disciples in Jerusalem ? Why?

2. What did Saul need at this stage of his Christian life?

3. How did Barnabas support Saul?

4. What might the results have been if Barnabas had not taken this action?

Group Two: Read Acts 11:19-30 and discuss:

1. What exciting developments took place in Antioch?

2. What was Barnabas's response when he arrived in Antioch?

3. Why do you suppose Barnabas recruited Saul to assist in the Antioch ministry?

Allow groups ten minutes for discussion. Then ask group leaders to summarize their group's observations for the rest of the class.

Into Life

Add this principle to the leadership poster you began last week: *To be effective as Christian leaders, we must cooperate with God as He develops the necessary qualities in us.*

Suggest that God used many factors in developing Saul for leadership in the church. Then lead the class in discussing these questions, which can be found in the student book:

1. What role did Barnabas play in Saul's development as a Christian leader?

2. What role did rejection and persecution play in Saul's development?

3. What role did time play in Saul's development?

State that God wants us to have a greater impact on the world around us. Then ask students to form groups of three. Write these questions on the chalkboard and have students share their responses in their groups:

1. What is happening in your life that God might use to make you a more effective servant for Him?

2. How can you cooperate with God in this?

Let's Talk It Over

The questions on this page are designed to encourage review of the lesson Scriptures and to promote discussion of the lesson by the class. The answers provided are only discussion starters. Let your class talk it over from there.

1. What did Saul do following his call and conversion? How does that relate to periods of transition in our lives?

Saul spent several days with the disciples in Damascus (Acts 9:19); then he began preaching in the synagogues there. Acts 9:23 states, "After many days had gone by the Jews conspired to kill him" (*New International Version*). Actually, nearly three years had passed. After his brief preaching stint at the outset, Saul went into Arabia, seemingly for almost three years, and then returned to Damascus (Galatians 1:13-13). It was then that his preaching aroused the violent opposition of the Jews.

Times of transition are marked by an end to the old experience, a neutral zone, then a new beginning. Many persons want to go immediately from old endings to new beginnings. They fail to see that the neutral zone is the time when God prepares them for the new beginnings. Paul did not move immediately from being a persecutor of the church to being a missionary to the Gentiles. His three years in the desert, like Jesus' forty days and nights in the wilderness following His baptism, were a time of preparation for his task.

2. Why was Saul rejected by the disciples in Jerusalem when he first tried to join them?

The disciples were afraid of Saul and did not believe that he really was a disciple. After all, this was the infamous persecutor of Christ's followers just a few years earlier. How could they be sure of his honesty and sincerity? They may have felt that Saul was attempting to infiltrate the fellowship in Jerusalem in order to find out who the disciples were and continue his persecution.

3. What role did Barnabas play in this drama?

Barnabas took the role of the advocate! Contrary to the position and suspicions of the disciples at Jerusalem, Barnabas stood up for Saul. He brought Saul to the apostles and affirmed the genuineness of his conversion and the subsequent transformation of his life. This role involved significant risk—it was not the popular stand. Barnabas knew that if the apostles were convinced, they, as leaders in the church, would sway the attitudes and responses of the people. How crucial was Barnabas's role!

4. What kind of person was Barnabas?

The Scriptures speak very highly of Barnabas's character. Acts 11:24 lauds him as a "good man, full of the Holy Spirit and faith," (*New International Version*). He was an enthusiastic, joyous servant of the Lord. This is attested to by the fact that when he first came to Antioch and saw the grace of God bestowed on the church there, "he was glad and encouraged them all to remain true to the Lord with all their hearts: (v. 23, *New International Version*). Not only so, but he went to Tarsus to find and bring Saul to Antioch. Then for an entire year, the two of them labored tirelessly to establish the brethren in the faith. Earlier the apostles assessed the character of Barnabas, who, at the time, was known as Joses, or Joseph. It was they who named him "Barnabas," which means, "son of consolation," or "encouragement" (Acts 4:36). The Biblical record bears out that he lived up to the name the apostles gave him.

5. List some barriers in churches that may exclude certain persons from fellowship in those churches. What do you think a Christian's attitude should be toward such barriers?

Most barriers are social and cultural. Some congregations may appeal only to certain groups within society, and by this means they exclude those of other groups. Persons who are well educated may be welcome in some churches, whereas the opposite may be true in other churches. Whether or not a person possesses wealth may be a barrier of exclusion from certain congregations, as may be one's social standing in the community. All such attitudes are divisive and only harm the church's witness to those persons who are lost in sin. The example of Barnabas in promoting the unity of the diverse peoples who made up the church in Antioch should challenge us all.

6. How can the church today be like the church at Antioch in caring for the needy?

The Christians at Antioch shared their resources with famine victims. Congregations today can assist in feeding the hungry in their own communities and participate in inter-congregational efforts on a national and international level.

A Sermon at Antioch of Pisidia

LESSON SCRIPTURE: Acts 13:1-3, 13-52.

PRINTED TEXT: Acts 13:26-39.

Acts 13:26-39

26 Men and brethren, children of the stock of Abraham, and whosoever among you feareth God, to you is the word of this salvation sent.

27 For they that dwell at Jerusalem, and their rulers, because they knew him not, nor yet the voices of the prophets which are read every sabbath day, they have fulfilled them in condemning him.

28 And though they found no cause of death in him, yet desired they Pilate that he should be slain.

29 And when they had fulfilled all that was written of him, they took him down from the tree, and laid him in a sepulchre.

30 But God raised him from the dead:

31 And he was seen many days of them which came up with him from Galilee to Jeru-salem, who are his witnesses unto the people.

32 And we declare unto you glad tidings, how that the promise which was made unto the fathers,

33 God hath fulfilled the same unto us their children, in that he hath raised up Jesus again; as it is also written in the second psalm, Thou art my Son, this day have I begotten thee.

34 And as concerning that he raised him up from the dead, now no more to return to corruption, he said on this wise, I will give you the sure mercies of David.

35 Wherefore he saith also in another psalm, Thou shalt not suffer thine Holy One to see corruption.

36 For David, after he had served his own generation by the will of God, fell on sleep, and was laid unto his fathers, and saw corruption:

37 But he, whom God raised again, saw no corruption.

38 Be it known unto you therefore, men and brethren, that through this man is preached unto you the forgiveness of sins:

39 And by him all that believe are justified from all things, from which ye could not be justified by the law of Moses.

GOLDEN TEXT: Be it known unto you therefore, men and brethren, that through this man is preached unto you the forgiveness of sins.—Acts 13:38.

From the Damascus Road to Rome
Unit 2. Emerging Leader
(Lessons 3-5)

Lesson Aims

After this lesson students should be able to:
1. Give a short summary or outline of Paul's sermon at Antioch of Pisidia.
2. Describe the results of that sermon.
3. Give a sound reason for believing in Jesus.

Lesson Outline

INTRODUCTION
    A. A New Enterprise
    B. Lesson Background
I. JESUS DIED AND ROSE (Acts 13:26-31)
    A. Death (vv. 26-29)
       A Clear Understanding
    B. Resurrection (vv. 30, 31)
       A Shocking Demonstration of Power
II. PROPHECY FULFILLED (Acts 13:32-37)
    A. Good News! (vv. 32, 33)
    B. Death's Defeat (vv. 34-37)
III. THE MESSIAH'S OFFER (Acts 13:38, 39)
    A. Forgiveness (v. 38)
    B. Justification (v. 39)
CONCLUSION
    A. Incredible Truth
    B. What Can We Believe?
    C. Prayer
    D. Thought to Remember

Visual 3 from the visuals packet shows reasons why we can believe in Jesus. Refer to the visual when appropriate during this session, and especially when presenting the thoughts in part B of the Conclusion. The visual is shown on page 27.

Introduction

As we read of the church in Antioch, of Syria, we learn that "a great number believed, and turned unto the Lord" (Acts 11:21). Reading on, we twice find the phrase "much people" (11:24, 26). In today's English we might say "many people." That phrase tells us the church in Antioch was a big and a growing church.

This big church had many Gentiles among its members, as we saw last week. We saw also that it was a generous church, sending help to famine-stricken Jewish brethren in Judea. (*Refer to the map—visual 1—from the visuals packet.*)

Barnabas and Saul took the offering to Jerusalem; and when they came back, John Mark came with them. He was a kinsman of Barnabas.

A. A New Enterprise

With Barnabas and Saul back from Jerusalem, the Antioch church was well blessed with prophets and teachers. The Holy Spirit said it was time to share. He named Barnabas and Saul to be sent as missionaries, and the church obediently sent them (Acts 13:1-3).

Taking young John Mark along as a helper, the two launched their campaign on the island of Cyprus. This was Barnabas's old home (Acts 4:36, 37). Not many details of their work are recorded, but at this point we see Saul's name changed to Paul (Acts 13:9). The reason for the change is not explained, and probably it is useless to speculate about it; but through the rest of Acts we read the name *Paul* instead of *Saul.*

At this point we see also that Paul was emerging as captain of the team. He took the lead in the striking incident told in Acts 13:6-12. It was "Barnabas and Saul" that came to Cyprus (Acts 13:2, 7); it was "Paul and his company" that left it (Acts 13:13).

From the west end of the island they sailed north to the mainland of Asia Minor. For reasons unknown to us, John Mark left them and went back home to Jerusalem. Paul and Barnabas went inland and came to the great city of Antioch. This is called "Antioch in Pisidia" to distinguish it from the Antioch where the missionaries had worked before they began their journey (Acts 13:13, 14).

When the Sabbath Day came, Paul and Barnabas went to the regular meeting in the Jewish synagogue. After the customary readings from the Scriptures, the visitors were invited to speak. Paul responded (Acts 13:14-16).

B. Lesson Background

He emphasized God's leading and God's care from the time of Moses to the time of David. He declared that God, according to His ancient promise, had given Israel a Savior who was a descendant of David. He named the Savior: Jesus (Acts 13:16-25). Our text gives us the next part of Paul's sermon.

How to Say It

ANTIOCH. *An*-tee-ock.
CHALDEANS. Kal-*dee*-unz.
HABAKKUK. Hu-*bak*-kuk.
PISIDIA. Pih-*sid*-ee-uh.

I. Jesus Died and Rose
(Acts 13:26-31)

Paul probably said much more than is recorded. He may have explained at some length that Jesus' death atoned for the sins of the world and His resurrection brought life and immortality to light. Luke's short summary gives just the facts of His death and resurrection.

A. Death (vv. 26-29)

26. Men and brethren, children of the stock of Abraham, and whosoever among you feareth God, to you is the word of this salvation sent.

Some among the Gentiles had lost confidence in the imaginary gods and traditional myths and had come to believe in the one true God. Without becoming Jews, they went to the synagogue meeting to worship with the Jews and listen to the teaching. Paul saw the mixed group of Jews and Gentiles. He addressed the Jews as *children of the stock of Abraham;* but he also addressed the God-fearing Gentiles: *whosoever among you feareth God.* Likewise in the beginning of his sermon he spoke both to "men of Israel" and to other God-fearing men (v. 16).

To you is the word of this salvation sent. Paul had said that God had sent a Savior, Jesus (v. 23). Now he added that the message of His salvation was sent both to people of Israel and to God-fearing Gentiles.

27. For they that dwell at Jerusalem, and their rulers, because they knew him not, nor yet the voices of the prophets which are read every sabbath day, they have fulfilled them in condemning him.

Paul may have explained this in some detail. The people and rulers of Jerusalem did not recognize Jesus as the promised Savior, because they misinterpreted the prophecies in the Scriptures. They thought the Savior must sit on a throne in Jerusalem and rule with military might. The rulers thought the promised Savior would work with them. Jesus was not what they thought the Savior would be, so they rejected Him and killed Him—and in doing this they fulfilled the prophecies that said He would be despised and rejected and led as a lamb to the slaughter (Isaiah 53).

A CLEAR UNDERSTANDING

Have you ever tried making sense of your insurance policies? Most of us who lack training in *legalese* find it difficult, if not impossible. This is not a new problem. In 1596, an English judge grew so upset with the wordiness of a 120-page document filed in his court that he ordered a hole cut through its center. Then the head of the lawyer who wrote it was stuffed through the hole, and he was led through the court to be exhibited to all in attendance.

Recently, attempts have been made to simplify and clarify legal language. It may be hopeless, however. Defenders of legalese argue that it is necessary to make the language so precise as to withstand any legal challenge. Opponents counter by saying that much of it is imprecise and unnecessary to make legal writing clear.

The legal minds of Jesus' time were intent on arguing about the Scriptures, and more particularly their interpretations of it. They had so clouded the Scriptures' prophecies concerning the Messiah that when Jesus came and said, "I am He," they rejected Him.

As we try to know God's will and tell others about it, we must not make the faith so profound that we miss its simple truth and keep others from seeing Jesus.   —C. R. B.

28. And though they found no cause of death in him, yet desired they Pilate that he should be slain.

Jesus was not a criminal. He could not be convicted of crime, not even by perjured testimony (Mark 14:55-59). Pilate repeatedly declared Him innocent (John 18:38; 19:4, 6). Still the rulers increased their pressure till Pilate sent Jesus to His death (John 19:12-16).

29. And when they had fulfilled all that was written of him, they took him down from the tree, and laid him in a sepulchre.

By the people and rulers in Jerusalem Jesus was despised and rejected and slain just as the prophets had foretold. He was dead and buried, and His enemies thought they were through with Him. But God was not through.

B. Resurrection (vv. 30, 31)

30. But God raised him from the dead.

Nobody defeats God. Nobody! It was necessary for the Savior to die to atone for the sins of men, but it was necessary for Him to live and rule forever. With God nothing is impossible.

visual 3

31. And he was seen many days of them which came up with him from Galilee to Jerusalem, who are his witnesses unto the people.

Even those who believed in God might find it hard to believe that He had restored Jesus to life, but the testimony was certain. The risen Jesus was seen many times by people who knew Him well, and those people were still living to bear witness to the truth.

A SHOCKING DEMONSTRATION OF POWER

"Shock art" is a recent fad among those who seek to promote themselves into fame (or at least notoriety) as artists. The intent seems to be to see who can be the most outrageous in flouting convention—or good taste—in the name of "art."

One such "artist" dances and slides around barefoot on broken glass. A defender tries to dignify such foolishness by saying, "He is actually composing on the glass." Another "artist" ran afoul of the law recently when he set off fireworks on his chest and the audience was hit with burning shards.

God has done some surprising things, too, but not for the same reasons as the "artists" we've mentioned. When God raised Jesus from the dead, there were a lot of shocked people. Jewish leaders were shocked, because they thought they had rid themselves of a nuisance. Jesus' followers were amazed, because the events leading up to the crucifixion seemed to indicate Jesus really didn't have the power to establish His kingdom.

When the gospel was eventually preached to the Gentiles, they were overwhelmed that the life-giving benefits of the resurrection extended even to them. The resurrection of Christ is an astonishing demonstration to everyone that He is God.
—C. R. B.

II. Prophecy Fulfilled
(Acts 13:32-37)

We have seen that prophecy was fulfilled in the death of Jesus (v. 27), but that was only one item among many. Other prophecies were fulfilled in His birth, in His life and work, and in His resurrection. Paul mentioned especially the resurrection.

A. Good News! (vv. 32, 33)

32, 33. And we declare unto you glad tidings, how that the promise which was made unto the fathers, God hath fulfilled the same unto us their children, in that he hath raised up Jesus again; as it is also written in the second psalm, Thou art my Son, this day have I begotten thee.

Unto the fathers, the ancestors of the Jewish people, God had promised a Messiah, a Savior, a Redeemer, a Ruler. Through centuries of history He had repeated that promise many times. Jews everywhere knew and treasured the promise. Now Paul brought good news. At last God had kept His promise. Jesus was the promised Messiah.

He hath raised up Jesus may be taken to mean that God raised Jesus from the dead, but in this verse it may have a wider meaning. *Raised up* may be used as it is in Judges 2:16 and Acts 7:37, meaning that God provided Jesus, sent Him to fulfill the promise of a Savior.

The second psalm is one of the many prophecies of the Messiah. To the Messiah God said, *Thou art my Son*. This was literally fulfilled when God spoke from Heaven to say to Jesus,"Thou art my beloved Son" (Mark 1:11). Paul was speaking in the synagogue. Many people that were there were well acquainted with that psalm. They would remember its promise that the Messiah would overcome the mighty ones who would oppose Him. He would rule a worldwide realm. The psalm also carries a warning against rejecting Him.

B. Death's Defeat (vv. 34-37)

34. And as concerning that he raised him up from the dead, now no more to return to corruption, he said on this wise, I will give you the sure mercies of David.

Now Paul spoke specifically of the resurrection: *he raised him up from the dead*. That too had been foretold. Paul alluded to Isaiah 55:3: "I will make an everlasting covenant with you, even the sure mercies of David." In mercy God had given David victory and dominion over a great kingdom, but He had given more than that. He had given "an everlasting covenant," a promise of an eternal kingdom ruled by David's descendant, the Messiah (Psalm 89:2-4). That promise now was fulfilled in Jesus the Messiah and the people who accepted and obeyed Him.

35. Wherefore he saith also in another psalm, Thou shalt not suffer thine Holy One to see corruption.

Psalm 16 is another one that foretold the Messiah. Paul quoted verse 10 from it.

36. For David, after he had served his own generation by the will of God, fell on sleep, and was laid unto his fathers, and saw corruption.

Psalm 16 is one of David's songs. With God's help that great king served well in his own time. But that time was long past when Paul spoke. *Fell on sleep* means David died. *Laid unto his fathers* means he was buried as his forefathers had been. *Saw corruption* means his body decayed in the tomb. This made it plain that the quotation in verse 35 was not describing David.

37. But he, whom God raised again, saw no corruption.

Jesus too was laid in a tomb, but only for a short time. His body did not decay. God restored it to life, never to die again (Romans 6:9). The promise of no corruption is fulfilled in Him and in no other. This is powerful evidence that Jesus is indeed the promised Messiah.

III. The Messiah's Offer
(Acts 13:38, 39)

It was not easy for Jews to believe that Jesus was the Messiah. He had not freed them from the rule of Rome. He had not taken over the government of Israel. He had not subdued any of the other nations. He had not done any of the things they hoped the Messiah would do. If Jesus was the Messiah, what would anyone gain by following Him? Very briefly Paul explained. The Messiah offered more than military victory and earthly rule.

A. Forgiveness (v. 38)

38. Be it known unto you therefore, men and brethren, that through this man is preached unto you the forgiveness of sins.

It is sad that most of the people of the world do not realize how great a thing it is to be forgiven. This is a matter of life and death. "All have sinned" (Romans 3:23). "The wages of sin is death" (Romans 6:23). The only way to escape death is to be forgiven, and forgiveness can be announced only *through this man,* Jesus. He and no one else died for our sins. He and He only suffered the death that we deserve, and so set us free from sin and death. Only because He died for us can we escape death and live forever. "There is none other name under heaven given among men, whereby we must be saved" (Acts 4:12).

B. Justification (v. 39)

39. And by him all that believe are justified from all things, from which ye could not be justified by the law of Moses.

Forgiveness and justification are two sides of the same thing. Forgiveness takes away our sins, and that is how we are justified, made just. The law of Moses prescribed sacrifices to be offered to atone for sins, but the lives of animals cannot really atone for the sins of people (Hebrews 10:4). By the prescribed sacrifices the sins of men were acknowledged and remembered (Hebrews 10:3), not removed. The sacrifice of Jesus, however, can and does take away sins (Hebrews 10:14). It is enough to atone for all the sins of the world (1 John 2:2). It actually does atone for the sins of *all that believe.* Believing in Jesus makes the difference between being guilty and being justified, between being lost and being saved, between dying and living. Just saying we believe is not enough. "Not every one that saith unto me, Lord, Lord, shall enter into the kingdom of heaven; but he that doeth the will of my Father which is in heaven" (Matthew 7:21). We are "justified by faith" (Romans 5:1), but "not by faith only" (James 2:24). We must trust and obey.

Some people do not care about forgiveness and justification because they do not take their sins seriously. "I'm not such a bad guy." "Lots of people are worse than I am." "I'm as good as you are." "I'm a pretty good sort of person." "I'm good enough without Jesus." Wrong! No one is good enough till the Savior takes his sins away. Jesus is the only hope.

Conclusion

What happened next? We can hardly leave this lesson without a glance at the rest of the story. What more did Paul have to say? What was the result?

A. Incredible Truth

We have long been accustomed to think of the meek and lowly Jesus, the prince of peace, the king of a spiritual kingdom, ruling with love and not with military power. It is hard for us to imagine what a shock it was to the Jews to be told that the Messiah had come, but that He was not going to demolish all the enemies of Israel and rule a vast empire from His capital in Jerusalem.

Paul knew very well how hard it was for the Jews to accept Jesus. He himself had been a stubborn unbeliever till he had seen Jesus. In Damascus and in Jerusalem he had faced unbelief as stubborn as his own. Certainly he would not be surprised if he faced some of the same in Antioch.

There was nothing wrong with the message Paul brought. It was God's message. It was exactly right. It was what the hearers needed. But it seemed incredible to many hearers because their expectations were wrong. They were not willing to give up their own wishes and accept God's way, and so they denied that God's way was really His.

Think of the twentieth-century unbelievers you know. What mistaken expectations do they have, what wrong preconceptions, what selfish wishes that keep them from accepting the gospel? How can you help them?

How often God does things that seem incredible to many people! In ancient times there was evil in Judah—such evil that Habakkuk could hardly believe God was tolerating it (Habakkuk 1:2-4). God was going to end that evil with something even more incredible, an act so horrible that many would not believe the announcement of it (Habakkuk 1:5). He was going to bring the Chaldeans to destroy Judah (Habakkuk 1:6, 7). Incredible as it seemed, the Chaldeans came, and unbelieving Judah was destroyed.

Paul knew many in Antioch would not believe his teaching about Jesus. Solemnly he warned them with words from Habakkuk 1:5, quoting the Greek version: "Behold, ye despisers, and wonder, and perish: for I work a work in your days, a work which ye shall in no wise believe, though a man declare it unto you" (Acts 13:40, 41).

What incredible work was God doing in the days of Paul? He sent Jesus the Messiah, not to crush Rome and deliver Israel by a mighty military campaign, but to save His people from their sins by dying in their place. That was unbelievable to the Jews whose hearts were set on military conquest, but those who would not believe would die in their sins. With that warning Paul ended his sermon in Antioch.

So it is today. Whatever the reason for unbelief, those who do not believe in Jesus must die. "In none other is there salvation" (Acts 4:12, *American Standard Version*).

B. What Can We Believe?

"Don't believe all you hear." That's good advice. Advertisers, politicians, propagandists, and gossips bombard us with half truths and whole falsehoods.

"Don't reject all you hear." That's good advice too. In a changing world we cripple ourselves if we don't keep on learning.

What can we believe? That's a hard question. We can't be sure a statement is true just because we hear it from a friend or someone we admire. Friends and fine people can be mistaken, and so can popular entertainers, excellent athletes, scholars, scientists, and statesmen.

On the other hand, we can't reject a statement just because it comes from a crook or a scoundrel.

"When in doubt, check it out." That also is good advice. We can look up some things in the dictionary or the encyclopedia or the Bible. But some things can't be checked so easily, and we don't want to make up our minds too quickly. It's better to be in doubt than to be wrong. As Will Rogers put it, being ignorant ain't so bad as knowing things that ain't so.

It's bad to be unstable, always changing our minds, "tossed to and fro, and carried about with every wind of doctrine" (Ephesians 4:14). On the other hand, it's bad to be so stubbornly fixed in our opinions that we even resist the Holy Spirit, "Ye stiffnecked and uncircumcised in heart and ears, ye do always resist the Holy Ghost: as your fathers did, so do ye" (Acts 7:51).

What can we believe? We can believe what is supported by good and ample evidence. We can believe Jesus rose from the dead. There is abundant testimony to prove it (Acts 13:30, 31). Paul gives a list of witnesses in 1 Corinthians 15:3-8. The resurrection is a fact. And since God raised Jesus from the dead, it is reasonable to believe that Jesus had God's approval. If He was approved of God, it is reasonable to believe He is all he claimed to be: the Son of God, the Savior of the world, the final judge, the king eternal. We can believe in Jesus.

C. Prayer

Our Father in Heaven, holy and righteous and almighty forever, humbly we confess that we have sinned and have come short of Your glory. How good it is to know that You have sent a Savior for us and that You have given us a sure basis for believing in Him! Thank You for announcing Him clearly through the ages before He came. Thank You for approving Him while He lived on earth and for showing Your approval again by raising Him from the dead. With grateful hearts we pledge our loyalty to Jesus, and we ask Your help in being true. In Jesus name, amen.

D. Thought to Remember

We can believe in Jesus.

Home Daily Bible Readings

Monday, Sept. 9—The Gospel Preached at Cyprus (Acts 13:4-12)

Tuesday, Sept. 10—The Gospel Preached at Antioch (Acts 13:13-25)

Wednesday, Sept. 11—A Savior From David's Posterity (Acts 13:26-39)

Thursday, Sept. 12—Paul and Barnabas Preach to Gentiles (Acts 13:40-52)

Friday, Sept. 13—Redeemed by Faith, Not Works (Galatians 3:10-14)

Saturday, Sept. 14—The Promise to Abraham Fulfilled in Christ (Galatians 3:15-20)

Sunday, Sept. 15—Freedom Forever, Slavery Never!

Learning by Doing

*This page contains an alternate lesson plan emphasizing learning activities. Classes
desiring such student involvement will find these suggestions helpful.*

Learning Goals

This lesson, should equip students to:

1. Sift out the main points of Paul's sermon at
Antioch of Pisidia.

2. List core truths of the Christian faith.

3. Share these truths with another person during the coming week.

Into the Lesson

Write this question on the chalkboard: *What
would it take for most Christians to be more effective
in communicating their faith to non-Christians?* Then
ask your class members to pair off and discuss
this question. Give each pair a piece of paper
and a pen. Challenge them to think of at least
five ideas.

Allow two minutes for this. Then ask everyone to come together as a large group. As volunteers share the ideas they compiled, write their
suggestions on the chalkboard.

Make the transition into the Bible study by
saying, "One of the factors that enables the apostle Paul to be an effective leader is that he was
able to communicate his faith with accuracy,
clarity, and power. Today we will look at an example of how he communicated the gospel of
Jesus Christ."

Into the Word

To connect this lesson with last week's lesson,
present a brief lecture based on the information
from the Introduction section. (Limit this to
three to five minutes.)

After establishing this background, direct
class members to form groups of four to six. Appoint a leader for each group and provide each
group with paper and a pen. Instruct the groups
first to read Acts 13:17-39. Then have them examine each of the following sections and write a
summary of it in fifteen words or less:

verses 17-20
verses 21, 22
verses 23-25
verses 26-31
verses 32-37
verses 38, 39

Allow twelve to fifteen minutes for this activity. When the time is up, ask each group for
their summary for the first section, then for the
second, and so on until you have covered all
sections in the passage.

Into Life

Focus on the fact that when Paul was invited
to speak in the synagogue (v. 15), he was prepared to communicate his faith accurately and
clearly. The third principle for effective leadership, therefore, is this: *Effective Christian leaders
are able to communicate the basic truths of the faith.*
Add this principle to the chart you began in lesson one.

Emphasize that whether or not we consider
ourselves to be leaders, God wants all of us to
grow in our ability to communicate our faith.
We may not be able to speak before groups, but
we can speak to individuals. Every Christian
possesses, and is expected to share, the life-giving message of Christ.

Help your class members to zero in on the
core truths of the Christian faith by asking this
question: "What key truths would you need to
share with a non-Christian to introduce that person to the salvation God offers? As students volunteer their answers, list them on the
chalkboard. Here are a few core truths that you
will want to be sure is included: God exists,
Jesus is God's Son, every person has sinned
against God, Jesus died for our sins and rose
from the dead for our justification.

After you complete the list, give each student
a piece of paper and a pen. Ask them to imagine
that they are writing to a friend to explain their
faith and to encourage their friend to accept
Jesus as Savior and Lord. Then have them write
the letter. Let them know that this activity is a
means for them to practice communicating their
faith. Allow ten to fifteen minutes, depending
on your class schedule.

Suggest to your students that they practice
witnessing with another Christian. Expressing
their faith to a person who is non-threatening
will help them to be better prepared when they
encounter an opportunity to witness to a non-
Christian.

Ask students to think of someone with whom
they will try to share their faith in the coming
week, whether that person is someone who
needs to be saved, or is a Christian who is willing to help them practice.

Close the session by praying that God will
help your class members share their faith with
courage and confidence, and that He will create
opportunities for each person to do so.

Let's Talk It Over

The questions on this page are designed to encourage review of the lesson Scriptures and to promote discussion of the lesson by the class. The answers provided are only discussion starters. Let your class talk it over from there.

1. Why did Paul and Barnabas go to the synagogue on the Sabbath during their missionary journey?

Paul and Barnabas went to the synagogue because there they would find an appropriate audience for their message. Jews and "God-fearing" Gentiles gathered every Sabbath to worship God and to study the Scriptures. These people believed in God and looked for the coming of the Messiah spoken of by the prophets. It was only natural, therefore, that the message about Jesus Christ should be taken to those with such a background of preparation.

2. According to Paul's sermon, what is the pivotal and conclusive fact of the gospel? Why is it so important?

Paul focused on the historical fact of the bodily resurrection of Jesus Christ, which was verified by many witnesses. If God did not raise Jesus from the dead, then prophecy is incorrect, His personal claims were false, the Christian religion has but a dead martyr like many other world religions, and all who believe in Him have no hope of living beyond this life. *Everything* hinges on the fact that Jesus triumphed over death and the grave, and that He is alive and in God's presence now. We worship and serve a risen and living Lord.

3. Paul says that through Jesus we receive forgiveness of sins and we are justified from all things that we could not be justified from by the law of Moses. Describe "forgiveness" and what it means to be "justified." How are they related?

"Forgiveness" relates to sin, which alienates a person from God. Forgiveness removes a person's sin, thus releasing one from the guilt that sin produces and from the penalty that it demands.

To be "justified" is to be considered righteous. It is a legal term, and it implies that a person is declared guilty and unrighteous by law, but is treated as "not guilty" by the forgiving grace and love of God. To be justified means that a person stands before God "just as if" he or she had not sinned.

Forgiveness and justification are two sides of the same thing. Forgiveness removes our sins, and that is how we are justified, made just.

4. The Jews expected the Messiah to come as an earthly potentate, to conquer and to rule. Their perspective was invalid. What are some perspectives that people today have about Jesus Christ?

Some see Jesus as "healer" and expect Him to heal them of all their sickness and disease. Some see Him as "rescuer" and expect Him to rescue them from trouble and crisis. Some see Jesus as "benefactor" and expect Him to give them all the good things they want. Others see Him as "protector," expecting Him to protect them from all harm and injury. The list goes on, but one common thread runs through all of these expectations. People maintain dominant perspectives that distort the character and ministry of Jesus. Their expectations are tied more to their own desires and manipulations than to the revealed nature and mission of Jesus. He *does* heal, rescue, benefit, and protect His people, but none of these is His dominant or sole purpose. He wants to be Lord of all of life. Many people seem to want Him for what they deem He can do for them, but they are slow to make Him Lord!

5. What is the difference between belief and faith?

Belief involves intellectual assent to something that is offered for acceptance. Faith results when belief is coupled with trust. The formula is: belief plus trust equals faith. There were those in Jesus' day who believed He was who He claimed to be (God), but they did not have faith in Him—they would not trust themselves to Him. James 2:19 reveals that even demons believe, and tremble—but they do not have faith.

6. What is the basis for faith?

Faith is based on witness and testimony. It differs from credulity, which is readiness to believe, especially on slight or uncertain evidence. Credulity arises out of speculation, guesses, and imagination. Faith involves none of these. It arises out of historical evidence. For this reason, Paul marshals his evidence and witnesses for Jesus' resurrection. Faith is not some "grand guess," but rather believing and trusting Jesus Christ on the basis of reliable witnesses who had seen the risen Lord (Acts 13:30, 31).

A Healing in Lystra

LESSON SCRIPTURE: Acts 14.

PRINTED TEXT: Acts 14:8-18.

Acts 14:8-18

8 And there sat a certain man at Lystra, impotent in his feet, being a cripple from his mother's womb, who never had walked:

9 The same heard Paul speak: who steadfastly beholding him, and perceiving that he had faith to be healed,

10 Said with a loud voice, Stand upright on thy feet. And he leaped and walked.

11 And when the people saw what Paul had done, they lifted up their voices, saying in the speech of Lycaonia, The gods are come down to us in the likeness of men.

12 And they called Barnabas, Jupiter; and Paul, Mercurius, because he was the chief speaker.

13 Then the priest of Jupiter, which was before their city, brought oxen and garlands unto the gates, and would have done sacrifice with the people.

14 Which when the apostles, Barnabas and Paul, heard of, they rent their clothes, and ran in among the people, crying out,

15 And saying, Sirs, why do ye these things? We also are men of like passions with you, and preach unto you that ye should turn from these vanities unto the living God, which made heaven, and earth, and the sea, and all things that are therein:

16 Who in times past suffered all nations to walk in their own ways.

17 Nevertheless he left not himself without witness, in that he did good, and gave us rain from heaven, and fruitful seasons, filling our hearts with food and gladness.

18 And with these sayings scarce restrained they the people, that they had not done sacrifice unto them.

GOLDEN TEXT: Paul . . . steadfastly beholding him, and perceiving that he had faith to be healed, said with a loud voice, Stand upright on thy feet. And he leaped and walked.—Acts 14:9, 10.

Lesson Aims

After this lesson students should be able to:

1. Recall the main features of Paul's adventure in Lystra (preaching, healing, attempted worship, stoning).

2. From Paul's work seen in this and previous lessons, make at least three suggestions for modern missionaries.

3. Specify one thing the students themselves will do this week in Christian service.

Lesson Outline

INTRODUCTION
  A. Two Antiochs
  B. Lesson Background
  I. MIRACLE (Acts 14:8-10)
  A. Hopeless Case (v. 8)
  B. Faith (v. 9)
  C. Healing (v. 10)
 II. MISUNDERSTANDING (Acts 14:11-13)
  A. Heathen Error (vv. 11, 12)
  B. Heathen Action (v. 13)
III. EXPLANATION (Acts 14:14-18)
  A. Correction (vv. 14, 15)
      A Proper Sense of Humility
  B. Evidence (vv. 16, 17)
  C. Result (v. 18)
 IV. THE REST OF THE STORY (Acts 14:19-23)
  A. Opposition
  B. Success
  C. Follow-up
CONCLUSION
  A. Messages for Missionaries
  B. Stones for You
  C. Getting Personal
  D. Prayer
  E. Thought to Remember

Display visual 4 from the visuals packet as you present the thoughts in part B of the Conclusion section. The visual is shown on page 36.

Introduction

"When they persecute you in this city, flee ye into another" (Matthew 10:23). That was what Jesus told His apostles when He sent them out to preach while He himself was still teaching on earth. Paul later followed those instructions. He fled from Damascus (Acts 9:22-25) and from Jerusalem (Acts 9:28-30). In both of those cases his life was in danger.

A. Two Antiochs

It seems that there was no such violent opposition in Antioch of Syria, where Paul and Barnabas worked effectively till the Holy Spirit called them away. Last week we studied Paul's sermon in the synagogue of Antioch of Pisidia. Sometime afterward there was persecution again. Jews who rejected the gospel were angry with the preachers. This time they used their influence with civic leaders and had Paul and Barnabas thrown out of town. The missionaries then moved on to another city, Iconium (Acts 13:44-51).

B. Lesson Background

The synagogues of Damascus, Jerusalem, and Antioch were the places where Paul had found violent opposition. Nevertheless he and Barnabas promptly began to preach in the synagogue at Iconium. God's plan was to offer the gospel to all the world, but to the Jews first (Romans 1:16). The synagogue was the place to reach the Jews. Repeated persecution should not make us think synagogue preaching was useless. In Antioch many Jews followed Paul and Barnabas (Acts 13:43), and in Iconium "a great multitude both of the Jews and also of the Greeks believed" (Acts 14:1). There was opposition, but not enough to keep Paul and Barnabas from preaching there a "long time." People were the more ready to listen to these preachers because "the Lord . . . granted signs and wonders to be done by their hands" (Acts 14:3). Seeing the work of God done by them, many believed that the word of God was spoken by them. Their success made the opposition more bitter. When the enemies planned to stone Paul and Barnabas, the preachers went on to Lystra and Derbe (Acts 14:4-7). As we study our lesson text for today we will find out what happened at Lystra.

I. Miracle
(Acts 14:8-10)

There is no mention of a synagogue in Lystra, probably because there were not enough Jews to have one. The city seems to have been thoroughly Gentile and thoroughly pagan. We are not told where Paul and Barnabas found a place for preaching there. Later in Athens Paul taught in both synagogue and market (Acts 17:17). Perhaps he and Barnabas found an audience in the marketplace of Lystra.

How to Say It

ANTIOCH. *An*-tee-ock.
DERBE. *Der*-be.
HERMES. *Hur*-mez.
ICONIUM. Eye-*ko*-nee-um.
LYCAONIA. *Lik*-uh-*o*-ni-uh (strong accent on *o*.)
LYSTRA. *Liss*-truh.
MERCURIUS. Mur-*koo*-ri-us.
PISIDIA. Pih-*sid*-ee-uh.
ZEUS. Zoose.

A. Hopeless Case (v. 8)

8. And there sat a certain man at Lystra, impotent in his feet, being a cripple from his mother's womb, who never had walked.

This reminds us of another lame man who sat begging by the temple gate in Jerusalem (Acts 3:1-10). Perhaps the lame man in Lystra was a beggar too, or possibly he was sitting in a market booth and selling merchandise. We have no information about what he was doing; but we know his feet were powerless, he could not walk, and he had been in that condition all his life. Doctors could do nothing in such a case. Today, with all the marvels of science and technology, he probably would have a wheelchair.

B. Faith (v. 9)

9. The same heard Paul speak: who steadfastly beholding him, and perceiving that he had faith to be healed.

How we would like to know just what the crippled man heard Paul say! No doubt he was talking about Jesus. Perhaps he was saying that God approved of Jesus and showed His approval by the remarkable miracles of healing done by Him (Acts 2:22). He may have said this so convincingly that the lame man believed he too could be healed. Perhaps that conviction was plain in the man's eager face—but the Biblical record gives us no such details. It says Paul looked at the man and perceived that he had faith to be healed. Paul's perception may have been prompted by the Holy Spirit, but the record does not say so.

In many Scriptures we see faith associated with miracles (Matthew 8:13; 9:22, 29; Mark 9:23; 10:52; Luke 8:50; 17:19). That does not mean God is unable to do a miracle for someone who has no faith. Miracles were done to show God's approval of the one through whom or in whose name they were done (Acts 2:22). They were done whenever God willed, but many of them were done in response to faith.

C. Healing (v. 10)

10. Said with a loud voice, Stand upright on thy feet. And he leaped and walked.

Paul gave the command *with a loud voice* so the crowd could hear it. The man had faith enough to try to obey, and God gave him strength enough to succeed. His lifelong handicap was ended; he was free of it.

II. Misunderstanding (Acts 14:11-13)

God was unknown in Lystra. The people worshiped the imaginary gods of the Greeks who had conquered them several centuries earlier. They interpreted the miracle in the light of their mistaken belief, and so misunderstood the meaning of what they saw.

A. Heathen Error (vv. 11, 12)

11. And when the people saw what Paul had done, they lifted up their voices, saying in the speech of Lycaonia, The gods are come down to us in the likeness of men.

Lycaonia was the region where Lystra was situated. Alexander the Great and his Greek army had subdued that country more than three hundred years prior to the time of Christ. The Greeks then had made a strenuous effort to impose their language and culture on the conquered people. Lystra had adopted the Greek religion, or perhaps had merely given the names of Greek gods to their own ancient tribal deities. Most of the people were able to use the Greek language as fluently as their own. Paul probably spoke Greek while he was among them, but they used their own language when they cried out in excitement that gods in human form were visiting them.

12. And they called Barnabas, Jupiter; and Paul, Mercurius, because he was the chief speaker.

Zeus was the name the Greeks gave to the supposed father of their mythical family of gods, but in Roman mythology the father of gods was called Jupiter. In seventeenth-century England the Roman myths were more popular than the Greek, and so in the *King James Version* we read *Jupiter* instead of *Zeus*. Likewise we see *Mercurius* or *Mercury* instead of the Greek *Hermes*. This was the name of the mythical messenger of the gods. The people of Lystra supposed Paul was Hermes, *because he was the chief speaker*. It is generally supposed that Barnabas was a bigger man physically, and therefore more likely to be recognized as the father and chief of the gods.

visual 4

B. Heathen Action (v. 13)

13. Then the priest of Jupiter, which was before their city, brought oxen and garlands unto the gates, and would have done sacrifice with the people.

It seems that Zeus or Jupiter was the patron deity of Lystra, supposed to be the special protector of the city. *Jupiter, which was before their city,* may refer to a statue of the god that had been placed at the main entrance as watchman and defender. Some students think a temple had been built there for the god, perhaps along with his statue. Since a sacrifice was planned, we suppose there was an altar there. It is possible that statue, altar, and temple were there together. Whatever was to be seen before their city, the people thought their special god now was visiting them in the flesh. A sacrifice and a celebration were in order. The priest of Jupiter hurried to bring *oxen* decorated with *garlands* of flowers.

III. Explanation
(Acts 14:14-18)

It may have taken some time for Paul and Barnabas to find out what was going on. The people were shouting in their own language, and the priest may have had his oxen at the gate before anyone translated the shouting for the preachers. But Paul and Barnabas were Jews. The thought of sacrifice to anyone but Jehovah was abhorrent to them, and so was the idea that any man except Jesus could be divine. As soon as they knew what was going on, they protested with vigor.

A. Correction (vv. 14, 15)

14. Which when the apostles, Barnabas and Paul, heard of, they rent their clothes, and ran in among the people, crying out.

Among the Jews, tearing one's own clothes was a traditional expression of grief and shock. Whether the Lystrans knew what it meant or not, they could not miss the fact that their supposed gods were dashing among them and shouting protests.

15. And saying, Sirs, why do ye these things? We also are men of like passions with you, and preach unto you that ye should turn from these vanities unto the living God, which made heaven, and earth, and the sea, and all things that are therein.

The protest was a three-part sermon in one sentence:

1. We are men, not gods. We are no more divine than you are.

2. We are here for the express purpose of turning you away from these vanities. A vanity is something worthless, a nothing. Such were Jupiter and Mercury and all the paraphernalia and ceremonies of their worship. Paul and Barnabas had come to help the Lystrans abandon their baseless beliefs and practices. (What vanities do modern people put instead of God?)

3. We are calling you to give your worship to the only God who is alive, the one who made sky and earth and sea and everything in them.

A PROPER SENSE OF HUMILITY

The praise of men tempts us to think we are invincible. When things go well, the world gives us its acclaim, and we often believe what it tells us about our "greatness."

In that state of mind, a person may believe that he is above all law. If he were thinking clearly, however, he would know that foolish mistakes (or worse yet, deliberate sins) can and usually do come back to haunt those who commit them.

Events of recent years give ample testimony. How often have we seen those who were highly acclaimed in the realm of politics, business, even religion, disgraced because of pride and the delusion of self-importance that public acclaim fosters.

We cannot help but notice how differently Paul and Barnabas reacted to the adulation of the people of Lystra. Their response was, "We are men like you." These two early Christian leaders set us an excellent example. Humility is always becoming to the great. It is just as becoming to those who are less than great. As someone has said, "What's hard is to be humble when you're a nobody." No one is a "nobody" in God's eyes, but only God merits our adulation.

—C. R. B.

B. Evidence (vv. 16, 17)

16. Who in times past suffered all nations to walk in their own ways.

For ages the living God had been tolerant. He had let the Lystrans worship Jupiter and Mercury and the other so-called gods of the Greeks. Before that, He had let them worship their own tribal gods. But the phrase *in times past* implies that those times were ended. God now was calling all nations to walk in His way, not their own.

17. Nevertheless he left not himself without witness, in that he did good, and gave us rain from heaven, and fruitful seasons, filling our hearts with food and gladness.

Through all those past ages there was evidence enough to let thoughtful people know the living God. Year after year He did good. Year after year He gave the rain in its season, and at the proper time He gave the harvest. Year after year people ate of His bounty, and were glad. Everybody ought to know that God is good; everybody ought to walk in His way, ought to be good, to be generous, to be helpful.

Later the apostle Paul would expand that thought in a marvelous letter. The invisible things of God—His nature, His goodness, His love—are clearly shown by His creation. People were without excuse when they turned from His way to their own. Why did they do it? It was because "they did not like to retain God in their knowledge." They preferred their own cruel and greedy ways. So God gave them up to their depravity (Romans 1:18-32). But that was in times past (v. 16). Now He is sending out His good news, His power to bring salvation (Romans 1:16). Now He commands all men everywhere to repent, for He has set a day when He will judge the world righteously—and He will judge it by the man He has ordained, Jesus. To assure us of that, He raised Jesus from the dead (Acts 17:29-31).

C. Result (v. 18)

18. And with these sayings scarce restrained they the people, that they had not done sacrifice unto them.

Home Daily Bible Readings

Monday, Sept. 16—The Gospel Preached at Iconium (Acts 14:1-7)
Tuesday, Sept. 17—A Healing at Lystra (Acts 14:8-18)
Wednesday, Sept. 18—The Gospel Spreads and Grows (Acts 14:19-23)
Thursday, Sept. 19—Paul and Barnabas Make Their Report (Acts 14:24-28)
Friday, Sept. 20—No Excuse for Not Knowing God (Romans 1:18-25)
Saturday, Sept. 21—God's Law Written Upon Human Hearts (Romans 2:12-16)
Sunday, Sept. 22—Reconciled to God Through Christ (Romans 5:6-11)

Paul and Barnabas stopped the people from offering sacrifice to them, but it was hard to do. The people had their hearts set on a celebration, and they did not want to give it up. They said Paul and Barnabas were gods, but they would rather have a feast in their honor than do what they asked. Likewise many of the Jews called Jehovah their God, but would not submit to the Son He sent to save them. And we who accept God's Son—do we sometimes want to honor Him more than we want to obey Him?

IV. The Rest of the Story
(Acts 14:19-23)

We have a short text chosen to focus attention on one phase of the missionary campaign in Lystra. We have considered the healing of a crippled man and the mistaken attempt to worship Paul and Barnabas. Can we take time to note what else happened in Lystra, as well as to note what followed and what the lesson means to our daily living?

A. Opposition

It seems that there were few or no Jews living in the town of Lystra to oppose the gospel as Jews had done in other places. That did not mean there was no opposition in Lystra. Jews and Gentiles of Iconium had combined in a plot to stone the missionaries, and they were not content with driving them out of town. Jews from Iconium and Antioch came together to Lystra to carry out their plot. Enlisting people of Lystra to help them, they stoned Paul to death, they thought. But Paul was not dead—or if he was, the Lord restored him to life. Once again he and Barnabas left a city where they were persecuted and went on to another to continue their work (Acts 14:19, 20).

B. Success

Our text says nothing about the people of Lystra who accepted the gospel and turned from imaginary gods to the real and living one, but certainly some people did. We have two indications of this:

1. Not much later Paul and Barnabas came back to Lystra, as well as to other places, to strengthen and encourage the disciples (Acts 14:21, 22).
2. On a later trip Paul came again for the same purpose. From Lystra a fine young Christian went with him to help him in his work (Acts 15:41—16:5).

If the book of Acts had been written to glorify the missionaries, we would read more about their success. The facts are recorded very briefly. Only one convert on the island of Cyprus is mentioned (Acts 13:12). There must have been more. At Antioch "as many as were ordained to eternal life believed" (13:48), but we are not told how many there were. At Iconium "a great multitude both of the Jews and also of the Greeks believed" (14:1), but the fact is mentioned briefly with no fanfare. There is a hint here, not only for missionaries, but for all of us who work for the Lord. These workers were more interested in doing their job than in getting credit for it.

C. Follow-up

Paul and Barnabas did not consider their work to be finished when they got a church started. They made it a point to come back later and help it. How they helped is told briefly in Acts 14:21-23.

1. They strengthened the souls of disciples.
2. They urged them to be true to the faith.
3. They warned that trials must be endured.
4. They helped each church get organized.
5. They prayed with and for the disciples.
6. They committed them to the Lord's care.

Conclusion

How times have changed! Jupiter and Mercury are out of style, and stoning is not often directed at preachers. Does this lesson have any message for us? Indeed it has.

A. Messages for Missionaries

Every Christian is a missionary, or ought to be. Whether our mission is to the other side of the world or only to the other side of the street, we can see some hints for us in the methods of Paul and Barnabas.

1. They risked their lives, but they did not do it recklessly or stubbornly. Their Master had said, "When they persecute you in this city, flee ye into another" (Matthew 10:23).

2. They sometimes suffered violence, but they did not use violence against others. They did not throw stones at Jews or pagans or police. They did not burn a synagogue or a heathen temple. Their Master had told them to be harmless as doves (Matthew 10:16).

3. They preached Jesus, not civics or economics, not sociology or philosophy, not psychology or mathematics. They knew "there is none other name under heaven given among men, whereby we must be saved" (Acts 4:12).

4. They did not forget new Christians, but went back to help them and be sure they had capable leaders (Acts 14:21-23).

5. They went back and reported to the home church that had sent them (Acts 14:26, 27).

B. Stones for You

It is not likely that anyone reading this book will be pelted with literal stones, but all of us may suffer from figurative stones. Various people may say and do things that not only will give us pain, but also will hinder our Christian work. Which of the following are likely to be in your experience? Think about what you will do when they come.

1. The enemy's stone. Once in a while we meet someone who really hates Christianity and takes every possible opportunity to insult Jesus and His people.

2. The unbeliever's stone. Many unbelievers are scornful rather than hateful. They belittle us instead of insulting us.

3. The wise man's stone. A college professor said to his class, "If any of you want to believe those silly miracle stories, all right. But if you think about it, you will find a more mature satisfaction in realizing that there are no miracles."

4. The hypocrite's stone. A famous evangelist, a preacher, a deacon, or an ordinary church member is involved in a sex scandal, an embezzlement, or some other obvious sin. All sincere Christians are both hurt and handicapped in their work for the Lord.

5. The quitter's stone. A Christian drops out. He stops worshiping and serving and giving. This not only gives us pain, but also makes it harder to win others.

6. The careless stone. Many church members neither drop out nor work earnestly. They are neither hot nor cold. They are quick to criticize and slow to help. This too both pains us and makes our Christian work more difficult.

7. What other stones have you encountered?

C. Getting Personal

1. Whom do you know who needs either to be led to Christ or to be encouraged in Christian work?

2. How can you help him or her?

3. When will you do it?

D. Prayer

What an honor it is, our Heavenly Father, and what a pleasure to be servants of the Savior who gave His life for us! Please lead us so that we shall not be stopped by stones, but rather in love will win those who throw them. In Jesus' name, amen.

E. Thought to Remember

"I'll live for Him who died for me."

Learning by Doing

This page contains an alternate lesson plan emphasizing learning activities. Classes desiring such student involvement will find these suggestions helpful.

Learning Goals

As a result of this lesson, students will:

1. Analyze Paul's ability to overcome persecution.

2. Develop a strategy for increasing their spiritual power to overcome persecution.

Into the Lesson

Have class members form groups of four. Give each person a copy of the persecutions below and the questions that follow. Allow eight minutes for the groups to discuss the questions.

Form of Persecution
Ridicule
Slander
Loss of job
Imprisonment,
Torture,
Threat of death
Confiscation of home and possessions,
Threat of death to a loved one, harassment.

Discuss

1. If you were persecuted for your faith in Christ, which of these forms of persecution would you be most likely to withstand?

2. Which would be the hardest for you to withstand?

3. How would you maintain a strong faith in God during times of severe persecution?

When the time is up, lead into the Bible study portion of the lesson by saying, "We are continuing our study of the life of the apostle Paul. As we progress, we are looking for principles that enable leaders to be effective. Of course, each principle is relevant for all Christians, even if they aren't leaders. Today we will explore how effective Christian leaders overcome persecution."

Into the Word

Have your class members remain in their groups to discuss the following questions. Give each group a set of the questions, and appoint a discussion leader for each group. Before they discuss the questions, instruct each group to have someone read aloud Acts 14:8-23. Point out that some of the questions require speculation.

1. Why did the crowd at Lystra want to worship Paul and Barnabas?

2. Why did Paul and Barnabas refuse their worship?

3. Why were some Jews from Antioch and Iconium so intent on opposing Paul and Barnabas? (Consider Acts 13:45.)

4. Why would the people of Lystra so soon be willing to stone Paul and Barnabas?

5. Compare Acts 14:8-23 with Paul's reference to the same events in 2 Timothy 3:10-13. Note especially 2 Timothy 3:12 and compare it with Acts 14:22. Why must we "go through many hardships to enter the kingdom of God?" (Acts 14:22, *New International Version*)

After fifteen minutes, write this week's *Principle for Effective Leadership* on your leadership poster: *Effective Christian leaders have spiritual power to overcome persecution.*

Lead the entire class in discussing this question: "What factors in Paul's life enabled him to overcome persecution?" The lesson text doesn't deal with this issue, so your students' analysis will need to be based on what they know about Paul. These factors should be mentioned: he had an intimate relationship with God; he relied upon God, not himself; he was more committed to obeying God than to protecting his own life; he had a powerful prayer life; he walked by faith, not by sight. Although students will still be seated in their groups, they should discuss the question with the rest of the class.

Students should work on the next activity in their small groups. Assign one or two of the passages below to each group and have them answer this question: *What principles from this passage will enable you to have greater spiritual power to overcome persecution?*

The passages are: 2 Corinthians 4:7-11, 16-18; Ephesians 6:10-18; Philippians 1:27-30; 2 Timothy 1:7-14; 2 Timothy 3:10-17; Hebrews 10:32-36; Hebrews 12:1-13; 1 Peter 2:19-23; 1 Peter 3:13-17, 4:1, 2; 1 Peter 4:12-19.

After ten minutes, ask group leaders to summarize the principles their groups identified. List them on the chalkboard.

Into Life

At this point distribute a piece of paper and pen to each student. Ask, "What two things can you begin doing this week to increase your spiritual power to overcome persecution?" Ask students to write their intentions on the paper and share them with their group. Have each group close with prayer.

Let's Talk It Over

The questions on this page are designed to encourage review of the lesson Scriptures and to promote discussion of the lesson by the class. The answers provided are only discussion starters. Let your class talk it over from there.

1. What can modern missionaries learn from the conduct of Paul and Barnabas as seen in this lesson?

At least five insights or guidelines may be gained from the experience of these early missionaries in today's lesson. (1) God's messengers should go to receptive, potentially fruitful areas. In the background of the lesson, Paul and Barnabas "shook off the dust of their feet" as a symbolic expression of their decision to leave Antioch because of its resistance to the gospel (Acts 13:51). They then sought new territory. (2) The needs of people should not be ignored. Preaching the gospel is the Christian's primary task, but people's needs may be so severe as to prevent them from giving the gospel a fair hearing. In healing the crippled man, Paul set an example of ministering to the whole person. Missionaries today need to meet as many significant needs as possible. (3) A missionary's approach should be adapted to the specific situation that is faced. Paul did not approach his audience in Lystra as he did in Antioch. The background and orientation of the audiences were different. (4) Opposition should not be responded to in kind. For example, violence should not be met with violence, nor abuse with abuse). (5) Opposition should not be allowed to be a deterrent to the preaching of the gospel. Paul and Barnabas provide sterling examples of perseverance in the face of radical opposition.

2. How did Paul and Barnabas respond to the Lystrans' attempt to worship them as gods?

When Paul and Barnabas realized that the people of Lystra were preparing to offer sacrifices to them, they reacted in the customary Jewish manner of expressing shock or grief by tearing their clothes. Rushing among the would-be worshipers, they shouted their protests to what the Lystrans planned to do. Even though God empowered Paul and Barnabas to perform miracles, these messengers responded humbly by saying, "We too are only men, human like you" (Acts 14:15, *New International Version.*)

3. Why do people tend to "idolize" religious leaders?

The immature, the naive, the emotionally unstable tend to focus on the one whom they can see, who speaks for God, rather than on God, whom they cannot see. Often too such persons need a "father figure" to tell them what to do, to order their lives for them. As that respect turns into adulation, and even reverence, they center their lives more and more in that leader. Often religious leaders *feed* that kind of relationship. Unlike Paul, they enjoy being treated like deity. These leaders may begin to experience personal feelings of omnipotence and omniscience, and they play the game with their worshiping followers.

4. What was the purpose of the healing miracles in the ministry of Jesus and the missionary endeavors of Paul.?

These miracles were also called "wonders" and "signs" (see Acts 2:22; 14:3). They created wonder in the minds of those who saw them, and as signs, pointed to their divine source. Their basic purpose was to offer divine confirmation of the messenger and the message. This intent stands out in Acts 14:3, which states that Paul and Barnabas spoke "boldly for the Lord, who confirmed the message of his grace by enabling them to do miraculous signs and wonders" (*New International Version*). Although concern for hurting and disabled people existed, the *fundamental* purpose was not just to relieve suffering. Obviously, if that were the purpose, God's servants would have spent most of their time healing the sick and disabled.

5. What evidence has God given mankind of His existence and nature?

Essentially, revelation falls into two categories: general and special. General revelation refers to the witness of God that Paul cited: evidences in the created order. Although creation testifies of God, it does not speak specifically of God's grace and love for us. The goodness of God can be seen, but nature also can be terrifying, for example, in natural disasters. It remains for special revelation to *focus* our picture of God. In the messages of God's spokesmen (prophets and apostles) God reveals himself and His will. But ultimately, the special revelation is perfectly and completely focused in Jesus Christ. When we see Jesus Christ, we know who God is and what He is like. The picture is perfect!

A Conference in Jerusalem

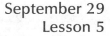

LESSON SCRIPTURE: Acts 15:1-35.

PRINTED TEXT: Acts 15:1-12.

Acts 15:1-12

1 And certain men which came down from Judea taught the brethren, and said, Except ye be circumcised after the manner of Moses, ye cannot be saved.

2 When therefore Paul and Barnabas had no small dissension and disputation with them, they determined that Paul and Barnabas, and certain other of them, should go up to Jerusalem unto the apostles and elders about this question.

3 And being brought on their way by the church, they passed through Phoenicia and Samaria, declaring the conversion of the Gentiles: and they caused great joy unto all the brethren.

4 And when they were come to Jerusalem, they were received of the church, and of the apostles and elders, and they declared all things that God had done with them.

5 But there rose up certain of the sect of the Pharisees which believed, saying, That it was needful to circumcise them, and to command them to keep the law of Moses.

6 And the apostles and elders came together for to consider of this matter.

7 And when there had been much disputing, Peter rose up, and said unto them, Men and brethren, ye know how that a good while ago God made choice among us, that the Gentiles by my mouth should hear the word of the gospel, and believe.

8 And God, which knoweth the hearts, bare them witness, giving them the Holy Ghost, even as he did unto us;

9 And put no difference between us and them, purifying their hearts by faith.

10 Now therefore why tempt ye God, to put a yoke upon the neck of the disciples, which neither our fathers nor we were able to bear?

11 But we believe that through the grace of the Lord Jesus Christ we shall be saved, even as they.

12 Then all the multitude kept silence, and gave audience to Barnabas and Paul, declaring what miracles and wonders God had wrought among the Gentiles by them.

GOLDEN TEXT: We believe that through the grace of the Lord Jesus Christ we shall be saved, even as they.—Acts 15:11.

From the Damascus Road to Rome
Unit 2. Emerging Leader
(Lessons 3-5)

Lesson Aims

After studying this lesson a student should be able to:

1. Describe the controversy in the church at Antioch and tell how it was settled.

2. Tell how controversy may be ended among Christians now.

Lesson Outline

INTRODUCTION
    A. Correcting the Error
    B. Another Error
    C. Lesson Background
  I. QUARREL AT ANTIOCH (Acts 15:1, 2)
    A. Teachers From Judea (v. 1)
    B. Challenge (v. 2)
 II. QUARREL AT JERUSALEM (Acts 15:3-5)
    A. Spreading Good News (v. 3)
    B. Welcome at Jerusalem (v. 4)
    C. Falsehood Again (v. 5)
      They Have to Be Like Us
III. DISCUSSION AND DECISION (Acts 15:6-12)
    A. Apostles and Elders (v. 6)
    B. Some Known Facts (vv. 7-9)
    C. Peter's Conclusion (vv. 10, 11)
      Removing the Yoke of Bondage
    D. Clincher (v. 12)
CONCLUSION
    A. Settled Questions
    B. Unsettled Questions
    C. How to Quarrel
    D. Prayer
    E. Thought to Remember

Display visual 5 from the visuals packet and let it remain before the class throughout the session. The visual is shown on page 43.

Introduction

The Jews were a separated people, and proud of it. Since the time of Abraham they had been set apart by their devotion to the one real God; They claimed as their own the promise made to Abraham (Genesis 12:1-3).

When Israel was subdued by Rome and made a part of the Roman empire, the Jews longed for the promised Messiah to come. They thought He would defeat the Romans and make Israel the dominant nation it had been when Solomon was king.

When some Jews were convinced that Jesus was the Messiah, they had to revise their thinking about what He would do. He did not slaughter their enemies to free them from Rome; He gave His own life to save them from sin. To some extent they revised their thinking about whom He would save. They saw that He would save only those who would accept Him and obey Him. But they continued to assume that His salvation was for Jews only.

A. Correcting the Error

It took several special acts of God to convince the early Christians that salvation was for Gentiles as well as Jews. We read about them in the tenth chapter of Acts.

1. God sent an angel to Cornelius, a Roman of noble character who believed in the real God. The angel told Cornelius to send for Simon Peter and get instructions from him (Acts 10:1-6).

2. God used a vision to remind Peter that God, not man, decides what is clean and what is unclean (Acts 10:9-16, 28).

3. The Holy Spirit told Peter to go with the messengers of Cornelius (Acts 10:19, 20).

4. In those ways the Lord convinced Peter that people of every nation can be acceptable to Him (Acts 10:34, 35).

5. God sent the Holy Spirit to Cornelius and other Gentiles even before they were baptized into Christ. That was the crowning evidence, and Peter was convinced that believing Gentiles were acceptable to God just as believing Jews were (Acts 10:44-48).

Jewish Christians in Jerusalem challenged Peter, not only because he had won Gentiles to Christ, but even because he had entered their house and eaten with them. But Peter told how God had convinced him, and the challengers were convinced too (Acts 11:1-18).

B. Another Error

After that time no one said Gentiles should be barred from salvation, but some of the nationalistic Jewish Christians put forth another error. They said those Gentiles who became Christians must become Jews also. They said Gentiles could not be saved just by believing in Jesus, turning away from sin, being baptized, and obeying Christ's commands. All this would be useless, they said, unless the Gentile Christians would be circumcised according to the law of Moses and would keep all the commandments of that law. This error persisted longer than the other, and disturbed Christians in many places.

C. Lesson Background

Last week's lesson brought us some of the adventures of Paul and Barnabas on the trip that has become known as Paul's first missionary journey. At the trips close the two went back to their starting point in Antioch of Syria. After reporting to the church, they stayed there for a "long time" (Acts 14:24-28). Now we shall look at some events of that "long time."

I. Quarrel at Antioch
(Acts 15:1, 2)

From the beginning of the church at Antioch, its fellowship with the brethren in Jerusalem had been cordial. The church at Jerusalem had sent Barnabas, famous for encouragement, and he had brought Saul to help (Acts 11:19-26). The brethren in Antioch had sent famine relief to Judea (Acts 11:27-30). But now some self-appointed teachers came from Judea, and they were not like Barnabas.

A. Teachers From Judea (v. 1)

1. And certain men which came down from Judea taught the brethren, and said, Except ye be circumcised after the manner of Moses, ye cannot be saved.

It is not hard to follow the thinking of these teachers from Judea. From infancy they had been taught that Jews and no others are God's people. Perhaps they had been shocked when they learned that Cornelius and other Romans had become Christians, but in that case the leading of God was too plain to be questioned. Now there was a big church in Antioch, perhaps with more Gentiles in it than Jews. Besides, Paul and Barnabas had been traveling through Cyprus and Asia Minor to bring uncounted Gentiles to Christ. It looked as if the Jews might soon be only a minority of God's people. That was incompatible with the lifelong belief of nationalistic Jews. The Jews were God's chosen! To these teachers it seemed very clear that all the Gentiles who became God's people must become Jews.

B. Challenge (v. 2)

2. When therefore Paul and Barnabas had no small dissension and disputation with them, they determined that Paul and Barnabas, and certain other of them, should go up to Jerusalem unto the apostles and elders about this question.

Paul and Barnabas promptly challenged this teaching from Judea because they knew it was false. Paul especially was in a position to know this beyond any shadow of doubt. Jesus himself

visual 5

had sent him to the Gentiles as a minister and a witness (Acts 26:16-18). Jesus himself had told him what to preach (Galatians 1:11, 12), and the message was not that all Christians must be Jews. Paul could not be mistaken, for he was taught by Jesus and inspired by the Holy Spirit. But the teachers from Judea probably denied this. After all, Paul was not one of the original apostles. The Judean teachers probably claimed to represent the teaching of the original twelve and the belief of the whole church in Jerusalem. Wisely the disciples in Antioch decided to send a committee to see if that was true.

II. Quarrel at Jerusalem
(Acts 15:3-5)

We are not told how many members the committee had. We are not told whether the Judean teachers went along or not. But there were some good men and true to be sure Paul and Barnabas would not misrepresent the controversy or bring back a false report of the decision. Apparently they went promptly.

A. Spreading Good News (v. 3)

3. And being brought on their way by the church, they passed through Phoenicia and Samaria, declaring the conversion of the Gentiles: and they caused great joy unto all the brethren.

Scattered disciples had established churches all along the way, so the committee was greeted by brethren at every stop. Paul and Barnabas delighted in telling how many Gentiles had turned to Christ, both in Antioch and in other cities where they had preached; and disciples along the way were delighted to hear it.

B. Welcome at Jerusalem (v. 4)

4. And when they were come to Jerusalem, they were received of the church, and of the apostles and elders, and they declared all things that God had done with them.

The welcome was cordial. Barnabas had always been a favorite at Jerusalem. No doubt some of the Christians remembered how Paul had persecuted them, but he had become such an earnest and energetic Christian that they no longer held any bitterness toward him. Again the two told of their adventures and success among the Gentiles. It is notable that they did not tell of what they had done, but of what *God had done with them.* They told of His success, not their own.

C. Falsehood Again (v. 5)

5. But there rose up certain of the sect of the Pharisees which believed, saying, That it was needful to circumcise them, and to command them to keep the law of Moses.

These *Pharisees* were Christians: they *believed* in Jesus. But they had not lost their zeal for the law of Moses and the traditions of the elders—the zeal that was a hallmark of Pharisees. Their position was the same as that of the teachers who had disturbed the brethren in Antioch. They held that Gentiles could not be saved just by becoming Christians: they must become Jews also.

THEY HAVE TO BE LIKE US

"Water wars" are not uncommon in areas where water is in short supply. To have water means life and prosperity; not to have it is unthinkable.

In the early 1900s, Los Angeles developers bought up land in the Owens Valley east of the Sierra Nevada, and with it, gained control of the mountain water that would fuel the growth of their burgeoning metropolis. Area farmers, ranchers, and environmentalists went to "war" with city dwellers, battling in court for legal rights to the precious stuff of life. Each side was sure its view was correct. Finally, in the early 1990s, some workable compromises seem to be on the way.

It's the way life has always been: "If only those people were like us, there would be no problems. Why won't they change?" The early church faced the same issue. Christian Pharisees wanted Gentile Christians to become Jews ("like real Christians should be," they probably said).

How to Say It

ANTIOCH. *An*-tee-ock.
CORNELIUS. Kor-*nee*-lih-us or Kor-*neel*-yus.
PHARISEES. *Fair*-ih-seez.
PHOENICIA. Fih-*nish*-uh.

There is no end of classes into which we may divide, if we are so inclined. But the gospel calls us just to be Christians—and then to find ways to be like Christ, not more like each other.
—C. R. B.

III. Discussion and Decision (Acts 15:6-12)

The difference of opinion was as sharp at Jerusalem as it had been at Antioch. For the sake of peace in the church, this problem needed a solution in accord with the will of God. The brethren faced the problem and looked for the solution.

A. Apostles and Elders (v. 6)

6. And the apostles and elders came together for to consider of this matter.

The whole congregation had met with the apostles and elders to welcome the group from Antioch (v. 4). That does not necessarily mean that all the members were present. The church must have numbered many thousands then, for it had been growing rapidly after the violent persecution ended (Acts 9:31). Now the leading men, *the apostles and elders*, got together to discuss the matter among themselves. It seems that they carried on their discussion in the presence of the whole congregation, however, for before it was over "all the multitude" was listening to Paul and Barnabas again (v. 12).

B. Some Known Facts (vv. 7-9)

7. And when there had been much disputing, Peter rose up, and said unto them, Men and brethren, ye know how that a good while ago God made choice among us, that the Gentiles by my mouth should hear the word of the gospel, and believe.

There was *much disputing.* The Christian Pharisees felt strongly about the position they had taken (v. 5). Paul and Barnabas felt no less strongly that the Pharisees were wrong. After both sides had been heard, Peter stood up to call attention to some well-known facts, (Acts 10). First, everyone knew Peter had been first to take the gospel to Gentiles, and that had been by God's choice, not Peter's.

8. And God, which knoweth the hearts, bare them witness, giving them the Holy Ghost, even as he did unto us.

A second fact known to all was that God had given the Holy Spirit to the Gentiles who heard Peter. By that act, God testified that those Gentiles were acceptable to Him.

9. And put no difference between us and them, purifying their hearts by faith.

God *put no difference* between circumcised Jews who followed the law and uncircumcised Gentiles who did not. He forgave the sins of both and purified their hearts because they believed in Jesus. Circumcision and the law had nothing to do with it.

C. Peter's Conclusion (vv. 10, 11)

10. Now therefore why tempt ye God, to put a yoke upon the neck of the disciples, which neither our fathers nor we were able to bear?

Keeping of the law was *a yoke*, a load that had been too much for every generation of Jews since the time of Moses. No one had succeeded in obeying the law fully. The Pharisees were most meticulous in observing a multitude of details, but they neglected the weightier matters (Matthew 23:23). The Jews had never been able to carry the load, and all their trying had not been enough to save them. Then why did they want to put that same load on the shoulders of the Gentiles?

11. But we believe that through the grace of the Lord Jesus Christ we shall be saved, even as they.

Some of the Jews had kept much of the law and some had kept little, but none could be saved by his keeping of the law. All had to depend on *the grace of the Lord Jesus Christ* to pardon their sins. Only thus could they be saved, and Gentiles who knew nothing of the law could be saved in exactly the same way.

REMOVING THE YOKE OF BONDAGE

In 1989 tumultuous events occurred within the Soviet empire. Many who remembered the fall of the "iron curtain" over Europe thought they would never live to see such startling changes.

One after another, Communist governments loosened their grip as long-entrenched "hard-liners" were forced to remove the yoke of political repression from their people. A new era of history dawned all across Europe within just a few weeks' time.

Christ has freed us from the bondage of sin, from the burden of keeping the law, and from the requirements that others might attempt to place upon our behavior. Nevertheless, the church has often had its "hard-liners," who have attempted to keep the thoughts and behavior of other Christians under their control. The circumcision faction in our text is but one example of such persons.

The early church exposed the error of those who insisted that Christians must keep the law. What yokes of bondage would some require Christians to bear today? From all such, we are free. Let us use our freedom responsibly, guided by the teachings of Christ and His apostles, so that the church advances. —C. R. B.

D. Clincher (v. 12)

12. Then all the multitude kept silence, and gave audience to Barnabas and Paul, declaring what miracles and wonders God had wrought among the Gentiles by them.

Now Barnabas and Paul spoke again, telling what God had done. Verse 4 records that they had done this before. Perhaps then they had told of the many Gentiles who had responded to the gospel. Now they emphasized the *miracles and wonders* that God had done. That clinched Peter's declaration that it was not necessary for Gentile Christians to become Jews. Everybody knew miracles were not done just to make sick people well. They were done to show that God was working through men, and thus to show that God approved what those men were doing. Thus Jesus was "approved of God" (Acts 2:22). Thus God confirmed the word as the apostles preached the gospel (Mark 16:20). Likewise by miracles God showed His approval of the work of Paul and Barnabas. With God's approval they said to Gentiles as Peter said to Jews, "Repent, and be baptized every one of you in the name of Jesus Christ for the remission of sins, and ye shall receive the gift of the Holy Ghost" (Acts 2:38). Jews and Gentiles were saved in the same way, and the law had nothing to do with it.

When Paul and Barnabas finished their recital, James spoke (Acts 15:13-21). He was a half-brother of Jesus (Galatians 1:19). He claimed no honor on that account, however, but called himself "a servant of God and of the Lord Jesus Christ" (James 1:1). By his wisdom and goodness he had become an outstanding leader in the church (Galatians 1:18, 19; 2:9).

From the Greek version of the Old Testament, James quoted Amos 9:11, 12, foretelling the time when Gentiles would seek the Lord. He then stated the obvious conclusion: Gentiles who became Christians should not be troubled with the Jewish law. As Christians they should abstain from some things that were common among the heathen, not because those things were forbidden by Jewish law, but because they were forever wrong. They were wrong before the law was given and after it was done away (v. 20).

This conclusion met the approval of apostles and elders and congregation. A letter was prepared for the Gentile Christians in Antioch and other places as well (Acts 15:22-29). It repudiated the unauthorized teachers who had misrepresented Christian teaching in Antioch. It presented the conclusion that had been stated by James. It claimed the approval of the Holy Spirit as well as that of apostles and elders and brethren.

The committee carried that letter back to Antioch (Acts 15:30, 31). Paul and Silas later carried it to other churches among the Gentiles (Acts 16:4). Some of the Christian Pharisees continued to spread the false teaching, but in so doing they contradicted not only the apostles and elders, but also the Holy Spirit. Vigorously Paul rebuked the Galatians for being led astray by such a perversion of the gospel (Galatians 1:6-9; 3:1-5). It is Jesus who saves. To seek salvation by keeping the law is to forsake the faith and fall from grace (Galatians 5:4).

Conclusion

A. Settled Questions

As we have seen in our lesson, some teachers who came from Judea caused great unrest in the church at Antioch with their teaching. They probably said they represented the position of the original apostles of Jesus, and Paul and Barnabas said they did not. The church sent people to ask those original apostles. The question was settled definitely and finally. Those who continued to dissent were in opposition to God himself.

Some of today's quarrels can be settled just as simply, not by sending to living apostles, but by examining their writings. For example, teachers arise from time to time to say that dead people stay dead, that Jesus did not rise actually, literally, physically. What do the apostles say? Matthew and John were there, and the Holy Spirit inspired their writing. Jesus did rise. The question is settled.

B. Unsettled Questions

Some disputes among Christians are not settled so easily. For example, some earnest brethren vigorously object to the popular observance of Christmas. There was no such observance in the early church, they say, and no one knows the date of Jesus' birth. But other devoted Christians ignore the protest and happily observe the day.

What can be done about that disagreement? The apostolic writings neither command nor forbid us to keep Christmas. But the apostle Paul did comment on a difference of opinion about special days: "One man esteemeth one day above another: another esteemeth every day alike." What is to be done about that disagreement? "Let every man be fully persuaded in his own mind" (Romans 14:5). In other words, every person has a right to his own opinion. We may argue with one another, but only with friendly persuasion, not

with angry accusation. This is true of many differences of opinion on which there is no decisive word from the inspired apostles.

C. How to Quarrel

Before we had TV to entertain us, interested people developed debating into a fine art. In some forensic societies there was a standing rule that a debater must not attack the character or motive of an opponent. It was legitimate to expose factual errors or unsound reasoning, but not to say the opponent was a greedy wretch who took his position for the sake of personal profit. An opponent might indeed be such a wretch, but that was not the point at issue. Even a person of bad character and bad motives might tell the truth, though he did it for selfish motives. So debaters were required to stick to the issues, and one who violated the rule was promptly called to order.

Such a rule might improve our Christian debating. The heat of conflict does not excuse us from the obligation to be "likeminded, compassionate, loving as brethren" (1 Peter 3:8, *American Standard Version*). If we maintain a Christian attitude through all our differences, perhaps we can settle some questions and leave others unsettled and still be "of one heart and of one soul" (Acts 4:32). Be a peacemaker! (Matthew 5:9).

D. Prayer

Each day, our Heavenly Father, we recall that Jesus so loved us that He gave His life for us. Both in harmony and in dispute, may we love one another as He has loved us. In His name we pray. Amen.

E. Thought to Remember

"Love the brotherhood" (1 Peter 2:17).

Learning by Doing

This page contains an alternate lesson plan emphasizing learning activities. Classes desiring such student involvement will find these suggestions helpful.

Learning Goals

As a result of studying this lesson students will be able to:

1. Explain why the controversial issue recorded in Acts 15 posed a threat to the church.

2. Determine how church leaders should deal with teachings that oppose the gospel.

3. Suggest ways they can protect themselves from false teachings.

Into the Lesson

Give each student a copy of the statements below. Tell them, "The twelve statements represent prevalent religious beliefs that are false according to the Bible. On a scale of one to five, rate how dangerous you think each statement is. One means that it is spiritually harmless for a person to believe it; five means that it is spiritually destructive."

1. Jesus was a good teacher, but He isn't God.

2. God was once a mere man. Someday we might become a god.

3. Jesus did not rise from the dead.

4. God is in everything, and everything is a part of God, including me. I am God.

5. Everyone will ultimately be saved.

6. We can get to Heaven by being good.

7. God is dead.

8. When we die we are reincarnated.

9. All religions lead to God.

10. It doesn't matter what you believe as long as it works for you.

11. The Bible is filled with many errors.

12. Jesus is one of many gods.

After students have finished, ask, "Which ones did you mark with a one?" Allow them to respond. Then ask, "Which ones did you mark with a five?" Next ask, "What determines how dangerous a false teaching is?" Discuss.

Make the transition to today's study by saying, "In our lesson today we will focus on how leaders—and every Christian—should deal with dangerous teachings."

Into the Word

After reading Acts 15:1-21 aloud, present a three-minute lecture based on the Introduction section in this lesson manual.

Have class members form groups of six. Provide each group with a copy of the questions below and ask them to discuss them.

1. What issue brought controversy to the church at Antioch? (vv. 1, 2)

2. How did the church deal with the controversy? (v. 2)

3. How did the leaders at the Jerusalem church deal with the controversy? (vv. 4-21)

4. What did the leaders conclude about the issue? (See especially vv. 7-11.)

5. What was at stake in this issue?

Bring the groups together following their discussion. Ask, "What did your group conclude for question five?" Allow feedback. You will want to be sure your class recognizes that what was at stake was the issue of how we are saved. Are we saved by keeping the law, as the Christian Pharisees taught, or are we saved through Jesus Christ? Are we saved by our own works, or by what Christ did for us? The apostles taught that we are saved through Christ. If we reject their teaching, we forsake the faith, fall from grace, and imperil our souls. (See Acts 4:12; Galatians 1:6-9, 3:1-5; 5:4)

Into Life

The fifth *Principle for Effective Leadership*, which we learn from this text, is, *Effective Christian leaders are committed to teaching the truth—as well as protecting the truth.* Write this principle on the poster you mounted in lesson one.

Direct students to gather in their previous groups. Write this question on the chalkboard: *What is the responsibility of church leaders when dangerous teachings emerge in their church?* Assign several of the following passages to each group, making sure that all the passages are covered: Acts 20:28-32; 1 Timothy 1:3-7; 1 Timothy 6:20, 21; 2 Timothy 4:2-5; Titus 1:9-11; Titus 3:9-11; Revelation 2:12-16; Revelation 2:18-25. Ask the groups to read their assigned passages and answer the question.

After eight minutes have the groups report their discoveries to the rest of the class. Then discuss these questions:

1. How do we know when a false teaching is important enough to oppose?

2. How can we protect ourselves from being led away by false teachings?

Of the answers suggested for question two, have the students select one that they will carry out this week.

Let's Talk It Over

The questions on this page are designed to encourage review of the lesson Scriptures and to promote discussion of the lesson by the class. The answers provided are only discussion starters. Let your class talk it over from there.

1. In the incident recorded in today's lesson, what did the church in Antioch do to resolve controversy? What does their example teach us?

They sought the guidance and wisdom of authority and maturity, namely, the inspired apostles and the elders of the church in Jerusalem. That same principle applies today. Whenever controversy arises in spiritual matters, we should seek insight and resolution by searching the Scriptures, the inspired revelation from God, for in them resides the ultimate authority. The apostles shared it in oral form; we have access to it in written form. Also, we should seek the wisdom of mature Christian leaders (represented by the elders in Jerusalem).

2. What attitudes are crucial for resolving disputes in a healthy way?

The first attitude is *openness*. This involves a person's willingness to consider options other than the one he or she has chosen. The willingness to listen becomes a high priority. A second attitude is *sincerity*. Maintaining or attacking positions on the basis of gaining or retaining control sabotages the healthy resolution of disputes. Being sincere and accepting the sincerity of the other person is necessary, although sincerity will never determine the validity or truth of a position. A third attitude is *humility*. Humility acknowledges the source of all knowledge and wisdom—God. Humility corrects the arrogant, "know-it-all" perspective that frustrates resolution of controversy. But most important of all is *love*. Only as there is love for the brethren, love for the truth, can there be a healthy resolution of disputes. The leaders of the Jerusalem conference exemplified these four attitudes.

3. What are some different ways in which people view conflict?

At least three views may be mentioned. (1) Threat. Most people fear conflict; the danger overwhelms them. The possibility of pain and divisiveness raises their anxiety level. They respond with the primal urges, either flight or fight. (2) Challenge. There are those who "love a good fight." They tend to be competitive, often control-oriented persons. These persons view conflict as the opportunity to assert themselves,

to prove they are powerful; they need "to win!" (3) Opportunity for growth. Few understand this perspective of conflict. Conflict reveals needs, and ministry must always match up with needs. Dr. David Mace calls conflict, "a friend in disguise." Note that the conflict that led to the Jerusalem conference provided a significant opportunity for growth in the life of the early church.

4. What are the major causes of conflict in congregations today?

Very little conflict involves essentials (what God has revealed and commanded); much centers around "incidentals." Incidentals focus on methods, materials, priorities, etc. Too many people, however, treat "incidentals" as though they were essentials. Most conflict revolves around opinions and personal agendas. One dominant dynamic surfaces, though, and it has to do with control. It centers around the question, "Who has the power?" Strip away the veneer of the holy phrases that enshroud opinions and pet proposals ("God's will" or "what's best for this church") and you will find the alarming reality that *power* is the basic consideration. Control towers over all other dynamics and issues.

5. What facts considered at the Jerusalem conference led the apostles, elders, and the whole church to conclude that Gentiles could be saved just by becoming Christians, without also becoming Jews?

After hearing of what God had accomplished among the Gentiles through Paul and Barnabas, Peter recounted his own experience when he took the gospel to Gentiles under God's clear direction. The fact that God had given the Holy Spirit to the Gentile Cornelius and his family and friends testified to the fact that those Gentiles were acceptable to Him. Additional testimony to God's approval of the Gentiles who accepted Christ was given by Barnabas and Paul. They declared that God had worked miracles and wonders among the Gentiles by them. Furthermore, James pointed out that the prophet Amos foretold the time when Gentiles would seek the Lord. These facts convinced the church that Gentiles who accepted Christ should not be burdened with keeping the Jewish law.

A Call From Macedonia

LESSON SCRIPTURE: Acts 15:36—16:24.

PRINTED TEXT: Acts 16:9-12, 16-24.

Acts 16:9-12, 16-24

9 And a vision appeared to Paul in the night; There stood a man of Macedonia, and prayed him, saying, Come over into Macedonia, and help us.

10 And after he had seen the vision, immediately we endeavored to go into Macedonia, assuredly gathering that the Lord had called us for to preach the gospel unto them.

11 Therefore loosing from Troas, we came with a straight course to Samothracia, and the next day to Neapolis;

12 And from thence to Philippi, which is the chief city of that part of Macedonia, and a colony: and we were in that city abiding certain days.

. . . .

16 And it came to pass, as we went to prayer, a certain damsel possessed with a spirit of divination met us, which brought her masters much gain by soothsaying:

17 The same followed Paul and us, and cried, saying, These men are the servants of the most high God, which show unto us the way of salvation.

18 And this did she many days. But Paul, being grieved, turned and said to the spirit, I command thee in the name of Jesus Christ to come out of her. And he came out the same hour.

19 And when her masters saw that the hope of their gains was gone, they caught Paul and Silas, and drew them into the market place unto the rulers,

Oct 6

20 And brought them to the magistrates, saying, These men, being Jews, do exceedingly trouble our city,

21 And teach customs, which are not lawful for us to receive, neither to observe, being Romans.

22 And the multitude rose up together against them; and the magistrates rent off their clothes, and commanded to beat them.

23 And when they had laid many stripes upon them, they cast them into prison, charging the jailer to keep them safely:

24 Who, having received such a charge, thrust them into the inner prison, and made their feet fast in the stocks.

GOLDEN TEXT: A vision appeared to Paul in the night. . . . And after he had seen the vision, immediately we endeavored to go into Macedonia, assuredly gathering that the Lord had called us for to preach the gospel unto them.—Acts 16:9, 10.

From the Damascus Road to Rome
Unit 3. Traveling Preacher
(Lessons 6-9)

Lesson Aims

After studying this lesson a student should be able to:

1. Tell how a girl was rescued from a demon, and relate the events that followed.

2. Discuss the motives of Paul, the girl's owners, and the magistrates of Philippi.

3. Search his own heart and life for any unworthy motives of selfishness, prejudice, or love of the easy way.

Lesson Outline

INTRODUCTION
  A. Starting the Second Journey
  B. Lesson Background
 I. CALL TO ACTION (Acts 16:9-12)
  A. Vision (v. 9)
  B. Meaning (v. 10)
      A Call for Help
  C. Action (vv. 11, 12)
 II. RESCUE (Acts 16:16-18)
  A. A Girl Possessed (vv. 16, 17)
  B. A Girl Set Free (v. 18)
III. REVENGE (Acts 16:19-24)
  A. Harsh Accusation (vv. 19-21)
  B. Mob Response (v. 22)
  C. Unjust Imprisonment (vv. 23, 24)
CONCLUSION
  A. Blinding Greed
  B. Blinding Prejudice
  C. Blinding Speed
  D. Prayer
  E. Thought to Remember

The map from the visuals packet—visual 6— shows the location of the places mentioned in lessons 6-10. The map is shown on page 54.

Introduction

Lessons 3 and 4 brought us some highlights of Paul's first missionary journey, in which he and Barnabas worked on the island of Cyprus and on the mainland of Asia Minor. (*Refer to the map—visual 1—from the visuals packet.*) After that trip, the two missionaries went with other men of Antioch to confer with the apostles and elders at Jerusalem, as we saw in last week's lesson.

Returning to Antioch, Paul and Barnabas worked there awhile before planning a second missionary journey (Acts 15:1-35).

A. Starting the Second Journey

This time Paul and Barnabas did not go together. Barnabas and John Mark went to Cyprus. This was Barnabas' homeland and the area the missionaries had covered in the first part of their former trip. Paul's companion now was Silas, a Christian prophet from Jerusalem. These two headed for Derbe and Lystra on the mainland of Asia Minor. At Lystra young Timothy joined them, and the three went on to Iconium and Antioch of Pisidia.

B. Lesson Background

After spending some time with the churches in Asia Minor, they went on to the west. It seems that they expected to preach the gospel in the Roman province called Asia, which was west of Antioch; but the Holy Spirit vetoed that plan. (*Locate Asia and the places mentioned in the rest of this lesson on the map—visual 6—from the visuals packet.*) Then they thought of going north to Bithynia; but again the Spirit said no.

Then what did the Spirit want them to do? Why didn't He tell them, instead of just saying no to some ideas that seemed good to them? They must have been deeply perplexed. But certainly there was no reason to sit idly in some town of Asia where they were not allowed to preach. They pushed on to the west till they came to the seacoast at Troas.

I. Call to Action
(Acts 16:9-12)

How did Paul know the Holy Spirit had forbidden him to preach in Asia or Bithynia? (Acts 16:6, 7). Did he hear a voice speaking in Hebrew, as he did at another time when Jesus spoke to him? (Acts 26:14). Or did the Spirit living in Paul give the message to Paul's mind without words? We who are not inspired prophets have only a vague idea of how inspiration was accomplished. God has different ways of imparting information, and in any case He uses the way He chooses. The important thing is that God's prophet understood the message and knew from whom it came. When at last it was time to tell Paul what to do next, the Lord used a vision.

A. Vision (v. 9)

9. And a vision appeared to Paul in the night; There stood a man of Macedonia, and prayed him, saying, Come over into Macedonia, and help us.

How to Say It

AEGEAN. A-*jee*-un.
ANTIOCH. *An*-tee-ock.
BITHYNIA. Bih-*thin*-ee-uh.
DERBE. *Der*-be.
ICONIUM. Eye-*ko*-nee-um.
LYSTRA. *Liss*-truh.
MACEDONIA. Mass-eh-*doe*-nee-uh.
NEAPOLIS. Nee-*ap*-o-lis.
PHILIPPI. Fih-*lip*-pie or *Fil*-ih-pie.
PISIDIA. Pih-*sid*-ee-uh.
SAMOTHRACIA. Sam-o-*thray*-shi-uh.
SILAS. *Sigh*-luss.
TROAS. *Tro*-az.

We are not told whether Paul was awake or asleep or in a trance, but he seemed to see and hear *a man of Macedonia* inviting him to go on to that country and help the people there.

B. Meaning (v. 10)

10. And after he had seen the vision, immediately we endeavored to go into Macedonia, assuredly gathering that the Lord had called us for to preach the gospel unto them.

Paul told his companions about the vision, and they agreed that it was the Lord's call. They had come to the western limit of Asia. If they were to go farther west, it must be southwest to Greece or northwest to Macedonia. Now the Lord had made the choice for them, and they promptly looked for a ship bound for Macedonia.

Notice the significant little pronouns *we* and *us*. We read that *they*—Paul and Silas and Timothy—came to Troas (v. 8), but *we* looked for a way to Macedonia. Obviously the writer of this record joined the party at this point. This writer was Luke, who also wrote the book we call by his name.

A CALL FOR HELP

Listen, my children, and you shall hear of the midnight ride of Paul Revere . . .

Those immortal lines from the pen of Henry Wadsworth Longfellow remind us of one of the great "calls" of history. Paul Revere, a skilled silversmith, was ready when the hour came for him to take action in the cause of freedom.

On that midnight, April 18-19, 1775, when the light in the Old North Church signaled that the British were coming, Revere charged his horse from Boston to Lexington, Massachusetts. Through sleeping villages he rode, shouting the warning to the minutemen, calling them to arise

and meet the British challenge to the freedom of her New World colonies. It was a moment of great significance in the American Revolution.

Seventeen centuries earlier, the apostle Paul received a call in the night. A man from Macedonia appeared to him, calling him to come and sound the gospel-cry of freedom to his people. Paul responded to the call and took the gospel to the West. In time, Europe became the principal arena where the gospel battled for the minds and hearts of the human race. It was a significant moment: the history of the next two thousand years was greatly influenced by Paul's acceptance of the Macedonian call.

Pay attention when God calls. We never know how great the results may be.   —C. R. B.

C. Action (vv. 11, 12)

11. Therefore loosing from Troas, we came with a straight course to Samothracia, and the next day to Neapolis.

Paul and his companions soon obtained passage on a ship bound for Macedonia. The ship was loosed from its mooring to put out to sea. The wind was favorable, so it was able to sail *a straight course* instead of a zigzag one. So it came *to Samothracia*, an island in the Aegean Sea. It stopped there for the night, *and the next day* went on to *Neapolis*, a seaport in Macedonia.

12. And from thence to Philippi, which is the chief city of that part of Macedonia, and a colony: and we were in that city abiding certain days.

Paul liked to preach the gospel and establish a church in a big city, from which the message would spread throughout the region. Therefore his group did not stay in the seaport, but pushed inland about ten miles to *Philippi*, which was *the chief city of that part of Macedonia*. Readers of Roman history or Shakespeare's *Julius Caesar* will recall that the plains of Philippi were the battleground where Antony and Octavian defeated the conspirators who had assassinated Julius Caesar. Many Romans made their homes in Philippi later, and the city became *a colony* of Rome. Its people had the rights and privileges of the citizens of Rome itself. This was the kind of place where Paul liked to plant the gospel, and the missionaries stayed there *certain days*.

Paul sometimes preached in synagogues, but apparently there was no synagogue in Philippi. That meant that not many Jews lived there, perhaps none at all. But the missionaries learned of a Sabbath prayer meeting near the city. Going to the meeting, they found a group of women. Prominent among them was Lydia, described as one who "worshipped God." This indicates she was not a Jew by birth, but had come to believe in the true God whom the Jews worshiped. Lydia was "a seller of purple." Purple was a rare dye, and fabrics colored with it, and garments made from such fabrics. All of these were costly, so the lady must have had a prosperous business. She and "her household" readily accepted the gospel and were baptized to become the first members of the church in Philippi. Whether Lydia had any family or not, her household probably included employees who worked in her business. Grateful for the message of salvation, Lydia invited the missionaries to make her house their home while they stayed in town (Acts 16:13-15).

II. Rescue
(Acts 16:16-18)

We are not told how the missionaries continued with their campaign in Philippi. Perhaps they talked with people in the marketplace, as Paul later did in Athens (Acts 17:17). Possibly they got enough attention to have daily evangelistic meetings in the place of prayer. In any case, our text now takes up the story as they were going to prayer.

A. A Girl Possessed (vv. 16, 17)

16. And it came to pass, as we went to prayer, a certain damsel possessed with a spirit of divination met us, which brought her masters much gain by soothsaying.

Not much is known about the spirits who took possession of certain people and caused various physical and mental disorders. It seems plain in the New Testament that such possession was frequent and sometimes easily recognized. The possessing spirits sometimes are called "devils" in the *King James Version* (Matthew 8:28), though

---

Home Daily Bible Readings

Monday, Sept. 30—Paul Begins Another Missionary Journey (Acts 15:36-41)
Tuesday, Oct. 1—Timothy Joins Paul and Silas (Acts 16:1-6)
Wednesday, Oct. 2—Paul Travels to Philippi (Acts 16:11-15)
Thursday, Oct. 3—Paul and Silas are Imprisoned (Acts 16:16-24)
Friday, Oct. 4—Paul's Prayer for the Colossian Christians (Colossians 1:1-8)
Saturday, Oct. 5—Lead a Life Worthy of Christ (Colossians 1:9-14)
Sunday, Oct. 6—Christ is Pre-eminent in All Things (Colossians 1:15-20)

---

other versions translate the word as "demons." They are also called "evil spirits" (Luke 7:21) and "unclean spirits" (Mark 5:13). Many students ancient and modern have thought the demons were Satan's angels (Matthew 25:41), though some have thought they were spirits of wicked dead people who were allowed to roam the earth instead of being confined in torment as was the rich man of Luke 16:23.

In the case recorded in our text, the spirit knew things unknown to people on earth. Speaking with the girl's voice, he was a capable fortune teller. Examples of his usual soothsaying are not recorded. Possibly he gave advice, located lost articles, and predicted future events as modern "psychics" are reputed to do. Many people wanted such services and paid well for them; but the girl was a slave, and the gain went to her owners.

17. The same followed Paul and us, and cried, saying, These men are the servants of the most high God, which show unto us the way of salvation.

In the Gospel records it appears that the demons instantly recognized Jesus (Luke 4:41). This demon at Philippi recognized His messengers and announced who they were. We have no hint of why he wanted to announce this, or why he wanted to help people by telling fortunes.

B. A Girl Set Free (v. 18)

18. And this did she many days. But Paul, being grieved, turned and said to the spirit, I command thee in the name of Jesus Christ to come out of her. And he came out the same hour.

Jesus quickly silenced the demons who testified about Him (Luke 4:41). We wonder why Paul waited *many days* before acting against this one. No reason is given, but it is well to note that the choice of time was not Paul's . He did not do this miracle, or any miracle, at his own whim. If he could do that, surely he would have healed the ills of his fellow workers and himself (Philippians 2:25-27; 2 Timothy 4:20; 2 Corinthians 12:7-9). But Paul did each miracle at the direction of the Holy Spirit who inspired him. This girl was known as an accurate soothsayer. Perhaps the Lord wanted her testimony to be heard for a time. But there may have been a different reason for waiting. The Lord knew what would follow when the girl was rescued from the spirit who possessed her. Paul's work in Philippi would be ended. Perhaps the rescue was delayed to give Paul more time for his preaching.

Paul was *grieved,* and we need not suppose he was merely annoyed by the continual shouting behind him. He was saddened by the girl's plight. Her mind and will were displaced by the spirit's; her feet and voice were used by him, not her. *In the name of Jesus Christ* the messenger of Jesus Christ ordered the spirit to set the girl free, and he did. She was still the slave of human masters, but she was no longer in bondage to an evil spirit.

III. Revenge
(Acts 16:19-24)

The masters of the slave girl were free men, they thought. They were not the slaves of men, nor were they in bondage to demons. But they were enslaved by greed. What a monster this is! It forbids human kindness and generosity and helpfulness; it drives its slaves to seek only gain. These greed-driven masters could take no joy in a girl rescued from a demon; they felt only anger at their loss of profits.

A. Harsh Accusation (vv. 19-21)

19. And when her masters saw that the hope of their gains was gone, they caught Paul and Silas, and drew them into the market place unto the rulers.

These *masters* cared nothing for truth or justice. They cared for gain, and *the hope of their gains was gone,* and they wanted revenge. We do not know how many of them there were. Perhaps they had some strong slaves to help them, or hired some thugs who were loafing around the market. They had manpower enough to seize Paul and Silas, and to drag them *into the market place unto the rulers.* How convenient! They did not have to go to the police station and file a complaint. They did not have to wait for a hearing in court the next week. The rulers were easily accessible, right there in the marketplace where complaints were likely to come from. There is much to be said for speedy justice—but quick injustice is not to be praised.

Timothy and Luke were not seized, probably because they had not attracted attention by public preaching. They may have talked with people privately, but we have no record of that. Paul and Silas were the obvious leaders of the group, the vocal ones. Paul alone had ordered the demon to leave, but Silas was notable enough to be grabbed along with him.

20. And brought them to the magistrates, saying, These men, being Jews, do exceedingly trouble our city.

We wonder about the setup of this court in the marketplace. What were the functions of rulers (v. 19) and magistrates (v. 20), or were they the same people? Luke does not explain, but makes it clear that judges were on hand to hear the owners' complaint.

The complainers began by saying Paul and Silas were *Jews.* We wonder if there was some vigorous prejudice against Jews in Philippi. Was that why there were no Jews living there, or not enough of them to have a synagogue? Be that as it may, these Jews were accused of troubling the city *exceedingly.* Actually they had troubled no one but a few slave owners, but a charge of freeing a girl from a demon would hardly get a conviction in court. The accusers had to fabricate some other charge.

21. And teach customs, which are not lawful for us to receive, neither to observe, being Romans.

This was the heart of the accusation. Paul and Silas were said to be subversive, teaching against Roman law—and that right there in a city that was proud of being a Roman colony. The preachers may in fact have praised the kingdom of God. They may have said Jesus was King. That was the accusation hurled against them in the next town where they preached (Acts 17:7). Given a chance to explain, Paul and Silas might have said, as Jesus did, that Jesus' kingdom is not of this world and poses no threat of armed rebellion (John 18:36). But there was no chance to explain.

B. Mob Response (v. 22)

22. And the multitude rose up together against them; and the magistrates rent off their clothes, and commanded to beat them.

The furious response of the marketplace crowd makes us wonder again if anti-Jewish prejudice was especially strong in Philippi. But certainly the city was proud of its status as a Roman colony, and the people would resent any suggestion that Caesar was not supreme. *Rose up together against them* suggests a threat of mob violence. That was the last thing the magistrates wanted. Rome insisted that local officials keep the peace in their cities. A riot in Philippi might mean the magistrates would lose their jobs. The quickest way to quiet the crowd was to deal severely with the supposed culprits. The magistrates ordered them stripped and beaten.

C. Unjust Imprisonment (vv. 23, 24)

23. And when they had laid many stripes upon them, they cast them into prison, charging the jailer to keep them safely.

If the magistrates had known those Jews were also Roman citizens, they certainly would not have beaten and imprisoned them as they did. See verses 35-39 and compare Acts 22:25-29. It was unjust to punish anyone without a hearing,

visual 6

but Roman officials were not careful about the rights of people who were not Romans. It seems that the main concern of these magistrates was to placate the angry people and keep them from taking the law into their own hands. When the accused men were severely punished, the danger of a riot was ended. The slave masters who had lost some income now had their revenge.

24. Who, having received such a charge, thrust them into the inner prison, and made their feet fast in the stocks.

The jailer did not judge the guilt or innocence of his prisoners. He was ordered to keep them securely, and such an order suggested that they were desperate and dangerous criminals who might try to escape. The jailer would forfeit his own life if he let them get away. He put them in the maximum security section of his prison and locked their feet in the stocks besides.

Conclusion

By long tradition, justice is pictured as blind. This means a court is blind to the wealth and position and reputation of those who appear before it. Each decision is based on the facts and the law, regardless of who is involved. The Philippian magistrates had things in reverse. Blind to the facts and the law, they based their decision on prejudice and pressure. Also blind were the accusers and the crowd that threatened to become a lynch mob.

A. Blinding Greed

Look at the masters of the demon-possessed slave girl. They wanted money, and they were getting it. They cared nothing about the welfare of the girl. Greed blinded them to human need. Greed left no room for sympathy and kindness.

Easily we condemn the greed of merchants of death who peddle illegal drugs in our streets. Some of us denounce the liquor industry because it loves its profits more than the thousands of lives snuffed out by drunken drivers. Some of us are grieved because cigarette makers get rich while smokers get emphysema and cancer. Popular cartoons picture a used-car dealer

misrepresenting his overpriced merchandise.

But let's turn the spotlight on ourselves. Does love of money ever blind us to truth when we have something to sell, or when we make out our tax return? Does it ever blind us to kindness and generosity when a neighbor is in need?

B. Blinding Prejudice

"Those Jews teach customs that are not lawful for us Romans." Without waiting for evidence, the crowd rose up against those Jews.

If the accused is a foreigner, do we instantly suppose he is guilty? If a quarrel is between black and white, do we decide it without listening to the evidence? Do we denounce the umpire whenever his decision is against the home team? When workers go on strike, do we blame the employer or the union before we know what the issues are? When a marriage falls apart, do we automatically say the fault is the husband's, or the wife's? Prejudice is not dead in our time.

C. Blinding Speed

The magistrates of Philippi could not wait to hear the defense. Threatened by a marketplace full of protestors, they had to make a quick and popular decision. They closed their eyes to everything else. So the best men in town lay in jail with bruised and bleeding backs, greedy and heartless slave owners had their revenge, and a thousand citizens who knew nothing about the case went home satisfied because they were able to force their will on the magistrates.

We may be impatient with the slow course of justice in our courts, but too slow is better than too fast. What if the jury would make up its mind before hearing the evidence? What if the demand for a quick decision were louder than the demand for a just one? What if the decision of the court could be swayed by the shouts of protestors in the streets? In settling a lawsuit or a family quarrel, in punishing a criminal or disciplining a child, in making gravy or repairing an automobile, it is more important to do it right than to do it quick.

D. Prayer

Heavenly Father, You have been more than just with us. You have taken away our sin and given us an inheritance among the sanctified. Dear Father, we would copy Your goodness. Help us to conquer selfishness and prejudice; give us wisdom and strength and courage to find and follow the right way rather than the easy way, the popular way, or the profitable way. Amen.

E. Thought to Remember

Do it right.

Learning by Doing

This page contains an alternate lesson plan emphasizing learning activities. Classes desiring such student involvement will find these suggestions helpful.

Learning Goals

By the end of this lesson students will:

1. Identify the cost Paul and his companions paid for doing what was right in the incident recorded in our lesson text.

2. Explore choices Christians may have to make that involve paying a price.

3. Express a desire to do what is right regardless of the cost.

Into the Lesson

Begin the lesson by asking, "What are some situations when doing what is right might cost a Christian something?" Ask class members to work in pairs and to think of at least five such situations. Provide each pair with a sheet of paper and a pencil.

After two minutes, ask for the situations they listed. Then say, "In our study of the apostle Paul, we are considering principles of effective Christian leadership, principles that apply also to every Christian. Today we will focus on this principle: *Effective Christian leaders seek to do what is right regardless of the cost.*" Write the principle on the poster you began in lesson one.

Into the Word

Present a four-minute lecture based on the Introduction section of this lesson.

Ask for five volunteers to read Acts 16:1-24 aloud, following these verse divisions: 1-5, 6-10, 11-15, 16-18, and 19-24. Then ask students to form groups of six to eight. Give half of the groups Assignment One below, and the other half Assignment Two. Provide written questions for all groups. (These assignments are provided in the student book.)

Assignment One

Read Acts 16:6-12 and discuss these questions:

1. As recorded in these verses, what right choice(s) did Paul and his companions make?

2. What price did they have to pay for making the right choice?

3. What might have been the result if they had chosen not to do what they knew was right?

Assignment Two

Read Acts 16:16-24 and discuss these questions:

1. As recorded in these verses, what right choice(s) did Paul make?

2. What price did he have to pay for making the right choice?

3. What might have been the result if he had chosen not to do what was right?

Appoint a discussion leader for each group. After ten minutes ask the groups to report their conclusions to the rest of the class.

Into Life

Have students remain in their groups. Give one of the following situations to each group. More than one group may consider the same situation. Groups should read the situation and discuss the questions.

Situation One

A controversial issue has come to a head in your community. It involves an activity that you and other Christians feel will have detrimental moral and spiritual effects if it is sanctioned. The city council is considering this issue. Because you are well-informed on the issue, and are articulate, you have been asked to address the city council, asking them to prohibit this activity.

What is the right thing for you to do?

What price may you have to pay for your choice?

Situation Two

This is your first year to lead your church's youth group, and you are just now getting to know and be accepted by the teens. Lately a new teenager has been coming to the group, and the group has not made her feel welcome. In fact, they virtually ignore her. She dresses differently than the others and is socially awkward. You are distressed as you observe the teens crack mean jokes about her and leave her out of their fellowship circle.

As a youth leader, what is the right thing for you to do?

What price may you have to pay for taking this action?

After eight minutes, ask each group to read their situation and report their suggestions.

Then give to each class member a pencil and a sheet of paper. Ask them to jot down one situation they sometimes face that requires paying a price for doing what is right. Then ask them to write a prayer to God, asking for His strength in helping them do what pleases Him, regardless of the cost.

Let's Talk It Over

The questions on this page are designed to encourage review of the lesson Scriptures and to promote discussion of the lesson by the class. The answers provided are only discussion starters. Let your class talk it over from there.

1. What motivates people to give help when they see a need?

Several motivations for helping people in need may be noted. The highest is care that arises out of genuine love. But not all people (even most?) are so purely motivated. Sympathy may cause some to help. They either feel sorry for the person in need, or they remember when they themselves were in a similar situation. Other motives are less commendable. Some are motivated by guilt. They may reason, "What will people think if I don't help? I'll feel like a shirker; I'll feel that I'm not behaving as a good person ought to." The basest motivation is to achieve personal advantage. There *are* those who give to get, who want to obligate people to themselves, who want to feel superior. Paul and his companions healed the slave girl because of concern for her welfare. The love of Christ caused them to reach out to her in compassion.

2. Describe the perspective of the owners of the slave girl concerning her possession by a demon and her subsequent release at Paul's command.

Their perspective was completely opposed to Paul's. Whereas Paul had compassion for the girl in her bondage to the demon, her owners viewed her possession by a demon as a good thing—for *them*. They owned her. They had a good thing going as long as she was under the demon's control. By the spirit of divination, she attracted many customers, and her owners gained great wealth. Greed was the name of their gain. Hence, when the girl was released from possession by the demon, they resented it. They had no concern for her pathetic condition. All they could see was their loss of profits. Infuriated over their financial loss, they took revenge on Paul and Silas.

3. What elements in the account of Paul's ministry in Philippi suggest that there may have been anti-Jewish prejudice in that city?

Philippi prided itself in being thoroughly Roman, in fact, a Roman colony. Apparently no synagogue had been built in Philippi, since Paul and his companions went outside the city to the river bank, where they knew a few God-fearing people gathered for prayer on the Sabbath. That meant that few, if any Jews, lived in Philippi. When Paul and Silas were dragged before the magistrates (in a miscarriage of justice), the first statement made against them was that they were Jews. Furthermore, one cannot help but notice how quickly and furiously the marketplace crowd rose up against Paul and Silas on this occasion. Anti-Jewish sentiment could have been a factor in this drama.

4. What are some responses people may make when help is given to them in a time of need?

(1) One response, and the most natural, is thanksgiving. The recipient may be genuinely grateful for assistance given. (2) However, just the opposite—ingratitude—may be the response of others. The help may go unappreciated and unacknowledged. (3) Rejection. Some may not only be ungrateful, but may respond with hostility toward the one giving help. (4) Misunderstanding. The recipient may attribute hidden motives to the act of generosity. (5) Manipulation. Those receiving help may feel that they can work on the giver to get more for themselves. The moral: give help, not for expected personal benefits or advantage, but as ministry in the name and spirit of Jesus Christ. You never know what response will be made, nor if the response will be positive or desirable. Give—*regardless* of potential response!

5. How can you know what God's will is when you must make decisions and choices that may affect the course of your life?

First, saturate your mind with pertinent guidance and truth from the Bible. Then commit this matter to God in fervent prayer. Seek out a mature Christian friend whose wisdom you value and talk it out. Wait on the Lord. Observe circumstances surrounding this experience. As Elton Trueblood suggests, "When 'coincidences' cluster, often God is trying to tell you something." If no clear direction seems to be forthcoming, continue doing what you have been convinced is God's will for your life until other guidance is given. Trust God to open and close doors on His timetable. He *will* lead if you genuinely and trustingly submit yourself to His leading.

A Song at Midnight

October 13
Lesson 7

LESSON SCRIPTURE: Acts 16:16–40.

PRINTED TEXT: Acts 16:25-34.

Acts 16:25-34

25 And at midnight Paul and Silas prayed, and sang praises unto God: and the prisoners heard them.

26 And suddenly there was a great earthquake, so that the foundations of the prison were shaken: and immediately all the doors were opened, and every one's bands were loosed.

27 And the keeper of the prison awaking out of his sleep, and seeing the prison doors open, he drew out his sword, and would have killed himself, supposing that the prisoners had been fled.

28 But Paul cried with a loud voice, saying, Do thyself no harm: for we are all here.

29 Then he called for a light, and sprang in, and came trembling, and fell down before Paul and Silas,

30 And brought them out, and said, Sirs, what must I do to be saved?

31 And they said, Believe on the Lord Jesus Christ, and thou shalt be saved, and thy house.

32 And they spake unto him the word of the Lord, and to all that were in his house.

33 And he took them the same hour of the night, and washed their stripes; and was baptized, he and all his, straightway.

34 And when he had brought them into his house, he set meat before them, and rejoiced, believing in God with all his house.

GOLDEN TEXT: [The keeper of the prison] brought them out, and said, Sirs, what must I do to be saved? And they said, Believe on the Lord Jesus Christ, and thou shalt be saved, and thy house.—Acts 16:30, 31.

From the Damascus Road
to Rome
Unit 3. Traveling Preacher
(Lessons 6-9)

Lesson Aims

After studying this lesson a student should be able to:

1. Tell in his or her own words the facts recorded in our lesson text.

2. Tell why the jailer decided to become a Christian.

3. Identify someone whom the student himself or herself will try to lead to Christ.

Lesson Outline

INTRODUCTION
    A. A Christian's Work
    B. Lesson Background
  I. EARTHQUAKE! (Acts 16:25-28)
    A. Midnight Prayer Meeting (v. 25)
        Praising God at Midnight
    B. Freedom! (v. 26)
    C. Despair and Reassurance (vv. 27, 28)
 II. GOOD QUESTION (Acts 16:29-32)
    A. The Question (vv. 29, 30)
        Upsetting the Rhythm of Life
    B. The Answer (vv. 31, 32)
III. BESIDES BELIEVING (Acts 16:33, 34)
    A. Baptism Without Delay (v. 33)
    B. Joyous Faith (v. 34)
CONCLUSION
    A. This Unhappy World
    B. Be Happy
    C. The Crowning Joy
    D. Prayer
    E. Thought to Remember

Visual 7 from the visuals packet expresses a thought that is developed in the conclusion of this lesson. The visual is shown on page 59.

Introduction

"I am not ashamed of the gospel of Christ: for it is the power of God unto salvation" (Romans 1:16). So wrote Paul, and it was an understatement. Not only was he unashamed of the gospel; he devoted his life to its proclamation. He told the good news in the synagogue (Acts 13:14-16) and elsewhere (Acts 13:43). He told it in the marketplace (Acts 17:17), and even in jail he was not silenced.

A. A Christian's Work

Jesus called Paul to be a servant and a witness (Acts 26:16), and he served by giving his testimony far and wide. Jesus sent the other apostles to all the world (Mark 16:15). The Bible tells but little of their response, but it must have been great. Old traditions tell marvelous stories of them. For example, Thomas is said to have done a magnificent work in India, and Matthew is said to have served in Ethiopia, Persia, and many areas between.

Our heritage is not only the good news, but also the unfinished task of giving it to all the world. How are we doing?

B. Lesson Background

Last week's lesson provides the background for this one. Look there for comments on Acts 16:16-24. Paul released a slave girl from a demon who had taken possession of her, and the owners of the slave were angry. They took Paul and Silas to the magistrates in the marketplace, accusing them of teaching customs that were not lawful for Romans. The marketplace crowd joined the accusers in their fury, and the magistrates hastily had Paul and Silas beaten and jailed.

I. Earthquake!
(Acts 16:25-28)

Paul and Silas were in the maximum security prison. With their feet locked in stocks they could not sit comfortably on the floor, and certainly they could not lie down in comfort on backs bruised and bleeding from their beating. It was midnight in the dark dungeon.

A. Midnight Prayer Meeting (v. 25)

25. And at midnight Paul and Silas prayed, and sang praises unto God: and the prisoners heard them.

There were several other prisoners in that dark dungeon, perhaps as uncomfortable as Paul and Silas. It seems no one could sleep, and they heard sounds such as were never heard there before. We are not told what Paul and Silas said in their prayers, but they *sang praises unto God*. At an earlier time the other apostles rejoiced "that they were counted worthy to suffer shame for his name" (Acts 5:41). Like Paul, they were not ashamed. One of them later wrote, "If any man suffer as a Christian, let him not be ashamed" (1 Peter 4:16). So Paul and Silas were not ashamed, but rejoicing. The condition they were in was shameful, but the shame was not theirs. It belonged to the people who had put them there.

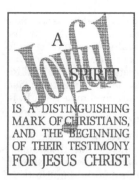

visual 7

A Joyful SPIRIT IS A DISTINGUISHING MARK OF CHRISTIANS, AND THE BEGINNING OF THEIR TESTIMONY FOR JESUS CHRIST

PRAISING GOD AT MIDNIGHT

"The Dark Night of the Soul" is the title of an essay by the sixteenth-century poet, John of the Cross. The phrase has a ring to it that resonates within the hearts of most of us.

The ministry of a Christian teacher in the public school system was cut short by the onslaught of pain that racked her body. Snatched from her were twenty more years of anticipated joy in opening children's minds to knowledge. In the dark night of her soul, she searched for answers: Why? What does this mean? Will the pain ever go away? Should I end my life and find release?

As she wrestled in the dark with her relentless assailant, she found the light of God's love gradually pushing back the edges of the blackness. A new grandchild came! A new business in her home brought the world to her. All who entered her circle of influence found strength and encouragement in her. Her faith took wings and her life gave God praise. her testimony was this: "What happens to me is of far less importance than how I respond to it." She was saying what the beaten, enchained apostles demonstrated as they sang in prison at midnight.   —C. R. B.

B. Freedom! (v. 26)

26. And suddenly there was a great earthquake, so that the foundations of the prison were shaken: and immediately all the doors were opened, and every one's bands were loosed.

This was no tiny temblor; it was *a great earthquake* that shook the massive *foundations* of the prison. It shook down no walls, but it opened all the locked doors. Most remarkable of all, *every one's bands were loosed.* The prisoners were free from the stocks, the fetters, the chains.

C. Despair and Reassurance (vv. 27, 28)

27. And the keeper of the prison awaking out of his sleep, and seeing the prison doors open, he drew out his sword, and would have killed himself, supposing that the prisoners had been fled.

It would be frightening enough to wake up on a shaking bed, to try to stand up and find no solid floor to stand on. But the jailer had a worse fright when the shaking stopped and he saw the open doors. How long had they been open while he was sleeping? He did not know, but he supposed the prisoners were gone. Romans had no mercy on a jailer who let the prisoners escape. Death would be the normal punishment, and a Roman thought it was more honorable to kill himself than to be executed.

28. But Paul cried with a loud voice, saying, Do thyself no harm: for we are all here.

Paul was in the inner prison (v. 24). How did he know what the jailer was doing? In the jailer's office there must have been a light. The jailer could see the open doors. Perhaps Paul was in a position where he could look through those open doors and see the jailer in the light while the jailer could not see him in the darkness. Or perhaps the jailer told someone what he was going to do, and Paul heard him. *With a loud voice* Paul called to reassure the jailer and save his life.

II. Good Question
(Acts 16:29-32)

We know nothing about his jailer's religion, and only a little about what he knew of Paul and Silas. From what he did, however, we can make some guesses about his thinking.

A. The Question (vv. 29, 30)

29. Then he called for a light, and sprang in, and came trembling, and fell down before Paul and Silas.

As already noted, there must have been a light in the jailer's office. Otherwise he could not have seen the open doors. But that light could not illumine the inner prison, and the jailer was not going in among the prisoners in the dark. He called for a light, and someone, perhaps a subordinate, was there to answer the call. Probably that one took a torch and lighted it from the little lamp in the office. Then the jailer *sprang in,* leaped in. The word suggests that he felt the utmost urgency. He had been waiting impatiently for the light, and now he went into the prison as fast as he could. We might expect his first care would be to count the prisoners. But no, it seems that he ignored the others and *fell down before Paul and Silas.* This does not necessarily mean he thought they were gods to be worshiped. It was not unusual to prostrate oneself before a human being who was in a superior position. This jailer probably had heard some of the prayers and hymns of Paul and Silas before he went to sleep.

Then came the miraculous earthquake that opened doors and unlocked fetters. The jailer must have concluded that these praying prisoners were in touch with the power that sent the earthquake. *Trembling* with fear, he fell down before them in humility and reverence.

30. And brought them out, and said, Sirs, what must I do to be saved?

We are not told what the jailer said as he fell prostrate, or as he arose and conducted the two prisoners out of the dungeon. Perhaps he was back in his office when he asked the crucial question, *What must I do to be saved?*

What did the jailer mean by that question? The earthquake was past; he was not asking to be saved from that. He was not asking to be saved from suicide; he had already been saved from that. We might guess he was hoping to be saved from the vengeance of Paul and Silas, but the next verse indicates that the jailer was asking about the salvation that Paul and Silas preached—salvation from sin and death and Hell.

How could the jailer know Paul and Silas were preaching such a salvation? There were several possible ways. He may have learned it from the prayers and hymns he heard before he went to sleep. And for days a fortune teller had been shouting around town, "These men are the servants of the most high God, which show unto us the way of salvation" (Acts 16:17). The jailer may have heard her, or heard about her. It is even possible that the jailer had heard Paul and Silas preaching in the marketplace or elsewhere. Whatever convinced him, the jailer was convinced that Paul and Silas could tell him how to be saved, and he wanted to know.

UPSETTING THE RHYTHM OF LIFE

Travelers often fall prey to an ailment unknown a generation ago. We call it "jet lag."

Traveling across several time zones at airliner speed produces this condition, which is often characterized by fatigue and irritability. It is thought that in the disruption of the amount of daylight we experience, our "circadian rhythms" are broken; we are thrown off pace. As a result, business deals can go sour; political summit conferences can be affected.

Even a jailer dealing with criminals day after day can develop a rhythm, a predictable response to life. One can get used to even the most bizarre circumstances. But the Philippian jailer's rhythm of life was shaken by the earthquake and the subsequent revelation that none of his now-unshackled prisoners had fled. To his credit, he saw in these extra-ordinary events the hand of God, to whom Paul and Silas prayed and of whom they sang.

God may use unsettling circumstances to shake us loose from our patterns of unconcern or disobedience. He may use such forces to alert us to new opportunities for service. He may thus awaken in us a new understanding of His will for our lives. May we, like the jailer, respond to God in a spirit of submission and obedience.—C. R. B.

B. The Answer (vv. 31, 32)

31. And they said, Believe on the Lord Jesus Christ, and thou shalt be saved, and thy house.

Anyone asking about eternal salvation should realize first of all that saving faith is not faith in the apostle Paul or Silas or any twentieth-century preacher. It is faith in Jesus the Son of God. This is not the whole answer. It is the beginning of the answer, and a summary of it. But there is much more to be said, as the next verse shows.

32. And they spake unto him the word of the Lord, and to all that were in his house.

The jailer's house probably was located not far from the prison, and the people in it had been wakened by the earthquake. They were gathered quickly to hear *the word of the Lord.* That message is basically the same to all mankind, but the way of presenting it may be changed to fit the hearers.

Speaking to Jews who knew and loved the Old Testament, a preacher led them through some prophecies of the Messiah and showed that those prophecies were fulfilled in Jesus. Thus he proved that Jesus was the Christ, the Messiah the Jews had been longing for (Acts 2:22-36; 13:16-41). Speaking to Gentiles who believed in God, Peter said God had raised Jesus from the dead and appointed Him to judge all people and to forgive the sins of those who believe in Him (Acts 10:34-43). Speaking to Gentiles who did not know God, Paul first introduced God as Cre-

Home Daily Bible Readings

Monday, Oct. 7—The Jailer Believes (Acts 16:25-34)

Tuesday, Oct. 8—Paul and Silas Are Set Free (Acts 16:35-40)

Wednesday, Oct. 9—Paul's Thanks for the Thessalonians (1 Thessalonians 1:1-5)

Thursday, Oct. 10—Faith Examples to Other Believers (1 Thessalonians 1:6-10)

Friday, Oct. 11—Paul's Love for the Thessalonians (1 Thessalonians 2:1-12)

Saturday, Oct. 12—Remain Faithful Despite Temptations (1 Thessalonians 2:17—3:5)

Sunday, Oct. 13—Continue to Grow in Faith and Love (1 Thessalonians 3:6-13)

ator and Sustainer of the world and mankind. Then he explained that God will judge the world by Jesus, and has given assurance of that by raising Jesus from the dead (Acts 17:11-31). Probably he spoke in a similar way to the jailer and his household. In a city with few Jews or none, those hearers probably knew little or nothing about the real God.

However the word is presented, the call to all people is that summarized in verse 31: "Believe on the Lord Jesus Christ." To put it another way, all people are called to believe that Jesus Christ is Lord (Philippians 2:11).

In our country the word *Lord* is seldom used except for God or His Son. In Paul's world, however, there were human lords everywhere. A man who owned a house was lord of that house; one who owned a slave was lord of that slave. The word *lord* meant the owner, the controller, the boss. When we take Jesus as our Lord we pledge ourselves to obey Him twenty-four hours a day and seven days a week. Such was the word that Paul and Silas spoke to the jailer and *all that were in his house.*

III. Besides Believing (Acts 16:33, 34)

Believing is faith. In the language in which Luke wrote this record, the verb *believe* and the noun *faith* are two forms of the same word.

Faith cannot live by itself. It is dead if it is not accompanied by appropriate action (James 2:20). If we believe Jesus is Lord, we obey Him; if we do not obey, we show that we do not believe.

So the believing jailer was different from the unbelieving jailer. His actions at dawning were not like his actions of the day before.

A. Baptism Without Delay (v. 33)

33. And he took them the same hour of the night, and washed their stripes; and was baptized, he and all his, straightway.

Less than twenty-four hours earlier, this jailer had thrust two men into the inner prison and locked them in the stocks without regard to their smarting backs. Now he washed away the caked blood and perhaps sponged the stripes with wine or some other simple antiseptic.

He and all his, or "all that were in his house" (v. 32), believed the message and were baptized. Obviously "the word of the Lord" that they heard (v. 32) included some teaching about baptism. Doubtless they understood that it was for the remission of sins (Acts 2:38), and they may have heard much more (Romans 6:3-11).

We are not told how many were in this household. Probably the number included household slaves as well as family members, but it included none who did not understand the word of the Lord (v. 32), none who did not believe on the Lord Jesus Christ (v. 31), and none who did not find joy in believing (v. 34).

B. Joyous Faith (v. 34)

34. And when he had brought them into his house, he set meat before them, and rejoiced, believing in God with all his house.

In the *King James Version,* the word *meat* means food of any kind; and probably the jailer provided the best in his larder. It was a happy breakfast because the jailer and his household were *believing in God* and believing in the Lord Jesus Christ (v. 31). Jesus had said, "he that believeth and is baptized shall be saved" (Mark 16:16).

Conclusion

Our children sing a chorus that declares "I've got the joy, joy, joy, joy down in my heart." It is a simple and sincere expression of the same rejoicing that made breakfast joyous in the jailer's house. This is a joy meant for the whole world and offered to the whole world. Then why is the world so unhappy?

A. This Unhappy World

The President of the United States has presented a multi-billion-dollar plan to combat the rising tide of illegal drugs. The Congress probably will enact some such plan before this lesson is published, but at this writing some congressmen are declaring that it will take many more billions than the President has suggested. Why is such a massive campaign needed? It is because millions of unhappy people are willing to spend their last dollar, willing to steal or defraud, willing to do any illegal or shameful thing, just to mask their unhappiness for a while in a "high" induced by a forbidden drug.

Other millions are getting drunk in neighborhood bars, flocking to wild parties, indulging in illicit sex, all in the hope of bringing a bit of pleasure into their unhappy lives.

Millions more are working overtime or moonlighting, embezzling funds, cheating customers, and robbing banks in the mistaken belief that money brings happiness. Among these people are unhappy millionaires who still hope to become happy by multiplying their millions.

There is a better way. The jailer and his household found it. It is a way still open to everybody. Why doesn't the whole unhappy world turn to Jesus and sing with the children, "I've got the joy, joy, joy, joy down in my heart"?

B. Be Happy

To the jailer and his household, Paul and Silas showed the joyous way with the help of an earthquake. If we wait for that kind of help, our world may be unhappy for a long time. But we must remember that Paul and Silas started to show the way before the earthquake helped them. In prison and in pain, they had joy in their hearts; and their joy had its effect on those who heard their glad song in the dark.

Be happy. This is a distinguishing mark of Christians, and the beginning of their testimony. We are not guaranteed trouble-free lives because we follow Jesus. His life was not free from trouble, and "the disciple is not above his master, nor the servant above his lord" (Matthew 10:24). "In the world ye shall have tribulation," said Jesus, "but be of good cheer; I have overcome the world" (John 16:33). Earth has no trouble that can overwhelm the joy of serving Jesus and being assured of "an inheritance incorruptible, and undefiled, and that fadeth not away, reserved in heaven for you" (1 Peter 1:4).

C. The Crowning Joy

Paul's joy was not crowned by his own salvation; it was crowned by others whom he led to Christ. To some of them he wrote, "What is our hope, or joy, or crown of rejoicing? Are not even ye in the presence of our Lord Jesus Christ at his coming? For ye are our glory and joy" (1 Thessalonians 2:19, 20). Likewise the crowning joy of every happy Christian is to lead others to find joy in Christ.

If we would lead a neighbor to Christ, our approach to him is governed by where he is now. Paul's approach to pious Jews in the synagogue (Acts 13:16-41) was different from his approach to the heathen philosophers on Mars Hill (Acts 17:22-31).

Perhaps a neighbor is a humanist who does not believe that God exists. We may need to help him see that creation had a Creator. The things we see are powerful evidence of God's everlasting power and divinity (Romans 1:20). Look at a pair of pliers. This is a very simple tool—just two bits of shaped steel and a pin to hold them together. But no one thinks that simple tool came into existence without being designed and manufactured. Then look at your hand. That tool is far from simple. It has nineteen bones precisely fitted and hinged, not counting eight wrist bones that might be considered parts of the hand. It has twenty muscles, plus the fifteen more powerful muscles of the forearm that operate the hand. The thumb is placed opposite the fingers for a powerful grip on a shovel handle or baseball bat; the fingers are separated so they can play a piano or violin, or do fine needlework. Nails make the fingertips firm so they can pick up a paperclip or a pin. Who can believe this complicated mechanical device was not designed and made as surely as a pair of pliers was? If the hand was designed and made, a superhuman designer and maker did it. So who can deny that God exists?

A neighbor may believe in God, but not in Christ. Perhaps we can get him to look at the evidence. A man was born without a human father, literally the Son of God (Luke 1:35). He showed a superhuman ability to heal the sick (Matthew 4:23, 24), to control the wind (Matthew 8:23-27), to walk on water (Matthew 14:22-27). He worked with God's power; can we not be sure He spoke with God's truth?

These things were recorded by Matthew and John, who were there; also by Mark and Luke, who gathered the facts from people who were there. Can we imagine that someone living nineteen hundred years later knows more about what happened?

Jesus and His trained apostles assure us that His death atones for our sins, that in Christ we can live after death, and live forever. Don't let anyone tell you it isn't so!

Perhaps a neighbor does not deny the facts that God exists and Jesus is His Son, and yet that neighbor does not feel motivated to give his life to Christ. If it is worth while to spend twelve to twenty years in school to get ready for another fifty to seventy years of life on earth, is it not wise to spend those fifty or seventy years in getting ready for a life that has no end?

Why are we so timid, so slow to speak to a neighbor about God and Christ and salvation? If we had a doctor who had safely removed a cancer from us, would we not mention his name to a friend who had a similar cancer? We do have the joy of serving Jesus day by day. We do have the assurance of eternal life. Shall we not tell our neighbors about these?

D. Prayer

Thank you for Your mercy, our Father who art in Heaven. Thank You for Your kindness and love. Thank You for Jesus, who died for us.

Weak as we are, our Father, we need Your strength to keep us walking in Your way. Foolish as we are, we need Your wisdom to guide our neighbors to the way that leads to life. Supply our need out of the riches of Your grace, we pray not for our sake alone, but also for the sake of our neighbors and for Jesus' sake. Amen.

E. Thought to Remember

Jesus saves!

Learning by Doing

This page contains an alternate lesson plan emphasizing learning activities. Classes desiring such student involvement will find these suggestions helpful.

Learning Goals

In this lesson students will:

1. Analyze why Paul and Silas saw their predicament as an opportunity to witness.

2. Anticipate situations they may encounter that could present witnessing opportunities.

Into the Lesson

Ask your class members to pair off. Tell them you are going to present some situations to analyze and discuss. Allow them two minutes to discuss each situation with their partners. Present the first situation: "You are eating in a restaurant. The service is slow. The waitress is gruff. How can you use this situation to create a positive influence for Christ?"

After two minutes ask the class, "What are some ideas you and your partner suggested?"

Then present the second situation:

"You are playing softball. You slide into third base and are clearly safe, but the umpire calls you out. Your teammates come to your defense and scream at the umpire. How can you use this situation to create a positive influence for Christ?"

	What would be a normal response to this situation?	How did Paul and Silas respond?	Why did they respond this way?
vv. 22-25 Paul and Silas are beaten and imprisoned			
vv. 26-28 Earthquake opens jail door and frees Paul and Silas			
vv. 27, 28 Jailer fears for his life			
vv. 29-34 Jailer bows before Paul and Silas			

Again, allow students two minutes to discuss with their partners. Then ask the class, "What ideas did you consider?"

Lead into the Bible exploration by saying, "The *Principle for Effective Leadership* that we will focus on today is this: *Effective Christian leaders seize opportunities to witness for Christ that other Christians miss.*" Write the principle on your leadership poster.

Into the Word

Help your class understand the setting of today's Bible passage by presenting a brief lecture based on the lesson Introduction.

Prepare a copy of the chart shown in the left column for each of your students. (The chart is included in the student book.)

Lead your class members in discussing the three questions at the top of the chart for each passage in the left column. Encourage students to write down answers the class suggests.

After completing the chart, have students form groups of six to eight. Write this question on the chalkboard: *What attitude enabled Paul to see many situations as opportunities for witnessing?* Assign each group one or two of these passages to investigate: Acts 20:22-24; Romans 1:16; 1 Corinthians 9:19-22; 2 Corinthians 2:14-17; 2 Corinthians 5:14-20; Philippians 1:12-18; Philippians 1:20-24.

Allow eight minutes for group discussion. Then ask each group to report their conclusions.

Into Life

Refer again to the *Principle for Effective Leadership* you wrote on the poster earlier. Then ask, "What will it take for us to see our daily situations as opportunities for witnessing?" Encourage students to think of as many ideas as they can while you write them on the chalkboard.

Give each student a piece of paper with the following questions written on it. Allow space for their answers.

1. What situations do I frequently encounter that could become opportunities for witnessing?

2. How can I respond in these situations to create a positive influence for Christ?

After students have finished writing their answers, close by praying that all will courageously witness for Jesus this week.

Let's Talk It Over

The questions on this page are designed to encourage review of the lesson Scriptures and to promote discussion of the lesson by the class. The answers provided are only discussion starters. Let your class talk it over from there.

1. In general terms, what are the two responses a person may make when experiencing a distressful situation?

Essentially, the options boil down to these: one can become bitter or better, weaker or stronger, in responding to difficulty. The final outcome will be determined in large measure by whether a person is externally or internally controlled. External control occurs when we allow things, events, or people to dictate our response in both attitude and behavior. Internal control occurs when we are Spirit-controlled, self-controlled (Galatians 5:23). It is clear from the event recorded in our lesson text that Paul and Silas were *not* externally controlled. In attitude and behavior they demonstrated that they were Spirit-controlled. They came through the experience better, not bitter; stronger, not weaker.

2. Paul and Silas had been severely beaten, put in a dark, inner prison, and restricted in movement by having their feet locked in stocks. In such circumstances, why would they pray and sing?

We can understand why they would pray. Most Christians would pray fervently in a situation such as these missionaries experienced. Crisis motivates people to pray. But what about singing? Can you imagine yourself *singing hymns* in a situation such as this one? Paul and Silas sang because Christian hymns give eloquent voice to faith, hope, and love. Hymns give release to our deepest feelings; they express our profoundest convictions. In singing Christian hymns, not only do we express our convictions; we also reinforce them. Thus as Paul and Silas sang, each encouraged himself and the other to hold on to his faith in Christ.

3. How did the jailer respond to the good news of salvation in Jesus Christ, which Paul and Silas announced to him?

The jailer responded with action. First, he wanted others to hear the good news also. So he gathered all that were in his household, and together they listened as Paul and Silas spoke unto them the word of the Lord. Second, he washed the wounds of his former prisoners, caring for their needs. Third, he was baptized immediately after caring for the wounds of Paul and Silas.

Fourth, He extended the hospitality of his home to Christ's messengers. And finally, he rejoiced because of his new faith and life.

4. Identify some of the reasons Christians give for not witnessing to non-Christians about Jesus Christ. What is the appropriate response to them.

Some reasons offered are these: (1) "I'm not well-informed about my religion. I don't know what to say or how to go about it." (2) "Religion is a very private matter, and I don't want to intrude on another's privacy." (3) "Others may think I'm some kind of fanatic. I know how they talk about religious 'kooks'." (4) "That's the job of professionals. The preachers are supposed to do the evangelistic work of the church." (5) "That's not my gift. I can serve in many ways in the church, but I'm not an evangelist." (6) "There's a time and place for everything. The right situation doesn't present itself."

The appropriate response to these rationalizations is that witnessing is *every* Christian's responsibility! It is not reserved for "clergy," or for specially trained personnel. Obviously, one who has a thorough understanding of God's Word will feel more comfortable in sharing its truths with others. And Christians should increase in their knowledge of the Bible. But you do not have to possess great knowledge of Biblical content or methods of evangelism to tell another about Jesus Christ. You can simply begin by telling that person what Jesus Christ has done for you; *that* is personal witnessing! Of course, there are appropriate times and places for witnessing; but the truth is that most of us who are Christ's followers do not utilize the many varied opportunities that *do* present themselves daily. Until *all* Christians take seriously the responsibility to tell the world about Jesus Christ, the world will not be won to Christ.

5. What is the difference between joy and happiness?

Happiness depends upon external circumstances. If things go well for you, you will most likely be happy. But joy is a constant, inner state that continues *despite* external circumstances. Paul and Silas sang because they knew the joy of the Lord.

A Proclamation in Athens

LESSON SCRIPTURE: Acts 17.

PRINTED TEXT: Acts 17:22-34.

Acts 17:22-34

22 Then Paul stood in the midst of Mars' hill, and said, Ye men of Athens, I perceive that in all things ye are too superstitious.

23 For as I passed by, and beheld your devotions, I found an altar with this inscription, TO THE UNKNOWN GOD. Whom therefore ye ignorantly worship, him declare I unto you.

24 God that made the world and all things therein, seeing that he is Lord of heaven and earth, dwelleth not in temples made with hands;

25 Neither is worshipped with men's hands, as though he needed any thing, seeing he giveth to all life, and breath, and all things;

26 And hath made of one blood all nations of men for to dwell on all the face of the earth, and hath determined the times before appointed, and the bounds of their habitation;

27 That they should seek the Lord, if haply they might feel after him, and find him, though he be not far from every one of us:

28 For in him we live, and move, and have our being; as certain also of your own poets have said, For we are also his offspring.

29 Forasmuch then as we are the offspring of God, we ought not to think that the Godhead is like unto gold, or silver, or stone, graven by art and man's device.

30 And the times of this ignorance God winked at; but now commandeth all men every where to repent:

31 Because he hath appointed a day, in the which he will judge the world in righteousness by that man whom he hath ordained; whereof he hath given assurance unto all men, in that he hath raised him from the dead.

32 And when they heard of the resurrection of the dead, some mocked: and others said, We will hear thee again of this matter.

33 So Paul departed from among them.

34 Howbeit certain men clave unto him, and believed: among the which was Dionysius the Areopagite, and a woman named Damaris, and others with them.

Oct 20

GOLDEN TEXT: God that made the world and all things therein, seeing that he is Lord of heaven and earth, dwelleth not in temples made with hands; neither is worshipped with men's hands, as though he needed any thing, seeing he giveth to all life, and breath, and all things.—Acts 17:24, 25.

Lesson Aims

After this lesson a student should be able to:
1. Summarize Paul's message in Athens.
2. Recall three kinds of response.
3. Plan a way to approach someone with the gospel this week.

Lesson Outline

INTRODUCTION
    A. Men on the Move
    B. Men Who Stayed
    C. Lesson Background
  I. INTRODUCING GOD (Acts 17:22-29)
    A. God the Unknown (vv. 22, 23)
    B. God the Creator (vv. 24-26)
    C. God the Father (vv. 27-29)
       Groping for God
 II. GOD'S CALL (Acts 17:30, 31)
    A. Call to Repent (v. 30)
    B. Warning of Judgment (v. 31)
       Seven Million Missing Children
III. THE RESULT (Acts 17:32-34)
    A. Mockery (v. 32a)
    B. Polite Interest (vv. 32b, 33)
    C. Acceptance (v. 34)
CONCLUSION
    A. Prayer
    B. Thought to Remember

Visual 8 from the visuals packet highlights the thoughts presented in section "III. The Result." The visual is shown on page 68.

Introduction

Last week we left Paul and Silas enjoying a happy breakfast in their jailer's house, though technically they were prisoners. When the magistrates went to work that morning, the first order of business was to set those prisoners free. The magistrates did this with apologies, and begged them to leave town.

A. Men on the Move

At times Paul and Silas must have felt that the whole world was against them. At Philippi some greedy heathen stirred up trouble, and frightened magistrates put the preachers in jail. When they were released they went to Thessalonica. There they found a good response till envious Jews enlisted some "lewd fellows of the baser sort" and stirred up a mob (Acts 17:1-9). At Berea the Jews were nobler. They listened to the message and studied the Scriptures to see if it was true. But troublemakers from Thessalonica followed the missionaries and went to work to rouse a mob (Acts 17:10-13). Paul then moved on to Athens.

B. Men Who Stayed

Looking back to the lesson of two weeks ago, we are reminded that "we" came to Philippi. The pronoun *we* includes Luke, the writer of this record. He came to Philippi with Paul, Silas, and Timothy (Acts 16:9-12). But when Paul and Silas were set free, "they" departed (Acts 16:40). Paul, Silas, and Timothy went on; Luke stayed in Philippi. This leads us to suppose that he was not a new convert, but a well-taught Christian who stayed there to guide the new church with his knowledge and experience.

Then in Berea, when troublemakers were stirring up a mob, Paul left town, "but Silas and Timothy abode there still" (Acts 17:14). The opposition was most fierce against Paul because he was the most notable of the evangelists. When he was gone, the others were able to teach and strengthen the new Christians in peace.

C. Lesson Background

At Athens Paul saw "the city wholly given to idolatry" or "the city full of idols," as the *American Standard Version* has it. Stirred by what he saw, he reasoned with worshipers in the synagogue and with others who met him in the marketplace (Acts 17:16, 17).

Athens was a center of Greek culture, a favorite haunt of philosophers who liked to discuss everything. Hearing Paul in the market-place, some of them realized that he was

---

How to Say It

ARATUS. *Air*-uh-tus.
AREOPAGITE. Air-ee-*op*-uh-gite.
AREOPAGUS. Air-ee-*op*-uh-gus.
BEREA. Beh-*ree*-uh.
CLEANTHES. Klee-*an*-theez.
DAMARIS. *Dam*-uh-ris.
DIONYSIUS. Die-oh-*nish*-ih-us.
PHILIPPI. Fih-*lip*-pie or *Fil*-ih-pie.
THESSALONICA. *Thess*-uh-lo-*nye*-kuh
   (strong accent on *nye*; *th* as in *thin*).
ZEUS. Zoose.

talking about matters unknown to them. A group of them invited him to a meeting place on Mars' Hill, called *Areopagus* in the Greek. In this place quieter than the market, they asked him to tell them more about the new doctrine he was bringing to Athens (Acts 17:18-21).

I. Introducing God
(Acts 17:22-29)

Paul's hearers now were not Jews who knew the Scriptures and believed them, but they were scholars and thinkers. Paul addressed them as such when he began to tell them about God.

A. God the Unknown (vv. 22, 23)

22. Then Paul stood in the midst of Mars' hill, and said, Ye men of Athens, I perceive that in all things ye are too superstitious.

Most students agree that *too superstitious* is not the best translation here. Several English versions have *very religious*. Paul was recognizing that the people of Athens were devout: they were people who worshiped. Evidence of this was seen in the images of imaginary gods and the altars dedicated to them that abounded in the city.

23. For as I passed by, and beheld your devotions, I found an altar with this inscription, To THE UNKNOWN GOD. Whom therefore ye ignorantly worship, him declare I unto you.

Your devotions means the things to which you are devoted, the objects of your worship. The Athenians recognized many mythical gods and goddesses, but they acknowledged that there probably was at least one god they did not know. An altar was erected to pay homage to him, whoever he might be. Paul proposed to tell them about the God they did not know.

B. God the Creator (vv. 24-26)

24. God that made the world and all things therein, seeing that he is Lord of heaven and earth, dwelleth not in temples made with hands.

Thus briefly Paul told the Athenians three things about the God unknown to them.

1. He is the Creator. He made the world and everything in it. There was not one maker of the land, another of the sea, another of the air, another of the trees, and another of the animals. One God made them all.

2. *He is Lord*, the owner, the controller, the boss of all He made. When we know this, it is easy to see that the best way to live on earth is to live by God's plan, to do His will.

3. He does not live in the temples we build with our hands. This was a statement to challenge the thinking of Athenian philosophers, and it challenges the thinking of Jews and Christians as well. The temples of Athens were famous, and tourists flock to see the ruins of them even now. Of course the real God would not live in temples made to honor mythical gods. But the temple at Jerusalem also was made with hands, and Jesus called it His Father's house (John 2:16). In earlier times it housed the ark of the covenant, symbol of God's presence and power and providence and law. Upon the ark were two golden cherubim, and between them was the spot where God promised to meet the appointed leader of His people (Exodus 25:22). In a sense, God did dwell there between the cherubim (Psalm 99:1). Then what did Paul mean when he said God does not live in temples made with hands? The next verse will help us understand.

25. Neither is worshipped with men's hands, as though he needed any thing, seeing he giveth to all life, and breath, and all things.

Some versions have *served* instead of *worshipped*. The Greek word can have either meaning, but we usually think of hands as serving rather than worshiping. It is evident that we do serve God with hands: hands that build a house of worship, hands that take food to the hungry in His name, hands that earn money and put it in the offering on Sunday. Then how can Paul say God is not served by men's hands? The explanation is in the next phrase. We do serve God, but not *as though he needed any thing*. The temple or church house we build is not to meet His need; it is to meet our own need and the need of our fellowmen. God does not need the food we carry to the hungry; the hungry need it. God does not need the money we put in the offering; we and our fellowmen need the things that money buys. Since God gives us everything we have, including life and breath, it is plain that He has abundance. He does not need our gifts, but we need to give. Paul is emphasizing the unlimited wealth and greatness of God. He made everything; He rules everything; He owns everything.

26. And hath made of one blood all nations of men for to dwell on all the face of the earth, and hath determined the times before appointed, and the bounds of their habitation.

One blood here is used in the sense of one race, one kind of people. Some ancient manuscripts and some modern versions leave out the word *blood*, saying God hath made of one all nations of men. That can mean either that He made all nations from one nation or that He made all nations from one man, Adam. In any case, the statement tells us that all humans are basically of the same kind. There are no exceptions: this

includes all who *dwell on all the face of the earth.*
God, who made the nations, determined when
they would live and die, and where they would
live on earth. His rule is supreme. Nations may
think they fix their boundaries by means of wars
and treaties; but a nation cannot take a foot
more territory than God allows, nor can it endure a day beyond the time He has allotted.

C. God the Father (vv. 27-29)

**27. That they should seek the Lord, if haply
they might feel after him, and find him, though
he be not far from every one of us.**

God created the people of all nations in such a
way that they feel a need of Him and search for
Him. Even people who are not guided by His
revelation *seek* Him, but they can only *feel after
him,* like people in darkness groping for something without knowing what it is. When we are
enlightened by His Word, we see that creation itself is enough to reveal "his eternal power and
Godhead" (Romans 1:20); but without His Word
most seekers fail to find Him. The Greeks imagined a large number of gods and goddesses, perhaps because the parts of creation are so many
and varied. But all these did not satisfy them.
They were still groping for a god unknown to
them. Paul was trying to help them find that unknown God and realize that He was the only
one. It seems strange that the real God is so hard
to find, for he is *not far from every one of us.* The
next verse shows how near He is.

GROPING FOR GOD

The town of Mt. Ida, Arkansas, prefers to call
itself the "Crystal Capital of the World," home of
the annual Quartz Crystal Festival and the
World's Championship Quartz Crystal Dig. Some
see it as New Age nirvana.

Mt. Ida sits on top of the largest deposit of
pure quartz crystal in the world. For years, people thereabouts dug up the beautiful geological
formations and sold them to the occasional rock
collector who came by. Then came the New Age

visual 8

movement, whose adherents put crystals on top
of air conditioners to save on electricity, or in
their cars to save gasoline, or sleep near crystals
to absorb the ancient knowledge that they suppose is contained in them. Now Mt. Ida is on the
map and making money, too!

The New Age movement is just one more of
man's attempts to find God. When we reject
God's revelation of himself in Scripture and
(most expressively) in Jesus Christ, we are left to
our own designs. We grope about, grasping at
one spiritual straw after another, to keep from
drowning in a tide of hopelessness.

The personal God has revealed himself to us.
When will we learn to quit groping and acknowledge Him?   — C. R. B.

**28. For in him we live, and move, and have
our being; as certain also of your own poets
have said, For we are also his offspring.**

God did not create mankind and then abandon
it. He is with each person daily, supplying life
and breath (v. 25). He gives us our strength; without Him we could not move a muscle. Greek
poets groping for God had come close to this
idea. Paul quoted a line from Aratus, who wrote
more than two hundred years earlier. Cleanthes
wrote a very similar line. Both of these poets
were of the Stoic school of philosophy. Stoics
were among the philosophers Paul was addressing (v. 18), so he fittingly spoke of *your own poets.*
These poets were writing of Zeus or Jupiter, the
supposed father of the imaginary gods; but Paul
applied the thought to the real God, the one unknown to Athenian philosophers.

**29. Forasmuch then as we are the offspring of
God, we ought not to think that the Godhead is
like unto gold, or silver, or stone, graven by art
and man's device.**

The Godhead means the divine nature, the
essence of God. Surely God's offspring, God's
children, cannot think He is an object of metal
or stone. Such images produce no offspring. Furthermore, such a man-made object cannot adequately represent or picture God. It is true that
man is made in God's image (Genesis 1:27), but
it does not follow that a man-like statue can represent God. God the Creator is more than the
image He created. God is a Spirit (John 4:24),
and no material form can properly portray Him.

II. God's Call
(Acts 17:30, 31)

Man's groping leaves him with the feeling that
God is still unknown. That was the feeling of
the people of Athens. Man is not satisfied with
that result, and neither is God. Man wants to
know God, and God wants to be known. It takes

a special revelation to bridge the gap and make God known to man.

A. Call to Repent (v. 30)

30. And the times of this ignorance God winked at; but now commandeth all men every where to repent.

Instead of *winked at* some versions have *overlooked*, which is a precise translation of the Greek word. Through centuries men have failed to know God, and through centuries God has patiently tolerated their ignorance. But now God has given a new revelation. The Son of God has appeared in human form. He has taught the nature and the will of God in words and demonstrated them in His own life. He has sacrificed His life to atone for the sins of men. Now His apostles inspired by the Holy Spirit, are taking His revelation to the world. Now is the time for *all men every where to repent.* Now is the time for people to end their groping and their ignorance, to know God as He has been revealed by His Son. Now is the time for people to turn away from the sins they committed because they did not know God (Romans 1:28-32). Now *all men every where* ought to be godly men, acknowledging God's Son and obeying Him.

B. Warning of Judgment (v. 31)

31. Because he hath appointed a day, in the which he will judge the world in righteousness by that man whom he hath ordained; whereof he hath given assurance unto all men, in that he hath raise him from the dead.

Why should everybody repent and do right? Because judgment is coming. God has set the day, He has not told us when it will be, but today it is a day nearer than it was yesterday. In that day God will judge the world. No one will be overlooked. "Every one of us shall give account of himself to God" (Romans 14:12). Even for "every idle word" we shall give account (Matthew 12:36). God will *judge the world in righteousness.* There will be no favoritism and no injustice. At last there will be a judge who will know the whole truth and will not be deceived by any excuse. There will be no appeal. His judgment will be final. God will judge *by that man whom he hath ordained.* That man is Jesus. With His own voice He plainly warned that He would judge the people of all nations, and He will. He will call some to the eternal kingdom, and He will consign some to eternal fire (Matthew 25:31-46). How do we know Jesus told the truth? God showed His approval by doing great miracles by Jesus (Acts 2:22). As an outstanding sign of approval, God *raised Him from the dead.* The resurrection is God's seal of approval on all that Jesus did and said.

SEVEN MILLION MISSING CHILDREN

Can you imagine seven million American children simply vanishing *in one year?* It happened in 1987! That was the year the IRS began requiring taxpayers to list the Social Security numbers for all children age five and over whom they were claiming as exemptions on their tax returns. And so, on April 15, the IRS's annual day of reckoning, there were seven million fewer children "alive" in 1987 than there had been in 1986! Do you suppose the "parents" of those seven million "children" suddenly saw the error of their ways and repented in a mass flurry of new-found spiritual insight? Perhaps. Or did the fact of stringent new laws result in their increased honesty? Much more likely!

The Bible makes it clear that God has appointed a day in which He will judge the world. Jesus has stated that the obedient will be blessed of God in His kingdom, but the disobedient will be banished from His presence. Do we obey God, however, simply because we fear His punishment? God doesn't want us merely to fall grudgingly into line and shape up. He wants something better from us (and for us): He calls on us to repent—to take the moral step away from evil and toward godliness because in our hearts we desire to be right with Him. —C. R. B.

III. The Result
(Acts 17:32-34)

At Thessalonica and Berea, envious Jews had opposed Paul's message with violence (Acts 17:1-15). In Athens, the reaction of educated

Greeks was more like that of educated Gentiles to whom we present the gospel today. There was mockery; there was polite interest; there was acceptance.

A. Mockery (v. 32a)

32a. And when they heard of the resurrection of the dead, some mocked.

How like the reaction of some educated hearers in the twentieth century! These hearers believe in science. Scientific observation discovers no spirit that survives the death of the body, and finds no evidence that dead bodies will ever be resurrected. Observation indicates that dead people stay dead, and that is regarded as a scientific fact. Belief in a resurrection therefore is labeled unscientific nonsense.

But the resurrection of Jesus is a fact. It is attested by testimony abundant and competent (1 Corinthians 15:3-8). It is not scientific to deny a fact just because we cannot reproduce it at will. The resurrection of Jesus is a sign of God's approval. It has value as such a sign because we cannot reproduce it. It is an act of God.

B. Polite Interest (vv. 32b, 33)

32b. And others said, We will hear thee again of this matter.

Some hearers were not so rude as to scoff openly when Paul spoke of the resurrection, but neither were they convinced. Politely they expressed a wish to hear more about it.

The record does not tell us whether they were sincere in that wish or not. If they were, probably they arranged a time and place for another meeting. If not, probably they went away to ignore the matter.

Every personal evangelist has met people who politely speak of hearing more of what he has to say, but who artfully dodge any opportunity to do so. On the other hand, every personal evangelist can recall people who made an appointment for another meeting and listened with interest.

33. So Paul departed from among them.

The meeting adjourned, and Paul went his way. Perhaps it was time for lunch, or supper. How many evangelistic meetings end with some hearers scornful and others unconvinced!

C. Acceptance (v. 34)

34. Howbeit certain men clave unto him, and believed: among the which was Dionysius the Areopagite, and a woman named Damaris, and others with them.

Some hearers were convinced. They were sincerely eager to hear more, so they went with Paul without delay.

The title *Areopagite* indicates that *Dionysius* was a prominent and respected man in Athens, one of the judges of a court that met on the Areopagus, Mars' Hill. That was the place where Paul had been speaking, but it seems that he was not addressing the court. A group of philosophers were using the meeting place when the court was not in session (vv. 18-21).

The subordinate position of women in ancient times is sometimes exaggerated. It is interesting to see that *a woman* was in the meeting of philosophers. The fact that she is named along with Dionysius suggests that she too was a person of prominence and influence.

We are not told how many *others* believed along with the two who are named. Neither are we told how many were in the meeting. But again we see how the experience of a modern evangelist is like that of Paul. We are happy if two or three are won from an audience of fifty.

Conclusion

Let's note some features of Paul's ministry that appear in our own.

Paul had *one message* for everybody. He preached Christ, with emphasis on His death and resurrection. In our world today there are many good causes to support and many evils to denounce, but let's not lose sight of the heart of our message.

Without changing his message, Paul *adapted* it to worshiping Jews, the marketplace crowd, or philosophers. We must meet people where they are in order to lead them to higher ground.

Paul's preaching produced *mixed results.* He met violence, scoffing, indifference, and success. Most of us see no violence. Grateful for that, we are the more ready to endure scoffing and indifference in order to win some for Christ.

Finally, Paul persisted. He was not discouraged by violence, scoffing, and indifference. Neither was he satisfied with his success. He kept on taking his one message to more people. Let's not give up when we fail nor stop when we succeed. There is more to be done.

A. Prayer

Thank You for our Savior, Father. Thank You for Paul and other heroes of the faith who have passed on His message till it has come to us. As we give it to others, grant us courage and wisdom and persistence to be as faithful and effective as Your people before us have been. In Jesus' name we pray. Amen.

B. Thought to Remember

"Preach the word" (2 Timothy 4:2).

Learning by Doing

This page contains an alternate lesson plan emphasizing learning activities. Classes desiring such student involvement will find these suggestions helpful.

Learning Goals

As a result of studying this lesson, your students will be able to:

1. Identify ways in which Paul adapted his method of presenting the gospel to various audiences.

2. Specify Christian words and phrases that may not be clear to secular people.

3. Express at least two of these phrases in language a secular person would understand.

Into the Lesson

Write the following words and phrases on your chalkboard.

Born again	Salvation
Repent	Justification
Trust Jesus	Grace
Blessing	Praise the Lord
Believe in Jesus	Receive Jesus
Discipleship	Follow Jesus
The Spirit's leading	God's will
The Messiah	Lord

Ask students, "Which of these Biblical ideas would the average unsaved person in our community understand accurately?" Circle the words as the students call them out.

Then say, "If we are committed to sharing the gospel with the lost, we will seek to communicate it to them as accurately as possible. We can never compromise the content of the message; but that does not mean we will never alter our method of presenting it. "In truth, many people who are outside of Christ do not understand some of the terms that are familiar to Christians. Therefore, we should select carefully and thoughtfully the words we use to convey Biblical concepts.

"As we examine the sermons recorded in the New Testament, we see that Christ's messengers communicated the gospel in a manner that was meaningful to their audiences. When speaking to a Jewish audience, they made reference to Jewish law and history. But when speaking to a Gentile audience, these Jewish ideas usually were not mentioned.

"In our lesson today, we will explore how Paul approached a totally secular audience in Athens. In addition, we will consider how we should speak about our faith to our friends who have little Bible background."

Into the Word

Ask for a volunteer to read Acts 17:16-34 aloud. Then lead your class in discussing the questions below.

1. Look at verses 16-21. What indicates that many at the marketplace did not understand what Paul was talking about?

2. Look at verses 22, 23. How did Paul establish a rapport with these idol worshipers?

3. Look at verses 24-31. What was Paul's main point in each of these sections?

vv. 24, 25

vv. 26-28

vv. 29-31

4. Observe that Paul made no reference to ideas or events that would be familiar only to Jews. What are some facts, phrases, or events that Jews would understand, but which would be unfamiliar to his Athenian audience? (For help, see Paul's sermon delivered in the synagogue at Antioch—Acts 13:16-41.)

5. Note that in verse 28 Paul quoted pagan poets. Why would he interject views from pagans in telling the Athenians about God?

Into Life

Write the following principle on your "Effective Leader" poster (you may have needed to begin a new poster by now, but be sure to keep the first one posted also): *Effective Christian leaders seek to communicate in language their hearers can understand.* Read the statement aloud. Then say, "Let's see if we can prepare ourselves to do this more consistently."

Refer to the list of phrases on the chalkboard from the beginning of class. Ask, "What are some additional phrases we Christians use that may not be clear to non-Christians?" List their suggestions on the chalkboard.

Ask class members to form groups of four to six. Appoint a discussion leader for each group and provide each with paper and a pen. Have each group select two of the phrases from the chalkboard and "translate" them into the language of non-Christians. Ask them to define or explain each phrase without using any "religious-sounding" language. Perhaps they can think of an illustration to convey the meaning. Allow ten to twelve minutes. Then ask each group to read their definitions to the class. Conclude with a time of prayer.

Let's Talk It Over

The questions on this page are designed to encourage review of the lesson Scriptures and to promote discussion of the lesson by the class. The answers provided are only discussion starters. Let your class talk it over from there.

1. List some responses that different people make to the gospel.

Indifference. This person says, "The gospel may be helpful to some, but it doesn't grab me. I'm not into that right now. I have other priorities. At some future time I might be interested, but not now."

Rejection, expressed perhaps as follows: "Talk about Jesus' death and resurrection is for children and old people! You don't expect me to buy that collection of fairy tales, do you? Catch up with the twentieth century—that antiquated nonsense went out with high-button shoes and hoop skirts."

Curiosity. This seeker of new ideas may respond, "I've always been interested in studying the major world religions. Maybe there's something of value in Christianity. I might be interested in hearing how it compares with Zen."

Belief. This person recognizes his sinfulness and rejoices to learn of the Savior. He responds, "I believe that Jesus Christ is the Son of God. I can't go on living the way I have, ignoring Him. What do I do next?"

Paul's audience at Athens reflected all of these responses. Some shrugged their shoulders, some sneered, others were curious, and a few believed and became followers of the Lord.

2. What "contact points" did Paul use to build a "bridge" with his audience in Athens?

Paul was skilled in the art of public speaking. As any effective communicator would do, Paul started with his audience where they were, in their own context. He made mention of their life-style. Noting the multiplicity of their idols, he remarked that they were a very religious people. In contemporary terms, he "plussed" them right away. In the process of establishing some key points of his message, Paul quoted from their own poets. Thus he acknowledged both his acquaintance with their own culture and heritage, and appealed to it. Paul set a masterful example for any today who would take the gospel to persons of a different culture.

3. In this sermon at Athens, why didn't Paul appeal to the history and the prophecies contained in the Old Testament Scriptures, as he did in his sermon at Antioch (Acts 13:16-41)?

The answer to this question builds on the previous one. In Athens Paul was speaking to Greeks steeped in philosophy, probably with little direct knowledge of the Hebrew Scriptures. In Antioch, he addressed Jews, Jewish proselytes, and God-fearing Gentiles in a *synagogue* service. Naturally, that message would be saturated with references to, and quotations from, the Hebrew Scriptures.

4. In Paul's message, what did he affirm about God?

Paul's affirmations may be put into six groupings: (1) God is Creator. He made the world and everything in it; He gives to mankind life and breath and everything he has; and He established the nations and their boundaries. (2) God is Lord. He rules over all the created order. (3) God is not an idol. He does not live in man-made temples, nor does he need anything from man. The fatal flaw of an idol (of any idol!) is that it cannot communicate life. God gives life; He has offspring. (4) God wants a relationship with mankind. He is not far off; He wants man to find Him. (5) God calls to repentance or judgment. He has patiently drawn mankind to repentance, but a day of judgment is coming. (6) God raised His appointed representative (His Son, Jesus Christ) from the dead. This final affirmation of Paul triggered the sneers of some and the belief of others.

5. Where do people today place their trust for their safety and security?

Some rely on the nation's military strength. They feel safe only when their nation holds military dominance. Others feel secure only in their personal possession of weapons and their ability to use them.

Some persons look to science and technology. Their motto is, "Science is my shepherd, I shall not want." They believe whatever they need will be provided by modern science and technology.

Money and material goods are the source of security for many. Their goal is to accumulate money and the things money can buy. Without these "things," these people know only unrest.

Other persons, recognizing the proper place of the above, anchor their lives for the present and the future only in Jesus Christ.

Disciples in Ephesus

LESSON SCRIPTURE: Acts 18:1—19:20.

PRINTED TEXT: Acts 18:24—19:6.

Acts 18:24-28

24 And a certain Jew named Apollos, born at Alexandria, an eloquent man, and mighty in the Scriptures, came to Ephesus.

25 This man was instructed in the way of the Lord; and being fervent in the spirit, he spake and taught diligently the things of the Lord, knowing only the baptism of John.

26 And he began to speak boldly in the synagogue: whom when Aquila and Priscilla had heard, they took him unto them, and expounded unto him the way of God more perfectly.

27 And when he was disposed to pass into Achaia, the brethren wrote, exhorting the disciples to receive him: who, when he was come, helped them much which had believed through grace:

28 For he mightily convinced the Jews, and that publicly, showing by the Scriptures that Jesus was Christ.

Acts 19:1-6

1 And it came to pass, that, while Apollos was at Corinth, Paul having passed through the upper coasts came to Ephesus; and finding certain disciples,

2 He said unto them, Have ye received the Holy Ghost since ye believed? And they said unto him, We have not so much as heard whether there be any Holy Ghost.

3 And he said unto them, Unto what then were ye baptized? And they said, Unto John's baptism.

4 Then said Paul, John verily baptized with the baptism of repentance, saying unto the people, that they should believe on him which should come after him, that is, on Christ Jesus.

5 When they heard this, they were baptized in the name of the Lord Jesus.

6 And when Paul had laid his hands upon them, the Holy Ghost came on them; and they spake with tongues, and prophesied.

Oct
27

GOLDEN TEXT: When Paul had laid his hands upon them, the Holy Ghost came on them; and they spake with tongues, and prophesied.—Acts 19:6.

> *From the Damascus Road
> to Rome*
> Unit 3. Traveling Preacher
> (Lessons 6-9)

Lesson Aims

After this lesson a student should be able to:

1. Briefly tell what Apollos did for Christians in Ephesus and Achaia, what Aquila and Priscilla did for Apollos, and what Paul did for disciples in Ephesus.

2. List three ways of helping that are seen in our text. (Some are mentioned under B in the conclusion.)

3. Help somebody this week.

Lesson Outline

INTRODUCTION
    A. Paul in Europe
    B. Lesson Background
  I. TEACHING A TEACHER (Acts 18:24-26)
    A. Enthusiastic Teacher (vv. 24, 25)
    B. Willing Learner (v. 26)
       Not Embarrassed to Change
 II. HELPING THE BELIEVERS (Acts 18:27, 28)
    A. Recommended (v. 27a)
    B. Helpful (vv. 27b, 28)
III. BACK IN EPHESUS (Acts 19:1-6)
    A. Important Question (vv. 1, 2)
    B. Another Baptism (vv. 3-5)
       The Price of Ignorance
    C. The Holy Spirit (v. 6)
CONCLUSION
    A. Teaching and Learning
    B. Helping
    C. Prayer
    D. Thought to Remember

Visual 9 from the visuals packet highlights a principal thought in A of the conclusion of this lesson. The visual is shown on page 75.

Introduction

In this series of lessons on Paul, the Scripture texts are bringing us samples of the apostle's work rather than covering all he did. Lessons 6-8 brought incidents in his second missionary journey. In lesson 6 we saw that he crossed from Asia to Europe, along with Silas, Timothy, and Luke. (*Trace Paul's movements mentioned here on the maps—visuals 6 and 1—from the visuals packet.*)

A. Paul in Europe

In lesson 7 we saw a bit of the adventures in Philippi. When the party moved on after Paul and Silas were released from jail, Luke stayed behind. He could give the new Christians the help of one more mature in the faith.

We passed over the adventures in Thessalonica and Berea, where unbelieving Jews opposed Paul so violently that he soon went on to Athens. Silas and Timothy both stayed in Berea to guide the new Christians. From Athens Paul sent word for them to come as soon as they could (Acts 17:15); but before they came, he went on to Corinth (Acts 18:1).

Apparently Paul was out of money. He got a job as tentmaker, working with a Jewish couple named Aquila and Priscilla. Paul worked through the week with them, and taught in the synagogue every Sabbath Day (Acts 18:2-4).

Silas and Timothy caught up with Paul in Corinth. Probably they brought funds contributed by the churches, so Paul was able to leave his secular job and give all his time to preaching. The unbelieving Jews opposed him so vigorously that Paul finally gave up trying to preach in the synagogue. He found a place next door where he kept on preaching for a year and a half (Acts 18:5-11).

B. Lesson Background

When we read that Paul went back to the east, we see nothing about Silas and Timothy. Perhaps they stayed at Corinth. Aquila and Priscilla went with Paul across the Aegean Sea to Ephesus. There they stayed; but after a brief stop, Paul went on to attend one of the Jewish feasts at Jerusalem (Acts 18:18-21).

How to Say It

ACHAIA. Uh-*kay*-yuh.
ALEXANDRIA. Al-ex-*an*-dri-a.
ANTIOCH. *An*-tee-ock.
APOLLOS. Uh-*pol*-luss.
AQUILA. *Ack*-wih-luh.
CAESAREA. Sess-uh-*ree*-uh.
CORNELIUS. Kor-*nee*-lih-us or Kor-*neel*-yus.
DERBE. *Der*-be.
EPHESUS. *Ef*-eh-sus.
ICONIUM. Eye-*ko*-nee-um.
LYSTRA. *Liss*-truh.
PHILIPPI. Fih-*lip*-pie or *Fil*-ih-pie.
PISIDIA. Pih-*sid*-ee-uh.
THESSALONICA. *Thess*-uh-lo-*nye*-kuh
   (strong accent on *nye*, *th* as in *thin*).

The record says no more about that feast, but probably Paul did attend it. Then he went to Antioch in Syria (Acts 18:22). Thus his second missionary journey ended at the city where it had begun (Acts 15:35-41).

After some time in Antioch, Paul set out on his third missionary journey. In the first part of it he revisited some of the churches he had started on his first journey and visited on his second one (Acts 18:23).

I. Teaching a Teacher
(Acts 18:24-26)

Now we go back to see what happened at Ephesus while Paul was completing his second journey and starting his third.

A. Enthusiastic Teacher (vv. 24, 25)

24. And a certain Jew named Apollos, born at Alexandria, an eloquent man, and mighty in the Scriptures, came to Ephesus.

Alexandria, a great city of Egypt, was a center of learning that rivaled Athens. In its university Apollos could have gotten an education second to none. Some versions say he was a *learned man* rather than *an eloquent man.* Very probably he was both. A Jew who lived in a pagan city, Apollos was *mighty in the Scriptures.* This indicates that he knew the Old Testament thoroughly and used it well.

25. This man was instructed in the way of the Lord; and being fervent in the spirit, he spake and taught diligently the things of the Lord, knowing only the baptism of John.

The Lord can mean either Jesus or God the Father. Here it seems to mean Jesus. Where *the Lord* appears the second time in this verse, some ancient manuscripts and some modern versions have the name *Jesus* instead. Apollos knew the way of God as taught in the Old Testament (v. 24). He had been so well taught that he now *spake and taught diligently the things of the Lord.* Some versions say he taught *accurately* instead of *diligently.* So far as we know, there was only one flaw in his teaching. He did not know about Christian baptism, but *only the baptism of John.* The two were not the same, as we shall see from the words of Paul in the latter part of our text.

We do not know when, where, or by whom Apollos had been taught about Jesus. Possibly he had been in Jerusalem for some of the Jewish feasts and had heard the teaching there. Or perhaps he had learned of Jesus from Jews who had gone to Alexandria.

Apollos was *fervent in the spirit:* he was on fire with the message, eager to tell it. He must have been enthusiastic and vigorous in his preaching.

B. Willing Learner (v. 26)

26. And he began to speak boldly in the synagogue: whom when Aquila and Priscilla had heard, they took him unto them, and expounded unto him the way of God more perfectly.

Visiting Jewish teachers were welcome in synagogues everywhere. Paul had spoken in that Ephesian synagogue not long before (Acts 18:19). Now it provided a hearing for Apollos's fervent preaching.

Aquila and Priscilla had been taught by Paul in Corinth, and may have been taught by others in Rome before they went to Corinth. They quickly saw the flaw in Apollos's preaching. Neither of them stood up to contradict him in the meeting, but *they took him unto them* for a private conference. Apparently the humble tentmakers presented the truth convincingly, and the brilliant scholar was humble enough to listen and learn from them. So the brilliant scholar became a better preacher.

NOT EMBARRASSED TO CHANGE

It's very difficult to admit we have been wrong about something, especially when we have publicly made our commitment to it. Just a few years ago, a book predicting the return of Christ on September 1, 1988, became quite popular. Four million copies of the book were sold and distributed by many churches. The day came, but the Lord did not.

The author then wrote another book, saying he had been off by a year—it should have been September 1, 1989. Not surprisingly, this book sold only thirty thousand copies. After the second failed prediction, the author said he wouldn't write another book about the end times, adding, "I guess God doesn't always do things the way man thinks He will." We should give the author credit for his integrity, if not for his Bible scholarship.

It takes character for one to admit that he or she has been wrong. Apollos possessed that attribute. When corrected by Priscilla and Aquila, he accepted the truth they shared with him. He then continued his ministry with even greater

A Wise Person IS HUMBLE ENOUGH TO LEARN FROM EVERYONE EVEN THOSE WHO KNOW LESS THAN HE DOES.

visual 9

power, because he was not embarrassed to change.

Do we stubbornly hold to our position because it is our position, or are we like Apollos, ready to follow where the truth leads? —C. R. B.

II. Helping the Believers
(Acts 18:27, 28)

We know but little about Apollos. Apparently he was a traveling evangelist, a missionary. Had some church sent him, as the church at Antioch had sent Paul? We do not know. Was he wealthy enough to pay his own expenses? We do not know. Where had he taught before he came to Ephesus? The record gives no hint. But after some time in Ephesus, he was ready to move on.

A. Recommended (v. 27a)

27a. And when he was disposed to pass into Achaia, the brethren wrote, exhorting the disciples to receive him.

Achaia was the region around Corinth, the southern part of what is now Greece. Apollos chose it as his next field of work. It was just across the Aegean Sea west of Ephesus.

The Christian brethren in Ephesus had been helped by Apollos. Now they wrote a letter to their fellow Christians in Achaia, urging them to welcome the traveling preacher.

Apparently the church in Ephesus was well established by this time. Perhaps Paul had won a few people to Christ in his short stay there (Acts 18:19). Aquila and Priscilla probably had won others, and so had Apollos. And of course the new Christians probably had been winning their neighbors.

B. Helpful (vv. 27b, 28)

27b. Who, when he was come, helped them much which had believed through grace.

We read nothing about what Silas and Timothy did after Paul left them in Corinth near the end of his second missionary journey. (Acts 18:18). Perhaps they were still working in Achaia. It seems that they were teachers of a quiet sort. Apollos was eloquent, fervent. His preaching stirred the Christians, encouraged them, aroused them. Thus he *helped them much.*

The Christians in Achaia are described in an unusual way: they *had believed through grace.* Through the grace of God Paul and Silas had brought them the gospel so they might believe and be saved. By God's grace Jesus came to earth, died, and rose again so there was a gospel to preach. Some students suggest that *through grace* goes with *helped* instead of *believed:* that is, through grace Apollos helped them. That can

mean that God's grace brought Apollos with his help, or it can mean that Apollos himself was gracious and graceful in helping. With any of these meanings the statement is true. The Christians did believe through grace, and Apollos did help them both graciously and by God's grace.

28. For he mightily convinced the Jews, and that publicly, showing by the Scriptures that Jesus was Christ.

Here we see one way in which Apollos helped the Christians. He not only knew the Old Testament prophecies, but also had an accurate knowledge of Jesus (vv. 24, 25). He could present the prophecies of the Christ and show how Jesus fulfilled them, thus showing by the Scriptures that Jesus was Christ. With eloquence and power added to his learning, he overwhelmed the unbelieving Jews in public debate.

III. Back in Ephesus
(Acts 19:1-6)

Leaving Apollos helping the Christians in Achaia, we go back to Ephesus to see what happened after Apollos left. In the background of this lesson we noted that Paul set out from Antioch of Syria on his third journey. As he had done on his second trip, he visited churches in Derbe, Lystra, Iconium, and Antioch of Pisidia; then he went on westward through the province of Asia.

A. Important Question (vv. 1, 2)

1. And it came to pass, that, while Apollos was at Corinth, Paul having passed through the upper coasts came to Ephesus; and finding certain disciples.

The upper coasts were not seacoasts, but the highlands of Asia east of Ephesus. On his second trip Paul was not allowed to preach in Asia (Acts 16:6). This time it seems that he did not stop to preach at the towns inland, but came on to Ephesus as he had promised (Acts 18:21). On his arrival he found *certain disciples*, Christians whom he did not know.

2. He said unto them, Have ye received the Holy Ghost since ye believed? And they said unto him, We have not so much as heard whether there be any Holy Ghost.

Today we usually say *the Holy Spirit* instead of *the Holy Ghost* because the word *ghost* has come to be used of imaginary phantoms supposed to live in graveyards and haunted houses. The Holy Spirit is very real, though unseen. He is a gift from God to each new Christian (Acts 2:38), and thereafter lives in the Christian (1 Corinthians 6:19). He is invisible, however, though He shows His presence by the fruit described in

Galatians 5:22, 23. In Paul's time some Christians received the Holy Spirit in such a way that they could work miracles. Probably Paul was asking those disciples if they had received the Spirit in that way. Paul may have asked other questions, too, but this one was important because it disclosed a lack in the teaching those disciples had received. They had not received the Spirit with any miraculous power. More than that, they had not even heard that there was a Holy Spirit.

B. Another Baptism (vv. 3-5)

3. And he said unto them, Unto what then were ye baptized? And they said, Unto John's baptism.

Since these disciples had not heard of the Holy Spirit, it was evident that they had not been baptized as Jesus ordered, "in the name of the Father, and of the Son, and of the Holy Ghost" (Matthew 28:19). They had been baptized in the way John the Baptist did it before Jesus gave that order. It seems probable that Apollos had baptized them before Aquila and Priscilla had taught him the way of the Lord more perfectly. Then he had gone on to Achaia without telling them what he had learned from the tentmakers.

4. Then said Paul, John verily baptized with the baptism of repentance, saying unto the people, that they should believe on him which should come after him, that is, on Christ Jesus.

John's baptism was "the baptism of repentance for the remission of sins" (Mark 1:4). He baptized people who repented so their sins would be forgiven. Christian baptism also is the baptism of repentance for the remission of sins (Acts 2:38). Besides, it is baptism into Christ, who died to atone for the sins of sinners (Romans 6:3, 4). In baptism we put on Christ (Galatians 3:27). When we are in Him we no longer trust our own faulty goodness, but we have His faultless righteousness (Philippians 3:9). Thus we are free from sin and its penalty.

5. When they heard this, they were baptized in the name of the Lord Jesus.

The disciples were baptized as Jesus had commanded. Then they were in Christ, members of His body (1 Corinthians 12:27; Ephesians 5:30).

THE PRICE OF IGNORANCE

Built in A. D. 1060, a twenty-five story bell tower in Pavia, Italy, collapsed in March, 1989. A newspaper kiosk was crushed, cars on the street were squashed, and nearby buildings were damaged. Three people were killed and several more injured.

The city authorities, who had been thinking about restoring the tower and making it a museum, said they had no idea that the tower was unsafe. Apparently the foundation had eroded to the point that it could not carry the weight of the tower.

Many such disasters occur because we are unaware of how dangerous a structure has become, or because we cannot adequately predict the coming of earthquakes or other destructive forces of nature. The response is often the regret-filled words, "If only we had known."

The believers whom Apollos had taught were unaware that the Holy Spirit had been promised to those who believed in Jesus and were baptized in His name. As a result, they were missing out on a great spiritual blessing.

The same thing happens today. Many do not realize how much their sinful habits and attitudes endanger their spiritual lives. Some may even have plans to make some changes and get their lives straightened out some day. But, without warning, life's foundations may crumble, bringing destruction with eternal consequences.

—C. R. B.

C. The Holy Spirit (v. 6)

6. And when Paul had laid his hands upon them, the Holy Ghost came on them; and they spake with tongues, and prophesied.

Now it is clear that the Holy Spirit came in such a way that He brought miraculous powers. Speaking in tongues is described in the second chapter of Acts. There we read that the Holy Spirit came on the apostles and enabled them to speak in languages they did not know before, but languages that were understood by some of the hearers. To prophesy is to speak by inspiration of the Holy Spirit. He gives the prophet such information as He wants the prophet to give others. Sometimes a prophet predicted future events (Acts 11:27, 28). Probably more often he guided the Christians in doing God's will. Before the New Testament was written to guide God's people, it was very helpful to receive God's instructions through the prophets. Such inspired men wrote the New Testament to guide Christians in later ages as well as their own.

Acts 2:38 indicates that the gift of the Holy Spirit is received by all who are baptized into Christ, but only a few of them received the power to speak in tongues and prophesy. Note that the Ephesians did not receive that power when they were baptized, but *when Paul had laid his hands upon them*. The apostles themselves received the Spirit with miraculous power without hands (Acts 2:1-4), and so did Cornelius and his household (Acts 10:44-48). But in other cases, miraculous powers were received when the apostles laid their hands on certain Christians. Philip the evangelist worked miracles (Acts 8:6) after the apostles laid their hands on him (Acts 6:1-6). But when Philip won many Samaritans to Christ, the Spirit gave them no miraculous ability till apostles from Jerusalem laid hands on them (Acts 8:1-8, 14-17). This seems to indicate that special gifts of the Spirit were given along with the apostles' hands.

This does not suggest that the Spirit's power is limited. No hands were laid on the apostles before He started them speaking in tongues. He gave the like gift to Cornelius and his household when it was neither asked nor expected. Gifts of the Holy Spirit are given as God chooses (Hebrews 2:4). But in Acts 8 and again in our text, we see that God chose to give special gifts to people touched by the apostles. Is it too much to infer that this was His custom?

Conclusion

Our text is a simple record of events long ago and far away, but it is loaded with lessons for the here and now.

A. Teaching and Learning

Teacher: Draw the class's attention to visual 9 as you present the following thoughts.

Will Rogers remarked that all of us are ignorant, but we are ignorant about different things.

Apollos was a learned man, not the kind we call ignorant. He was "mighty in the Scriptures" and "instructed in the way of the Lord." He may have studied mathematics, philosophy, and rhetoric in the University of Alexandria. But he was ignorant about Christian baptism.

Aquila and Priscilla may have been ignorant about many things. Probably they learned their trade from their parents. But on the subject of baptism they knew more than the learned Apollos did.

Fortunately the tentmakers had courage enough to teach the scholar, and sense enough to do it privately and tactfully instead of confronting him in the synagogue. Fortunately the brilliant scholar was wise enough and humble enough to learn from ignorant tentmakers. So a wise scholar became wiser, a great teacher became greater, and a good man became better.

Let's think of ourselves. Are we brave enough to teach people who know more than we do? Probably I know something that is unknown to the wisest man in town. Are we humble enough to learn from people who know less than we do? Perhaps the most ignorant person in town knows something that I need to learn.

B. Helping

When Apollos went to Achaia, our text says, he "helped them much which had believed." But that is only one item of many. This Scripture is full of helpfulness.

1. Aquila and Priscilla helped Apollos by expounding unto him the way of God more perfectly.

2. Apollos helped the Christians in Ephesus before he helped those in Achaia.

3. The Christians in Ephesus helped Apollos by recommending him to the Christians in Achaia.

4. Apollos "helped much" the Christians in Achaia, as our text says.

5. The Christians in Achaia helped Apollos by listening to his teaching and following it.

6. We are left to wonder if the Christians in Ephesus and Achaia helped Apollos with food and clothing and shelter, or a love offering, or even a salary; but we know the Lord has ordained that those who preach the gospel should have their living from it (1 Corinthians 9:14).

Whom do you know who needs help? Can you be a helper this week?

C. Prayer

Thank You for the faithful persons through the centuries who have served You and us so well that the gospel of salvation has come to us. Thank You for the gospel, and for the inspired teaching about how we ought to live and serve. Give us minds to see the abilities You have given us, hearts to reach out to those who need our help, and hands to help them. In Jesus' name, amen.

D. Thought to Remember

Serve.

Learning by Doing

*This page contains an alternate lesson plan emphasizing learning activities. Classes
desiring such student involvement will find these suggestions helpful.*

Learning Goals

Help students to accomplish the following as
they participate in today's class session.

1. Explore how Aquila, Priscilla, and Paul led
people from error to truth.

2. Suggest principles to guide Christians as
they try to lead people from error to the truth as
revealed in God's Word.

Into the Lesson

Write the following incomplete sentences on
the chalkboard before your class members arrive:

The difficulty in correcting someone else is—
The difficulty in being corrected is—
The best way to correct another person is—
The value of correction is—

Give students a sheet of paper and a pencil as
they arrive. Ask them to write the incomplete
sentences on their paper and complete them as
they think best.

After students have done so, ask them to pair
off and share their sentence completions with
their partners. Allow several minutes for this
"neighbor nudge."

Lead into the Bible study by saying, "Although
correction is sometimes necessary, it is never
easy. This is true whether one is being corrected
or doing the correcting. Today we will examine a
passage in which several people successfully
corrected others in error."

Into the Word

Prepare a brief lecture to explain the background of today's passage. You will find the information in the introduction to this lesson
helpful.

Ask a volunteer to read Acts 18:24-28, aloud
and another volunteer to read Acts 19:1-6. Then
have class members form groups of four to six.
Provide each group with a chart fashioned after
the one shown in the next column. Allow room
for writing in each section. (The chart is included in the student book also.) Assign half of
your groups the left portion of the chart (Acts
18:24-28) and the other groups the right portion
(Acts 19:1-6).

Allow the groups about ten minutes to complete their charts. Then have them report their
conclusions to the rest of the class.

Acts 18:24-28	Acts 19:1-6
Apollos showed these strong points:	The disciples showed these strong points:
Apollos's error was:	The disciples' error was:
Aquila and Priscilla's approach to correcting Apollos was:	Paul's approach to correcting them was:
The apparent results of the correction were:	The results were:

Comment on the subject of the error of both
Apollos and the disciples in Ephesus. Their understanding and experience of baptism were
limited to the baptism of John. They were not
aware of Christian baptism, in which a person is
united with Christ (Romans 6:3, 4; Galatians
3:27). Other Scriptures dealing with baptism are
Matthew 28:18-20; Mark 16:15, 16; Acts 2:38;
22:16; Colossians 2:11-13; 1 Peter 3:21.

Into Life

Write this principle on your "Effective Leader"
poster: *Effective Christian leaders possess wisdom to
correct in an appropriate way.*

After reading the principle, have students
form their small groups again. Give one of the
following situations to each group.

1. A Christian sincerely believes anti-Christian teaching.

2. A Christian is trying to overcome a sinful
habit, but keeps slipping back into the sin.

3. A Christian is irresponsible in his daily life
and habits.

4. A Christian spreads malicious gossip.

Ask the groups to discuss the best way to
guide this person into Christ's way concerning
this matter. Allow eight minutes for discussion.
Then bring the class together as one group and
ask, "What are some principles we should follow in helping others to see the error of their
ways?" Write suggestions on the chalkboard.
Then ask, "Which principle from this list do
you need to remember the next time you try to
help someone in this way?" Have them write it
on the paper given them earlier. Then close
with prayer asking for wisdom and grace, not
only in giving such instruction, but also in receiving it.

Let's Talk It Over

The questions on this page are designed to encourage review of the lesson Scriptures and to promote discussion of the lesson by the class. The answers provided are only discussion starters. Let your class talk it over from there.

1. What does Apollos's experience with Aquila and Priscilla reveal about him?

From this experience we learn that Apollos possessed more than knowledge; he had wisdom also. He was wise enough to realize that he did not possess all the truth; in fact, he lacked at least one very important truth relating to the gospel of Christ. Second, in this experience, Apollos's humility shines through. He did not arrogantly assume a "know-it-all" stance, but submitted himself to the teaching of two disciples who, most likely, were not nearly as well educated as he. Wisdom and humility are two significant traits for which every Christian should strive.

2. How did the Ephesian disciples receive the power of the Holy Spirit to speak in tongues and prophesy?

Acts 19:6 reveals that these spiritual gifts were received when the apostle Paul laid his hands on them. These gifts were given for the common good of the church (1 Corinthians 12:7).

3. Cite some important characteristics that should be found in one who instructs another in the way of the Lord.

The first characteristic that should be noted is *concern*. One might say, "I'm not responsible for what another teaches." God's servant, however, does not take such a position. This lesson demonstrates a legitimate concern on the part of Aquila and Priscilla for Apollos and his defective teaching. Their concern was for both the person and the truth.

A second characteristic is *sensitivity*. Aquila and Priscilla did not contradict Apollos publicly, but took him aside privately and tactfully. Then they explained to him "the way of God more perfectly."

The third characteristic of those who proclaim God's revealed truth is *accuracy*. They recognize their responsibility to transmit to others God's message as He has revealed it. Aquila and Priscilla called Apollos to a full and accurate presentation of the truth.

4. What qualities did Apollos possess that enabled him to be especially helpful in the Lord's work in Achaia?

First, of course, is the fact that he had a thorough knowledge of both the Old Testament Scriptures and the teachings of Christ, and he was able to teach them accurately. In addition, he had been educated in the world-renowned center of Greek culture, Alexandria. He may well have attended the university there. All of that stood him in good stead in Corinth, the area of Achaia where he directed his efforts. Acts 18:24 states that he was an eloquent speaker, and verse 28 records that "he vigorously refuted the Jews in public debate." An able and eloquent speaker appealed to the Greeks. His qualities made Apollos the kind of "vessel" that the Lord could use with great effectiveness in Greece.

5. Often, Christians are resistant to "correction," such as Apollos received from Aquila and Priscilla. Why is this so?

Our egos get in the way! To admit that we are wrong, that we are "lacking" in any way, assaults our pride. In religious circles, particularly, many are reluctant to confess any lack of understanding of God's revelation. In their thinking, to make such a confession would be an admission of weakness. Many Christians view dogmatism as a sign of great spiritual strength, but it really is a sign of weakness. Strong Christians are willing to be open, to listen, to weigh and consider differing positions in the light of God's Word. Weak Christians need to feel they are right and anyone who disagrees with them are wrong.

6. On Paul's missionary journeys, what generally influenced his decision to either remain with a synagogue and continue sharing the gospel with them, or to leave and go elsewhere?

As has been noted in previous lessons, Paul went to synagogues on the Sabbath to preach and teach about Jesus Christ. There he would find those who were knowledgeable about the Scriptures and who might be open to learning of how God had fulfilled the prophecies of the Old Testament. His "stop and go" signal focused on the responsiveness of his audience. As long as the response was encouraging, as long as the people remained open-minded to consider the message he brought them, he would stay. When obstinacy surfaced and the response was negative, he left (Acts 19:8, 9).

A Sad Farewell

LESSON SCRIPTURE: Acts 20.

PRINTED TEXT: Acts 20:17-31.

Acts 20:17-31

17 And from Miletus he sent to Ephesus, and called the elders of the church.

18 And when they were come to him, he said unto them, Ye know, from the first day that I came into Asia, after what manner I have been with you at all seasons,

19 Serving the Lord with all humility of mind, and with many tears, and temptations, which befell me by the lying in wait of the Jews:

20 And how I kept back nothing that was profitable unto you, but have showed you, and have taught you publicly, and from house to house,

21 Testifying both to the Jews, and also to the Greeks, repentance toward God, and faith toward our Lord Jesus Christ.

22 And now, behold, I go bound in the spirit unto Jerusalem, not knowing the things that shall befall me there:

23 Save that the Holy Ghost witnesseth in every city, saying that bonds and afflictions abide me.

24 But none of these things move me, neither count I my life dear unto myself, so that I might finish my course with joy, and the ministry, which I have received of the Lord Jesus, to testify the gospel of the grace of God.

25 And now, behold, I know that ye all, among whom I have gone preaching the kingdom of God, shall see my face no more.

26 Wherefore I take you to record this day, that I am pure from the blood of all men.

27 For I have not shunned to declare unto you all the counsel of God.

28 Take heed therefore unto yourselves, and to all the flock, over the which the Holy Ghost hath made you overseers, to feed the church of God, which he hath purchased with his own blood.

29 For I know this, that after my departing shall grievous wolves enter in among you, not sparing the flock.

30 Also of your own selves shall men arise, speaking perverse things, to draw away disciples after them.

31 Therefore watch, and remember, that by the space of three years I ceased not to warn every one night and day with tears.

Nov
3

GOLDEN TEXT: They all wept sore, and fell on Paul's neck, and kissed him, sorrowing most of all for the words which he spake, that they should see his face no more.—Acts 20:37, 38.

From the Damascus Road to Rome

Unit 4. Destination: Rome
(Lessons 10-13)

Lesson Aims

After this lesson a student should be able to:

1. Briefly tell the story of Paul's trip from Macedonia to Miletus and his meeting with the elders from Ephesus.

2. Describe an elder's duty as revealed in this text.

3. Describe the corresponding duty of a church member.

Lesson Outline

INTRODUCTION
   A. Slow Travel
   B. Lesson Background
  I. LOOKING BACK (Acts 20:17-21)
   A. Elder's Meeting (v. 17)
   B. Diligent, Dangerous Service (vv. 18, 19)
   C. Full Service (vv. 20, 21)
 II. LOOKING AHEAD (Acts 20:22-27)
   A. Foreboding (vv. 22, 23)
   B. Determination (v. 24)
     A Sense of Purpose
   C. Declaration (vv. 25-27)
III. DUTY AND DANGER (Acts 20:28-31)
   A. Duty (v. 28)
   B. Danger (vv. 29-31)
     True Leaders and False
CONCLUSION
   A. The Elders
   B. The Rest of Us
   C. Prayer
   D. Thought to Remember

Visual 10 centers attention on the points in the conclusion of the lesson. The visual is shown on page 84.

Introduction

Last week's lesson concluded with Paul in Ephesus. After staying there three years, he went to Macedonia and encouraged the churches in that area. He then made his way to Greece, where he remained three months.

While on this his third missionary journey, Paul encouraged many churches to gather an offering for the poverty-stricken Christians in Judea (Romans 15:25-27). He planned to end his journey by going with representatives of the churches to carry the offering to Jerusalem. See 2 Corinthians 8 and 9 for more about the offering.

A. Slow Travel

Turning toward Jerusalem, Paul met delay after delay. He learned that hostile Jews were planning an ambush, so he took a long way through Macedonia instead of sailing from Greece (Acts 20:3). When he went to sea, the sailing vessel was slow. At an earlier time he had sailed from Troas to Macedonia in two days (Acts 16:11). Now it took five days to cover the same course in the other direction (Acts 20:6). There was a seven-day layover in Troas, perhaps waiting for the regular weekly meeting of the brethren (Acts 20:6, 7). When he went to sea again, the vessel made slow progress along the coast (Acts 20:13-15).

B. Lesson Background

Paul had made many dear friends in Ephesus in his three years there. After months of absence, he must have longed to spend some time with them on his way to Jerusalem. But time was running out. He wanted to be in Jerusalem for the feast of Pentecost. The Passover season was past before they left Macedonia (Acts 20:6). Paul decided not to stop in Ephesus at all (Acts 20:16).

I. Looking Back
(Acts 20:17-21)

Acts 20:4 lists seven men who were traveling with Paul. In the next two verses the pronouns *us* and *we* show that the group also included Luke, the writer of this record. With Paul, there were nine in the group. It seems they found passage on a ship that was scheduled to bypass Ephesus and stop for several days at Miletus, thirty miles farther south.

A. Elders' Meeting (v. 17)

17. And from Miletus he sent to Ephesus, and called the elders of the church.

From Miletus Paul sent men with an invitation to their good friends, *the elders of the church* in Ephesus. Vigorous walkers could cover the thirty miles in a day. If any of the elders were old enough to be feeble, it may have taken them two days to make the trip to Miletus.

B. Diligent, Dangerous Service
(vv. 18, 19)

18. And when they were come to him, he said unto them, Ye know, from the first day that I came into Asia, after what manner I have been with you at all seasons.

LESSON 10. NOVEMBER 3

Only a few months had passed since Paul had left Ephesus. The elders could easily remember what he had done throughout his three-year ministry there, *from the first day*. He had served diligently *at all seasons*— no vacations.

19. Serving the Lord with all humility of mind, and with many tears, and temptations, which befell me by the lying in wait of the Jews.

As an apostle of Jesus, Paul was well qualified to issue orders; but he chose to serve *with all humility of mind*. Paul did not have to tell the elders what had brought him to *tears*. Probably they had wept along with him when he could no longer teach in the synagogue (Acts 19:8, 9), when his good friends were seized by an angry mob and other good friends would not let him share their danger (Acts 19:29, 30), and at other times they remembered well. The vocal opposition of Jews is recorded (Acts 19:9), but *lying in wait* suggests a plot to do physical injury to Paul. Such plots were made by angry Jews in other places (Acts 9:23-25, 29, 30; 13:50; 14:5, 6, 19; 17:5, 13; 18:12, 13), and perhaps in Ephesus.

C. Full Service (vv. 20, 21)

20. And how I kept back nothing that was profitable unto you, but have showed you, and have taught you publicly, and from house to house.

Those who were apostles before Paul were told to make disciples, and to teach them to do all that Jesus had commanded (Matthew 28:19, 20). Paul likewise was diligent in teaching. He taught publicly in the synagogue and then in another place (Acts 19:8, 9), and he went from house to house to teach people privately.

21. Testifying both to the Jews, and also to the Greeks, repentance toward God, and faith toward our Lord Jesus Christ.

Paul's message was for all persons. Here *Greeks* is a general term for Gentiles, everyone who was not Jewish. They were to repent, to change their mind and attitude *toward God*, worshiping Him only. Jews were to repent of their misunderstanding, to acknowledge that God was offering salvation through Christ to all people.

How to Say It

EPHESUS.   *Ef*-eh-sus.
GALATIANS.   Guh-*lay*-shunz.
MACEDONIA.   Mass-eh-*doe*-nee-uh.
MILETUS.   My-*lee*-tus.
TROAS.   *Tro*-az.

II. Looking Ahead
(Acts 20:22-27)

From memories of his past service with the Ephesians, Paul turned to thoughts of the future. Those thoughts were dark with foreboding, but bright with determination to continue his service, regardless of the cost.

A. Foreboding (vv. 22, 23)

22. And now, behold, I go bound in the spirit unto Jerusalem, not knowing the things that shall befall me there.

Bound in the spirit. As we see this in the *King James Version*, it indicates that Paul felt in his spirit that he was bound to go to Jerusalem, that he must go. The *New International Version* has a different interpretation: "Compelled by the Spirit." This indicates that the Holy Spirit who controlled Paul was now directing him to Jerusalem. From either translation we see that Paul was going to Jerusalem, not just because he wanted to, but because he had to. He and his companions were carrying funds for the poverty-stricken Christians in Judea, as we have already noted. This gift was designed to do more than relieve the poverty of the poor. It would be a bond of brotherhood; it would tie the Jewish Christians in Judea with Gentile Christians in other places; it would tend to unify the churches everywhere. Paul was a Jew specially commissioned to take the gospel to Gentiles (Acts 26:15-18). He had to go with the gifts because no one else was so well fitted to help the Christians in Judea see their unity with Gentile brethren all over the world. So he was on the way to Jerusalem, not knowing what would happen there, but with the warnings mentioned in the next verse.

23. Save that the Holy Ghost witnesseth in every city, saying that bonds and afflictions abide me.

If we understand verse 22 as the *New International Version* has it, the Holy Spirit was specifically sending Paul to Jerusalem. But the Spirit did not want him to be surprised by trouble there. At every stopping place along the way, He warned that prison and hardship were to be expected.

B. Determination (v. 24)

24. But none of these things move me, neither count I my life dear unto myself, so that I might finish my course with joy, and the ministry, which I have received of the Lord Jesus, to testify the gospel of the grace of God.

Paul had a *ministry*, a service, a job to do. *The Lord Jesus* himself had given it. Paul was going to continue his service to the end, regardless of the cost. The assurance of jail and trouble could not turn him from his course. He would continue even at the cost of his life.

A SENSE OF PURPOSE

In the latter part of the 1980s, Americans seemed finally to decide to get serious about what was happening to the environment. Warmer than normal temperatures made the dire predictions of the "greenhouse effect" seem plausible. Ground water supplies in many places were found to have been contaminated by seepage from toxic waste dumps. Topsoil was discovered to be blowing and washing away at an increasingly rapid rate. In short, we didn't know what the future held. From what we could see of it, however, the future wasn't going to be pleasant unless we took severe measures to change the way we were dealing with our world. Even today, most of those needed measures are still undefined.

As Paul faced Jerusalem, he was unsure of what would happen to him there. The Holy Spirit was telling him through various means that what awaited him was not pleasant. This, however, did not deter him from facing the future boldly. He had a sense of purpose—a sense of what his life was about. He knew that what made his life count was his service for Christ. When the moment came, he would do what the situation required and what his Lord called for. We can do no better than to have such a sense of divine purpose for our lives as well.   —C. R. B.

C. Declaration (vv. 25-27)

25. And now, behold, I know that ye all, among whom I have gone preaching the kingdom of God, shall see my face no more.

It is generally thought that Paul did return to Ephesus years later (1 Timothy 1:3; 3:14). Some students conclude that Paul was mistaken in saying the elders would not see him again, and therefore that he was not inspired by the Holy Spirit. These are not necessary conclusions. The brief references to Paul's later travels do not conclusively prove that he ever returned to Ephesus; and if he did return after more than four years, there is nothing to prove that these elders were still there. A literal translation of Paul's words is *no more will see my face you all.* This would be true if even a part of them died or moved away before Paul returned. The evidence does not require the conclusion that Paul was mistaken. This was his last chance to talk with these men, or at least with some of them, and therefore he wanted to say some things as plainly and forcefully as he could.

26, 27. Wherefore I take you to record this day, that I am pure from the blood of all men. For I have not shunned to declare unto you all the counsel of God.

I take you to record may be translated *I testify to you.* Its purpose is to emphasize what follows. With a like purpose Jesus said, "Verily, verily:" In our day we say, "I tell you this for sure?" For three years in Ephesus Paul had declared *all the counsel of God.* He had not held back one word of what the Holy Spirit had inspired him to say. He had told the good news of Jesus and His offer of salvation. He had urged people to believe the gospel, to repent and be baptized. He had taught the Christians to do all that Jesus had commanded. If anyone in Ephesus was doomed to the terrible second death (Revelation 20:14, 15), his blood was on his own head. Paul could not be blamed.

III. Duty and Danger
(Acts 20:28-31)

No more would Paul be in Ephesus to guide God's people with his inspired teaching. We are not told whether any of the elders were inspired prophets or not. Inspired or not, they were in charge. Solemnly Paul impressed them with their duty and warned them of dangers.

A. Duty (v. 28)

28. Take heed therefore unto yourselves, and to all the flock, over the which the Holy Ghost hath made you overseers, to feed the church of God, which he hath purchased with his own blood.

Take heed. This is a call to pay attention, to keep watch, to be alert, to apply the mind. No Christian should go to sleep on the job, but elders especially must be watchful and concerned. *Unto yourselves.* It is easier to see the faults and misdeeds of others than it is to see our own. Each person should put himself under the microscope, give careful and minute attention to

SHEPHERD
LEADS
FEEDS
PROTECTS
WARNS

SHEEP
FOLLOWS/EATS
IS CAREFUL/HEEDS

visual 10

his own behavior, and talk, and thoughts. This is especially important for elders and others in positions of leadership. Their job requires them to be forever thinking of others, but one engrossed with others must not forget to watch himself. Most of us can recall the names of some noted Christian leaders who have scandalized the world in recent years. Every leader should be warned by their fall. Don't let it happen to you!

Besides watching themselves, the elders must be concerned about *all the flock,* every member of the church. Men inspired by the Holy Spirit directed that elders be chosen (Acts 14:23) and told what kind of men would be chosen (1 Timothy 3:1-7; Titus 1:5-9). Paul therefore could say, *The Holy Ghost hath made you overseers.* The Greek word for *overseer* is the word from which we have our English word *bishop.* That is why the *King James Version* calls the overseer a bishop in 1 Timothy 3:1, 2.

Our version reads *over the which the Holy Ghost hath made you overseers,* but the phrase is literally *in which* rather than *over which.* The overseers were not over the flock in the sense of being separate or apart; they were in the flock, members of the congregation. Nevertheless they were over the flock as a shepherd is over the sheep. Their work is *to feed the church.* An elder is to be "apt to teach" (1 Timothy 3:2) so the flock will be well nourished by "words of faith and of good doctrine" (1 Timothy 4:6). He must carefully adapt the teaching to the needs of the hearers (1 Corinthians 3:1, 2). But *to feed* means more than to provide food. The *New International Version* aptly translates, "Be shepherds of the church." A shepherd not only sees that the sheep have food; he also protects them from wild animals and human thieves, guides them in safe pathways, and finds a sheltered place in time of storm. No good shepherd puts his own safety or comfort ahead of the welfare of the flock. See Ezekiel 34:1-10 for the Lord's rebuke to selfish shepherds of Israel who fed themselves rather than the flock. It may well apply to leaders who care more for power or prestige or gain than for the welfare of the church.

The church does not belong to the elders who supervise its work; it is *the church of God.* It is costly and very precious to Him—the church *which he hath purchased with his own blood.* Some ancient manuscripts read *the church of the Lord* instead of *the church of God,* and some modern translators prefer that reading because it was the Lord Jesus who shed His blood to redeem men for His church. We need not pause to argue about which reading to choose, for Jesus and the Father are one (John 10:30). Together they gave Jesus' life, together they love and cherish the church, and an elder who does not love and cherish it sins against both Father and Son.

B. Danger (vv. 29-31)

29. For I know this, that after my departing shall grievous wolves enter in among you, not sparing the flock.

Elsewhere Paul warned of "men of corrupt mind, who have been robbed of the truth and who think that godliness is a means to financial gain" (1 Timothy 6:5, *New International Version*). We think of the Dark Ages, when rulers of the church lived in luxury by extorting money from the poor. We think of the twentieth century, when some smooth talkers have lived no less luxuriously and no less immorally by gathering the gifts of earnest Christians. Part of the elders' duty is to protect the flock against such unscrupulous operators, and all of us can make the elders' task easier by thinking twice before we send our savings to some powerful preacher of unknown character who comes with a tearful plea or a smiling promise.

30. Also of your own selves shall men arise, speaking perverse things, to draw away disciples after them.

Not only do wolves invade the flock from outside; sheep also turn out to be wolves. A trusted church member, even an elder, may *arise, speaking perverse things.* Jesus warned against "false prophets, which come to you in sheep's clothing, but inwardly they are ravening wolves." He said one who claims to be a prophet should be judged by results rather than claims (Matthew 7:15-20). Jude thought it was necessary to urge us to contend for the faith because "certain men whose condemnation was written about long ago have secretly slipped in among you. They are godless men, who change the grace of our God into a license for immorality and deny Jesus Christ our only Sovereign and Lord" (Jude 4, *New International Version*). Anyone who denies that Jesus is the Christ marks himself as a liar. In denying Jesus he denies the Father as well (1 John 2:22). But there are some who "profess that they know God; but in works they deny him, being abominable, and disobedient, and unto every good work reprobate" (Titus 1:16). The church has never been free from perverters, and the multitude of sects is evidence that they do *draw away disciples after them.* The elders must protect us against every perverter; and again all of us can help by knowing God's Word well enough to recognize perversion when we hear it, and by refusing to be drawn away, no matter how appealing the perversion or the perverter may be.

31. Therefore watch, and remember, that by the space of three years I ceased not to warn every one night and day with tears.

To *watch* is to be wide awake, alert, on guard. The elder is both shepherd and watchman. If the sheep have no warning against wolves, the elder is at fault. If the sheep are warned, but still choose to go away with the wolf, their blood is on their own heads (Ezekiel 3:16-19). But shall not every sheep be as alert as the shepherd? Shall not each of us study the Word of truth and take it to heart? Shall we not recognize a wolf in his wooly disguise? Shall we not faithfully follow the good shepherd, refusing to be turned aside?

TRUE LEADERS AND FALSE

There seems to be no end of people who will follow some self-proclaimed "messiah," even though he doesn't live what he teaches.

On the California coast, the guru of one cult lives in leisure on a large sailing vessel, where he is free to meditate about the universe. Most of his followers live in the desert and work long hours for minimal pay in the cult's businesses to support him. While preaching an ascetic life-style, he became addicted to alcohol and drugs. Extolling the virtues of poverty for others, he lives in extravagance.

The apostle Paul warned about this very kind of person. The cults prey upon the church by making exaggerated claims of spirituality, by professing to have knowledge available to only a few, or by challenging people to a rigorous, "works-righteousness" type of discipline. Christians with unstable personalities, those who are not well-grounded in Christian teaching, or those whose faith has grown cold are tempted to follow the new leader who claims to have the "real" answers to life's problems.

It's the same old story: whoever would draw us away from the historic Christian faith will destroy us. We must be ever vigilant.   —C. R. B.

Conclusion

In closing, let's think about duties. What duties of the elders appear in our text? What duties of the rest of us are implied?

A. The Elders

1. An elder is an overseer (v. 28). He is a foreman, a boss. His job is to direct the rest of us so that we will work harmoniously and effectively.

2. An elder is a shepherd (v. 28). That means he is a servant of the rest of us as well as a boss. His job is to feed us with sound teaching, help us when the going is rough, defend us from wolves.

3. An elder is a watchman (v. 31). His job is to warn us against false teaching and wrong living—warn us loudly and clearly.

B. The Rest of Us

1. If an elder is an overseer, our job is to accept his direction and follow it cheerfully. "Obey your leaders and submit to their authority. They keep watch over you as men who must give an account. Obey them so that their work will be a joy, not a burden" (Hebrews 13:17, *New International Version*). Are our elders happy in their work because of our cooperation?

2. If an elder is to feed us with God's Word, we are to "desire the sincere milk of the word" and grow by it (1 Peter 2:2). If the elder is to help us, we are to do our best. If the elder is to defend us, we are to stay within the bounds he sets. Are we as hardworking as our elders are?

3. If an elder is to warn us, our duty is to heed his warning and keep out of trouble. Are we as concerned as we expect our elders to be?

When it is time to choose elders, we look again at 1 Timothy 3:1-7 and Titus 1:5-9 to see what is proper for an elder to be and do. What do you see in those passages that is not proper for all of us to be and do? Our elders will be better at their jobs when we are better at ours.

C. Prayer

Our Father in Heaven, we thank You for our overseers, those godly men who do so much to guide us, help us, and protect us. May they have strength and courage and wisdom to guide us well, and may we have strength and courage and wisdom to follow. In Jesus' name we pray. Amen.

D. Thought to Remember

Follow the leaders.

Home Daily Bible Readings

Monday, Oct. 28—Idol Makers Organize Against the Gospel (Acts 19:21-27)
Tuesday, Oct. 29—The Idol Makers Incite a Riot (Acts 19:28-34)
Wednesday, Oct. 30—The Town Clerk Defends Paul (Acts 19:35-41)
Thursday, Oct. 31—Paul Travels Through Macedonia (Acts 20:1-6)
Friday, Nov. 1—The Journey Continues (Acts 20:7-16)
Saturday, Nov. 2—Paul's Farewell Address (Acts 20:17-24)
Sunday, Nov. 3—Paul Bids Farewell to the Ephesians (Acts 20:25-38)

Learning by Doing

This page contains an alternate lesson plan emphasizing learning activities. Classes desiring such student involvement will find these suggestions helpful.

Learning Goals

As a result of this lesson your students will:

1. Demonstrate evidence that Paul took Christian leadership responsibility seriously.

2. Summarize the responsibilities of church leaders based upon Acts 20:17-38.

3. Specify one way in which they will show support this week for a church leader.

Into the Lesson

Give each student a copy of the following statements. Ask students to read each statement and write *A* in front of it if they agree with it, and *D* if they disagree.

Allow several minutes. Then take a tally of each statement. Ask students to defend their views, but do not allow more than ten minutes for this activity. Here are the statements:

1. In God's eyes a church leader has more responsibility than a church member does.

2. If the church is ineffective, God will hold only the leaders responsible.

3. If church leaders are to be effective, the members must submit to them and support them.

4. God expects church members to be as serious about their involvement in ministry as He expects church leaders to be.

After discussion, tell the class, "Today we will focus on some responsibilities for church leaders. In addition, we will explore what our responsibilities are to our church leaders."

Into the Word

Three study options are presented below. You may choose one option for everyone to do in small groups of four to six. Or you may choose more than one, and give different assignments to different groups. Have students read Acts 10:17-38 prior to their activity.

Option One

Prepare copies of these questions for students to discuss. (They are in the student book.)

1. How does Paul describe his ministry among the Ephesians (vv. 17-21, 25-27, 31, 33-35)?

2. What responsibilities of the elders are mentioned in verses 28-32?

3. What phrases indicate that Christian leadership is demanding?

4. Based upon this passage, how would you summarize the responsibility of church leaders?

Option Two

Students are to prepare a sermon on church leadership based on this passage. The group will prepare the ideas together, and a spokesperson for the group will present the "sermon" to the class. Allot two to three minutes for the sermon. Students can build on the outline provided below, or create their own:

I. Paul's Example for the Ephesians Elders
   (Acts 20:17-21, 25-27, 31, 33-36)

II. Paul's Exhortation to the Ephesian Elders
   (Acts 20:28-32)

You will need to provide the group(s) with paper and pencils.

Option Three

Students are to work together in groups to create a picture of a faithful Christian leader. Using Acts 20:17-38, they are to draw a person (stick figure is adequate) and label relevant body parts as the passage identifies them or implies them. For example, they might note the following: eyes that keep watch (v. 28); feet that finish the race (v. 24); mouth that declares the whole counsel of God (vv. 20, 21, 27); eyes that shed tears (vv. 19, 31); hands that supply needs (v. 34); heart of humility (v. 19); no blood on his hands (v. 26). Provide one or two of these ideas if students have difficulty getting started.

Into Life

Write the following Principle for Effective Christian Leadership on the poster in your classroom: *Effective Christian leaders take their leadership responsibilities seriously.* Then ask, "What in today's passage indicates that Paul took leadership seriously?" Discuss.

Then say, "This quarter we've been looking at Christian leadership. In truth, leaders can be effective only to the extent that their followers enable them to be." Ask, "What responsibilities do church members have toward their leaders?" Have students read the following passages for some answers: Hebrews 13:7, 17; 1 Thessalonians 5:12, 13. Then ask, "How can we show our support for our leaders?" Allow time for discussion. Write the class's suggestions on the chalkboard.

Conclude by encouraging class members to select one item from the list and do it this week to show support for one or more of their leaders. Close with prayer for your leaders.

Let's Talk It Over

The questions on this page are designed to encourage review of the lesson Scriptures and to promote discussion of the lesson by the class. The answers provided are only discussion starters. Let your class talk it over from there.

1. On the basis of Paul's farewell address to the elders of the church in Ephesus, from which today's lesson text is taken, what were some characteristic marks of Paul's ministry to the church at Ephesus?

Humility. As a servant leader, following the Servant Lord, Paul ministered in Ephesus with great humility (Acts 20:19). He did not seek any personal gain; rather, he lived among the Ephesians as a humble servant.

Vulnerability. Paul lived in the presence of constant threats from the enemies of the gospel; he was no stranger to pain and tears (20:19). He did not minister by putting concern for his own safety and well-being first.

Perseverance. Paul could testify that from his first day in their midst, he persisted in ministering, preaching, and teaching (20:18, 20). He invested time, energy, indeed his very life in them and for them, regardless of contrary circumstances.

Openness. He ministered publicly among the Ephesians, and did not hold back anything that was helpful to them (20:20). He excluded no one from hearing the gospel; he preached to both Jews and Gentile alike (20:21).

Involvement. Paul lived among the Ephesians, fulfilled his ministry of the gospel, and built warm and genuine relationships with them. At the time of his parting from the elders of the church, the tears and the embraces were testimonies of his deep involvement in the lives of these people.

Testimony. In word and deed, Paul testified eloquently to the love and grace of Jesus Christ. Today's text exudes the vibrant testimony of a life transformed and totally committed to Jesus Christ as Lord.

Clear conscience. Paul could in all honesty say that his conscience was clear; no man's blood was on his hands. He fulfilled his responsibility to preach the gospel to all and call them to repentance (20:26, 27).

2. Why was Paul so determined to go to Jerusalem?

First, he was "bound in the spirit" to go there, which seems to mean that he was compelled by the Holy Spirit (20:22). Second, he must complete his ministry, fulfill his responsibility, regardless of threat. He had received his ministry from Jesus, and he saw his going to Jerusalem as necessary to the completion of his task. Third, he must deliver the contributions of the Gentile Christians to aid the poverty-stricken Christians in Judea. He had accepted the responsibility of carrying these funds to Jerusalem.

3. What responsibilities of elders are cited in this lesson?

(1) They are called to live faithfully, keeping watch over themselves, first of all. Those who are elders are expected to be mature Christians, exemplifying Christlike character and behavior at all times.

(2) Elders are to be overseers of the flock. Themselves members of the church, they are responsible for watching over the life of the church.

(3) Elders are to be shepherds of the flock. Shepherds are entrusted with the complete care of their sheep. It is so in the church, God's flock. Elders are to feed, guide, shelter, and protect the church. Ever watchful, they are to be on guard against threat from outside ("wolves") and inside ("those who distort the truth"—Acts 20:28, *New International Version*).

4. What are the dangers that face churches today?

The more things change, the more they remain the same! Present dangers are identical to those Paul warned of in his farewell address to the elders of Ephesus. The church today faces threat from without—there are those who would destroy the church and its influence. Most likely, however, the greater threat is from within. Those who would subvert the church from being what Christ would have it to be, those who seek their own power and exaltation, those motivated by self-interest, pose the greatest threat.

5. What is grief?

Grief is the feelings and emotions that accompany significant loss. The Ephesian elders *grieved* when Paul told them that they would not see him again. This represented significant loss to them. How appropriately they wept—they would not see him again!

Arrested and Accused

LESSON SCRIPTURE: Acts 21:17-40; 22:25 — 23:11.

PRINTED TEXT: Acts 21:26-33, 37-39a.

Acts 21:26-33, 37-39a

26 Then Paul took the men, and the next day purifying himself with them entered into the temple, to signify the accomplishment of the days of purification, until that an offering should be offered for every one of them.

27 And when the seven days were almost ended, the Jews which were of Asia, when they saw him in the temple, stirred up all the people, and laid hands on him,

28 Crying out, Men of Israel, help: This is the man, that teacheth all men every where against the people, and the law, and this place: and further brought Greeks also into the temple, and hath polluted this holy place.

29 (For they had seen before with him in the city Trophimus an Ephesian, whom they supposed that Paul had brought into the temple.)

30 And all the city was moved, and the people ran together: and they took Paul, and drew him out of the temple: and forthwith the doors were shut.

31 And as they went about to kill him, tidings came unto the chief captain of the band, that all Jerusalem was in an uproar:

32 Who immediately took soldiers and centurions, and ran down unto them: and when they saw the chief captain and the soldiers, they left beating of Paul.

33 Then the chief captain came near, and took him, and commanded him to be bound with two chains; and demanded who he was, and what he had done.

· · · · · · · · · · · · · ·

37 And as Paul was to be led into the castle, he said unto the chief captain, May I speak unto thee? Who said, Canst thou speak Greek?

38 Art not thou that Egyptian, which before these days madest an uproar, and leddest out into the wilderness four thousand men that were murderers?

39a But Paul said, I am a man which am a Jew of Tarsus, a city in Cilicia, a citizen of no mean city.

GOLDEN TEXT: The night following the Lord stood by him, and said, Be of good cheer, Paul: for as thou hast testified of me in Jerusalem, so must thou bear witness also at Rome.—Acts 23:11.

From the Damascus Road to Rome

Unit 4. Destination: Rome
(Lessons 10-13)

Lesson Aims

After this lesson a student should be able to:

1. Retell the story found in the lesson introduction and the printed text.

2. Recall a modern example of thoughtlessness that led to wrongdoing.

3. Resolve to think things through and do right.

Lesson Outline

INTRODUCTION
- A. Stopping Slander
- B. Lesson Background
I. ASSAULTED (Acts 21:26-30)
- A. Purification (v. 26)
   - *Regarding Tradition*
- B. Accusation (vv. 27-29)
- C. Action (v. 30)
II. ARRESTED (Acts 21:31-33)
- A. Rescue (vv. 31, 32)
- B. Arrest (v. 33)
III. IDENTIFIED (Acts 21:37-39a)
- A. Request (v. 37a)
- B. Surprise (vv. 37b, 38)
   - *Aren't You Someone Else?*
- C. Identity (v. 39a)
CONCLUSION
- A. Gossip
- B. Propaganda
- C. Hysteria
- D. Prayer
- E. Thought to Remember

Visual 11 is an overhead view of the temple and its courts. Refer to it as you relate the events of today's lesson. The visual is shown on page 93.

Introduction

The first Christians were Jews, and for some time they invited only Jews to accept Christ. In lesson 5 we reviewed the extraordinary means God used to convince them that the gospel was for Gentiles too. When all were convinced that Gentiles might become Christians, some still insisted that they could not be saved unless they became Jews as well. The Holy Spirit and the church together decided that salvation was through Christ, and Gentiles had no need to take up Jewish customs. Paul proclaimed that decision throughout the wide area where he served.

A. Stopping Slander

Last week we read that Paul and others were on the way to Jerusalem, carrying a large offering for the poor Christians there. When they arrived, Paul learned that he was being slandered in that area. People were saying he was teaching Jews everywhere to turn away from the law of Moses and the ancient Jewish customs. That was not true. Paul taught that Gentile Christians need not become Jews, but he did not tell Jews to give up their ancient customs. Christian leaders in Jerusalem suggested that Paul could stop the slander by joining heartily in observing Jewish customs.

One well-known custom was to take a vow of consecration. A Jew might do this in gratitude for his blessings, or just as a means of drawing closer to God. He might consecrate himself for thirty days, or any length of time he chose. During that time he would not cut his hair, would not drink wine or eat anything from a grapevine, would not touch a dead body, not even if a member of his own family would die. At the end of the period of consecration there were specified sacrifices to be made (Numbers 6).

B. Lesson Background

At that time, four Christian Jews were nearing the end of a period of consecration. Christian leaders suggested that Paul could join them by undergoing the regular ceremony of purification and paying for the sacrifices that would be offered. That would be very helpful, since most Christians in that area were poor. Besides, it would show everybody that Paul himself kept the honored Jewish customs (Acts 21:17-24).

I. Assaulted
(Acts 21:26-30)

In making their suggestion, the leaders reaffirmed the earlier declaration that Gentiles need not take up the Jewish customs. Paul's action would be simply to help the men who had made the vow and to show that Paul himself was still a loyal Jew (Acts 21:25). It seemed to be a good plan, and Paul readily accepted it.

A. Purification (v. 26)

26. Then Paul took the men, and the next day purifying himself with them entered into the temple, to signify the accomplishment of the days of purification, until that an offering should be offered for every one of them.

Apparently there was some act or ceremony of purification for Paul and the four men who were nearing the end of the time of their vow. They went to the priests in the temple to arrange a schedule for all the offerings and ceremonies that would mark the completion of their time of special consecration.

REGARDING TRADITION

In 1988 the National Nihilist Party explored the possibility of entering a candidate in the presidential race. One claim to fame of the proposed standard-bearer was that he sponsored the 1984 Nihilist Olympics, which featured an art defacing competition! Nothingness, indeed!

The Nihilist platform policies included a proposal for the United States and U. S. S. R. to exchange governments for one month each year, and the relocation of the nation's capital to Los Angeles. The Nihilist theme is found in one statement by the candidate: "My candidacy is not frivolous. *Traditional* politics is frivolous."

We live in an age when all manner of nonsense is proposed as a replacement for values and institutions that people in the past have deemed to be good or useful. The assumption by some is that anything traditional is bad.

Paul was not such a person. Even though he uncompromisingly preached salvation through Christ only, he could observe the traditional ceremonies of the Old Covenant where there was no conflict with the principles of the New.

We should not worship the past, but we should give it due respect. Let us not be so proud of our innovations that we belittle all that has gone before us.   —C. R. B.

B. Accusation (vv. 27-29)

27. And when the seven days were almost ended, the Jews which were of Asia, when they saw him in the temple, stirred up all the people, and laid hands on him.

Apparently the ceremonies and sacrifices were to take seven days. Near the end of that time there was an interruption. *Asia* was the province where Ephesus was located, and probably some or all of these Jews of Asia were from that city. They knew about Paul's three-year ministry there. These were non-Christian Jews like those who had forced Paul to stop teaching in the synagogue at Ephesus (Acts 19:8, 9). Such Jews hated Paul for two reasons. First, they hoped the Messiah would defeat the Romans and build a triumphant Jewish kingdom, but Paul said the Messiah had been crucified and was building a spiritual kingdom rather than a worldly one. Second, Paul was calling Gentiles as well as Jews into God's kingdom. Nationalis-

---

tic Jews thought this would end their special place as God's chosen people. These Jews from Asia probably had been in Jerusalem for national festivals before this one. They knew the festival crowd was easily stirred up. They saw an opportunity to get rid of Paul so they took advantage of it.

28. Crying out, Men of Israel, help: This is the man, that teacheth all men every where against the people, and the law, and this place: and further brought Greeks also into the temple, and hath polluted this holy place.

The people meant the Jewish people; *the law* meant the Jewish law; *this place* meant the Jewish temple. As noted earlier, Paul did nothing to keep Jews from honoring the people, the law, or the temple according to their ancient customs. He did teach that Gentiles could be saved without being Jews and without keeping the Jewish law or honoring the Jewish temple. To some non-Christian Jews it seemed that he was teaching against the people, the law, and the temple. The accusers added that Paul not only taught against the temple, but also defiled it by bringing in people who were not Jews. *Greeks* here means Gentiles, non-Jewish people. They were allowed in the big outer court of the temple, but the inner court had a wall with inscriptions declaring any Gentile venturing within would do so on pain of death.

29. (For they had seen before with him in the city Trophimus an Ephesian, whom they supposed that Paul had brought into the temple.)

Trophimus was a Gentile Christian from Ephesus. He had come with Paul to bring gifts to the poor Jewish Christians in Judea (Acts 20:4). The hostile Jews from Asia had seen him with Paul somewhere in Jerusalem. On that slender basis they now shouted their charge that Paul had brought Greeks into the temple.

C. Action (v. 30)

30. And all the city was moved, and the people ran together: and they took Paul, and drew him out of the temple: and forthwith the doors were shut.

The shout of Asian Jews was taken up by others, the uproar was heard beyond the temple walls, and people of the city came running to see what was going on. The enemies who had accused Paul of defiling the temple with Greeks would not themselves defile it with murder, so they dragged Paul outside. Probably that means out of the restricted inner courts to the big outer court. That was considered much less sacred. Gentiles were allowed there. The accusers of Paul would not think that court was defiled by his death. The crowd surged through the gate with Paul in the midst, and probably the temple police hurried the stragglers outside before *the doors were shut* to keep the sacred area undefiled.

II. Arrested
(Acts 21:31-33)

The Roman overseers of Judea also knew the holiday crowds in Jerusalem could easily be stirred up. They had a stout fort at the northwest corner of the temple area. At festival times they kept enough soldiers there to deal quickly with riots. From the fort a flight of stairs ran down inside the wall of the big outer court so the troops could arrive quickly at any scene of trouble in that area.

A. Rescue (vv. 31, 32)

31. And as they went about to kill him, tidings came unto the chief captain of the band, that all Jerusalem was in an uproar.

The accusers meant to kill Paul, but they were handicapped by lack of weapons. They must have been beating him (v. 32) with their fists and feet. A man is not killed quickly in that way, and no doubt sentries at the fort were on the watch for just such trouble. Word very quickly reached the commander.

32. Who immediately took soldiers and centurions, and ran down unto them: and when they saw the chief captain and the soldiers, they left beating of Paul.

No doubt the soldiers were on full alert whenever many people were in the temple court. They sprang into action *immediately.* A centurion commanded a hundred men. More than one centurion came with the soldiers, so we can be sure it was a formidable fighting force that ran down the stairs and charged into the mob. Those who were beating Paul now stopped, for Roman soldiers had no mercy for anyone who resisted them.

B. Arrest (v. 33)

33. Then the chief captain came near, and took him, and commanded him to be bound with two chains; and demanded who he was, and what he had done.

Probably Paul's bruised and disheveled condition made it plain that the mob's fury was focused on him. The commander put him under arrest and had him *bound with two chains.* Perhaps he was chained to a soldier on each side. At one point, however, soldiers picked him up and carried him (v. 35). This suggests that one chain may have fettered his feet while the other handcuffed him. In any case, the two chains would assure the mob that the commander took their charges seriously and did not mean to let Paul get away. Having made the prisoner secure, the commander asked *who he was, and what he had done.* The accusers knew the Romans would not think it was any great crime to teach against the Jewish people and law and temple, so they gave no intelligent answer. Nothing could be learned from a furious, screaming mob. The commander told his men to take Paul up the steps to the fort (vv. 34-36).

III. Identified
(Acts 21:37-39a)

No one could be happy with the situation at that point. The would-be killers saw their victim snatched away from them. The commander had a prisoner and did not know who he was or why the people were angry with him. Paul was saved from death, but had no opportunity to speak in his own defense. He was the one who spoke up with a request.

A. Request (v. 37a)

37a. And as Paul was to be led into the castle, he said unto the chief captain, May I speak unto thee?

Now Paul was far enough up the stairway to be above the crowd, and he was *led* rather than carried (v. 35). If his feet were fettered, they were not held tightly enough to keep him from walking up the stairs. Being free from the pressure of the mob, he and the soldiers were relaxed enough so he could ask permission to speak to the commander.

B. Surprise (vv. 37b, 38)

37b, 38. Who said, Canst thou speak Greek? Art not thou that Egyptian, which before these days madest an uproar, and leddest out into the wilderness four thousand men that were murderers?

The *murderers* were terrorists who were numerous in Judea at that time. In the Greek they were called *sikarioi,* dagger men, because they carried concealed daggers and murdered their enemies in the midst of festival crowds. Sometimes they burned whole villages that displeased them. Apparently, not long before the time of Paul's capture an Egyptian led such a band in a small revolt. The revolt was crushed, but the Egyptian escaped. Seeing the mob's fury, the commander jumped to the conclusion that its victim was that Egyptian. He was surprised to hear the supposed Egyptian speaking Greek.

AREN'T YOU SOMEONE ELSE?

In 1981, a successful engineer in El Segundo, California, left his job and never came back. He was discovered in 1989 in Houston, Texas, living under an assumed name.

In 1982, a college president in Maryland told his wife as he left home that he might be back for lunch. He withdrew $28,000 from a bank account, drove to Washington, D. C., mailed farewell letters to his family and friends, and disappeared. Years later, he was discovered alive, well, and employed in Texas.

Life apparently had become just too much for these men to cope with, so they "bailed out." They went somewhere else and started life over as someone else. The college president kept his same name, but he was still a different person than he had been in his "former life."

The Roman commander mistook the apostle Paul for an Egyptian revolutionary who had given the Romans trouble. (We know that the Paul the commander saw was not the same man that Saul of Tarsus had been years earlier.) Most of us, like Paul, have become "different people" as we have matured spiritually. Each day ought to find us becoming "someone else" as we identify more and more with Christ.   —C. R. B.

C. Identity (v. 39a)

39a. But Paul said, I am a man which am a Jew of Tarsus, a city in Cilicia, a citizen of no mean city.

Far from being an obscure Egyptian terrorist, Paul was a Jew from Tarsus, a prominent city of the Roman Empire. Later he added that he was a citizen of Rome as well. That citizenship carried privileges, and it saved Paul from being scourged (Acts 22:24-29). But at that moment on the stairs, Paul identified himself and asked per-

mission to speak to the crowd below. Permission was granted, and he explained his preaching and the reason for it (Acts 21:39b—22:21). Once he had opposed the followers of Jesus as vigorously as did those men who now wanted to kill him. But he had seen Jesus, alive from the dead and appearing in Heavenly light. He then had no choice but to obey the living Lord, and the Lord had sent him to carry the gospel of salvation to the Gentiles. That last statement sent the crowd into a screaming rage again. To them it was intolerable to speak of sharing the blessings of salvation with any who were not Jews. There was no longer any hope of reasoning with the people, so the soldiers left the howling mob behind and led Paul into the fort (Acts 22:22-24).

Conclusion

Jerusalem was full of danger. Before he arrived there, Paul knew he was in danger of arrest (Acts 20:23; 21:10, 11), but he soon found that he was in danger of death as well.

Paul was not the only one in danger. There was danger from gossip and propaganda, and many were deceived. Those who wanted to kill Paul were endangered by Roman swords. Even the commander of the troops was in danger of being disciplined because he mistreated a prisoner who was a citizen of Rome.

A. Gossip

"They are informed of thee: (Acts 21:21). Jewish Christians in Jerusalem were being told that Paul was teaching Jews to stop obeying the Jewish law, to give up the ancient Jewish customs. Who was telling them all this? That question has no answer. Often the source of gossip is hard to find. "They say . . ." says the gossip, not telling who "they" are. Even a respected newspaper or TV newsman may give us a report from a "source" who is not named. Does the reporter ever make up the story he reports? We do not know.

A few years ago, media in the United States were excited briefly by a story from a newspaper in the Soviet Union. It reported that a spaceship had landed in a public park and that small-headed aliens twelve feet tall had been seen strolling in the vicinity. Someone was concerned enough to do some checking, and the furor quickly died when it was disclosed that the reporter had gotten the story from imaginative children.

Any Jewish Christian in Jerusalem could have learned that the gossip about Paul was false. Leaders of the church knew. Any member could have asked them. But there were "many thou-

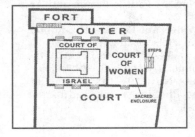

visual 11

sands" of Christians in that area, and it seems
that most of them did not check the story.

Paul's response to the gossip was not an announcement but a demonstration. He joined
some of the Jewish Christians in keeping an old
Jewish custom. It involved ceremonies carried
out publicly in the temple where Jews gathered.

Some students think Paul was wrong in doing
this, but the Bible does not say so. What is the
source of that rumor? We know Paul's action
was mistaken, some critics say, because it failed.
Where does the Bible say it failed? It did not
convince the mob of non-Christian Jews, but
that was not its purpose. It was designed to convince Christian Jews, and there is nothing to indicate that it failed to do that.

Some critics say Paul's action contradicted his
own teaching that people are saved by faith in
Christ, not by keeping the ceremonies prescribed by the Jewish law. But where is the contradiction? He taught that Jewish ceremonies
were not necessary for salvation, yes: but that
does not mean they were wrong.

We know Paul's actions sometimes were
guided by the Holy Spirit (Acts 16:6, 7). Where
such guidance is not specifically stated,
shouldn't we wait for positive proof before we
suppose Paul did wrong?

B. Propaganda

"Men of Israel, help: This is the man, that teacheth all men every where against the people,
and the law, and this place: and further brought
Greeks also into the temple, and hath polluted
this holy place" (Acts 21:28). Not a word of it
was true, but it was enough to rouse a mob and
try to take a life. This was not idle gossip; it was
a deliberate attempt to destroy.

"Don't believe all you hear." We know that is
good advice, but do we always apply it thoughtfully? It is bad to believe a lie; it is bad to reject
the truth. How can we tell a lie from the truth? It
takes time and care and effort.

We know news stories and TV interviews can
be slanted for purposes of propaganda. We know
a multitude of pressure groups are working for
selfish purposes rather than the common good.
Do we take time to hear the other side before we
support any effort to build or to destroy?

C. Hysteria

"All the city was moved, and the people ran
together" (Acts 21:30). Perhaps fifty or a hundred people heard what the men from Asia said
about Paul. Others arrived too late for that. They
heard only the confused shouting of many people. As the soldiers took Paul away, probably a
majority of the people did not know either who
he was or what accusation was made against
him. Still they pressed on the soldiers, screaming with the crowd, "Away with him!"

In technical language *hysteria* has a more specific meaning, but in popular speech it means
emotional excitement out of control. In Europe
the fans at a soccer match went berserk, irra-
tionally assaulting people and destroying property. In Cincinnati a throng was waiting to
attend a rock concert. When the gates opened,
the crowd surged forward so madly that people
were trampled to death. In big cities on several
continents peaceful meetings have turned into
destructive riots because emotional excitement
has gotten out of control.

A thoughtless crowd jumped to the conclusion that Paul deserved the beating he was getting. A Roman commander jumped to the
conclusion that he was a rebel from Egypt.
When that proved false, he jumped to the conclusion that Paul was a Jewish criminal who
could be whipped till he confessed. All these
hasty conclusions were wrong.

Why can't we all be sensible? Why can't we
wait to get the facts, hear both sides, think
things through—and then do right?

D. Prayer

Almighty God, the strength of our bodies is
Your gift, and so is the power of our minds. In
gratitude we want to use these gifts in Your service. So guide us that the actions of our bodies
will be controlled by the thinking of our minds,
and the thinking of our minds will be controlled
by Your Word, we pray in Jesus' name. Amen.

E. Thought to Remember

Think.

Home Daily Bible Readings

Monday, Nov. 4—Acts 21:1-6 Paul Travels
to Tyre (Acts 21:1-6)
Tuesday, Nov. 5—Agabus Predicts Paul's
Arrest (Acts 21:7-14)
Wednesday, Nov. 6—Paul Reaches
Jerusalem (Acts 21:15-26)
Thursday, Nov. 7—Paul is Beaten and Ar-
rested (Acts 21:27-39)
Friday, Nov. 8—Paul Reveals His Roman
Citizenship (Acts 22:25-29)
Saturday, Nov. 9—Paul's Conflict With the
Jewish Council (Acts 22:30—23:5)
Sunday, Date Nov. 10—Discussion Be-
tween the Pharisees and Sadducees
(Acts 23:6-11)

Learning by Doing

This page contains an alternate lesson plan emphasizing learning activities. Classes desiring such student involvement will find these suggestions helpful.

Learning Goals

This lesson will help students:

1. Describe the events surrounding Paul's arrest in the temple.

2. Explain why Christian leaders can anticipate being slandered at times.

3. Suggest appropriate responses to slander.

Into the Lesson

Prepare a copy of this matching quiz for each class member. (You will find it in the student book.) The quiz lists six persons and a false accusation made against each. Students are to try to match the person with the accusation made against him. Encourage them to read the Scripture passages to check their answers. (Answers: 1-c; 2-b; 3-e; 4-f; 5-a; 6-d.)

1. Moses
   (Numbers 16:12, 13)

   a. He was called a troubler of Israel

2. David
   (2 Samuel 16:5-8)

   b. Shimei called him a scoundrel

3. Jeremiah
   (Jeremiah 43:2, 3)

   c. Dathan and Abiram claimed he intended to kill the Israelites

4. Jesus
   (Matthew 26:64-66)

   d. He was accused of conspiring against the king of Israel

5. Elijah
   (1 Kings 18:17)

   e. Azariah and Johanan accused him of lying in order to have them killed

6. Amos
   (Amos 7:10)

   f. He was accused of blasphemy

Lead into the Bible study by writing this principle on your quarterly poster: *Effective Christian leaders must be prepared to experience opposition and slander.* Point out that although this principle is somewhat negative, the Scriptures indicate it to be a reality.

Into the Word

Deliver a brief lecture based on the information included in the introduction of this lesson.

Ask a volunteer to read Acts 21:17-39 aloud. Then have students form groups of six, and provide a copy of the following questions for each group to discuss.

1. What false accusations had the Christian Jews heard concerning Paul? (vv. 20, 21).

2. What did the elders suggest Paul do to prove that the rumors were false? (vv. 22-24).

3. What damage might have resulted from these false accusations?

4. When Paul went to the temple, how was he slandered? (vv. 26-29).

5. What happened to Paul as the result of the slander (vv. 30-39)?

As students discuss the questions, there may be some confusion regarding the accusation against Paul (vv. 20-26). Be prepared to clear the issue.

Point out that Paul was accused of teaching Jews everywhere to stop observing the ceremonies and customs of the law of Moses. That charge was false. Paul taught that the law could not save anyone, and Christians, whether of Jewish or Gentile background, were not *required* to keep it. By his own example, however, Paul showed that Christians of Jewish background were free to continue participating in the ceremonies of the law as a means of expressing their devotion to God.

Into Life

Lead students in discussing the following questions:

1. Why should those who follow Jesus expect to be slandered and opposed? (See Matthew 10:24, 25; John 15:18-21; 2 Timothy 3:12.)

2. How should Christians respond when they are slandered?

3. How should Christians respond when they hear accusations against other Christians?

4. How can Matthew 5:10-12 encourage those who are slandered for the kingdom's sake?

5. How can Christians prepare themselves for opposition without becoming paranoid?

Before class concludes, ask for one or two volunteers to read a selected book and report on it during class in two weeks. Their report should focus on how the individual in the book turned an obstacle into an opportunity to serve Christ. The books they can choose from include *Joni*, by Joni Eareckson and Joe Musser, *The Hiding Place*, by Corrie Ten Boom, or *Born Again*, by Charles Colson. Be sure to get a copy of one or more from your local or church library, or from a local Christian bookstore.

Let's Talk It Over

The questions on this page are designed to encourage review of the lesson Scriptures and to promote discussion of the lesson by the class. The answers provided are only discussion starters. Let your class talk it over from there.

1. Why did Paul, who was now a Christian, observe a Jewish ceremony in the temple at Jerusalem?

When Paul arrived in Jerusalem, a rumor concerning him was circulating among Jewish Christians. It was being said that he had taught Jews everywhere to abandon their ancient Jewish customs, and this rumor was a threat to the unity of the church. James and the elders in Jerusalem urged Paul to participate with four Christian brothers in a temple ceremony to demonstrate that he was not anti-Jewish, that he did not advocate the destruction of Jewish customs. Paul taught that it was not necessary to keep Jewish ceremonies for salvation; he did not teach, however, that it was wrong for Jewish Christians to worship God in the manner to which they were accustomed. While standing firm on the *essentials* of the Christian faith, Paul could bend on incidentals for others.

2. What was behind the intense hostility of the Jews toward Paul that would cause some to want to kill him?

Paul's offense was that he believed that God wanted to save all men, not just the Jews, and that He would do this through the sacrificial death of Jesus Christ. Therefore Paul preached the gospel to all. This was too broad for some Jews who would restrict God's love to themselves.

3. What are some of the dynamics of "mob psychology," which cause people in a mob to behave as they do?

One dynamic present in a crowd is that feelings are easily stirred, whether on a legitimate basis or not, and can soon get out of hand. A second dynamic is that the individual can hide in a crowd and feel brave and strong, drawing these feelings from the sheer numbers of people present. A third dynamic is that responsibility (and guilt) can be thrown off by the individual. It becomes easier to say that the responsibility belongs to "the crowd," not to me. Fourth, the dark, seamy side of human personality can take over in a mob. A mob *does not* bring out the best in people!

4. How was Paul's Roman citizenship an asset to him in his ministry?

On two occasions recorded in the New Testament, Paul called attention to his Roman citizenship to influence his treatment at the hands of officials: in Philippi (Acts 16: 37, 38) and in Jerusalem, immediately following the event recorded in our lesson text (Acts 22:25-29). On both of these occasions all he had to do was mention that he was a Roman citizen and changes occurred—quickly.

5. What is the cause and the effect of gossip?

Gossip is caused by the intent to shape opinion negatively. Most of the time, that intent is malicious; however, some pass on the gossip without that conscious intent. *Always* the dynamic is present to make the gossiper feel better than others or to gain some perceived advantage. The root cause of gossip is Satan—gossip is sin.

The effect of gossip is seen in the distortion of truth, damage to the reputation of the person gossiped about (it can damage more than that; it can even lead to death), and damage to the gossiper. Most people do not think of this last effect, but the gossiper demeans *self* as well as the object of the gossip. Gossip may hurt another person, but it certainly damages the character and integrity of the gossiper.

6. How should we respond when we are falsely accused?

The most basic response must be one of love, not a response in kind. It is legitimate most of the time to attempt to correct the false information. Paul did this, as we have seen in today's lesson. However, there are circumstances in which it is counter productive to attempt to answer false charges. Such a situation is "no win"; getting into the arena where mudslinging is occurring will only mean that one will get covered with more mud. Frequently, the target of false accusations must trust to his or her reputation and evident track record to carry the weight of defense. The people who know the reputation and character of the one who is being attacked will recognize that the accusations against the person are false.

Before Agrippa

LESSON SCRIPTURE: Acts 25:13 — 26:32.

PRINTED TEXT: Acts 26:1-8, 22, 23, 27-29.

Acts 26:1-8, 22, 23, 27-29

1 Then Agrippa said unto Paul, Thou art permitted to speak for thyself. Then Paul stretched forth the hand, and answered for himself:

2 I think myself happy, king Agrippa, because I shall answer for myself this day before thee touching all the things whereof I am accused of the Jews:

3 Especially because I know thee to be expert in all customs and questions which are among the Jews: wherefore I beseech thee to hear me patiently.

4 My manner of life from my youth, which was at the first among mine own nation at Jerusalem, know all the Jews;

5 Which knew me from the beginning, if they would testify, that after the most straitest sect of our religion I lived a Pharisee.

6 And now I stand and am judged for the hope of the promise made of God unto our fathers:

7 Unto which promise our twelve tribes, instantly serving God day and night, hope to come. For which hope's sake, king Agrippa, I am accused of the Jews.

8 Why should it be thought a thing incredible with you, that God should raise the dead?

· · · · · · · · · · · · · · ·

22 Having therefore obtained help of God, I continue unto this day, witnessing both to small and great, saying none other things than those which the prophets and Moses did say should come:

23 That Christ should suffer, and that he should be the first that should rise from the dead, and should show light unto the people, and to the Gentiles.

· · · · · · · · · · · · · ·

27 King Agrippa, believest thou the prophets? I know that thou believest.

28 Then Agrippa said unto Paul, Almost thou persuadest me to be a Christian.

29 And Paul said, I would to God, that not only thou, but also all that hear me this day, were both almost, and altogether such as I am, except these bonds.

GOLDEN TEXT: Having therefore obtained help of God, I continue unto this day, witnessing both to small and great, saying none other things than those which the prophets and Moses did say should come.—Acts 26:22.

From the Damascus Road to Rome

Unit 4. Destination: Rome
(Lessons 10-13)

Lesson Aims

After this lesson a student should be able to:

1. Name the three main characters in our lesson text and tell what each of them wanted.

2. Think seriously about what he himself wants most of all.

3. Identify one thing his greatest wish will lead him to do this week.

Lesson Outline

INTRODUCTION
    A. Alive but in Prison
    B. Lesson Background
 I. PRELIMINARIES (Acts 26:1-3)
    A. Permission to Speak (v. 1)
    B. Address to the King (vv. 2, 3)
 II. A JEW ACCUSED (Acts 26:4-8)
    A. Paul the Jew (vv. 4, 5)
    B. Unreasonable Accusation (vv. 6-8)
III. APPEAL TO THE KING (Acts 26:22, 23, 27-29)
    A. Preaching From the Prophets (vv. 22, 23)
    B. Almost Persuaded (vv. 27-29)
    Indecision or Lack of Faith?
CONCLUSION
    A. Festus the Governor
    B. Agrippa the King
    C. Paul the Prisoner
    D. Prayer
    E. Thought to Remember

Visual 12 from the visuals packet lists thoughts relating to God's promise referred to in verses 6 and 7. The visual is shown on page 100.

Introduction

As a Jew who did not believe in Jesus, Paul harassed Jews who did (Acts 8:3). He was an energetic persecutor, but not a happy one. Jesus said to him, "It is hard for thee to kick against the pricks: (Acts 26:14). This seems to mean that what Paul was doing was painful to him, but he did it because he thought it was his duty.

Then when Paul did believe in Jesus, the unbelieving Jews persecuted him. They opposed him with argument in the synagogues and with violence in other places (Acts 9:23, 29; 13:45, 50; 14:2, 19; 17:5, 13; 18:12; 19:9; 20:3).

A. Alive but in Prison

Last week we read that a mob of unbelieving Jews tried to kill Paul. Roman troops rescued him and made him their prisoner. Lysias, commander of the troops, took him to the ruling council of the Jews; but the council argued so violently that Lysias took him back to the Roman fort for safety (Acts 22:30—23:10).

Then the unbelievers made a daring plot. They would ask Lysias to bring Paul to the council again, but a band of men would ambush and kill him on the way. The plot was frustrated when Lysias learned about it. He sent Paul under heavy guard to Caesarea, the headquarters of the Roman governor of Judea.

Felix the governor took an interest in Paul's case, but took no action. He simply kept the prisoner in prison, hoping to be offered a bribe for his release. But no bribe was offered. After two years Felix was replaced by Festus. So there was a new governor, but Paul was still in prison (Acts 23:12—24:27).

B. Lesson Background

The new governor soon learned of Paul's case. Leading Jews asked that the prisoner be brought back to Jerusalem to answer to their council. Paul did not want to go back to Jerusalem, for he knew the plot to kill him would be reactivated. So Paul appealed to the emperor, as a Roman citizen had a right to do. That meant he had to be sent to Rome for a hearing.

Now Governor Festus had a problem. The case of Paul seemed to be a purely Jewish matter. How could he send a prisoner to Rome without some evidence of a crime against Roman law?

Then Agrippa came to Caesarea. He was king of all Palestine, and he graciously came to greet the new governor who would be serving under him. Could the king help with the troublesome problem of a prisoner with no crime? Agrippa readily agreed to listen to Paul. So the stage was set for a great affair of state. About the king and his consort were gathered the civil and military dignitaries of Caesarea, and Paul was brought before them. (Acts 25:1-23).

I. Preliminaries

(Acts 26:1-3)

It was a glittering array of power and prestige that Paul faced, but Paul was not one to be intimidated. He was ambassador of the King of kings. He may have been told years earlier that Jesus was sending him to kings, among others (Acts 9:15). Certainly he was told that he was to be a witness to all men (Acts 22:15).

A. Permission to Speak (v. 1)

1. Then Agrippa said unto Paul, Thou art permitted to speak for thyself. Then Paul stretched forth the hand, and answered for himself.

Read Acts 25:24-27 to see how Festus introduced the prisoner to the king. The king then formally permitted Paul to speak in his own behalf. We are left to imagine what sort of gesture Paul made as he *stretched forth the hand* and began to speak.

B. Address to the King (vv. 2, 3)

2. I think myself happy, king Agrippa, because I shall answer for myself this day before thee touching all the things whereof I am accused of the Jews.

Paul was always glad to present a defense when he was accused. He had asked permission to speak to a riotous mob of Jews intent on killing him (Acts 21:39). Only the pleas of friends had kept him from trying to speak to a mob of heathen who also were hostile (Acts 19:30, 31). He was glad not only to have a chance to defend himself, but also to have an opportunity to present the claims of Christ.

3. Especially because I know thee to be expert in all customs and questions which are among the Jews: wherefore I beseech thee to hear me patiently.

In this case there was a special reason for gladness. Paul was speaking to a man who was well acquainted with the background of Jewish *customs and questions.* Men of Agrippa's family had been prominent in government for generations. They had tried hard, though not always successfully, to win the favor of the Jews they ruled. Agrippa's great grandfather was the Herod who slew the babies of Bethlehem (Matthew 2:16). His great-uncle was Herod Antipas, who beheaded John the Baptist (Matthew 14:1-12). His father was Herod Agrippa I, who killed the apostle James to please the Jews (Acts 12:1-3). Now Agrippa II was hearing Paul's defense, and he would understand it much better than Festus would. The new governor would conclude that Paul had lost his mind (Acts 26:24-26).

II. A Jew Accused
(Acts 26:4-8)

Agrippa's great grandfather was Edomite rather than Jewish: that is, he was a descendant of Esau rather than Jacob; but the Jewish nation had annexed the land of Edom in the time between the Old Testament and the New. Besides, Agrippa's great grandmother was a Jewess of the high priest's family. This helped to make Agrippa acceptable to the Jews. Though he was educated in Rome, he never lost touch with the homeland. Paul could speak to him as a Jew speaking to a Jew, and the king would understand.

A. Paul the Jew (vv. 4, 5)

4. My manner of life from my youth, which was at the first among mine own nation at Jerusalem, know all the Jews.

Paul was a native of Tarsus in Cilicia, but he came to Jerusalem at such an early age that he could say he was brought up there (Acts 22:3). He was taught by the honored Gamaliel, and was an outstanding student (Galatians 1:14). Perhaps twenty years had passed since he had left Jerusalem; but many people there remembered him well, and younger people had heard of him.

5. Which knew me from the beginning, if they would testify, that after the most straitest sect of our religion I lived a Pharisee.

The Pharisees were the strictest sect of the Jews. The name means separated, and the members of this sect took great care to separate themselves from the ordinary people by being more zealous about keeping the Jewish law and the added traditions. Paul himself was among the strictest of that strict sect, "being more exceedingly zealous of the traditions" (Galatians 1:14). There were many people in Jerusalem who knew that very well.

B. Unreasonable Accusation (vv. 6-8)

6. And now I stand and am judged for the hope of the promise made of God unto our fathers.

Now this ardent Jew, one of the strictest of the strict, was a prisoner standing in judgment because he held the hope that God's promise made to their forefathers would be kept. Agrippa and all the Jews knew that God had promised a great deliverer and ruler, the Messiah. The Jews treasured such passages as Isaiah 9:6, 7 and Daniel 2:44; and they treasured the hope of the promised kingdom. That was the very hope that Paul cherished, and for his devotion to it he was a prisoner.

7. Unto which promise our twelve tribes, instantly serving God day and night, hope to come. For which hope's sake, king Agrippa, I am accused of the Jews.

Our twelve tribes, all the Jews, were hoping to see the promise of God fulfilled, hoping to come to the kingdom that was promised. In that hope they were serving God *instantly,* which means earnestly. Now they were accusing Paul of terrible crimes because he cherished the same hope they did. What could be more unreasonable? The conflict arose because Paul understood the promise and the kingdom better than the non-Christian Jews did. He knew the Messiah was not going to wrest His people from Roman rule by the use of military force; He was going to buy them from sin and death by His sacrificial death. The Messiah had risen from the dead to rule His kingdom by love and from Heaven, not by force and from the city of Jerusalem. The Messiah's kingdom was not for Jews only; it was for all the people of the world. Paul proclaimed a kingdom that fulfilled the prophecies of Scripture; but it did not meet the expectation of the Jews, and they hated Paul for proclaiming it.

8. Why should it be thought a thing incredible with you, that God should raise the dead?

Paul had been speaking directly to King Agrippa (v. 7), but the *you* here in verse 8 is plural. It challenged the whole audience, Jews in the king's entourage and Gentiles in Festus's company. Agrippa and the Jews especially should not doubt that God can raise the dead. They all believed in God. They all knew He was the giver of life (Genesis 2:7). They all knew He had restored life to dead people in ancient times (1 Kings 17:17-22; 2 Kings 4:32-35). Yet the resurrection of Jesus was at the very center of the Jews' quarrel with Paul. They said Jesus was dead; Paul said He was alive (Acts 25:19). Those who accepted the fact of Jesus' resurrection were His devoted followers; those who would not follow Him denied He had risen from the dead.

III. Appeal to the King
(Acts 26:22, 23, 27-29)

After raising the question about the resurrection, Paul went on to explain how he himself had become a staunch believer in Jesus (Acts 26:9-21). Once he had been like the Jews who now opposed him. He had thought Jesus was dead and the preaching of His resurrection was false. But then Paul saw Jesus. No longer could he deny that Jesus was alive, nor could he deny that Jesus was Lord.

The Lord then gave him a commission, a special task, a job to do. He was to be a minister

visual 12

and a witness of the risen Lord. Jesus sent him especially to the Gentiles, "to open their eyes, and to turn them from darkness to light, and from the power of Satan unto God, that they may receive forgiveness of sins, and inheritance among them which are sanctified by faith that is in me" (v. 18).

Paul accepted the task. Far and wide he proclaimed to Jews and Gentiles "that they should repent and turn to God, and do works meet for repentance." That was why the Jews tried to kill him (vv. 19-21).

A. Preaching From the Prophets
(vv. 22, 23)

22. Having therefore obtained help of God, I continue unto this day, witnessing both to small and great, saying none other things than those which the prophets and Moses did say should come.

By God's help Paul survived the Jews' attempt to kill him. As we saw in our lesson text last week, Roman soldiers helped too, snatching him from an angry mob that was about to beat him to death (Acts 21:31, 32). Paul's nephew helped when he detected a murderous plot against him and reported it (Acts 23:12-22). Roman soldiers helped again when they escorted Paul to Caesarea (Acts 23:23, 24). Still Paul gave the credit to God. By His will Paul had survived. The other helpers were His instruments. Even the heathen Romans who did not know Him were tools in His hand to accomplish His purpose.

With such help Paul survived *unto this day,* and *unto this day* he kept on *witnessing both to small and great.* The small were the common people of the mob to which he gave his testimony (Acts 22:1-21). By ordinary human standards Agrippa the king was greatest of the great in that part of the world, and now he was hearing Paul's testimony.

The main point of this verse is that Paul was announcing the very events that the prophets had foretold. For that the Jews were trying to kill him. It was preposterous!

23. That Christ should suffer, and that he should be the first that should rise from the

dead, and should show light unto the people, and to the Gentiles.

Paul now mentioned specific things foretold by the prophets and fulfilled in Jesus, things that the unbelieving Jews were not willing to hear. They did not want to believe *that Christ should suffer.* They wanted Him to trample their enemies under His feet and rule in triumph forever, as suggested in Daniel 2:44. But look at the fifty-third chapter of Isaiah: "Despised and rejected . . . wounded for our transgressions . . . oppressed . . . afflicted . . . brought as a lamb to the slaughter . . . cut off out of the land of the living." The Jews hid from that prophecy, saying that it was not written of the Christ but of someone else, perhaps the prophet himself (Acts 8:32-34).

The Jews did not want to hear that Christ *should be the first that should rise from the dead,* for they were confident that He would never die (Isaiah 9:7). But with the first public proclamation of the risen Lord, Peter pointed to the prophecy of His resurrection in Psalm 16:8-11 (Acts 2:25-36).

The Jews welcomed the declaration that the Christ would *show light unto the people:* that is, the Jewish people. However, they fiercely resented the announcement that He would show light also *to the Gentiles.* Even Christian Jews resented that for a time; but from the prophets they came to understand that the blessings of Christ were for all people who would accept them (Acts 13:46, 47; Isaiah 49:6; Acts 15:14-18; Amos 9:11, 12).

The Jews who opposed Paul most violently were not present, and it was the heathen Festus who raised a loud objection (v. 24). Perhaps the talk of rising from the dead made him think Paul was out of his mind. Paul answered that objection with brief courtesy (vv. 25, 26) and turned back to the king, who knew more about the Scriptures, and Jewish ways, and the beginning and growth of the church.

B. Almost Persuaded (vv. 27-29)

27. King Agrippa, believest thou the prophets? I know that thou believest.

Both this Agrippa and his father were educated in Rome and favored by Roman emperors, but to the Jews they took care to show themselves as Jews. They did in fact do much to secure better treatment for their people. Eager as he was to appear as a loyal Jew, Agrippa certainly would not express any doubts about the prophets whom the Jews revered. If the king would plainly accept the prophets, that would give Paul an opening to press the claim of Jesus, who fulfilled so many prophecies.

28. Then Agrippa said unto Paul, Almost thou persuadest me to be a Christian.

We would understand the king better if we could hear the tone of his voice and see the expression on his face. Some students take his words seriously, thinking he really was close to becoming a Christian at that moment. Others think he spoke with sarcasm and scorn, ridiculing the idea that anyone could be so easily persuaded. Some students read Agrippa's words as a question instead of a statement. To add to the difficulty, the Greek text is somewhat ambiguous. *Almost* is literally *in little* or *with little.* Some think it means in a little time or with a little persuasion. Various possible meanings are seen in different English translations:

American Standard Version: "With but little persuasion thou wouldest fain make me a Christian."

Revised Standard Version: "In a short time you think to make me a Christian!

The Living Bible: "With trivial proofs like these, you expect me to become a Christian?"

New International Version: "Do you think that in such a short time you can persuade me to be a Christian?"

New American Standard Bible: "In a short time you will persuade me to become a Christian."

Moffat: "At this rate it won't be long before you believe you have made a Christian of me!"

The New English Bible: "You think it will not take much to win me over and make a Christian of me."

New American Bible: "A little more, Paul, and you will make a Christian out of me!"

29. And Paul said, I would to God, that not only thou, but also all that hear me this day, were both almost, and altogether such as I am, except these bonds.

Whatever the king's attitude was, Paul's was utterly serious. Earnestly he wished that everyone in that audience would be a Christian and share Paul's benefits, but not his bonds. And whatever the king's tone was, it is clear that he wanted to hear no more. He stood up and ended the meeting. Still it is plain that Paul had made a good impression. King and governor agreed that there was no reason to hold this prisoner. But Paul himself had appealed to the emperor, and they had to send him to Rome (vv. 30-32).

INDECISION OR LACK OF FAITH?

James Thurber once remarked, "It is better to know some of the questions than all of the answers." How many people in our time resist making a decision because they can't pin down every facet of the future with absolute assurance?

How many people resist the decision to marry because they are not certain that they will escape the unhappiness they observe in so many marriages? How many are stuck in a job that is a lifelong rut because they are afraid to risk what little is in their hand for the possibility of something much greater slightly beyond their grasp?

We don't know for sure what caused King Agrippa's curt response to Paul. Perhaps, as some have suggested, he felt Paul was "pushing" him to make a hasty decision. Or maybe he was fearful of his position as king of the Jews. Or maybe it was something else: maybe he wanted to have all the answers before making a commitment to Christ.

Regarding Christ's call, we'll never have all the answers. If we did, we'd be walking by sight, not by faith. God calls us to trust him, to take one more step with our hearts beyond what we can see with our eyes.   —C. R. B.

Conclusion

Three men stood out in that roomful of important people in Caesarea: Festus the governor, Agrippa the king, and Paul the prisoner. Each of them wanted something.

A. Festus the Governor

Festus wanted an answer. He had to send a prisoner to the emperor, and he had to send a paper to explain why. As far as he could see, however, the man was not even accused of any crime against Rome. What could he say to the emperor? Quite sensibly, Festus consulted an expert. The visiting king was well acquainted with Jewish ways. Perhaps he could help.

We all depend on experts. In sickness we go to the doctor; with legal problems we consult a lawyer; with car trouble we seek a mechanic; with a theological question we go to the preacher. This is the sensible thing to do. But can't we all recall a time when the doctor's diagnosis was wrong, the lawyer's advice was bad, the mechanic was incompetent, or the preacher couldn't answer? Likewise Festus got little help from the king.

Fortunately we have infallible help with our most important problems. The Bible is clear about right and wrong. It tells us how to get rid of our sins and live forever. Experts may disagree about some of its teachings; but if we try, each of us can become expert enough to find out what we really need to know.

B. Agrippa the King

Agrippa wanted out. Paul's clear reasoning drove him into a corner. He could not doubt the prophecies of Scripture. That would make him unpopular with the Jews he ruled, and he was trying hard to be popular with them. But the prophecies supported the claim that Jesus was the Christ, and Agrippa did not want to admit that. Such a stand would make him unpopular with the Jews, for most of them rejected Jesus' claim. Being the king, Agrippa easily found a way out. He got up and made for the door. The discussion was over.

Do you know people who take the same way out? They don't want to discuss religion. They don't want to hear the evidence that Jesus is the Lord. They don't want to know what the Bible says. But a Day of Judgment is coming, and all of us will be judged by what the Bible says.

C. Paul the Prisoner

Paul wanted to win souls for Christ. King and commoner alike were lost without the Savior. So Paul spoke directly to the King about his belief. The king evaded the question, and so do many people we know. But there are many today who will be saved if we keep on pressing the claims of Jesus.

Think about the people you will be seeing this week. Some of them need to hear about the Savior. Will you be the one to tell them?

D. Prayer

Our Father, in all this world's confusion, how good it is to have a sure and certain guide! Your Word is a lamp unto our feet, and a light unto our path. We thank You for the Bible, and ask that you will help us to walk in its light. In Jesus' name, amen.

E. Thought to Remember

Jesus saves.

Home Daily Bible Readings

Monday, Nov. 11—Festus Tells the Emperor About Paul (Acts 25:13-17)

Tuesday, Nov. 12—The Emperor Asks to Hear Paul (Acts 25:18-22)

Wednesday, Nov. 13—Paul Appears Before King Agrippa (Acts 25:23-27)

Thursday, Nov. 14—Paul Begins His Defense (Acts 26:1-8)

Friday, Nov. 15—Paul Describes His Encounter With Christ (Acts 26:9-18)

Saturday, Nov. 16—Paul Describes His Ministry (Acts 26:19-23)

Sunday, Nov. 17—Paul Concludes His Defense (Acts 26:24-32)

Learning by Doing

*This page contains an alternate lesson plan emphasizing learning activities. Classes
desiring such student involvement will find these suggestions helpful.*

Learning Goals

As a result of this lesson, your students will:

1. Summarize Paul's personal testimony to King Agrippa.

2. Develop their own personal testimony of how Jesus has changed their lives.

Into the Lesson

Begin today's session by asking your class members, "In what ways are personal testimonies used in society to persuade or motivate people?" Allow students to respond. They will probably mention that celebrities often endorse commercial products, suggesting that if someone who is successful and well known uses the product, it must be valuable. Testimonies are given at corporate sales meetings to motivate others in their sales. Testimonies may be given in goal-oriented endeavors, such as weight-loss groups, to persuade people that they can achieve their goals, just as others have done. Other examples will probably be suggested.

After a few minutes of discussion, point out that the personal testimonies of some Christians have been effective in helping others see their need for Christ.

Write this principle on the effective leadership poster you have been making this quarter: *Effective Christian leaders have been changed by Jesus and are eager to tell others about it.* Read the principle aloud, and then comment: "In our study today we will observe how Paul gave his personal testimony to a king."

Into the Word

Present a brief lecture explaining the background for today's passage. You will want your students to understand the events that occurred between the Scripture text of last week's lesson and this lesson's text (that section includes Acts 21:40—25:27). Be sure to explain the circumstances that led to Paul's giving his testimony in Acts 26. You can base your lecture on the information in the introduction to this lesson.

Before the beginning of class, reproduce the chart that is shown in the next column. If possible, spread the chart over an entire page to allow plenty of room for writing. Give each student a copy of the chart at this time. If your class uses the student book, you will find the chart included in it.

	Paul's Life	My Life
Description of life before encountering Jesus	vv. 4-11	
Circumstances/ people that influenced coming to Jesus	vv. 12-18	
Changes in life made by Jesus	vv. 19-23	

Have class members form groups of six. Appoint a discussion leader for each group and provide pencils for each class member. In their groups, students are to analyze Paul's testimony in Acts 26 and fill in the column of the chart that pertains to Paul's life.

After twelve minutes call the groups together and ask the leader from each group to report the group's observations. After the groups have reported, mention that Paul's testimony before Agrippa did not result in any recorded conversions. Point out that our testimonies for Christ may not produce any immediate results either, but God can use them as one of many influences in bringing others to Christ.

Into Life

Ask students to write their own testimony following the outline shown on the chart. They can write it in the appropriate column on the chart or on blank sheets of paper. Allow at least ten minutes for this. Students will need to work alone.

When time has expired, ask for volunteers to share their testimony with the class. Be sure to encourage and thank each person who shares. If you prefer, have students form their groups again and let several volunteers in each group share their testimony with the group.

Before you conclude, have students discuss this question:

1. How can you share your personal testimony with non-Christians in a sensitive, yet effective way?

2. Close with a prayer that each member of your class will possess courage like Paul to share his or her testimony with a non-Christian.

Let's Talk It Over

The questions on this page are designed to encourage review of the lesson Scriptures and to promote discussion of the lesson by the class. The answers provided are only discussion starters. Let your class talk it over from there.

1. What excellent psychological and logical approaches did Paul use in his address before Agrippa?

First, he "plussed" Agrippa, expressing his gratitude for the opportunity to speak before him, acknowledging Agrippa as an expert on Jewish customs and questions. Second, he traced his way of life as an ardent Jew and strict Pharisee, which, he stated, his accusers knew full well. Furthermore, it was a life-style his accusers themselves shared. Third, he introduced God's promise made to the fathers regarding the Messiah, a hope shared by the accusers, Agrippa, and Paul. No one would deny Israel's longing for the fulfillment of that promise. *Then* Paul presented Jesus, the hope of Israel, raised from the dead by God's power. Paul had *seen* Him—alive! Then he reminded his audience that his preaching consisted only of what the prophets and Moses had said should come to pass—that the Messiah would suffer, be raised from the dead and proclaim light to all people. This speech is both an excellent legal defense and a powerful personal testimony.

2. What did Festus, Agrippa, and Paul want from the encounter in today's lesson?

Festus wanted an answer to a knotty problem. Paul had appealed to Caesar for a hearing of his case, and Festus had to send a letter to Rome explaining the charges against the prisoner. Knowing that Paul was guilty of no crime, Festus hoped Agrippa could help him out of a tough spot.

Agrippa wanted to "play both sides of the fence." He wanted to build and maintain his base of popularity with his Jewish subjects and also maintain Roman justice with Paul. He saw that Paul was innocent, but the appeal to Caesar must be honored. What Agrippa finally wanted, though, was "out." When Paul's address got too personal, Agrippa terminated it by simply leaving.

Paul wanted *everyone* to believe in Jesus Christ and to share his hope of eternal life in Him.

3. List some of the things people want most out of life.

Happiness. Ask the majority of people what they want and they will reply, "I want to be happy." That may seem to be an innocent enough desire, but essentially it is extremely self-centered. In popular thinking, happiness results when one's external circumstances are desirable and pleasurable. Americans have been assured of the inalienable rights of "life, liberty, and the pursuit of happiness." In reality the *pursuit* of happiness seems only to thwart the possession of it. Many have found this to be true and have discovered instead that happiness is, as God's Word suggests, a by-product of sharing and giving to others.

Success. In a culture of "rugged individualism," where the opportunity beckons to climb to the top, success becomes the goddess of many. Upward mobility marks the path of those who are striving for success. Yet for many, success (when achieved) turns to ashes, rather than sweetness, in their mouths.

Wealth. The dream of many persons is to escape from poverty and build their own fortune. Many are obsessed with making money, feeling that money, and the things that money can buy, will satisfy. But those who desire wealth seem never to get enough.

Power. In a society that values power, whether in politics, automobiles, athletics, or business, the appeal of personal power is strong and pervasive. Many persons want to feel powerful, to feel that they are in control of others. Most of the time, though, power is abused, rather than used in a healthy way, showing the truth of the expression, "Power corrupts, and ultimate power ultimately corrupts."

Meaning. Underneath all the other desires, it may well be that most people want to find some kind of meaning in life. If life has meaning, it is livable and fulfilling. They search for meaning in relationships, philosophies, service, religion. Ultimate meaning, however, can be found only in Jesus Christ.

4. What issue was at the heart of the conflict between Paul and the Jews?

The central teaching of the gospel is that Israel's hope, and indeed the hope of all mankind, is found in Jesus Christ, risen from the dead, in fulfillment of the teachings of Moses and the ancient prophets of Israel. Various charges were hurled at Paul by the Jews, but this was at the heart of them all.

Paul in Rome

LESSON SCRIPTURE: Acts 27, 28.

PRINTED TEXT: Acts 28:21-31.

Acts 28:21-31

21 And they said unto him, We neither received letters out of Judea concerning thee, neither any of the brethren that came showed or spake any harm of thee.

22 But we desire to hear of thee what thou thinkest: for as concerning this sect, we know that every where it is spoken against.

23 And when they had appointed him a day, there came many to him into his lodging; to whom he expounded and testified the kingdom of God, persuading them concerning Jesus, both out of the law of Moses, and out of the prophets, from morning till evening.

24 And some believed the things which were spoken, and some believed not.

25 And when they agreed not among themselves, they departed, after that Paul had spoken one word, Well spake the Holy Ghost by Isaiah the prophet unto our fathers,

26 Saying, Go unto this people, and say, Hearing ye shall hear, and shall not understand; and seeing ye shall see, and not perceive:

27 For the heart of this people is waxed gross, and their ears are dull of hearing, and their eyes have they closed; lest they should see with their eyes, and hear with their ears, and understand with their heart, and should be converted, and I should heal them.

28 Be it known therefore unto you, that the salvation of God is sent unto the Gentiles, and that they will hear it.

29 And when he had said these words, the Jews departed, and had great reasoning among themselves.

30 And Paul dwelt two whole years in his own hired house, and received all that came in unto him,

31 Preaching the kingdom of God, and teaching those things which concern the Lord Jesus Christ, with all confidence, no man forbidding him.

GOLDEN TEXT: Paul dwelt two whole years in his own hired house . . . preaching the kingdom of God, and teaching those things which concern the Lord Jesus Christ, with all confidence, no man forbidding him.—Acts 28:30, 31.

From the Damascus Road to Rome
Unit 4. Destination: Rome
(Lessons 10-13)

Lesson Aims

After this lesson students should be able to:

1. Tell what Paul did during his two years as a prisoner in Rome, also to recall such parts of the introduction and conclusion as the teacher chooses to include in the lesson.

2. Admire Paul's vigorous work when he was handicapped by imprisonment.

3. Find at least one way of adding vigor to his own Christian work.

Lesson Outline

INTRODUCTION
  A. Paul and Felix (Acts 24)
  B. Paul and Festus (Acts 25, 26)
  C. Paul at Sea (Acts 27)
  D. Paul on Melita (Acts 28:1-10)
  E. Paul in Italy (Acts 28:11-16)
  F. Lesson Background (Acts 28:17-20)
 I. HEARERS AND MESSAGE (Acts 28:21-23)
  A. Eager Listeners (vv. 21, 22)
      The Value of an Open Mind
  B. About the Kingdom (v. 23)
 II. PROPHECY ABOUT THE HEARERS (Acts 28:24-27)
  A. Agreement and Disagreement (v. 24)
  B. Resisting God's Message (vv. 25-27)
III. A WIDER AUDIENCE (Acts 28:28-31)
  A. Salvation for All (v. 28)
  B.   Continuing Debate (v. 29)
  C. Preaching Prisoner (vv. 30, 31)
CONCLUSION
  A. The Rest of the Story
  B. Prayer
  C. Thought to Remember

Display visual 13 from the visuals packet and let it remain before the class throughout this session. The visual is shown on page108.

Introduction

Paul was a perplexing prisoner to the Romans. To begin with, they seized him to save his life, not because they saw anything wrong with him. Second, they found that he was a Roman citizen, and therefore entitled to secure protection and special privileges. Third, only confusion came from trying to find why the Jews hated him. Fourth, a murderous plot against him was unveiled, and they took the more care to keep him safe (Acts 21:27—23:35).

A. Paul and Felix (Acts 24)

Governor Felix was not greatly perplexed. He had a prisoner with no substantial charge against him. As this governor saw it, the only thing to do was to hold the prisoner till a bribe was offered for his release. That was neither puzzling nor surprising to anyone accustomed to the ways of corrupt officials. But no bribe was offered, and Paul stayed in prison.

B. Paul and Festus (Acts 25, 26)

Festus was perplexed. He was new in that area. He saw no substance in the charges against Paul. He did not know about the plot to assassinate the prisoner. He did not understand why Paul appealed to Caesar. Worst of all, from his point of view, he had to send a prisoner to Rome and he had no adequate reason for his imprisonment. He appealed to Agrippa for help, but it seems that he got none.

We are not told what Festus finally wrote to the emperor. It must have been similar to what he told King Agrippa. (1) Festus had not arrested Paul, but had found him in prison when he came into his office. (2) The charges against him seemed to be Jewish matters of no interest to Roman justice. (3) Paul himself had appealed to the emperor, and that was the only reason for sending him.

C. Paul at Sea (Acts 27)

For a record of the long voyage toward Italy we are indebted to Luke. He was not a prisoner, but he went along with Paul. A Thessalonian named Aristarchus also went with them.

Paul provided surprise after surprise for the ship's crew. He was a landlubber, but he alone predicted a storm at sea and advised that the ship stay in port. When his advice was ignored and the ship was tossed by a tempest, Paul was the one who cheered the despairing sailors with an angel's promise of survival. He was the one who predicted shipwreck on an island. His warning kept the sailors from deserting. To save Paul, the centurion in charge kept his men from killing all the prisoners.

D. Paul on Melita (Acts 28:1-10)

When the ship broke apart on a beach, crew and passengers found themselves on the island of Melita, the one now called Malta. There they had to stay for the winter, and there again Paul was full of surprises. He survived the bite of a poisonous snake. He healed the sick of the is-

<table>
<tr><td colspan="2">

How to Say It

AGRIPPA. Uh-*grip*-puh.
ANTIOCH. *An*-tee-ock.
ARISTARCHUS. Air-iss-*tar*-cuss.
CAESAREA. Sess-uh-*ree*-uh.
ERASTUS. E-*rass*-tus.
FESTUS. *Fes*-tus.
MELITA. *Mel*-i-tuh.
MILETUS. My-*lee*-tus.
NICOPOLIS. Ni-*cop*-o-lis.
ONESIMUS. O-*ness*-ih-muss.
PUTEOLI. Pew-*tee*-o-li.
THESSALONIAN. *Thess*-uh-*lo*-nee-un (strong
    accent on *lo*; *th* as in *thin*).
TROAS. *Tro*-az.
TROPHIMUS. *Troff*-ih-muss.

</td></tr>
</table>

land. The residents were grateful, and Luke says they "honored us with many honors; and when we departed, they laded us with such things as were necessary."

E. Paul in Italy (Acts 28:11-16)

When the winter storms were over, passengers and crew found passage on another ship. They landed at Puteoli on the west coast of Italy. Paul the prisoner had been treated as an honored guest on the island; now his captors gave him similar treatment. At Puteoli he and Luke and Aristarchus were greeted by Christians and allowed to stay a week. As they went on toward Rome, Christians of that city came to meet them and escort them as if they were conquering heroes instead of a prisoner and his friends. At Rome the favored treatment continued. Paul was not locked in jail, but allowed to rent a house to live in. To be sure he did not escape, a soldier stayed with him, probably fastened to him with a chain (Acts 28:20).

F. Lesson Background (Acts 28:17-20)

In some cities Paul took his message first to the Jewish synagogues. It seems that he was confined to his rented house in Rome, but allowed to receive visitors. Therefore he sent word to leading Jews of the city and asked them to meet with him. When they came, he told them frankly that Jews at Jerusalem were responsible for his imprisonment. Without making any accusations against those persons, he insisted that he had done nothing contrary to Jewish law or custom. He shared Israel's hope of deliverance by a Messiah, and for that hope he was a prisoner. Our lesson text begins with the response of the Jewish leaders.

I. Hearers and Message
(Acts 28:21-23)

It is notable that Jews everywhere were willing to listen—for a while. When they did not like what they heard their objection was vociferous and sometimes violent, but they listened first. So Jesus at Nazareth was allowed to speak in the synagogue, and then threatened with death (Luke 4:16-30). So Paul and Barnabas at Antioch were invited to speak (Acts 13:13-15), but later they were run out of town (Acts 13:50). Even the murderous mob at Jerusalem listened for a time (Acts 21:40—22:22). Likewise at Rome Paul was received cordially.

A. Eager Listeners (vv. 21, 22)

21. And they said unto him, We neither received letters out of Judea concerning thee, neither any of the brethren that came showed or spake any harm of thee.

Leading Jews at Jerusalem were hostile to Paul, hostile enough to plot murder (Acts 25:1-3); but apparently they did not think it worth while to warn those in Rome against him. Several months had passed since Paul had left Caesarea, and neither by letter nor by word of mouth had the Jews at Rome heard anything bad about him from those in Judea.

22. But we desire to hear of thee what thou thinkest: for as concerning this sect, we know that every where it is spoken against.

From Judea the Roman Jews had heard nothing against Paul, but from everywhere they had heard much against Christians. Still they were eager to hear Paul's thoughts from his own mouth.

THE VALUE OF AN OPEN MIND

The world's moldiest piece of cheese—all one hundred pounds of it—was found a few years ago in a peat bog in County Tipperary, Ireland. The workmen were harvesting peat at a depth of about five feet when they came upon the ball of cheese wrapped in wickerwork.

An archaeologist was called. Judging from the depth at which the cheese was found, he said it was probably fourteen hundred years old and might still be edible. He said it might be butter instead of cheese, but he wasn't keen on tasting it to determine either!

Most of us wouldn't blame the archaeologist. A spirit of scientific inquiry is admirable, but risking serious illness or death to see if an ancient piece of cheese (or butter) is edible is above and beyond the call of duty.

There are more important things in life, and regarding them an open mind and an inquiring spirit are virtues. The Jews who came to Paul had heard that Christianity was criticized "everywhere," but they wanted to hear for themselves what Paul had to say about it. The fact that some of them accepted his testimony is proof that they had open minds.

An open mind is a necessity for anyone today who would experience spiritual growth.

—C. R. B.

B. About the Kingdom (v. 23)

23. And when they had appointed him a day, there came many to him into his lodging; to whom he expounded and testified the kingdom of God, persuading them concerning Jesus, both out of the law of Moses, and out of the prophets, from morning till evening.

Obviously the Jews were sincere in their wish to hear Paul. They *appointed him a day* when they could bring more of their number and spend more time with him. On that day *there came many* and they spent the entire day, *from morning till evening.* The subject of discussion was *the kingdom of God.* That was what the Jews were hoping for—the world-conquering, everlasting kingdom foretold in Daniel 2:44. Its ruler, they felt sure, would be the marvelous king described in Isaiah 9:6: "Wonderful, Counselor, The mighty God, The everlasting Father, The Prince of Peace." Paul's task was to persuade them that Jesus was that mighty, eternal king. He took his evidence *out of the law of Moses, and out of the prophets,* explaining that Jesus did and would do what was foretold in many Scriptures. In writing the record, Luke did not pause at this point to cite any of the Scriptures Paul used. Earlier in the book he had several times summarized the same line of reasoning by Paul and others (Acts 2:14-36; 3:11-26; 7:1-53; 8:26-38; 13:16-41).

II. Prophecy About the Hearers (Acts 28:24-27)

Paul did not deliver an all-day monologue, of course. A lively discussion must have taken place.

A. Agreement and Disagreement (v. 24)

24. And some believed the things which were spoken, and some believed not.

This was the usual reaction to the kind of reasoning Paul was using. Acts 2:41 records that three thousand believed; but uncounted thousands did not, and among them were the leaders at Jerusalem. Acts 13:43 says, "many of the Jews and religious proselytes followed Paul and Barnabas"; but others "were filled with envy, and spake against those things which were spoken

visual 13

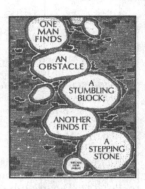

by Paul, contradicting and blaspheming" (Acts 13:45). Paul certainly was not surprised to find his audience sharply divided in Rome.

B. Resisting God's Message (vv. 25-27)

25. And when they agreed not among themselves, they departed, after that Paul had spoken one word, Well spake the Holy Ghost by Isaiah the prophet unto our fathers.

We need not take this to mean *they departed* because *they agreed not among themselves.* Probably they had been doing that all day. More likely they departed because the day was over and it was time to go home. At the end of the meeting Paul had the last word, and it was not his word. He called attention to the word of *the Holy Ghost,* a word written in Isaiah 6:9, 10.

26. Saying, Go unto this people, and say, Hearing ye shall hear, and shall not understand; and seeing ye shall see, and not perceive.

Isaiah was sent to give God's message to Israel seven hundred years before Jesus came, and he was sent with the warning that most of the hearers would not understand and accept the message they would hear. They would hear the words, but would not absorb the message and change their way of living. They would see the speaker, but would not perceive that he was God's prophet speaking God's message.

27. For the heart of this people is waxed gross, and their ears are dull of hearing, and their eyes have they closed; lest they should see with their eyes, and hear with their ears, and understand with their heart, and should be converted, and I should heal them.

God's message by Isaiah was true; it was understandable; it was reasonable. It failed to make the people change their ways, not because they could not understand it, but because they did not want to believe it. They closed their eyes and ears and minds; they disregarded God's message and went on in selfish and sinful ways till they were taken in captivity to Babylon. That was a matter of history. Paul's audience knew it well. Paul simply called attention to the well-known facts and left his hearers to make the application for themselves. Some of them were doing exactly what their forefathers had done. They were rejecting God's message. This time the result would not be seventy years in Babylon, but eternity in Hell.

III. A Wider Audience
(Acts 28:28-31)

On the heels of the Holy Spirit's word through the prophet Isaiah came the Holy Spirit's word through the apostle Paul. To some of the hearers it was as unwelcome as anything Paul said that day.

A. Salvation for All (v. 28)

28. Be it known therefore unto you, that the salvation of God is sent unto the Gentiles, and that they will hear it.

This too was foretold by the prophets, but the Jews had been overlooking it. Abraham was the beginning of a separated people, but even as he was separated he heard that the separated people would bring a blessing to the whole world (Genesis 12:3). Even Christian Jews were slow to believe that salvation was literally for all people (Mark 16:15, 16). But when they stopped to think about it, they saw that it was taught by the prophets (Acts 15:16, 17). Still many closed their hearts to that part of the prophetic message. Eagerly they looked for a Messiah to deliver them, but they refused to think that He would deliver anyone else. Paul insisted that salvation was for Jews and Gentiles alike, and that was one reason the unbelieving Jews hated him (Acts 22:21, 22).

B. Continuing Debate (v. 29)

29. And when he had said these words, the Jews departed, and had great reasoning among themselves.

Many of the ancient manuscripts do not have this verse, and so it is left out of some English versions. Still we can hardly doubt that what it says is true. After arguing through most of the day, the Jews did not let the matter drop. The debate may have gone on for weeks or years, unless it became so sharp that those among them who believed that Jesus was the Christ were evicted from the synagogue.

C. Preaching Prisoner (vv. 30, 31)

30. And Paul dwelt two whole years in his own hired house, and received all that came in unto him.

Paul had come to Rome for Caesar's judgment. Caesar was a busy man, however, and in no hurry to take up an unimportant case from Judea. It was easy to postpone a matter that had no influential person at court asking for attention to it. We who are impatient with the slow course of justice are reminded that it is not new in our time. Paul could not even be released on bail. Still his situation had its bright side. He was not in jail, but *in his own hired house.* He was not sequestered, but allowed to see *all that came in unto him,* and certainly they were many. The Jews who believed his message surely came back for more instruction, and probably brought their friends with them. The Christians who came to meet him as he approached Rome (Acts 28:15) certainly came to him at other times, and probably brought heathen friends. Onesimus, for example, seems to have been led to be born again while Paul was a prisoner (Philemon 10). So Paul was under house arrest, but his house was a schoolhouse and evangelistic center.

Incidentally, this verse tells us when Luke finished writing this record. It was when Paul had been two years in Rome as a prisoner. If the record had been finished earlier, it could not have included those two years; if it had been written later, it would have included more. This places the writing about A. D. 63.

31. Preaching the kingdom of God, and teaching those things which concern the Lord Jesus Christ, with all confidence, no man forbidding him.

Month after month Paul continued *preaching the kingdom of God, and teaching those things which concern the Lord Jesus Christ.* This must have included teaching like that given to the Jewish leaders on that long day of discussion, plus much teaching about how Christians ought to live, teaching such as we find in Paul's letters. Four of those letters were written during this imprisonment: Philippians, Ephesians, Colossians, and Philemon. He carried on his teaching *with all confidence, no man forbidding him.* Among the hearers, of course, were the soldiers who guarded him (Acts 28:16). Thus his teaching became well-known where they were quartered, and there were Christians in Caesar's own household (Philippians 4:22). Paul's confidence encouraged the free Christians to preach more energetically, and he could say his imprisonment actually had helped the progress of the gospel (Philippians 1:12-14).

Paul was getting old (Philemon 9). He might have said, "I've done my part. It's time for younger people to take over. I need to rest." But he gave no high priority to rest, even if age slowed him down. Since he was not tramping

long miles, he had more time and energy for
Christian work. "Paul the aged" was as active as
Paul the youth. Does our ministry to senior citizens include finding ways for them to minister
to others?

Paul was shut in. He might have said, "There's
nothing I can do. I can't even go to church." But
there were things he could do. He held Bible
classes, evangelistic meetings, counseling sessions in his home. He wrote letters that are a
part of our treasure even now. Is there among us
a shut-in whose home might house a Bible-study
group, whose wisdom might be helpful in a
committee meeting, from whom a troubled soul
might seek advice?

Conclusion

Since we have devoted three months of study to
the work of Paul, it may be well to conclude this
final lesson by noting what he may have done
after the two years of imprisonment in Rome.
Some students think he was held for another year
and then put to death in the frightful persecution
of Christians that began in A. D. 64. It seems more
probable that he was released and resumed his
travels for several years. This is deduced from
hints in his letters to Timothy and Titus.

A. The Rest of the Story

Perhaps Paul's case came to trial in A. D. 63,
after Luke finished the book of Acts. Since there
was no substantial charge against him, he was
set free before the great persecution began.

At an earlier time Paul had expected to go to
Spain (Romans 15:28). Some students think he
may have gone there as soon as he was released.
While he was a prisoner, however, he seemed
eager to return to friends in Macedonia and Asia
(Philippians 1:25, 26; Philemon 22). Perhaps he
went there when he was set free. Possibly he visited Spain between two tours of places farther
east, but the indications of such a visit are not
enough to make us sure.

We will not try to make an itinerary of Paul's
travels after he left Rome, but the following
places may have been included.

He left Titus in Crete to help the churches
there (Titus 1:5). It is not recorded that Paul had
been there before, except briefly on his eventful
voyage to Rome.

He left Trophimus sick at Miletus (2 Timothy
4:20).

He visited Troas and left some things with a
friend there (2 Timothy 4:13).

He may have been at Ephesus with Timothy (1
Timothy 1:3) and at Corinth with Erastus (2
Timothy 4:20).

He said he was going from Asia to Macedonia
(1 Timothy 1:3), and there is no reason to think
he did not go.

He expected to spend a winter at Nicopolis
(Titus 3:12). Probably this means the city of that
name on the west coast of Greece.

Nero's fierce persecution of Christians began
in A. D. 64. It began in Rome, but probably
spread abroad. Somewhere Paul was arrested,
and again he was imprisoned in Rome. From
there he wrote his second letter to Timothy.

This time Paul was not released but executed,
probably not later than A. D. 68. This we know
only from old traditions, but probably they are
correct. These state that as a Roman citizen Paul
was not crucified, but allowed a more honorable
death by beheading. The greater honor, however,
was that he gave his life for Christ.

The great apostle can hardly have a finer epitaph than a few lines from his last letter: "I have
fought a good fight, I have finished my course, I
have kept the faith: henceforth there is laid up
for me a crown of righteousness, which the
Lord, the righteous judge, shall give me at that
day: and not to me only, but unto all them also
that love his appearing" (2 Timothy 4:7, 8).

B. Prayer

For the magnificent work of Paul we give
thanks, our Father in Heaven. Thank You also
for other heroes who have passed down the
gospel through centuries so that we also may be
Jesus' disciples. May we also fight a good fight
and keep the faith till we finish our course and
take a crown of righteousness from the hand of
our Savior. In His name we pray. Amen.

C. Thought to Remember

Keep the faith.

Home Daily Bible Readings

Monday, Nov. 18—The Voyage to Rome
Begins (Acts 27:1-8)
Tuesday, Nov. 19—Storm at Sea (Acts
27:9-20)
Wednesday, Nov. 20—Paul Predicts Ship-
wreck (Acts 27:21-32)
Thursday, Nov. 21—Shipwreck, but No
Loss of Life (Acts 27:33-44)
Friday, Nov. 22—Paul Mistaken for a God
(Acts 28:1-10)
Saturday, Nov. 23—Paul Arrives at Rome
(Acts 28:11-22)
Sunday, Nov. 24—Paul Preaches and
Teaches at Rome (Acts 28:23-31)

Learning by Doing

This page contains an alternate lesson plan emphasizing learning activities. Classes desiring such student involvement will find these suggestions helpful.

Learning Goals

As a result of this lesson, your students should be able to do the following:

1. Explain how Paul used the obstacle of his imprisonment as an opportunity to advance God's kingdom.

2. Explore how apparent obstacles may be opportunities to advance God's kingdom.

3. Seek to develop a perspective that redefines obstacles as spiritual opportunities.

Into the Lesson

If you asked any of your students to read and prepare a brief report on one of the suggested books (lesson 11), have the reports presented now. Be sure to contact the students during the week to remind them. Emphasize that they are to report how the person in the book used his or her obstacles as an opportunity to serve God.

If you did not assign those books, begin the lesson by distributing copies of the following chart. (The chart is included in the student book.)

Obstacle	Potential for Good	Person Who Turned Obstacle Into Opportunity
Failure		
Handicap		
Poverty		
Rejection		
Pain		
Danger		

Have students consider the obstacles in the left column. For each one ask, "What potential for good does this obstacle have?" Allow time for class discussion. Then ask students to think of an individual they know or have heard about (it could be someone in the Bible) who turned that obstacle into an opportunity for good. If they don't think of someone for each obstacle, that's okay.

Lead into the lesson by saying, "Our study today encourages us to look at obstacles as opportunities for God's kingdom. We'll see how the apostle Paul was able to do this, and discuss how we can do it too."

Into the Word

Present a brief lecture on the background of today's passage, using information from the introduction to this lesson.

Lead the class in discussing these questions.

1. Read Acts 28:16-31. What obstacles did Paul face in this passage?

2. How did Paul turn the obstacles into opportunities for God's kingdom?

3. Read Philippians 1:12-21. (Note: Philippians was written by Paul while he was a prisoner at Rome.) How was God's kingdom advanced as a result of Paul's imprisonment?

4. What was Paul's attitude toward his imprisonment?

5. Paul was able to view his imprisonment as an opportunity, not an obstacle. What perspectives of Paul recorded in verses 19-21 enabled him to take that view?

At this point, write this *Principle for Effective Leadership* on your poster: *Effective Christian leaders define obstacles as opportunities for God's kingdom.*

Into Life

Below are several situations persons may encounter. All of them are obstacles. Select several of them and have your class discuss this question for each: *How may this obstacle become an opportunity to advance God's kingdom?* Write the question on the chalkboard. It is possible that someone in your class has recently experienced one of these situations. Therefore, you will need to use wisdom and sensitivity in selecting the ones to discuss.

Here are the situations:

1. You are in the hospital for major surgery.

2. You have become unemployed.

3. A loved one dies.

4. Your teenage daughter runs away.

5. Your spouse tells you that he/she wants a divorce.

6. You are told you have terminal cancer.

Have class members personalize the lesson by answering the following question to themselves:

On a scale of one to ten, how consistently do you view obstacles as spiritual opportunities? (One equals never; ten equals all the time.)

Then discuss this question: How can we develop the ability to view obstacles as spiritual opportunities?

Let's Talk It Over

The questions on this page are designed to encourage review of the lesson Scriptures and to promote discussion of the lesson by the class. The answers provided are only discussion starters. Let your class talk it over from there.

1. Describe the kind of treatment Paul received on Malta, at Puteoli, and in Rome.

We must not assume that Paul consistently was maltreated on his journeys. In all three instances cited here, he was received hospitably. On Malta he was shown great kindness by the islanders. Publius, the chief official of the island, provided courteous hospitality for Paul for three days. After Paul healed many of the island's diseased residents, they honored him and his companions and furnished them with needed supplies when they sailed.

At Puteoli and in Rome, Paul was greeted warmly and enthusiastically by the brethren. In Rome, rather than kept in a prison, he was permitted to live in a rented house with a soldier as guard. Visitors were permitted to come and go freely, and doubtless the Christians there, as well as from other places, ministered to his needs (see Philippians 4:18).

2. How did Paul use his "prison," his rented house?

There he established a base for preaching, teaching, and ministering. The soldiers who guarded him learned of Jesus Christ, and the gospel became known throughout the imperial guard (Philippians 1:13). There were even some in Caesar's household who had been won to Christ (Philippians 4:22). Paul may have been "imprisoned," but he was free in Christ, to be powerfully used of God. Although he referred to himself as "Paul the aged" (Philemon 9), he still vigorously fulfilled his stewardship of life and ministry.

3. How may we apply to our situation the principles of Paul's experience in Rome?

We too can use our homes as a base of kingdom work. We can have groups in our homes for Bible study, prayer, sharing, and caring for one another. Groups from within the church and groups involving non-Christians can thrive in the home setting.

We can also learn from Paul, the aged servant of the Lord. If we see the aging in our congregations as a source of wisdom, leadership, and ministry, the potential enrichment is enormous. We should value the aging among us, and minister *with* them, not just *to* them.

We can use *every* circumstance for furthering the cause of Christ. If we begin to see life with the eyes of Christ, as Paul did, we will find opportunities for witnessing and serving that previously may have gone unnoticed.

4. In what ways do people tend to react to limitations?

There are three prevailing reactions. (1) Some persons fret, stew, and lament. These responses all involve chafing under the limitations, in some measure resisting them. These are nonproductive responses that only increase a person's sense of limitation and irritation. (2) Others submit. They allow the limitations to determine everything. They give in, convinced that there is nothing they can do about them. Capitulation, "caving in," expresses the "victim" mentality and ultimately expresses weakness. (3) Some transcend and transform the limitations. They have the view that limitations often can be used as building blocks rather than barriers. By the grace and power of the Lord, limitations can be transcended. Witness the way that Joni Eareckson has transcended her quadriplegic condition, has transformed her limitations into a powerful witness for Jesus Christ. When we transcend and/or transform our limitations, we are strengthened for future challenges and our witness to others is multiplied.

5. What would be a fitting epitaph on Paul's tomb?

It is believed by many Bible students that Paul was released from prison in Rome, perhaps not long after Luke finished the book of Acts. Certain comments in his letters to Timothy and Titus suggest that he once again traveled, preaching and teaching as he had done for so many years. Arrested once more, he was taken to Rome again as a prisoner, where, tradition tells us, he was finally beheaded. Perhaps no more appropriate epitaph can be penned than the words Paul himself wrote in summing up his life since meeting Jesus that day on the road to Damascus: "I have fought a good fight, I have finished my course, I have kept the faith" (2 Timothy 4:7). If the same may be said of us, we too shall receive a crown of righteousness from our Lord.

Winter Quarter, 1991-92

Theme: Songs and Prayers of the Bible

Special Features

Lessons

Unit 1: Songs From Ancient Israel

Unit 2: Songs From Festive Occasions

Unit 3: Songs and Prayers of the Church

Related Resources

The following publications are suggested to provide additional help on the subjects of study presented in the Winter Quarter. They may be purchased from your supplier. Prices are subject to change.

Help! I've Got Problems, by Dean Dickinson. This book contains ideas and problem solutions for adult teachers and leaders. Order #14-03663, $1.95.

Guidelines for Growing Christians, by LeRoy Lawson. This book offers help for improving one's attitude, relationships, and prayer life. Order #18-39950, $5.95.

Philippians—Thessalonians (Standard Bible Studies), by Gary Weedman. This book illuminates Paul's message of hope, encouragement, and joy found in these letters. Order #11-40110, $9.95.

Revelation (Standard Bible Studies), by Lewis Foster. A study of Revelation broken down into three aspects: interpretation, verification, and application. Order #11-40116, $12.95.

Dec 1
Dec 8
Dec 15
Dec 22
Dec 29
Jan 5
Jan 12
Jan 19
Jan 26
Feb 2
Feb 9
Feb 16
Feb 23

Voices Raised in Song

by John W. Wade

THERE ARE NUMEROUS WAYS one might teach the Bible. One could, for example, begin with Genesis 1:1 and proceed one verse at a time through Revelation 22:21. No doubt this method has been tried and perhaps even successfully. But such an approach is likely to leave most modern students hopelessly stranded among the Old Testament "begats" with little interest or energy to continue.

Across the years, the International Sunday School Lesson Series has used a number of approaches to Bible study. Sometimes studies have concentrated on one book—the book of Genesis or the Gospel of John, for instance. Or perhaps the lessons have concentrated on one writer such as Luke in a study of the Gospel of Luke or the book of Acts. Some quarters feature a person such as Moses in his leadership of the Israelites or Paul and his missionary journeys. Or a topical study might give emphasis to a specific theme. In any event, it may be fairly stated that the International Lessons present variety in their approach.

This quarter features "Songs and Prayers of the Bible." Some of the songs are exaltations over victory, while one (Lesson 3) is a funeral dirge. Three others (Lessons 5-7) are hymns of praise to God. Lesson 8, "Lyrics of Love," is unusual. For perhaps the first time in its one-hundred-twenty-year history, the International Lesson Series has based a lesson on a Biblical passage taken from the Song of Solomon. Other lessons are based on more familiar passages such as the Model Prayer (Lesson 10), Jesus' high priestly prayer in John 17 (Lesson 11), and Philippians 2, which tells of Christ's humbling himself. You can readily see that you will not lack for variety as you teach the lessons in this quarter.

Songs From Ancient Israel

Three of the first four lessons are based on events from Israel's early days. The first lesson features Moses' song of praise to God just after the Israelites had passed safely through the Red Sea, escaping the oppressive Egyptian Pharaoh. The song gives in rather graphic detail the defeat of the over-confident Egyptians as they recklessly plunged into the sea in their pursuit of the Israelites. It is a song of thanksgiving to God for Israel's deliverance and an acknowledgment of God's power over nature and nations.

Modern readers may be a bit shocked at Moses' reaction to the destruction of Israel's enemies. We need to remember that the people of Israel had experienced many years of terrible oppression at the hands of the cruel Egyptians. Had we lived under such circumstances, we could better understand Israel's attitude. We need to remember also that these Egyptians had been storing up judgment for themselves for centuries. Certainly it is God's prerogative to call any of us before the bar of judgment at any time He sees fit. The Pharaoh and his people had had many opportunities and many unmistakable warnings to turn from their opposition to God, but they had arrogantly chosen to ignore these. Now came judgment, certain and severe. Moses' song describes in some detail the progress of that judgment.

Lesson two, dealing with the song of Deborah and Barak, also is a song of victory over oppressive foes. The period recorded in the book of Judges was a difficult time for the Israelites. Although they had entered the promised land, they had not been able to drive out the Canaanites and claim all the territory. Worse, they had become divided in the face of their enemies. In addition, they had often borrowed some of the religious practices of their pagan neighbors and fallen into idolatry. As a result, God permitted some of these neighbors to plague them. But these oppressive neighbors in their treatment of the Israelites had gone beyond what God had intended, and as a result they too were called to judgment. The result was an astounding victory for the Israelites, led by Deborah, over the Canaanites. In the wake of this victory, she and Barak raised their voices in praise to God.

In lesson three national triumph turns to personal tragedy as David mourns the death of Saul and Jonathan. Both had been killed in battle against the Philistines. David's grief at the death of Jonathan, his best friend, is quite understandable. Some have difficulty, however, understanding his equal grief at the death of Saul, who sought on several occasions to kill him. David's lament reveals two things about him. First, he held the kingship in high regard, even when Saul did not always conduct himself properly in that office. Second, David had a forgiving heart. Many might sing a song feigning sorrow at the death of a personal enemy. There is nothing hypocritical about David's song, however, for while Saul was still alive, David had been just as magnanimous toward him.

Lesson four, the Christmas lesson, allows us to hear the joyful songs of two mothers—Hannah in the Old Testament and Mary in the New. Both raise their voices to God in praise because of His intervention in their lives. Hannah rejoiced because although she had been barren, God gave her a son. Mary's joy came because the Son she was to bear was miraculously conceived and was to be the fulfillment of the promises given to Abraham.

Songs From Festive Occasions

Lesson five, six, and seven are all based on selections from the book of Psalms. This book served as the hymnal for the ancient Israelites. Like our modern hymnal, it contained a variety of songs. We find that variety in the lesson selections. Lesson five is a hymn to the Creator. It is interesting to note that today we sing a chorus drawn from the words of this psalm. Lesson six is the song of a worshiper who finds great joy in coming into the house of the LORD. Lesson seven praises God as man's redeemer. It is a song of gratitude for God's tender mercies that are from everlasting to everlasting, a refreshing contrast to other relationships that seem temporary.

Lesson eight is based upon a selection from the Song of Solomon, a book that we rarely study in our churches. One reason we have avoided this book is that it deals with the physical aspects of love. Many of us feel a bit uncomfortable in discussing sexual love in public. Yet we need to remember that God created us physical as well as spiritual beings. Sexual love was a part of God's plan, not only for the perpetuation of the race but for enhancing relations between a husband and wife. The tragedy is that what God intended to be pure and holy has been defiled by the world. This lesson can serve as a wholesome antidote to much that we see on television and hear in contemporary music.

Lesson nine, featuring the "Song of the Vineyard," is a musical parable. It tells of the Beloved (God) who planted a vineyard and tended it carefully. Yet the vines brought forth sour grapes. As a consequence, God lays waste the vineyard. This lesson demonstrates that God's prophets may couch their message in a variety of literary forms.

Songs and Prayers of the Church

The third unit in this quarter, "Songs and Prayers of the Church," begins with two familiar prayers of Jesus. Lesson ten studies the Model Prayer, popularly known as the LORD's Prayer. Lesson eleven features Jesus' high priestly prayer found in John 17. In an age that tends to neglect prayer, these two lessons can remind us of the power of prayer. The Model Prayer deals with the fundamentals of life—such things as reverence toward God, thanks for one's daily bread, and forgiveness of sins. Our Master's intercessory prayer deals with the specific subject of unity among His followers. In a Christendom that has been divided a thousand times over, this prayer is extremely relevant.

Lesson twelve is based on Philippians 2:1-11. These verses are not a prayer nor are they a song. Rather, they hold Jesus up as a model of a humble and obedient servant, a model that Paul urges his readers to follow. Modern Christians need this model just as much or more than those who lived in the first century, for the qualities of humility and servanthood do not rank very high in the modern world.

The final lesson, appropriately enough, is based on two passages selected from the book of Revelation. The hallelujah chorus celebrates the marriage of Christ and His church. This event signals the ultimate consummation of the church and the final victory of Christ over all His enemies. It extends a message of hope that can sustain the downtrodden and disconsolate in every life situation.

Some may find the lessons this quarter somewhat difficult to teach. For one thing, several of the lessons treat passages that are not very familiar to many students. The fact that several of the lessons draw on Old Testament texts will "turn off" some students. For some reason, there are those persons who have the idea that the Old Testament is not very relevant for today's needs. How wrong they are! As the teacher you may have to do a selling job to convince them of its pertinence to their lives.

Some of the lessons deal with worship. This too is a subject that does not arouse a great deal of interest among many people. Again, this is most unfortunate, for a natural result of our commitment to God is a desire to worship and adore Him. Sometimes we have trouble in worship because we do not know how to worship Him, but at other times our trouble may stem from a lack of commitment and a sense of awe in the presence of the Almighty.

A teacher will find it wise to consult the sections of the lesson development that suggest various ways to present each lesson. A new approach or a new teaching method may help overcome some of the difficulties that may arise in teaching these lessons. Try to instill a sense of adventure and enthusiasm as you begin this series of lessons. It may very well turn out to be one of the most profitable you have ever taught.

An Appeal for Joy

by Charles E. Cook

CHRISTIANITY IS A RELIGION of joy. It is rooted in the very nature of God himself, His creative work, His holiness, His mercy, and His love. The contemplation of God is an occasion for joy.

Three of the lessons in this quarter of study are based on psalms. as we consider these psalms, we will see that the psalmist is contemplating God and that in doing so his heart overflows with joy. He rejoices when He considers God as Creator. So, as he treads out the grapes and reflects upon God's creative work, and His great love and kindness to mankind, the psalmist sings, "O LORD, our LORD, how majestic is your name in all the earth!" (Psalm 8:1).

On his pilgrimage to the temple, the psalmist rejoices as this beautiful place of worship comes in view. He sings, "How lovely is your dwelling place, O LORD almighty! . . .Blessed are those who dwell in your house; they are ever praising you" (Psalm 84:1, 4).

A song of joy fills the psalmist's heart as he reflects upon the LORD's forgiveness, His mercy, and His compassion. Coming from the depths of his being is his song, "Praise the LORD, O my soul; all my inmost being, praise his holy name. Praise the LORD, O my soul, and forget not all his benefits" (Psalm 103:1, 2).

Someone has observed that the heart of any religion is expressed in the songs it produces. If that is true, then at the very heart of Christianity is this note of joy. It is in Mary's song known as the Magnificat: "My soul praises the LORD and my spirit rejoices in God my Savior: (Luke 1:46, 47). It is in the song Zechariah sang at the birth of his son John, later known as John the Baptist: "Praise be to the LORD, the God of Israel, because he has come and has redeemed his people" (Luke 1:68). It is in the announcement and song of the angels to the shepherds in the fields near Bethlehem: "Do not be afraid. I bring you good news of great joy that will be for all the people . . . "Suddenly a great company of the heavenly host appeared with the angel, praising God and saying, 'Glory to God in the highest, and on earth peace to men on whom his favor rests" (Luke 2:10, 13, 14).

How unfortunate that this note of joy is so often missing in our lives, in our worship, and in our service for Christ! Jesus taught that His joy could be in us and that our joy might be full. He assured His disciples that they would have a joy that no circumstance of life would be able to take away (John 15:11).

Have you ever noticed that little children will often awaken with a fresh, radiant kind of joy. Sometimes when it is very quiet you will hear their excited, joyful expressions in their play. I have a granddaughter who, from her earliest childhood, has customarily awakened in the morning singing little tunes to herself. There is a deep, inner joy that bubbles forth in song. That is how Jesus would affect us. Recently a young college student responded to the invitation to receive Christ as her personal Savior and LORD. I expressed my joy in her decision, and she responded, "I'm so excited. It's going to be such fun being a Christian." Granted, that may be a bit naive, but it has an important element of truth in it that I wish some Christians hadn't forgotten. Why is it that we seem to feel that, as Christians, we must be somber and restrained instead of joyous and exuberant?

The writers of the New Testament were certainly aware of the joy that characterized the lives of the early Christians. They use the words *joy, rejoice, glad, happy,* or *blessed* more than two hundred times in relating the thoughts and experiences of Jesus and His disciples. Paul wrote his epistle to the Philippians when he was in prison, and the letter is chiefly concerned with suffering and hardship; yet his favorite word in that letter is the word *joy.* The Bible makes it clear that the life of the early Christians was a joyful life, in spite of its perils and difficulties.

How did we lose this precious attribute? Why do we so often convey to the world the impression that the Christian life is anything but joyful? Paul Tillich, in his book, *The New Being,* described what the lack of joy in Christian people he knew almost did to him. He wrote, "The suppression of joy, and guilt about joy in Christian groups, almost drove me to a break with Christianity." Tillich was not alone in this experience. Friedrich Nietzsche, the son of a Protestant minister, once commented, "His (Jesus') disciples should look more redeemed."

One of the reasons a Christian might lose his or her joy is found in our tendency to associate joy with the circumstances of life. We so often find our delight in such things as having enough money to get whatever we want, good weather for a boating excursion, or a quick and easy solution to a difficult problem. Christian joy, however, is a higher happiness. It is a blessedness not to be confused with the pursuit of pleasure. It does not consist of the joy a person pursues, but the ability to enjoy the pursuit even when it has reverses. It does not consist of the things that might interest us, but our interest in the things that are of eternal worth. it is not what you find at the end of the rainbow, but your state of mind on those days when there is no rainbow to be seen.

Long before she became a hymn writer, Fanny Crosby, a blind little girl of eight, wrote these lines:

> O what a happy soul am I!
>   Although I cannot see,
> I am resolved that in this world
>   contented I will be;
> How many blessings I enjoy
>   That other people don't!
> To weep and sigh because I'm blind
>   I cannot, and I won't.

This is the joy that does not depend upon our good fortune. It is our joy in the LORD, and it puts a song in our hearts and upon our lips. This is the joy that we should cultivate.

Joy and Goodness

The Christian life is a life of joy because it is a life of goodness. No person who is given to doing evil can truly rejoice and praise God. This is the world's con game—to make us believe that we can find joy and happiness in doing the wrong things. The person who chooses this route will be bothered inevitably by remorse and regret, admonished by the voice of his own conscience, shamed by his own failures, and deprived of the satisfaction that comes from a life of goodness. In Paul's listing of the Holy Spirit's fruit in our lives, both joy and goodness are included. They are inseparably linked together. Where there is not goodness there is no genuine, lasting joy. David's plea to the LORD was that He might restore the joy of his salvation. (Psalm 51:12). The reason David's joy was missing was that he had sinned against the LORD and had done what was evil in His sight (v. 4).

It is important to understand that real joy grows out of positive, constructive goodness, not out of negative, legalistic prohibitions. The psalmist said, "I desire to do your will, O my God; your law is within my heart" (Psalm 40:8). Is it any wonder that the LORD had put a new song in his mouth (v. 3)? His heart and his will had joined together in praising and serving God. Jesus seems to teach that a man can be as good as he wishes, only if he wishes to be good. Goodness will fill your heart with joy and cause you to desire even more to live the good life.

Joy and Our Hope

The Christian life is a joyful life because of its hope. Joy fills the heart of the person who anticipates something worthwhile in the future. One needs only to observe the joy and excitement in a small child who is anticipating a birthday party or a picnic in the park to realize how much joy comes from hope. Paul wrote in Colossians 1:5, 6 of "the faith and love that spring from the hope that is stored up for you in heaven and that you have already heard about in the word of truth, the gospel that has come to you." Of all the reasons for the joy of those early Christians, none is more understandable than their hope of future glory. It enabled them to endure the worst of life's experiences and still maintain their joy.

Consider the Beatitudes. They would be preposterous if it were not for the hope upon which they are based. In each one, men and women are "blessed" or filled with joy, not because of what is, but because of what *will be*. Those who mourn are filled with joy because they will be comforted. Those who hunger and thirst for righteousness experience joy because they will be filled. Those persons who are pure in heart are joyful because they will see God. The persecuted are filled with joy because they will receive the kingdom of heaven. Thus Paul wrote, "I consider that our present sufferings are not worth comparing with the glory that will be revealed in us" (Romans 8:18).

There is every reason for Christians to be hopeful, even today. No matter how depraved a particular generation has been, Christ has prevailed. People have always looked beyond the tragedy of the hour to the hope of tomorrow. We will "receive the crown of life" if we are faithful and do not lose our hope. Reinhold Niebuhr is reported to have said to Harry Emerson Fosdick, on one occasion, "If you will be a pessimist with me decade by decade, I will be an optimist with you century by century." Decade by decade evil wins some battles, but when we look to the centuries, Christ's truth is victorious. Decade by decade pessimism and despair may seem to be in order, but with the perspective of the centuries, the Christian rejoices, remembering the assurance of Jesus, "Take heart! {be of good cheer} I have overcome the world" (John 16:33).

As Christians, we should be radiantly joyous, because ours is a way that is good, a truth that will not be disproved, and a life that is eternal. "Rejoice in the LORD always. I will say it again: Rejoice!" (Philippians 4:4).

All Scripture passages are taken from the *New International Version*.

The Servant Teacher

by Victor Knowles

EVERY CHRISTIAN should be involved in service. Bud Wilkinson, former college and professional football coach, was once asked what contribution football had made to the overall physical conditioning of the United States.

"Absolutely none," Bud answered. "I define football as twenty-two men on the field desperately in need of rest and seventy-five thousand people in the stands desperately in need of exercise."

Let it not be said of us who are Christians that we allow such a numerical imbalance to exist in the church regarding Christian service. We are not to be spectators—we are to be *participants*. It is not a matter of who can serve us, but whom can we serve? To paraphrase John F. Kennedy, "Ask not what your church can do for you; ask what you can do for your church."

Through the blood of Jesus we have been purged from dead works to *serve* the living God (Hebrews 9:14). Many churchgoers have very little concept of what that means. They think *service* means "serve us." But service is not being served—it is serving. Christian service is not waiting for others to serve you—it is personally getting involved in ministry.

Christ, Our Great Example

Jesus is our finest example of what it means to serve. In a truly remarkable passage we read, "Let this mind be in you which was also in Christ Jesus, who, being in the form of God, did not consider it robbery to be equal with God, but made Himself of no reputation, *taking the form of a servant*, and coming in the likeness of men. And being found in appearance as a man, He humbled Himself and became obedient to the point of death, even the death of the cross" (Philippians 2:5-8, *The New King James Version*, italics mine).

The greatest teachers are those who have a humble heart and a servant spirit. This is why Jesus is still the greatest teacher the world has ever known!

Our LORD is remembered not merely for the truths that He taught, although He taught as no other teacher ever has. The oral teaching of Jesus was so impressive that the chief priests and Pharisees once sent officers to arrest Him. This was a great mistake on the part of those who hated Jesus because the soldiers were absolutely mesmerized by the eloquence of Christ.

They forgot to arrest Him! When they returned, empty-handed, to their superiors, they were asked, "Why have you not brought Him?" Still dazed, they replied, "No man ever spoke like this Man!" (John 7:46).

Why was Jesus' teaching so powerful and persuasive? The answer lies in the concluding statement by Matthew after Jesus delivered the Sermon on the Mount: "And so it was, when Jesus had ended these sayings, that the people were astonished at His teaching, *for He taught them as one having authority, and not as the scribes*" (Matthew 7:28, 29, italics mine).

Authority left to itself, however, is not enough. Someone has said that power (authority) corrupts and absolute power absolutely corrupts. Not so with Jesus. Though He had "all authority," He humbled himself, taking the form of a servant, and taught by example as well as by word. Perhaps the greatest lesson our LORD ever taught was the unforgettable night He took a towel, poured water into a basin, and began to wash the disciples' feet. No teaching, no lecture, no preaching (until Peter began to preach to the LORD). The lesson that Jesus wanted them to learn is one that we must also receive: "A servant is not greater than his master; nor is he who is sent greater than he who sent him" (John 13:16).

Never a teacher spoke like Jesus. Never a teacher *served* like Jesus. He practiced what He preached. He backed up His lesson with servant living. We are not successful teachers until we do the same.

Modeling the Servant Jesus

When I was a little lad growing up in the church in Hamburg, Iowa, where my father was serving as minister, the Sunday-school teachers were among those in whose lives I saw Jesus modeled. That is one big reason why I am preaching the gospel today. After graduation from Bible college, I returned to serve in the role of an assistant minister.

One Sunday afternoon I went calling with one of the elders, who was also an adult Bible-school teacher. It was a fine summer day, and as we walked up the sidewalk to old Mrs. Dankof's house, we could see into the living room through the screen door. Before we could knock on the door, we heard pitiful groans coming from the living room.

Poor Mrs. Dankof was sitting in her rocking chair, crying quietly. "What's wrong, Sister?" asked the kindly elder as he knelt by her chair. "Oh, Brother Emberton" she said "it's my toenails. They've grown so long and they're hurting me so much."

What will he do? I wondered to myself as I sat down on the couch. I didn't have to wait long to find out. Speaking words of comfort to the suffering woman, he took out a pocket knife, opened it, and gently began to trim the old woman's toenails. I sat there in rapt fascination. I was seeing Christ in action all over again, especially when Brother Emberton went to the kitchen, filled a basin, and proceeded to wash her feet!

I learned a valuable lesson that day: the great teachers are humble servants. Teaching is not ministry until it comes out one's fingertips. Matthew 4:23 has always impressed me: "Now Jesus went about all Galilee, teaching in their synagogues, preaching the gospel of the kingdom, *and healing all kinds of sickness and all kinds of disease among the people*" (italics mine). Great teachers go beyond the classroom and become involved in the lives of people.

Someone has captured the spirit of the teacher who is willing to leave his or her classroom in search of "The Absentee."

"Someone is absent," the Shepherd said,
As over my class-book He bent His head;
"For several Sundays absent, too,
So tell me, Teacher, what did you do?"

"I didn't call as perhaps I should,
I wrote some cards, but they did no good;
I've never heard and she never came,
So I decided to drop her name."

He answered gravely, "A flock of mine,
A hundred—no, there were ninety and nine;
For one was lost in the dark and cold,
So I sought the sheep which had left the fold.

"The path was stony and edged with thorns,
My feet were wounded and bruised and torn,
But I kept on seeking, nor counted the cost,
And oh, the joy when I found the lost."

Thus spoke the Shepherd in tender tones,
I looked and lo, I was all alone;
But God a vision had sent to me
To show His will toward the absentee.

The Greatest Work in the World

Teaching is the greatest work in the world. John Steinbeck said, "School is not easy and it is not for the most part very much fun, but then, if you are very lucky, you may find a teacher. Three real teachers in a lifetime is the very best of luck. I have come to believe that a great teacher is a great artist and that there are as few as there are any other great artists. Teaching might even be the greatest of the arts since the medium is the human mind and spirit.

"My three had these things in common. They all loved what they were doing. They did not tell—they catalyzed a burning desire to know. Under their influence, the horizons sprung wide and fear went away and the unknown became knowable. But most important of all, the truth, that dangerous stuff, became beautiful and very precious."

Those of us who have seen the award-winning film, "Molder of Dreams," produced by Focus on the Family, will never forget the Guy Doud story. Little Guy came from a dysfunctional family and had many personal obstacles to overcome. But several loving teachers helped shape and mold the life of Guy Doud into something very special. In fact, he became Teacher of the Year in 1986 and was personally received at the White House by President Ronald Reagan. Doud gives all the credit to those loving teachers in his formative years. He doesn't remember much of what they taught, but he certainly remembers what he caught from them—genuine concern and interest, compassion, a loving hand on the shoulder, and time spent outside the classroom with him. Indeed, it was a public school teacher, a devout believer, who introduced Guy to the Lord Jesus.

Want to be a great teacher? Be a servant teacher!

Scripture quotations are from *The New King James Version*.

Answers to Quarterly Quiz on page 120

Lesson 1—1. drowned. 2. heap. **Lesson 2**—1. highways, byways. 2. avenging. **Lesson 3**—1. Gilboa. 2. eagles, lions. **Lesson 4**—1. Hannah. 2. blessed. 3. proud. **Lesson 5**—1. God's heavens, the moon and the stars. 2. glory and honor. **Lesson 6**—1. the courts of the Lord. 2. a doorkeeper. **Lesson 7**—1. the eagle's. 2. as far as the east is from the west. **Lesson 8**—1. hills. 2. spoil. **Lesson 9**—1. wild. 2. Israel and Judah. **Lesson 10**—1. vain repetitions. 2. we must forgive the trespasses of others. **Lesson 11**—1. life eternal. 2. that the world might believe that He was sent by the Father. **Lesson 12**—1. form, equal. 2. servant. **Lesson 13**—1. true. 2. the righteousness of saints.

Quarterly Quiz

The questions on this page may be used in several ways: as a pretest at the beginning of the quarter; as a review at the end of the quarter; or as a review after each lesson. The questions are based on the Scripture text of each lesson (King James Version). **The answers are on page 119.**

Lesson 1

1. Pharaoh's chariots and his host and his chosen captains pursued Israel, and they _____ in the Red Sea. *Exodus 15:4*
2. By God's power the waters of the Red Sea were parted and stood upright as a _____. *Exodus 15:8*

Lesson 2

1. In the days before Deborah became a judge, the conditions in Israel were so bad that the _____ were unoccupied and the travelers walked through _____. *Judges 5:6*
2. Deborah and Barak praised the LORD for the _____ of Israel. *Judges 5:2*

Lesson 3

1. On what mountain in Israel were Saul and Jonathan slain in battle against the Philistines? *2 Samuel 1:21*
2. In eulogizing Saul and Jonathan, David said they were swifter than _____ and stronger than _____. *2 Samuel 1:23*

Lesson 4

1. The mother of Samuel was _____. *1 Samuel 2:1*
3. Mary stated that God had scattered the _____ in the imagination of their hearts *Luke 1:51*

Lesson 5

1. What did the psalmist contemplate that led him to exclaim to God, "What is man, that thou art mindful of him? *Psalm 8:4*
2. According to Psalm 8, what did God crown man with? *Psalm 8:5*

Lesson 6

1. The writer of the Eighty-fourth Psalm said that his soul longed, even fainted, for what? *Psalm 84:2*
2. The psalmist said that he would rather be this in God's house than to dwell in the tents of wickedness. *Psalm 84:10*

Lesson 7

1. In Psalm 103, the psalmist said that God satisfies our mouth with good things so that our youth is renewed like whose? *Psalm 103:5*
2. In describing God's mercy, the psalmist said that God has removed our transgressions from us how far? *Psalm 103:12*

Lesson 8

1. Describing her lover's joyful approach to her home, the maiden in the Song of Solomon said he came "leaping upon the mountains, skipping upon the _____." *Song of Solomon 2:8*
2. What are little foxes said to do to grapevines? *Song of Solomon 2:15*

Lesson 9

1. In Isaiah's song of the vineyard, the owner did all he could to ensure an excellent harvest, but the vineyard produced what kind of grapes? *Isaiah 5:2*
2. Who did the vineyard in Isaiah's song represent? *Isaiah 5:7*

Lesson 10

1. Jesus taught that when His disciples pray, they are not to use _____ _____ as the heathens do. *Matthew 6:7*
2. When Jesus gave the Model Prayer, what condition did He say we must meet if we desire God to forgive us? *Matthew 6:14*

Lesson 11

1. Jesus said that to know the only true God and Jesus Christ, whom He sent to earth, is what? *John 17:3*
2. In His prayer in John 17, Jesus stated a reason why He desired all of His followers to be one. What was that reason? *John 17:20, 21*

Lesson 12

1. When Christ Jesus was in the _____ of God, He thought it not robbery to be _____ with God. *Philippians 2:6*
2. Relinquishing His glories in Heaven, Jesus took upon Him the form of a _____ and was made in the likeness of men. *Philippians 2:7*

Lesson 13

1. The redeemed, who sing the song of Moses and the song of the Lamb, say that all nations will come and worship God. T/F *Revelation 15:4*
2. In heaven, the fine linen worn by the wife of the Lamb is what? *Revelation 19:8*

Song of Moses

LESSON SCRIPTURE: Exodus 14:19—15:21.

PRINTED TEXT: Exodus 15:1-10, 13.

Exodus 15:1-10, 13

1 Then sang Moses and the children of Israel this song unto the LORD, and spake, saying, I will sing unto the LORD, for he hath triumphed gloriously: the horse and his rider hath he thrown into the sea.

2 The LORD is my strength and song, and he is become my salvation: he is my God, and I will prepare him a habitation; my father's God, and I will exalt him.

3 The LORD is a man of war: the Lord is his name.

4 Pharaoh's chariots and his host hath he cast into the sea: his chosen captains also are drowned in the Red sea.

5 The depths have covered them: they sank into the bottom as a stone.

6 Thy right hand, O LORD, is become glorious in power: thy right hand, O LORD, hath dashed in pieces the enemy.

7 And in the greatness of thine excellency thou hast overthrown them that rose up against thee: thou sentest forth thy wrath, which consumed them as stubble.

8 And with the blast of thy nostrils the waters were gathered together, the floods stood upright as a heap, and the depths were congealed in the heart of the sea.

9 The enemy said, I will pursue, I will overtake, I will divide the spoil; my lust shall be satisfied upon them; I will draw my sword, my hand shall destroy them.

10 Thou didst blow with thy wind, the sea covered them: they sank as lead in the mighty waters.

. . . .

13 Thou in thy mercy hast led forth the people which thou hast redeemed: thou hast guided them in thy strength unto thy holy habitation.

GOLDEN TEXT: The LORD is my strength and song, and he is become my salvation: he is my God, and I will prepare him a habitation; my father's God, and I will exalt him.—Exodus 15:2.

Lesson Aims

As a result of studying this lesson, the students should:

1. Have a growing appreciation for God's power and wisdom demonstrated in His interventions in human history.

2. Be able to recount the events that led Moses to raise this song of victory to God.

3. Trust God as the strength of their lives.

Lesson Outline

INTRODUCTION
    A. God Uses Small Things
    B. Lesson Background
  I. GLORIOUS TRIUMPH (Exodus 15:1-3)
    A. Praise to the Lord (v. 1)
    B. The Source of Israel's Strength (v. 2)
    C. Leader in War (v. 3)
 II. THE TRIUMPH DESCRIBED (Exodus 15:4-10)
    A. Pharoah's Forces Destroyed (vv. 4, 5)
        A Song of Victory
    B. The Lord's Power Described (vv. 6-8)
    C. The Egyptians' Arrogance Shown (vv. 9, 10)
III. GOD'S CONCERN FOR HIS PEOPLE (Exodus 15:13)
    A. Merciful Redemption (v. 13a)
    B. Strong Guidance (v. 13b)
        The Way Home
CONCLUSION
    A. A God When We Need Him
    B. Help Is All Around Us
    C. Let Us Pray
    D. Thought to Remember

Visual 1 from the visuals packet relates to thoughts included in the lesson introduction and conclusion. The visual is shown on page 124.

Introduction

A. God Uses Small Things

Robert Bruce, one of Scotland's great heroes, was once fleeing from his enemies, who sought to take his life. Thoroughly exhausted, he crawled into a cave, hoping to get a little rest until darkness came. In a short while, however, he heard his enemies approaching. He listened in dread as they neared the cave, for he knew there was no other exit and that he was trapped.

To his amazement, his pursuers paused a few moments at the mouth of the cave and then went on. After a while, Bruce ventured out to see what had happened. There he saw a spider web across the cave's entrance. Apparently a spider had busily spun the web after he had entered the cave. The enemies, seeing the spider web, reasoned that no one could have entered the cave without destroying the web, and so they had gone on. Seeing what had happened, Bruce paused to give thanks to God for using a spider to save his life.

As we see in today's lesson, Moses led Israel in praising God, for in a mighty fashion God saved the Israelites from the wrath of the Egyptians. As God used the forces of the winds and the waves to accomplish His purpose, it was, indeed, a dramatic rescue. As we marvel at the great power at God's disposal, let us remember that He can also use small things to accomplish His purpose. Something as small as an act of kindness can start a lost soul on the road to eternal salvation.

B. Lesson Background

At long last God had responded to the cries of His people in bondage in Egypt. Moses, assisted by His brother Aaron, had stood before the mighty Pharaoh and demanded, "Let my people go!" But Pharaoh stubbornly had refused this request. God then had visited the ten plagues, one after another, upon the land, sparing the Israelites, who lived in the land of Goshen.

After the tenth plague—the death of the firstborn in every household that was not protected by the blood of the Passover lamb—Pharaoh agreed to let the people go. They had not traveled far, however, until once more Pharaoh's heart was hardened. Gathering his chariots, he set out in pursuit of the slow-moving Israelites and finally caught up with the people. Apparently it was a place where they were trapped by mountains and the Red sea. With the Egyptian chariots converging upon their only route of escape, the Israelites thought that their situation was hopeless.

Terror gripped the people and they turned against Moses. Moses reassured them, however, that they had nothing to fear. At God's command, Moses lifted up his rod and stretched his

---

How to Say It

PHARAOH.   *Fair*-o or *Fay*-ro.
YAHWEH (Hebrew).   *Yah*-weh.

hand over the sea. Miraculously the waters divided, allowing the people to walk through the sea on dry ground. The Egyptian chariots and horsemen then went in after them. When the last of the Israelites had reached the safety of the other shore, Moses again stretched his hand over the water, and it closed upon the hosts of Pharaoh, destroying them.

I. Glorious Triumph
(Exodus 15:1-3)
A. Praise to the Lord (v. 1)

1. Then sang Moses and the children of Israel this song unto the LORD, and spake, saying, I will sing unto the LORD, for he hath triumphed gloriously: the horse and his rider hath he thrown into the sea.

We can well understand the overwhelming joy and gratitude that Moses and the people of Israel felt at this time. The Israelites had been slaves in Egypt for many decades. Moses himself had lived half of his life in the desert as a fugitive from Pharaoh's wrath. Now, finally, by the mighty power of God they had been set free. The swift and deadly cavalry forces of the Egyptians had been wiped out, and with it Israel's fear of being recaptured and enslaved again.

We are left to speculate about the details of the event recorded in our text. It would seem that the Israelites remained encamped near the shore of the Red Sea for several days. During this time Moses composed his song of praise to God. We do not know if all the people sang the song. It may be that a specially trained choir joined Moses in singing it. The only instruments mentioned were the timbrels (tambourines or small hand drums) that Miriam and the other women used as they danced and sang a response at the end of each stanza of the song.

This verse introduces the song, spelling out its subject. It was sung to and about the Lord. The word here used for *Lord* is *Jehovah* or *Yahweh*. This is the unique name of God that identifies Him as the covenant God. (See Exodus 3:14, 15.)

The Lord's victory over the enemies of His chosen people was glorious because it was complete. Pharaoh's troops had pursued the Israelites with an arrogance born of their certainty that they would quickly force them into submission. How quickly that arrogance turned to dismay as the waters of the sea closed over them!

B. The Source of Israel's Strength (v. 2)

2. The LORD is my strength and song, and he is become my salvation: he is my God, and I will prepare him a habitation; my father's God, and I will exalt him.

The Israelites, in their own right, were weak. They did not hesitate to acknowledge this. They just as readily acknowledged that their present strength came from the Lord. Only a short time before, they had been quivering in fear. Now they could stand and sing of their strength.

Most of us have had similar experiences. When faced by serious dangers, we have often found ourselves without strength to meet the challenge. How reassuring it is to turn to God when those times come! But we should remember that God is always the source of our strength, whether we are facing serious challenge or enjoying success, and that our strength does not come from our own resources.

He is my God, and I will prepare him a habitation. This is a possible meaning of the Hebrew text, but most modern versions translate it differently. They are all similar to the *New International Version*, which has, "He is my God, and I will praise him." Thus translated, it stands in literary parallelism with the sentence that follows. This repetition of thought expressed in different terms is a characteristic of Hebrew poetry.

My father's God. Sustaining the Israelites through their many difficulties was their awareness of their history. Their faith in Jehovah God was not just a faith for their own generation; it was rooted in Him who had revealed himself to Abraham, Isaac, and Jacob centuries earlier. Since He had been the God of the Israelites in the past, Moses and his generation had every reason to believe that he would be their God in the future as well.

C. Leader in War (v. 3)

3. The LORD is a man of war: the LORD is his name.

The Lord is a man of war. Ascribing to God the qualities of a human being is called an anthropomorphism. Here Moses depicts God as a warrior. This is an apt description of God in this particular situation, for by His power He had just destroyed the armed force of a mighty nation; of course, this figure does not attempt to encompass all of God's attributes. While God is a God of justice and judgment, He is also a God of love, and mercy, and peace.

VISUALS FOR THESE LESSONS

The *Adult Visuals/Learning Resources* packet contains classroom-size visuals designed for use with the lessons in the Winter Quarter. The packet is available from your supplier. Order no. ST 292.

II. The Triumph Described
(Exodus 15:4-10)

A. Pharaoh's Forces Destroyed
(vv. 4, 5)

4. Pharaoh's chariots and his host hath he cast into the sea: his chosen captains also are drowned in the Red sea.

The chariots were in the vanguard of Pharaoh's army. From the Egyptian monuments, we have a good idea of what these chariots looked like compared to the heavy armored chariots of the Assyrians. They were of strong, but very light construction, capable of attaining great speed very quickly. Made of wood and leather, they usually carried two men—a driver and an archer—and were drawn by two horses. In battle the chariots normally led the attack. Their purpose was to shatter the enemy's lines, striking fear and confusion into the hearts of the opposing foot soldiers. The infantry that followed the chariots would then attack, killing the wounded and routing the enemy that still remained.

Apparently the Egyptians followed the normal battle plan with the chariots leading the way. The cavalry, and perhaps some infantrymen, also entered the dry bed of the sea in pursuit of the Israelites. The officers often rode in the chariots in the front of the army so that they would be in a position to direct the army's actions. The majority of the officers may have been in the chariots, since they felt that the Israelites offered no serious threat. They failed to understand that their fight was not with the Israelites but with almighty God.

At the appointed time, God slowed the progress of the pursuers—presumably causing the wheels of the chariots to sink into the sand. Sensing their danger, the Egyptians attempted to flee; but the receding waters came together so quickly and with such force that the warriors were hurled into the furious sea and all drowned.

visual 1

5. The depths have covered them: they sank into the bottom as a stone.

The charioteers and horsemen wore armor, which consisted of plates of bronze sewn to a linen undergarment. These warriors had no time even to attempt to remove this armor, and so they sank like stones. Ironically, the very equipment that they hoped would protect them proved to be their undoing. Even today men and women are constantly tempted to look to wealth, or power or position for security in life. But how often is the pursuit or possession of them the cause of their downfall!

A SONG OF VICTORY

Every college and most high schools have a victory song that they sing after a triumph by their athletic teams. Most of these songs exalt the stamina, courage, prowess, and achievements of the school's players and praise the faithfulness and support of their followers to bring the victory.

When the victory or fight song is played or sung, the students and the alumni stand and share in the celebration of triumph. Most of us have rejoiced and sung along with gusto when "our" team won!

Faith in God as the victor creates a different hymn of celebration. Moses set a pattern for all time when he exalted the Lord for overthrowing the Egyptian army in the Red Sea. Moses' song is a song praising God for Israel's deliverance.

Believers in Christ have victory songs, too. "Faith Is the Victory" heads my list. What is yours?

We sing from our hearts. Our hymns need something of the "Song of Moses" in their content and expression. We are winners in the Lord, and we should sing as victors through His love and grace. To Him be the glory, for He has triumphed over Satan, who is our enemy!   —W. P.

B. The Lord's Power Described (vv. 6-8)

6. Thy right hand, O LORD, is become glorious in power: thy right hand, O LORD, hath dashed in pieces the enemy.

Thy right hand. This is another of the anthropomorphisms found in this poem. This expression is frequently used as a symbol of God's unequaled power, and mostly used in the book of Psalms. God's power was displayed against the Egyptians, whom He *dashed in pieces.* The victory over the forces of Pharaoh was so complete than none could doubt His power.

7. And in the greatness of thine excellency thou hast overthrown them that rose up against thee: thou sentest forth thy wrath, which consumed them as stubble.

The idea of God's might, set forth in the previous verse, is restated in this verse. The figure of God consuming His enemies as stubble was a reference to the common practice of burning the stubble that remained after a wheat field had been harvested. Nothing in the field escaped. The smoke and flames was a convincing picture of the complete destruction wrought by God's judgment.

8. And with the blast of thy nostrils the waters were gathered together, the floods stood upright as a heap, and the depths were congealed in the heart of the sea.

In this verse we are given yet another picture of God's power. Here we are shown His dominance over nature. *With the blast of thy nostrils.* Moses depicts God as a man exhaling. But the power of this blast, described in 14:21 as a "strong east wind," was so great that the waters of the sea were rolled back and retained as if by a wall.

The depths were congealed in the heart of the sea. If this expression is to be taken literally, this miracle must have caused the water to cease its movement as a fluid and to become a hard substance. But this is a poetical description, and Moses may have been speaking figuratively, suggesting that the wall of water was so straight and upright that it appeared to have been solid.

C. The Egyptians' Arrogance Shown (vv. 9, 10)

9. The enemy said, I will pursue, I will overtake, I will divide the spoil; my lust shall be satisfied upon them; I will draw my sword, my hand shall destroy them.

This verse shows the vicious hatred of the Egyptians as they pursued the Israelites in their desire for revenge. They had no doubt that with their speedy chariots they could quickly overtake the slow-moving multitude ahead of them. *I will divide the spoil.* In ancient times, it was a common practice for victorious soldiers to loot their defeated enemies. In this case, the spoils would be large, for the Israelites had taken substantial treasures from the Egyptians as they left (See Exodus 3:22; 12:36).

My lust (literally, "my soul") *shall be satisfied upon them.* The words that follow show that the Egyptians' dominant passion was not lust, but rage. *I will draw my sword, my hand shall destroy them.* Pharaoh had been concerned about the loss of all this slave labor, but by this time his anger and the anger of his army was so aroused that they sought not to capture the Israelites and return them to slavery but to completely destroy them. This is the reason that God so vehemently loosed His wrath upon them. In our own times, we are reminded of Adolf Hitler, whose rage seemed to increase with each victory, not only against the Jews, but against any people he deemed to be "inferior."

10. Thou didst blow with thy wind, the sea covered them: they sank as lead in the mighty waters.

It took but one breath from God to bury the arrogant Egyptians beneath the sea. God had caused a wind to blow, opening a pathway across the sea for the fleeing Israelites. Now all He had to do was to cause the wind to blow in the opposite direction and what had been a pathway of safety for the Israelites became a death trap for the Egyptians.

III. God's Concern for His People (Exodus 15:13)

A. Merciful Redemption (v. 13a)

13a. Thou in thy mercy hast led forth the people which thou hast redeemed.

The first part of this verse states that God's mercy was the reason that He led His people out of bondage in Egypt. The *Revised Standard Version* has "steadfast love," while the *American Standard Version* renders it "lovingkindness." This suggests that God did not redeem the Israelites because they particularly deserved it or because they were superior to any other people. He did it out of mercy.

B. Strong Guidance (v. 13b)

13b. Thou hast guided them in thy strength unto thy holy habitation.

God's mercy did not end once He had led the people through the sea. He had no intention of abandoning them on the edge of the desert. By the eye of prophecy, Moses could look forward to God's continued guidance until He brought them safely into the promised land. In typical prophetic language Moses spoke of this future event in the past tense, knowing that its fulfillment was certain.

THE WAY HOME

Grandfather Phillips was a man of integrity and faith. At an early age he accepted Jesus Christ as his Lord and Savior. He lived the ninety-four years of his life by the teachings of the Bible and the commands and example of his Lord.

In his final years the Word of God was a constant companion. At age ninety-four he could still work. The day he died he chopped wood, sat down to read the Scripture, and fell asleep. He awoke, not in this life, but at home with his Lord. The example of Grandfather Phillips helped many to discover the life of faith that could give peace and triumph here and forever.

In mercy the Savior he served had finally brought him to His "holy habitation."

The "Song of Moses" expressed the assurance that the people of Israel would one day enter God's holy habitation, the land promised to their forefathers centuries earlier. That promised land serves as a figure of the eternal home God has prepared for His faithful people (see Hebrews 3:7—4:13).   W. P.

Conclusion

A. A God When We Need Him

On one occasion, so the story goes, the town atheist, who had spent his life denying that there was a God, fell into a mill pond. The water was over his head, and, unable to swim, he quickly sank. In a moment he came to the surface sputtering, "O God, help me!" Once more he sank and again he came up uttering the same cry: "O God, help me!"

A preacher heard his cry and jumped in and pulled him to safety. As the atheist lay on the bank recovering from his ordeal, his rescuer asked him, "Since you don't believe in God, why were you calling for Him to save you?"

"Preacher," came his reply, "if there isn't a God, there ought to be when a man needs Him." Exactly. There ought to be a God when we need Him. As Christians, we don't have the problem that the atheist had. We know that there is a God, and we know that He will be there when we need Him.

B. Help Is All Around Us

Few things characterize our times more than change and instability. There was a time when we could look to our families for security, but today our families are scattered across the country, or even around the world. Thus they are not immediately at hand to give a bit of wise advice or needed encouragement.

A couple of generations ago, when most of our population lived in rural areas or small towns, we could look to the community for support in time of trouble. But no more. We move on the average about once every five years, and many move more often than that. This high transciency rate makes it difficult if not impossible to put down reassuring roots.

If God chose miracles as the method of providing support for us, He would indeed be busy. But God is not limited to such spectacular deliverances as we see in His rescue of the Israelites from the Egyptians. He can work through the small, everyday events to give us help. He can work through individuals who in their commitment to God are also committed to serve their fellowmen. Only God can count the number of times that a kind word, a timely gift, a quiet favor, or a needed loan has helped a person through a crisis.

The church provides a base to encourage its members to be helpers. Only a few years ago the critics of the church were saying that its time had passed, that it was an outmoded institution providing advice that was equally out of date. No doubt some of the criticism was deserved; but after all the shots have been fired and the smoke has cleared, the church is still there doing its job.

May we be able to sing with Moses, "The Lord is my strength and song, and he is become my salvation . . . and I will exalt him." Let us exalt Him when things are going well for us. Let us also exalt Him when our fragile world seems to be collapsing about us. Let us exalt Him because for our lives He provides a solid foundation that will remain secure no matter how swiftly the tides of time may swirl about us.

C. Let Us Pray

We thank You, Our Heavenly Father, for showing us Your might as You delivered the Israelites from their bondage in Egypt. Even as You set them free from their physical bondage, so may we be set free from the bondage of fear and uncertainty when things go wrong. We pray that You will give us assurance and lead us to exalt You. In the name of our Master we pray. Amen.

D. Thought to Remember

I know not where His islands lift
Their fronded palms in air;
I only know I cannot drift
Beyond His love and care.
—John Greenleaf Whittier

Home Daily Bible Readings

Monday, Nov. 25—Let All Creation Praise God! (Psalm 98)
Tuesday, Nov. 26—Give Thanks to the Lord (Psalm 105:1-6)
Wednesday, Nov. 27—God Is Dependable Forever (Psalm 105:7-15)
Thursday, Nov. 28—God Leads Israel to Egypt (Psalm 105:16-25)
Friday, Nov. 29—God Leads Israel Out of Bondage (Psalm 105:26-36)
Saturday, Nov. 30—God Protects Israel in the Wilderness (Psalm 105:37-45)
Sunday, Dec. 1—Praise the Faithful, Loving God! (Psalm 106:1-5)

Learning by Doing

This page contains an alternate lesson plan emphasizing learning activities. Classes desiring such student involvement will find these suggestions helpful.

Learning Goals

As students participate in today's class session, they should:

1. Reflect on the place of singing in their Christian lives.

2. Preview all of this quarter's lessons to decide which could have the greatest impact on their own lives.

Into the Lesson

Introduce this quarter's theme with music. Bring a tape player to class and have Christian music playing as students arrive.

To begin this session, play short sections of three or four different Christian songs, each of them in a completely different style (contemporary, classical, heavy metal, choir, instrumental, orchestra, vocal solo; etc.). Make sure that at least one of the choices is not your personal preference. Ask class members to discuss, in twos or threes, which of the selections they liked best and why. Then discuss some or all of the following questions as a class:

1. What kinds of emotions are expressed with music? Can you name some examples of each emotion you've listed? (Examples may include "secular" songs as well as religious.)

2. Share a favorite hymn or Christian song. What makes it your favorite? The message? The melody? A personal experience? Other?

3. How would you evaluate the role of music in your Christian experience (choose one): essential; important; interesting; doesn't matter. Why? Does a person need to be musical in order to highly value Christian hymns?

4. When do you feel most like singing? Can you think of a time or experience in your life when music was especially meaningful to you?

Tell students that today's session will set the stage for this whole quarter of study. Explain that you're challenging them to think about the place of music in their experience, and especially in their worship, to help them identify with the persons whose songs we will be studying in coming weeks.

Into the Word

Rather than look at today's lesson specifically, why not use your Bible-study time to introduce students to the whole quarter? By showing students how these lessons relate to life, you will stimulate interest in studying them. (The "Learning by Doing" section for next week's lesson suggests activities for studying both this week's and next week's texts.)

The following sentences summarize this quarter's lessons. Use them in one of several ways:

Read them. Copy each sentence onto a slip of paper and distribute the slips among students in your class. Ask each student to read his sentence aloud as a preview of what's coming.

Choose them. As the sentences are read, students are to choose the three or four they would most like to study.

Scramble them. Mix up the sentences without the lesson numbers before each one and give each student a copy of them. Ask them to look through the upcoming lessons and to decide which sentence goes with which lesson. (Give them a list of lesson topics and Scriptures if they do *not* have the student book. If they *do,* this activity is provided there.) Here are the sentences:

1. God can deliver us from our enemies.

2. God gives victory against His foes to those who trust Him.

3. God comforts us when we are grieving for the loss of someone close to us.

4. God sometimes intervenes in life to bring events and people that fill us with joy.

5. God made the whole universe, and yet He is interested in you and me.

6. In God's presence—and in His will—we find the greatest joy.

7. When we trust God, He brings us up from the depths of sin and shares His love with us forever.

8. God gives us the love shared by married partners.

9. God loves humankind, but sometimes His love for humans is not returned by them.

10. God wants to hear and answer our prayers.

11. God has perfect unity with Christ and wants His followers to have unity with each other.

12. Someday everyone will bow at Jesus' feet.

13. Heaven will be filled with songs to God.

Into Life

Challenge students to read texts from this quarter's study at home, especially those they chose as the most meaningful to them.

Let's Talk It Over

The questions on this page are designed to encourage review of the lesson Scriptures and to promote discussion of the lesson by the class. The answers provided are only discussion starters. Let your class talk it over from there.

1. The song recorded in Exodus 15 seems to have been the product of some reflection and preparation following the event it celebrates. What does this suggest regarding the expression of praise and thanksgiving to God?

We sometimes sing about "counting our blessings," but we tend to offer praise to God that is of a general nature. We offer thanks for our salvation, our church, our families, our national freedom, etc., and we are sincere in doing so. Blessings such as these, however, deserve our careful consideration and a more detailed expression of our gratitude. Concerning our salvation, for example, we could join Paul in extolling God for the magnificence of His plan of redemption (Romans 11:33-36); we could offer praise for Jesus' willingness to go to Calvary for our sins; we could express to God our gratitude for apostles, prophets, missionaries, preachers, and teachers who have communicated the gospel in spite of suffering. Pondering the various elements of our blessings in this manner will surely increase our appreciation for all God has done for us.

2. How may our Christian heritage help us through difficult times?

Besides having a thorough knowledge of the Bible, we should gain a broad understanding of the history of the church. In so doing, we will find many examples of men and women whose faith shone brightly during dark times. If our own congregation is a comparatively older one, we can benefit from meditating on the previous generations and the laborers who served as ministers, elders, deacons, teachers, etc. before us. We may also ponder what the faith of our parents, grandparents, and other relatives has contributed to our own faith. In those times when we feel alone as Christians, such deliberations can strengthen our Christian resolve.

3. How is the Bible's frequent reference to God's powerful right hand a source of assurance for us?

When we think of our experiences with the hands of our parents, this symbol becomes rich in meaning. Like God's right hand, our father's or mother's right hand gave us *protection*. We

may be able to recall occasions when they protected us against bullies or threatening animals or weather-related hazards. It may have seemed to us that when we were ill our mother's soothing hand on our brow was a guarantee that we would soon feel better. Like God's right hand, our father's or mother's hand sometimes meted out *punishment*. At the time we could not fully appreciate the love that guided that hand in administering discipline, but later it became clear to us. It is the same with God's discipline—unsettling at first, but later reassuring.

4. God often has dealt rather harshly with human arrogance, as He did with the Egyptian army. What lesson may we draw from this fact?

It is wise to use the "mirror of God's Word" regularly to detect the possible development of an unhealthy pride. That pride could cause us to exalt ourselves above our fellowman (see Luke 18:9-14). Jesus observed that "every one that exalteth himself shall be abased" (Luke 18:14). Unhealthy pride could lead us to depend too much on our own cleverness or goodness or forceful personality, and not allow God's wisdom and power to work in us. It is better to let God's Word work gently within us to cultivate an appropriate humility than to become proud and suffer the downfall to which it can lead.

5. If God can use our small, everyday efforts and gifts to bring help and comfort to our fellow human beings, how should this affect our attitude regarding what we do and give?

To visit a sick person, to offer a word of encouragement to someone who is bereaved or depressed, or to express gratitude or praise when it is due may appear to be a small and unimportant gesture. For that reason, some may neglect doing such acts. These brief expressions of concern, however, can be and have been used by God to work wonders in people's lives. Whoever we are, whatever our circumstances, we are in a position to influence someone else for good or ill. We might well begin each day echoing the famous prayer of Francis of Assisi, which begins with the plea, "Lord, make me an instrument of Thy peace!"

Song of Deborah and Barak

LESSON SCRIPTURE: Judges 4:4—5:31.

PRINTED TEXT: Judges 5:1-11.

Judges 5:1-11

1 Then sang Deborah and Barak the son of Abinoam on that day, saying,

2 Praise ye the LORD for the avenging of Israel, when the people willingly offered themselves.

3 Hear, O ye kings; give ear, O ye princes; I, even I, will sing unto the LORD; I will sing praise to the LORD God of Israel.

4 LORD, when thou wentest out of Seir, when thou marchedst out of the field of Edom, the earth trembled, and the heavens dropped, the clouds also dropped water.

5 The mountains melted from before the Lord, even that Sinai from before the LORD God of Israel.

6 In the days of Shamgar the son of Anath, in the days of Jael, the highways were unoccupied, and the travelers walked through byways.

7 The inhabitants of the villages ceased, they ceased in Israel, until that I Deborah arose, that I arose a mother in Israel.

8 They chose new gods; then was war in the gates: was there a shield or spear seen among forty thousand in Israel?

9 My heart is toward the governors of Israel, that offered themselves willingly among the people. Bless ye the LORD.

10 Speak, ye that ride on white asses, ye that sit in judgment, and walk by the way.

11 They that are delivered from the noise of archers in the places of drawing water, there shall they rehearse the righteous acts of the LORD, even the righteous acts toward the inhabitants of his villages in Israel: then shall the people of the LORD go down to the gates.

GOLDEN TEXT: I, even I, will sing unto the LORD; I will sing praise to the LORD God of Israel.—Judges 5:3.

Songs and Prayers of the Bible
Unit 1: Songs From Ancient Israel
(Lessons 1-4)

Lessons Aims

As a result of studying this lesson students should:

1. Have a better understanding of the historical setting of this lesson.

2. Appreciate the importance of capable leadership in difficult times.

3. Be better able to face threatening situations because of their growing faith in God.

Lesson Outline

INTRODUCTION

    A. Backing Up Is Dangerous

    B. Lesson Background

I. A SONG OF PRAISE (Judges 5:1-5)

    A. The Singers (v. 1)

    B. Responsible Action (v. 2)

       Working Together

    C. Past Victories (vv. 3-5)

II. A SONG OF DISASTER (Judges 5:6-8)

    A. Dangerous Travel (v. 6)

    B. Failure of Leadership (v. 7)

    C. Reason for the Disaster (v. 8)

III. A RENEWED SONG OF PRAISE (Judges 5:9-11)

    A. For the Leaders (v. 9)

    B. For God's Righteous Acts (vv. 10, 11)

       Remembering!

CONCLUSION

    A. Leaders Needed

    B. Let Us Pray

    C. Thought to Remember

Display visual 2 from the visuals packet and let it remain before the class throughout the session. The visual is shown on page 132.

Introduction

A. Backing Up Is Dangerous

The airplane is different from all other means of transportation—the automobile, the train, the ship, and even the blimp. These all can go forward, stop, or even back up. The airplane can only go forward. If the jets were to be reversed in an effort to stop the plane or back up, it would immediately fall from the sky. It can stay in the air only if it continues to go forward fast enough to keep from stalling.

This is rather like the situation in ancient Israel. So long as the people were faithful to God and continued to grow spiritually, God blessed them. If they failed to go forward, they soon fell into distress, being oppressed by their neighbors. At times, the people of Israel did more than slow down; they came to a halt and even tried to back up. They did this by turning to "new gods." Such a course could only bring severe chastening from God.

B. Lesson Background

Between the events recorded in last week's lesson and the events dealt with in today's lesson, more than two hundred years had passed. During that time the Israelites had enjoyed some good times, but more often than not they had experienced bad times. After the death of Moses, Joshua had led the people into the promised land. Under his leadership, they had defeated the Canaanites and driven most of them out. But here and there, pockets of Canaanites and other peoples had managed to survive the conquest. Their presence was a constant source of trouble, for the Israelites were tempted again and again to follow after their gods.

Joshua had succeeded in keeping the people united during the conquest, but once the people settled down in their own allotted areas, they went their separate ways. On occasion they fell to fighting among themselves, which made them ready prey for the surrounding nations.

The people also fell into moral anarchy, each man becoming a law unto himself. The closing words of the book of Judges state it this way: "Every man did that which was right in his own eyes."

It is not surprising that under these conditions the Israelites became alienated from God. As a result, He allowed them to be oppressed by their hostile neighbors. When they repented and turned back to God, He sent special leaders, whom we call judges, to guide them out of their difficulties. The Israelites learned slowly, however, and this process was repeated several times.

On the occasion of today's lesson, the Israelites were suffering under the hand of the Canaanites, whose king was Jabin. He reigned in Hazor, a city north of the Sea of Galilee. His army, under the command of Sisera, was equipped with nine hundred iron chariots. Because of their military superiority, the Canaanites had cruelly oppressed Israel for twenty years.

God's people cried out to Him for help, and He heard their cries. He raised up a woman named Deborah to free His people. We read that this outstanding woman was a "prophetess" (Judges 4:4). Specially chosen by God, she announced His commands and promises to the people (Judges 4:6, 7). She also "judged Israel at that time" (v. 4).

During the period of the judges, the Israelites had no unified judicial system. Probably in each community there were respected men who served as arbiters to settle disputes. It is likely that the reputation for wisdom and fairness of some of these persons went beyond their own community, and people would come from some distance to have their cases heard. Apparently Deborah was one of these persons. It is said that "the children of Israel came up to her for judgment" (Judges 4:5).

Deborah held court in the mountain region about ten miles north of Jerusalem, between Ramah and Bethel. This was on the main road that ran north and south along the backbone of the central highlands. Thus Deborah was readily accessible to those who needed her advice.

The office of judge in ancient Israel involved more than settling civil disputes, however. It was a position of leadership combining both civil and military jurisdiction. It was rare for a woman in the Old Testament period to exercise such authority as Deborah did. The shortage of capable male leaders, however, made her leadership necessary, and the people seemed to have accepted it without protest.

God used Deborah to challenge Barak to lead the people against Jabin. Barak, however, was afraid to face the Canaanites alone and refused to lead the people unless Deborah went with him. Deborah agreed to this arrangement, and the Israelites won a resounding victory over their enemies. Deborah's song of victory that followed is the basis for today's lesson.

How to Say It

ABINOAM. A *bin*-o-am.
ANATH. A-nath.
BARAK. *Bay*-ruk or *Bair*-uk.
CANAANITES. *Kay*-nan-ites.
HAZOR. *Hay*-zor.
JABIN. *Jay*-bin.
JAEL. *Jay*-ul.
LAPIDOTH. *Lap*-uh-doth.
NAPHTALI. *Naf*-tuh-lye.
RAMAH. *Ray*-muh.
SEIR. *See*-ir.
SHAMGAR. *Sham*-gar.
SISERA. *Sis*-er-uh or *Sis*-uh-ruh.
ZEBULUN. *Zeb*-you-lun.

I. A Song of Praise
(Judges 5:1-5)
A. The Singers (v. 1)
1. Then sang Deborah and Barak the son of Abinoam on that day, saying,

This song in celebration of God's triumph over Israel's enemy is in a class with the song of Moses sung by Israel after the crossing of the Red Sea. Joining Deborah in this song was Barak. His name means "lightning," but in facing the threat of the Canaanites, he hardly lived up to his name. He had not taken the initiative in this matter, and was reluctant to do so until Deborah called him into service.

B. Responsible Action (v. 2)
2. Praise ye the LORD for the avenging of Israel, when the people willingly offered themselves.

The translation that most modern translations have for verse 2 is similar to this: "That the leaders took the lead in Israel, that the people offered themselves willingly, bless the Lord!" (*Revised Standard Version*). Thus the verse expresses a patriotic joy that leaders had responded to the threat of the Canaanites and that the people had been willing to follow them. This action was worthy of recognition, for the participants had responded to the call to duty even though no one had the authority of a king to call them into service.

WORKING TOGETHER

A popular song of World War II was "Praise the Lord and Pass the Ammunition." It was written shortly after Pearl Harbor, when our nation needed a lift after the disaster of that attack that brought the United States into the war.

The words were attributed to a U. S. Navy chaplain on a battleship under attack in the early days of the conflict. His feelings as he spoke the words and his personal involvement carrying them out are only of historic importance. What needs to come through to us is the truth portrayed in this popular lyric.

When God's people praise Him and involve themselves in doing His work, they are following the example of Deborah and Barak and the people of their generation. Deborah's song of praise spoke of leaders who willingly led and of people who willingly offered themselves in the work of the Lord at a time when heroism was desperately needed.

The church needs leaders who will turn the hearts of all believers to God and give them a sense of ultimate victory for their cause. Deborah and Barak sang after the battle was won. We are already overcomers in Jesus, and the best is

still ahead for us. Praise the Lord, and keep working!   —W. P.

C. Past Victories (vv. 3-5)

3. Hear, O ye kings; give ear, O ye princes; I, even I, will sing unto the LORD; I will sing praise to the LORD God of Israel.

The kings and princes mentioned here are the rulers of the nations of the earth. These rulers were called to give heed to the mighty acts of God in delivering His people. This special relationship between God and the Israelites hearkened back to the covenant that God established with them at Mount Sinai.

4, 5. LORD, when thou wentest out of Seir, when thou marchedst out of the field of Edom, the earth trembled, and the heavens dropped, the clouds also dropped water. The mountains melted from before the LORD, even that Sinai from before the LORD God of Israel.

This recent victory recalled earlier victories that Israel had experienced through the power of the Lord. Their victory over the Canaanites was not a historical accident; it was but a continuation of God's past intervention on behalf of His people.

Seir sometimes refers to a mountain (Genesis 14:6). On other occasions, it refers to a land (Genesis 32:3; 36:21) or the people who lived there. It was located in the area south of the Dead Sea, where the Edomites made their home. During their wandering in the wilderness, the Israelites wanted to pass through Edom to reach the territory east of the Jordan River. But the Edomites refused to allow them to do this (Numbers 20:14-21), and so the Israelites had to take a long detour around this territory. From there God led them in a triumphant march to the land of Canaan, overthrowing those nations east of the Jordan that fought against them (Numbers 21:21-35).

The earth trembled, and the heavens dropped, the clouds also dropped water. The forces of nature were used by God to display His power, as at

Sinai when the mountain "quaked greatly" (Exodus 19:18), and to save His people. We saw this in last week's lesson, as we considered the miraculous crossing of the Red Sea. It appears that God used a rainstorm, and its resultant flood, to bring about the defeat of the Canaanites before the forces of Deborah and Barak (see Judges 5:20, 21).

II. A Song of Disaster
(Judges 5:6-8)

A. Dangerous Travel (v. 6)

6. In the days of Shamgar the son of Anath, in the days of Jael, the highways were unoccupied, and the travellers walked through byways.

Deborah's song shifts from a praise of God's deliverance in the past to the miserable plight of the Israelites in recent years. In the days of Shamgar, who lived shortly before the time of Deborah, Israel was oppressed by the Philistines. We are told he killed six hundred Philistines with an ox goad (Judges 3:31). Apparently, however, the relief was only temporary.

The Canaanites had succeeded the Philistines as the oppressors of Israel. *Jael,* the woman who had a part in the overthrow of the Canaanites (Judges 4:17-22), was, of course, contemporary with Deborah. Conditions in Israel were so bad that the people were afraid to travel the main highways. This may have been because the Canaanites themselves occupied the land, or because their raids had so disrupted the stability of local communities that brigands roamed the highways attacking travelers at will. We today know it can be unsafe traveling some of our city streets even in the daytime. In our case, however, the oppressors are not foreign invaders but the forces unleashed by the use of illicit drugs. Our tragedy is compounded because our wounds are self-inflicted.

B. Failure of Leadership (v. 7)

7. The inhabitants of the villages ceased, they ceased in Israel, until that I Deborah arose, that I arose a mother in Israel.

The inhabitants of the villages ceased. The *American Standard Version* translates this "the rulers ceased in Israel," and this seems a better translation. Clearly the inhabitants of the villages had not been destroyed, for they still remained when they were called into service against the Canaanites. Certainly, though, the leadership in Israel had failed. The lack of leadership left the people open to the raids of the enemies. This is often the case. When the leadership is inadequate, the people suffer.

C. Reason for the Disaster (v. 8)

8. They chose new gods; then was war in the gates: was there a shield or spear seen among forty thousand in Israel?

The real cause for the disaster was not the lack of leadership, as serious as that was. The root of their problem was that they had abandoned Jehovah and sought *new gods*, the gods of the idolatrous peoples who surrounded them. The worship of these gods often involved sexual orgies that appealed to their worshipers' lower nature. We are appalled that so many of the Israelites would succumb to these temptations, yet the situation is not much different today. Men and women today will risk their reputations, their careers, and even their lives in the pursuit of lust.

Deborah makes it clear that when the people turned away from God, they left themselves open to His judgment. The judgment came in the form of raids by neighboring tribes, raids that brought the violence and destruction of war to the gates of their cities. The people were helpless against this onslaught because they lacked the weapons—shields and spears—needed to defend themselves. Armed only with clubs and stones, they were hardly a fair match for well-trained and well-equipped troops.

Some interpreters understand the reference to weapons differently. They say that the people had the weapons but kept them out of sight because without leadership they were afraid to display them. Regardless of which interpretation is correct, the final result is the same—the people were defenseless before the enemy.

III. A Renewed Song of Praise
(Judges 5:9-11)

A. For the Leaders (v. 9)

9. My heart is toward the governors of Israel, that offered themselves willingly among the people. Bless ye the LORD.

Although many of the people had turned away from Jehovah and followed after other gods, not everyone had done this. When the call had been issued for volunteers against the Canaanites, some had come forward to serve. Some of these volunteers were *governors* (which might be better translated "leaders" or "commanders"), who led the people against their enemies. God gave the victory, but He used human instruments to accomplish His purpose. God has not changed His method of operation. He still uses human leaders in His program.

Israel's leaders were commended because they had willingly offered their services when the

call went out for them. The tribes of Zebulun and Naphtali were especially mentioned (4:10; 5:18) for their response, and their heroism called forth from Deborah the grateful shout, *Bless ye the Lord.*

B. For God's Righteous Acts (vv. 10, 11)

10, 11. Speak, ye that ride on white asses, ye that sit in judgment, and walk by the way. They that are delivered from the noise of archers in the places of drawing water, there shall they rehearse the righteous acts of the LORD, even the righteous acts toward the inhabitants of his villages in Israel: then shall the people of the LORD go down to the gates.

In these verses Deborah challenges people of all classes to join in telling of the great victory the Lord has given. Those *that ride on white asses* and *sit in judgment* were the well-to-do, the upper class. The asses were probably not white but were tawny or reddish with white spots. Asses with such coloration were quite rare and so only the rich could afford them. These same people were usually the magistrates or village leaders who dispensed justice. Some modern translations render *sit in judgment* as "sit on rich carpets." Regardless of which translation is followed, it refers to the privileged class.

The expression *walk by the way* refers to the common people, who were too poor to own asses and so had to walk.

Verse 11 has provided some difficulties for translators. *They that are delivered from the noise of archers* is translated "the voice of the singers" in the *New International Version* and "to the sound of musicians" in the *Revised Standard Version*. Regardless of which translation is preferred, the meaning is clear. Those who gather at the watering places—wells or springs—should tell of Jehovah's victory. In the villages of Israel the well or spring that supplied the water was a popular meeting place for the inhabitants. Sooner or later, everyone had to go there, whether they were housewives needing water for cooking and laundry or herdsmen watering their flocks.

Then shall the people of the Lord go down to the gates. The city fathers met in the city gates to discuss business matters and mete out justice. Merchants often gathered to sell their wares just outside the city gates. The fact that these activities could be conducted in and about the gates indicated that these areas were now safe. The threat of the Canaanites had been removed by the great victory over Sisera and his forces.

REMEMBERING!

It was early December; the nights were cold, and the snow already covered the Sierra Nevada range of California. Along the highway stood a monument to the pioneers of the ill-fated Donner party. We stopped to read it.

Beginning their passage through the mountains too late in the season in 1846, this group was entrapped in heavy snows before they could reach the top of the pass now bearing their name. There was no way forward and no way back. Somehow a few of the Donner group survived that terrible winter, and in the spring they finally crossed over the pass to the mild climate of the California valleys.

As we paused, our minds went back to those days of incredible hardship during which California, and, indeed, much of this nation, were settled. Only by remembering the acts of bravery and courage of our forebears will we continue to appreciate our blessings as a nation.

The song of Deborah and Barak appealed to Israel to remember and speak of God's acts that brought their freedom. Let us recount regularly all that our Lord has done for us in this land and in our life in Christ, lest we and those who follow us forget.

—W. P.

Conclusion

A. Leaders Needed

When congregations are asked what their greatest need is, more often than not they reply that they need more and better trained leaders. It should come as no surprise, then, that the same problem faced ancient Israel. Because they lacked leadership, they spent many years under the heavy hand of their enemies. Without leaders they could not marshall their resources nor plan strategy against their oppressors. Even the leaders they had lacked the courage to face the enemies.

It is appropriate to ask why there was such a shortage of leaders in ancient Israel. At the very heart of their problem was the fact that they had lost their faith in God. Oh, they still offered sacrifices to Jehovah and went through the motions of serving Him, but the compelling fires that had burned in the hearts of their fathers had cooled. The parallels with our own times are all too obvious. The faith that sent the Pilgrims across the stormy Atlantic to find a refuge on the inhospitable shores of New England, that sent the circuit riders across the Appalachians in search of lost souls, is largely missing from our churches today.

Once their love for God had cooled, the Israelites turned increasingly to their own interests, ignoring the needs of their neighbors. Again we see parallels. The "me" attitude that causes people to do their own thing regardless of the needs of the larger society is all too obvious.

To become leaders, young people need models who will set the right kind of examples for them and encourage them as they develop their leadership skills. As we read the rather dismal history of Israel, the lack of worthy models is apparent. Our times are no different. In general, young people look to sports stars, movie and television performers, and political leaders for models. But what do they find? In most cases men and women who are involved in drugs and gambling, who sneer at Biblical standards for marriage, and who wantonly waste the resources that have come to them.

If we are to have the kind of leadership the church needs, as the church moves into the 21st century, we must have good models to attract them. More than this, however, we must diligently recruit people for service and then provide them the training, experience, and encouragement they need to become capable leaders. What is your class, your church, doing to prepare men and women for effective leadership?

B. Let Us Pray

We thank You, O God, for the example of intelligent and dedicated leadership we see in the life of Deborah. Move us to seek to imitate her example. Instill in us the faith that will give us the courage to face the enemies of the truth, even when those enemies seem too numerous and too strong for us. Above all, dear God, let us never waver in the assurance that the truth will eventually triumph over error. In Jesus' name, amen.

C. Thought to Remember

Those who would lead God's people must first heed God's voice.

Learning by Doing

*This page contains an alternate lesson plan emphasizing learning activities. Classes
desiring such student involvement will find these suggestions helpful.*

Learning Goals

Help students to accomplish the following as
they participate in today's class session:

1. Discover how God brought victory to His
people in each of the texts examined today.

2. Consider how they need victory from Him
in their lives this week.

3. Choose one example of past deliverance
and one need for future deliverance to bring before God in prayer.

Into the Lesson

Choose one of the following ideas to introduce
the theme of *"victory"* to your students:

Neighbor nudge. Ask students to turn to their
neighbors and share this thought: "A time in my
life when victory was particularly sweet. A time
in my life when defeat was especially bitter."
Each student has ninety seconds to share with a
neighbor. After three minutes call "time" and
ask volunteers to share.

Hymn search. Provide hymnals for this activity.
In pairs, students are to find hymns and gospel
songs that have the theme of victory. Give students about five minutes to find some; then let
volunteers share what they've found. Choose
one to sing as a whole class.

Brainstorm. Write the word *VICTORY* on your
chalkboard and ask students, "Can you think of
any victory songs?" They may list songs associated with war or with athletic victories or Christian songs about spiritual victory. List as many
as students can think of in about two minutes.
Then discuss, "What is it about victory that
makes us want to sing? What do victory songs
usually praise?"

After any one of these options, tell students
that today's lesson will examine the theme of
victory by looking at two songs of praise to God.
Each one thanks Him for delivering His people
from their enemies. Each one honors Him as the
source of victory.

Into the Word

Explain the material under "Lesson Background" both for this week's and last week's lesson. (You may want to assign this minilecture to
one or two class members during the week before class.) Then ask half of the class to study
last week's text and the other half to study this
week's.

Give each student pencil and paper. Students
assigned last week's text should make two
columns with these headings: "What God Did"
and "Why He Did It." They should read the text
to find items for a list under each heading.

Students assigned this week's text should outline the text, using the three main headings from
the lesson outline on page 130: "A Song of
Praise": (vv. 1-5), "A Song of Disaster" (vv. 6-8),
"A Renewed Song of Praise" (vv. 9-11). Their assignment is to paraphrase each section of Scripture in one sentence if possible.

Give each group ten minutes or more to complete their assignment. Then ask them to share
with the whole class what they have written.

After the first half has reported, ask the whole
class to identify the anthropomorphic references
in the text. That is, how does this song attribute
human characteristics to God in order to make
Him more understandable? What do each of
these teach about God?

Discuss: What did the Israelites learn about
God from this experience? What should the
Egyptians have learned about Him? What does
this event teach about Him that our culture
needs to learn?

After the second half has reported, share any
explanations of difficult-to-understand verses
that you wish. If the students' paraphrases revealed any misunderstandings, clarify them.

Discuss with students: Suppose you had never
studied the Bible before today. What do these
passages teach you about God?

Into Life

Ask students to identify as many *enemies of the
church* as they can think of in ninety seconds.
Write their answers on the chalkboard as students call them out. When the time is up, ask
students to look at the list and decide which is
the biggest threat for your congregation.

Then do the same for *enemies that threaten individual Christians.*

Discuss: Can you share a testimony about how
God has shattered an enemy you were facing?
What is the enemy chasing you this week?

Ask volunteers to participate in a time of sentence prayers. Some should ask God for deliverance from particular enemies that the class has
singled out. Others should thank Him for the deliverance He has already provided.

Let's Talk It Over

The questions on this page are designed to encourage review of the lesson Scriptures and to promote discussion of the lesson by the class. The answers provided are only discussion starters. Let your class talk it over from there.

1. Israel's circumstances in Deborah's time illustrate that God's people must continue to grow spiritually or else spiritual stagnation and decline will result. How does this truth relate to the church?

The church as a body, and its individual members, need to broaden their vision as to what they can accomplish for the Lord, and they need to set sensible goals and devise plans for reaching them. The church tends to stagnate when it fails to do this, and individual Christians who stop growing in Christ will often drift away from the church. In missionary gatherings it is often observed that "the church is always one generation away from extinction." This is true of the church that supports world missions as well as the church on the mission field. If it neglects evangelism, teaching, training of leaders, and the like through a complacent, self-satisfied attitude, it can in a few years' time fall into a decline that will be extremely difficult to reverse.

2. Deborah is unique as a woman who apparently occupied the most prominent position of leadership in Israel in her time. What aspects of her leadership may be applicable to Christian women today?

It is noteworthy that while Deborah was a wife and mother, she also served God outside of her home. This situation is paralleled in the lives of many Christian women, who faithfully perform domestic duties and also teach, serve as musicians, sponsor youth programs, and in other ways labor in the church. Also, it is interesting to draw a comparison between Deborah's widespread influence in giving spiritual and practical counsel as a judge and the ministry many women have today as speakers and writers. Their talks and writings have benefited both men and women. Further, while men and women are sometimes at odds today over women's proper role in the church, it is pleasing to see that Deborah and Barak were united in giving glory to God for the victory.

3. Travelers faced danger on the roads in Deborah's time. In our time, it has become unsafe to travel on some city streets. What can Christians do to help make the streets of their communities safe?

We live in an era when respect for those who enforce our laws has diminished. Since every civil authority is "ordained of God" and the "minister of God" (Romans 13:1, 4), we owe such authorities our respect and cooperation. Christians should take the lead in encouraging law enforcement officers in the performance of their duties. Also, since drug and alcohol abuse is a major contributor to the fearful condition of our streets, Christians should be very vocal in their opposition to such abuse. Many communities with drug and alcohol problems have organized groups to combat them. One way Christians can function as "salt of the earth" (Matthew 5:13) is to participate in such groups.

4. How can we encourage more volunteers for leadership in the church?

In asking volunteers to assume leadership positions in the church, we may give them the impression that they are merely cogs in the church's machinery. The New Testament, on the other hand, frequently pictures Christian work in exciting terms of waging warfare or competing in athletic events. Perhaps it would stir up more members to a spirit of voluntarism if they could see Christian work in these Scriptural terms. Futhermore, a soldier or athlete knows precisely what is expected of him. If volunteers in the church could be shown clearly what their task is to be, they would be more likely to respond to a call for leadership recruits.

5. Why do we need stronger role models for our youth, and where can the church find them?

Christian role models in society at times prove disappointing. Movie stars who claim to be Christians take roles in films that are morally questionable. Christian athletes make public statements that reveal an un-Christlike pride or greed. Prominent religious leaders suffer moral lapses. Almost any local congregation has men and women in it whose faith, devotion, and moral integrity make them excellent models for the young people in the congregation. These adults may shy away from being placed on a kind of "pedestal," but they must see that a legitimate humility can be balanced with a conscious effort to provide a godly example for our youth.

David's Lament for Saul and Jonathan

LESSON SCRIPTURE: 2 Samuel 1.

PRINTED TEXT: 2 Samuel 1:17-27.

2 Samuel 1:17-27

17 And David lamented with this lamentation over Saul and over Jonathan his son:

18 (Also he bade them teach the children of Judah the use of the bow: behold, it is written in the book of Jasher:)

19 The beauty of Israel is slain upon thy high places: how are the mighty fallen!

20 Tell it not in Gath, publish it not in the streets of Askelon; lest the daughters of the Philistines rejoice, lest the daughters of the uncircumcised triumph.

21 Ye mountains of Gilboa, let there be no dew, neither let there be rain, upon you, nor fields of offerings: for there the shield of the mighty is vilely cast away, the shield of Saul, as though he had not been anointed with oil.

22 From the blood of the slain, from the fat of the mighty, the bow of Jonathan turned not back, and the sword of Saul returned not empty.

23 Saul and Jonathan were lovely and pleasant in their lives, and in their death they were not divided: they were swifter than eagles, they were stronger than lions.

24 Ye daughters of Israel, weep over Saul, who clothed you in scarlet, with other delights; who put on ornaments of gold upon your apparel.

25 How are the mighty fallen in the midst of the battle! O Jonathan, thou wast slain in thine high places.

26 I am distressed for thee, my brother Jonathan: very pleasant hast thou been unto me: thy love to me was wonderful, passing the love of women.

27 How are the mighty fallen, and the weapons of war perished!

GOLDEN TEXT: Saul and Jonathan were lovely and pleasant in their lives, and in their death they were not divided: they were swifter than eagles, they were stronger than lions.—2 Samuel 1:23.

Songs and Prayers of the Bible

Unit 1: Songs From Ancient Israel

(Lessons 1-4)

Lesson Aims

After this lesson, each student should:

1. Understand that most lives are touched sooner or later by the loss of loved ones.

2. Appreciate the great sorrow that David felt at the loss of Saul and Jonathan.

3. Be better able to minister to others in times of grief.

Lesson Outline

INTRODUCTION
  A. Grief Is Universal
  B. Lesson Background
 I. DAVID'S LAMENT INTRODUCED (2 Samuel 1:17, 18)
  A. The Subjects (v. 17)
  B. Instruction (v. 18)
 II. CONTENT OF DAVID'S LAMENT (2 Samuel 1:19-27)
  A. Cause of Mourning (v. 19)
  B. Concern About the Enemy (v. 20)
  C. Curse Upon the Battle Site (v. 21)
  D. Praise of the Fallen Warriors (vv. 22, 23)
    Fallen Leaders
  E. Reminder of Saul's Gifts (v. 24)
  F. Love of a Friend (vv. 25, 26)
    A Lost Love
  G. Closing Words (v. 27)
CONCLUSION
  A. The Inevitable Visitor
  B. Memories
  C. Let Us Pray
  D. Thought to Remember

Display visual 3 from the visuals packet and refer to it as you discuss each point that it contains. The visual is shown on page 141.

Introduction

A. Grief Is Universal

The Chinese have a story about a woman whose son died suddenly, leaving her alone in the world. The woman was devastated by her son's death and refused to be consoled by her friends and neighbors. Finally one of them suggested that she go to see the wise old philosopher who lived in the next village.

The woman went to visit him and poured out her heart to him. The wise man attempted to console her and finally promised that he could bring her son back. This immediately caught her attention, and she stopped her sobbing. "Yes," he assured her, "I can bring back your son. There is but one thing you must do. You must bring me a mustard seed from some home in your village that has not lost a loved one."

This seemed simple enough, and so she hurried back to her village to find the required mustard seed. As she went from house to house, however, her search proved vain. Mustard seeds she found, but every home she visited had known the sorrow of the loss of a loved one. Thus she was not able to get her son back, but in the process she learned that grief is universal and that others had learned to cope with it. Such a valuable lesson should find a lodging place in our own hearts.

B. Lesson Background

The book of 1 Samuel ends with the death of King Saul and three of his sons, including David's good friend, Jonathan. Historians date this event about 1010 B. C., approximately two hundred years after the time of Deborah, the subject of last week's lesson. The death of Saul brought to a tragic end a reign that began with great potential. In spite of his physical prowess, Saul had some serious flaws in his character. These began to come to light in his dealings with Samuel (see 1 Samuel 13:8-14; 15:10-23).

Because of Saul's disobedience, God sent Samuel to anoint David to take his place. Even though David was completely loyal to Saul, the king developed a jealousy of him that bordered on paranoia. On several occasions Saul tried to kill David, but each time David escaped. Finally, David was forced to flee and go into hiding in the hill country south of Bethlehem. Saul continued to pursue David, and at least twice David had the opportunity to kill Saul, but he spared him because Saul was "the Lord's anointed" (see 1 Samuel 24; 26:23).

Gathered about David were men who were dissatisfied with Saul as king. Before long, his band became a formidable fighting force and they came and dwelt with Achish, king of the Philistines. When Achish decided to launch a campaign against Saul, he sought to enlist David and his men in the effort. Some of the Philistine lords did not trust David, however, and so Achish sent him back to Ziklag, a town located on the border between Philistia and Israel that Achish had given David for his base of operations.

While David was at Ziklag, he received the tragic news of the death of Saul. The messenger who brought the news, an Amalekite, claimed to have killed Saul, expecting David to reward him for his actions. Actually the man lied, for Saul had committed suicide. His lie cost him his life, because David had him executed for slaying "the Lord's anointed" (2 Samuel 1:1-16).

I. David's Lament Introduced (2 Samuel 1:17, 18)

A. The Subjects (v. 17)

17. And David lamented with this lamentation over Saul and over Jonathan his son.

We can understand David's lament over the death of Jonathan, who had interceded with his father on behalf of David (1 Samuel 19:4-7; 20:27-33), and helped him escape Saul's anger (1 Samuel 20:34-42). On the other hand, we might expect David to have rejoiced at the death of Saul. Saul had tried to kill David on several occasions and had mistreated him in other ways. If David were a lesser man with personal ambitions, he would have found the death of Saul and his three sons a reason to celebrate, for it presented him the opportunity to become king. David, however, was a man of integrity, and he held the office of kingship in high regard. There was no way that he was going to cheapen that office by making it the object of his personal ambitions.

We can learn a lesson from David's example in this situation. Our society is characterized often by dog-eat-dog competition in business and sometimes in our churches. Let us pray that God will give us the integrity to escape such attitudes.

In the Hebrew, *lamentation* is something of a technical word used to indicate a dirge or a poem commemorating the dead. Old Testament laments are characterized not so much by the rhythm of sound as by the rhythmic pulsation of thought. David's lamentation for Saul and Jonathan was "a song of sorrow which for tenderness and intensity has never been surpassed" (B. Dale).

B. Instruction (v. 18)

18. (Also he bade them teach the children of Judah the use of the bow: behold, it is written in the book of Jasher.)

He bade them teach the children of Judah the use of the bow. The words *the use of* are not in the Hebrew text. They were inserted by translators attempting to clarify the meaning of this verse. Some Bible students, however, feel that an instruction to teach Judah how to use the bow would not have been put between the sentence that says David composed "this lamentation" and the lamentation itself. The *American Standard Version* inserts "the song of" instead.

How to Say It

ACHISH.   A-kish.
AMALEKITE.   *Am*-uh-leck-ite.
ASKELON.   *As*-ke-lon.
GILBOA.   Gil-*bo*-uh.
GOLIATH.   Go-*lye*-uth.
JASHER.   *Jay*-sher.
JEZREEL.   *Jez*-re-el.
PHILISTIA.   Fih-*liss*-tih-uh.
PHILISTINES.   Fi-*liss*- teens or *Fil*-iss-teens.
ZIKLAG.   *Zick*-lag.

This suggests that this lament was referred to as "the bow," being so named from the mention of Jonathan's bow in verse 22. Teaching the children of Judah a song honoring two fallen national heroes, rather than how to use the bow, seems more fitting in this context. The book of Jasher is mentioned also in Joshua 10:13. It may have been a collection of national songs that has long since been lost.

II. Content of David's Lament (2 Samuel 1:19-27)

A. Cause of Mourning (v. 19)

19. The beauty of Israel is slain upon thy high places: how are the mighty fallen!

Some take *the beauty of Israel* to refer to all those who were slain in the battle against the Philistines. Since Saul and Jonathan are the subjects of this lament, however, it seems best to limit the expression to them. Even though Saul had fallen out of favor with God because of his disobedience, many in Israel still respected him. Even today when we remember the dead, we tend to recall the good things, and not the evil, they have done.

Thy high places. This expression refers to the places where Saul and Jonathan died—on the slopes of Mount Gilboa. This mountain, rising to a height of nearly seventeen hundred feet, overlooks the valley of Jezreel. The northern and eastern slopes are rather steep, with precipices in many places, and so it is likely that Saul and Jonathan met their death on the western slopes.

How are the mighty fallen! This refrain is repeated in verses 25 and 27. It seems to sum up the dismal theme of the entire song.

B. Concern About the Enemy (v. 20)

20. Tell it not in Gath, publish it not in the streets of Askelon; lest the daughters of the Philistines rejoice, lest the daughters of the uncircumcised triumph.

Gath and Askelon were two of the five principal cities of the Philistines. Gath was the royal city of the Philistine king, Achish, with whom David was briefly allied. Gath was also the home of Goliath, whom David had slain earlier.

David knew very well that the news of the death of Saul and Jonathan would be told and gloated over throughout these two cities. It was the common practice of the women to come out of the cities to greet the return of their victorious men. With singing and dancing they celebrated the skill and bravery of the nation's warriors. David had experienced a similar greeting from the women when he had returned from slaying Goliath (1 Samuel 18:6-9). It pained him greatly when he thought about how the Philistines would rejoice at the news.

C. Curse Upon the Battle Site (v. 21)

21. Ye mountains of Gilboa, let there be no dew, neither let there be rain, upon you, nor fields of offerings: for there the shield of the mighty is vilely cast away, the shield of Saul, as though he had not been anointed with oil.

The depth of David's emotion led him even to pronounce a curse upon the place where the two men had died. He was asking that God withhold the life-giving dew and rain from the slopes of Gilboa. The barrenness of the mountain would remain a constant memorial of the terrible deed that had happened there. In mentioning *fields of offerings,* David expressed his desire that the fields would be so barren that they would not even produce the first fruits that would be sacrificed.

Vilely cast away. This expression is forceful in its description of Saul's violent death. This Hebrew word, however, may also be translated "defiled," and many Bible students feel that that is its proper meaning here. The meaning then would be that the shield of Saul was defiled, stained, with his own blood. *As though he had not been anointed with oil.* This conveys the meaning that Saul fell in battle just as if he had not been a king. The sense of this is good. We must note, however, that the words *as though he had been* are not in the Hebrew text; they have been supplied by translators. The translators of most modern translations believe the inserted words change the intended meaning of the original text. They render the second half of verse 21 somewhat as follows: "There the shield of the mighty is defiled, the shield of Saul not anointed with oil." It was the custom of ancient warriors to anoint their shields with oil in preparation for battle (see Isaiah 21:5). Therefore, Saul, having been slain, would no longer be able to polish his shield in preparation for combat. His shield had been defiled instead with his own blood.

D. Praise of the Fallen Warriors

(vv. 22, 23)

22. From the blood of the slain, from the fat of the mighty, the bow of Jonathan turned not back, and the sword of Saul returned not empty.

In this verse David sings the praises of the prowess of Saul and Jonathan. Elsewhere, Jonathan is associated with the bow, probably indicating that he had developed great skill with it (1 Samuel 20:20, 36, 37). Saul, on the other hand, is associated with the sword. His great size would have given him a definite advantage with that weapon in combat. The ancients sometimes spoke of the arrow as drinking the blood of its victim while the sword ate his flesh. David's association of these two weapons with Jonathan and Saul indicates that they were a formidable combat team. Even if Saul had not been king, their deaths were a serious blow to the army of Israel.

23. Saul and Jonathan were lovely and pleasant in their lives, and in their death they were not divided: they were swifter than eagles, they were stronger than lions.

Even though Saul had turned away from God, this should not obscure the fact that he had many fine qualities. He had been a courageous and victorious leader in Israel's struggle against the Philistines. His leadership, flawed though it was, still had given the people some relief from the attacks of their enemies. David himself had felt the wrath of Saul's jealous rage, and yet he could see his king's good qualities.

Some Bible students feel that the phrase *in their lives* belongs with the words that follow rather than those that precede them. For example, the *New English Bible* reads, "In life, in death, they were not parted." It was obvious to everyone that father and son were united in their deaths. David wanted also to emphasize that they were united in their lives. Jonathan was a remarkable man, torn by his love for David and his sense of loyalty to his father. His life is all the more remarkable when we realize that he was able to maintain his loyalty to both men without compromising his integrity.

The eagle and the lion are renowned for swiftness and strength. In eulogizing these qualities of Saul and Jonathan, David could call on no more appropriate figures.

FALLEN LEADERS

When John F. Kennedy died by an assassin's bullet in Dallas, Texas, our nation went into mourning. Even President Kennedy's bitterest political foes, and they were many, mourned his tragic and unexpected death. His funeral service and procession were a pageant of family, personal, and national grief. We, as a people, were stunned at such an act of malice in a country dedicated to peace and fraternity.

In the days and weeks that followed, President Kennedy was eulogized, idolized, made larger than life, and transformed from an elected head of government into a martyred hero honored and revered.

It is not unnatural that such adulation should occur. We weep over our fallen leaders and overlook reality in our intense desire to lift them up and hold their lives and works in greatest esteem.

This is what David did in eulogizing Saul, his enemy, and Jonathan, his closest friend, when they died in battle. Animosities were forgotten. Only the honor due to those holding high office, and the glories of past accomplishments, were to be remembered. —W. P.

E. Reminder of Saul's Gifts (v. 24)

24. Ye daughters of Israel, weep over Saul, who clothed you in scarlet, with other delights; who put on ornaments of gold upon your apparel.

Early in the reign of Saul, the conditions of life in Israel were miserable (see 1 Samuel 13:19-22). Under Saul's strong leadership, Israel won freedom from this oppression, and the women were among those who enjoyed the benefits of it. Even though the closing years of Saul's life were a tragedy, David insisted that the women should mourn Saul's death in remembrance of what he had done for them in the earlier and happier years of his reign. *Scarlet* refers to brilliant crimson clothing worn by the wealthy, which was made even more expensive by being adorned with ornaments of gold. This single example represented the increase in prosperity Israel enjoyed under Saul's leadership. It was only natural that the death of such a benefactor be attended by mourning.

F. Love of a Friend (vv. 25, 26)

25, 26. How are the mighty fallen in the midst of the battle! O Jonathan, thou wast slain in thine high places. I am distressed for thee, my brother Jonathan: very pleasant hast thou been unto me: thy love to me was wonderful, passing the love of women.

Once more we read the refrain that marks the theme of this lament. Here it introduces the section of David's song that deals specifically with Jonathan. Nowhere in the Bible do we find a richer, purer friendship than that between Jonathan and David. David acclaims him as a

visual 3

brother, a deeply meaningful relationship in that day. Our great emphasis upon individualism makes it difficult to develop or even appreciate the powerful bonds that existed between members of families in Bible times.

This relationship is all the more remarkable when we realize what it cost Jonathan. David and Jonathan became fast friends after David had slain Goliath. We are told that "the soul of Jonathan was knit with the soul of David, and Jonathan loved him as his own soul" (1 Samuel 18:1). Jonathan's affection was demonstrated when he gave David his own robe, sword, and bow.

Soon it became apparent that Saul, by his rebellion, had forfeited the crown of Israel, not only for himself but for his family. David had been anointed Saul's successor. Jonathan, the logical heir apparent to the throne, never seemed to resent the fact that he would be supplanted by David. Instead, their love for one another only increased through growing difficulties.

David now reflected on Jonathan's noble character, his loyalty, his self-effacement, his willingness even to risk death at the hand of his father in defense of David's innocence. All of these thoughts, no doubt, and more rushed through David's mind causing him to utter the words of endearment recorded here.

A LOST LOVE

Romeo and Juliet is Shakespeare's play of enmity, intrigue, passion, and lost love. Few can view this drama without feeling the intensity of passions ranging from family power and pride to young love that is lost through a dramatic series of mistakes in human judgment and communication.

The climactic scene shows Juliet appearing dead from a potion Romeo does not know she has received. She has simulated death to join her exiled Romeo. In despair over her apparent death, Romeo kills himself. A little later, Juliet awakes to discover that her young husband is dead. She then commits suicide in her grief over his loss.

Losing someone we desperately love in real life is like Shakespeare's play. The events may unfold in a few days or hours of time, and death terminates the longed-for relationship.

David sang of his love for Jonathan in this touching lament over his friend's death. David's pain and distress are evident. Each of us too may experience the hurt and confusion over a lost love, but we need not despair. Jesus has opened the gates to eternal life. Even in the time of our greatest loss, His love will sustain us.

—W. P.

G. Closing Words (v. 27)

27. How are the mighty fallen, and the weapons of war perished!

For the third and final time David uses the refrain to conclude his lament. Many understand the *weapons of war* to be figurative, not referring to bows, swords, and shields, but to Saul and Jonathan. Such an interpretation makes this expression parallel in thought to that of the first part of the verse.

Critics generally have hailed the verses included in this lesson as one of the most moving and powerful laments in all of ancient literature. Certainly this song deserves such a ranking. Not only is it sublime poetry, but it gives us insights to the character of David. He was a man who loved his great friend, but who also respected and praised his avowed enemy.

Conclusion

A. The Inevitable Visitor

Nothing in our lives is more certain than death. A good genetic inheritance and a sensible life-style may prolong life, and modern medical technology may give us a few more months or even years, but no one cheats death forever. He is the inevitable visitor. Since none of us can escape death, the best we can do is to prepare ourselves for it.

The sorrow that accompanies death stems from several different causes. We sorrow when a good person dies. A person who lived a life of service to others will be missed by all whom he or she has touched. The passing of a close friend or a family member will leave an emptiness that only time can heal. The greatest sorrow comes at the death of one who has never accepted the loving invitation of Christ.

Different cultures deal differently with the sorrow brought by death. The ancient Stoics and some American Indian tribes were conditioned to show no outward signs of emotion when death came to their loved ones. In other cultures loud and exaggerated displays of emotion were

considered the norm. This was true in Israel in Jeremiah's time (see Jeremiah 9:17, 18) and in Jesus' day (see Matthew 9:23, 24). In David's time it was common for mourning to be loud and prolonged. We do not see that, however, in his behavior. His mourning for Saul and Jonathan, though intense, was restrained and dignified.

B. Memories

When a loved one dies, memories are certain to linger. No doubt David had many pleasant memories of Jonathan, memories of times spent together in army camps, of times together in the court of King Saul. Memories of the past can bring sadness if we allow them to dominated our minds.

On the other hand, pleasant memories can inspire us to live nobler lives. We remember a parent or a child or a friend whose life was a model of faithful commitment to God and loving compassion for others. The memory of such a life can move us to similar commitment and compassion. Longfellow wrote, "Lives of great men all remind us we can make our lives sublime."

C. Let Us Pray

Dear God, we know sorrow is often a part of this life. Teach us to prepare ourselves for that time when it comes to us or our loved ones. Teach us to rely on You. Teach us also to help bear the burdens of others in their times of sorrow. In Jesus' name we pray. Amen.

D. Thought to Remember

"But I would not have you to be ignorant, brethren, concerning them which are asleep, that ye sorrow not, even as others which have no hope."   —1 Thessalonians 4:13

Home Daily Bible Readings

Learning by Doing

This page contains an alternate lesson plan emphasizing learning activities. Classes desiring such student involvement will find these suggestions helpful.

Learning Goals

Help students to accomplish the following as they participate in today's class session:

1. Survey David's song of lament to discover his attitude toward Saul and Jonathan.

2. Compare David's attitude with attitudes toward authority and obedience today, both inside and outside the church.

Into the Lesson

Begin by telling the story found under the heading "A. Grief Is Universal" in the introduction section. Then ask students to discuss in pairs, "What have you learned about coping with grief from the example of others you've known?" Allow about five minutes for discussion before asking for volunteers to share with the rest of the class.

If you have time, and in keeping with the theme of this quarter, ask students to think of songs they associate with death or grieving. Is sadness a time for singing too?

Tell your class members that, as they study today, they will consider lessons about grief and lessons about life as they look at the grieving of David.

Into the Word

Before class, prepare two flash cards with these words: "David and Saul" and "David and Jonathan." Display them and ask students to tell you what they know about each pair. You may want to summarize their comments on your chalkboard. Fill in any gaps with information from "B. Lesson Background" and the commentary under verse 17.

Divide the class into groups of three or four students each. Assign two of the questions below to each group. Ask them to read the mourning song of David and answer the questions as completely as possible.

1. *How and where did Saul die?*

2. *How did David feel about Saul?*

3. *How did David feel about Jonathan?*

4. *What kind of warriors were Saul and Jonathan?*

5. *How did David feel Israel should react to the deaths of Jonathan and Saul?*

Allow plenty of time for the students to share and for you to fill in any insights they may have missed.

Into Life

If students worked in groups to answer the questions above, you may keep them in groups for this part of the lesson. Ask each group to write a sentence or two under one of the following headings in response to it. (You may assign a heading to each group or allow them to choose.)

1. *What David's song teaches about death.*

2. *What David's song teaches about respect for authority.*

3. *What David's song teaches about love for a friend.*

4. *What David's song teaches about obedience to God.*

Be prepared to add insights from your study to the comments of class members when you allow them to share, group by group, with the whole class.

Ask class members, "What surprises you about the attitude of David here? How may we have expected him to react to the death of Saul, considering the trouble Saul had caused him? Why did David view Saul with such respect? Why did he feel such grief at his passing?"

Option. Instead of assigning these topics to groups, assign each topic to a different class member in the week before class. Each should be prepared to talk about his assigned topic for two minutes at this point in today's lesson.

After either of these activities, discuss with students, "What does this lesson teach *you?* Which of the four 'lessons' above that we have discussed could make the biggest impact on your life?"

You may want to focus on the relationship between respect for authority and obedience to God. What should be our attitude toward the office that government leaders hold, even if we sometimes do not agree with the leader himself or herself? Is there an application here for the church? What should be our attitude toward the ministry, even though we may not always agree with the person who is the minister?

Close with prayers of thanks for those in authority, including requests for God's guidance in their lives. You may want to focus on government leaders (especially if your church membership includes such leaders). Or you may want to list several of your congregation's leaders and ask volunteers to pray for each leader by name.

Let's Talk It Over

The questions on this page are designed to encourage review of the lesson Scriptures and to promote discussion of the lesson by the class. The answers provided are only discussion starters. Let your class talk it over from there.

1. Should the word *lamentation* be descriptive of a Christian's funeral? Why or why not?

Unlike David, we possess clear teaching about the resurrection and eternal life. Therefore, we should "sorrow not, even as others which have no hope: (1 Thessalonians 4:13). Still, we are likely to be shocked and saddened when a Christian relative or friend dies. We may lament over the fact that the deceased person left a young wife (or husband) and children behind. It may strike us as tragic that the individual died before completing some significant personal task. There may have been certain conditions, such as severe or prolonged suffering, that made death a more terrible experience. We may lament, therefore, over such circumstances, even while we rejoice that our relative or friend has become "absent from the body, and . . . present with the Lord" (2 Corinthians 5:8)

2. Some may consider it hypocritical to speak well of an enemy after his death, as David did in the case of Saul. What shall we say about this?

We know that David spoke well of Saul while the king was alive, so his sentiments expressed in his song of lamentation did not constitute a radical change. Whatever we may have thought or said in the past about a person with whom we were at odds, our harsh feelings are usually softened when that individual dies. Also, many people tend to forget the bad experiences and hold onto the good associations they shared with the deceased. To speak well of the dead under such circumstances, therefore, is not necessarily an act of hypocrisy. How much better, though, to speak well in life and death of even those people with whom we have experienced a measure of conflict.

3. What are some aspects of Jonathan's friendship with David that we would do well to imitate in regard to our friends?

The expression "faithful friendship" is well illustrated by Jonathan. His father's jealous hatred of David could have swayed him, but Jonathan remained David's loyal friend in spite of the pressure. From the Biblical record it appears that Jonathan gave more than he received in his relationship with David. We also should aim to be bigger givers than receivers in our friendships. Jonathan's friendship was free of jealousy. He knew that David was going to occupy the throne that could have been his, but he did not let that alter his affection for David. We must likewise avoid letting jealousy erode the beauty of our friendships.

4. Christians are noted as people who are making spiritual preparations for death. What are some practical preparations we should also be making?

The Biblical principle of stewardship applies to every aspect of our lives. This includes the distribution of our material properties when our lives on earth have ended. Churches, Bible colleges, Christian retirement homes, and other church-related institutions have benefited from the estates of thoughtful believers. We should also keep these in mind in estate planning. Where our families are concerned, it should be our aim to keep their adjustment as simple as possible in the event of our death. How often do we hear, for example, of a widow who has little knowledge of the handling of family finances or the maintenance of the home or automobile? Love dictates also that we make provision for the welfare of loved ones in the event of our untimely death.

5. How can our memories of deceased family members or friends make us better persons?

In Hebrews 11:4 it is said of righteous Abel "he being dead yet speaketh." Even so should we let our deceased loved ones speak to us. We can do this by focusing on the deceased's virtues, such as godliness, generosity, patience, or cheerfulness. The living often go to great lengths to fashion elaborate tributes to those who have died. The decorating of graves on special days, the publishing of memorial notices in the newspaper, the donation of money to a religious or charitable cause in the name of the deceased are among these. But what better tribute can we offer than to imitate the positive qualities we saw in our loved one's life?

Songs of Hannah and Mary

LESSON SCRIPTURE: 1 Samuel 2:1-10; Luke 1:26-56.

PRINTED TEXT: 1 Samuel 2:1-5; Luke 1:46-55.

1 Samuel 2:1-5

1 And Hannah prayed, and said, My heart rejoiceth in the LORD, mine horn is exalted in the LORD; my mouth is enlarged over mine enemies; because I rejoice in thy salvation.

2 There is none holy as the LORD: for there is none besides thee: neither is there any rock like our God.

3 Talk no more so exceeding proudly; let not arrogancy come out of your mouth: for the LORD is a God of knowledge, and by him actions are weighed.

4 The bows of the mighty men are broken, and they that stumbled are girded with strength.

5 They that were full have hired out themselves for bread; and they that were hungry ceased: so that the barren hath borne seven; and she that hath many children is waxed feeble.

Luke 1:46-55

46 And Mary said, My soul doth magnify the Lord,

47 And my spirit hath rejoiced in God my Saviour.

48 For he hath regarded the low estate of his handmaiden: for, behold, from henceforth all generations shall call me blessed.

49 For he that is mighty hath done to me great things; and holy is his name.

50 And his mercy is on them that fear him from generation to generation.

51 He hath showed strength with his arm; he hath scattered the proud in the imagination of their hearts.

52 He hath put down the mighty from their seats, and exalted them of low degree.

53 He hath filled the hungry with good things; and the rich he hath sent empty away.

54 He hath holpen his servant Israel, in remembrance of his mercy;

55 As he spake to our fathers, to Abraham, and to his seed for ever.

GOLDEN TEXT: My soul doth magnify the Lord, and my spirit hath rejoiced in God my Saviour.—Luke 1:46, 47.

Lesson Aims

As a result of studying this lesson, each student should:

1. Have a better understanding of why both Hannah and Mary praised God.

2. Have a deeper sense of gratitude for the salvation God has provided through His Son.

Lesson Outline

INTRODUCTION

  A. Putting Music in the World

  B. Lesson Background

 I. HANNAH'S SONG (1 Samuel 2:1-5)

  A. Rejoicing in the Lord (v. 1)

  B. God's Holiness (v. 2)

  C. God's Knowledge (v. 3)

  D. God Humbles the Proud (vv. 4, 5)

    Trust and Triumph

II. MARY'S SONG (Luke 1:46-55)

  A. Praise to the Lord (vv. 46, 47)

  B. Reasons for Praise (vv. 48, 49)

  C. God's Mercy (v. 50)

  D. God's Judgment (vv. 51-53)

  E. Help for Israel (vv. 54, 55)

    A Promise Fulfilled

CONCLUSION

  A. Revealing Songs

  B. Let Us Pray

  C. Thought to Remember

Display visual 4 from the visuals packet throughout this session. The visual is shown on page 149.

Introduction

A. Putting Music in the World

According to an old Jewish legend, God, after creating the world, called the angels in to look it over and evaluate it. Naturally they were excited by this bright new creation and spoke in complimentary terms about it. But one angel had one small reservation. "O mighty God," he said, "there is yet one thing lacking."

"And what might that be?" asked the Lord.

"Sir, there is no music to sound Your praise as Creator," came the reply.

So God gave the winds a voice, and the birds a song, and finally He gave man the power to sing.

Ever since then, the forces of nature, the animals, and mankind have used their musical powers to praise God.

Hannah and Mary were no exception. Hannah could sing her praises because she had received a son she had long prayed for, and Mary could sing because the child she would give birth to was God's long-promised Savior. Does not each one of us also have a song of praise and thanksgiving that we can raise to our Lord?

B. Lesson Background

Hannah, who lived about 1100 B. C., was carrying a heavy burden—she was childless. In that culture a married woman without children was an object of pity and shame. Hannah had prayed that God would allow her to have a child. On one occasion she was praying so earnestly in the tabernacle that old Eli, the high priest, thought that she was drunk. When he learned otherwise, he gave her his blessing and prayed that God would answer her prayer. Later a son, whom she named Samuel, was born to Hannah. She had promised to dedicate her child to the Lord, and so when the child was weaned, she brought him to Eli to be reared by the old priest. As she prepared to leave him, she praised God with a song, the first half of which forms the first part of our lesson text.

Mary's situation was quite different. She had been visited by an angel who informed her that she would bear a son whom she would call Jesus. This Son was destined to inherit the throne of David in a kingdom that would never end. Overwhelmed with joy, she journeyed to the hill country of Judah to visit her relative, Elisabeth, who was then six months pregnant with John. The song that Mary raised came during this visit.

I. Hannah's Song
(1 Samuel 2:1-5)

A. Rejoicing in the Lord (v. 1)

1. And Hannah prayed, and said, My heart rejoiceth in the LORD, mine horn is exalted in the LORD; my mouth is enlarged over mine enemies; because I rejoice in thy salvation.

When Samuel had been weaned, which in ancient Israel usually occurred when a child was between two and three years old, Hannah and her husband, Elkanah, brought him to the house of the Lord, that is, the tabernacle, which was then located at Shiloh. As a mother, she must have felt the pangs of sorrow at the thought of leaving her son. Yet she did not hesitate to raise her voice to God in praise for the great blessing He had bestowed on her.

This verse contains four elements. In the first section is Hannah's statement that she rejoiced in the Lord. God had answered her prayer and given her a son. In the concluding verse of chapter one she stated that she had "lent him to the Lord." She had not really lost her son but had given him to the Lord's service. Each year she returned to Shiloh to visit Samuel and bring a new coat she had made (1 Samuel 2:19)

Parents are sometimes reluctant to see their grown children go into Christian service because some are called into distant places, even overseas, to serve. Perhaps if more parents felt as Hannah did, more young people would be recruited for Christian service. Even though she missed her son, she found great comfort knowing that he was growing up in service to God.

Mine horn is exalted. In ancient Israel the horn was often a symbol of strength and power. The weakness Hannah had felt because she was childless was now gone, and she felt new strength in the Lord.

In the third element, Hannah enjoys her triumph over her enemies, which is the meaning of the rather unusual expression, *my mouth is enlarged over mine enemies*. The enemies may have been Elkanah's other wife, Peninnah, and her friends. Peninnah is described as Hannah's "adversary, who provoked her sore" because of her barrenness (1 Samuel 1:6). The *salvation* that Hannah mentions in the fourth element may refer to her being saved from the shame of being childless.

B. God's Holiness (v. 2)

2. There is none holy as the LORD: for there is none besides thee: neither is there any rock like our God.

Hannah's joy is based upon God's holiness. The attribute of holiness distinguished Jehovah God from all of the imaginary deities worshiped by the nations surrounding Israel. These gods might be characterized as having power or even showing mercy, but the quality of holiness was never ascribed to any of them. In fact, they were anything but holy!

There is none besides thee indicates Hannah's belief that Jehovah is the only true and living God. He is described as a *rock*. Moses first described God in this way (see Deuteronomy 32:4, 15), and it is quite possible that Hannah was familiar with

---

this use of the term. This expression indicates that God is strong and immovable, always available to His people in their time of need.

C. God's Knowledge (v. 3)

3. Talk no more so exceeding proudly; let not arrogancy come out of your mouth: for the LORD is a God of knowledge, and by him actions are weighed.

Because God is holy and human beings are not holy, none should be proud or boastful. There is always a temptation for us to compare ourselves with other persons and to feel justified and even proud of who and what we are. This is the wrong comparison, however; we should compare ourselves to God. When we do, we see there is no room for pride.

God is *a God of knowledge*. Other Scriptures ascribe to Him omniscience. He is all-knowing; He can weigh and properly evaluate all human actions.

D. God Humbles the Proud (vv. 4, 5)

4, 5. The bows of the mighty men are broken, and they that stumbled are girded with strength. They that were full have hired out themselves for bread; and they that were hungry ceased: so that the barren hath born seven; and she that hath many children is waxed feeble.

These two verses contain several examples of how God works in human affairs, often bringing dramatic reversals in the lives of men. *The bows of the mighty men* may actually refer to the men themselves, not the bows. Those who have waged war victoriously can never be certain that their good fortunes will continue. Napoleon and Hitler, for example, won great victories, and yet in the end both went down to crushing defeat. On the other hand, those who *stumbled*, suffered defeat, have been strengthened by God. Time and again history has demonstrated that the race is not always won by the swiftest, nor is a war always won by the strongest.

Other examples of reversal in fortune follow. The rich have lost their wealth and have been humbled by having to hire themselves out as day laborers. The poor, on the other hand, have *ceased* from their labors because they have gained wealth. With her own situation in mind, Hannah mentions the barren woman who became mother of seven. By contrast, the mother who had given birth to many children saw them all die, leaving her weak and helpless in her old age. All of these examples illustrate how God weighs actions in order to bring justice. Since her own situation is similar to these other cases, she feels that she has been vindicated and thus has a reason to rejoice.

How to Say It

ELKANAH.   *El*-kuh-nuh or El-*kay*-nuh.
PENINNAH.   Pe-*nin*-uh.
SHILOH.   *Shy*-lo.

TRUST AND TRIUMPH

"Simply Trusting Every Day" is a beautiful poem written by Edgar Stites. It was first published in a newspaper, a copy of which was given to the great nineteenth-century evangelist Dwight L. Moody. Mr. Moody was so impressed by the poem that he asked his song leader, Ira D. Sankey, to set it to music. Sankey did so, and thus the church has been blessed ever since by this hymn of practical faith.

Each stanza ends with the words, "Trusting Jesus, that is all." This confidence is what leads sinners to salvation and enables believers to triumph in their times of testing and trial.

Bearing the shame of being childless though married, Hannah continued year after year to worship and trust God. Fervently she prayed, "O, Lord . . . look on my affliction and give me a male child." In time, God answered her prayer, and she bore Samuel, who grew to become one of Israel's greatest leaders. Out of Hannah's trust came the triumph she desired.

Trust precedes triumph when we make request of the Lord. His answer may not always be what we expect or desire, but it will always be for our ultimate good.   —W. P.

II. Mary's Song
(Luke 1:46-55)

A. Praise to the Lord (vv. 46, 47)

The scene now changes, moving from the time of Samuel to just before the birth of Christ, a period of more than a thousand years. In the verses preceding the lesson text, Elisabeth had hailed Mary and pronounced a blessing upon her because of the child she was about to bear.

46, 47. And Mary said, My soul doth magnify the Lord, and my spirit hath rejoiced in God my Saviour.

The words of Luke 1:46-55 comprise Mary's beautiful poem known as the "Magnificat." It is so named because this is the first word of the poem in the Latin version. The word means "magnify," just as it is translated in most English versions.

We may note some resemblance between the song of Mary and that of Hannah. Since from early childhood children were taught the Scriptures, it would have been natural for Mary to remember some phrases from Hannah's song and to include them in her own song.

Mary's praise of God issues from her heart and soul for the great favor God has granted her. She also rejoices because God is her Savior. In the Old Testament, terms such as *Savior, save, and salvation* refer to God's deliverance of persons from sickness or physical danger. But the Old Testament also uses these terms in the sense of salvation from sin and a growing fellowship with God. We cannot say for sure what Mary had in mind when she used the term, but either or both would be appropriate here.

B. Reasons for Praise (vv. 48, 49)

48, 49. For he hath regarded the low estate of his handmaiden: for, behold, from henceforth all generations shall call me blessed. For he that is mighty hath done to me great things; and holy is his name.

Hath regarded the low estate. Mary was an obscure young woman who lived in a despised village of Galilee. Yet God had looked upon her and had seen fit to bless her in a way no woman had ever been blessed before. She knew that she had done nothing to merit this great privilege. Mary's attitude was one of humility and submissiveness before God, the same as when the angel appeared to her to announce that she was to become the mother of the Son of God.

From henceforth all generations shall call me blessed. How prophetic were her words! From the first century on, people have considered Mary especially happy and honored. Yet there is nothing in these words or any other passage in the New Testament that suggests that Mary should be given adoration that belongs only to God.

For he that is mighty hath done to me great things. By God's power He had chosen Mary to become the mother of the long-awaited Messiah. By His power she, a virgin, had become pregnant and would bear His Son. *Holy is his name.* In the same breath, Mary praised God's holiness, that quality that separates Him from all other beings. He is high and lifted up; He alone is worthy of all worship.

C. God's Mercy (v. 50)

50. And his mercy is on them that fear him from generation to generation.

God is not only holy; He is also merciful. Mary's words remind us of those in Psalm 103:17: "But the mercy of the Lord is from everlasting to everlasting upon them that fear him."

God's mercy reaches out to the whole human race. Every day we experience His mercy in countless ways that we don't even know about. His special mercy, however, is reserved for those *that fear him.* To fear God is not to cringe before Him in mortal dread; it is to recognize His holiness and purity and to reverence Him for what He is. Such awe and reverence naturally lead a person to devote his life in faithful service to God. The mercy that extends to God-fearing people is not limited to any one nation or racial group or to any one period in history. It is not bound by time or place.

D. God's Judgment (vv. 51-53)

51. He hath showed strength with his arm; he hath scattered the proud in the imagination of their hearts.

He hath showed strength with his arm. Here we have another instance in which an attribute of God is described in human terms. To say that God *showed strength with his arm* means that He has power to do what man would need an infinitely strong arm to accomplish. The arm of God can uphold and deliver, or bring down and drive out. In this section of Mary's song we see examples of both. *He hath scattered the proud.* The proud are especially the target of God's judgment for two reasons. First, in their arrogance they look to themselves for their strength rather than to God. Second, they lord it over their fellowmen, often oppressing them and taking advantage of them. Mary notes that God has punished these persons in the past and will continue to do so in the future.

52. He hath put down the mighty from their seats, and exalted them of low degree.

The term *mighty* is often used to designate kings, nobles, or conquerors. When Mary spoke these words, she may have had in mind specific rulers to whom this had happened. In the centuries that have passed since her time, many mighty rulers have been similarly *put down*.

In His teaching, Jesus emphasized the importance of humility. This emphasis stood in sharp contrast with the general attitudes of His day. A person who was humble was looked down upon and often taken advantage of. The proud who boasted to the world of their achievements were the ones who won great acclaim. Jesus rejected all of this, saying instead, "Whosoever shall exalt himself shall be abased; and he that shall humble himself shall be exalted" (Matthew 23:12). Indeed, God's choice of Mary herself is an example of His lifting the lowly to the heights of importance.

53. He hath filled the hungry with good things; and the rich he hath sent empty away.

The previous verses dealt with those who occupied high political positions. Now Mary speaks in terms of social and economic status. Beginning with the poor, she notes that God in His mercy has fed them. Of course, God does not always feed all of the poor. He does, however, provide the resources by which all may enjoy the necessities of life. Unfortunately, through men's greed and stupidity these resources are often wasted, and people, especially innocent little children, are made to suffer. When

famine does come, it should be noted that Christians take the lead in providing for the needy.

The rich, those who have acquired great wealth at the expense of others, will suffer quite a different fate. Even what they have will be taken away. God has a variety of tools to strike down the rich—a storm, ill health, a failing market, a political turn of events. We must keep in mind that full and complete justice is not always achieved in this life. In fact, the wicked often prosper while the faithful suffer. Yet in the final judgment, the demands of justice will be met in full.

E. Help for Israel (vv. 54, 55)

54, 55. He hath holpen his servant Israel, in remembrance of his mercy; as he spake to our fathers, to Abraham, and to his seed for ever.

Mary knew the history of her people, how time and again across the centuries God had intervened to help them. She also knew of the times that God had chastened them for their disobedience, but this was not the emphasis she was making at this point. God's help for Israel had not happened at random or without a purpose. He had blessed them because of the covenant He had made with Abraham two thousand years earlier. Time and again Israel had broken the covenant, but God had always been faithful to His word. The people of Israel had been blessed and they had become a great nation, but most importantly through them the whole world would be blessed (Genesis 12:1-3)

This last great promise was in the process of being fulfilled through Mary, who was chosen by God to give birth to the child who was to be the Savior of His people. His people were to be not only the physical descendants of Abraham, but also those of all races who would have a faith like Abraham's (Galatians 3:7-9). On this joyous note Mary ends her song of faith.

A PROMISE FULFILLED

Warsaw, Poland, is an amazing city. Near the end of World War II, as the German army re-

visual 4

treated from the Polish capital under the pressure of the advancing Soviet forces, Hitler put into effect a demented scheme. Bombing and artillery fire had already badly damaged the city. Now a total destruction was ordered. No building was to be spared. When it was over, much of Warsaw lay in ruins.

The amazing tenacity and resilience of the Polish people are seen in their promise that they would restore Warsaw as it had been. Taking the plans of the inner city that had been built long ago, they set about to preserve the heritage and history of their capital city. The decades that have passed since the end of the war have witnessed the fulfillment of the Poles' promise to themselves. A new and beautiful Warsaw has arisen from the ashes of the old city. Believing in God and in their right to be free, they are now in the process of rebuilding politically.

Mary spoke of God's promise to Abraham and his seed forever. That promise was now to be fulfilled in the birth of Jesus, who would be the Savior of His people. Through all the pain and loss of Israel, God remained faithful and fulfilled His word. He will also rebuild our shattered lives if we will believe and trust in His promises.   —W. P.

Conclusion
A. Revealing Songs

It is possible to tell a great deal about a nation by the songs it sings. In the *Iliad* the ancient Greeks sang of heroism to right a wrong, the kidnapping of Helen. In the *Odyssey*, they sang of a hero who was both clever and courageous, qualities that the Greeks admired. In the *Aeneid*, the Romans sang of a hero who gave status to their history; but they also recited the poems of Ovid with their sexual overtures, which spoke of a nation that was beginning to lose its respect for family ties that had made Rome strong.

Of all the ancient peoples, none had nobler songs than the Hebrews. Of course, we don't have all of their songs, but in the book of Psalms, and in the songs we have considered in the first four weeks of this study, we have a wealth of material that reveals their national character. They exalted God as their Savior, and they fell before Him in recognition of His holiness. Sometimes they complained because He allowed them to suffer, yet even then their complaints were to a God who they knew cared about them. These songs of Hannah and Mary are but two examples of the greatness of Israel's lyrical recognition of God.

What about the songs of our nation? A study would certainly reveal a wide range of tastes in the songs we have sung. We have sung patriotic songs in which the honor of flag and nation have been held high. Some of these we still sing, and we feel a tingle up our spines when we do. We have sung spirituals, whose haunting melodies and words tell of a faith that sees beyond immediate suffering. In earlier years we sang love songs, sometimes maudlin and even silly, but still songs that extolled love that was pure and faithful.

What about our contemporary songs? Set to a thunderous beat and raucous music, the lyrics are often incomprehensible. In many cases it is just as well that we don't understand the words, for they reflect a sickness of the soul. Illicit sex, drugs, perversions, and violence are the dominant themes. Even much of our contemporary religious music is shallow and repetitive, lacking in the qualities that produce awe and reverence in those who sing them and those who hear them.

Hebrew songs lived on to shape future generations, insuring that they would never forget that Jehovah was their God and Father. How will our songs shape us?

B. Let Us Pray

We thank You, Father, for giving us the songs of these two women, who sang out of their gratitude for the blessings You had given them. May these songs teach us reverence, humility, and gratitude as we consider Your holiness and the salvation You have provided through Your Son. In His name we pray. Amen.

C. Thought to Remember

"The Lord is my strength and my shield; my heart trusted in him, and I am helped: therefore my heart greatly rejoiceth; and with my song will I praise him." —Psalm 28:7

Home Daily Bible Readings

Monday, Dec. 16—Hannah Exulted in God's Salvation (1 Samuel 2:1-5)

Tuesday, Dec. 17—Hannah Praised the Lord (1 Samuel 2:6-10)

Wednesday, Dec. 18—Jesus' Birth Announced (Luke 1:26-38)

Thursday, Dec. 19—Elizabeth Blessed Mary (Luke 1:39-45)

Friday, Dec. 20—"My Soul Magnifies the Lord" (Luke 1:46-55)

Saturday, Dec. 21—The Lord Is Good (Psalm 34:1-10)

Sunday, Dec. 22—God Sent Redemption (Psalm 111)

Learning by Doing

This page contains an alternate lesson plan emphasizing learning activities. Classes desiring such student involvement will find these suggestions helpful.

Learning Goals

Lead students to accomplish the following as they participate in today's lesson:

1. Compare and contrast the situations of Hannah and Mary.

2. Discover how God can use ordinary physical experiences to accomplish His spiritual purposes.

3. Consider how God has helped them reach goals during 1991 and/or how they want Him to help them reach goals in the coming year.

Into the Lesson

Duplicate the chart below and give each student a copy. Ask them to check which of the listed experiences they have had in 1991 (column 1), in the last two years (column 2), and in their lifetimes (column 3).

To the left of each item, they should write an S or a P to indicate whether each was a *spiritual* or a *physical* victory.

Finally, they should check each item for which they could say, "This caused me to sing!"

When they are finished, tell them that our lesson is about two women who experienced a great blessing from God. It was both a spiritual and a physical victory, and it caused both of them to sing!

Item	1	2	3
Having a baby			
Reaching a goal			
Getting a job			
Buying a house			
Becoming a Christian			
Winning someone to Christ			
Overcoming a temptation			

Into the Word

Ask students if they can think of any Bible mothers whose sons were born surrounded by unusual circumstances. They will probably be able to name more than one, among them the main characters of today's Bible study, Hannah and Mary.

Ask volunteers to share as much of Hannah's and Mary's stories as they can remember. Fill in the facts of the Bible background after class members have spoken. (See 1 Samuel 1 and Luke 1:26-45.)

Next, have two class members read the lesson text aloud, one the passage from 1 Samuel and the other the passage from Luke. As the text is read, have class members look for similarities and differences in the two women and their situations. As class members identify these when the readings are concluded, list the similarities and differences on the chalkboard.

Ask class members to work in groups for the following assignment. (Each group should have between four and six members.) As a group, they are to assume the role of one of the following professions as they analyze today's texts:

Psychologist: Write a profile of Hannah and Mary, based on what you learn about them in this passage. What kind of person was each?

English professor: List the figures of speech each woman used in her song. What does each figure represent?

Bible commentator: Be ready to explain troublesome terms in the text. (You may want to provide study resources for this group.) Especially consider the following: *horn* (1 Samuel 2:1); *bows* (1 Samuel 2:4); *magnify* (Luke 1:46); *arm* (Luke 1:51).

Allow students to choose which of the roles they want to take. After about ten minutes for group work, ask them to share. If two groups did the same assignment, they can compare their conclusions during the sharing time.

Into Life

Look at the list of items the students considered in the lesson introduction. Ask which of these is physical and which is spiritual. Lead them to see that each can be a spiritual experience, a reason to praise and thank God. Ask students to think of goals they have reached in the last year. Have they thanked God for them? Ask them to think of spiritual goals they would like to set for the coming year. Would they be willing to share any of these with the whole class?

If so, these can become prayer requests for the class to consider. If there are several, you may want to write them on three-by-five cards and distribute them among class members who would promise to pray for the person and his or her goal in the coming weeks.

Let's Talk It Over

The questions on this page are designed to encourage review of the lesson Scriptures and to promote discussion of the lesson by the class. The answers provided are only discussion starters. Let your class talk it over from there.

1. Hannah's readiness to yield her son to a lifetime of service to God is one of the most striking facets of her story. Why are many Christian parents today reluctant to have their children enter vocational Christian service?

It seems clear that even if Hannah had not made her vow concerning the then-unborn Samuel, she still would have acknowledged that he belonged to the Lord. Christian parents need the regular reminder that their children belong to the Lord and that the Lord's will must be determinative in the children's future plans. Also, one of the considerations that causes parents to discourage their children from full-time Christian service is their concern for the children's financial security. Wise is the parent who understands that those persons who put God's kingdom first in their lives know the greatest security, in this life *and* the next. (See Matthew 6:25-34; Mark 10:29, 30.)

2. What are some examples of the way God puts down the proud and lifts up the humble?

The local, national, and international news on any given day will feature examples of proud people brought low: political dictators overthrown, criminals brought to justice, dishonest businessmen caught in their crooked schemes, and the like. Thankfully the news also focuses at times on quiet, self-sacrificing people who are blessed with honors or material rewards from their peers. We see this Biblical principle at work also in our place of employment, in our neighborhood, and in the church. It is well for us to be alert for these reminders of God's concern for and control over human affairs.

3. How can we increase our appreciation for the kind of woman Mary was?

Character studies are made of Abraham, Moses, Peter, John, and other Bible persons. A wealth of Biblical material exists on which to base such a study of Mary. Her humanness stands out in such verses as Luke 2:48, which records her questioning the boy Jesus' decision to stay behind in Jerusalem, and in John 2:3-5, where we see her apparently urging Jesus to perform a miracle at Cana. In this lesson's text and in Luke 1:26-38, which records her conversation with the angel Gabriel, we are made aware of

the strength of her faith and the completeness of her commitment. Her presence at the cross (John 19:25) and with the apostles in the days leading up to Pentecost (Acts 1:14) testifies to a steadfast allegiance to her son and God's son. A comprehensive study of the Biblical record of Mary's life would yield significant benefit to men and women alike today.

4. How can we cultivate the godly fear that is a requirement for receiving God's mercy and blessing?

The psalmist recorded God's admonition, "Be still, and know that I am God" (Psalm 46:10). The hectic nature of our lives makes it difficult for us to be quiet enough to think seriously about God. When we do, however, we experience awe in contemplating His greatness as Creator, His eternality, His holiness, and His love. We do not even need Scripture to begin such meditations, for it is awesome in itself to ponder how one could be great enough to create the universe, or how this one could have existed from eternity. The teaching of the Bible impresses us with its emphasis on how this Almighty One expects obedience from His creatures, but loves us and saves us in spite of our failure to render such obedience.

5. We sometimes hear complaints about contemporary religious music. What can we do about the objectionable aspects of it?

It may trouble us that some religious musicians seem intent on patterning their songs too closely after those in the popular field. The beat is much the same; the monotonous repetition of certain lines or phrases is there; and the attire and antics of the musicians in live performances are often similar. We need to ponder just what message is being communicated. Is the beat so strong that it overpowers the words? Are the words at best a weak presentation of truth, or at worst theologically inaccurate? Do the artists convey the sense of glorifying God or themselves? Without question there are some excellent contemporary religious songs and some truly dedicated Christian musicians. We should be discriminating in attending concerts and purchasing tapes to support what is spiritually sound.

A Hymn to the Creator

LESSON SCRIPTURE: Psalm 8.

PRINTED TEXT: Psalm 8.

Psalm 8

1 O LORD our Lord, how excellent is thy name in all the earth! who hast set thy glory above the heavens.

2 Out of the mouth of babes and sucklings hast thou ordained strength because of thine enemies, that thou mightest still the enemy and the avenger.

3 When I consider thy heavens, the work of thy fingers, the moon and the stars, which thou hast ordained;

4 What is man, that thou art mindful of him? and the son of man, that thou visitest him?

5 For thou hast made him a little lower than the angels, and hast crowned him with glory and honor.

6 Thou madest him to have dominion over the works of thy hands; thou hast put all things under his feet:

7 All sheep and oxen, yea, and the beasts of the field;

8 The fowl of the air, and the fish of the sea, and whatsoever passeth through the paths of the seas.

9 O LORD our Lord, how excellent is thy name in all the earth!

GOLDEN TEXT: O LORD our Lord, how excellent is thy name in all the earth!
—Psalm 8:9.

Songs and Prayers of the Bible

Unit 2: Songs From Festive Occasions

(Lessons 5-9)

Lesson Aims

After this lesson each student should:

1. Have a better understanding of the wonders of God's creation.

2. Be moved to praise God, who is seen through His works in nature.

3. Have a greater appreciation for his or her place in God's creation.

4. Be able to suggest one thing he or she can do to protect nature.

Lesson Outline

INTRODUCTION

    A. Man Is the Astronomer

    B. Lesson Background

I. GOD'S GLORY REVEALED IN NATURE (Psalm 8:1-3)

    A. God Praised (v. 1)

    B. Praise by Children (v. 2)

    C. Praise by the Heavens (v. 3)

II. GOD'S GLORY REVEALED IN MAN (Psalm 8:4-9)

    A. Man's Seeming Insignificance (v. 4)

    B. Man's Exalted Position (v. 5)

    God Made Us Too!

    C. Man's Dominion (vv. 6-8)

    Special Assignment

    D. Closing Refrain (v. 9)

CONCLUSION

    A. "A Little Lower Than the Angels"

    B. Exercising Dominion

    C. Let Us Pray

    D. Thought to Remember

Display visual 5 from the visuals packet and let it remain before your class throughout this session. The visual is shown on page 157.

Introduction

A. Man Is the Astronomer

A group of amateur astronomers was visiting an observatory. The director of the observatory discussed with them some of the things they would be seeing that night. He explained the huge size of some of the stars they would look at and some of the vast expanses of space that they could span through the telescope.

After taking her turn at the eyepiece of the telescope, one lady stepped back in great amazement and exclaimed, "Why, astronomically speaking, man is just a speck of dust, nothing!"

"Madam," responded the director, a man of devout Christian faith, "astronomically speaking, man is the astronomer!" Precisely. Man, specially endowed by the Creator, is the seeing, knowing observer. Like the ancient psalmist, we may stand in breathless wonder as we consider the vastness of the physical universe; yet a million suns a million light years away are nothing compared to a human being, who is made in God's own image.

B. Lesson Background

This, the fifth lesson of the quarter, begins Unit 2, which deals with songs from festive occasions. Today's lesson is a hymn of praise to the Creator. Other lessons in this unit include a song for those who worship in the temple, a hymn to the Redeemer, lyrics to love and marriage, and a song of harvest—all raised in celebration of happy occasions.

The superscription on Psalm 8 identifies it as a psalm of David. It is inscribed "To the chief Musician upon Gittith." "Gittith" is believed to have been the instrument upon which the accompaniment was to be played for the singing of the psalm. A psalm of praise and thanksgiving, it was probably sung by the congregation in public worship. Some have referred to this psalm as the astronomer's song, but actually the real center of focus is man, not the starry heavens. The writer of the psalm stands in amazement as he contemplates the vast expanse of night sky and then realizes that in the eyes of God man is more important. In his amazement he then does the only thing he can do—lift his voice in praise of the Lord.

I. God's Glory Revealed in Nature (Psalm 8:1-3)

A. God Praised (v. 1)

1. O LORD our LORD, how excellent is thy name in all the earth! who hast set thy glory above the heavens.

The psalmist opens and closes this psalm with a refrain that exalts God through the universe He has created. God is addressed by His personal name, Jehovah or Yahweh, which is represented by the first *Lord* of this verse. This was the name by which God revealed himself to Moses at the burning bush (Exodus 3:13, 14). By the name of Jehovah God revealed himself to Abraham, Isaac, and Jacob, and by this name God called out a special people and entered into a covenant relationship with them. Thus, when the psalmist addresses Him, it is as the covenant God who is also the Creator.

The New English Bible translates the opening of this psalm, "O Lord our sovereign, how glorious is thy name in all the earth." God is thus recognized as the ruler, not only of man but of the earth. The peaks of the highest mountains and the depth of the deepest sea attest to His excellence. But His glory extends beyond this globe; it extends beyond the most distant star into the far reaches of space that even our most powerful telescope has not penetrated.

These awesome wonders of the physical universe lead some to belief in the Creator. Others, however, observe these same wonders and see nothing but blind matter and energy and the laws that govern their interactions. We must recognize that some persons have so hardened their hearts (often under the guise of sophistication) that they cannot see the most obvious lessons from nature.

B. Praise by Children (v. 2)

2. Out of the mouth of babes and sucklings hast thou ordained strength because of thine enemies, that thou mightest still the enemy and the avenger.

Babes. This word is used of young children rather than infants. Jeremiah used it to refer to children old enough to play in the streets (Jeremiah 6:11). *Sucklings* refers to younger children, those not yet weaned but capable of the beginnings of speech. It should be noted that children were not weaned as young then as they are now. David may have used these terms figuratively to refer to the simple, the unlearned. These have often borne testimony to the glory of the Lord when the scholars and the leaders have rejected Him. We think of when Jesus cleansed the temple after the triumphal entry. The children cried "Hosanna" while the religious leaders rejected Him (Matthew 21:15, 16). In responding to the criticisms of the chief priests and scribes, Jesus quoted Psalm 8:2.

God has never had to depend upon the wisdom or strength of men to advance His cause. Indeed, He has often used the weak to confound His enemies. Paul wrote to this point: "God hath chosen the foolish things of the world to confound the wise; and God hath chosen the weak things of the world to confound the things which are mighty" (1 Corinthians 1:27).

C. Praise by the Heavens (v. 3)

3. When I consider thy heavens, the work of thy fingers, the moon and the stars, which thou hast ordained.

For centuries men have gazed heavenward on a clear night and felt the wonder and awe of the diamond-studded sky. As children, surely we all did this. How long, though, has it been since you have looked at the stars and contemplated their silent message? The psalmist is saying "whenever I consider" or "as often as I consider." This seems to suggest not a one-time occurrence but a regular practice.

As we have developed spacecraft and more sophisticated instruments, we have been able to probe deeper into space and in greater detail. Everything that we have recently learned only serves to intensify our sense of awe as we look heavenward. Our universe is much larger than we earlier thought and it is much more intricately designed. Only the God revealed in the Scriptures could have designed and created such a universe.

II. God's Glory Revealed in Man (Psalm 8:4-9)

A. Man's Seeming Insignificance (v. 4)

4. What is man, that thou art mindful of him? and the son of man, that thou visitest him?

What is man, that thou art mindful of him? When we contemplate the vast heavens bejewelled with a million points of light or stand and watch the shimmering rays of the moon reflecting from the waters of a lake, we can scarcely avoid being awed by the beauty and the immensity of what we see. At the same time, even if we give it a brief thought, we can't avoid realizing how small and how finite we are. This was exactly the feeling that the psalmist expressed in this verse.

Two different words are used for man in this verse. The fist expresses the idea of man's mortality, a frail and limited creature, a mere speck of dust in the vast universe and a tiny blip against the background of eternity. The second word literally means the "son of Adam," the human race. This would seem to emphasize that man is a created being made from the dust of the earth. It would also suggest that he is heir to all the frailties and foibles of Adam's fallen nature.

Man is only one of the thousands of creatures living on a rather small planet, revolving around a medium-sized star, our sun, in the Milky Way galaxy, only one of countless galaxies. If man is such an insignificant part of the creation, why should the almighty God, the creator of all things, be concerned about him? The psalmist does not answer the question. In fact, it is not a question to be answered. It is an expression of wonder and awe that the Creator really does care about human beings.

The son of man, that thou visitest him. This is a restatement of the thought in the first part of the verse, a common feature of Hebrew poetry. The "visitation" of God is an expression of the fact that He is "mindful" of man. Some see a reference here to God's "visiting" mankind in the person of His only begotten Son, Jesus, who was "made flesh, and dwelt among us" (John 1:14).

B. Man's Exalted Position (v. 5)

5. For thou hast made him a little lower than the angels, and hast crowned him with glory and honor.

In the few words of this verse, David states man's exalted position. Such a statement can be meaningful only when a comparison is made to something or someone else. A baseball is quite small when compared to the earth, but quite large when compared to an atom. The writer begins his comparison with an absolute standard—God himself.

Thou hast made him a little lower than the angels. The word that is translated *angels* is *elohim,* which is ordinarily translated "God." Most modern versions so translate it. Perhaps the meaning could be expressed this way: "Man is a little less than divine." This would be in harmony with the account of man's creation. "God created man in his own image, in the image of God created he him" (Genesis 1:27). Some would have us believe that man is but another animal, the end product of an evolutionary process. But man is different from every other earthly creature *by nature.* The difference between man and animals is not a matter of degree; it is a difference in *kind.* Man alone is created in God's image.

Crowned him with glory and honor. Man has been honored by God in several ways. First, the record of man's creation shows that he was made in the image and likeness of God and given rule over all God's creation. Man has also been honored by being given freedom of will. Man is free, free to obey God or free to rebel against Him. Unfortunately, that freedom may be and often has been abused with resulting disaster. Man has been greatly honored in another sense. When God chose to send His Son into the world, He sent Him not as an animal nor as an angel but as a man.

Because God has crowned man with glory and honor, man has no reason to feel proud or boastful. At the very heart of the human predicament is human arrogance. When we realize that all that we have and all that we are comes from God, there is no room for this attitude.

At the same time, because God has crowned man with glory and honor, he is endowed with a dignity and worth that transcends the dignity

and worth of either the starry heavens or members of the animal kingdom. For this reason, we as Christians place a high value on human life, whether it be an unborn fetus, a growing teenager, a mature adult, or an octogenarian. We must protect the dignity of life at every stage. We ought to insist that every human being have adequate food, shelter, clothing, and access to medical care. That is a tall order for a world that is beset by sin in every form, but it ought to be our goal, nevertheless.

GOD MADE US TOO!

The new mother proudly displayed her baby girl. "Isn't she beautiful," the baby's adoring grandmother proclaimed. "Such lovely eyes! Perfect skin—and look at that smile! I think she is the most wonderful little girl in the world!" Words couldn't fully express the delight of the baby's parents and grandparents as this tiny, newborn creation of almighty God.

The wonders of procreation, development, birth, and growth of a human child defy description. In just a few years the totally dependent baby becomes capable of discovering the unlimited possibilities placed into us by our Creator. Communication, social interaction, dreaming, writing, invention—all the multiplicity of skills man knows can be that child's.

In recent years the creativity of man has multiplied our knowledge and potential. We are "fearfully and wonderfully made" (Psalm 139:14). It is more than accident or evolutionary chance. David wrote of God's creation, "For thou hast made him a little lower than the angels, and hast crowned him with glory and honor."

We are made in God's image to think and act with the divine potential He breathed into us in the beginning. Let us sing of God's greatness and give Him glory for making us so we are able to communicate with our Maker.   —W. P.

C. Man's Dominion (vv. 6-8)

6. Thou madest him to have dominion over the works of thy hands; thou hast put all things under his feet.

As the Creator of the universe, God has complete sovereignty over it. He has chosen, however, to delegate some of that responsibility to man. When God created man, He placed him in the Garden of Eden and told him to "be fruitful and multiply, and replenish the earth" (Genesis 1:28). Adam was to "dress" the garden and "keep" it (Genesis 2:15). Sadly, man has not always lived up to this responsibility. He has used his dominion to ravage and waste the resources God put here. He has exploited nature with little regard for future generations. Some of the drastic results of man's actions may not wait until the next generation. At the rate we are fowling the air, the water, and the soil, we ourselves may have to pay some of that price.

7, 8. All sheep and oxen, yea, and the beasts of the field; the fowl of the air, and the fish of the sea, and whatsoever passeth through the paths of the seas.

Man has been given dominion over all living creatures, even though many are stronger or swifter than he. Man has succeeded in mastering the animals because he is far more intelligent than any animal. Even the most intelligent animal has the intelligence of only a normal three-year-old human being. Some animals, such as elephants, horses, and camels, man has tamed and used to lighten his work. Others he has domesticated, using them for food and clothing—cattle, sheep, hogs, and chickens. Still others he has brought to extinction or near extinction either by hunting or by destroying their habitat. The mighty elephant, for example, killed by the hundreds each year for its ivory tusks, is now among the endangered species. Other animals and birds have disappeared forever. Obviously, the dominion that God has given man over other living creatures entails moral responsibility. When man ruthlessly slaughters any of them, so as to jeopardize the very existence of any species, he abuses the dominion given to him.

SPECIAL ASSIGNMENT

"Jim, I have a very special assignment for you." Mr. Carson's words sounded impressive, so Jim stopped shooting baskets and came over to where his dad was standing. As he did so he thought to himself, "This is something new."

"Son," continued Mr. Carson, "I believe you can handle this job. The well-being of all our family depend on it." That did sound important. "I have provided everything you need to do the task, and I will trust you completely. If you do a good job, I'll have a reward for you on your next birthday that you will enjoy. If you fail, I will be disappointed; but I know you can do it."

Mr. Carson's words made Jim stand a little taller than his five feet five inches and his thirteen years really demanded. There was a determined set to his walk as he and his dad strode toward the barn. There in the lot it lay! The several cords of firewood needed splitting and stacking before they could be used to supply the Carsons' fuel for the winter. Jim stopped, a little stunned, and then said, "OK, Dad, I can do it, and I'll be looking for the surprise on my birthday. Jim fulfilled his dad's assignment, and a new bicycle was his on his next birthday.

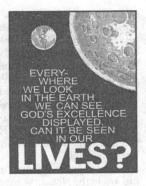

God has given man a special assignment—that of ruling over all of God's created earth. If man does the job well, the created order yields incredible blessings for him. Abuse of that dominion, however, brings disappointment to God and the loss of blessings.
—W. P.

D. Closing Refrain (v. 9)

9. O Lord our Lord, how excellent is thy name in all the earth!

The psalmist has stood in awe as he viewed the starry heavens. He has contemplated the glory and honor with which God has crowned man. Yet God is greater than all His creation. Appropriately, then, the psalmist closes with the refrain that once more exalts the excellence of God's name.

Conclusion

A. "A Little Lower Than the Angels"

Whether the human race is a little lower than the angels or "but little lower than God," as the *American Standard Version* translates verse 5, does not alter the point that the writer is making. The point is that man is more important than the heavenly bodies floating in outer space, or our own physical globe, or the animals that inhabit it along with us. Man is the centerpiece of God's creation. Only after God created man and viewed everything He had made was creation described as "very good" (Genesis 1:31). A picture in a children's home recently caught my eye. It showed a little crippled youngster dressed in tattered clothing and supporting himself on a crutch. Obviously life had not dealt gently with him in his few short years. Yet there was a gleam in his eyes and a smile on his face. The caption read, "I'm worth something! God ain't made no junk!"

Since man is the crowning glory of God's creation, certain implications logically follow. Surely, one of the most important is that every human being deserves concern and respect from other human beings. As we look around us we see that many persons' evaluations of the worth of others are based instead on carnal considerations. Most notable, perhaps, is the tendency to judge others on the basis of their perceived economic worth. For example, a graduate of a prestigious university would be considered worth more than an illiterate dweller in a city ghetto. A person who has acquired wealth, whether by inheritance, good luck, illegal means, or hard work is considered worth more than one who is impoverished.

Other factors influence the evaluation of people's worth. National bias is one of these. Members of an advanced, civilized nation may think themselves more important than natives of southern Patagonia, or almost any other place, for that matter. Race is also a matter that we take into consideration. Many persons are more likely to trust those of their own race than members of another race.

Sex has been the basis of determining human worth also. We think of how women have been oppressed across the centuries. In many societies men have looked upon women as property or playthings to be used as they chose. In war, women were the helpless prizes who were ravished or carried off as slaves.

In countless other ways people have been guilty of debasing other members of the human race. Only recently have our media called to our attention the problem of child abuse. We have been appalled both by its brutality and by its wide extent. It has been discovered in neighborhoods of all economic classes. Appallingly, it often comes from the hands of parents and family members who by law and by nature ought to work hardest to protect little children. As Christians we ought to work for laws that will have the effect of reducing child abuse. We need to provide care for bruised children and battered wives. And we need to find ways to minister to the villains as well as the victims.

Perhaps the worst abuse of all is abortion. A helpless child is murdered even before it has a chance to draw its first breath. No amount of clever sophistry can change the fact that an unborn fetus bears the image of God just as much as a child or a mature adult. What is even worse is that a million or more unborn babies are sacrificed every year in America upon the altar of personal convenience. How long will God withhold His judgment upon a nation that so disregards the crown of His creation, only "a little lower than the angels"?

B. Exercising Dominion

God gave man dominion over His works, including the animals of the field, the birds of the air, and fish of the sea. All of these creatures were put here for man to use, but man's wanton and thoughtless wastefulness has caused some animals to become extinct and has brought many others to the verge of extinction.

In many cases there is little that we can do to change these destructive practices. We can, however, work for and obey laws that are designed to protect our environment. We can find ways to recycle many of the things we now throw away, which clutter up our landscape and fill up our waste disposal systems. We can avoid those practices that poison our atmosphere, pollute our water supplies, and erode our tillable soil. And finally, we can work to help others understand the importance of these issues.

Having been given dominion over the world and everything in it, man sustains a relationship and responsibility to the world. He is obligated to care for the physical world, its resources and life forms, so that future generations may receive the blessings from them that God intended. To do less is to be faithless in executing the dominion that God has entrusted to him.

C. Let Us Pray

O Lord, how excellent is Your name in all the earth! Teach us to honor Your name by honoring the world You have created. Teach us to walk with dignity, respecting the dignity of others, because we all bear Your image. Teach us also to walk with humility, aware of our weaknesses. In our Master's name we pray. Amen.

D. Thought to Remember

Everywhere we look in the earth we can see God's excellence displayed. Can it be seen in our lives?

Home Daily Bible Readings

Monday, Dec. 23—The Birth of Jesus (Luke 2:1-7)

Tuesday, Dec. 24—Shepherds and Angels (Luke 2:8-20)

Wednesday, Dec. 25—The Visit of the Wise Men (Matthew 2:1-12)

Thursday, Dec. 26—Presentation in the Temple (Luke 2:21-38)

Friday, Dec. 27—"The Lord God Comes" (Isaiah 40:1-11)

Saturday, Dec. 28—Praise God All Creation (Psalm 148)

Sunday, Dec. 29—Scripture Fulfilled (Luke 4:16-21)

Learning by Doing

This page contains an alternate lesson plan emphasizing learning activities. Classes desiring such student involvement will find these suggestions helpful.

Learning Goals

As students participate in today's lesson, lead them to:

1. Summarize the relationship between man and nature, as it is taught in Psalm 8.

2. Apply this summary to some popular misconceptions that are held by some persons in our society.

Into the Lesson

Conduct an informal debate to begin today's class session. One half of the class should think of reasons to support this statement: "Man is at the center of life on earth." The other should think of reasons to support, "God is at the center of life on earth."

If your class is not any larger than fifteen or twenty, divide into two groups, one group to discuss each sentence. If the class is larger, divide the class into several groups. One-half of the groups can discuss one sentence and the other half the other.

After five or six minutes, allow the class to conduct a discussion "point-counterpoint" style. After several minutes of this debate, tell the class that there is a measure of truth in each statement, and that today's text will show how the two ideas harmonize.

Into the Word

Point out to students that today's session begins the second unit in this quarter's study of Bible songs and prayers. This unit is different from the first in that these texts are not associated with a particular person or familiar Bible story as the first ones were.

Instead, these texts, called "Songs From Festive Occasions," may have been sung or repeated again and again by God's people as they praised Him for His goodness.

The writer of the first lesson plan has outlined today's text under two headings: "God's Glory Revealed in Nature" and "God's Glory Revealed in Man." Ask students if they can think of examples in which people have tended to emphasize man at the expense of nature or nature at the expense of man. (Don't spend too much time on this, because it relates to the suggested "Into Life" activity.)

Tell students that their assignment today is to decide on a Biblical reconciliation of the two extremes. How, according to God and according to this text, are man and nature to relate to each other?

Read Psalm 8 slowly and dramatically as students listen. Then divide the students into the same groups that met for the opening activity. Have each group write one sentence that summarizes what this text teaches about man and nature.

After several minutes, let the groups read their sentences. Allow students to use verses from Psalm 8 to defend or sharpen the sentences that are read.

Into Life

Print or type each of the following sentences on a separate slip of paper. Make enough slips of paper so that every two or three members of your class can have one. Distribute the slips among the students, and ask every student without a piece of paper to group himself with someone who does have one. The groups formed should have an equal number of students. Students are to read the statement on their slip and decide how to refute it using truths from Psalm 8. In some cases other Scriptures may also apply to the sentences, but encourage the class members to concentrate especially on the teaching of today's text.

1. All this environment hullabaloo is just so much hype. God did give us the world to *use*, didn't he?

2. Of course, I wouldn't wish those people any harm; but they are so *different* from us. They just haven't been raised the way my children have, and I'm not sure I want my family around them.

3. The universe is so vast, and man is simply an insignificant speck, an accident of creation, a meaningless blip in the expanse of the heavens.

4. The drives and urges within our bodies are natural and good, given to us for our enjoyment. We can be thankful that we have the ability to satisfy our sex drive and other appetites in so many creative ways. Other animals on earth cannot be so creative.

5. Every woman has the right to control her own destiny, her own body, her own future. It is a profound tragedy when an unwanted pregnancy occurs, but the resolution of this tragedy should be the woman's choice alone.

Let's Talk It Over

The questions on this page are designed to encourage review of the lesson Scriptures and to promote discussion of the lesson by the class. The answers provided are only discussion starters. Let your class talk it over from there.

1. Some intelligent people find no evidence of God's handiwork when they look out upon the universe. Why should that be no hindrance to our faith?

Several years ago a Russian cosmonaut made much of the fact that he did not see God when he ventured out into the vastness of space. It was obvious that he had been blinded to the reality of God by having grown up in a system that was godless and materialistic. Our society is not so pervaded by godlessness, but many individuals within it have chosen to view the universe without reference to God. Whether we call it blindness or nearsightedness, they refuse to acknowledge that "the invisible things of [God] from the creation of the world are clearly seen . . . so that they are without excuse" (Romans 1:20). They may be intelligent and learned, but they have chosen to be fools where God is concerned (see Romans 1:21, 22).

2. To "consider the heavens" seems a legitimate aspect of a well-rounded Christian education. How can the church incorporate instruction about the physical universe in its overall teaching program?

Perhaps we simply need to hold some Bible classes or informal worship services under an evening sky! Excessive study would not be required for a teacher or preacher to point out constellations, stars, and planets and to call attention to the work of the Master Designer. Such an emphasis would fit in well with men's and women's retreats or with young people's camping programs. There are also special speakers available who can use visual aids to make us more aware of God's handiwork in the heavens. If we neglect this area of knowledge in the church, we miss out on teaching that can be very impressive and inspiring.

3. The natural world contains many lessons and illustrations of spiritual truth. How can we incorporate these into our church's program of Biblical teaching?

Since the Bible refers to lessons from nature (see Proverbs 6:6-8; 30:24-31; Matthew 6:25-34; John 15:1-8), we will encounter them in the course of a normal Bible study. Trees and other plants, animals, birds, and insects, however, are worthy of something more than a casual look. Why not encourage teachers and speakers in our Christian camps to utilize object lessons from the plant and animal life at hand? Also, cannot the Sunday-school display animals, fish, plants, insects, etc. within the classrooms, and use these in connection with Biblical instruction?

4. What can Christians do to help stop child abuse?

When we remember the tender regard Jesus had toward children and the grave warning He uttered concerning any who would mistreat them (Matthew 18:1-6; 19:13-15), we can see that Jesus' followers should be in the forefront of the campaign against child abuse. Because of its various teaching programs for children, the church may have contact with families in which abuse is taking place. We must be alert to this, prompt to report it to the proper authorities, and prepared to minister to the abusers as well as the abused. It may be said also that we oppose child abuse when we promote Christian values in the home. Since alcoholic beverages often play a role in child abuse, their elimination from the home can be a positive step. The establishing of sound communication in the home can help prevent the misunderstandings and frustrations that escalate into abuse.

5. What can Christians do to help protect our environment?

It may seem a small thing, but Christians should refrain from being the same kind of careless litterbugs as some of their non-Christian neighbors. There is something particularly distressing about seeing a Christian family tossing out soft drink cans and candy wrappers from the windows of their moving automobile. Since "The earth is the Lord's, and the fulness thereof" (Psalm 24:1), and we are the Lord's servants, we should exhibit an exemplary concern for preservation of the earth. After we have "cleaned up our own act," we should be ready to lend our support in opposing specific instances in which our environment is being polluted and destroyed.

A Song for Temple Visitors

LESSON SCRIPTURE: Psalm 84.

PRINTED TEXT: Psalm 84.

Psalm 84

1 How amiable are thy tabernacles, O LORD of hosts!

2 My soul longeth, yea, even fainteth for the courts of the LORD: my heart and my flesh crieth out for the living God.

3 Yea, the sparrow hath found a house, and the swallow a nest for herself, where she may lay her young, even thine altars, O LORD of hosts, my King, and my God.

4 Blessed are they that dwell in thy house: they will be still praising thee. Selah.

5 Blessed is the man whose strength is in thee; in whose heart are the ways of them.

6 Who passing through the valley of Baca make it a well; the rain also filleth the pools.

7 They go from strength to strength, every one of them in Zion appeareth before God.

8 O LORD God of hosts, hear my prayer: give ear, O God of Jacob. Selah.

9 Behold, O God our shield, and look upon the face of thine anointed.

10 For a day in thy courts is better than a thousand. I had rather be a doorkeeper in the house of my God, than to dwell in the tents of wickedness.

11 For the LORD God is a sun and shield: the LORD will give grace and glory: no good thing will he withhold from them that walk uprightly.

12 O LORD of hosts, blessed is the man that trusteth in thee.

GOLDEN TEXT: My soul longeth, yea, even fainteth for the courts of the LORD: my heart and my flesh crieth out for the living God.—Psalm 84:2.

Lesson Aims

After this lesson, the students should:

1. Sense the psalmist's overwhelming joy in worshiping in the temple at Jerusalem.

2. Experience a similar joy in the fellowship and worship of the church.

3. Make worship of God a regular and significant part of their lives.

Lesson Outline

INTRODUCTION
    A. Blankets or No Blankets
    B. Lesson Background
  I. THE HOUSE OF GOD (Psalm 84:1-4)
    A. A Place of Joy (v. 1)
    B. A Place Longed For (v. 2)
    C. A Sanctuary for Birds (v. 3)
    D. A Sanctuary for People (v. 4)
       The Right Location
 II. FINDING STRENGTH IN GOD (Psalm 84:5-8)
    A. A Heart Set on God (v. 5)
    B. Strength for Difficult Times (vv. 6, 7)
    C. Supplication (v. 8)
III. TRUSTING IN GOD (Psalm 84:9-12)
    A. Prayer for Israel's Leader (v. 9)
    B. Joy in Serving God (v. 10)
       A Better Choice
    C. Blessings From God (vv. 11, 12)
CONCLUSION
    A. Patterns of Worship
    B. When the Service Begins
    C. Let Us Pray
    D. Thought to Remember

Display visual 6 from the visuals packet and let it remain before the class throughout this session. The visual is shown on page 165.

Introduction

A. Blankets or No Blankets

An aged, devout Christian, whom everyone knew as "Aunt" Thelma, loved the Lord and never missed an opportunity to praise Him. Occasionally during worship services her exclamations of praise became rather loud, and some of the members began to complain to the minister. The minister explained the situation to Aunt Thelma, who agreed to be a bit more restrained in her "Praise the Lords." But try as she might, Aunt Thelma just couldn't keep her enthusiasm to herself when she agreed with some statement in the preacher's sermon.

Finally the preacher made an offer to her that he thought would solve the problem. He knew that the dear old lady wanted to buy two warm blankets for her bed but didn't have the money to purchase them. He promised to buy them for her if she would keep quiet during the worship service. With winter coming on she needed the blankets and agreed to his offer.

For several weeks Aunt Thelma kept her part of the bargain. Then one Sunday the preacher brought a sermon on the joys and blessings of Heaven. This was just too much, and in a voice that everyone heard, she cried out, "Blankets or no blankets, praise the Lord. I've got my faith to keep me warm."

No doubt the psalmist who wrote Psalm 84 had a similar feeling when he contemplated worship in the temple of the Lord.

B. Lesson Background

According to the superscription, Psalm 84 was "for the sons of Korah." The Korahites were singers in the temple (2 Chronicles 20:19). Members of the tribe of Levi, they were descendants of the infamous Korah, who led a rebellion against Moses and Aaron while the Israelites were in the wilderness. In addition to serving as musicians in the temple, they also were gatekeepers and bakers for the sanctuary (1 Chronicles 9:19, 31; 26:1, 19). Whether this psalm was written by one of the Korahites or written for them is a matter of conjecture.

Some have suggested that Psalm 84 was written while the writer was exiled from Jerusalem and unable to worship at the temple. The thoughts expressed, therefore, would have been his precious memories of times past when he had experienced the joy of worship in God's house. It seems better, however, to regard this as one of the songs sung by pilgrims to Jerusalem, both on their way to the temple and upon their arrival. The psalm breathes an air of joy, confidence, and a longing to be in God's presence, which has found fulfillment.

I. The House of God
(Psalm 84:1-4)

A. A Place of Joy (v. 1)

1. How amiable are thy tabernacles, O LORD of hosts!

How amiable. "How lovely; how beautiful!" *Are thy tabernacles.* This word is plural in form but is single in meaning and may be translated "dwelling." To express greatness or majesty, the Hebrews often used the plural. Understood in this manner, the statement lends emphasis to the majestic nature of God's dwelling. Thus the *New International Version* translates this "How lovely is your dwelling place." The sight of the beautiful temple of God was thrilling to the psalmist.

The psalmist was not merely admiring the physical beauty of God's temple. He had in mind also the deep joy he felt in meeting God there through worship. Speaking of the temple as a dwelling place, he was not suggesting that God actually lived there. Instead, he considered the tabernacle amiable or lovely because the acts of worship that brought him into a proper relationship with God were performed there.

As Christians, we recognize that God does not actually dwell in the church buildings that we erect to His honor. At the same time, we do regard these buildings as helpful in providing a place where we can meet as the body of Christ to worship God and find rest for our souls. We also find our church buildings amiable because there we meet our friends, receiving from them loving support and encouragement as we strive to live the Christian life.

B. A Place Longed For (v. 2)

2. My soul longeth, yea, even fainteth for the courts of the LORD: my heart and my flesh crieth out for the living God.

Absence does not always make the heart grow fonder, but in this case absence made the heart of the psalmist long for the courts of the Lord. So intense was his desire to be there that it seemed that his very soul would faint. Someone has suggested that he suffered holy homesickness to be in God's presence. The psalmist would have trouble identifying with those modern church members who look for almost any excuse to be absent from the worship services in God's house. His *heart* knew no greater love than the love for God, and to appear before Him was his greatest joy. Often our flesh leads us into the wrong actions, but for the writer even his *flesh* cried out for the living God.

C. A Sanctuary for Birds (v. 3)

3. Yea, the sparrow hath found a house, and the swallow a nest for herself, where she may lay her young, even thine altars, O LORD of hosts, my King, and my God.

The sparrow is probably the common house sparrow that still is found in Palestine. The swallow is different from the sparrow. It is readily recognized by its swift, darting flight. Several

How to Say It

ABSALOM.   *Ab*-suh-lum.
BACA.   *Bay*-ka.
KORAH.   *Ko*-ra.
KORAHITES.   *Ko*-ra-ites.
SELAH (Hebrew).   *See*-luh.

species of this bird are still found in Palestine, where it nests in clefts in the rocks and in niches in houses and mosques.

The psalmist found himself almost envying these birds because they had found a home in the house of God. They built their nests, laid their eggs, and raised their young within the temple grounds and buildings. *Thine altars* is a figure referring to the sacred place set apart for the living God. The actual altars—the altar of sacrifice and the altar of incense—were in constant use and so would hardly have provided a safe place for the birds to build their nests.

O Lord of hosts. This expression is used nearly three hundred times in the Old Testament. It often refers to God in a military context and indicates his power and might.

D. A Sanctuary for People (v. 4)

4. Blessed are they that dwell in thy house: they will be still praising thee. Selah.

Certain of the priests and others who ministered about the holy things in the temple lived in the chambers that were a part of the temple complex. To these persons the psalmist's thoughts now turn. The worshipers came, they enjoyed the blessing of being in God's presence, but soon they had to leave His sanctuary and return to their own homes. These others, however, were privileged to remain, to praise God still, and to enjoy the experience of worshiping Him continually. In the psalmist's estimation, they were privileged and blessed indeed.

Selah. This word, appearing here and after verse 8, divides the psalm into three equal parts of four verses each. It seems certain that this term is a musical or liturgical sign of some kind, but its precise meaning is not known. It means "to lift up." This has led some to conjecture that it was an instruction for the musicians to play louder.

THE RIGHT LOCATION

Several large landowners in Jamaica were having serious problems raising cattle. The grass, though green and lush, apparently lacked some nutrients essential for good cattle production.

One of the owners decided to find out what could be done to improve the situation. He wanted better cattle for greater profits. He sent samples of his soil, grass, water, and feeding procedures to experts in England, feeling certain that some fertilizers, properly applied, could change the food value of his pastures.

After several weeks the owner received the report from the experts. Their opening comment was puzzling. "Sir," it read, "we suggest you quit raising cattle and start producing aeroplanes." The soil analysis contained the explanation. Some of the richest bauxite ore in the world lay under his pasture lands. Refined, it would produce aluminum. For years he had been in the right location, but he had received none of the potential benefits of being there.

The right place to be to praise and worship God is in His house with His people. Many attend the services of the church who never know all the blessings that are there for them to possess. They need to look, listen, and know that by accepting Jesus as their Savior and Lord, all they will ever need can be theirs.   —W. P.

II. Finding Strength in God
(Psalm 84:5-8)

A. A Heart Set on God (v. 5)

5. Blessed is the man whose strength is in thee; in whose heart are the ways of them.

Some persons base their security on their physical prowess, or material possessions, or social position. The person who truly is strong, however, is the godly person. David declared, "The God of Israel is he that giveth strength and power unto his people" (Psalm 68:35).

The latter part of this verse is a bit obscure and is variously translated. The *New International Version* reads, "who have set their hearts on pilgrimage." This suggests that those who go on a pilgrimage to Zion to worship God will be blessed. Devout Israelites made a pilgrimage to Jerusalem two or three times a year to worship in the temple. Those who undertook these arduous journeys did so with joy in their hearts and with the confident expectation that God would sustain them on their journey.

B. Strength for Difficult Times (vv. 6, 7)

6. Who passing through the valley of Baca make it a well; the rain also filleth the pools.

The pilgrimage to Jerusalem was not an easy trip. For those coming from any distance, it meant days of plodding along dusty roads, sleeping out on the ground, and eating plain meals from the rations that could be carried along with them. Yet for the true believers these were but minor inconveniences compared to the joys that would be theirs when they reached the

house of God. This idea is expressed in the expression the *valley of Baca*. A place by this name cannot be identified. The word *baca*, meaning weeping, is also the name of a mulberry or balsam tree that grew in dry places. Hence, the psalmist may have had reference to arid places through which the pilgrims must pass on their way to Jerusalem. The pilgrims' joy made the arid places seem like an oasis. It was as if a refreshing rain had filled the pools.

7. They go from strength to strength, every one of them in Zion appeareth before God.

Other travelers might tire as they journeyed toward Jerusalem, but godly pilgrims who went there with the expectation of coming into the presence of God in the temple only became stronger as they approached the city of Zion. We are reminded of the words of Isaiah 40:29-31.

C. Supplication (v. 8)

8. O Lord God of hosts, hear my prayer: give ear, O God of Jacob. Selah.

Verse 8 introduces the prayer in verse 9. As in the opening verse of this psalm, God is addressed as "Lord of hosts." Then in the latter part of the verse He is addressed as *God of Jacob*. God is not only the God of strength and power. He is also the covenant God who never forgets His own people. Regardless of what they were doing or what they were involved in, God's spokesmen never let the people forget their history. This sense of history held the Israelites together and sustained them through many difficult situations.

III. Trusting in God
(Psalm 84:9-12)

A. Prayer for Israel's Leader (v. 9)

9. Behold, O God our shield, and look upon the face of thine anointed.

There is some ambiguity in this verse. As the *King James Version* interprets it, the psalmist is praying to God, whom he considers his shield and protector. God is called a shield in verse 11, and so using the term in the same way would not be out of place in this verse. However, the *New International Version* interprets the meaning differently: "Look upon our shield, O God." This makes *shield* apply to God's *anointed*, who is usually thought to be the king.

Regardless of whether God is the shield or the "anointed" is the shield, the prayer apparently is for the king. It was certainly appropriate for the writer to pray for the king. A strong king provided protection for the pilgrims as they made their way to Jerusalem to visit the temple. A good king also set the spiritual atmosphere that helped make a visit to the temple a high and holy experience.

It is possible that the psalmist was praying, not for the king, but for the high priest, who was also anointed when he took office. If this is the case, then the prayer was for spiritual leadership that guided its worshipers rather than civil leadership that protected its citizens.

In the same way we ought to pray for our leaders. Not only was this an accepted practice under the Old Covenant; it is also enjoined upon Christians (1 Timothy 2:1, 2). Citizens in a democracy have an even greater responsibility in this regard, for we have a part in choosing our leaders.

B. Joy in Serving God (v. 10)

10. For a day in thy courts is better than a thousand. I had rather be a doorkeeper in the house of my God, than to dwell in the tents of wickedness.

The writer had his priorities straight. He did not allow the glitter of worldliness to blind him to true values. A day in the service of the Lord was worth a thousand dwelling in the comfortable tents of wickedness. Actually, the contrast is even stronger. The place of service he had in mind was not one of prominence or great honor. He would be happy serving in a humble position—as a doorkeeper in the house of God. As we look about us, we see that a great majority of the people have chosen the things of this world that all too quickly pass, or at least lose their allure. The spiritual things, the things that will last through eternity, have been shunned.

A BETTER CHOICE

Bob Devin stood in front of the nightclub where he played the piano. It was a Wednesday evening and his night off. Usually he would "drop in" at the club, talk with a few friends, and then go home. Most of his days were alike, and he had little purpose in living.

A few weeks earlier, however, Bob had taken a Gideon Bible from a hotel room in Eugene, Oregon, and he had been reading it each day. The conviction had grown in his heart that Jesus was the Savior, but Bob knew nothing of Christian fellowship.

Walking to the club that Wednesday evening in Dunsmuir, California, Bob passed by a little church and noticed people going in. Now, standing in front of the club, he came to a decision. Resolutely he walked the short distance to the church and went in. He liked the singing and the Bible study, and he was moved deeply by the prayers of those in attendance. Sunday morning Bob was back. He gave himself to Jesus

visual 6

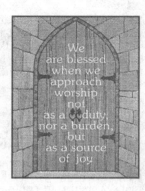

and became part of that small congregation's rich fellowship.

In a few months Bob was in college in Texas. No more nightclubs for him. His music was now dedicated to the Lord. In time Bob Devin became a minister of the gospel and he served in the church until his death.

That night, in front of the club in Dunsmuir, Bob made the right decision. He could testify with the psalmist that it is better to serve in the "house of . . . God than to dwell in the tents of wickedness."

—W. P.

C. Blessings From God (vv. 11, 12)

11, 12. For the LORD God is a sun and shield: the LORD will give grace and glory: no good thing will he withhold from them that walk uprightly. O LORD of hosts, blessed is the man that trusteth in thee.

For those who were on a pilgrimage to Jerusalem, *a sun and shield* were essential in their travels. The sun not only provided light for their travel, it provided warmth on cold days. Protection against bandits and wild animals was needed also if the pilgrims were to complete their journey successfully. So, in life, God is a *sun and shield* to His people. He is the sustainer of our physical bodies; but more, He provides life and light and warmth to our souls. More than the protection that the king could provide travelers (v. 9), God keeps our souls as we make our journey to His Heavenly dwelling.

God gives *grace and glory* to those who make their way to His place of worship. We are not told all that this may involve, but it would certainly include the joys that come from fellowship with other pilgrims. It would also include the peace that comes to those who join in worship of God. These blessings are not reserved alone for a few favored saints but are available to all those who *walk uprightly*.

No good thing will he withhold from them is not to be understood principally in the sense of physical blessings, although certainly these are not to be excluded. Far more important are the spiritual blessings that God pours out upon those who trust Him and walk after His commandments. Those who trust in God know countless blessings in this life, but, even more important, they have assurances of blessings beyond measure in the life to come.

Conclusion

A. Patterns of Worship

The Old Testament spells out in rather great detail some activities that were involved in Israel's worship. In contrast, the New Testament gives little in the way of instructions about how Christians should worship. This contrast is significant. The Mosaic covenant was for a specific people living in a specific place at a particular time in history. Christianity, on the other hand, is not so limited. It has been and is yet today open to all people of every climate, race, or time.

As a result, worship activities have varied widely from place to place and culture to culture. Some people worship God by following a very structured liturgy that may even be in a language that the people do not understand. Others approach God in a service that appears to outsiders to be so spontaneous as to border on the chaotic. Yet one cannot doubt that worshipers in both situations are able to draw close to God and find strength in Him.

As one studies worship patterns around the world, it is obvious that the manner in which people prefer to worship depends largely upon their particular culture and educational level. Some may prefer the solemn cadences of Bach or Handel. Others feel at home with simpler rhythms and the latest tunes. The quiet, soul-searching moments that some cherish as the very epitome of reverence would be rejected as cold and lifeless by others.

What can we conclude from all of this? Just this. We learned in today's lesson that pilgrims making their way to Zion experienced great joy and blessing in their anticipation of worshiping in God's house. If we can learn to approach our worship, not as a duty to be fulfilled or a burden to be borne, but as a source of joy, then we can know the blessings they knew.

B. When the Service Begins

Years ago a person who knew nothing about the Friends happened by chance to visit a service. This was an old-fashioned Quaker meeting in which there was no specific order of service. The members simply sat around in quiet meditation until one or more of them were "moved by the spirit" to speak. In this particular meeting, no one was so moved for several minutes. The stranger, not understanding this long silence, turned to a member sitting beside him and asked, "When does the service begin?"

"Brother," responded the Quaker, "the service begins right after the benediction."

Exactly! In worship we are drawn into the presence of almighty God and ever so briefly, so inadequately we come into contact with His holiness. Those brief moments should drive us to our knees as we humbly acknowledge our sinfulness (see Isaiah 6:1-8). Through our prayers, our songs, and the Lord's Supper, we commit ourselves anew to God and His holy purposes. As with Isaiah, repentance of sin brings cleansing. Once we are cleansed, and only then, are we really prepared to respond to God's call to service.

Our worship of God should cause us to depart from His house with hearts full of joy and gratitude, with spirits brightened with hope, and with hands ready to serve our fellowmen for the sake of our Master. It is true, the service begins after the benediction. The validity of our worship is measured by how lovingly and freely we serve God and others when we enter once again into a world that is lost and dying.

C. Let Us Pray

Almighty God, as we come before Your throne of grace, may we do so with awe and reverence. May our hearts be filled with joy as we meditate about You. Cleanse us from all our iniquities. Send us forth better prepared to serve. In Jesus' name we pray. Amen.

D. Thought to Remember

"It is only when men begin to worship that they begin to grow."—President Calvin Coolidge.

Home Daily Bible Readings

Monday, Dec. 30—In the House of the Lord (Psalm 122)

Tuesday, Dec. 31—All Shall Praise God (Psalm 138)

Wednesday, Jan. 1—Sing for Joy (Psalm 63:1-8)

Thursday, Jan. 2—Hope in God (Psalm 43:3-5)

Friday, Jan. 3—Worship With a Pure Heart (Psalm 24)

Saturday, Jan. 4—God's New Dwelling (Revelation 21:1-7)

Sunday, Jan. 5—The Glory of God (Revelation 21:22-27)

Learning by Doing

This page contains an alternate lesson plan emphasizing learning activities. Classes desiring such student involvement will find these suggestions helpful.

Learning Goals

As students participate in today's lesson, lead them to:

1. Compare the attitudes about God and worship recorded in Psalm 84 with attitudes prevalent in the church today.

2. Choose one way they can pursue worship more intensely and enjoy it more completely.

Into the Lesson

Before class write each of the words of the brief "Thought to Remember" (shown on the preceding page) on a different note card or flash card. To begin today's lesson, give each of the cards to a different student; ask the students to stand in random order in front of the whole class.

Class members should put the students into the right order so that their words make a sensible sentence. (If you prefer, you may write the words, in scrambled order, on the chalkboard and ask class members to jot them in correct order on scrap paper.)

Next, ask students to turn to their neighbor and decide three ways that worship helps us grow. Allow ninety seconds for this. After you call time, ask the class to call out their answers as you list them on the chalkboard. If you wish, let the class choose the best three answers from those you have listed.

Tell your students that the psalm that is the text for this lesson will help us grow, and how our worship can be more effective.

Into the Word

Choose one of the following Bible learning activities to involve students with today's text. You may decide to present all of these options to students and allow them, in groups, to choose which one they would like to do.

Write a hymn. Today's Scripture has been used as the text for more than one hymn or contemporary anthem. Perhaps some students would like to use this psalm as the basis for a new worship hymn. They can use a familiar hymn tune and write new words, based on the ideas in this Scripture.

Make a list. Students should look at Psalm 84 and list as many answers as they can find there to this question: How should God's people feel about worship?

Mark the verses. Each of the verses in Psalm 84 could fit under one of the following headings:

1. Worship Gives Us Strength.
2. Anticipating Worship Brings Us Joy.
3. Worship Makes Life Fulfilling.

As students discuss the text, they should put at least one of the numbers above beside each verse, to designate the idea the verse is conveying.

Pass the flash cards. What does today's psalm say about TRUSTING GOD, HUNGERING FOR GOD, STAYING CLOSE TO GOD, and WORSHIPING GOD? Write each of these labels on a separate piece of paper or flash card. Divide the students into groups and give each group a different flash card. Each group is to consider what the Scripture says about its assigned topic. After a designated period of time, each group switches cards with another group and they all consider the new topic they have received. After all the groups have considered all four topics, discuss them as a whole class. Fill in gaps in their understanding with information you gleaned from your study before class.

Into Life

Ask class members, "Why do people come to church today?" List their answers on the chalkboard. Look at the answers and compare them with the attitudes toward God and His worship that you discovered in today's text.

Discuss, "What can we do to build a hunger for God among Christians today? How can the Christian heighten personal anticipation for worship experiences?" Suggest the following answers to this question. (To aid the students' memory, you may write the italicized parts on the chalkboard.)

1. *Develop the habit* of private worship.
2. *Prepare for Sunday worship* on Saturday evening.
3. *Actively participate* in group worship.
4. *Keep a journal* that lists prayer requests, spiritual concerns, and evidences of how God is working in your life.

As you suggest each item, or after you have listed them all, ask students to suggest more specific ideas for each point. Challenge students to choose at least one of these ideas as their method for improving their worship experiences and becoming closer to God.

Let's Talk It Over

The questions on this page are designed to encourage review of the lesson Scriptures and to promote discussion of the lesson by the class. The answers provided are only discussion starters. Let your class talk it over from there.

1. What are some things we can do to cultivate a sense of God's presence in our church building?

"The Lord is in his holy temple: let all the earth keep silence before him" (Habakkuk 2:20). Our church building may differ in many ways from the temple in Jerusalem, but silence before God in our meeting place is as appropriate as it was in the temple. We enjoy visiting with fellow worshipers, but at certain times (such as in the moments before the service begins, Communion, and occasions of silent prayer) quietness is necessary if we are to focus our thoughts on the Almighty. Also, our selection of hymns needs to be examined. Gospel songs, with their emphasis on personal experience, occupy a very important place in many churches. Without belittling these, we can still say that the use of hymns that focus on God's greatness, power, wisdom, and love will help us be more aware of Him when we worship together.

2. Why do many Christians suffer from an apparent lack of "holy homesickness" for the worship services of their church?

Various attendance patterns may be discerned among the members of an average church. Besides those who are present every Sunday, there are those who show up every other Sunday, once a month, once or twice a year, or one of several other variations. If Christians are healthy and growing spiritually, and if the church is truly offering worshipful services, perfect or near-perfect attendance should be expected. It is clear, however, that many Christians are not growing spiritually as they should. We must look for ways to stir them up to a broadening faith, a deeper commitment, and a greater sense of urgency to worship God. Perhaps the church's services of worship are not always conducive to genuine worship. If so, we must constantly evaluate them and improve them.

3. To what extent should the church design its worship services to make the worshipers "feel good," or is this a legitimate aim in any way?

People feel good when they are entertained, but entertainment is obviously not our goal in worship. People are made to feel good when their egos are bolstered, but that is clearly not what we should be doing when we worship God. It may not produce pleasurable feelings when we call worshipers to repentance or to a holier life or to more zealous service, but these are aspects of Biblical worship. Worship can legitimately encourage a sense of relief in reminding us that our sins are forgiven; it can also stimulate in us a feeling of anticipation for the promised glories of Heaven. If we want to help the worshipers to feel good in these ways, we can quite appropriately stress such Biblical themes.

4. What kinds of prayers should be offered for preachers and others who lead in worship?

Paul asked for prayer "that utterance may be given unto me, that I may open my mouth boldly, to make known the mystery of the gospel" (Ephesians 6:19). We should pray for the preachers of today that they may proclaim the gospel with boldness to capture people's attention. It is appropriate to pray for wisdom for modern church leaders, who must consider differences in opinion, personality conflicts, and the like when conducting worship services that will meet divine requirements and minister to human needs. Leaders can be particularly vulnerable to the peril of pride. Therefore, prayers regarding their cultivation of humility and a true Christ-centeredness are needed.

5. How may worship services be conducted so as to provide worshipers with a stronger incentive to witness and to serve?

Second Corinthians 5:14, 15 records Paul's incentive for service: "For Christ's love compels us . . . he died for all, that those who live should no longer live for themselves but for him who died for them and was raised again" (*New International Version*). Our weekly worship gives us opportunities to explore and experience that self-sacrificing love of Christ. The Communion service especially should cause the worshiper to have a fresh realization of what Christ in love has given for them. Surely our singing should not be a formal exercise, but a thoughtful and emotional celebration of Christ's love. Sermons should be designed to influence the head, the heart, and the will. Worshipers should be sent forth with hearts aflame for their Lord.

A Hymn to the Redeemer

LESSON SCRIPTURE: Psalm 103.

PRINTED TEXT: Psalm 103:1-17.

Psalm 103:1-17

1 Bless the LORD, O my soul: and all that is within me, bless his holy name.

2 Bless the LORD, O my soul, and forget not all his benefits:

3 Who forgiveth all thine iniquities; who healeth all thy diseases;

4 Who redeemeth thy life from destruction; who crowneth thee with lovingkindness and tender mercies;

5 Who satisfieth thy mouth with good things; so that thy youth is renewed like the eagle's.

6 The LORD executeth righteousness and judgment for all that are oppressed.

7 He made known his ways unto Moses, his acts unto the children of Israel.

8 The LORD is merciful and gracious, slow to anger, and plenteous in mercy.

9 He will not always chide: neither will he keep his anger for ever.

10 He hath not dealt with us after our sins; nor rewarded us according to our iniquities.

11 For as the heaven is high above the earth, so great is his mercy toward them that fear him.

12 As far as the east is from the west, so far hath he removed our transgressions from us.

13 Like as a father pitieth his children, so the LORD pitieth them that fear him.

14 For he knoweth our frame; he remembereth that we are dust.

15 As for man, his days are as grass: as a flower of the field, so he flourisheth.

Jan 12

16 For the wind passeth over it, and it is gone; and the place thereof shall know it no more.

17 But the mercy of the LORD is from everlasting to everlasting upon them that fear him, and his righteousness unto children's children.

GOLDEN TEXT: The LORD is merciful and gracious, slow to anger, and plenteous in mercy.—Psalm 103:8.

Lesson Aims

As a result of studying this lesson, the students should:

1. Understand that God loves all his children and offers them forgiveness.

2. Be thankful that God does not treat us as our sins deserve.

3. Share with lost sinners the message of God's mercy and forgiveness.

Lesson Outline

INTRODUCTION
    A. The Smoothing Tide
    B. Lesson Background
I. THE SINNER'S BLESSINGS (Psalm 103:1-5)
    A. Praise to God (vv. 1, 2)
       Bless the Lord
    B. Forgiveness and Healing (vv. 3, 4)
    C. Renewal (v. 5)
II. GOD'S ATTRIBUTES (Psalm 103:6-13)
    A. Justice (vv. 6, 7)
    B. Mercy (vv. 8-13)
       Extended Mercy
III. MAN'S FRAILTY (Psalm 103:14-17)
    A. Man Is Dust (v. 14)
    B. Man's Life Is Brief (vv. 15, 16)
    C. God's Mercy Is Everlasting (v. 17)
CONCLUSION
    A. Great Is His Mercy
    B. Let Us Pray
    C. Thought to Remember

Visual 7 from the visuals packet highlights the central teaching of this lesson. The visual is shown on page 172.

Introduction

A. The Smoothing Tide

Some children visited a lonely stretch of beach. The tide was out, and they played in the sand at the water's edge. Soon the smooth surface of the sand was marred by their many footprints. One of the children noticed this and commented to the others about how they had ruined the smooth beach. "Let's make it smooth again," said one of the youngsters, and they all went to work trying to smooth the sand. But try

as they might, they couldn't restore the smooth surface to the sand. Even when they got it reasonably leveled out, they still left their footprints.

Finally they gave up their task as hopeless and turned to other things. Then the tide began to come in. As the water rose, the restless waves swept across the sandy beach, erasing all the footprints and leaving it smooth again.

That's the way God deals with us. We rebel against God and as we do we leave ugly footprints behind us. Our efforts to erase them are to no avail. Then the rising tide of God's mercy sweeps across our lives, leaving them smooth again.

B. Lesson Background

Psalm 103, by its superscription, is attributed to David. Some scholars believe that it was written by a later author. There is nothing in this psalm, however, that is foreign to the spirit of David that we see expressed in other psalms that clearly are his. This psalm seems to be the work of a mature man, one who has experienced many of life's vicissitudes. Some believe that it logically follows Psalm 51, which records David's prayer of forgiveness for his sin with Bathsheba. In it he acknowledged his sin, and then asked God to create in him a clean heart. In Psalm 103, the terrible anguish of guilt seems to have passed, and in the relief and joy of forgiveness he raises his voice in praise to God.

I. The Sinner's Blessings (Psalm 103:1-5)

This psalm consists of an introduction (verses 1 and 2); a main section (verses 3-5) in which the writer expresses his thankfulness for forgiveness and healing; a second main section (verses 6-18) in which he extols God's righteousness; and a conclusion (verses 19-22).

A. Praise to God (vv. 1, 2)

1, 2. Bless the LORD, O my soul: and all that is within me, bless his holy name. Bless the LORD, O my soul, and forget not all his benefits.

Many of the psalms begin with an exhortation for the congregation to join in the praise and worship of God. In this psalm, the writer is exhorting himself to praise God. In his soliloquy, he urges his *soul*, his inner being, to honor God, to exalt Him, to acknowledge His greatness, His holiness, His goodness. He desired to praise God with everything he had. No part of his being was to be left out of this worship experience.

Do we sometimes worship God only halfheartedly, allowing things of the world to interfere?

Do we find ourselves resenting it when the service runs too long? If so, we will fail to experience the joy that David did when he came into the presence of God.

BLESS THE LORD

One of the world's greatest composers was Franz Joseph Haydn. Born in Austria in 1732, he was the son of a poor wheelwright. Haydn displayed great musical talent at a very early age, and when he was eight years old he was taken into the cathedral choir in Vienna. Here he received the musical education he desired.

When Haydn was twenty-eight years old, Prince Esterhazy made him the musical director of his court, a position he held for thirty years. During this time he composed many of his great symphonies, which gave him the title of "Father and Inventor" of the symphonic form as we know It.

At age sixty-five, Haydn composed the oratorio *The Creation*. Near his death twelve years later, he was carried into the concert hall where, for the last time, he heard this oratorio. When the opening section climaxed with "Let There be Light," the audience rose and cheered. Haydn, the musical genius, waved his hand toward Heaven and cried, "It comes from there! It comes from there!"

Haydn knew the source and inspiration for the masterpiece he had written. He had been given great gifts by the Lord, and with them he had blessed God's holy name. For all the benefits we have received from the Lord, may we never cease praising Him.   —W. P.

B. Forgiveness and Healing (vv. 3, 4)

3. Who forgiveth all thine iniquities; who healeth all thy diseases.

In his soliloquy David writes as if he is speaking to another person, which explains his use of the second person pronouns. In this verse he begins to enumerate some of the benefits he has received from God. As a devout person, he quite naturally thinks first of the forgiveness he has experienced. Without the sense of relief that forgiveness brings, none of the other blessings can really be enjoyed or appreciated. A soul burdened by unforgiven sin can never fully understand God's grace in other areas of life.

We have invented all kinds of ways to try to escape the blight of sin. Sometimes we redefine it so that our transgressions are only minor indiscretions or social maladjustments. Or we blame it on someone else, a ploy that Adam introduced. "The devil made me do it," or "everybody's doing it," or "it's society's fault," we argue. Sometimes we even cover our sins with a blanket of righteousness, insisting that it is all for a good cause. At other times we drown ourselves in pleasure or busy ourselves with work in order to try to numb the nagging feeling that all is not right.

None of these devices really works, for deep down we know what we really are and how we stand in the presence of God's holiness. The psalmist knew this, and he knew that the only safe route was to turn to God and rely upon His grace for cleansing.

Who healeth all thy diseases. Among the greatest blessings we receive from God is recovery from physical illness. David was thinking of the times when he had been restored to health. Some students object to confining the psalmist's words here to bodily ailments and would broaden his meaning to include ailments of the mind and spirit as well.

4. Who redeemeth thy life from destruction; who crowneth thee with lovingkindness and tender mercies.

Some believe that the writer here is referring to a serious illness that brought him to the very gates of death. Many who are living today have experienced such a rescue from death, either from illness, accident, earthquake, or tornado. But much more may be implied. *The New English Bible* translates the first part of the verse this way: "He rescues me from the pit of death," which conveys better the idea the writer is expressing. We who are in Christ were, at one time, dead in our trespasses (Ephesians 2:1) and headed for eternal damnation, a justly deserved punishment. We were helpless to save ourselves. But then God's mercy intervened to spare us. So abundant are the manifestations of God's *lovingkindness and tender mercies* to us that David speaks of them as a crown.

C. Renewal (v. 5)

5. Who satisfieth thy mouth with good things; so that thy youth is renewed like the eagle's.

According to our version, the writer acknowledges that God provides all manner of good things to satisfy his appetite. This food not only sustains his life, it also enables him to retain his youthful vigor as he advances in age. However, the meaning of the Hebrew word translated *mouth* is uncertain. Some Bible students think it means "desire." The meaning therefore would be that God provides the reasonable desires of His people, so that they have from Him all that is necessary for a rich and full and happy life (see 1 Timothy 6:17). Thus their *youth is renewed:* they stay young. David compares this youthful strength to an eagle's strength.

II. God's Attributes
(Psalm 103:6-13)

In the first five verses of this psalm, David has told of the blessings he has received from God. The following verses remind us of God's love and concern for Israel and for all mankind. Two of God's attributes are highlighted.

A. Justice (vv. 6, 7)

6. The LORD executeth righteousness and judgment for all that are oppressed.

This verse summarizes certain of God's activities in history. The wickedness of men is seen in government, in business, and in day-to-day personal relationships. We may tend to grow impatient seeing that righteousness does not always prevail in this life, and that the oppressed are not always rescued from the injustice they must suffer. Yet as one looks back over the long sweep of history, a certain pattern does begin to emerge. Precise and equitable judgment is not always meted out, but many things are evened up. The Hitlers and the Stalins may have their day, but the oppressive regimes they institute eventually crumble, often carrying their perpetrators to their destruction. The freeing of the oppressed may take years, even generations, but eventually God puts an end to injustice.

7. He made known his ways unto Moses, his acts unto the children of Israel.

Here we see an example of how God deals with injustice and oppression. The people of Israel were enslaved in Egypt and had been mistreated for years. God revealed himself to Moses and guided his efforts to effect Israel's release from Pharaoh's power. God's *acts* were witnessed by *the children of Israel*, from the sending of the plagues on the Egyptians to the crossing of the Red Sea and the subsequent destruction of Pharaoh's forces. Release from oppression was many years in coming, but it finally came, and the oppressors were severely punished.

B. Mercy (vv. 8-13)

8. The LORD is merciful and gracious, slow to anger, and plenteous in mercy.

Just as the study of history leads one to understand that God executes justice, so also a study of history will reveal many examples of His mercy. This verse reflects the sentiment expressed in Exodus 34:6, a sentiment that God had made known to the people hundreds of years earlier.

Through His mercy God stays the punishment of sin, even though it is due us as sinners. Through His grace, He grants us favors that we do not deserve. He is patient with us, hoping that His patience will lead us to see the error of our ways and repent. Peter warns us that we should not mistake His patience for negligence or carelessness: "The Lord is not slack concerning his promise, as some men count slackness; but is longsuffering to us-ward, not willing that any should perish, but that all should come to repentance" (2 Peter 3:9).

9. He will not always chide: neither will he keep his anger for ever.

The verb translated *chide* means "to contend, to quarrel, to go to law." Although God has constant cause for bringing us before the bar of justice, yet he will not always do this. Nor *will he keep his anger for ever,* that is, He doesn't bear grudges. When He forgives, He also forgets. Once our sins are forgiven, they are not thrown up to us in some future situation.

10. He hath not dealt with us after our sins; nor rewarded us according to our iniquities.

God does not deal with us *after* (according to) *our sins.* If he did, we would all be consigned to Hell with no chance for a reprieve. A worldly person will never be able to comprehend this. Only the spiritually mature can really begin to understand the nature of sin and what a terrible violation of God's holiness it is. Understanding this, he can begin to appreciate God's mercy and grace.

11. For as the heaven is high above the earth, so great is his mercy toward them that fear him.

The psalmist seeks some kind of measuring rod by which he can convey to others his understanding of God's mercy. Turning to the starry heavens he feels he has an adequate standard. In the ancient world, a person could conceive of no greater distance than that from the earth to the heavenly bodies. If the ancients, using only the unaided eye, thought this a breathtaking distance, then what about us today, who, with the aid of instruments, can see thousands of times farther. Yet even this is inadequate to measure God's mercy.

IMMEASURABLE!

The height of the sky above the earth

The distance from east to west

The extent of God's mercy and forgiveness.

visual 7

The writer explains however, that God's mercy is qualified. It is extended to those who *fear Him.* To fear God is to give Him reverence, worship, and obedience. This is not to suggest that God is harsh in His judgment, but it does point up the fact that to gain mercy we must be in a position to receive it. We must come before Him with faith and penitent humility if we are to know the joy of mercy. The writer of the Hebrew epistle stated it this way: "But without faith it is impossible to please him: for he that cometh to God must believe that he is, and that he is a rewarder of them that diligently seek him" (Hebrews 11:6).

12. As far as the east is from the west, so far hath he removed our transgressions from us.

David uses another measuring rod to try to help us understand just what forgiveness means. *As far as the east is from the west*—as far as the sunrise is from the sunset—that is how far God has removed our sins from us. The thought the psalmist is trying to convey is that our sins are removed from us as far as possible. We need not worry about them again. It is hard for us to understand this. In our own lives we sometimes hold grudges for years, and even when we forgive someone for a sin against us, we still remember it, keeping it for ammunition to use in some future argument. It is not so with God; His forgiveness is complete.

Verses 11 and 12 are closely tied together. Verse 11 gives the cause—God's mercy, and verse 12 gives the result—God's forgiveness. One is impossible without the other.

EXTENDED MERCY

The Spanish writer Cervantes wrote, "Among the attributes of God, although they are all equal, mercy shines with even more brilliance than justice." Cervantes showed that he grasped clearly man's unending need.

Truth is powerfully portrayed through art. We have all seen justice depicted as a blindfolded woman holding balance scales that must measure truth accurately. The fact that she cannot see proclaims her impartial judgment and refusal to be swayed by circumstances or bribery. Mercy, on the other hand, is depicted with eyes wide open and arms extended to reach out with caring and concern when we are not our best. We demand justice but long for mercy.

Mercy is that everlasting attribute of God that tempers justice to give us hope. This hope becomes ours through God's love extended to us in Jesus Christ.

David's words beautifully express the wonder of this: "For as the heaven is high above the earth, so great is his mercy toward them that

fear him. As far as the east is from the west, so far hath he removed our transgressions from us." Cast yourself on the mercy of God. He will accept Jesus' sacrifice in place of our death, which justice demands for our sins. No wonder Cervantes wrote, "Mercy shines with even more brilliance than justice." Mercy meets our need!
—W. P.

13. Like as a father pitieth his children, so the Lord pitieth them that fear him.

The writer invokes yet another figure to express God's compassion upon us, a figure that is both nearer and more personal. A loving Father suffers when his children suffer; he worries when they worry, and sometimes even when they don't worry. A father is close by, within easy reach when he is needed. If this figure is less compelling now than when the psalmist wrote, it is because many fathers fail to measure up to the high standards that they should.

III. Man's Frailty
(Psalm 103:14-17)
A. Man Is Dust (v. 14)

14. For he knoweth our frame; he remembereth that we are dust.

Our frame. That is, the manner in which we were formed. God knows, for it was He who "formed man of the dust of the ground" (Genesis 2:7). Furthermore, He stated, "For dust thou art, and unto dust shalt thou return" (Genesis 3:19). Man is frail, and God's mercy toward us is based on His love for us and His awareness of our every need.

B. Man's Life Is Brief (vv. 15, 16)

15, 16. As for man, his days are as grass: as the flower of the field, so he flourisheth. For the wind passeth over it, and it is gone; and the place thereof shall know it no more.

The impact of this simile would have been more immediately felt by those who lived in the writer's day than by modern readers. Most of us are accustomed to seeing some kinds of green plants the year around. But in Palestine, the sparce rain that fell during the winter and early spring caused the grass to spring up. Then when the rains ceased and the searing winds of the summer season came, the grass quickly withered and died. The brilliant flowers that carpeted the desert floor lasted only a short while and then were gone. The grass and the flowers were often gathered and used as fuel, leaving nothing behind as a reminder that they had even been there.

Are not our lives like this? Even if we are granted a few years beyond the familiar threescore and ten, few of us will leave lasting memorials. Friends and family who knew us will soon join us, and even the granite markers will be lost or weathered into the soil that surrounds it. Some may protest that this is a quite morbid outlook on life. Actually it is a most realistic outlook. It becomes morbid only when we fail to include our faith in God, His mercy toward us, and the hope that this engenders. That is exactly what the psalmist is trying to tell us in these verses.

C. God's Mercy Is Everlasting (v. 17)

17. But the mercy of the LORD is from everlasting to everlasting upon them that fear him, and his righteousness unto children's children.

Contrasted with man's brief life span is the Lord's mercy that extends for ever and ever. Our feeble intellects, limited as they are by our physical existence, have no way of comprehending God's eternity. But thanks be to Him, we don't have to understand all the mysteries of the universe to enjoy the blessings that are held in store for us. And these blessings are not for us alone, but for many generations to come, our *children's children*.

This lays upon each of us a dual responsibility. God's mercy does not come upon us automatically. It is promised here, as in verses 11 and 13, to *them that fear him*. Our first obligation, then, is to commit our lives to Him in faith. Our second responsibility is to share that faith with our children so that they also may know these blessings. Given all the temptations that surround us today, the family and the church must work closely together if this goal is to be realized.

Conclusion

A. Great Is His Mercy

Most people hold one or the other of two extreme attitudes about sin. One attitude toward sin, and probably the prevalent one, is that sin is only a minor matter. Sin is regarded as a slight matter of social maladjustment, scarcely more important than a sneeze, and certainly not as significant as a cold. To these people, sin becomes a matter of concern only when it brings disappointment, pain, embarrassment, or a confrontation with the legal system. Even then such persons are not likely to have more than a faint understanding of the theological implications of sin. It rarely occurs to them that sin is more than a temporary inconvenience, that its implications are eternal.

People who hold this view of sin feel little or no need to seek forgiveness. In fact, they are likely to reject with an attitude of contempt any suggestion that to gain forgiveness they must come to God in faith and with a contrite and penitent heart.

Another extreme attitude, and one that is unbiblical also, is the position that one's sins are so terrible that God cannot forgive them. Persons who have committed gross sins such as murder or treason may hold such a view, but sometimes persons whose lives seem rather commendable may feel the same. Their problem is not that they have a misunderstanding of sin. They quite correctly understand that sin—any sin and all sin—is a rebellion against God and deserves severe punishment. Their problem is that they don't understand God's mercy. Oh, they may acknowledge that God extends His mercy to sinners, but they just can't quite believe that it extends to them. Psalm 103 has good news for them! "As the heaven is high above the earth, so great is his mercy toward them that fear him." Amen and Amen!

B. Let Us Pray

Dear loving and forgiving Heavenly Father, please help us take to heart the message of this psalm. May it help us to realize that we are sinners, hopelessly lost without You. Let us also understand that Your grace is full and free, reaching down into the depths of sin and raising us up to the heights of forgiveness. In our Master's name we pray. Amen.

C. Thought to Remember

There's a wideness in God's mercy,
Like the wideness of the sea;
There's a kindness in His justice,
Which is more than liberty.
—Frederick W. Faber

Home Daily Bible Readings

Monday, Jan. 6—"Bless the Lord, O My Soul" (Psalm 103:1-5)
Tuesday, Jan. 7—God Is Gracious (Psalm 103:6-14)
Wednesday, Jan. 8—God's Love Is Everlasting (Psalm 103:15-22)
Thursday, Jan. 9—God's Greatness Extolled (Psalm 104:1-13)
Friday, Jan. 10—Praise for God's Creation (Psalm 104:14-23)
Saturday, Jan. 11—God Sustains Life (Psalm 104:24-30)
Sunday, Jan. 12—The Lord Delivers (Psalm 107:1-16)

Learning by Doing

This page contains an alternate lesson plan emphasizing learning activities. Classes desiring such student involvement will find these suggestions helpful.

Learning Goals

As students participate in today's lesson, lead them to:

1. Decide why sin is so awful as they examine the psalm that is today's printed text.

2. Consider the appeal of sin and the reasons some people decide not to forsake it.

3. Deal with their own sin by renewing their faith in God according to at least one of the images of Him presented in this week's lesson text.

Into the Lesson

Begin today's session by dividing the whole class into pairs. Challenge students to list as many "benefits" of sin as they can think of in sixty seconds. They should jot their list on scrap paper that you have provided.

Call time and then tell students to turn over their papers and write four more "benefits" that they did not list the first time. Give sixty more seconds for the second listing. Students may protest that they have thought of all the possible answers, but push them to come up with at least four more. This will stretch their thinking and more successfully prepare them for the discussion to follow.

Ask a few volunteers to read some of the items from their lists. Ask class members how they felt about listing *benefits* of sin. Did it seem an awkward or difficult assignment?

Point out that while we are at church, we expect to hear about the evils of sin; but outside of the church, the world is always inviting us to participate in sin's temporary pleasures.

Discuss with the class, "Have you ever found yourself wishing you could participate in something that is forbidden?"

Tell class members that today's lesson will help them see why and how sin is really so bad. Perhaps they will become better prepared to answer temptation and respond to friends who seem to see sin as something good.

Into the Word

Divide the students into groups of three or four to participate in the following Bible study activities. Let half of the groups do the first activity while the other half does the second.

List making. Students are to read today's text three times and make a different list after each reading:

1. All the images of sin that are conveyed in this psalm.

2. All the images of God that can be found in this psalm.

3. All the descriptions of humankind that can be found in this psalm.

Question answering. Ask students, in their groups, to find answers to the following questions in today's text. (You may want to write these on the chalkboard or a poster. Or point students to the student book, where the questions are listed.) A recorder in each group should jot down the groups thinking as members find answers to the questions:

1. Why should we worship God?
2. What's so bad about sin?
3. Why does God react to our sins as He does?
4. Why do we need a God like this?

Into Life

Ask students, "What are the extreme ways that people might react to sin?" Hear several answers, and then summarize the ideas stated under "Great Is His Mercy" in the conclusion to the first lesson plan. If you have time, ask students to share examples from their acquaintances who illustrate these extreme ways of dealing with sin.

Propose two questions to the class. Half of the class, in the groups formed for Bible study earlier in the lesson, should discuss, "What does this psalm say to the person who believes sin is not important?" The other half should discuss, "What does this psalm say to the person who feels defeated by his sin?"

If you have time, ask each class member to choose one of the images of God suggested by this psalm, which they feel is especially meaningful: (Healer, verse 3; Renewer, verse 5; Forgiver, verses 9-12; Father, verses 13, 14; or "Forever Lover," verse 17). Each member should find a partner and share why he or she chose this image as especially meaningful. Challenge the students to write a prayer to God emphasizing the image chosen.

Ask five volunteers to offer prayers in closing this class session. Each person who prays should emphasize one of these images of God. Challenge students to pray briefly, no longer than about one minute.

Let's Talk It Over

The questions on this page are designed to encourage review of the lesson Scriptures and to promote discussion of the lesson by the class. The answers provided are only discussion starters. Let your class talk it over from there.

1. What can we do to keep distractions from interfering with our Lord's Day worship?

We encounter at least two distractions as we enter into worship. They are our worries and our anticipation of approaching pleasures. In regard to the latter it may help if we will make Sunday more of a "Lord's Day" than we do. When we emphasize Sunday socializing or television sports or shopping, we create unnecessary distractions from our worship. As for our worries, perhaps some mental exercise would help. When we leave our homes on Sundays, we may picture ourselves leaving our worries behind, lying on a desk or table where we can take them up again and deal with them when we return home. If we center our thoughts on God, on His love, His power, His promises, etc., as we worship, we may discover we have a renewed strength to deal with those worries.

2. David says the Lord blesses us so that our "youth is renewed like the eagle's." What aspects of our youth might we want renewed?

A restoration of some of the idealism of youth could be beneficial. As we grow older, we may grow more cynical because of the failure of our plans, the hypocrisy of associates, the general undependability of human heroes, etc. A fresh spark of idealism could encourage us to make new plans and to regain an appreciation for what is good in other human beings. Another desirable youthful characteristic is energy—mental or physical. Isaiah 40:29-31 is similar to Psalm 103:5. It speaks of how by waiting on the Lord we may "mount up with wings as eagles." Energy is described there, a reservoir of strength that any of us could long for.

3. The Bible has many illustrations of God's wrath against sin. How can we reconcile these with His mercy and willingness to forgive?

The great flood, the destruction of Sodom and Gomorrah, and the total destruction commanded for the inhabitants of Canaan are some examples of the divine wrath. These Biblical examples show the seriousness of sin. If God had not dealt decisively with human sin in times past, civilization might not have survived to the present day. It may help if we ponder the fact that in His death on the cross Jesus endured God's wrath against sin, but that was God's means of bringing us mercy.

4. Psalm 103:13 compares God's compassion toward us with that of a father toward his children. Why is that a sobering and challenging statement for fathers today?

Many fathers today fall short of the kind of compassion that reflects the Heavenly Father's gracious care for us. We hear too often of children who have been beaten or sexually abused by their fathers, and we know that in other homes fathers are generally absent. Christian fathers especially must fulfill their fatherhood in such a way as to enrich and enhance their children's appreciation of God as Father. That means providing for and protecting children, being patient and understanding toward them, administering consistent discipline, and encouraging them to become the best they can be.

5. How can we impress people with the fact that sin is not a minor matter?

While sin harms our relationship with God, many people will be better able to see how it affects our relationships with other human beings. All around us are examples of the effects of sin: broken homes, destroyed friendships, and damaged personalities. It would be beneficial for us to examine our own experience and trace how some specific sin we have committed has resulted in pain, grief, or confusion for other individuals. After we have probed the damage sin does on the human level, we can better appreciate how it offends our Heavenly Father, who loves us, and has given generously to us.

6. How can we impress people with the fact that their sins are forgivable?

Some people feel that their sins, or some specific sin they have committed, cannot be forgiven. But the Bible contains some impressive illustrations of God's willingness to forgive even the most heinous sins. David received forgiveness for adultery and murder. Wicked King Manasseh repented in the latter days of his reign (see 2 Chronicles 33:1-20) and found healing from the Lord. Jesus' prayer for those who were crucifying Him (Luke 23:4) indicates that forgiveness was possible for even so terrible a sin.

Lyrics of Love

LESSON SCRIPTURE: Song of Solomon 2:8-17.

PRINTED TEXT: Song of Solomon 2:8-17.

Song of Solomon 2:8-17

8 The voice of my beloved! Behold, he cometh leaping upon the mountains, skipping upon the hills.

9 My beloved is like a roe or a young hart: behold, he standeth behind our wall, he looketh forth at the windows, showing himself through the lattice.

10 My beloved spake, and said unto me, Rise up, my love, my fair one, and come away.

11 For, lo, the winter is past, the rain is over and gone;

12 The flowers appear on the earth; the time of the singing of birds is come, and the voice of the turtle is heard in our land;

13 The fig tree putteth forth her green figs, and the vines with the tender grape give a good smell. Arise, my love, my fair one, and come away.

14 O my dove, that art in the clefts of the rock, in the secret places of the stairs, let me see thy countenance, let me hear thy voice; for sweet is thy voice, and thy countenance is comely.

15 Take us the foxes, the little foxes, that spoil the vines: for our vines have tender grapes.

16 My beloved is mine, and I am his: he feedeth among the lilies.

17 Until the day break, and the shadows flee away, turn, my beloved, and be thou like a roe or a young hart upon the mountains of Bether.

Jan 19

GOLDEN TEXT: Many waters cannot quench love, neither can the floods drown it.
—Song of Solomon 8:7.

Songs and Prayers of the Bible

Unit 2: Songs From Festive Occasions

(Lessons 5-9)

Lesson Aims

As a result of this lesson each student should:

1. Have a better understanding of God's plan for relations between a man and a woman.

2. Have a growing appreciation for the beauty and sanctity of marriage.

3. Be able to avoid some of the hindrances to meaningful and lasting relationships with others.

Lesson Outline

INTRODUCTION

    A. Seeing With the Eyes of Love

    B. The Song of Solomon

    C. Lesson Background

  I. THE BELOVED'S ARRIVAL (Song of Solomon 2:8, 9)

    A. Happy Anticipation (v. 8)

    B. Timid Approach (v. 9)

      It's Fun to Be in Love!

 II. THE BELOVED SPEAKS (Song of Solomon 2:10-14)

    A. Invitation (v. 10)

    B. Appeal to Nature (vv. 11-13a)

    C. Invitation Repeated (v. 13b)

      Come With Me!

    D. Persistence (v. 14)

III. THE MAIDEN RESPONDS (Song of Solomon 2:15-17)

    A. She Seeks to Avoid Troubles (v. 15)

    B. Her Confidence (vv. 16, 17)

CONCLUSION

    A. A Many-Splendored Thing

    B. Let Us Pray

    C. Thought to Remember

Display visual 8 from the visuals packet and let it remain before the class throughout this session. The visual is shown on page 181.

Introduction

A. Seeing With the Eyes of Love

Life had not dealt kindly with George. As a boy he had been awkward and homely. He was not very athletic and so he was the last one to be chosen in the playground games. His head was misshapen with one ear higher than the other. A shock of unruly hair and a nose, twisted to one side as the result of an accident, gave him a grotesque look. When he spoke, he stammered, making it hard for him to carry on a conversation. Children are often cruel, and they were to George, making him the butt of their jokes. As he grew to manhood, he became increasingly withdrawn and often sullen. He had few acquaintances and no close friends.

When he became a teenager, no girl would date him, and by the time he reached thirty, he had no hope of ever marrying. Then a new family moved to town. The parents were middle aged, and they had a daughter in her early twenties still living at home. Linda was a very attractive young lady, but she was blind. Linda and George, two lonely people, met at church. In their loneliness they became friends. In a few months their friendship blossomed into romance. George was a changed man. He became friendlier and more outgoing, and his stammer seemed less obvious. His mop of hair, now neatly cut and combed, added to his appearance.

As the wedding day approached, a "friend" took Linda aside for a talk. (Every congregation seems to have at least one person like this who just can't bear to see other people happy.) "What do you see in George?" she asked. "Don't you know he's the homeliest man in town, and the laughingstock of the whole community. A beautiful girl like you could surely find someone else."

"My dear," replied Linda, "Even though I am blind, God has enabled me to see. I am able to see the real George, the one that your physical eyes keep you from seeing."

Our modern culture places a great deal of emphasis on physical beauty and physical love. These are important, of course, but we should never allow them to blind us to spiritual beauty and spiritual love. The sexual revolution has tried to sell us a bill of goods that physical love is all that matters. The Song of Solomon does dwell on physical love, but it does so in the larger context of God's love, which gives meaning to everything else.

B. The Song of Solomon

Probably few books in the Bible are the subject of more controversy than the Song of Solomon, the basis of today's lesson. First, there is disagreement about its authorship. Traditionally, it has been attributed to David's son, King Solomon. The title verse (1:1) and other references (3:7, 9, 11, and 8:11) would support this view. Some, however, believe that the work has multiple authorship and date it later than the time of Solomon. But there is no compelling reason to reject the view that it was written either by Solomon or as a tribute to him.

Methods of interpreting this book have given rise to even more numerous disputes. Across the centuries both Jewish and Christian scholars have interpreted it allegorically. A literal interpretation of the book, because of its erotic lyrics and absence of any obvious religious theme, has been deemed offensive by some. By giving a figurative meaning to the book, these offensive elements could be avoided. Jews interpreted this poem to refer to God's love for Israel. God is seen as a lover wooing His people under a variety of circumstances. Christian scholars have followed along a similar line, except they have seen it illustrating Christ's love for His church.

Another view is that this book is a collection of love poems or a series of nuptial songs used at wedding celebrations. It is our feeling, however, that this book is not a mere collection of isolated poems or songs, but it is a poem with a unified structure and definite aim.

A fundamental rule for understanding what the Bible means is to take every passage literally unless there is a compelling reason to do otherwise. Obviously, many Bible passages must be understood in a figurative sense. If we come to the Song of Solomon without any preconceived ideas about it, however, there is no good reason why we should not understand it in its literal sense. Some in the past have approached the book with the idea that physical love was evil or, at the very best, that which was necessary for the propagation of the race but certainly not something to be enjoyed or celebrated. It needs to be pointed out that this view is not derived from either the Old or New Testaments, but has its origins in pagan religion and philosophy.

Ancient Israelites expressed themselves in bold and vivid language, including language about marital love. Westerners have often found this distasteful or even shocking. One good thing that has come of the so-called sexual revolution is that we can speak more freely of the love between a man and a woman. This will allow us to see the book in its original light—a rich and wholesome expression of marital love.

C. Lesson Background

The Song of Solomon opens with the heroine, Solomon's bride, in the king's chambers with her admiring companions and attendants. The bride is conversing with them and reminiscing of her first intense longings for her beloved (1:2-4b) and they respond (1:4cd). She explains that her dark complexion is due to the fact that her brothers had made her work in the vineyards

---

How to Say It
Bether. *Be*-ther.
Canaanites. *Kay*-nan-ites.
Shulamite. *Shoo*-la-mite.

---

under the hot sun (vv. 5, 6). The bride then recalls her first meeting with Solomon while she was working in the vineyard (vv. 7, 8), and the exchanges of endearing expressions between them as their romance blossomed (1:9—2:2). She then expresses her complete delight and satisfaction in the king's love (vv. 3-7). As we begin our study, the bride reminisces about the occasion when she was in her home in the hill country of Israel and her beloved came to her seeking her company.

I. The Beloved's Arrival (Song of Solomon 2:8, 9)

A. Happy Anticipation (v. 8)

8. The voice of my beloved! Behold, he cometh leaping upon the mountains, skipping upon the hills.

The name of the heroine of the Song of Solomon is uncertain. Some believe it was Shulamite (6:13); others, however, take this to designate the town from which she came. Recalling a day of her courtship with her bridegroom, she sees her beloved coming to her in her native home. His pace is not as one plodding toward an undesirable destination. Rather he comes leaping and skipping as one not only in a hurry but as one with a merry heart.

B. Timid Approach (v. 9)

9. My beloved is like a roe or a young hart: behold, he standeth behind our wall, he looketh forth at the windows, showing himself through the lattice.

The maiden awaits in her house for the coming of her beloved. As she watches, she catches a glimpse of him. His beauty of form and graceful movement remind her of a *roe* or *a young hart*. The roe is the gazelle, a small antelope still found in Palestine. It is noted for its speed and graceful beauty. The hart is translated "stag" in the *New International Version,* and "wild goat" in *The New English Bible*. We cannot precisely identify the animal today.

Having come near, her beloved now stands behind the *wall*, which is probably a wall of the house rather than a garden wall. It would appear that he is trying to avoid being seen. He peers through the window, looking through the lattice work that protects the opening.

We are not told why the young man approached the house so furtively. Perhaps his actions reveal a shyness. On the other hand, it is possible that he had not yet gained permission from the maiden's father to court her and therefore wanted to remain unseen.

IT'S FUN TO BE IN LOVE!

Love can be heroic, stalwart, brave, sacrificial, giving, and much more. True love is characterized by these noble and sublime qualities. Also, love can be fun!

The older couple walked slowly hand in hand along the beach at Santa Cruz. They were in no hurry and seemed hardly to notice the other people there at the shore. They looked at the sea, the sky, the far distant Monterey hills, and the dominant wharf nearby. Mostly, however, they looked at each other. Their eyes spoke more than words as they strolled along the water's edge on the firm, wet sand. You could see they were in love and enjoyed sharing all their surroundings together.

As they came to the steps going up to the pier, the old man slipped his arms around his wife, just touched her hair with his lips, and lighted her face with a smile. Watchers knew that for this couple love was a joyful adventure and that their years together had only enriched their sharing of all they were to each other. One young woman, who had been watching, turned to her companion with these words: "It must be wonderful to be in love like that!"

Solomon spoke of such love. It is holy and good when preserved and sanctified in a marriage that is alive with laughter and commitment through the years. It is fun to be in love! —W. P.

II. The Beloved Speaks (Song of Solomon 2:10-14)

A. Invitation (v. 10)

10. My beloved spake, and said unto me, Rise up, my love, my fair one, and come away.

The young man becomes bolder and speaks. He invites the young lady to leave the house and join him outside in the beautiful spring sunshine. It seems obvious that this is not the first meeting between the two lovers, but we get the impression that they have been separated for some time.

B. Appeal to Nature (vv. 11-13a)

11. For, lo, the winter is past, the rain is over and gone.

The winters in Palestine are not terribly cold, but since most of the year's rain falls during the winter months, those months are not pleasant to

be outside. The winter months are not a good time for a young couple to be courting. Now, however, spring has arrived and the beloved invites his loved one outside to enjoy the earth's verdure and beauty. In addition to the cessation of rain, other signs of the spring season are mentioned in the two verses that follow.

12. The flowers appear on the earth; the time of the singing of birds is come, and the voice of the turtle is heard in our land;

Spring is a beautiful time in Palestine. The landscape that is brown and lifeless suddenly becomes green almost overnight and then bursts into an array of brilliant colors as the spring flowers bloom. The spirits that have been burdened and dreary through the winter months now rejoice—the time of singing is at hand. Our version has *the singing of birds*, which makes this clause parallel to the one that follows. The words *of birds*, however, are not in the Hebrew text. This leads some to think the reference is to human beings singing or humming or making music. Some scholars suggest the root of this word can also mean "to prune," which gives another interesting possibility to this verse. For certain plants, early spring is the time for pruning. While this meaning can't be demonstrated conclusively, at least it would fit into the general context.

The *turtle* is actually the turtle dove, which is a migratory bird, ordinarily in Palestine only in the spring and summer. It's characteristic cooing was taken as a sign of spring.

13a. The fig tree putteth forth her green figs, and the vines with the tender grape give a good smell.

The fig tree grows throughout Palestine and was highly prized by the ancients. Normally a fig will bear two crops. The spring crop grows on branches of the previous year's growth and ripens about June. The fruit is considered inferior. The appearance of these small green figs signaled the coming of spring.

Grapevines were cultivated throughout the ancient Near East. The Canaanites had productive vineyards before the land was conquered by the Israelites (Numbers 13:21-24). *The tender grape.* Most Bible students understand this Hebrew term to mean the blossom of the grapevine, which preceded the tender grape. Its delicate but distinctive fragrance was yet another harbinger of spring.

C. Invitation Repeated (v. 13b)

13b. Arise, my love, my fair one, and come away.

The beloved repeats his invitation for the maiden to join him for a tryst among the beauties of the awakening spring. We can only guess as to why a second invitation was necessary. Perhaps the maiden's reluctance was due to her shyness; or perhaps it was only a playful bit of coquetry, familiar to all lovers.

COME WITH ME!

The English poet, Joseph Addison, in his writing of *Rosamond* included these words:

"Mysterious love, uncertain treasure,
Hast thou more or pain or pleasure!
Endless torments dwell about thee:
Yet who would live, and live without thee!"

This intensity of love is seen in the Song of Solomon as the suitor entreats, "Arise, my love, my fair one, and come away!" The exclusive relationship love demands is one of its great virtues. The ache of the loving heart is in not knowing if the object of its affection truly belongs only to the one who pleads, "Come away with me! Set all others aside that we can share our lives, our total beings, with each other."

This need makes loving such painful pleasure. It is something less than love to pass easily from one intimacy to another without commitment to an exclusive relationship.

The Lord our God asks, in the ways of the spirit, that we love Him with all our heart, soul, mind, and strength. Such love endures and is enriched with the passing years. It is a relationship that all may enter into and enjoy through faith in Jesus Christ.   —W. P.

D. Persistence (v. 14)

14. O my dove, that art in the clefts of the rock, in the secret places of the stairs, let me see thy countenance, let me hear thy voice; for sweet is thy voice, and thy countenance is comely.

Earlier the maiden watched for the coming of her beloved. He furtively approached, but she caught only glimpses of him as he hid behind the wall and gazed through the window. Now it is her turn to become coy as she hides from his

visual 8

view in the house. He addresses her as *my dove.* This is the rock dove, a different bird from the turtle dove mentioned in verse 12. It often found refuge in clefts of rocks in mountainous areas. *That art in the clefts of the rock.* This, together with the preceding designation of the maiden, suggests that her home was situated on a rather steep hillside and was surrounded by rocks. *The secret places of the stairs* makes it seem that the maiden is hiding in the house, perhaps in some closet near the stairs.

He pleads for the maiden to show her face and speak to him. Absence has indeed made his heart grow fonder, and now he desperately wants to see her and be with her. Her sweet voice and lovely face will soothe the pains their separation has brought.

III. The Maiden Responds (Song of Solomon 2:15-17)

A. She Seeks to Avoid Troubles (v. 15)

15. Take us the foxes, the little foxes, that spoil the vines: for our vines have tender grapes.

Various explanations have been given to this statement, which, on the surface, seems inappropriate in the middle of a courting scene. Some think the maiden is refusing her beloved's invitation to join him because of the duties her brothers had imposed on her of caring for the vineyards (1:6). Others think the beloved is speaking to the maiden, suggesting that together, in playful pleasure, they attempt to catch the little foxes that might do damage to the blossoming grapevines. Still others seek a figurative meaning. We must recognize that in departing from a literal understanding of a passage, we open the door to all kinds of imaginative interpretations.

It seems best to understand that the speaker is the maiden. The previous verse indicates that she was hiding from her beloved, perhaps as the result of a slight tiff. Whatever their differences were about, he was seeking to make amends, addressing her with terms of endearment. Recognizing his good intentions, she then takes steps to bring about a reconciliation. In this case the *foxes, the little foxes, that spoil the vines* could refer to the problems and differences that often arise in a courtship. These must be taken or captured so that the lovers' blossoming relationship is not destroyed. In the vineyard it was a serious matter when foxes (or jackals, as the word may also mean) invaded and damaged the blossoming vines. In the same way, it was a tragedy if petty annoyances or even serious disagreements prevented their love from developing and maturing.

B. Her Confidence (vv. 16, 17)

16. My beloved is mine, and I am his: he feedeth among the lilies.

Whatever shadows may have crept across their love for one another have been chased away. Once more they are united. This reunion reassures the maiden and renews her confidence. *He feedeth among the lilies* may be a poetic way of saying that once more they share embraces and kisses.

17. Until the day break, and the shadows flee away, turn, my beloved, and be thou like a roe or a young hart upon the mountains of Bether.

The meeting of the two lovers, pleasurable though it was, must be brief. *Until the day break* is better rendered "until the day breathe." This is a reference to the evening breeze when the day cools. *The shadows flee away* as the sun is setting and the lengthening shadows finally disappear into night. The maiden must now tend to her duties in the vineyard, and so she bids him leave and return again in the evening. *The mountains of Bether* have never been identified, although several possibilities have been suggested. Actually, this may not refer to a geographical location at all. *Bether* comes from a word meaning "to divide." Perhaps she is speaking figuratively of the time that they will be separated and is urging him to return to her quickly like a gazelle.

Conclusion

A. A Many-Splendored Thing

Love is a many-splendored thing, finding its expression in many different ways. Love is physical, and physical love is expressed by a touch, an embrace, a kiss, and through sex. Love is emotional, and its emotional expression can run the whole gamut of feelings, from the heights of joy to disappointment, fear, hatred, and jealousy. Spiritual love transcends all of these, and ultimately finds its expression in eternity, for it is rooted in the love of God.

A true marriage must involve physical, emotional, and spiritual dimensions. The law recognizes that a physical union must take place before a legal marriage exists. But sexual union alone can never make a marriage. Our divorce courts are filled with disappointed couples who have made the tragic mistake of believing that sex and marriage are synonymous.

If we as a nation had deliberately set out to undermine the family, it is hard to imagine what more we could have done that we have not already done to accomplish this. Through motion pictures, television, and literature we have made premarital sex and adultery not only acceptable but the "in" thing to do. We have been taught to snicker or sneer at God's standards for marriage and the home.

What is worse, we have felt helpless to stem the tide of the so-called sexual revolution, and so we have done little but wring our hands and complain. It is time for Christians to take definite action. We can boycott those companies that exploit sex to sell their products. We can teach our children God's standards for sex and marriage. And perhaps most important of all, we can set the right kind of examples for our children. If we do less than this, we can look forward to the continued destruction of our families and ultimately the destruction of our nation.

The Song of Solomon does emphasize the physical aspects of marriage. The writer makes no effort to conceal the fact that men and women are physically attracted to one another. Yet this physical attraction must always be set against the background of divine love. This lesson must be thoroughly learned by this and future generations if the family is to survive in our society.

B. Let Us Pray

Dear loving Heavenly Father, teach us how to love. Teach us to love faithfully, to love purely, and to love enduringly. Above all Father, teach us to love You in all Your holiness that we in turn may love our fellowmen. In Jesus' name we pray. Amen.

C. Thought to Remember

"Many waters cannot quench love, neither can the floods drown it" (Song of Solomon 8:7)

Home Daily Bible Readings

Monday, Jan. 13—A Time for Everything (Ecclesiastes 3:1-8)

Tuesday, Jan. 14—A Song of Love (Song of Solomon 2:8-13)

Wednesday, Jan. 15—Joy in Mutual Love (Song of Solomon 2:14-17)

Thursday, Jan. 16—Love Is Life (1 John 3:11-18)

Friday, Jan. 17—"Love Is of God" (1 John 4:7-12)

Saturday, Jan. 18—Love Forgives (Ephesians 4:25-32)

Sunday, Jan. 19—"Let Love Be Genuine" (Romans 12:9-21)

Learning by Doing

*This page contains an alternate lesson plan emphasizing learning activities. Classes
desiring such student involvement will find these suggestions helpful.*

Learning Goals

As students participate in today's lesson, lead
them to:

1. Compare the love portrayed in the Song of
Solomon with that which they see in life today.

2. Decide how to express love as the lovers in
this Bible book do.

Into the Lesson

Write, "I know my spouse loves me, because—" on the chalkboard. Ask class members
to complete the sentence on small slips of paper,
but not to sign their names. Collect the slips and
read the answers to the class. Tell class members
that today's lesson looks at a unique section of
Scripture, a passage that records the expressions
of love between a young man and a maiden.
And there is no doubt that each of them is sure
of the other's love.

Into the Word

Explore today's printed text by means of a
"color study." In a color study, students do *not*
draw pictures. Instead they choose colors and
shapes and textures to convey their impression
of the text they are studying.

Students may do a color study of the text by
following the instruction below. They may draw
their answers in the student book (where this
activity is included). Or you may duplicate the
questions and give them blank paper to use.
(Provide crayons or markers.)

1. With no more than three colors, draw a
pattern or series of lines to show how the young
woman feels about the approach of the young
man (vv. 8, 9).

2. With one line, depict the lover's invitation
to his beloved (v. 10).

3. Why did the lover want his beloved to join
him? Draw a colorful answer (vv. 11, 13).

4. How did the lover feel about his beloved?
(vv. 14, 15). Use two colors: one to represent
him, and one to represent her.

5. How does the beloved respond to her
lover's invitation? (vv. 16, 17).

Have the students do this exercise individually. Then discuss the text, allowing students to
explain their drawings.

Option. You may want to acquaint your students with more of the Song of Solomon than is
in today's lesson text. To do this, ask two of the

class members, a man and a woman, to present
the following reading as a dialog. (Give this assignment to the members during the week before class.)

She: 1:1-4 (through "chambers")
He: 1:9-11
She: 2:1
He: 2:2
She 2:3-10a
He: 2:10b-14
She: 2:15-17
He: 4:1-4, 7, 9-12
She: 5:10-16
He: 6:4-9
She: 7:10-13
He: 8:6, 7

As students hear the reading, they should listen for the following:

(1) How does the woman feel about the man?
(2) How does the man feel about the woman? (3)
What images do you hear to describe married
love? After the reading is finished, discuss these
questions.

Into Life

If your class is made up mostly of singles, discuss the following questions:

1. How would you characterize the relationship of the lovers in this Bible book?

2. How does their relationship compare or
contrast with the relationships of couples we see
portrayed on television or in the movies?

3. How does their relationship compare or
contrast with the relationships of couples you
know in real life?

4. Why do you suppose this book is included
in the Bible?

If your class is mostly married couples, you
may discuss the following questions, in addition
to those above:

1. When was your relationship with your
spouse most like that depicted between the husband and wife in the Song of Solomon?

2. What factors from modern life conspire to
undermine this kind of relationship?

3. Notice the verbal admiration in this song,
that is, how much each partner expresses appreciation for the other. How long has it been since
you have expressed this kind of appreciation for
your spouse? What makes this kind of expression difficult?

Let's Talk It Over

The questions on this page are designed to encourage review of the lesson Scriptures and to promote discussion of the lesson by the class. The answers provided are only discussion starters. Let your class talk it over from there.

1. What are some Biblical principles that are applicable to dating and courtship?

One of the most noteworthy principles of Christian behavior that Paul mentions is "Whatsoever ye do, do all to the glory of God" (1 Corinthians 10:31). That consideration should affect the kind of relationship a couple has and the activities they share together. One way a Christian insures that his or her relationship with the opposite sex will be conducted unto God's glory is to heed another principle stated by Paul: "Be ye not unequally yoked together with unbelievers" (2 Corinthians 6:14). Some may object that dating non-Christians is not a binding act; but since dating is a step that may lead to marriage, it seems wise for Christians to limit their dating to those who share their faith in Christ. The fact that one's body belongs to the Lord and is the temple of the Holy Spirit (1 Corinthians 6:12-20) is a principle that should govern sexual behavior. We need to impress young people in the church with such principles as these.

2. By its frequent reference to beautiful flowers and graceful animals, the Song of Solomon seems to emphasize the beauty of romantic love. Why is it appropriate to find this theme in the Bible?

Sometimes it seems that romance is the exclusive concern of popular musicians, novelists, and moviemakers. However, as with all other aspects of life, the attraction between two persons of opposite sex is a matter of importance to God. He created us with this sexual attraction, in part as a means to the propagation of the human race (Genesis 1:26-28), and this aspect of His creation was among those things He regarded as "very good" (Genesis 1:31). We can say, therefore, that there is something divinely beautiful in human courtship. We should speak out for the preserving and enhancing of this beauty by adhering to God's standards and by avoiding the popular view that distorts the role of sexual relations.

3. We are told that a lack of communication is one of the major hindrances to happiness in marriage. How can a couple develop a healthy communication within their marriage?

In his much-discussed description of marriage relationships (Ephesians 5:22-33), Paul commanded wives to submit to their husbands and husbands to demonstrate a sacrificial love toward their wives. One aspect of this mutual obligation should be the continual sharing of needs and desires, of expectations and disappointments, of appreciation for one another. Many families struggle with hectic schedules that tend to eliminate opportunities for genuine communication. One way to overcome this is to work into the schedule frequent days or evenings or weekends when the husband and wife can be free to talk.

4. What are some actions we can take to combat sexual immorality in our society?

In Matthew 5:27-30 Jesus emphasized the peril of mental adultery. Lust is a sin in itself, and its sinfulness is compounded when it leads to immoral and criminal acts. In our society influences abound that promote illicit sexual desires, and Christians should work to eliminate them. Many Christians are already engaged in a united effort to influence television networks and advertisers to clean up the offending programs. There are other Christians who are battling to curb the distribution of pornography. We can become involved in these efforts, and we can no doubt find similar problem areas where we need to make our voice heard.

5. Should the subject of sex be discussed frankly in church? Why or why not?

This subject is discussed quite openly elsewhere—on television, in magazines, in sex education classes in public schools, and in countless private conversations. In many of these discussions sex is presented without any clear moral guidelines as to its practice. It only makes sense that in the church, where we have access to the Biblical standards regarding sex, we will speak of it in classrooms and from the pulpit to make those divine standards known. The Bible often deals with sexual matters. Therefore, when we are studying subjects such as creation (Genesis 1-3), the debased worship of the Canaanites with its appeal to the sexual appetites, and the moral purity to which early Christians were called, we can quite naturally discuss the Biblical purpose and plan for this gift God has granted us.

Song of the Vineyard

LESSON SCRIPTURE: Isaiah 5:1-7.

PRINTED TEXT: Isaiah 5:1-7.

Isaiah 5:1-7

1 Now will I sing to my well-beloved a song of my beloved touching his vineyard. My well-beloved hath a vineyard in a very fruitful hill:

2 And he fenced it, and gathered out the stones thereof, and planted it with the choicest vine, and built a tower in the midst of it, and also made a winepress therein: and he looked that it should bring forth grapes, and it brought forth wild grapes.

3 And now, O inhabitants of Jerusalem, and men of Judah, judge, I pray you, betwixt me and my vineyard.

4 What could have been done more to my vineyard, that I have not done in it? Wherefore, when I looked that it should bring forth grapes, brought it forth wild grapes?

5 And now go to; I will tell you what I will do to my vineyard: I will take away the hedge thereof, and it shall be eaten up; and break down the wall thereof, and it shall be trodden down:

6 And I will lay it waste: it shall not be pruned, nor digged; but there shall come up briers and thorns: I will also command the clouds that they rain no rain upon it:

7 For the vineyard of the LORD of hosts is the house of Israel, and the men of Judah his pleasant plant: and he looked for judgment, but behold oppression; for righteousness, but behold a cry.

Jan 26

GOLDEN TEXT: The vineyard of the LORD of hosts is the house of Israel, and the men of Judah his pleasant plant: and he looked for judgment, but behold oppression; for righteousness, but behold a cry.—Isaiah 5:7.

Lesson Aims

As a result of studying this lesson the students should:

1. Have a growing appreciation for Isaiah's faithfulness and courage.

2. Be able to list some parallels between ancient Israel and our own society.

3. Choose one fruit God desires in their lives and increase it in the coming week.

Lesson Outline

INTRODUCTION

    A. Recent Favors

    B. Lesson Background

I. PREPARATION OF THE VINEYARD (Isaiah 5:1-4)

    A. Location (v. 1)

    B. Lavish Care (v. 2a)

    C. Disappointing Results (v. 2b)

    D. Searching Questions (vv. 3, 4)

       Why?

II. JUDGMENT UPON THE VINEYARD (Isaiah 5:5-7)

    A. Withdrawal of Protection (v. 5)

    B. Withholding of Blessings (v. 6)

    C. Explanation (v. 7)

       A Lost Heritage

CONCLUSION

    A. Payday Someday

    B. Let Us Pray

    C. Thought to Remember

Display visual 9 from the visuals packet to establish the theme of this lesson. The visual is shown on page 188.

Introduction

A. Recent Favors

Alben Barkley, when he was a U. S. Senator from Kentucky, told about one of his constituents who had been one of his staunchest supporters for years. But in a recent election, the man had come out in support of Barkley's opponent. After the election, the senator confronted the man and reminded him of all the favors he had done for him.

"When you were out of work, didn't I get you a government job?" asked the senator.

"Yep, you did."

"And when your uncle was in jail, didn't I persuade the judge to waive his bill?"

"You sure did."

"And didn't I recommend your son for the Naval Academy?"

"Yes, you did."

"Well, then, after all I have done for you and your family, why did you work for my opponent?"

"But, Senator," complained the man, "what have you done for me lately?"

The ingratitude of this man was matched and even surpassed by the ingratitude of the ancient Israelites. The people to whom Isaiah ministered had for many generations accepted God's blessings, and yet time and time again they had stubbornly rebelled against him. No doubt there was a limit to Senator Barkley's patience. And certainly there was a limit to God's patience. When God's patience is exhausted, the time of judgment is at hand. This is the message that Isaiah delivered.

B. Lesson Background

The prophet Isaiah's ministry was a long one, beginning about 740 B. C. and extending down to about 698 B. C. He ministered during the reigns of four different kings: Uzziah, Jotham, Ahaz, and Hezekiah. He was a member of a noble family, and he may even have been a member of the royal family. As a result, he had ready access to the throne, and on occasion his message was addressed directly to the king.

His ministry was carried out in a time of rapid social and political change. When he began his ministry, both Judah and Israel were enjoying solid prosperity. In part, the prosperity of both kingdoms came because of the decline in Egypt and Assyria. Soon, however, Assyria began to revive as a great power, a revival that was to have a traumatic impact on the two little kingdoms in Palestine. Indeed, most of Isaiah's life was spent under the threat of invasion by this fierce nation from the east, and he lived to see the ruin of the kingdoms of Israel and Judah, with the exception of Jerusalem itself.

In about 725 B. C. the Assyrians laid siege to Samaria, the capital of the northern kingdom. In 721 B. C. the city fell, and the invaders carried the people away into captivity, bringing an end to the kingdom of Israel.

The Assyrians soon turned their attention to Judah, and under Sennacherib, besieged Jerusalem. During this threat Isaiah was providing counsel to Hezekiah, king of Judah. As a result of divine intervention, the city was spared and Isaiah's ministry was vindicated (see 2 Kings 18:13—19:36; Isaiah 36, 37).

In his preaching, Isaiah got to the very heart of Judah's problems. The nation's problems came because the people had forgotten God and turned away from Him. The immediate threat came from Assyria, true enough, but Assyria was only the instrument God used to bring judgment upon His people.

There are many prophecies in the book of Isaiah, some of which are not dated. We cannot be certain when Isaiah first presented the song that is the text for this lesson. Since both Israel and Judah are mentioned in it, it would seem that it was before Samaria was destroyed in 721 B. C.

I. Preparation of the Vineyard (Isaiah 5:1-4)

When we think of God's prophets of old delivering their messages to the people, we usually envision them standing in a public place, arm upraised, shouting their warnings of doom and urging their listeners to turn back to God in sincere repentance. Not every prophetic message, however, was delivered in such a manner. The text for today's lesson was a message of terrible judgment that was to come, but Isaiah presented this truth in an unusual way. He related a parable and presented it in the form of a song.

Given the agricultural setting of the song, it is thought by many that Isaiah first presented it at the grape harvest, which was a time of feasting and rejoicing. On this happy occasion songs and folk ballads were popular. By presenting his teaching in this manner, Isaiah would have been able to capture the attention of his listeners and involve them before they realized the outcome of the parable.

A. Location (v. 1)

1. Now will I sing to my well-beloved a song of my beloved touching his vineyard. My well-beloved hath a vineyard in a very fruitful hill.

My well-beloved. Isaiah was referring to God, who was the owner of the vineyard. At the first the prophet did not reveal His identity. This permitted the parable to have a greater impact on the hearers. The meaning here is that Isaiah was singing concerning the One he loved in regard to His vineyard.

How to Say It

AHAZ.   A-haz.
HEZEKIAH.   Hez-ih-*kye*-uh.
JOTHAM.   *Jo*-tham.
SENNACHERIB.   Sen-*nack*-er-ib.
UZZIAH.   Uh-*zye*-uh.

The vineyard was situated *in a very fruitful hill.* Hillsides, especially hillsides facing south, are a favorite place for vineyards. This provides better exposure to the sun, which produces sweeter, richer-flavored grapes. The place chosen for the vineyard was ideal for the growth of grapes. With a vineyard in such a choice spot, who could blame the owner for anticipating a wonderful harvest from the vines he would plant?

B. Lavish Care (v. 2a)

2a. And he fenced it, and gathered out the stones thereof, and planted it with the choicest vine, and built a tower in the midst of it, and also made a winepress therein.

Not only did the owner select a choice location for his vineyard, he went to great lengths to be sure that it would be fruitful. *He fenced it.* Some Bible students feel that "dug" is a better translation of the Hebrew word used here. This would fit in with the next part of the sentence. It is clear from verse 5, however, that the vineyard did have a fence about it. *Gathered out the stones.* A worker preparing a spot for a vineyard would dig out any rocks that were in the ground so the searching roots of the vines would find only soft, rich soil. It is quite possible that the stones so removed could be used to fence off the vineyard.

Planted it with the choicest vine. Not just any vine would do for this vineyard owner. He planted only the best vine. The word describing the vine indicates that it was deep red in color. Since grape vines are usually reproduced from cuttings, the plants can be expected to produce true to their original stock.

It was a common practice to build a watchtower in a vineyard. From the top of the tower those who were tending the vines could survey the whole vineyard to protect it both from thieves and from foraging animals. The owner *also made a winepress therein.* Well suited was this hill for a vineyard. In addition to its rich soil, there was an outcropping of limestone, which was ideal for a winepress. The owner cut a basin into this rock. A channel cut in the rock connected this basin to another basin, which was cut deeper into the rock. Grapes were placed in the upper basin and trampled by the workers. The juice then flowed through the channel and was collected in the lower basin. This vineyard was well situated, cared for, and equipped.

C. Disappointing Results (v. 2b)

2b. And he looked that it should bring forth grapes, and it brought forth wild grapes.

The owner anticipated a good crop, but he never got to enjoy the product of his effort. The

visual 9

"*The wages of sin is death*"

WARNING
...to the wicked

PAYDAY WILL COME!

vines *brought forth wild grapes,* unfit for use. The disappointment of the owner in such a situation would certainly be understandable. With these sad words Isaiah's parable ends.

D. Searching Questions (vv. 3, 4)

3, 4. And now, O inhabitants of Jerusalem, and men of Judah, judge, I pray you, betwixt me and my vineyard. What could have been done more to my vineyard, that I have not done in it? Wherefore, when I looked that it should bring forth grapes, brought it forth wild grapes?
In presenting the facts in the situation, Isaiah had caught the attention of his listeners, the *inhabitants of Jerusalem, and men of Judah.* Probably few of them had as yet caught the drift of his song. It was still just a vineyard festival song to them.

Judge, I pray you, betwixt me and my vineyard. Here Isaiah changed to the first person pronoun—"I, " "me," "my." The speaker was not the prophet but his beloved, the owner of the vineyard. The owner asked the people of Jerusalem to judge in this situation. What more could he have done to make his vineyard productive? The answer was plain. There was nothing the men could have said but to agree that the owner had done everything possible to insure a good crop. Why then, the owner asked, didn't the vineyard produce the kind of grapes it should have produced? The answer to this question was not so easy. It was plain, however, that the fault lay with the vineyard itself, and not with the owner.

WHY?

Football is a recurring theme in American comedy, jokes, cartoons, and stories. We all have our heroes and our goats to praise or criticize. One of the most unique of the game's players is Lucy, the character in the "Peanuts" cartoon strip.

Lucy always wants Charlie Brown to kick her football while she holds it for him. From past experience, Charlie Brown has learned that doing

as she asks always leads to disaster. No matter how much she promises, faithfully vows, or commits herself to hold the ball steady, Lucy, at the last moment, pulls it away. Each time Charlie Brown kicks with all his might and falls flat on his back, wondering once more why he ever agreed to trust Lucy. A thoughtful reader may also ponder why Lucy goes back on her word each time.

Israel was like Lucy. Their vows to God were solemnly given, but their performance seldom measured up to their promises. Time and again God forgave them and continued to expect more faithfulness and stability in their lives. His feelings are echoed in Isaiah's "Why?" Why were they unfaithful generation after generation when God had blessed them abundantly as His chosen people? Why did they return to the Lord only when disaster overtook them and He removed their blessings? When we fall short of His glory, God must still ask, "Why?" What is your answer to God's inquiry?
—W. P.

II. Judgment Upon the Vineyard (Isaiah 5:5-7)

A. Withdrawal of Protection (v. 5)

5. And now go to; I will tell you what I will do to my vineyard: I will take away the hedge thereof, and it shall be eaten up; and break down the wall thereof, and it shall be trodden down.
The owner of the vineyard did not have to take any direct action against the vineyard. All he had to do was remove the protection with which he had surrounded it. The *hedge* was ordinarily of thickly planted thorns that grew so close together that they formed an almost impenetrable barrier. Even today one may see in Palestine thorns or cactus used to protect garden plots or sheepfolds. The second barrier, the wall of stone, would also be broken down.

With both barriers removed, sheep, goats, and cattle would quickly eat the green leaves and grapes from the vines. In a land that is so arid, any bit of greenery quickly attracts grazing animals. But the vineyard would suffer more damage than that. As the animals grazed, they would trample the vines into the ground.

B. Withholding of Blessings (v. 6)

6. And I will lay it waste: it shall not be pruned, nor digged; but there shall come up briers and thorns: I will also command the clouds that they rain no rain upon it.
The previous verse told how the vineyard owner would remove the hedge and wall that protected it, allowing it to be ravaged by ani-

mals. Here he states that he will neither prune nor hoe this vineyard. Grapevines need extensive pruning to keep them healthy and fruitful. To neglect pruning is to insure that the vines will suffer. Without pruning, they may grow rampant for a season or two, but the dense vegetation will prevent the production of good fruit.

The vineyard would also go uncultivated. The hoeing keeps out the weeds that deprive the vines of moisture and nutrients. It also loosens the soil so that it accepts and holds the moisture better. When cultivation is neglected, only *briers and thorns* grow. Since numerous species of plants in Palestine bear thorns, it is impossible to identify these plants here. Regardless of their identity, their presence in the vineyard would destroy its productivity.

Finally, the owner would withhold the rain. The cultivation of crops by irrigation was practically unknown in Palestine in ancient times, and so any shortage of rainfall would be devastating. Under the best of circumstances Palestine receives little rain, and crop cultivation is always rather risky. Even deep-rooted plants would not be able to survive a prolonged drought. We are reminded of an earlier occasion when God brought a draught upon the land in the time of the prophet Elijah (1 Kings 17:1-7).

If Isaiah's listeners had any doubts about the identity of the vineyard owner in this parable, the reference to withholding the rain should have removed that doubt. Men may talk about the weather, but only God can do anything about it.

C. Explanation (v. 7)

7. For the vineyard of the LORD of hosts is the house of Israel, and the men of Judah his pleasant plant: and he looked for judgment, but behold oppression; for righteousness, but behold a cry.

Isaiah's explanation of the parable comes with frightening swiftness. He puts aside the figurative language and speaks in plain terms that all can understand. The vineyard belongs to the *Lord of hosts.* This title for God denotes His power and authority. It is sometimes used in reference to a military context, but it is also used in reference to judgment. The latter would appear to be the case here.

The vineyard is the *house of Israel, and the men of Judah his pleasant plant.* It is possible that this is an instance of parallelism, a characteristic of Hebrew literature. If so, by mentioning *Israel* Isaiah meant God's people as a whole among whom *Judah* was preeminent. It seems best to understand Israel in the sense of the northern kingdom and Judah as the southern kingdom. The

northern kingdom was still standing in the early years of Isaiah's ministry. It would have been appropriate for him to speak of the northern kingdom's destruction, which would have been only a few years into the future. While Isaiah's ministry was primarily to Judah, Israel was still within the scope of God's concern.

Judah is described as God's *pleasant plant.* This would seem to indicate that Judah occupied a favored position. That may well have been the case, for it was Judah that produced the royal line of David, and from Judah that the Messiah would come. If this is the meaning of this phrase, Judah's responsibility to produce the kind of fruit God desired was only increased. Judah should have fulfilled God's expectations.

God looked for *judgment,* that is, for justice among His people; He saw *oppression* instead. Those who possessed economic and political power were guilty of unjust and cruel treatment of the poor and the weak. With all of the guidance and instruction He had given, the Lord expected to see a people devoted to *righteousness.* Instead He heard the *cry* of anguish arising from a mistreated people. Any nation guilty of such evils must certainly fall before God's judgment. How much more severe would be His punishment of a nation upon whom He had lavished such care and protection.

A LOST HERITAGE

The twenty acres lie just off Scenic Avenue in the Rogue River Valley. The present owner may know nothing of their earlier history.

In the 1920s, following the end of the First World War, that land, along with eighty more acres nearby, was carefully planted with Bartlett pear seedlings. These fruit trees were cultivated, sprayed, pruned, and nurtured by loving care and hard work. When the trees first began to bear, the pears were profuse and perfect, bringing top prices in the market.

The 1930s were different. The price of pears would not pay for pruning, irrigation, frost protection, spraying, picking, and packing. That beautiful orchard developed blight, and in a few more years it had to be pulled out. Cold winters, poor care, and lack of funds combined to turn a productive, healthy orchard into blighted worthless trees. The farm was lost!

God's vineyard, Israel, began as the carefully nurtured people of God. Failure to obey God brought their downfall. As His people turned from Him, He removed His blessing from them.

We, as believers, are now God's farm, his people. Let's preserve all that He has given us by grace and produce the fruit He wants to see in us.
                                                                    —W. P.

Conclusion

A. Payday Someday

Many who live in this, the "now" age, find it difficult to believe that anything that happened before yesterday morning can have any meaning for them. We who enjoy the blessings of modern technology are quite certain that those who lived in the horse and buggy age—or even earlier—could not have known very much about life. How wrong such conclusions are!

The prophet Isaiah, who lived twenty-seven hundred years ago, spoke words of wisdom that are as timely as if they had appeared in this morning's newspaper. The sins he denounced are as prevalent in our day as in his. And God's judgments, which he pronounced upon the sinners in his day, are just as appropriate today.

The study of history has many values, not the least of which are the insights it gives us by which we may draw parallels between our society and earlier ones. Once we recognize the parallels, hopefully we can learn to avoid the mistakes that these earlier societies made.

The verses that immediately follow today's printed text record several woes that Isaiah pronounced upon his people for their sins. It would pay us to look at these more closely. The first woe was spoken against the greedy (v. 8). There were those who joined "house to house" and laid "field to field." The acquisition of houses and lands in itself was not an evil, but it is clear from Isaiah's words that many were acquiring these illegally, or they were using them to oppress the poor. Greed is one of the besetting sins of our times. Someone has appropriately labeled ours the "Acquisitive Society." Even though greed has not as yet led to national disaster, personal disasters abound. The pathetic life of Howard Hughes is just one example that may be given.

The prophet next condemned those who "rise up early in the morning, that they may follow strong drink" (v. 11). This same warning is repeated in verse 22. Our generation has far surpassed the excesses of Isaiah's age. To wine, we have added a list of far more potent alcoholic beverages. But we haven't stopped there. To alcohol, we have added even more dangerous drugs—heroin, cocaine, crack, ice, and a number of hallucinogenic drugs. The violence that follows in the wake of drug use seems raging out of control.

Verse 18 contains Isaiah's pronouncement of judgment upon those who "draw iniquity with cords of vanity." This suggests that the people did not blindly stumble into sin or innocently fall victim to it. Rather, they deliberately sought it out, pulling "sin as it were with a cart rope."

The similarities between Isaiah's times and ours are obvious.

"Woe unto them that call evil good, and good evil!" Isaiah proclaimed (v. 20). How modern this practice is! We cleverly refrain from calling abortion what it really is—the deliberate taking of a human life. We talk instead about a woman's right to make decisions about her own body, which seems to make the process a noble act rather than the sin it is.

Isaiah's pronouncement of woe upon those who "are wise in their own eyes" is found in verse 21. Such persons set their own standards and boast when they are able to live up to them. No only do they reject God, but they lead many others into their wayward paths, all the while arrogantly affirming their righteousness.

Isaiah's song, which began with the happy strain of an idyllic poem ended as a pronouncement of judgment upon those who had abused God's benevolence. Just as the vineyard of Isaiah's song felt its owner's wrath, so there would be a payday for God's ungrateful and disobedient nation. Are we so foolish as to suppose that if we reject God's grace and live lives of rebellion against Him that we can escape our payday?

B. Let Us Pray

We thank You, dear God, for the inspired words of Isaiah. Help us to realize that though they were spoken long ago, they still bear a witness and a judgment to us today. In Jesus' name we pray. Amen.

C. Thought to Remember

"Judgment for an evil thing is many times delayed some day or two, some century or two, but it is sure as life, it is sure as death!"

—Thomas Carlyle

Home Daily Bible Readings

Monday, Jan. 20—What the Lord Requires (Micah 6:6-8)

Tuesday, Jan. 21—Parable of the Vineyard (Isaiah 5:1-7)

Wednesday, Jan. 22—Unfaithful Stewards (Mark 12:1-12)

Thursday, Jan. 23—God Will Judge (Isaiah 3:13-15)

Friday, Jan. 24—God Is Just (Isaiah 5:13-16)

Saturday, Jan. 25—Prayer for Restoration (Psalm 51)

Sunday, Jan. 26—A Vision of God's Holiness (Isaiah 6:1-8)

Learning by Doing

This page contains an alternate lesson plan emphasizing learning activities. Classes desiring such student involvement will find these suggestions helpful.

Learning Goals

As students participate in today's lesson, lead them to:

1. Compare the vineyard of Isaiah 5 with the church of today.

2. Compare the sins of Isaiah's society with the sins of ours.

3. Choose one sin and a specific way to combat it in their own lives.

Into the Lesson

Use one or both of the following activities to introduce this lesson:

A Song About Judgment. Write the following words on the chalkboard:

Praise	Rejoicing
Repentance	Adoration
Celebration	God's Judgment

Remind students of this quarter's "songs" theme. Ask the class members to work in pairs and to think of hymns that go with each of the above words.

After a few minutes, let the class members share their choices. Ask if they had trouble coming up with examples of the last one. Although we don't often think of singing about God's judgment, that's exactly what today's Scripture text is—a song about judgment!

Agree/Disagree. Distribute the following statements, or read them slowly for the whole class. Class members should indicate whether they agree or disagree with each one.

1. God's judgment is swift and final.

2. God's judgment is tempered by His mercy.

3. Man's sin tests God's mercy.

4. God warns before He punishes.

5. God explains His will before He punishes His people for disobeying it.

Tell class members that today's text gives a unique look at God's judgment and how His people can push Him to exercise it.

Into the Word

Share information from the "Lesson Background" section in the introduction to the first lesson plan.

Give each student a sheet on which the following five statements are written (minus the verse references). The statements are also listed in the student book. Ask students to jot down the words of Scripture and the number of the Scripture verse that each of these statements summarizes. They may also put the sentences into the correct order according to how they appear in the text.

1. The vineyard yielded a disappointing crop (v. 2).

2. The owner would turn his back on the vineyard (vv. 5, 6).

3. The vineyard was full of potential (v. 1).

4. The vineyard was God's people (v. 7).

5. The owner worked hard to prepare the vineyard (v. 2).

After a few minutes, ask class members to share their answers. Ask them how each of these statements was true for God's people in the time of Isaiah.

If you have time, divide the class into groups of four. Ask them to study Isaiah 5:8-23 to search for the specific sins of God's people that made Him so angry. They should list the sins and the verse references beside each. (See the conclusion section of the first lesson plan.)

Into Life

After each of the five statements above, have students write a sentence to explain in what sense the sentence could apply to the church.

On the chalkboard, list the sins from verses 8-23. They are greed, (v. 8), excesses (vv. 11, 22), deliberate sin (v. 18), confusing evil and good (v. 20), and arrogance and pride (v. 21).

Ask volunteers to share examples of how each of these sins is a problem in our society. Challenge them to give specific examples.

Refer back to the agree/disagree statements from the beginning of the lesson, and ask the class to evaluate them in the light of this study. (If you did not use them earlier, do so now.)

Challenge students to look again at the sins Isaiah lists and to decide which of them threatens to be the biggest problem in their own life. Can they take steps to overcome it or to protect themselves against it? Some students from your class may be willing to share their feelings and insights here.

Close with prayers of thanks for God's judgment—it teaches us the difference between right and wrong, which makes our lives better. Also thank Him for His mercy; all of us are guilty of some of these sins, but in Christ we are forgiven.

Let's Talk It Over

The questions on this page are designed to encourage review of the lesson Scriptures and to promote discussion of the lesson by the class. The answers provided are only discussion starters. Let your class talk it over from there.

1. Isaiah's song of the vineyard was in reality a song of judgment. There are songs of judgment in our hymnals. What are some of these, and why should we not neglect to sing them?

The familiar "Battle Hymn of the Republic" is one such hymn. The hymn traditionally used at Thanksgiving time, "Come, Ye Thankful People, Come," is another. We can also add the Gaithers' "The King Is Coming!" Many of the hymns we sing celebrate God's love and grace, and they speak of our joy in Christ and our hope of Heaven. It is natural and good that we should sing such hymns frequently. But this matter of judgment is a prominent Biblical theme that also should be reflected in the hymns we sing. As we worship God through the singing of hymns, it is appropriate that we acknowledge His justice along with His love. On those occasions when we edify one another through our hymn-singing, it is well that we remind one another of this vital Biblical truth.

2. God expects us to be productive and fruitful in accomplishing His work. What are some advantages He has given our generation that should make us more fruitful than previous generations?

One advantage we have is the amount of leisure time available to us. If we will utilize it in increased Bible study, evangelism, teaching etc., we can accomplish much more than Christians in past eras. Another advantage is the tools we possess for Christian work. Books and tracts, audio and video cassettes, computers and copy machines, and various other modern devices enable us to save time to enhance the effectiveness of our labors. Modern methods of transportation offer a further advantage. Time formerly spent simply in travel may be used more productively by the Christian worker. Modern transportation methods also enable us to extend our ministries over a wider area.

3. The lesson writer observes that "greed is one of the besetting sins of our times." What are some examples of this greed?

The news media carry daily reports of the happenings in state-supported lotteries. Many view these lotteries as a disturbing phenomenon of our time, a legalized monument to greed that encourages a wasteful use of the money people already possess. One can only wonder what percentage of lottery tickets is purchased by people who can least afford them. Another example of greed is provided by those who are victimized by "get-rich-quick" schemes or rackets. We even hear occasionally of Christians who have been so victimized. Also, there are families in which the members argue and permanently divide over money or property left as an inheritance. These examples show that the temptation to greed can touch any of us, not merely the wealthy members of society.

4. Our society may be characterized as one that engages in willful, deliberate sin. What are some examples of this practice?

In Romans 1 Paul lists various human sins and then points to those "who, knowing the judgment of God, that they which commit such things are worthy of death, not only do the same, but have pleasure in them that do them" (v. 32). In our time we have seen individuals scorn the Biblical standards of sexual morality, and their immoral life-styles are often celebrated in the media. We are aware that in some circles the use of illegal drugs is still glamorized, although the dangers of these have been amply demonstrated. We hear of many examples of people who cheat and deceive in order to achieve success, and their methods seem to gain a measure of approval in our "anything-goes" era.

5. What evidences of God's patient dealing with our society may be offered?

When we remember that God destroyed Sodom at least in part because of that city's perverted sexual practices (see Genesis 19), we must marvel at His forbearance in withholding judgment from our society. Another illustration is provided by the principle expressed in Proverbs 16:18: "Pride goeth before destruction, and a haughty spirit before a fall." The humanistic pride demonstrated by prominent people in our society is surely an abomination to God, but He patiently delays the punishment it deserves. Also, even though much of our society rejects the gospel, God continues to be "long-suffering to us-ward, not willing that any should perish, but that all should come to repentance: (2 Peter 3:9).

The Model Prayer

LESSON SCRIPTURE: 1 Chronicles 29:10-13;
Matthew 6:7-15.

PRINTED TEXT: Matthew 6:7-15.

Matthew 6:7-15

7 But when ye pray, use not vain repetitions, as the heathen do: for they think that they shall be heard for their much speaking.

8 Be not ye therefore like unto them: for your Father knoweth what things ye have need of, before ye ask him.

9 After this manner therefore pray ye: Our Father which art in heaven, Hallowed be thy name.

10 Thy kingdom come. Thy will be done in earth, as it is in heaven.

11 Give us this day our daily bread.

12 And forgive us our debts, as we forgive our debtors.

13 And lead us not into temptation, but deliver us from evil: For thine is the kingdom, and the power, and the glory, for ever. Amen.

14 For if ye forgive men their trespasses, your heavenly Father will also forgive you:

15 But if ye forgive not men their trespasses, neither will your Father forgive your trespasses.

GOLDEN TEXT: Now therefore, our God, we thank thee, and praise thy glorious name.
—1 Chronicles 29:13.

Lesson Aims

As a result of studying this lesson, the students should:

1. Have a better understanding of the simplicity and the majesty of the Model Prayer.

2. Incorporate the elements of the Model Prayer in their prayers.

Lesson Outline

INTRODUCTION
    A. Ceiling High prayers
    B. Lesson Background
I. VAIN REPETITIONS IN PRAYER (Matthew 6:7, 8)
    A. A Heathen Practice (v. 7)
    B. A Needless Practice (v. 8)
       Too Many Words
II. THE MODEL PRAYER (Matthew 6:9-13)
    A. Adoration of God (v. 9)
    B. Concern for God's Kingdom (v. 10)
    C. Physical Necessities (v. 11)
    D. Spiritual Needs (vv. 12, 13a)
       Asking for the Right Things
    E. Conclusion (v. 13b)
III. A PREREQUISITE FOR FORGIVENESS (Matthew 6:14, 15)
    A. One Must Forgive Others (v. 14)
    B. An Unforgiving Spirit Prevents Forgiveness (v. 15)
CONCLUSION
    A. To Forgive Is Divine
    B. Let Us Pray
    C. Thought to Remember

Display visual 10 of the visuals packet and refer to it especially in connection with verse 8. The visual is shown on page 197.

Introduction

A. Ceiling High Prayers

An old legend, coming from the Middle Ages, tells about a group of monks in a monastery in France. They were unusually devout men, giving themselves fervently to their prayers and their labor. But they had one problem: not one of them could carry a tune. Each evening when they sang the Magnificat as a part of their worship, the results were embarrassing, so embarrassing that they asked God to forgive them and to send them a brother who could sing.

Then one Christmas Eve a brother from another monastery was visiting them and joined with them in their evening worship. As they began to sing the Magnificat, the visitor's voice stood out, strong and melodious. He sang so beautifully that the other monks all stopped their singing and listened. When he finished, they were so delighted that they almost applauded.

According to the legend, as the abbot slept that night he was visited by an angel, who asked him why the Magnificat had not been sung during worship that evening. "Oh, it was sung," responded the abbot, "Sung more beautifully than I have ever heard it."

"I am sorry," responded the angel, "but your song this evening never reached Heaven. Before, we always heard you because your hymns were the outpouring of pure and sincere hearts. He who sang tonight sang for love of self and for the praise of men. Such songs never rise beyond the ceiling of the room."

And thus it is with our prayers.

B. Lesson Background

The text for this lesson is drawn from that portion of Matthew (chapters 5-7) referred to as the Sermon on the Mount. Jesus preached this sermon during His Galilean ministry, probably in the second year of His public ministry. It came just after His calling of the twelve apostles (Mark 3:13-19) at a time when His popularity was running at a high level. Although visitors to the land of Israel will be shown places where tradition says this sermon was preached, there is no way of verifying these claims. In all likelihood the place was somewhere near the city of Capernaum.

The Sermon on the Mount is a kind of a handbook describing the standards for the thought and behavior of those who would be Jesus' disciples. The Sermon begins with the Beatitudes, followed by numerous admonitions and prohibitions. In the midst of the Sermon is this precious gem we often call the Lord's Prayer. More appropriately, we refer to it as the Model Prayer, for it was not a prayer that Jesus prayed for himself but one that He gave as an example for His disciples.

Luke also gives us a version of this prayer but in a different setting (11:1-4). In Luke's account one of Jesus' disciples came asking Him to teach them how to pray. Jesus then gave the Model Prayer as an example. Some scholars hold that these are but two versions of the same incident. It is quite likely, however, that Jesus taught this same prayer more than once. Indeed, if people were then as they are today, most would have needed to hear the prayer several times before it finally sank in and they got the full impact of it.

Some among the Jews in Jesus' day made a great show of performing religious deeds. Standing in the synagogues and on the street corners they gave to the needy and uttered their prayers that they might receive the praise of men. Jesus took note of their hypocritical behavior and warned His disciples against it (Matthew 6:1-5). He suggested instead that they do their praying in private, for God is quite capable of hearing private prayers (v. 6). Our lesson text continues Jesus' instructions regarding the manner in which we should pray.

I. Vain Repetitions in Prayer (Matthew 6:7, 8)

A. A Heathen Practice (v. 7)

7. But when ye pray, use not vain repetitions, as the heathen do: for they think that they shall be heard for their much speaking.

In this verse, Jesus states a criticism of the prayer practices of the heathen. Such prayers are characterized by *vain repetitions*. The Greek expression here means "do not babble." The adherents of certain pagan religions pray repeating set phrases over and over again until they induce in themselves a hypnotic condition. We are reminded of the occasion on Mount Carmel when the prophets of Baal repeated the cry, "O Baal, hear us!" from morning until noon.

They think that they shall be heard for their much speaking. Those who approach prayer in this manner think that God has a higher regard for their prayer count than their prayer content.

B. A Needless Practice (v. 8)

8. Be not ye therefore like unto them: for your Father knoweth what things ye have need of, before ye ask him.

Our practices relating to God reveal a great deal about our theology. If we believe that we must repeat our prayers many times to get God's attention, then we are saying that God is (1) limited, (2) that He is too busy to give His attention to each one of us all the time, or (3) that He is reluctant to hear our prayers and must be wheedled and coaxed to do so. In response to (1), Jesus in His teaching made it very clear that God is all-knowing, omniscient. In answer to (2), Jesus made it plain that God is concerned about the minutest details of His creation. Not a sparrow falls to earth but that He is aware of it. He has even numbered the very hairs of our heads (Matthew 10:29, 30). And (3), in urging us "al

---

<table>
<tr><td colspan="2">How to Say It</td></tr>
<tr><td>BAAL.</td><td>Bay-ul.</td></tr>
<tr><td>CAPERNAUM.</td><td>Kuh-per-nay-um.</td></tr>
</table>

ways to pray" (Luke 18:1) Jesus was suggesting that God is more ready to answer our prayers than we are to pray. Obviously, one does not have to shout or pray repetitiously in order to get the attention of such a God as this.

Your Father knoweth what things ye have need of. This does not mean that we ought not to ask God for the things that we need, for the following prayer contains specific requests. In our asking, we are humbly acknowledging that we are dependent upon Him for all things. When we ask, we should do so with the attitude of seeking His will.

TOO MANY WORDS

At a meeting in Northern California a gentleman was asked to pray before the guest speaker brought his well-advertised topic for the waiting assembly. The praying brother must have felt his words were all important. Instead of reading the Biblical text that was selected for the occasion, and offering a brief prayer of blessing on the speaker, he prayed for more than ten minutes on subjects that were in no way related to the speaker or the text he had read.

Beginning with missionaries around the world and working around to persons in his home church and their special needs, his prayer, with many repetitious phrases, continued with no end in sight. Everyone became increasingly embarrassed and restless, and began to wonder who would bring the extended and inappropriate prayer to its conclusion.

Finally the chairman, a respected Christian leader, tugged gently at the prayer's coattail. When this elicited no response, the chairman strode to the podium and made this announcement: "Lets all stand and sing the Doxology while our brother concludes his prayer." This was effective, and the audience then sat down relaxed to listen to the guest speaker.

Too many words, unwisely spoken, rob prayer of both purpose and meaning.   —W. P.

II. The Model Prayer (Matthew 6:9-13)

Across the centuries probably no passage of Scripture has been repeated more often by more Christians than these five verses. One writer describes it as "a composition unequalled for comprehensiveness and for beauty."

As we have seen, in the verses preceding the Model Prayer Jesus instructed His followers not to offer vain, repetitious prayers. In these verses, He gives us an example of a brief, thought-filled prayer.

A. Adoration of God (v. 9)

9. After this manner therefore pray ye: Our Father which art in heaven, Hallowed be thy name.

Our Father. God is our Father because He is our Creator. He is our Father because He is our Sustainer. But most importantly in this prayer, He is addressed as Father because we have been adopted into His spiritual family. Unfortunately, not everyone can appreciate the warm and affectionate relationship that the word *Father* conveys because their physical fathers have not set good examples for them. We are appalled at accounts we hear of fathers who neglect, abandon, or abuse their own children. But even if one has not known a wholesome and happy relationship with his or her own father, that person can turn to the Heavenly Father and find the support, love, and assurance that has been missed.

Which art in heaven. Although we may address God as our Father, yet that relationship must never become so chummy that we forget that He is our Heavenly Father—high, holy, and lifted up. The fact that He is in Heaven, however, should not be taken to mean that He is confined exclusively to Heaven. His throne is in Heaven and He will spend eternity there with the saved, but the earth is still a part of his dominion.

Hallowed be thy name. "What's in a name?" we may cynically ask, suggesting that a name is not very important. To the ancients, however, a name was very important, and to God, His name was most important. The Scripture indicates strongly that God's name represents His person. The third Commandment makes this clear: "Thou shalt not take the name of the Lord thy God in vain." When we pray that God's name will be hallowed, we are praying that it will be held in reverence. This attitude of reverence is not confined just to our speech. It covers every aspect of our lives—words, deeds, and thoughts.

B. Concern for God's Kingdom (v. 10)

10. Thy kingdom come. Thy will be done in earth, as it is in heaven.

The two petitions recorded in this verse are closely associated. Jesus sometimes used the term *kingdom* almost synonymously with the church, which He would see established on Pentecost. On other occasions, He spoke of the kingdom in more comprehensive terms, including in it the idea of all of God's redemptive activities.

That seems to be the sense in which Jesus is using the term here. God's kingdom exists wherever His will is recognized and obeyed. That situation already exists in Heaven, and for His kingdom to come to earth means that the inhabitants of the earth would display the same enthusiastic obedience that the angels in Heaven now show. In a sense, this prayer is not so much a prayer for the coming of the kingdom, which is already an established certainty, as it is for the complete coming of that kingdom. It is a prayer that people everywhere will yield themselves to God and allow His will to prevail in their hearts and in all their activities.

C. Physical Necessities (v. 11)

11. Give us this day our daily bread.

This simple petition is fraught with all kinds of implications. It is first of all a recognition of our dependence upon God for our daily sustenance. Of course, human labor is involved. Someone must plow, plant, and harvest so that all may have food. It is God, however, who gives the rain and the sunshine that make food production possible. Most of us today are too remote from the field and the orchard to be aware of God's part in producing our food. We simply go to the supermarket and there we find the food we need. We should be aware, though, that God is just as involved in the complicated distribution system that enables us to buy our food from the store.

We are to pray for our daily food. Of course, this does not mean that we should be concerned for our food for only the next twenty-four hours. After all, the farmer must store the fruit of his harvest for many months before it can be used, and we should exercise equally good stewardship in our conserving of food. The real point is that we should not be so concerned about our food that we worry about it months in advance. We are to trust God that our daily need for sustenance will be met.

We are to pray for *bread*. Obviously, Jesus had in mind the whole range of foods that are essential to our health, but He chose as the symbol of this the simplest food, a common item in most diets. Perhaps He was suggesting that food to sustain life is sufficient and that we should not be concerned about lavish feasting.

D. Spiritual Needs (vv. 12, 13a)

12. And forgive us our debts, as we forgive our debtors.

The words *debts* and *debtors* are not, of course, to be taken literally. Jesus' concern is not about monetary matters, but about moral matters. The issue is God's forgiveness of sin. This is clear from verse 14, which speaks of "trespasses" rather than debts, while Luke's version of this prayer has "sins" (11:4). For this reason, one version of the Lord's Prayer that we sometimes use in public worship has *trespasses* instead of *debts*.

It would be a mistake to think of this as a mathematical transaction. In other words, the principle is not that if we are willing to forgive so many sins against us, then God will forgive a similar number of our sins. God's forgiveness is always a matter of grace, not something that can be earned in some precise, legalistic way.

The point Jesus was making is that the attitude we show others will affect our relationship with God. It is possible to love our fellowmen without loving God, but we cannot love God without loving our fellowmen. Later in the Sermon on the Mount, Jesus dealt again with the matter. "Judge not," He said, "that ye be not judged. For with what judgment ye judge, ye shall be judged" (Matthew 7:1, 2). This teaching is further reinforced in the parable of the unforgiving debtor (Matthew 18:23-35).

On one occasion, General Oglethorpe, the founder of Georgia, remarked to John Wesley, "I never forgive a man who has mistreated me."

Wesley's reply was swift and to the point: "I shall pray then, that you never commit a sin."

13a. And lead us not into temptation, but deliver us from evil.

Some people are bothered by this verse, for it seems to suggest that God is responsible for seducing one to sin. The word here translated *temptation* is often translated "test" or "trial." *The New English Bible* renders this verse, "Do not bring us to the test." James deals with a similar dilemma. On the one hand he writes, "Count it all joy when you fall into divers temptations" (James 1:2). At the same time, he insists that God never tempts any man (1:13).

God, because He has granted freedom to the human race, allows us to fall into temptation. Either through our own weaknesses or wickedness or the weaknesses and wickedness of oth-

ers, temptations will come our way. The force of the prayer, then, is that God will *deliver us from evil*, enabling us to pass through temptations without succumbing to them. Paul gives us a further assurance about temptations: "God . . . will not suffer you to be tempted above that ye are able; but will with the temptation also make a way to escape" (1 Corinthians 10:13). Even when temptations are especially severe, we know that through His grace we have the strength to escape them.

Asking for the Right Things

Tevye, the central character in the epic story *Fiddler on the Roof*, sings with feeling and gusto, "If I Were a Rich Man." In his song, he recites his dreams and desires, which he believes would be fulfilled with wealth. Unfortunately, Tevye remains a poor man, making his living delivering milk produced by his few cows.

The poignant tale reaches its climax when all the Jewish people of this Russian village, persecuted under the czar's anti-Jewish policy, are ordered to leave their homes and find new places to live. This means that most of them must move to new countries, learn another language, and earn their livings with new and different skills. The pain, passion, and problems of raising a family under these circumstances, and still trusting God, is both the pathos and glory of the film.

All of us dream of things we believe would benefit our lives, and quite often we have in mind material blessings. We may even make them significant parts of our prayers. In the Model Prayer, Jesus urges simplicity regarding material requests and emphasizes those matters of spiritual benefit. It is right to ask for "daily bread," which sustains our physical bodies, and that should suffice. Concern for material things beyond that should find no place in our prayers.

Petitions for the enlargement of God's kingdom and for right relationships with God and man, however, are never out of place. When we pray for these, we are asking for the right things.
—W. P.

E. Conclusion (v. 13b)

13b. For thine is the kingdom, and the power, and the glory, for ever. Amen.

This clause is not found in the oldest manuscripts, and thus has been omitted or placed in the margins of most modern translations. But even if these words were not a part of the original text, it is an excellent tribute to the faith of the early church. In the midst of difficulties and persecution, they could confidently affirm that the true kingdom along with its power

Prayer is not conquering God's reluctance, but taking hold of God's willingness

visual 10

and glory belonged to God. It certainly is a fitting close to this powerful prayer, or as one writer put it, "a final peal of trumpets."

III. A Prerequisite for Forgiveness (Matthew 6:14, 15)

A. One Must Forgive Others (v. 14)

14. For if ye forgive men their trespasses, your heavenly Father will also forgive you.

Human forgiveness and divine forgiveness are always intertwined. If we are willing to forgive others, we can receive forgiveness from God. It is true that we are saved by grace, and not by works, even the good works of forgiveness. Yet in a way our willingness to forgive others reveals what is really in our hearts.

B. An Unforgiving Spirit Prevents Forgiveness (v. 15)

15. But if ye forgive not men their trespasses, neither will your Father forgive your trespasses.

These last two verses in our printed text are given as further explanation of verse 12. Perhaps Jesus appended these in order that no one would misunderstand this verse.

This is the negative side of the previous verse. It is true that everyone of us must face God on Judgment Day; yet, in a very real sense, every day is Judgment Day, for every day we are doing or not doing the things that will determine the verdict He will pronounce upon us. Our unwillingness to forgive others leaves scars on them, but worse, it leaves scars on us. Fortunately, however, the unwillingness to forgive is not an unforgivable sin. At any time we can lay aside our stubbornness and extend forgiveness to those who have mistreated us. It sometimes takes a great deal of humility for us to do this, and it may take time. But it pays tremendous dividends, both in this life and, according to Jesus, in the life to come.

Conclusion

A. To Forgive Is Divine

In his "Essay on Criticism," Alexander Pope penned the familiar line, "To err is human, to forgive divine." How right he was! Since forgiving others is so difficult for most of us to do, following are some suggestions that may make it a little easier.

1. *Try to understand the other person.* Sometimes people mistreat us unintentionally. Some people's lack of social graces causes them to say or do things that are hurtful when that is not their intention. Others act in anger, and then are reluctant to admit their fault. Some are angry with themselves and with the world and they lash out at anyone who is nearby. When we understand why people act this way, it is easier to forgive them.

2. *We must learn to forget.* Sometimes we say, "I'll forgive that person, but I won't forget." While it is probably impossible to wipe something completely from our minds, yet we can avoid rehashing it and repeating it. If we dwell on a hurt, we will burn it indelibly into our minds. But if we busy ourselves with doing good to others, that bad memory will play an ever smaller part in our lives.

3. *We can learn to love that person.* If we understand that *agape* love, which Christ commands us to have for others, is a rational act not dependent upon emotion or whimsy, then we can bring ourselves to love others. One way to accomplish this is by doing good deeds for those who have mistreated us. Sometimes this is quite difficult both for us and the other person. And we can be misunderstood. But it is psychologically very difficult to keep on hating someone whom we are helping.

B. Let Us Pray

Our Heavenly Father, teach us how to reverence Your name. Show us how to work for the coming of Your kingdom. Keep us humbly dependent upon You for every bite we eat and every threat we hear. Grant us forgiving hearts. Guard us against temptation. Through our Master we pray. Amen.

C. Thought to Remember

"If you would have God hear you when you pray, you must hear Him when He speaks."
—Thomas Benton Brooks

Home Daily Bible Readings

Monday, Jan. 27—Seek the Lord (Isaiah 55:6-11)
Tuesday, Jan. 28—David's Prayer (1 Chronicles 29:10-13)
Wednesday, Jan. 29—Sincere Prayer (Matthew 6:5-8)
Thursday, Jan. 30—The Model Prayer (Matthew 6:9-15)
Friday, Jan. 31—Pray With Humility (Luke 18:9-14)
Saturday, Feb. 1—Pray With Thanksgiving (Philippians 4:4-7)
Sunday, Feb. 2—Effectual Prayer (James 5:13-16)

Learning by Doing

This page contains an alternate lesson plan emphasizing learning activities. Classes desiring such student involvement will find these suggestions helpful.

Learning Goals

As students participate in today's lesson, lead them to:

1. Paraphrase the words of the Model Prayer so they can examine its meaning in a fresh way.

2. Study the structure of the Model Prayer so that they can rediscover the proper place of God in our lives.

3. Choose one new insight about prayer to apply to their personal prayer lives.

Into the Lesson

Choose one of the following activities to begin today's class session.

Test your memory. Give students pencils and blank paper and challenge them to write the Model Prayer from memory. You may even want to give prizes—perhaps one for the first person who finishes and another for the person whose written prayer has the fewest errors.

Bible Pictionary. Divide into two teams. Players try to get their team members to guess the clue by drawing pictures on a newsprint tablet or chalkboard. The player drawing the picture may not talk at all during his turn. Give each player a sixty-second time limit.

Possible clues include "Our Father which art in heaven," "Hallowed be thy name," "Thy kingdom come, Thy will be done," "Give us this day our daily bread," "Forgive us our debts, as we forgive our debtors," etc.

After either of the above activities, discuss with students our familiarity with the Model Prayer. Do students remember when they first learned this prayer? Does it have some sentimental or nostalgic meaning to them? Does it have any real spiritual meaning? Today's class session will help students rediscover how this prayer can help us build our relationship with God.

I remember. Students should pair off and share their completions to this sentence: "I first learned to pray when—" Give students three minutes to tell each other their stories, and then allow volunteers to share with the whole class. Tell class members that today's text gives Christ's instructions to the disciples regarding how they should pray.

Into the Word

Prepare all of the following Bible-study activities. Divide students into groups of between four and six and allow each group to choose which activity they will do:

Word by word paraphrase. Those choosing this activity will work as a group to find new words for *every word* in the Model Prayer. By rephrasing the prayer in this way, they will be forced to grapple with its real meaning.

"Teach me to pray." Suppose you want to teach a young child how to pray. What would you tell the child, in the simplest language, based on what we learn about prayer from the Model Prayer? Students in this group should actually prepare a brief presentation as if they were going to deliver it to a class of six-year-olds.

Frieze. Students should draw a series of pictures to illustrate the meaning of this prayer. One student draws a picture to represent verses 7 and 8; another draws one for verse 9; another for verse 10; another for verse 11; another for verse 12; another for the first half of verse 13; another for the last half of verse 13. Later you will display the pictures in order on the classroom wall.

(If you prefer, you may choose just one of the above activities for the whole class to do.)

Duplicate the following inductive Bible-study questions (or have the student books available, where these questions are printed). As students complete their Bible-study activity, have them answer these questions while they are waiting for the rest of the class to finish:

1. Why does the Model Prayer begin as it does? How does this compare with how we typically begin our prayers? What does this teach us about praying?

2. William Barclay in *The Beatitudes and the Lord's Prayer for Everyman* says that the prayer's three petitions (verses 11-13) deal with the present, the past, and the future. How do you see that to be true?

3. Of what do we remind ourselves with the words that end the Model Prayer? How does such a reminder help our praying and build our faith?

Into Life

Allow each of the groups to share the results of their Bible-learning activity. Then discuss the above questions with the class. Ask class members to share some new thought or insight or help for their personal praying that today's discussion has prompted.

Let's Talk It Over

The questions on this page are designed to encourage review of the lesson Scriptures and to promote discussion of the lesson by the class. The answers provided are only discussion starters. Let your class talk it over from there.

1. What are some "vain repetitions" that we may tend to use in our prayers, and how can we avoid using them?

Most likely we learned how to pray, at least in part, by listening to the prayers offered aloud at church gatherings. As a result we may have adopted some phrases and expressions that sound quite pious, but hold little actual meaning for us. Some of these may be very broad petitions that need to be made more specific. For example, we often hear, "Lord, bless all the missionaries," or "Heal those who are sick." One can fill an entire prayer with such requests, and that type of prayer can be uttered without much thought or effort. Examining our prayers and eliminating anything that does not clearly express our faith and our specific desires for ourselves and others will help us to avoid using empty expressions.

2. How can we cultivate a proper reverence toward God's name when we pray?

As with the previous question, taking time to examine our prayers can help us to be sure that we maintain a high level of reverence. When we remember that prayer is an actual communication with almighty God, it makes sense to plan and prepare for such communication. Whether we are thinking about private or public prayers, we do well to consider beforehand how we want to express our trust in God, our humility before Him, our submission to Him, our thanksgiving for His gifts. We may find it helpful to incorporate phrases from the Bible in our prayers, so long as we really understand them and they express what is in our heart. Psalm 8:1, studied earlier this quarter, is a beautiful expression of reverence: "O Lord our Lord, how excellent is thy name in all the earth!" Many similar expressions are found in Psalms.

3. Why is it important that we pray for daily bread, even though we live in a society in which food is abundantly available?

We tend to take our food supply for granted, but it is not wise to do so. Even with modern methods of agriculture we are still vulnerable to weather conditions, such as drought and late freezes, that can damage crops. In spite of chemicals to combat them, insects and plant diseases remain threats to our food production. Even if this were not the case, it would still be important for us to pray for daily bread, since it is one way in which we express our dependence on God. As our Heavenly Father, He wants to protect us and provide for us, and He wants us to trust in Him and depend on Him. We should not be anxious about our food (Matthew 6:25-34) or smug in our possession of it (Luke 12:15-21), but gratefully dependent on our Father, who, in truth, is the one who provides food for our bodies.

4. How may we expand on the prayer regarding victory over temptation?

We can pray for discernment to recognize situations in which temptations can occur. Of course, such a prayer should be combined with a diligent study of the Scriptures, which help us to develop discernment. We can pray also for courage to say no to temptations. The Bible exhorts us, "Resist the devil, and he will flee from you" (James 4:7). It would be a worthy prayer to ask to be made strong enough to experience such a victory. Finally, we can pray for help in extricating ourselves when we do succumb to temptation. One sin can lead to another, or falling into sin can tempt us to cover up what we have done instead of repenting. Let us pray that we will be prompt to confess our sins in line with 1 John 1:8-10.

5. In spite of our desire to forgive others for wrongs done to us, we are sometimes unable to shake a lingering sense of resentment or bitterness. What can we do about this?

"Let all bitterness, and wrath, and anger, and clamor, and evil speaking, be put away from you, with all malice: and be ye kind one to another, tender-hearted, forgiving one another, even as God for Christ's sake hath forgiven you" (Ephesians 4:31, 32). The fact that Paul recorded this command indicates that it must be possible to fulfill. Perhaps the reference to acting in kindness holds the key. Some Bible teachers have pointed out that while we may not always be able to make a direct change in our feelings, we can change our actions, which in turn can influence our feelings. So if we go out of our way to be kind and loving toward someone who has hurt us, those actions may eventually melt our resentments.

Jesus' High Priestly Prayer

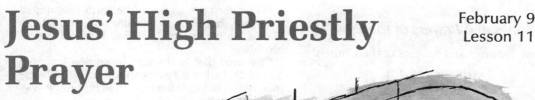

LESSON SCRIPTURE: John 17.

PRINTED TEXT: John 17:1-11, 20, 21.

John 17:1-11, 20, 21

1 These words spake Jesus, and lifted up his eyes to heaven, and said, Father, the hour is come; glorify thy Son, that thy Son also may glorify thee:

2 As thou hast given him power over all flesh, that he should give eternal life to as many as thou hast given him.

3 And this is life eternal, that they might know thee the only true God, and Jesus Christ, whom thou hast sent.

4 I have glorified thee on the earth: I have finished the work which thou gavest me to do.

5 And now, O Father, glorify thou me with thine own self with the glory which I had with thee before the world was.

6 I have manifested thy name unto the men which thou gavest me out of the world: thine they were, and thou gavest them me; and they have kept thy word.

7 Now they have known that all things whatsoever thou hast given me are of thee.

8 For I have given unto them the words which thou gavest me; and they have received them, and have known surely that I came out from thee, and they have believed that thou didst send me.

9 I pray for them: I pray not for the world, but for them which thou hast given me; for they are thine.

10 And all mine are thine, and thine are mine; and I am glorified in them.

11 And now I am no more in the world, but these are in the world, and I come to thee. Holy Father, keep through thine own name those whom thou hast given me, that they may be one, as we are.

.   .   .   .

20 Neither pray I for these alone, but for them also which shall believe on me through their word;

21 That they all may be one; as thou, Father, art in me, and I in thee, that they also may be one in us: that the world may believe that thou hast sent me.

Feb 9

GOLDEN TEXT: Neither pray I for these alone, but for them also which shall believe on me through their word; that they all may be one.—John 17:20, 21.

Lesson Aims

As a result of studying this lesson each student should:

1. Have a better understanding of Jesus' ministry as an intercessor for us.

2. Have a growing sensitivity and concern for the physical and spiritual needs of others.

3. Develop and maintain an attitude of unity with all of Jesus' followers

Lesson Outline

INTRODUCTION

    A. Divide and Conquer

    B. Lesson Background

I. JESUS' PRAYER FOR HIMSELF (John 17:1-5)

    A. Glorification (v. 1)

    B. Giving of Eternal Life (vv. 2, 3)

       Knowing the Right Person

    C. Glorification Again (vv. 4, 5)

II. JESUS' PRAYER FOR HIS DISCIPLES (John 17:6-11)

    A. Revelation Given (v. 6)

    B. Revelation Received (vv. 7, 8)

    C. Relationship Affirmed (vv. 9, 10)

    D. Request for Safekeeping (v. 11)

III. JESUS' PRAYER FOR OTHERS (John 17:20, 21)

    A. For All Believers (v. 20)

    B. For the Believers' Unity (v. 21ab)

       We Are One!

    C. For All the World (v. 21c)

CONCLUSION

    A. A Quest for Christian Unity

    B. Let Us Pray

    C. Thought to Remember

Display visual 11 of the visuals packet and let it remain before the class. The visual is shown on page 205.

Introduction

A. Divide and Conquer

There is a story that supposedly took place in Satan's headquarters in Hell. Satan, disturbed by the continued growth of the church, had called a conference of his chief lieutenants to discuss the crisis. "We must develop a new strategy to stop the church," he informed his fellow demons. "Does anyone have any suggestions?"

"Why don't we go up to the earth and spread the word that Jesus was a liar and that all the claims He made for himself as the Son of God are false?"

"We tried that in the very beginning," snarled Satan. "It fooled a few people, and we still use that tactic; but it won't stop the church the way it is growing now."

"I have a better idea," said another demon. "Let's encourage the enemies of the church to persecute Christians—put them in prison, beat them, exile them, and even better, burn them at the stake!"

"You haven't studied history very well," snorted Satan. "We tried that in the beginning too. Remember Saul of Tarsus. He was a real persecutor. But all the persecution did was scatter Christians all over the Roman Empire, and everywhere they went they started new churches. And to top it all, Saul became one of them. One of their leaders once wrote, 'The blood of the martyrs is the seed of the church.' Don't ever forget that!"

"I have another idea," said a third demon. "Let's go up and work among Christians and get them to argue and fight among themselves. It can be over petty matters such as how they cut their hair, the order of service, what color they paint the nursery, etc. I believe it will work."

"I agree," replied Satan with a sinister sneer. "And besides, it will thwart Jesus' prayer for the unity of all His followers." So the plan was put into operation—divide and conquer. It worked then, it has been working ever since.

B. Lesson Background

The text for this lesson is drawn from John 17, a portion we sometimes refer to as Jesus' intercessory prayer or the great high priestly prayer. This was offered on the night of Jesus' betrayal.

Earlier Jesus had joined with His disciples in eating the Passover meal, at the conclusion of which He had instituted the Lord's Supper. During this time with His disciples, Jesus gave many precious teachings, which are recorded in chapters 13 through 16 of John's Gospel. Leaving the upper room, Jesus and His disciples made their way toward the Garden of Gethsemane (John 14:31). Somewhere along the way, before they crossed the brook Kidron which ran between Jerusalem and the garden, Jesus offered the prayer that we find in John 17.

This is the longest and most personal of all of Jesus' prayers. One writer makes this observation: "No attempt to describe the prayer can give a just idea of its sublimity, its pathos, its touching yet exalted character, its tone at once of tenderness and triumphant expectation."

I. Jesus' Prayer for Himself
(John 17:1-5)

A. Glorification (v. 1)

1. These words spake Jesus, and lifted up his eyes to heaven, and said, Father, the hour is come; glorify thy Son, that thy Son also may glorify thee.

These words refers to Jesus' farewell discourse with His disciples in John 13-16. This discourse ended on an optimistic note: "Be of good cheer; I have overcome the world" (16:33). His remarks to His disciples now concluded, Jesus turned from them to speak to His Father.

As Jesus began His prayer, He *lifted up his eyes to heaven.* This was an accepted posture for prayer, one that Jesus took when praying at the resurrection of Lazarus (John 11:41) and when He healed the man who was deaf and also had an impediment of speech (Mark 7:34). Later this night Jesus knelt in prayer (Luke 22:41) and also prostrated himself (Matthew 26:39). It seems obvious that no one posture must be taken when we offer our prayers.

The hour is come. By this expression Jesus referred to His death on the cross. Earlier in His ministry, He had escaped death because the proper time had not yet come (John 7:30; 8:20). Now, however, that time had arrived. *Glorify thy Son.* To glorify means to honor or praise someone. Jesus knew that He was soon to die on the cross, a death that in human eyes was a mark of shame. Yet He could see beyond that. He knew that in His death salvation would be made possible for all humankind and that thereby He would bring "many sons unto glory" (Hebrews 2:10). Glory would thus come to Jesus for redeeming countless souls. The Father also would be glorified as Jesus obediently fulfilled the saving mission the Father gave Him.

B. Giving of Eternal Life (vv. 2, 3)

2. As thou hast given him power over all flesh, that he should give eternal life to as many as thou hast given him.

Christ had been given authority over *all flesh,* that is, the entire human race. While all men do not recognize Christ's authority, nevertheless, that power is His. In this verse the authority extended specifically to the power to give eternal life. Christ would soon glorify the Father by going obediently to the cross. By dying on the cross, He thus had the power to confer eternal life to all who came to believe on Him.

3. And this is life eternal, that they might know thee the only true God, and Jesus Christ, whom thou hast sent.

Jesus here gives us a brief definition of eternal life, which is to know the *only true God and Jesus Christ* whom He sent to us. There were many false gods, but only one true God. To know God is to have much more than an intellectual knowledge of Him. Saving knowledge of God involves loving, trusting, and obeying Him fully. We are led into this saving relationship through Jesus Christ. To know Jesus is to recognize Him as God's representative on earth and to worship and serve Him. Through Jesus' death, we see God's love. Through His resurrection we see His power over death. Through His obedience, we learn also to obey.

KNOWING THE RIGHT PERSON

It was 1980 in the East German city of Eisleben, the place of Martin Luther's birth and death. We were visiting churches and encouraging believers behind the iron curtain, and this would be my only opportunity to see Luther's birthplace, the church where he preached his last sermon, and the chamber where the great reformer died. On this day, however, the church and house were closed.

Across the street was a manse, so we decided to inquire about the locked doors. When I introduced myself as a Christian minister from the USA, the welcome mat came out. The Lutheran pastor of that congregation gave us a personal tour of the church and the high pulpit where Luther preached his final sermon. Then he took us to the house where Luther was carried when he became ill on his final visit to his home congregation. As the pastor told of these events, my heart was warmed. I am a history professor and a believer, indebted to Luther's stand on the Scripture as the authority for the church. It was a memorable day in my life.

What opened those closed doors? I had identified myself as a believer in Jesus Christ, and I was accepted as a fellow believer by the one who had the keys.

Knowing and being accepted by the one who has the keys helps both now and forever! Do you know God through Jesus Christ? Jesus is the only way to eternal life. Get acquainted with Him today!

—W. P.

C. Glorification Again (vv. 4, 5)

4. I have glorified thee on the earth: I have finished the work which thou gavest me to do.

Clearly, Jesus was referring to His three-year ministry that had been completed—not the final work He was yet to accomplish on the cross. In that ministry, He had taught people about a loving Heavenly Father. By His miracles He had shown the power of God, while the specific miracles of healing had shown God's loving concern. Beyond this, His teaching had shown that God had a plan for man that extended beyond this life—eternal life. In all of these things, Jesus had glorified the Father.

5. And now, O Father, glorify thou me with thine own self with the glory which I had with thee before the world was.

Jesus existed with the Father even before the creation, and, as a matter of fact, participated in the creation of the physical universe (John 1:3; Hebrews 1:2). Before the creation He shared divine glory in Heaven (John 1:1, 2). He emptied himself of that glory when He came to earth as a man and humbly served mankind (Philippians 2:5-8). Now He neared the time of His death, and He prayed that God would restore to Him the former glory that had been His. God did this after Jesus died and rose again (Philippians 2:9-11; Hebrews 1:3, 4).

II. Jesus' Prayer for His Disciples (John 17:6-11)

A. Revelation Given (v. 6)

6. I have manifested thy name unto the men which thou gavest me out of the world: thine they were, and thou gavest them me; and they have kept thy word.

From His prayer that He be glorified, Jesus now turns the focus of His petition for the disciples. To manifest God's name to men means to reveal Him to them, for in this context the name stands for the person. Through His teaching, His miracles, and His very life, Jesus had revealed the Father to them. Earlier that very evening Jesus had reminded His disciples that "he that hath seen me hath seen the Father" (John 14:9).

Which thou gavest me out of the world. The twelve, now reduced to eleven by the treachery of Judas, had been especially selected to serve as Jesus' followers. They had been with Him during His three-year ministry, during which time He prepared them to carry on His work through the church. *They have kept thy word.* They had been faithful to Him. Of course, they did not yet understand all of the implications of His teachings. Their hearts were right, though, even if their heads had catching up to do.

How to Say It

CAESAREA PHILIPPI. Ses-uh-*ree*-uh Fuh-*lip*-pie or *Fil*-uh-pie.
GETHSEMANE. Geth-*sem*-uh-nee.
KIDRON. *Kid*-ron.

B. Revelation Received (vv. 7, 8)

7. Now they have known that all things whatsoever thou hast given me are of thee.

In the years they spent with Jesus, the disciples saw firsthand the divine wisdom and power He possessed. But they were more than witnesses, for Jesus had conferred divine power on them when He had sent them on a preaching and healing mission (Mark 6:7-13, 30). Thus by observation and experience they had become convinced that whatever Jesus said or did came from the Father.

8. For I have given unto them the words which thou gavest me; and they have received them, and have known surely that I came out from thee, and they have believed that thou didst send me.

This verse sets forth four distinct actions involving Jesus and His disciples. First, Jesus had conveyed to the disciples the words that God had given Him. Jesus did not come into the world to "do His own thing," but to do the will of the Father. This He had done, faithfully and thoroughly.

The second action involved the disciples. They had *received* the words that Jesus brought. Of course, we need to understand that much more than words were involved. They were commingled with His miracles and the example of His life. Not everyone who heard Jesus had *received* His words. There were many who had heard Him teach and had seen His miracles and His manner of life, and yet had rejected Him.

Third, as a result of accepting Jesus' words, they had come to the conviction that He had come from God. He was more than a great teacher or even one of the inspired prophets. Peter's good confession at Caesarea Philippi was a public acknowledgment that Jesus was indeed "the Christ, the Son of the living God" (Matthew 16:16).

Fourth, the disciples believed that God had sent Jesus into the world to carry out a special mission. He had come to make known God's will for mankind, to offer himself as an atoning sacrifice for the sins of the world, and to establish the church by which the message of salvation could be taken to all persons. Since the disciples were to be the instruments through which the church was to be established, it was vitally important that they understand His mission.

If we are to be pleasing to Christ, upon hearing His words we must receive them, believe that He came from God, and believe that He came into the world to bring salvation to everyone. Since the church is the divine institution established to carry out God's redemptive work

CHRISTIAN
UNITY
BEGINS
IN
THE

HEART
OF
EVERY
BELIEVER

visual 11

on earth, it follows that we who are part of the church have certain obligations in regard to it.

C. Relationship Affirmed (vv. 9, 10)

9. I pray for them: I pray not for the world, but for them which thou hast given me; for they are thine.

At this point in His prayer, Jesus prayed specifically for the disciples. He knew that within a few hours they would be subjected to many different temptations and threats, and He knew that they would need extra help to withstand them. Already one of the chosen twelve had fallen to temptation.

I pray not for the world. Jesus' whole mission was to the world, and so these words are not to be understood in the sense that He was not concerned for the world. Rather, His concern at that particular moment was for the very special needs of the disciples. The disciples are spoken of as belonging to God, and because of this, He was free to give them to Christ.

10. And all mine are thine, and thine are mine; and I am glorified in them.

This verse gives evidence of the unity of the Father and Son. What belongs to the Son also belongs to the Father, and what is the Father's is also the Son's. *I am glorified in them.* By worldly standards, the eleven who remained with Jesus would not have been highly regarded. They were not well educated, they were not wealthy, and they lacked both political and religious prestige. How then could they bring glory to Him? In a few short weeks they would bring glory to His name by fearlessly proclaiming the message He had prepared them to bring. Their efforts then brought honor to His name, and two thousand years later their efforts still redound to His glory.

D. Request for Safekeeping (v. 11)

11. And now I am no more in the world, but these are in the world, and I come to thee. Holy Father, keep through thine own name those

whom thou hast given me, that they may be one, as we are.

I am no more in the world. Because in Jesus' mind His death was so certain, He spoke as if He were already returning to the Father. The disciples, however, had to remain in the world with all of its threats and temptations. Jesus prayed that the Father would keep watch over them through these trials. Then He prayed for the unity of His disciples. He knew that one of the most serious temptations they would have to resist was the temptation to go it alone. When the egos of God's servants become more important than the will of the Lord, that precious unity is shattered.

III. Jesus' Prayer for Others
(John 17:20, 21)

Verses 12-19 record Jesus' additional prayer requests for the eleven. Then He broadened His concern to include all future generations of believers, as we see in the final verses of our text.

A. For All Believers (v. 20)

20. Neither pray I for these alone, but for them also which shall believe on me through their word.

The disciples faithfully proclaimed God's message to their own generation, and from that time to this it has reverberated down through the halls of time. Each generation of believers has passed it on to the next. The continuation of this message has depended upon the willingness of the messengers to proclaim it without altering it. That is still the unchanged responsibility of our generation today.

B. For the Believers' Unity (v. 21ab)

21ab. That they all may be one; as thou, Father, art in me, and I in thee, that they also may be one in us.

Few things have been more damaging to the growth of the church through the centuries than divisions among followers of the Lord. Knowing that this would be a problem, Jesus prayed that His followers would be one. He desired that the unity among His followers resemble that which exists between the Father and Son. This unity is spiritual in nature. The parallel is not exact, of course, for the Father and Son are one in essence; believers, on the other hand, are to be one in mind, and will, and purpose. This unity is expressed in their love for God and for all who have accepted Christ. It is seen as they work together and present to the world the message of salvation that came from God, not one based on human opinion.

WE ARE ONE!

C. H. Spurgeon credited this parable to the great Reformation theologian, Melanchthon. With this story this German scholar mourned the divisions among Protestants.

There was war between the wolves and the dogs. The dogs were many, and the wolves few. Being afraid, the wolves sent out a spy to observe the dogs. His report said, "The dogs are many but they have only a few mastiffs among them. . . . What did cheer me was that as they came marching forward toward the battlefield, they were snapping right and left at each other. I could see that they hated wolves, but each dog also hates any other kind of dog with all his heart. The dogs may lose the battle by destroying each other instead of engaging the wolves, who are their real enemy."

Christians must accept and maintain the unity for which Christ prayed, so that the world may believe. Struggles among the members of Christ's body produce more doubt than faith. They also greatly encourage Satan, our true enemy, by the division they create among those who belong to the Lord.   —W. P.

C. For All the World (v. 21c)

21c. That the world may believe that thou hast sent me.

Jesus then gave the reason for the unity of believers in Christ: that the world might believe that God sent Him. A divided church cannot be a strong witness to one God. The world will be more likely to receive Christ as God's Son and the Savior of the world when all Christians, by their attitudes and actions demonstrate the unity for which Christ prayed.

Conclusion

A. A Quest for Christian Unity

Ours is not the first generation that has been concerned about divisions within the church. The church of the first century faced these same problems. Jewish Christians, for example, found themselves at odds with Gentile Christians. And Paul calls our attention to the problems of the church at Corinth, which was shattered into four factions.

Some have argued that Christ's prayer has been answered all along. Their contention is that even though factions of the church have worked and worshiped separately and sometimes even fought one another, still beneath it all, and invisible to human eyes, there is unity. But this kind of unity in an "invisible church" is not an answer to our Lord's prayer. The world

needs to see Christians united in order to be led to faith.

Others have said that we would have unity by bringing all the denominations together in some kind of a super denomination. Apart from the fact that such a union would be virtually impossible to achieve, a super denomination would only lead to other divisions—and what is worse, a super ecclesiastical bureaucracy.

The church will not find unity in a super church, nor will it find unity in human creeds, as helpful as they may be at times. Christian unity must begin in the heart of every believer with the desire and the determination to be one with all believers. The only basis for the unity that Jesus prayed for is the Bible. It alone contains the divine truths, which, if put into practice by all Christians, will bring all to "the unity of the faith" and to maturity, even "unto the measure of the stature of the fulness of Christ" (Ephesians 4:13) Let us then give ourselves to studying the Bible, living the Bible, and teaching the Bible that our Lord's prayer for unity may be answered in our time.

B. Let Us Pray

We thank You, Heavenly Father, for the strength that we derive from knowing that our Lord prayed for us. May we add our prayers to His for the unity of all His followers. We confess to You our guilt that at times we have been sectarian and divisive in our attitudes and actions. Please forgive us and grant us the wisdom and the courage to learn from our mistakes. In the name of Jesus we pray. Amen.

C. Thought to Remember

Let us become one that the world might be won.

Home Daily Bible Readings

Monday, Feb. 3—Jesus' Prayer for Himself (John 17:1-5)
Tuesday, Feb. 4—Prayer for Jesus' Disciples (John 17:6-19)
Wednesday, Feb. 5—Prayer for All Christians (John 17:20-26)
Thursday, Feb. 6—"Worthy Is the Lamb" (Revelation 5:9-13)
Friday, Feb. 7—Stand Firm (2 Thessalonians 2:13-17)
Saturday, Feb. 8—Pray for Strength (2 Thessalonians 3:1-5)
Sunday, Feb. 9—Live in Unity and Peace (Ephesians 2:11-22)

Learning by Doing

This page contains an alternate lesson plan emphasizing learning activities. Classes desiring such student involvement will find these suggestions helpful.

Learning Goals

As students participate in today's lesson, lead them to:

1. Discover the principles for unity revealed by Jesus in His prayer.

2. Choose one way in which they can help achieve Christian unity in our world.

Into the Lesson

Write this incomplete sentence on the chalkboard for students to see as they arrive:

"People best achieve a sense of unity when they"

Ask students to complete the sentence on slips of paper that you distribute to them. Collect the slips and read the answers to the class. State that today's lesson is a prayer, which includes Jesus' desire for unity among believers. Your discussion today will help your students see if their ideas for achieving unity match those in the prayer of Jesus.

Alternate idea. Ask three class members to stand and form a triangle. one of them represents Jesus; the other two represent two humans, "You" and "I." Along which path should "You" and "I" walk in order to find unity? If "You" and "I" walk directly toward each other, the two may get together, but what has happened to their relationship to Christ? (At best, they are no closer to Him. We know that in real life, when people concentrate on each other, they may forget about Christ.) But what happens when the two each walk closer to Jesus? (They get closer to each other as well!)

Tell class members that today's lesson will explore the kind of unity that not only brings people closer to each other, but closer to Jesus as well.

Into the Word

Each class member should find a partner so that students can work in twos to answer the following Bible-study questions. (They are printed in the student book without the answers, of course.) If time is short, let a third of the class answer each section, and then after several minutes go through all the questions with the whole class.

Jesus' prayer for himself (vv. 1-5)

1. What do these verses teach about Jesus? (His goal was to glorify God. God gave Him au-thority over all persons. His purpose was to offer eternal life to everyone. He was sent by God. He brought glory to God by doing His will.)

2. How does a person get eternal life? (By knowing God through Jesus Christ.)

3. What did Jesus pray for himself? (To be glorified by the Father.)

Jesus' prayer for the disciples (vv. 6-11)

1. What do these verses teach about the disciples? (God gave them to Jesus. They obeyed God's Word. They knew that Jesus came from God. They accepted the words of Jesus as the words of God.)

2. What did Jesus receive from the disciples? (Glory.) How was this true? (They obeyed Him. They would glorify Him in their future ministries.)

3. What did Jesus pray for the disciples? (That God would protect them so that they might be united.)

Jesus' prayer for future believers (vv. 20, 21)

1. How would future Christians become believers? (Through the message of the disciples.)

2. What did Jesus pray for concerning future believers? (Unity.) Why? (That the world might believe that Jesus came from God.)

Into Life

After you have discussed the Bible-study questions with the whole class, combine the pairs into groups of four class members each. Let these groups discuss the following application questions (also printed in the student book).

1. As He approached the end of His life, how did Jesus assess His ministry on earth (v. 4)? What did He mean? What work do you feel God has given you to do? If your life were to end this month, would you be able to make a statement similar to Jesus' statement?

2. What is the basis for the unity that Jesus prayed for? What obstacles are standing in the way of this unity? What can your church do to help build such unity? What can an individual Christian do?

Once again, allow time for the small groups to share their thoughts with the class. Close with sentence prayers by four students. Two should ask God to help class members do the work He has for them. Two others should pray for specific ways the class or individual members can help achieve unity among Christians.

Let's Talk It Over

The questions on this page are designed to encourage review of the lesson Scriptures and to promote discussion of the lesson by the class. The answers provided are only discussion starters. Let your class talk it over from there.

1. In His prayer recorded in John 17, Jesus gave priority to praying for His disciples. Do we need to give a similar priority to praying for Christian brothers and sisters, and if so, why?

Paul advised the Galatians, "As we have therefore opportunity, let us do good unto all men, especially unto them who are of the household of faith" (Galatians 6:10). Prayer is one form of doing good that we should exercise, with particular emphasis on the needs of fellow Christians. We should pray that our brothers and sisters in Christ may grow in faith, overcome Satan's temptations, and be effective witnesses for Christ. It may seem that our priority in prayer should be given to those who are yet outside of Jesus Christ, but prayer for Christians is a way of insuring that a strong witness will be maintained by the church to the non-Christian world.

2. The disciples brought glory to Jesus, even though they came from humble backgrounds. How may their example inspire us to work in such a way as to bring further glory to Jesus?

If our background is humble; if our family is not a prominent one; if we are not wealthy or highly-educated, we can still have an impact on the non-Christian world similar to what the apostles had. It is said in Acts 4:13 that when the Jewish leaders "saw the boldness of Peter and John, and perceived that they were unlearned and ignorant men, they marveled; and they took knowledge of them, that they had been with Jesus." Of course, the Lord can make mighty use of a learned man, as the example of Paul shows. But the fact that He was so glorified in the beginning of the church by the labors of common men should challenge the common folk of today to bring Him glory by their witness and work.

3. The message of Jesus Christ has been faithfully passed on from generation to generation, and now it is our turn. What is involved in our fulfilling this responsibility of passing it on to the next generation?

Paul instructed Timothy, "And the things that thou hast heard of me among many witnesses, the same commit thou to faithful men, who shall be able to teach others also" (2 Timothy 2:2). That means we must not only teach our own children and other young people in the church the truths of God's Word, but we must also equip them with the skills they will need to communicate those truths to their own children. It is important also that we pass our faith on in such a way that the next generation can make it their own faith, and not merely a weak copy of ours. An inherited faith may not be strong enough to withstand the temptations the next generation will face.

4. In what ways would Christian unity help promote the evangelizing of the world?

People have various ideas in mind when they use the term *Christian unity.* Some would make uniformity in doctrine a relatively unimportant aspect of it. If, however, the church were united in its message to the world, one area of confusion that hinders evangelism would be eliminated. Also, one can point to the overlapping of efforts in certain mission fields as different denominations compete to convert the same group of people. This overlapping of effort means that funds for missionary work are often utilized in a competitive way. True Christian unity could bring about the end of that overlapping. Finally, people who are outside of Christ need to see the followers of Christ united in love toward one another and edification of one another, rather than being rivals and opponents, as is often the situation now. Note John 13:34 in this connection.

5. What can each Christian do to promote unity on a personal, individual basis?

We can begin this answer at the point where the answer to question four left off—John 13:34. We are to love one another as Jesus Christ has loved us. How we need to personalize that principle and change our attitude and behavior toward fellow Christians with whom we are in conflict! It is certainly a form of hypocrisy to sound off about worldwide unity of believers while we continue to hold grudges or separate ourselves from brothers or sisters in our own congregation. By bringing the transforming love of Jesus to bear on the instances of disunity in which we are involved, we can do more for Christian unity than any number of denominational mergers or resolutions dealing with the horror of division.

Praise for Christ, God's Servant

LESSON SCRIPTURE: Philippians 2:1-11.

PRINTED TEXT: Philippians 2:1-11.

Philippians 2:1-11

1 If there be therefore any consolation in Christ, if any comfort of love, if any fellowship of the Spirit, if any bowels and mercies,

2 Fulfil ye my joy, that ye be likeminded, having the same love, being of one accord, of one mind.

3 Let nothing be done through strife or vainglory; but in lowliness of mind let each esteem other better than themselves.

4 Look not every man on his own things, but every man also on the things of others.

5 Let this mind be in you, which was also in Christ Jesus:

6 Who, being in the form of God, thought it not robbery to be equal with God:

7 But made himself of no reputation, and took upon him the form of a servant, and was made in the likeness of men:

8 And being found in fashion as a man, he humbled himself, and became obedient unto death, even the death of the cross.

9 Wherefore God also hath highly exalted him, and given him a name which is above every name:

10 That at the name of Jesus every knee should bow, of things in heaven, and things in earth, and things under the earth;

11 And that every tongue should confess that Jesus Christ is Lord, to the glory of God the Father.

Feb 16

GOLDEN TEXT: Let this mind be in you, which was also in Christ Jesus.
—Philippians 2:5.

Lesson Aims

After this lesson, each student should:

1. Have a better understanding of Christ's humiliation as an obedient servant.

2. Identify specific ministries in which a person may serve Christ.

3. Select one of these ways in which he or she will serve the Lord.

Lesson Outline

INTRODUCTION
   A. From Palaces to Poverty
   B. Lesson Background
I. EXHORTATION TO UNITY (Philippians 2:1-4)
   A. Desire for Unity (vv. 1, 2)
      Fulfill My Joy
   B. Way of Unity (vv. 3, 4)
II. CHRIST JESUS THE SERVANT (Philippians 2:5-8)
   A. Attitude (v. 5)
   B. Self-Emptying (vv. 6, 7)
   C. Sacrificial Death (v. 8)
III. EXALTATION OF THE SERVANT (Philippians 2:9-11)
   A. A Name Above All (v. 9)
   B. Submission by All (vv. 10, 11)
      All Will Bow
CONCLUSION
   A. J. O. Y.
   B. Let Us Pray
   C. Thought to Remember

Display visual 12 from the visuals packet and let it remain before the class throughout this session. The visual is shown on page 213.

Introduction

A. From Palaces to Poverty

In the little Dutch village of Saardam there is a small, wooden house, obviously very old. Protecting the little house is a roof supported by pillars. An interesting story is told about this house.

In the seventeenth century, Peter, who came to be called *the Great*, became czar of Russia. He realized that his country was very backward and lacked many of the skills needed for it to become a great power, and so he was determined to westernize his land. One of the skills the Russians lacked was knowledge about how to build ocean-going ships. To gain this knowledge, Peter gave up the luxuries of his court and, traveling incognito, went to the Netherlands. There he took a job in the shipyards, hoping to learn the secrets of shipbuilding. While working in the shipyards, he lived in the little cottage that is now protected as a historic site.

In a humble way, this represents what Jesus did. He left the courts of Heaven, and all the honor and glory that were His there, and became a human being. For thirty-three years He lived among men, and then He suffered and died. In one important way, however, Peter's and Jesus' trips differed. Peter came to the Netherlands to take something from them—their shipbuilding secrets. Jesus, on the other hand, came to bring something to earth—the hope of eternal life.

B. Lesson Background

On his second missionary journey, Paul and his companions left Troas in response to the Macedonian call and journeyed to the city of Philippi. There they established a church. Leaving Philippi, they made their way westward, establishing churches in other Macedonian cities as well. One of these cities was Thessalonica. While Paul was there, the Christians in Philippi sent aid to him on more than one occasion (Philippians 4:15, 16).

Years later, Paul was arrested as a result of his testimony for Jesus and was sent to Rome as a prisoner. The Philippians, learning of his imprisonment, sent a gift to him by the hand of Epaphroditus. Paul's letter to the Philippians, written in about A.D. 62 or 63, was a kind of thank-you note for the gift they had sent to him through Epaphroditus. In this letter Paul expressed his love for the Philippians, and the absence of any sharp criticism of the church indicates that the church was relatively free of the problems that plagued some of the other churches to which he wrote.

Yet the second chapter of Philippians, from which today's lesson is taken, does contain a hint of a problem. Paul's plea for unity ("that ye be likeminded") and his call for humility suggest that some disagreements had arisen within the congregation.

I. Exhortation to Unity (Philippians 2:1-4)

A. Desire for Unity (vv. 1, 2)

1, 2. If there be therefore any consolation in Christ, if any comfort of love, if any fellowship of the Spirit, if any bowels and mercies, fulfill

ye my joy, that ye be likeminded, having the same love, being of one accord, of one mind.

In the closing verses of chapter one, Paul acknowledged that the Philippian church had suffered some type of persecution. Urging them to continue to stand firm in the faith, he welcomed them into the fellowship of suffering.

The four clauses that make up verse 1, each beginning with *if,* may make it sound as if Paul were casting doubt on all of these things. But the grammatical construction of these clauses makes it possible to substitute *since* for *if.* Paul knew that all these things were true. Thus these expressions were affirmations of faith, not conditional clauses raising doubts. Since they were true, Paul's readers ought to do what verse 2 suggests.

Any consolation in Christ. The word translated *consolation* comes from a root meaning "to call along side of one" for the purpose of providing support or help. The same root word is used of Jesus as "an advocate with the Father" (1 John 2:1) and of the Holy Spirit (John 14:26).

Any comfort of love. The word translated *comfort* comes from two words that mean "speech" or "story" and "along side of." Thus it conveys the idea of speaking along side of a person for the purpose of providing solace or cheering him up. The solace, however, must not be just syrupy sentimentality, but must be based on *agape* love, that love that is both intelligent and helping.

Any fellowship of the Spirit. The abiding presence of the Holy Spirit is promised to every believer. The point Paul was making is that their common sharing in the Spirit ought to be a factor in the life of the congregation. *Any bowels and mercies.* The ancients spoke of the abdominal organs as the center of tender emotions, whereas we moderns speak of the heart. Paul's appeal was that they would show compassion in all of their dealings.

The Philippians had already brought much joy to the apostle Paul. They had readily received the gospel when he had preached it to them. As noted in the lesson background, they had expressed their love and concern for him in tangible ways on several occasions. Now he asked them to make his joy complete by being united in love and spirit and purpose.

That ye be likeminded. Literally, this means that they should "think the same thing." The emphasis is not so much upon intellectual agreement as it is upon their commitment to a common cause. The other three elements in the remainder of the sentence all point toward the goal of unity within the congregation. Whatever it was that was disrupting the congregation, Paul was

---

How to Say It

AGAPE (Greek).   uh-*gah*-pay.
EPAPHRODITUS.   E-paf-ro-*dye*-tus.
PHILIPPI.   Fih-*lip*-pie or *Fil*-ih-pie.
THESSALONICA.   *Thess*-uh-lo-*nye*-kuh
    (strong accent on *nye; th* as in *thin*).

---

determined to hold up unity as a desirable and attainable goal.

FULFILL MY JOY

The family was all there. This seldom happened, because the children's work and ministry had scattered them to three different continents. They had grown apart without even realizing it. Now that they were home again, the severed relationships were being repaired.

Marjorie, their mother, turned to her husband and said, "Honey, this reunion fulfills my dream of having all of our children home together at least one more time. Look at their faces and listen to them. They are happy with each other, happy to be here with us, happy to have their children playing and getting acquainted. My joy is full, for we are one family. Today is a day I have longed for and will never forget! Heaven must be something like this."

The family rejoices in that memory, for Marjorie died before they were ever all together in one place again.

The members of families can't always live close to each other, but they can be one in spirit, with love and appreciation for all members of the family.

Paul worked and prayed for the unity of love, purpose, and mind that Jesus came to give to His people. Fulfill Paul's joy by being of one spirit. Honor the church, the family of our Lord, until we are all finally home.   —W. P.

B. Way of Unity (vv. 3, 4)

3. Let nothing be done through strife or vainglory; but in lowliness of mind let each esteem other better than themselves.

In this verse Paul gives us some causes of disunity and suggests some ways to cure it. The word here translated *strife* is also used in 1:16, where it is translated "contention." It suggests self-seeking, that which is done with a partisan and factious spirit. When individuals in a group all seek to advance themselves, resentment soon plagues that group and it is torn with strife.

True honor is bestowed on a person because of his or her character or accomplishments. *Vainglory,* on the other hand, is empty honor. This kind of honor is given just because one is wealthy or is in a position to do favors for others. Those who compete for this kind of honor create an atmosphere of disharmony that leads to division.

Paul reminds the Philippians that there is a better way. This better way begins with humility. Humility causes one to consider others better than himself. A note of caution must be inserted here. This does not mean that one's self-esteem should be reduced to the point that a person practically hates himself. Psychologists tell us that many people's problems stem from a low self-esteem, which is the result of rejection and mistreatment in their childhood. One will never fall into the error of self-rejection if that person realizes that he or she is a child of God, and made for a purpose in God's kingdom. What Paul means, simply, is that instead of seeking honor for themselves, Christians should seek to honor others as much as possible. If every Christian does this, a spirit of unity will prevail in the church (see Romans 12:10).

4. Look not every man on his own things, but every man also on the things of others.

It is natural for a person to look after his or her own welfare and interests. Indeed, each Christian is instructed to provide for his own needs if he is able to do so (see 2 Thessalonians 3:11, 12). Furthermore, harsh words are directed to that person who does not provide for his own family (1 Timothy 5:8). The word *also* in the verse before us shows that Paul is saying in addition to looking out for our own concerns, we should *also* consider the interests of others. An attitude of concern for the welfare of others will manifest itself in those actions of helpfulness that promote harmony and unity in the body of Christ.

II. Christ Jesus the Servant (Philippians 2:5-8)

A. Attitude (v. 5)

5. Let this mind be in you, which was also in Christ Jesus.

Paul knew that people can understand abstract principles better when they are shown a model of the desired attitude or conduct. Christ Jesus was that model, the perfect model. The Philippian Christians were urged to imitate Jesus' mind, or attitude. The emphasis here is not on the intellectual aspects of the mind but on the attitudes that shape behavior. As a man "thinketh in his heart, so is he" (Proverbs 23:7). In a large measure, what we do is determined by what we think. If we can learn to think Christ's thoughts after Him, then we will begin to act like Him in our relations with others. If this is really to mean anything in our lives, however,

we must learn what Jesus' mind was like. That necessitates our serious study of the Scriptures.

B. Self-Emptying (vv. 6, 7)

6. Who, being in the form of God, thought it not robbery to be equal with God.

Paul's statement is beyond human ability to comprehend fully. He touches the very mystery of the identity of Jesus with God, stating that before Jesus became a man He was *in the form of God.* That is, He possessed the same nature, character, and essence of being as God. *Thought it not robbery to be equal with God.* Christ Jesus' equality with God was His by nature. It was His right, therefore, to claim this equality, and in doing so, He was not taking anything that did not belong to Him. This is the meaning of the expression as it stands in the *King James Version.* The *New International Version* translates this differently. It has "did not consider equality with God something to be grasped." This translation, which in similar wording is found in most modern versions, seems more in keeping with the context of Paul's thought in this chapter. The meaning, therefore, would be as follows: Though Christ was God, and in His Heavenly estate enjoyed all the prerogatives of deity, yet He did not grasp or cling tenaciously to His divine state. In obedience to God, He was willing to surrender the glories of deity that were His. Paul's purpose was to give the Philippians an example of humility. What greater example of humility could one find than this?

7. But made himself of no reputation, and took upon him the form of a servant, and was made in the likeness of men.

The *New American Standard Bible* translates the first part of this verse as "but emptied Himself." This is the key to the whole passage we are studying in this lesson. The humiliation and sacrifice of Christ were not forced upon Him; He chose and accepted them deliberately in order that we might be redeemed. In emptying himself, Christ laid aside glory, honor, and Heavenly station. In His willingness to become the Savior of mankind, He became a human being with all the weaknesses and limitations that this involved. In His physical body he experienced hunger, labor, fatigue, temptation, disappointment, and death.

It is clear, however, that He did not lay aside His divine nature. He retained the authority to forgive sins. He had miraculous power over nature, over disease, and over demons. He knew what was in the minds of men, fathoming their thoughts even as they thought them. And on the mount of transfiguration, His divine glory burst forth in such force that the three disciples were overwhelmed. Still, the condescension of Christ, which Paul portrays in this verse, is all but beyond our comprehension. From "being in the form of God," deserving to be worshiped and served, Christ *took upon him the form of a servant,* becoming as one who serves a superior.

C. Sacrificial Death (v. 8)

8. And being found in fashion as a man, he humbled himself, and became obedient unto death, even the death of the cross.

Christ humbled himself by leaving the courts of Heaven and becoming a man. His humiliation did not end with His incarnation, though. The depth of His humiliation came on the cross. Even citizens of the first century, who had much more immediate contact with brutality than we today, found death by crucifixion repulsive. Cicero described death on the cross as "this most cruel and hideous of punishments."

Crucifixion was reserved for the worst and most despised criminals. Those who were crucified had no choice, but were forced to face death in that manner. Jesus, however, did have a choice. But He had come as a servant, and He was obedient to God, even to the extent that He gave His life in this most painful and shameful way.

III. Exaltation of the Servant (Philippians 2:9-11)

A. A Name Above All (v. 9)

9. Wherefore God also hath highly exalted him, and given him a name which is above every name.

The word *wherefore* means that what follows is a result of what has gone before. God has exalted Christ because of His obedience. His exaltation comes as the natural consequence of His humility. During His ministry Jesus often stressed this theme. "And whosoever shall exalt himself shall be abased; and he that shall humble himself shall be exalted" (Matthew 23:12). "But many that are first shall be last; and the last shall be first" (Matthew 19:30). "He that loveth his life shall lose it; and he that hateth his life in this world shall keep it unto life eternal" (John 12:25).

And given him a name which is above every name. God bestowed on Christ "the name" (*New American Standard Bible*) supreme and divine. Some have suggested that this name was *Jesus;* others have said that it was *Lord.* Still others think that Paul was not referring to any particular appellation or title. It may be that Paul was referring to the station to which God has named Christ. God has given Christ Jesus all authority (Matthew

visual 12

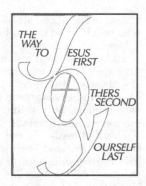

28:18); God has appointed Him heir of all things (Hebrews 1:2) and made Him head over all things to the church (Ephesians 1:22). Christ has been named (exalted) above all.

B. Submission by All (vv. 10, 11)

10. That at the name of Jesus every knee should bow, of things in heaven, and things in earth, and things under the earth.

This verse reveals the extent of the authority given Christ. Every knee shall bow before Him as an act of reverence and humility. Those showing this reverence are not limited to human beings on earth. Some take *things* in heaven, in earth, and under the earth to be neuter and thus to include inanimate objects and animals as well as human beings or other beings such as demons and angels. The words are actually masculine in gender, and the *New American Standard Bible* translates it more accurately: "of those who are in heaven, and on earth, and under the earth."

The book of Revelation records the songs of saints and angels in praise of the Lamb. And all persons, whether now living or dead, will bow the knee to Christ in the Day of Judgment.

11. And that every tongue should confess that Jesus Christ is Lord, to the glory of God the Father.

This verse reiterates the previous verse, confirming that every being will recognize Christ as Lord with tongue as well as with bended knee. The honor that was bestowed on Christ will also glorify the Father (see 1 Corinthians 3:21, 23; 15:24-28).

ALL WILL BOW

Protests, revolutions, assassinations, and coups have all testified to the unwillingness of people to bow before rulers whom they felt were not worthy of their allegiance.

Those who have come closest to gaining universal homage have not been the rich and the powerful. Hitler, Mussolini, and Stalin were despised, as were any other figures in history who attempted to force all to bow to their rule and who provided no care or human dignity in ruling.

Honored, instead, are those who have served mankind best. Leaders in medical research and discovery and all who have relieved human misery stand at the head of the list. Others who have served to overcome the ravages of famines, earthquakes, floods, and storms are acclaimed our heroes and heroines.

Think of Jesus. He fed the hungry, healed the sick, and restored the disabled. He taught us to love our enemies and to care for those in need: the poor, naked, starving, and abused. And most important, He overcame sin. Is it any wonder that in God's timing and by His word all will finally bow to Jesus and acclaim Him Lord?—W. P.

Conclusion

A. J. O. Y.

A teenager once put up a large poster in her room with these three letters on it: *JOY*. Noticing the sign, her mother asked her what it meant. The daughter told her that it was her life goal.

"That's a wonderful goal in life," commented her mother. "But I'm afraid it isn't practical."

"What do you mean?" asked the girl.

"Well, you want joy, but your motto doesn't tell how to find it."

"Oh, but it does Mother. The *J* means Jesus first. The *O* means others second, and the *Y* means yourself last. If people are willing to live their lives on those terms, then they'll have joy." And right she was!

The opening verses of the lesson seem to indicate that the Philippian church had been experiencing some strife and division. Apparently the problem arose because some had fallen victim to pride and had pushed their interests ahead of the interests of others. Instead of heaping a scathing indictment upon them for their selfishness, Paul held up before them the example of Christ. If the people had even the slightest idea of what was involved in Christ's leaving His Heavenly home and becoming a slave among men, then every last vestige of pride would be washed from them.

How can a person watch the Lord stoop to wash the dirty feet of His disciples and still loudly insist upon receiving his or her rights? How can one stand at the foot of the cross and look up into the face of the dying Savior and still become involved in the petty game of church politics? How can a person continue to think only of his or her own interests, knowing that the time will come when every knee shall bow and every tongue shall confess that Christ is Lord?

Dare we face these questions openly and candidly?

There is a great deal of truth in the teenager's formula for finding joy. Even though the church in Philippi had some problems and strife, still it was a church that had found satisfaction in Christian service. They had sent financial support to Paul as he preached the gospel, and, as a result, they could share in the fruits of his ministry.

Those individuals who think of their own interests first are certain to find such an attitude self-defeating. The satisfaction they hope to find in life will evaporate before their very eyes. We hear many people talk about "finding themselves." The surest way for people to find themselves is to lose themselves in service to others. What is true of individuals is also true of congregations. The most vibrant, joyous churches today are those that give themselves in service to the Lord and other people. They are active in evangelism, in supporting missions, and in helping the poor, the homeless, the sick, and the dying. The way to find joy is through J. O. Y.

B. Let Us Pray

Dear God, if we are inclined to demand our rights, bring us to our knees in humility. Daily we are tempted to selfishly pursue our own interests. Help us to learn that these will perish. In this "me-first" world, we are taught to push and shove to get to the head of the line. Teach us that the first shall be last and the last shall be first. May we learn these things while there is still time. In Jesus' name, amen.

C. Thought to Remember

"They that know God will be humble. They that know themselves cannot be proud."

—John Flavel

Home Daily Bible Readings

Monday, Feb. 10—New in Christ (2 Corinthians 5:16-21)

Tuesday, Feb. 11—Greatness Through Service (Mark 10:35-45)

Wednesday, Feb. 12—The Strong and the Weak (Romans 15:6)

Thursday, Feb. 13—The Mind of Christ (Philippians 2:1-11)

Friday, Feb. 14—Christ Became a Servant (John 13:1-20)

Saturday, Feb. 15—One in Christ (Galatians 3:23-28)

Sunday, Feb. 16—The Bread of Life (John 6:35-40)

Learning by Doing

This page contains an alternate lesson plan emphasizing learning activities. Classes desiring such student involvement will find these suggestions helpful.

Learning Goals

As students participate in today's lesson, lead them to:

1. List the servant attributes of Christ recorded in today's text.

2. Choose one of these attributes and decide how to better demonstrate it in their lives.

Into the Lesson

Divide the class into two teams. Students in one half of the class are to think of every positive idea they can possibly associate with the idea of *servanthood*. The other half is to think of every negative idea they can possibly associate with this word.

List their contrasting ideas beside each other on the chalkboard and discuss with your students how they really feel about the idea of being servants. Most of them realize that this is a Scriptural mandate, but many Christians have not come to terms with what servanthood demands. Today's lesson will help us incorporate the idea into our everyday living.

Into the Word

Ask your students to make four lists as they examine today's Scripture. They may do this as they work together in groups of three. Or they may make these lists individually as a class member reads the text aloud. (Space for this is provided in the student book.) Here are the four headings, with possible answers suggested for your reference:

What Jesus WAS—God (v. 6), man (v. 7), exalted as Lord (vv. 9, 10).

What Jesus DID—did not cling to equality with God (v. 6), made himself nothing (v. 7), took the form of a servant (v. 7), became human (vv. 7, 8), humbled himself (v. 8), was "obedient to death"—on a cross! (v. 8).

What we should BE— encouraged by our unity with Christ (v. 1), comforted by Christ's love (v. 1), in fellowship with the Spirit (v. 1), tender and compassionate (v. 1), unified with other Christians in love, spirit, and purpose (v. 2), humble (v. 3), servants (vv. 5-8).

What we should DO—nothing out of selfishness or conceit (v. 3), consider others better than ourselves (v. 3), look to the interests of others (v. 4), bow before Jesus and confess Him as Lord (vv. 10, 11).

In addition to this idea for Bible study, or instead of it, you may want to use the following suggestion:

Chart of contrasts. Write the following headings on your chalkboard:

The World's Success
The Servant's Success.

Ask class members to copy the headings on blank paper you give them, making a worksheet for analyzing today's printed text. First they should look through this passage, noting every characteristic for successful living that it mentions. These should be listed under the second heading, "The Servant's Success." Beside each of these attributes or actions that should characterize the Christian's life-style, students should write a contrasting characteristic that is often suggested by non-Christians as a means to success.

After students have completed this Bible study (in pairs or groups of four to six), discuss with them what they have written. Do your students agree with each other about the inadequate definitions of success that the world hands them? How have they tried to confront this faulty thinking? When your students have tried to live by Christian standards instead, how have their co-workers or supervisors or neighbors reacted? Which of the characteristics listed from this Scripture is the hardest to live by? (You may decide to let this discussion be an alternative to the "Into Life" activity that is suggested below.)

Into Life

Give students individual sheets of art paper and ask them to draw at least one "servant situation" for the rest of the class to see. They should think of a situation from everyday life in which we need to follow Jesus' example of humble service. Challenge them to think of their roles as parents, adult children, neighbors, employees, or church members as they think of times when it is difficult to consistently demonstrate a servant attitude.

After several minutes allow volunteers to share what they have drawn and to explain its significance. End the class session with sentence prayers. Encourage class members to mention specific situations where they need God's help to demonstrate a servant spirit.

Let's Talk It Over

The questions on this page are designed to encourage review of the lesson Scriptures and to promote discussion of the lesson by the class. The answers provided are only discussion starters. Let your class talk it over from there.

1. Christians are to be likeminded in commitment to a common cause. How does such a commitment promote unity in the church?

People with a common cause tend to pull together when there is an opportunity to advance their cause. In the church we need to emphasize that within the surrounding community are many persons who are lost in sin. The fields "are white already to harvest," and great opportunities exist for those who will help with reaping (see John 4:35, 36). When all the church is caught up in some aspect of evangelism, the members are more likely to experience unity. Also, people with a cause tend to pull together when that cause is threatened. Thus, when Christians are all involved in defending the church against unbelievers who degrade the name of Christ and distort the teachings of the Bible, a more unified church results.

2. We hear much today about the importance of self-esteem, while the Bible frequently urges us to humility and lowliness of mind. How can we achieve a proper balance between these two emphases?

Some Christians object to the use of the term *self-esteem* in the church because it seems to be at odds with the Bible's frequent admonitions against a proud, self-centered attitude. It is clear, however, that God does not want us to discount ourselves to the point that we abuse our bodies, or regard ourselves as unworthy of friendships, or express other forms of self-abasement. God's love is the key here. God loves us personally and powerfully, and this is the basis for a healthy view of ourselves. We must remember, however, that God has that same love for other human beings, so that none has justification for thinking of himself "more highly than he ought to think" (Romans 12:3).

3. It is striking to think of how Jesus emptied himself in coming to earth. How may we follow His example in this?

Jesus gave up certain divine prerogatives in order to dwell in human flesh for a time. He was willing to forego temporarily the rights that were His as the Son of God. His example should lead us to take inventory of our rights and to ask ourselves if God may not want us to give up some

of those to accomplish His will. We may say that we have a right to spend our money as we please or that it is our privilege to set aside a certain time for ourselves. But God may call on us to empty ourselves in the sense of relinquishing those rights for a while, so that we may serve and witness to other human beings in need.

4. There is something very compelling in the assurance that "at the name of Jesus every knee should bow." How can we respond to this?

As Christians, we should find satisfaction in anticipating that moment when we ourselves will be able to bow down before Jesus and show Him our gratitude, love, and devotion. As we consider that occasion, we should be stirred to share the gospel with others so that they also may bow the knee in reverent homage to the Savior. The statement above must include the unsaved, who apparently will bow in fear and horror, as they realize that the One they rejected and refused to follow is indeed Savior and Lord. It is disturbing to contemplate multitudes falling down before Jesus in sober realization of fiery judgment. How it should stir us to urge our friends and family to yield to Him now, so that their bowing to Him on that great day to come may be with joyful anticipation!

5. We sometimes hear the lament, "I'm not getting anything out of church." What does such a complaint reveal?

Those who complain in this way are on a self-defeating course. They may have a sense of desperation about finding some peace, encouragement, answers to problems, assurance of love, and the like through the church. If their focus, however, is primarily on getting as much as they can for themselves, they are unlikely to be satisfied for long in any church. Jesus showed us that dedicating ourselves to service is the key to the highest level of spiritual contentment. He told His disciples, "Whosoever will be great among you, let him be your minister; and whosoever will be chief among you, let him be your servant" (Matthew 20:26, 27). We should encourage every church member to seek this kind of greatness; in so doing they will also discover a sense of personal fulfillment within the church.

The Hallelujah Chorus

LESSON SCRIPTURE: Revelation 15:2-4; 19:1-8.

PRINTED TEXT: Revelation 15:2-4; 19:4-8.

Revelation 15:2-4

2 And I saw as it were a sea of glass mingled with fire: and them that had gotten the victory over the beast, and over his image, and over his mark, and over the number of his name, stand on the sea of glass, having the harps of God.

3 And they sing the song of Moses the servant of God, and the song of the Lamb, saying, Great and marvelous are thy works, Lord God Almighty; just and true are thy ways, thou King of saints.

4 Who shall not fear thee, O Lord, and glorify thy name? For thou only art holy: for all nations shall come and worship before thee; for thy judgments are made manifest.

Revelation 19:4-8

4 And the four and twenty elders and the four beasts fell down and worshipped God that sat on the throne, saying, Amen; Alleluia.

5 And a voice came out of the throne, saying, Praise our God, all ye his servants, and ye that fear him, both small and great.

6 And I heard as it were the voice of a great multitude, and as the voice of many waters, and as the voice of mighty thunderings, saying, Alleluia: for the Lord God omnipotent reigneth.

7 Let us be glad and rejoice, and give honor to him: for the marriage of the Lamb is come, and his wife hath made herself ready.

8 And to her was granted that she should be arrayed in fine linen, clean and white: for the fine linen is the righteousness of saints.

GOLDEN TEXT: Alleluia: for the Lord God omnipotent reigneth. Let us be glad and rejoice, and give honor to him.—Revelation 19:6, 7.

Feb 23

Lesson Aims

This lesson should help each student to:

1. Be assured that God will ultimately triumph over the forces of evil.

2. Be able to face the various threats and problems of life, knowing that those in Christ will share in God's victory over evil.

Lesson Outline

INTRODUCTION
  A. Singing in Triumph
  B. Lesson Background
  I. THE VICTORS' SONG (Revelation 15:2-4)
  A. The Setting (v. 2a)
  B. The Singers (v. 2b)
  C. The Song (v. 3a)
  D. The Subject (v. 3b)
  E. The Triumph (v. 4)
  II. A HALLELUJAH WEDDING (Revelation 19:4-8)
  A. The Worshipers of God (v. 4)
  B. A Call for Praise (v. 5)
  C. The Shout of the Multitude (v. 6)
      Hallelujah! God Reigns!
  D. The Wedding Is at Hand (v. 7)
  E. The Attire of the Bride (v. 8)
      Prepared to Be Wed
CONCLUSION
  A. To a Wedding We're Going
  B. Let Us Pray
  C. Thought to Remember

Display visual 13 from the visuals packet and let it remain before the class throughout the session. The visual is shown on page 220.

Introduction

A. Singing in Triumph

In the eighteenth century the Wesleyan Revival swept across the British Isles, and the Methodists, as Wesley's followers came to be called, became noted for their joyous outlook on life. The Methodists loved to sing, not only in their meetings but wherever they went. It is no accident that Charles, John Wesley's brother, wrote many hundreds of hymns.

On one occasion a lawyer in a Welsh mining town needed some information for a case. The only person who could provide this information was a miner who had already gone to work deep into the mine. The lawyer needed the information at once and could not wait until the miner came to the surface at the end of the work day. So he got permission to go down into the mine to find the man. As the lawyer and his guide descended into the mine, it became totally dark. "How will I ever find the man in this darkness?"

"Oh, you'll find him all right," came the guide's reply. "He's a Methodist; you'll hear him singing." The lawyer couldn't help asking himself how anyone could sing in such a dark, dank, dirty place. But as they moved down a tunnel, they heard a voice lustily singing one of Charles Wesley's hymns: "Love divine, all loves excelling."

So it will be with those battle-scarred veterans of God's war with Satan. Surrounded by the din of battle and covered with the scars of combat, they will lift their hallelujahs to the Lord God Almighty.

B. Lesson Background

The book of Revelation poses numerous problems for interpreters for at least two reasons. First, the book is cast in highly figurative language. At times we can only guess at some of the meanings intended in the figures that are used. When we are forced to speculate about the meaning of figures, we should not be dogmatic about our conclusions.

Second, differing interpretive methods are suggested for a proper understanding of the book. As a result some hold a postmillennial view, some a premillennial view, and others an amillennial view. Only the most optimistic person would ever believe that we could approach unanimity in our understanding of the details of the book of Revelation.

Even if we can never achieve total agreement about the details of the book, there are certain general conclusions that all may accept. For example, all will agree that the book shows the church going through times of terrible persecution. Further, there is complete agreement that the church will eventually emerge triumphant. It is also clear that those who have passed through suffering will raise their voices to God in songs of joy and victory.

I. The Victors' Song (Revelation 15:2-4)

The chapters immediately preceding this passage tell of great persecution of the church and suffering of the saints. Whether these chapters depict events that have already happened or whether they look to some future event may be debated. One thing, however, is clear from the text we are studying in this lesson—even though the forces of evil have made an all-out assault on the church, the faithful have survived through great difficulties. Now they are prepared to raise their voices in worship and praise.

A. The Setting (v. 2a)

2a. And I saw as it were a sea of glass mingled with fire.

A sea of glass was mentioned earlier (4:6), and there it was located before the Heavenly throne. We are not told that the sea of glass mentioned here in chapter 15 was in Heaven, but that seems certain. This is indicated by the fact that the four beasts (living creatures) mentioned in the scene in Heaven (4:6) were also present here (15:7). John does not actually write that he saw a sea of glass, but *as it were a sea of glass.* The *New International Version* has "what looked like a sea of glass." It is uncertain whether John means that the sea was pure in appearance like glass or whether the consistency of the sea was solid like glass.

The sea was mixed with fire. Fire is often emblematic of purity. In the scene in 4:6, the sea of glass was "like unto crystal," which also conveys the idea of purity. Fire, however, is also used in the Scriptures to designate God's judgment (2 Thessalonians 1:7, 8; 2 Peter 3:10). Some commentators point out that God's judgment is the theme of the song of the saints (v. 4).

B. The Singers (v. 2b)

2b. And them that had gotten the victory over the beast, and over his image, and over his mark, and over the number of his name, stand on the sea of glass, having the harps of God.

Over the beast. The word *over* is better translated "from" here and each time it appears in this verse. The singers were those who had suffered great persecution, and had been victorious by fleeing. *And over his image.* This may have reference to some form of idolatry that the beast had tried to force the faithful to accept. We remember that statues were erected to the Roman emperors and divine honors were paid to them. We are reminded also of Nebuchadnezzar's efforts to force the three Hebrew men to bow down before his golden image (Daniel 3). *And over his mark.* This phrase is not found in the older manuscripts, and thus is omitted from most modern translations. *And over the number of his name.* This may have reference to the number 666, which the beast required all to have written on their right hand and on their forehead (see Revelation 13:16-18). *On the sea of glass.* The

---

How to Say It

ISAIAH.   Eye-*zay*-uh.
NEBUCHADNEZZAR.   *Neb*-you-kud-*nezz*-er (strong accent on *nezz*).

Greek construction here may also be translated "*by* the sea of glass," and many versions read that way.

C. The Song (v. 3a)

3a. And they sing the song of Moses the servant of God, and the song of the Lamb.

The song of Moses is not verbatim the song that Moses sang when the people of Israel safely crossed the Red Sea and were delivered from the Egyptians (Exodus 15). The idea is that just as Moses sang praises to God for deliverance, so the redeemed should in a similar fashion raise their voices in thanksgiving. *The song of the Lamb.* This is not a second song, but is simply a second way of identifying the song.

D. The Subject (v. 3b)

3b. Saying, Great and marvelous are thy works, Lord God Almighty; just and true are thy ways, thou King of saints.

The subject of the victors' song is the *Lord God Almighty.* Its words clearly reflect numerous Old Testament expressions of praise to God, especially some of the psalms (see 1 Chronicles 16:9; Psalm 111:2; 139:14). He is *Lord* because He is Ruler, not only of men, but of the entire universe. He is *God* because He is the Creator of everything. He is *Almighty* because in the context He has conquered all his enemies.

Not only are the works of God vast in scope; they are also *marvelous* because they produce wonder in those who contemplate them. His ways are *just* because they are true and reflect His holy nature. The full weight of that justice is reserved for the forces of evil.

King of saints. Many Greek manuscripts have either "of the nations" or "of the ages." As a result, most recent translations prefer one or the other of these over "of saints." Any one of the three is fitting in the context.

E. The Triumph (v. 4)

4. Who shall not fear thee, O Lord, and glorify thy name? For thou only art holy: for all nations shall come and worship before thee; for thy judgments are made manifest.

Who shall not fear thee, O Lord? See Jeremiah 10:7. *Fear* here is used in the sense of reverence. The answer to this rhetorical question is obvious. Once men have witnessed God's might and

His justice, then all will hold Him in awe and reverence. But beyond that they will be overwhelmed by His holiness. This quality above all qualities distinguished Jehovah God from the gods of the pagan nations that surrounded Israel. Even a servant of God such as Isaiah felt himself undone in the presence of the holy God (Isaiah 6:1-6).

The basic meaning of *holy* is "to be set apart from" or "separated from." God is holy in this sense, in that He is separated from His creation, the work of His hands. But holiness also has an ethical quality, indicating moral excellence. Those who would serve God must demonstrate in their lives this same ethical quality, and thus bring glory to God. Yet human holiness cannot even begin to approach the holiness of God, which must ever remain an unattainable idea.

For all nations shall come and worship before thee. The ancient Israelites believed themselves especially chosen by God because of certain virtues they possessed. Chosen by God they certainly were, but not because they merited it in any sense. They were chosen to perform a special mission. That mission was to serve as a channel through which God would transmit His saving grace to all people.

When God called Abraham, He promised to bless him and make of him a great nation; but God's promise did not stop there. God also promised that through Abraham "all families of the earth" would be blessed (Genesis 12:1-3). By and large, Abraham's later descendants forgot this aspect of the promise. God's spokesmen, however, expressed this thought at various times (see Psalm 22:27; 66:4; 67:7; 86:9; Isaiah 66:23; Micah 4:1-4; Zechariah 8:22, 23).

Now once more that theme is sounded. As the end of all things approaches, people from all nations will come to worship God. This certainly looks to the great missionary enterprise of the church, for all nations will not come to worship God unless they know about Him. And they will not know unless we carry that message to them.

visual 13

For thy judgments are made manifest. God's judgments, His righteous acts, have been revealed. This may refer to the judgments that He has brought upon every nation, or to acts other than those in a judicial setting. The worshipers know of these judgments or acts either because of firsthand observation or because of the testimony of the Scriptures. The righteousness of God, which is thus revealed, draws people to worship Him.

II. A Hallelujah Wedding (Revelation 19:4-8)

This section of our printed text presents another scene in Heaven. Chapters 17 and 18 record the utter destruction of the harlot Babylon. Chapter 19 opens with Heaven praising God for taking vengeance on the great harlot, for she was guilty of the blood of God's people (see 18:24). Heaven's rejoicing then continues over the coming marriage of the Lamb and His bride.

A. The Worshipers of God (v. 4)

4. And the four and twenty elders and the four beasts fell down and worshipped God that sat on the throne, saying, Amen; Alleluia.

The scene depicted in this verse hearkens back to chapter 4, the great "throne room" vision. In that scene the twenty-four elders are seen sitting on twenty-four thrones and are wearing white garments and golden crowns. In Revelations 5:8 the twenty-four elders are also mentioned. There they fell down before the Lamb and proclaimed that He alone was worthy to take the book and open the seals. In the scene in chapter 19, they are not on thrones but have fallen down before God, who is seated on a throne.

The identity of the twenty-four elders has been the subject of considerable discussion among scholars. Perhaps the best conjecture is that they represent the twelve Hebrew tribes and the twelve apostles (Revelation 21:12-14). If that is the case, then together they represent the whole host, both those under the Old Covenant and those under the New Covenant, who will be saved.

The four beasts ("living creatures" may be a better translation) are also mentioned in chapter 4, where they are described in some detail. One was like a lion, another was like a calf, the third had the face of a man, while the fourth was like a flying eagle. They all had six wings and were "Full of eyes before and behind" (v. 6) and were "full of eyes within" (v. 8). There is even less agreement among scholars about the identity of these living creatures. Perhaps the wisest counsel is to acknowledge that we don't know their identity or what they represent.

One thing we are sure of, however, is that they join in the worship of God. *Alleluia* is another version of the Hebrew exclamation Hallelujah, which means "praise ye Jehovah."

B. A Call for Praise (v. 5)

5. And a voice came out of the throne, saying, Praise our God, all ye his servants, and ye that fear him, both small and great.

In the midst of this scene a voice is heard proceeding from the throne. The voice, which is not identified, offers an invitation to all of God's servants to praise Him. The invitation includes all who fear Him, *both small and great*, regardless of rank or wealth. This reflects the idea expressed in Psalm 115:13.

C. The Shout of the Multitude (v. 6)

6. And I heard as it were the voice of a great multitude, and as the voice of many waters, and as the voice of mighty thunderings, saying, Alleluia: for the Lord God omnipotent reigneth.

In response to the voice from the throne came the sound of the mighty choir of the redeemed raising their voices as one. Lacking modern instruments to measure the volume of the choir, John struggled to find means to convey the intensity of the sound to his readers. It was *as the voice of many waters*. One thinks of the roar that can be heard blocks away as the mighty Niagara hurls millions of gallons of water into the ravine below, or of standing at the top of a cliff as the angry waves pound the rocks below. But John wasn't satisfied with this. He tried again to express what he heard: *the voice of mighty thunderings*. One who has been on a mountaintop during a thunderstorm can have some appreciation of what John was trying to convey.

The volume was essential to express the idea of the choral response. *The Lord God omnipotent reigneth.* The word that is here translated *omnipotent* is elsewhere rendered "Almighty." Literally it means "one who holds all things in his control." Nothing could more accurately describe God's power.

HALLELUJAH! GOD REIGNS!

George Hayes was an elder and Bible teacher most of his adult life. In his later years he became deaf. It was a real blow, for he loved both the singing and preaching at the worship times in his church. When George was seventy-five, his eyesight began to fail. This made his daily Bible reading increasingly difficult, but with a magnifying glass and a large-print Bible he could enjoy his Bible study. No matter what physical problem occurred, George Hayes never missed the Bible study or worship services.

He was asked why he was so faithful in attendance when he couldn't hear, see, or walk well. Listen carefully to his answer. "I don't intend to be absent from worship, proclamation, or study of the Word at our church until it is a physical impossibility for me to attend. There is no other place on earth I can go where God is praised and adored in song and word as He is in the assembly of His saints. No other meeting makes the Holy Spirit a full partner in our minds as when we are in a church service. I may not hear or see all that goes on there, but I intend to be present. I plan to attend because worship will be my joy in Heaven, and I want to get a head start in that hallelujah time right now!"

God reigned in George Hayes's life. How important is worship in your life?   —W. P.

D. The Wedding Is at Hand (v. 7)

7. Let us be glad and rejoice, and give honor to him: for the marriage of the Lamb is come, and his wife hath made herself ready.

The voice of the multitude continues. The basis for the praise is the coming wedding of the Lamb. Marriage has often been used as a figure of God's relationship with His people. In the Old Testament, this imagery depicts Israel as the bride of Jehovah (see Isaiah 54:1-8; Ezekiel 16:8; Hosea 2:19). In the New Testament, the church is shown to be the bride of Christ (2 Corinthians 11:2; Ephesians 5:22-32).

The figure of the marriage of the Lamb in Revelation symbolizes the union between Christ and His faithful church. That union will be consummated at the last day when God's enemies are completely overthrown and sin is destroyed.

E. The Attire of the Bride (v. 8)

8. And to her was granted that she should be arrayed in fine linen, clean and white: for the fine linen is the righteousness of saints.

Some Bible students think that the Heavenly song ceased at the end of verse 7 and that all of verse 8 was a parenthetical statement by the Seer. Others think that the song ended with the words "clean and white," and that the remainder of the verse is the comment of John based on his remembrance of 7:14 (see also 3:18).

Verse 7 indicates that the bride had made herself ready for the coming of the Bridegroom. She was arrayed in white linen, a symbol of her purity and innocence. In this respect she stands in obvious contrast to the harlot, who was "arrayed in purple and scarlet" and "decked with gold and precious stones" (17:4).

The righteousness of saints is rendered in most modern versions as the "righteous acts of the saints." Giving themselves to Christ and becoming united with Him, the followers of Christ partake of his righteousness by the grace of God. In their lives the saints on earth reflect this righteousness and manifest their fidelity to Christ. Revelation 14:13, speaking of those who die in the Lord, states that "their works do follow them." In this scene they are clothed in fine linen, which is the righteous acts of the saints.

PREPARED TO BE WED

What is more lovely than a wedding when everything is prepared for a Christian celebration of marriage? At one west coast church, couples who desire to be married by a staff minister must complete prescribed training. This begins with eight lessons on marriage taught in a regularly scheduled marriage preparation class, and concludes with three sessions between the couple and the minister who will marry them. When this preparation has been completed, the rehearsal is held. Then comes the great day.

As the groom's party comes in, all is in place to begin. The organ sounds the chords of the wedding march, and the bride, fully prepared, is a vision of beauty. The audience stands as she walks down the aisle to join her groom.

Theirs is an hour worth waiting for! The bride is adorned for her husband, and his eyes reflect his love and desire to be one with her. She is arrayed in white, to portray purity, and each of them are prepared to be the best they are capable of being for one another.

We share the expected joy in the marriage of a prepared Christian couple. How much greater the joy we anticipate for the only marriage really "made in Heaven." There the church, pure and holy in the righteousness of Christ, becomes His bride. Don't miss being there for lack of preparation!   —W. P.

Conclusion

A. To a Wedding We're Going

Ordinarily weddings are happy occasions, although mothers have been known to cry, fathers often feel awkward, and brides and bridegrooms frequently feel a sense of panic. But those who share in the marriage of the Lamb and His bride will know only one emotion—triumphant joy. And why shouldn't they? This is the occasion toward which God's plan for human redemption has been building.

It is God's intention that all should be a part of this great wedding feast. Yet many will not be there because they refused the invitation. In Jesus' parable of the wedding feast (Matthew 22), many who had been invited refused the invitation, often for the most trivial excuses. Some

ridiculed the invitation. Others murdered the kings servants.

In the parable, the king who had issued the invitations refused to tolerate such conduct, and brought dire punishment on those wicked persons. Then he sent his servants out to bring in others, and these people came. It is very obvious that in this parable the king is God and the wedding is that of His Son and the church. Sad indeed will be the lot of any who deliberately ignore His invitation.

One of those who came to the wedding, however, was improperly dressed. Either he had not taken the wedding seriously, or he was careless. When the king saw the man, he ordered him to be removed and punished. The proper dress apparently is a symbol of lives of moral purity. For a member of the church, the bride of Christ, to live otherwise dishonors both the King and His Son, the bridegroom (see Ephesians 5:27).

As Christians we have a responsibility to lead people into a saving knowledge of Jesus Christ. Then we must help them to grow in that relationship so that when the marriage of Christ and church takes place, all will be ready for that happy and glorious occasion.

B. Let Us Pray

Almighty God, we give You thanks that we have been given a glimpse of the glorious victory that will be Yours when the last enemy is vanquished. May this knowledge give us strength and hope when we are surrounded by powerful enemies and we seem too weak to face them. In Jesus' name amen.

C. Thought to Remember

Heaven is a prepared place for prepared people.

Home Daily Bible Readings

Monday, Feb. 17—Praise to the Almighty (Revelation 15:1-4)

Tuesday, Feb. 18—Song of Triumph (Revelation 19:1-8)

Wednesday, Feb. 19—God's Kingdom (Revelation 11:15-19)

Thursday, Feb. 20—God Reigns Over All (Psalm 47)

Friday, Feb. 21—The City of God (Psalm 48)

Saturday, Feb. 22—Great is the Lord (Psalm 145:1-13)

Sunday, Feb. 23—Glory to God (Ephesians 3:14-21)

Learning by Doing

This page contains an alternate lesson plan emphasizing learning activities. Classes desiring such student involvement will find these suggestions helpful.

Learning Goals

Students in today's class session should:

1. Review the themes of all of this quarter's lessons.

2. List many of God's righteous deeds and mighty acts, for which we should praise Him.

3. List some of the righteous acts we should perform in response to Him.

Into the Lesson

This is the final lesson in a quarter in which we have been thinking about singing. So make sure music has some part in today's session. If nothing else, have Christian music playing as class members arrive.

You may find some song that relates to the praise of God that we will all someday offer in Heaven. If so, begin today's session by asking class members, "What is our greatest reason to praise God?" They may suggest several different ideas, all of them valid. Tell your students that today's printed text looks at praises we will sing in Heaven, and that the promise of Heaven is perhaps the best reason to always praise God.

Into the Word

Use the following list of lesson themes, introduced in lesson one, as a review for this quarter's study:

1. God can deliver us from our enemies.

2. God gives victory against His foes to those who trust Him.

3. God comforts us when we are grieving for the loss of someone close to us.

4. God sometimes intervenes in life to bring events and people that fill us with joy.

5. God made the whole universe, and yet He is interested in you and me.

6. In God's presence—and in His will—we find the greatest joy.

7. When we trust God, He brings us up from the depths of sin and shares His love with us forever.

8. God gives us the love shared by married partners.

9. God loves humankind, but sometimes His love for humans is not returned by them.

10. God wants to hear and answer our prayers.

11. God has perfect unity with Christ and wants His followers to have unity with each other.

12. Someday everyone will bow at Jesus' feet.

13. Heaven will be filled with songs to God.

Give these sentences to thirteen class members, one per class member, perhaps in the week before class. Ask each to be ready to read the sentence as well as the printed text for that lesson.

Put the following on the chalkboard:

! This lesson was important to me.

? I don't remember this lesson.

* I'd like to study this more.

Give each student a sheet of paper and ask them to number it from one to thirteen. As each passage is read, students should listen carefully and then put the appropriate symbol from the chalkboard on their sheet. After number thirteen is read (today's text), discuss it briefly with students: According to Revelation 15, why are we to praise God? (Because God is holy and His marvelous deeds and righteous acts have been revealed.) Ask students to suggest some of His righteous acts. (As they call them out, list them on the chalkboard.) Which of these acts are suggested by the texts we have examined this quarter? What other of God's deeds are mentioned in the texts that have been read aloud this morning?

While our text from Revelation 19 focuses on praising God, these verses also mention God's people. Where? (See verses 5 and 8.) How are the saints, who are the bride of Christ, clothed? (They are wearing fine linen, which stands for their righteous acts!) What righteous acts of God's people are suggested by the texts of this quarter? (If you have room, also list these on the chalkboard, or perhaps on a newsprint pad displayed beside the chalkboard.)

Into Life

If you have time, ask students to tell which lessons they marked with an exclamation point. Can they tell why the thoughts of their marked lessons are especially important to them?

Look again at the list of God's mighty deeds and the believers' righteous acts. For which of God's deeds are the class members especially grateful? Ask a few volunteers to mention these in a special prayer time that will close the session, each student emphasizing one. Which of the righteous acts would class members find most needed?

Perhaps some class members would mention these in the closing prayer time.

Let's Talk It Over

The questions on this page are designed to encourage review of the lesson Scriptures and to promote discussion of the lesson by the class. The answers provided are only discussion starters. Let your class talk it over from there.

1. Some Christians tend to neglect the book of Revelation because it contains so much that is difficult to understand. How can we encourage all Christians to benefit from this book?

Some persons enjoy speculating about the meanings of the various symbols in the book, but others do not. All, however, can benefit from features of the book that do not require extensive interpretation. The counsel given to the seven churches (chapters 2, 3) may be applied to the church today. We can adapt the praises found in such places as 4:11; 5:9-13; 7:10, 12. Many believers have honed their sense of anticipation for Heaven by reading chapters 21, 22, and these chapters are helpful in spite of their use of symbolism. It is accurate to say that Revelation contains matters of interest for every sincere Christian and that we all should read it regularly.

2. Revelation pictures people from all nations joining together in Heavenly worship. Why should we ponder this feature?

A detailed description of this appears in chapter 7. John saw "a great multitude, which no man could number, of all nations, and kindreds, and people, and tongues" worshiping God (Revelation 7:9). This needs to be kept in mind, since many are inclined to see the church in terms of their own nation and culture. They may forget that the gospel is universal in its appeal. This feature reminds us of the necessity of being active in supporting missionary work. One of the most exciting aspects of these descriptions of "multinational praise" is the thought that we shall be able to stand with the rest of Heaven's citizens, no longer separated by language or culture, but united in worship of our one Lord.

3. Revelation pictures people from all ranks and classes joining together in Heavenly worship. Why should we ponder this feature?

We may be inclined to overlook the fact that the early church was made up largely of poor people. If our own congregation is made up of middle-class families, we may see the church in those terms and fail to maintain an evangelistic outreach among the poor of our community. The scenes in Revelation remind us of how important it is for us to see that the gospel is communicated to persons of all ranks and classes. Just as it is a joy to anticipate worshiping with those of other nations and cultures, it is an exciting prospect to worship equally in Heaven with the wealthy and the poor, the highly educated and the uneducated, all bonded together through our devotion to Christ.

4. In what ways may the joys of a wedding be compared with the joys we shall know in Heaven?

A wedding is a celebration of love, and in Heaven we will rejoice in God's love, which led Him to plan our salvation, and in Christ's love, which resulted in His making atonement for our sin. A wedding ends a period of waiting and brings a long-anticipated uniting of two lives. In Heaven Christ's bride, the church, will at last be united with Him. Part of the joy of a wedding lies in each partner's vow to minister to the other's needs. Heaven will be a place of ministry, as God tenderly soothes the hurts we have known on earth (Revelation 21:3, 4) and as we who are his servants "serve him" (Revelation 22:3). At its best a wedding signifies a "till-death-do-us-part" commitment, a lifelong relationship. Heaven is even better, for it will bring us into an eternal relationship with God and Christ.

5. In what ways may we compare the preparations that go into a wedding with the preparations we must make for Heaven?

It is a matter of wedding tradition that the bride will go to great pains to make herself as beautiful as possible for her bridegroom. The church should likewise be developing "the beauty of holiness" (Psalm 96:9). Or we can say that we should be cooperating with the Lord's desire regarding the radiance and purity of the church, for He cleansed it "that he might present it to himself a glorious church, not having spot, or wrinkle, or any such thing; but that it should be holy and without blemish" (Ephesians 5:27). Another aspect of wedding preparation is the home the couple makes ready so that they may dwell there as husband and wife. Jesus was not speaking in wedding imagery when He said, "I go to prepare a place for you" (John 14:2), but this promise fits in with His role as Bridegroom of the church.

Spring Quarter, 1992

Theme: The Strong Son of God

Special Feature

Lessons

Unit 1: Mission and Message

Unit 2: Confession and Crucifixion

Theme: God's People in the World

Related Resources

The following publications give additional help for the lessons in the Spring Quarter. They may be purchased from your supplier. Prices are subject to change.

Check Your Discipleship, by Knofel Staton. This book can help a person become a better disciple of Jesus. The author not only shows what the apostles did and what we should do, but he also shows us how to do it. Order #11-39990, $2.50.

Check Your Relationships, by Knofel Staton. This study of the Gospel of Mark leads us to consider how Jesus related to people who were hurting, and invites us to compare how we relate to such persons. Order #11-39943, $2.95.

James—Jude (Standard Bible Studies), by William R. Baker and Paul K. Carrier. A detailed study of these Bible books with contemporary applications. Order #11-40115, $12.95.

Mark (Standard Bible Studies), by Paul R. McReynolds. This commentary is written for a general church audience, without technical notes, for ease of understanding. Order #11-40102, $9.95.

Mar 1
Mar 8
Mar 15
Mar 22
Mar 29
Apr 5
Apr 12
Apr 19
Apr 26
May 3
May 10
May 17
May 24
May 31

The Rock and the Church

by Edwin V. Hayden

WHICH IS MORE IMPORTANT, the foundation for a building, or the building itself? Jesus answered that question in His reference to a wise builder and a foolish one (Matthew 7:24-27). The building without foundation collapses at the first severe testing. The foundation without a building fails of its purpose. Both parts are necessary.

When the apostle Peter first formally acknowledged Jesus as the Christ, the Son of the living God, Jesus identified that confession as of divine origin and added, "Upon this rock I will build my church" (Matthew 16:18). Later, Paul named Christ himself as the one foundation upon which the church is, and always must be, built (1 Corinthians 3:11). This agrees with the Lord's promise, "The gates of hell (*hades*—death and the grave) shall not prevail against it." By His crucifixion and burial Jesus, the rock foundation for the church, invaded death and the grave, and in His resurrection He triumphed over it. So the Lord's promise was fulfilled. Will it be fulfilled again in the experience of the church? Certainly, as long as it is established in union with its divine foundation Rock.

The apostle Peter was and is prominently associated with the identification of Jesus as the Messiah and with the establishment of the church upon Him as its foundation. And Peter's testimony, preserved in the New Testament, provides essential instruction for the understanding of Jesus the rock and the church that is built upon Him. That testimony comes to our attention in the fourteen lessons before us in March, April, and May of 1992. Eight lessons, under the general title, "The Strong Son of God," find their Scriptural background in the Gospel written by John Mark, whom Peter referred to as his "son" (1 Peter 5:13). Ancient and respected tradition says that Mark recorded the gospel message as Peter preached it. Our last six lessons, under the title, "God's People in the World," describe the church as Peter addressed it in two epistles, First and Second Peter, written in his later years.

The Strong Son of God

The gospel story falls naturally into two parts. The first establishes Jesus' credentials as the "Christ, the Son of God" (Mark 1:1; Matthew 16:16), through His ministry of teaching, preaching, and healing, often under the most difficult circumstances and the most critical scrutiny. The first seven chapters of Mark develop this theme. The second part of the gospel reveals the "suffering Servant" nature of the Messiah who must die for men's sins, then rise in victory over death and return to the side of God the Father until He shall come again in glory and judgment.

This is the pattern for our first eight lessons, March 1 through April 19. They are presented under two unit titles—"Mission and Message," based on Mark's first seven chapters, and "Confession and Crucifixion," as developed in the latter part of the Gospel.

The "Mission and Message" portion of our study is introduced with the account of Jesus' baptism and temptation in Judea, leading to His ministry in Galilee. Controversy came in the Pharisees' questions about their Sabbath traditions. Next we study Jesus' rejection at Nazareth, and the extension of His ministry outside the land of the Jews.

The second division, "Confession and Crucifixion," opens with Peter's confession of Jesus as the promised Messiah, coupled with the Lord's teaching about the sacrificial nature of His messiahship. Then comes His statement of the commandment to love—to love God and one's fellowmen—as central in His kingdom. This is followed by His own loving self-sacrifice on the cross, and then His victory over death and the grave in the the resurrection.

God's People in the World

The *church* part of our study, from the epistles of Peter, begins with the apostle's presentation of the Christian's *hope* in the resurrection—our Easter theme. Then comes his insistence that Christians are *set apart* as God's people. The believer's testimony through *patience in suffering* comes next. That is followed by admonition to *leaders of the church* that they be humble, steadfast, and watchful in their responsibilities. The believer's *spiritual growth* to maturity in Christ receives major attention. The church's *focus on the future*—the end of the present material world and the establishment of God's new Heaven and earth—concludes the lesson series.

For the life and the church that are built firmly on the strong Son of God, we are entering a fourteen-weeks' study in triumph!

Identification and Testing

LESSON SCRIPTURE: Mark 1:1-15.

PRINTED TEXT: Mark 1:1-15.

Mark 1:1-15

1 The beginning of the gospel of Jesus Christ, the Son of God.

2 As it is written in the prophets, Behold, I send my messenger before thy face, which shall prepare thy way before thee.

3 The voice of one crying in the wilderness, Prepare ye the way of the Lord, make his paths straight.

4 John did baptize in the wilderness, and preach the baptism of repentance for the remission of sins.

5 And there went out unto him all the land of Judea, and they of Jerusalem, and were all baptized of him in the river of Jordan, confessing their sins.

6 And John was clothed with camel's hair, and with a girdle of a skin about his loins; and he did eat locusts and wild honey;

7 And preached, saying, There cometh one mightier than I after me, the latchet of whose shoes I am not worthy to stoop down and unloose.

8 I indeed have baptized you with water: but he shall baptize you with the Holy Ghost.

9 And it came to pass in those days, that Jesus came from Nazareth of Galilee, and was baptized of John in Jordan.

10 And straightway coming up out of the water, he saw the heavens opened, and the Spirit like a dove descending upon him:

11 And there came a voice from heaven, saying, Thou art my beloved Son, in whom I am well pleased.

12 And immediately the Spirit driveth him into the wilderness.

13 And he was there in the wilderness forty days tempted of Satan; and was with the wild beasts; and the angels ministered unto him.

14 Now after that John was put in prison, Jesus came into Galilee, preaching the gospel of the kingdom of God,

15 And saying, The time is fulfilled, and the kingdom of God is at hand: repent ye, and believe the gospel.

GOLDEN TEXT: There came a voice from heaven, saying, Thou art my beloved Son, in whom I am well pleased.—Mark 1:11.

The Strong Son of God

Unit 1: Mission and Message

(Lessons 1-4)

Lesson Aims

This lesson should enable the students to:

1. Summarize the basic facts of John's ministry, Jesus' baptism and temptation, and Jesus' earliest preaching in Galilee.

2. Recognize some way in which they will adjust their own lives to God's kingdom.

Lesson Outline

INTRODUCTION
  A. A Day of Good News
  B. Before the Beginning
 I. JOHN TESTIFIES TO GOD'S SON (Mark 1:1-8)
  A. Word From John Mark (v. 1)
  B. Word From the Prophets (vv. 2, 3)
  C. Work of the Baptizer (vv. 4-6)
   "I'm Sorry!"
  D. Words of the Baptizer (vv. 7, 8)
   True Greatness
 II. GOD ACKNOWLEDGES HIS SON (Mark 1:9-11)
  A. Jesus Seeks Baptism (v. 9)
  B. God Speaks His Pleasure (vv. 10, 11)
III. SATAN TESTS GOD'S SON (Mark 1:12, 13)
 IV. GOD'S SON ANNOUNCES HIS KINGDOM (Mark 1:14, 15)
CONCLUSION
  A. He Proved His Point
  B. Therefore!
  C. A Penitent's Prayer
  D. Thought to Remember

The map of Palestine in Jesus' day (visual 1 of the visuals packet) is designed for use with lessons 1-8 of the Spring quarter. The map is shown on page 230.

Introduction

A. A Day of Good News

"We're not doing right. This is a day of good news and we are keeping it to ourselves" (2 Kings 7:9, *New International Version*).

It's an old, old story about four leprous men who were starving. They, along with the citizens in the city of Samaria, were suffering from the siege by the Syrian army. Grasping desperately at a slim chance to live, the four left the city gates by night to throw themselves on the mercy of the enemy. But there was no enemy, only a

camp suddenly abandoned with all its supplies. The good news and supplies had to be shared with all in Samaria.

No less a responsibility rests upon folk who have discovered the miracle by which God has lifted the siege of sin from mankind through the gift of His one and only Son, Jesus. The discovery is *good news*, or *gospel*. The Biblical accounts of Jesus are rightly called Gospels. Mark wrote his account as a man in a hurry to tell swiftly what needed to be known, as spiritual food for starving sinners. Today we follow him as he plunges into the "beginning of the gospel."

B. Before the Beginning

If the gospel is the good news of God's grace to man through His Son, Jesus Christ, we would expect it to begin with the birth of Jesus, as it does in Matthew and Luke. Mark, however, elects to start with the public announcement of the good news, as it was made first by John the Baptizer and then by Jesus himself.

What took place before the public announcement? Matthew 1:18-24 and Luke 1 tell of God-given family events leading to the births of John the Baptist and of Jesus. Luke 2:1-38 recounts the birth of Jesus in Bethlehem and His being presented in the temple at Jerusalem. Matthew 2 tells of Wise-men coming to worship Jesus, and of the family's Egyptian refuge from the wrath of Herod. Luke 2:41-52 recalls Jesus' visit to Jerusalem at the age of twelve.

All four of the Gospels (Matthew 3:1-12; Mark 1:1-8; Luke 3:1-18; and John 1:19-28) tell the story of John the Baptizer and his ministry of preparation and announcement concerning the Messiah.

I. John Testifies to God's Son (Mark 1:1-8)

A. Word From John Mark (v. 1)

1. The beginning of the gospel of Jesus Christ, the Son of God.

The writer, John Mark, kinsman of Barnabas (Acts 15:37; Colossians 4:10) provides a *beginning* without introduction. The *gospel* is good news about Jesus. It shows Him to be *Christ*, the

VISUALS FOR THESE LESSONS

The *Adult Visuals/Learning Resources* packet contains classroom-size visuals designed for use with the lessons in the Spring Quarter. The packet is available from your supplier. Order no. ST 392.

promised anointed One—the *Son of God.* This is the theme for Mark's Gospel. It echoes the confession made by Simon Peter and blessed by Jesus: "Thou art the Christ, the Son of the living God" (Matthew 16:16). In turn it is echoed in the apostle John's reason for writing his Gospel: "That ye might believe that Jesus is the Christ, the Son of God; and that believing ye might have life through his name" (John 20:31).

Mark did not often repeat this theme in these exact words. *Son of God* appears four times in Mark; but fourteen times Mark records Jesus' references to himself as Son of Man. The Son of God, so acknowledged by men, was also Son of Man, so acknowledged by himself.

B. Word From the Prophets (vv. 2, 3)

2, 3. As it is written in the prophets, Behold, I send my messenger before thy face, which shall prepare thy way before thee. The voice of one crying in the wilderness, Prepare ye the way of the Lord, make his paths straight.

For Mark's purposes here, the gospel began with the fulfillment of Scriptural prophecies concerning Messiah's kingdom. Verse 2 quotes from Malachi 3:1: "Behold, I will send my messenger, and he shall prepare the way before me." Closely related is Malachi 4:5: "Behold, I will send you Elijah the prophet before the coming of the great and dreadful day of the Lord." John fulfilled the role of announcing forerunner.

Verse 3 quotes Isaiah 40:3, but not the next verse. Isaiah 40:3, 4 says, "The voice of him that crieth in the wilderness, Prepare ye the way of the Lord, make straight in the desert a highway for our God. Every valley shall be exalted, and every mountain and hill shall be made low: and the crooked shall be made straight, and the rough places plain."

Isaiah spoke in reference to the Jews' return from Babylonian captivity, and Malachi spoke of judgment to come upon sinners after the captivity; but these "primary references" seem blurred in contrast to the clearer applications to the Baptizer in his wilderness ministry of announcement and preparation for the Lord Jesus.

C. Work of the Baptizer (vv. 4-6)

4. John did baptize in the wilderness, and preach the baptism of repentance for the remission of sins.

John's ministry was active, and action is prominent in Mark's Gospel. John is named for his most significant action, immersing his responsive hearers "in the river of Jordan" (v. 5). The area immediately west of the Jordan and the Dead Sea is *wilderness* land of barren ridges, but the river provided ample water for the immer-

sion of those who heard and heeded John's demand for repentance. John preached baptism as a part of the process of turning toward God and away from sin. The mind must reject sin, the heart must abhor it, and the will must replace sin with righteousness. This repentance was in order to bring forgiveness and eternal relationship with God (see Acts 2:38).

"I'M SORRY!"

My youngest grandson is quick on the verbal trigger with his, "I'm sorry, Mommie." We often chuckle to ourselves as we hear him pleading his cause, because we suspect his repentance is more vocal than actual. When he gets into trouble he's likely to be sent to a lonely seat at the end of a hall, a fate that to him must seem equal to being drawn and quartered. Although he is young, he is smart. He has learned that a few tears coupled with an "I'm sorry" usually tip the scales of parental justice in his favor.

But repentance isn't true repentance if it remains merely vocal. True repentance results in a changed life. That was the kind of repentance John the Baptist demanded (see Luke 3:7-14), and Jesus preached (Mark 1:15).

I have never liked Eric Segal's oft-quoted definition of love, the one he popularized in *Love Story:* "Love means never having to say you're sorry." I think there is a sense in which the opposite is true: "Love means always being willing to say you're sorry," and then after saying it, living accordingly. I think my grandson is beginning to learn this. I hope we all understand it.
—T. T.

5. And there went out unto him all the land of Judea, and they of Jerusalem, and were all baptized of him in the river of Jordan, confessing their sins.

There was something impressive and exciting about this preacher and his message. Folk came out into the wilderness from cities and villages of Judea and the valley of the Jordan from the Sea of Galilee to the Dead Sea (Matthew 3:5). Many walked for several days just to hear him. They came from *all* the areas. Obviously some stayed at home, and some who came rejected his message (Matthew 21:23-27). The *all* in this verse is clearly general rather than absolute.

Isaiah's figure of road building for the King's approach—bringing down, building up, and straightening out (Isaiah 40:3-5)—fits perfectly to John's preparatory ministry. He rebuked the royal and the proud, he instructed publicans, he showed the straight way to Roman soldiers and Jewish commoners (Luke 3:7-14).

We need not suppose that every penitent one listed all his acts of misbehavior. But *all* did recognize and acknowledge themselves as sinners in need of cleansing and conversion.

6. And John was clothed with camel's hair, and with a girdle of a skin about his loins; and he did eat locusts and wild honey.

John was a rugged outdoorsman, wresting his living from a hostile environment (Luke 1:80). His robe was made from the coarse hair of camels, commonly used for rugs and tent coverings. It was caught in at the waist by a circling strip of undressed leather. Elijah and other Old Testament prophets had been so clad (2 Kings 1:8; Zechariah 13:4).

John's diet was such as the wilderness provided. Herbs and occasional wild berries were probably added to such staple items as *locusts and wild honey.* Leviticus 11:22 lists locust and other members of the grasshopper family as acceptable for eating, and they are still eaten by poor folk in the Middle East. They may be either roasted or fried. Wild bees are plentiful in the wilderness, and their combs may be found built into almost any convenient opening (Judges 14:5-9), including crevices in the rocks. "Honey out of the rock" is named as a provision of God (Psalm 81:16).

D. Words of the Baptizer (vv. 7, 8)

7. And preached, saying, There cometh one mightier than I after me, the latchet of whose shoes I am not worthy to stoop down and unloose.

The second phase of John's message is here introduced. Both were designed to prepare hearers to receive their Messiah. A moral and spiritual ground breaking resulted from the preaching of penitents' baptism for the remission of sins. A personal ground breaking lay in John's catching the people's attention, claiming their commitment, and then directing them to the greater One who should come after him.

John's hearers were familiar with the office of the lowliest slave, whose duty included removing his master's sandals, either at his arrival at

home or in preparation for his bath. The first act in either case was to *stoop down and unloose* the master's footwear. So John, although acknowledged by Jesus as the greatest of prophets (Matthew 11:7-15), felt unworthy to serve the coming One in even the most menial capacity.

TRUE GREATNESS

Years ago I was called to the ministry in Grayson, Kentucky, and also to serve as a part-time faculty member of Kentucky Christian College there. In these two roles I gained some interesting insights into J. Lowell Lusby. I saw him as the president of the college, efficiently administering the work of the school. I also saw him as an elder of the congregation where I ministered, a role that he filled well.

My wife and I have often commented that Lowell Lusby was never happier than when he was serving as an usher at the church. There he passed out bulletins, assisted people to their seats, and humbly sought other ways to create good will for the congregation and the Lord. Lowell was one of those persons who could move from a position of prestige to one of humble service and do it with ease. Perhaps you know others like him.

John the Baptist was a capable and popular leader, yet he openly and humbly acknowledged his unworthiness to perform even the lowliest task for the Messiah, whom he announced. Such a spirit in John no doubt contributed to Jesus' evaluation of him (Matthew 11:11).   —T. T.

8. I indeed have baptized you with water: but he shall baptize you with the Holy Ghost.

No contrast between the two would be greater than the contrast in their most significant works. John had immersed his converts in water; the Lord Jesus would overwhelm and infill them with the Holy Spirit. Jesus renewed the promise in His last conversation with His apostles (Acts 1:4, 5). It had not yet been fulfilled, but would be so within a few days. The promised overwhelming took place on the Day of Pentecost (Acts 2:1-4), when the infilled ones preached the gospel plainly in languages they had not learned (Acts 2:6-11). Some years later, when Gentiles first received the gospel, a similar Spirit baptism was visited upon the members of Cornelius' household, with similar results. Peter's report of the event indicated that nothing like it had happened between the two occasions (Acts 11:15-17). Ordinary Christian baptism, in water, performed by the hands of men, took place afterward in both instances. It was, and is, followed by its own "gift of the Holy Ghost" (Acts 2:38). The Spirit bestowal, in whatever measure, is still the work of the Lord.

visual 1

II. God Acknowledges His Son
(Mark 1:9-11)
A. Jesus Seeks Baptism (v. 9)

9. And it came to pass in those days, that Jesus came from Nazareth of Galilee, and was baptized of John in Jordan.

In those days John had been preaching for about six months, and Jesus was thirty years old (Luke 3:23). His home at Nazareth in Galilee was some seventy miles from where John was baptizing. Jesus made the several days' journey with purpose to be baptized, and upon arrival, after all other applicants present had received baptism (Luke 3:21), He persuaded John to baptize Him (Matthew 3:13-15). His was not a baptism of repentance for any sin committed by himself, for He had no sin (Hebrews 4:15; 1 Peter 2:22). It was a baptism of determination to fulfill righteousness.

B. God Speaks His Pleasure (vv. 10, 11)

10. And straightway coming up out of the water, he saw the heavens opened, and the Spirit like a dove descending upon him.

Straightway. Mark's record moves swiftly from one important event to another. What Jesus saw in that moment when He came up from the watery burial of baptism was seen also by the Baptizer, who remembered the event and its meaning to him: "He that sent me to baptize with water, the same said unto me, Upon whom thou shalt see the Spirit descending, . . . the same is he which baptizeth with the Holy Ghost. And I saw, and bare record that this is the Son of God" (John 1:33, 34). Luke 3:22 says the Spirit descended "in a bodily shape like a dove." The dove, harmless and peaceable (Matthew 10:16), here identified Jesus as the promised Messiah, at least to the Baptizer.

11. And there came a voice from heaven, saying, Thou art my beloved Son, in whom I am well pleased.

How many persons heard the voice that came from heaven and received its testimony? Matthew 3:17 quotes it as saying, "This is my beloved Son," as though addressed at least to John and perhaps also to others.

Jesus had always shaped His conduct to conform with what the Father chose and directed (Matthew 3:15; John 4:34; 6:38; Hebrews 5:8). That is vastly different from one's following the way he himself supposes to be right, and then expecting God to be pleased with his choice. Nothing pleased the Father more than Jesus' humble submission and self-sacrifice on behalf of those He came to save (Philippians 2:5-11). In this we see echoed the prophecy of Isaiah 42:1:

"Behold my servant, whom I uphold; mine elect, in whom my soul delighteth; I have put my Spirit upon him."

The three manifestations of God are notably present in the event before us. The *Father* expressed His pleasure in the *Son,* upon whom the *Spirit* had descended in visible form.

III. Satan Tests God's Son
(Mark 1:12, 13)

12. And immediately the Spirit driveth him into the wilderness.

Jesus' baptism was no light matter. He had determined upon it; He had traveled far to receive it; He had insisted upon it; He had been in prayer as it was completed (Luke 3:21); He had received God's spoken approval. Now what? This was a question immediately to be pondered prayerfully and alone. The Greek word translated *driveth* is better translated "sent" or "led." The Holy Spirit led Jesus into *the wilderness* to do battle with the devil. This would give Him further preparation for His ministry to humankind.

13. And he was there in the wilderness forty days tempted of Satan; and was with the wild beasts; and the angels ministered unto him.

Satan's temptation came immediately after the high and holy experience of Jesus' baptism. So a Christian may be most sorely tempted in the aftermath of a "mountaintop experience."

Mark suggests that temptations came to Jesus continually throughout the *forty days.* He does not mention the Lord's going without food during that time (see Matthew 4:2; Luke 4:2). But the continual battle with the tempter seems to have rendered Him unaware of hunger. At the end of the forty days, however, He was hungry enough to be sensitive to the first of three specific temptations described by Matthew and Luke—namely, to use His supernatural powers to turn a loaf-shaped stone into bread. Similarly He was invited to prove His divine sonship by leaping unharmed from a high point of the temple, or to gain instant control of the world and its kingdoms by recognizing Satan's dominion. Satan challenged, "If thou be the Son of God . . ." (Matthew 4:3; Luke 4:3). Then Jesus established His sonship, not on Satan's terms, but on His own. As the Son of God, He followed the will and the word of the Father.

Untamed animals such as snakes, lizards, and lions were His companions during the forty days in the wilderness. Whether they endangered Him physically as Satan endangered Him spiritually, we can only guess. But the spiritual danger was very real. When Jesus taught His disciples to pray, He included this fervent petition, "Bring us not into temptation, but deliver us from the evil one" (Matthew 6:13, *American Standard Version*).

Did the *angels* protect Jesus from the wild creatures, or sustain him throughout His long fast, or was their ministry, as Matthew 4:11 suggests, to revive Him after the temptations had ended ("Then the devil leaveth him, and, behold, angels came and ministered unto him")? In any case Jesus our great high priest "was in all points tempted like as we are, yet without sin" (Hebrews 4:15).

During the six weeks of Jesus' wilderness temptation, John the Baptizer continued to preach, identifying Jesus as the one to whom his own ministry led (John 1:15-34). Jesus came back to where John was preaching, and some of John's disciples followed Him (John 1:35-51). After a short visit to Galilee (John 2:1-12), the Lord went to Jerusalem for the Passover and continued to teach for several months in Judea (John 2:13—3:36).

IV. God's Son Announces His Kingdom (Mark 1:14, 15)

14, 15. Now after that John was put in prison, Jesus came into Galilee, preaching the gospel of the kingdom of God, and saying, The time is fulfilled, and the kingdom of God is at hand: repent ye, and believe the gospel.

At about this time Herod the tetrarch, being offended because John the Baptizer rebuked him for taking his brother's wife as his own, had the prophet *put in prison* (Luke 3:19, 20). Thereupon Jesus left Judea, where His growing popularity had attracted the attention of the Pharisees (John 4:1), and set out for Galilee, pausing for two days of teaching in Samaria (John 4:3-42).

Home Daily Bible Readings

Monday, Feb. 24—John's Witness to Jesus (Mark 1:1-8)

Tuesday, Feb. 25—God's Beloved Son (Mark 1:9-15)

Wednesday, Feb. 26—Jesus' Temptation (Matthew 4:1-11)

Thursday, Feb. 27—Kept From Falling (Jude 24-25)

Friday, Feb. 28—Christ Our High Priest (Hebrews 4:14-16)

Saturday, Feb. 29—Strengthened in Christ (Romans 16:25-27)

Sunday, Mar. 1—God's Discipline Brings Peace (Hebrews 12:3-11)

Galilee, the province in which Jesus had been brought up, was to be the scene for a large part of His ministry. For His early ministry there Jesus began where John the Baptizer had left off (compare Matthew 3:2).

The time for the coming of the *kingdom* prophesied in Daniel 2:44 had arrived, and it was about to be established. The hearers needed to *repent*—that is, change their minds from ignorance or rejection to belief and acceptance, and so to be ready to enter the kingdom. The other aspect of repentance—changing the active mind so as to work the righteousness that John demanded—would follow. The Son of God came to establish the reign of God. So He announced and so He taught.

Conclusion

A. He Proved His Point

"Jesus Christ, the Son of God," the subject and theme of Mark's Gospel, has been introduced to us in a few swift, bold strokes that establish Mark's assertion. Prophecy concerning Him is fulfilled (vv. 2, 3); needed adjustments (repentance) to His rule are prescribed (vv. 4-6); John's testimony concerning Him is heard (vv. 7, 8); the Holy Spirit signs His baptismal certificate (v. 10); God himself affirms His sonship (v. 11); forty days of testing in the wilderness establishes His position (vv. 12, 13); and He sets about immediately to do the work assigned to Him (vv. 14, 15). Mark has proved his point!

B. Therefore!

Since Jesus is the Christ, God's only begotten Son, and since He is the reigning Prince in the kingdom of Heaven, those who would be His people need to adjust their thinking to accept these facts, and they need to adjust their ways to His way. The adjustments are called *repentance*. Repentance is neither punishment nor an unkind burden. It is a privilege—a gift of God's grace—making possible a person's family relationship with God for time and for eternity.

C. A Penitent's Prayer

Thank You, God, for the gift of Your Son, who brings salvation and citizenship in Your kingdom within our grasp. Help us to accomplish that continuing repentance that will make us comfortable in Your loving presence forever. We pray in Jesus' name. Amen.

D. Thought to Remember

Jesus Christ is the way, the truth, and the life. No one comes to the Father except by Him (see John 14:6).

Learning by Doing

This page contains an alternate lesson plan emphasizing learning activities. Classes desiring such student involvement will find these suggestions helpful.

Learning Goals

This lesson will lead students to:

1. Summarize the basic facts of John's ministry, Jesus' baptism and temptation, and Jesus' earliest preaching in Galilee.

2. Share the gospel of Christ with those who are lost in sin.

3. Suggest one way in which they will be more pleasing to God.

Into the Lesson

Write the word *outstanding* on the chalkboard. As the students arrive, ask each one to think of someone who is well known for his or her faith, and is unusually dedicated to the Lord.

When you are ready to begin, ask for their suggestions, beginning with historical characters. Then add some contemporary Christians. Comment briefly on them. Then tell the class, "Today we are going to study one of the most outstanding and unusual characters recorded in the Gospels: John the Baptist. Perhaps his boldness for God will challenge us to be outstanding in our faith as well."

Into the Word

Introduce this study of Mark's Gospel by sharing the thoughts found under the heading "A Day of Good News" in the lesson introduction (page 228). Then read aloud the text or have a student read it. Discuss how this could be the "beginning of the gospel" (v. 1). After all, there are no angels, no shepherds, no stable, no Wisemen. See "Before the Beginning" in the lesson introduction and comments under verses 1-3.

Divide the class into three small groups. (If you have more than eighteen students, make more groups and give duplicate assignments.) Give the following assignments:

1. Examine Mark 1:4-8 and summarize the ministry of John the Baptist. Note the purpose of his ministry, the contrast between John and his culture, and the testimony he gave of Christ.

2. Examine Mark 1:9-13 and summarize the details of Jesus' baptism and temptation. Compare and contrast these events in Jesus' life and the baptism and temptations of Christians today.

3. Examine Mark 1:14 and 15 and summarize the early preaching of Jesus. Note especially the purpose of Jesus' ministry and the significance of the following expressions: "the time is fulfilled," "the kingdom of God," and "believe the gospel."

Have one person in each group serve as the group's reporter. Give the groups about ten minutes to work, and then ask for their reports. List on the chalkboard significant details from each report. (Or provide each group with a poster and a marker and let them list their own points as they discuss the assignment. Allow them to display their posters and summarize their discussion.)

Summarize this exercise by noting that each section points to Christ and shows that He is worthy of our faith. This, of course, is the purpose of Mark's Gospel.

Into Life

Point out again the contrast between John and his culture. Ask the class how such a person would be accepted by our own culture. How would such a one be accepted by the church? Discuss whether or not *all* Christians should stand out in stark contrast to their cultures. Why or why not? In what ways should a Christian differ from the world? Why is this difficult? What gives a person the courage to stand out?

Discuss Jesus' baptism with the class. Ask the students why they think God said He was "well pleased" with Jesus. In connection with this, read and briefly discuss these Scripture texts: Matthew 3:15; John 4:34; 6:38; Hebrews 4:15; 1 Peter 2:22.

Ask: "How can we be well pleasing to God?" Lead the class to understand that the beginning point is to accept the gracious provision God has made for us through His Son Jesus Christ. If we reject Christ, then all that God has done in our behalf has been for nought. Once we accept Christ as Savior and Lord, are there things we can do to please God? (See Philippians 4:18; Hebrews 13:15, 16, 20, 21.) Point out the difference between doing things that are pleasing to God—which is good and right—and doing things to "earn" salvation—which, of course, is impossible. See Ephesians 2:8-10.

Discuss the fact that temptation comes to every Christian. Make clear, however, that temptation is not sin. Point out that even Jesus was tempted, yet He was without sin (Hebrews 4:15). Close with a prayer that each of us will try to be more pleasing to God.

Let's Talk It Over

The questions on this page are designed to encourage review of the lesson Scriptures and to promote discussion of the lesson by the class. The answers provided are only discussion starters. Let your class talk it over from there.

1. The first sentence in a work sets the tone and the topic for the whole work. What does Mark's first sentence tell us about his book?

Mark's work is concise. His book clearly presents the work of Jesus without some of the extra details of the other Gospel writers. Mark focuses on the gospel (good news) of Jesus Christ. Jesus is the good news sent to earth from Heaven. As His name, *Jesus,* indicates, He is the Savior. *Christ* means anointed one. Jesus is prophet, priest, and king, anointed by God. *Son of God* identifies His source, which establishes Jesus' deity. This unadorned beginning to the profound truth of God challenges us simply to present the claims of Jesus to others.

2. Mark quotes Malachi 3:1 and Isaiah 40:3 as examples of prophecies fulfilled in Christ. Why is fulfilled prophecy important to faith in Jesus Christ?

Fulfilled prophecy is an important element for establishing faith in Jesus as the Christ. More than three hundred prophecies pointing to the Messiah (Christ) are included in the Old Testament, many of them dealing with details of His life, ministry, and death. The fact that all of these prophecies, given many centuries before Jesus was born, were fulfilled in Him is compelling evidence that He is the Messiah who was to come.

Fulfilled prophecy also helps us to see that God had planned to send Jesus as our Redeemer. It testifies to God's great love and concern for us and gives us strong reason to have confidence in Him for our future well-being.

3. John did not hesitate to call for repentance from those who gathered to hear him. Why is it important to challenge people to repent today?

Repentance involves recognizing one's sin, taking responsibility for the sin, having regret for the sin, reforming from the sin, restoring what was damaged by the sin, if possible, and resolving not to repeat the sin. Repentance means to change. We can no longer call sin a sickness or mistake for which we have no responsibility. If we accept Jesus as the Son of God, we must be willing to change and to let Him change us.

4. John drew great crowds to himself, but still he pointed those people to the coming Messiah. How does God use us in pointing people to Jesus?

We are only vessels; He is the content. We are servants; He is the Master. We are ambassadors; He is the King. We are sinners; He is the Savior. We are voices; He is the Word. Everything about our lives should point others to Jesus so that they may respond to His gospel.

5. Mark mentions several witnesses to establish the fact that Jesus is the Son of God. Who are they, and why are they important?

First are the prophets. God's special preparing of the way for His special messenger, His Son Jesus Christ, helps us to know that God's planning is sure.

Second is John the Baptizer. John is called the greatest of the prophets by Jesus (Matthew 11:7-11). John ministered in the wilderness, challenging the people to come out of the wilderness of sin and to prepare to enter God's kingdom. He faithfully pointed the way to Jesus.

Third, are God the Father and the Holy Spirit. At Jesus' baptism, the Holy Spirit descended upon Him in a bodily form like a dove, and God himself testified to His "beloved Son."

These witnesses assure Mark's readers of Jesus' claims. God was well pleased with His Son, and Mark lays a firm foundation for us to believe in His Servant.

6. Immediately after His baptism, Jesus was led by the Spirit into the wilderness where He was tempted by Satan. How may Christians today find encouragement from Jesus' experience?

Jesus' baptism was a spiritual high point in His life. And yet, very soon after His baptism He was severely tested by Satan to turn from God's will. We need to be aware that spiritual mountaintop experiences do not rule out the possibility of Satan's attacks on us. Furthermore, we can know that the presence of temptation following a high spiritual experience does not mean we have left the will of God. Satan is seeking all the harder to reclaim our allegiance. Like Jesus, we can overcome him by relying on the strength God supplies.

The Clash of Truth and Tradition

LESSON SCRIPTURE: Mark 2:23—3:6.

PRINTED TEXT: Mark 2:23—3:6.

Mark 2:23-28

23 And it came to pass, that he went through the corn fields on the sabbath day; and his disciples began, as they went, to pluck the ears of corn.

24 And the Pharisees said unto him, Behold, why do they on the sabbath day that which is not lawful?

25 And he said unto them, Have ye never read what David did, when he had need, and was ahungered, he, and they that were with him?

26 How he went into the house of God in the days of Abiathar the high priest, and did eat the showbread, which is not lawful to eat but for the priests, and gave also to them which were with him?

27 And he said unto them, The sabbath was made for man, and not man for the sabbath:

28 Therefore the Son of man is Lord also of the sabbath.

Mark 3:1-6

1 And he entered again into the synagogue; and there was a man there which had a withered hand.

2 And they watched him, whether he would heal him on the sabbath day; that they might accuse him.

3 And he saith unto the man which had the withered hand, Stand forth.

4 And he saith unto them, Is it lawful to do good on the sabbath days, or to do evil? to save life, or to kill? But they held their peace.

5 And when he had looked round about on them with anger, being grieved for the hardness of their hearts, he saith unto the man, Stretch forth thine hand. And he stretched it out: and his hand was restored whole as the other.

6 And the Pharisees went forth, and straightway took counsel with the Herodians against him, how they might destroy him.

GOLDEN TEXT: The sabbath was made for man, and not man for the sabbath: therefore the Son of man is Lord also of the sabbath.—Mark 2:27, 28.

The Strong Son of God

Unit 1: Mission and Message

(Lessons 1-4)

Lesson Aims

This study should enable the students to:

1. Summarize the two events reported in Mark 2:23—3:6.

2. State in their own words the principle set forth by Jesus in relation to each event.

3. Apply these principles to their own observance of the New Testament Lord's Day.

Lesson Outline

INTRODUCTION
    A. "No Longer a Child"
    B. The Sabbath and the Lord's Day
I. PURPOSE OF THE SABBATH (Mark 2:23-28)
    A. Pharisees Enforce Tradition (vv. 23, 24)
       Worship Service Variations
    B. Jesus Cites Scripture (vv. 25, 26)
    C. He Is Lord of the Sabbath (vv. 27, 28)
II. PRACTICE ON THE SABBATH (Mark 3:1-6)
    A. Pharisees Prepare a Test (vv. 1, 2)
    B. Jesus Proposes His Own Test (vv. 3, 4)
    C. Jesus Demonstrates His Principle (v. 5)
       Need Versus Tradition
    D. Pharisees Plot His Destruction (v. 6)
CONCLUSION
    A. You Be the Judge!
    B. Priority and Propriety
    C. Prayer of a Learner
    D. Thought to Remember

Display visual 2 of the visuals packet and let it remain before the class. The visual is shown on page 239.

Introduction

A. "No Longer a Child"

"I am beginning to suspect that you and I are going to find it a little hard to be friends for a year or two yet. But no matter how rough things may become occasionally, I want you to know that I love you very much, and I am really on your side in all the bigger battles."

Mother and Jennifer, who was entering adolescence as though she were already through it, had already experienced some monumental clashes of ideas. Some of Jennifer's understandings and judgments were really very good, and that made it harder to counter her continual in-

sistence that "I am no longer a child!" She was quite sure that on many issues her wisdom was at least equal to that of her mother and her perception of the real world was vastly superior. As almost any parent can testify, it was a problem not easily solved.

When Jesus was in Galilee, announcing the reign of God, teaching and demonstrating divine loving power, He found himself in a similar clash of ideas with the Pharisees, the nation's religious teachers.

Like Jennifer, the Pharisees who confronted Jesus were "no longer children." They were instructed in the law of God, and were respected for their commitment to the way of God. They were confident that their understanding and their commitment were superior to those of any around them.

Unlike Jennifer, who understood that her mother had the right to give her guidance, the Pharisees did not recognize in Jesus any special identity with the Father nor any right to teach ideas different from their own.

Their position was flawed, however, in two ways that they failed to recognize. Their zeal for the divine law had obscured their love for the divine Person, with His purpose to save all mankind. And their obsession with interpreting the law had led them to fabricate a vast network of opinions and precedents that they accepted as equal with the law itself. They and their followers would have been better off if they had been children, loving, learning, and responsive to the Father.

Jesus' clash with the Pharisees is introduced early in the Gospel of Mark. The Lord's public ministry was, in fact, into its second year when the events of today's lesson occurred.

B. The Sabbath and the Lord's Day

Controversy between Jesus and the Pharisees centered in the Sabbath laws. These were held in high priority by the Jews. The Ten Commandments dealt mostly with one's personal relationship to God, family relationships, and moral behavior. Only one—"remember the Sabbath day, to keep it holy"—was ceremonial. Leviticus 23:3 summarizes, "There are six days when you may work, but the seventh day is a Sabbath of rest, a day of sacred assembly. You are not to do any work; wherever you live, it is a Sabbath to the Lord" (*New International Version*).

Rest, or cessation from common work, was central in the observance of the Sabbath. The Commandments linked it to God's rest after six days of creation (Exodus 20:8-11), and also to the Israelites' rest from slavery in Egypt (Deuteronomy 5:12-15).

Constantly discussed and never entirely settled was the question as to what constituted the "work" that was prohibited on the Sabbath. Volumes were written, detailing such matters as how far one might walk or how many stitches a housewife might sew on the Sabbath. All of these became parts of divine law to the Pharisees.

Jesus observed the Sabbath law, but not all the traditions. Much of His teaching and healing was done on Sabbaths in the synagogues. After His resurrection, His followers continued to attend synagogue services to preach His gospel.

A new manner of observance came into being, however. On the Day of Pentecost—the first day of the week—Christ's church came into being, built on Him and His gospel. And when Christians came together in His name to remember Him in His sacrifice for their sins, they did so on the first day of the week (Acts 20:7; 1 Corinthians 16:2). This came to be known as the Lord's Day (Revelation 1:10). Its key was not physical rest, but spiritual refreshment, and its memorial connection was not the creation of physical life, but the giving of life eternal through Jesus' resurrection on the first day of the week. All of this lay in the future, however, when Jesus encountered the faultfinding Pharisees.

I. Purpose of the Sabbath
(Mark 2:23-28)

A. Pharisees Enforce Tradition (vv. 23, 24)

23. And it came to pass, that he went through the corn fields on the sabbath day; and his disciples began, as they went, to pluck the ears of corn.

Jesus and His disciples, perhaps on their way from the synagogue, were walking one of those paths that go along or through the unfenced fields of standing grain (called "corn" in the *King James Version*, although the maize that we call corn was not known in Israel). Whether barley, rye, or wheat, it was ripe enough to chew. Matthew 12:1 says the disciples were hungry, and that they ate the grain, having pulled the heads from some of the stalks, and rubbed out the grain in their hands (Luke 6:1).

Jesus' disciples were not accused of thievery, for the law made provision for gathering grain as they were doing (Deuteronomy 23:25). "When thou comest into the standing corn of thy neighbor, then thou mayest pluck the ears with thine hand; but thou shalt not move a sickle unto thy neighbor's standing corn."

24. And the Pharisees said unto him, Behold, why do they on the sabbath day that which is not lawful?

At this stage of His ministry, spies and critics were always present. Jesus had not committed any offense, but He was held responsible for what His followers did. How like the present day, when Christ and His church are blamed for the offenses of any who wear His name. We disciples need to walk worthily for His sake!

What, though, was the offense? Some rabbis taught that the pulling of a head of wheat from its stalk was harvesting, and rubbing out the chaff in one's hand was threshing, both of which were prohibited on the Sabbath. The Scripture did not identify these acts as such, but the rabbis' interpretations did, and that, to the Pharisees, was all the same.

WORSHIP SERVICE VARIATIONS

Picture this scene: It's Sunday afternoon, and the preacher has preached for about thirty minutes. An elderly lady in the audience decides it's time for a break. She stands and begins to sing, clapping her hands loudly. Others join her and the speaker, apparently unphased, joins in too. After a couple of songs of praise have been sung, the crowd sits again, and the preacher resumes his message.

It doesn't seem to bother him when a few people walk into the open-air service considerably late. Nor is he flustered when some of the worshipers get up, walk a few yards away, and start a fire upon which to cook a meal.

In Zimbabwe where I once lived, as well as in other parts of Africa, such scenes regularly occur as Christians assemble to worship Jehovah and sing the praises of the Lord Jesus.

Visitors or newcomers to Africa might feel that the Africans are being disrespectful of God by their conduct. Not so. They are merely worshiping God in a way that is natural to them, a way that fits their life-style.

Regarding worship, such things as time or place of meeting, and order of service are matters of opinion. If praise is God-centered, from the heart, and in harmony with His revelation, it pleases the Heavenly Father.   —T. T.

B. Jesus Cites Scripture (vv. 25, 26)

25, 26. And he said unto them, Have ye never read what David did, when he had need,

---

How to Say It

ABIATHAR. Ah-*bye*-uh-thar.
AHIMELECH. A-*him*-uh-leck.
BAAL. *Bay*-ul.
HERODIANS. Heh-*roe*-dee-unz.

and was ahungered, he, and they that were with him? How he went into the house of God in the days of Abiathar the high priest, and did eat the showbread, which is not lawful to eat but for the priests, and gave also to them which were with him?

Jesus addressed the questioners' spiritual need, rather than merely answering the question. In so doing, He showed the fallacy of their whole attitude.

The incident to which Jesus referred is found in 1 Samuel 21:1-9, and the Pharisees knew it well. David, with a few of his companions, was fleeing the murderous wrath of King Saul. Without food or weapons, they stopped at Nob, a town situated just north of Jerusalem, where the tabernacle was located at the time. David went in and persuaded the priest Ahimelech (Abiathar became high priest shortly thereafter) to give him the only food and the only weapon on the premises. Five loaves of the sacred bread of the divine presence, having been removed on the Sabbath when twelve fresh loaves were set out in the Holy Place, remained to be eaten by the priests. These became the supply for David and his friends. Leviticus 24:5-9 prescribes the making, the display, and the use of showbread.

David and Ahimelech collaborated here in two clear violations of the revealed law. David entered the Holy Place, and he and his companions were given the priests' bread to eat. Jesus did not say whether David was right or wrong in doing this, but it is clear that the Pharisees did not condemn the great King David. Why then did they criticize Jesus' disciples?

C. He Is Lord of the Sabbath (vv. 27, 28)

27. And he said unto them, The sabbath was made for man, and not man for the sabbath.

What a bold and even revolutionary statement! Even the sacred Sabbath, ordained by almighty God to memorialize His creative acts, was not an end in itself. Sabbath rest and Sabbath worship were given for the good of God's people, that they might live in health and peace with Him. God's rules were given to liberate and build up, not to bind and tear down, His people.

Is it possible, then, that man-made forms of worship may become so binding that they get in the way of worship itself? May we become so concerned about doing the right thing in the right way at the right time that we forget what we are doing it for?

It is even more obviously true that material possessions, power, and pleasures were made for man, and not man for possessions, power, and pleasure. The long weekend can readily be-

come a tyrant, dissipating and destroying the useful life in the name of "recreation." God's law, applied in God's way, is life more abundant.

28. Therefore the Son of man is Lord also of the sabbath.

Here was a pronouncement almost more radical than the other. In Daniel's night visions he had seen one "like the Son of man" in the presence of "the Ancient of days" (God) and there given a kingdom with unlimited glory and dominion (Daniel 7:13, 14). Jesus customarily referred to himself as Son of man, to indicate His identification with mankind, and still not to deny His divinity. Thus He had the authority to order even the sacred Sabbath in such a way as to bless, rather than to dominate, mankind. He also had the authority ultimately to set aside the Sabbath in favor of His own Lord's Day. So if anyone wishes to learn about the Sabbath, let him hear it from the Son of man!

II. Practice on the Sabbath (Mark 3:1-6)

A. Pharisees Prepare a Test (vv. 1, 2)

1. And he entered again into the synagogue; and there was a man there which had a withered hand.

Luke 6:6 introduces this incident with more detail: "And it came to pass also on another sabbath, that he entered into the synagogue and taught: and there was a man whose right hand was withered." There was nothing unusual about Jesus' presence and teaching in the synagogues of Galilee at this time (see Luke 4:15, 16), but the presence of a man with a shrunken and useless right hand is especially noted.

2. And they watched him, whether he would heal him on the sabbath day; that they might accuse him.

Luke 6:7 identifies the critical watchers as the "scribes and Pharisees"—the scholarly preservers and the zealous defenders of the law. Matthew 12:10 indicates that the watching was active and vocal: "And they asked him, saying, Is it lawful to heal on the sabbath days?" If Jesus said yes, as expected, they would accuse Him of Sabbath violation. If He said no, they could claim a victory over His usual compassion.

Would a healing, accomplished with a touch or a word, break the Sabbath rest? Perhaps it would. Even God's creative work, from which He rested on the seventh day, was accomplished with a word—"Let there be . . . and there was." And when a hemorrhaging woman gained healing by touching Jesus' garment in a crowd, He felt strength go out of Him (Mark 5:25-30). Challenged at this very point after a Sabbath healing

visual 2

GOD'S
RULES WERE GIVEN
TO LIBERATE AND
BUILD UP, NOT TO
BIND AND TEAR
DOWN, HIS
PEOPLE

at the Pool of Bethesda, Jesus said plainly, "My Father worketh hitherto, and I work" (John 5:17).

B. Jesus Proposes His Own Test (vv. 3, 4)

3, 4. And he saith unto the man which had the withered hand, Stand forth. And he saith unto them, Is it lawful to do good on the sabbath days, or to do evil? to save life, or to kill? But they held their peace.

Again Luke supplies significant details: "[Jesus] knew their thoughts, and said to the man which had the withered hand, Rise up, and stand forth in the midst. And he arose and stood forth" (Luke 6:8). Without waiting for the situation to develop on His critics' schedule, Jesus seized the initiative, issuing a public challenge to those who were attempting His public humiliation. Was He unkind in calling public attention to the cripple? Certainly not. That had been done already, but with less than forthright honesty, by those who would make a test case of his affliction. Jesus probably knew this man's thoughts, too, and anticipated his willing compliance. Now, with all eyes on the unfortunate man, Jesus faced His critics with the question recorded in Matthew 12:11, 12 "What man shall there be among you, that shall have one sheep, and if it fall into a pit on the sabbath day, will he not lay hold on it, and lift it out? How much then is a man better than a sheep?"

Silence! Then the key question: "Which is right on the Sabbath? To do good by relieving affliction, or to do evil by further neglect? To preserve and enrich life as I am about to do, or to plot a man's death, as you are about to do?" If healing on the Sabbath was a capital offense, Jesus was to give His critics plenty of ammunition. Mark 1:21-31 tells of His casting an unclean spirit out of a man and of His healing Peter's mother-in-law. Luke 13:10-14 and 14:1-6 recount His healing of an infirm woman and a dropsical man. John 5:1-9 and 9:1-14 tell of His healing life-long lameness and blindness. All of these took place on Sabbaths (Matthew 12:12).

C. Jesus Demonstrates His Principle (v. 5)

5. And when he had looked round about on them with anger, being grieved for the hardness of their heart,s he saith unto the man, Stretch forth thine hand. And he stretched it out: and his hand was restored whole as the other.

When Jesus gazed at His accusers, one by one, in the long silence that followed His questions, what did He see that so stirred His anger? It was not their hatred against himself. He did not so respond to personal injuries (1 Peter 2:21-23). No, His wrath was reserved for the "hypocrites. . . blind guides . . . fools and blind . . . [those] full of hypocrisy and iniquity . . . serpents . . . vipers" (Matthew 23:13-36) who used their position as professional religionists to advance themselves, to misrepresent God, and to betray the poor and the helpless. In this instance their grievous sin was *hardness of heart*, translated as "obstinate stupidity" (*The New English Bible*), "indifference to human need" (*The Living Bible*), or "inhumanity" (*Phillips*). Under the guise of protecting divine law and the holy day, they were guarding their own power and position.

The electric silence was broken at last with a firm directive to the cripple: "Stretch out your hand." Did the man expect to be healed? He had at least enough faith to attempt what he was told to do. And with the attempt came the ability to do it. Now he had two good hands!

Jesus, the Son of man, had done well on the Sabbath Day, and God the Father approved.

NEED VERSUS TRADITION

The church board was discussing a problem. Worship services were consistently exceeding sixty minutes, and folks were complaining. The chairman said, "Our people are busy and won't sit through a service that lasts an hour and ten minutes. Something must be cut."

The newest board member suggested that they not sing the "Doxology" following the offering. But someone scoldingly replied, "That's been a part of our service for over a hundred years, and people won't stand for such a change." "Well, how about dropping the birthday offerings?"he countered. "Singing 'Happy Birthday' every Sunday is time consuming." "Yes," the chairman replied, "but people are used to it."

Other suggestions were considered and dismissed. Finally someone said, "I think we ought to cut out the prayer requests. Who cares about Bill's aunt in the hospital a thousand miles away? We don't even know her. Let's save five minutes by not asking for any requests." The suggestion met with agreement and was adopted.

While the meeting may be fictitious, there have been many like it. Too often traditions have been valued more than human suffering and spiritual need. Christ was amazed and angered at the callousness of Israel's religious leaders. Observing the traditions regarding the Sabbath was more important to them than healing a man.

And what of us? Where does human need register on our scale of values?   —T. T.

D. Pharisees Plot His Destruction (v. 6)

6. And the Pharisees went forth, and straightway took counsel with the Herodians against him, how they might destroy him.

This incident took placed in the synagogue where many were gathered for instruction. But it was the *Pharisees*, stalwart guardians of the law and the holy day, who went out from the synagogue on that Sabbath Day to plot a murder! As Luke 6:11 says, "They were filled with madness." Frustrated, jealous rage deprived them of all sane judgment.

The Herodians were politicians advancing the cause of the Herods as Rome's representative rulers in Palestine. The Herods knew Jewish law and customs, which they respected insofar as it was to their political advantage. But one Herod had tried to kill Jesus at His birth, another had slain John the Baptist, and still another was later to move murderously against the apostles (Acts 12:1-4). The Herods' henchmen were thus ideally suited to the Pharisees' present purposes, though poles apart from them in piety and morals. Politics and pride do make strange partnerships and partners.

Conclusion

A. You Be the Judge!

Are we shocked at the Pharisees' audacity in judging, rejecting, and seeking to destroy the Son of God? Then let us consider the extent to which every one of us sits in judgment on the divine Savior whenever we hear Him say something we hadn't already believed. Between Him and us there is frequently a clash of ideas. We are seldom so violent as were the Pharisees in opposing Him; yet almost instinctively we sometimes respond, "That's all very interesting, but. . . ." It is a great deal easier to take exception to His teaching than it is to accept it completely and follow it wholly.

It is impossible, in fact, for a person to avoid judging God! It is that judgment to which Joshua called the children of Israel: "Choose you this day whom ye will serve" (Joshua 24:15). Elijah echoed the same challenge: "If the Lord be God, follow him: but if Baal, then follow him" (1 Kings 18:21). Jesus told of a would-be king whose citizens objected, "We will not have this man to reign over us"; and the king who answered their judgment with his own: "Those mine enemies, which would not that I should reign over them, bring hither, and slay them before me" (Luke 19:14, 27). Thus Jesus pictured His kingship and the judgment He will render.

Our first clash of ideas is a clash of claims to authority. Who is to rule? Who is Lord? When we once judge Jesus as worthy to be Lord, the remaining small skirmishes are but diminishing echoes of the original conflict.

B. Priority and Propriety

Jesus' clash with the Pharisees over Sabbath observance centered in questions of priority and propriety. Which is more important: humanly prescribed forms or personal values? Jesus answered, "The sabbath was made for man, and not man for the sabbath."

What, then, is proper to be done in observing the Sabbath or the Lord's Day? Jesus said, "It is lawful to do good on the sabbath." His own life is summarized by saying that "He went about doing good" (Acts 10:38). Let us honor Him by doing His kind of good in His name.

C. Prayer of a Learner

Thank You, Father, for the loving concern You displayed in establishing the Sabbath for the children of Israel. Thank You even more for the love that sent Your Son to be the Savior of all mankind, and for the resurrection we celebrate in the Lord's Day. May we honor You always by serving in His way in His name. Amen.

D. Thought to Remember

It is never wrong to do right!

Home Daily Bible Readings

Monday, Mar. 2—The Lord's Anointed (Isaiah 61:1-4)

Tuesday, Mar. 3—Desperate for Healing (Mark 2:1-5)

Wednesday, Mar. 4—Authority to Forgive (Mark 2:6-12)

Thursday, Mar. 5—Sick and the Sinners (Mark 2:15-17)

Friday, Mar. 6.—A Time to Fast (Mark 2:18-22)

Saturday, Mar. 7—The Lord of the Sabbath (Mark 2:23-28)

Sunday, Mar. 8.—Hardness of Heart (Mark 3:1-6)

Learning by Doing

This page contains an alternate lesson plan emphasizing learning activities. Classes desiring such student involvement will find these suggestions helpful.

Learning Goals

After this lesson the students will be able to:

1. Distinguish between human traditions and divine truth.

2. Explain how meeting human needs is important to the practice of true Christianity.

3. Express their commitment to the "Lord of the Sabbath."

Into the Lesson

Write the following statements on three slips of paper, one statement per slip: (1) Our worship services follow certain traditional procedures, and these are very important to the vitality of our worship." (2) "Our worship services follow certain traditional procedures, but these have little or no effect on the vitality of our worship." (3) "Our worship services would be a better reflection of our freedom in Christ if we would eliminate all the traditional practices." (If you expect more than eighteen students, prepare duplicates of one or all of these statements.)

Divide the class into three groups (more than three if each group exceeds six members). Give each group one of the statements and ask them to prepare a defense of the position. Each group should prepare a hypothetical defense of the stated position, even if the members do not agree with it. (Assure the students they will get a chance to share their true feelings later.)

After a few minutes, allow the groups to present their position papers. Then discuss how important tradition is to worship. Most will agree that *some* tradition has value (even starting at the same time each week is a tradition). As we shall see in this lesson, however, traditions must never be regarded as more important than the needs of people.

Into the Word

Share some of the background information that is included under the heading "The Sabbath and the Lord's Day" in the lesson introduction. Especially point out that "Jesus observed the Sabbath law, but not all the traditions." Emphasize that Jesus valued human needs more highly than tradition.

Read the text, Mark 2:23—3:6, aloud. The question of whether the disciples were stealing the grain in the first incident should not be allowed to confuse the issue at hand. Have someone read Deuteronomy 23:25 as soon as the text has been read and note that Jewish law permitted what the disciples did on this occasion.

Have the class work in the small groups formed earlier to discuss the following questions:

(1) What law were Jesus' disciples breaking in the first incident in our text, the law of God or a man-made regulation?

(2) What key principle did Jesus give about the Sabbath (v. 27), and how did that relate to the charge against His disciples?

(3) What principle is implied in Jesus' question recorded in Mark 3:4? Compare Matthew 12:12.

(4) What was the cause of Jesus' anger in Mark 3:5? What actions from those present would have appeased His anger?

(5) What do these two Sabbath events demonstrate concerning Jesus' view of human beings and human traditions?

Give the groups about ten minutes, and then ask for reports. Discuss the questions briefly.

Into Life

Call attention to Jesus' statement in Mark 2:27. This statement concisely sums up Jesus' priority of people over tradition (as the discussion of question 5 above will have made clear). State that everything we do in the name of the Lord Jesus should reflect this same priority.

Ask the students to reflect once again on Jesus' anger directed at the Pharisees in the synagogue. Their insisting on maintaining their human traditions concerning the Sabbath caused them to disregard the need of the man with the withered hand. And this heartless attitude provoked Jesus' wrath. Ask, "Is it possible that we as a church maintain certain human traditions that blind us to the needs of people? If so, may Jesus' anger be directed toward us also?"

Finally, note Jesus' claim to be "Lord also of the sabbath." Suggest that we can submit to the "Lord of the Sabbath" best when we combine following His commands with following His example of meeting human needs. Distribute three-by-five index cards and ask each student to write one thing he or she can do to express commitment to the "Lord of the Sabbath." It should be something that combines His love for the truth with His love for people.

Let's Talk It Over

The questions on this page are designed to encourage review of the lesson Scriptures and to promote discussion of the lesson by the class. The answers provided are only discussion starters. Let your class talk it over from there.

1. In the first incident recorded in our lesson text, the Pharisees criticized Jesus in the form of a question regarding His disciples conduct on the Sabbath. How can Jesus' response to their question be a model for us?

Jesus did not argue with the Pharisees about what constituted work on the Sabbath. He dealt with God's purpose for giving the Sabbath. In His response, Jesus addressed the questioners deeper spiritual need. He sought to change an attitude, not to win an argument.

When we are questioned, we must be careful to listen for the questioner's intent. We also need to become conversant in the Scripture so that we can cite appropriate Biblical teachings and examples to refute error. Instead of being defensive, we need to ask probing, appropriate questions of the inquirer in order to bring that person face-to-face with the truths of God's Word.

2. The Pharisees challenged Jesus because of the behavior of His disciples. Why was this so, and what does it say to Christians today?

The Pharisees felt that what a teacher's disciples did reflected the teaching they had received, so they held the teacher responsible. Even so, the attitudes and behavior exhibited by Christians today influence the way persons outside of Christ think of Him and the church. If we are guilty of offenses, Christ and the church suffer reproach. If, however, we reflect His character, He will be praised. Paul wrote, "As a prisoner for the Lord, then, I urge you to live a life worthy of the calling you have received. Be completely humble and gentle; be patient, bearing with one another in love. Make every effort to keep the unity of the Spirit through the bond of peace" (Ephesians 4:1-3, *New International Version*).

3. On the occasion when Jesus healed the man with the withered hand, how did Jesus show that He was both tough and tender?

Jesus showed tenderness and compassion on the man with the withered hand by healing him. Although He knew that a confrontation with the Pharisees would result, He still spoke the words of healing. He was tough in regard to the Pharisees, however, because of the hardness of their hearts. As leaders of the people, these men should have shown compassion toward the needy. Instead, they were more concerned with protecting their own position and power.

As disciples of Jesus, we too are to show compassion upon those who are struggling with sin and illness. But there are occasions when Christians must be firm. Those persons who, under the guise of preaching the gospel, are guilty of false teaching must be opposed. And those who seek to use their positions of influence to prey upon the weak or unsuspecting in order to advance themselves should be challenged.

4. The Pharisees challenged Jesus' right to do and teach what He did, and they sought to nullify His influence among the people. Do Christians challenge Jesus today and seek to nullify His influence? If so, how?

We who are Christians readily acknowledge Jesus as our Savior and Lord. But what is our response when we are confronted with new insights from Scripture regarding Christ's expectations of His followers? Do we say, "That's interesting, but I think . . ." or do we recognize His authority over our lives and obey? Each of these challenges is actually the clash of claims to authority. Will I truly allow Jesus to be the Lord of my life? Will I follow Him or will I live as I please? Joshua challenged the people of his day, "Choose you this day whom ye will serve" (Joshua 24:15). A similar choice is ours as we consider questions such as the following: "Am I willing to dress modestly? Will I live a consumptive life-style? Am I my brother's keeper? Can I do it just one more time?" We are challenging Christ today when we live life on the edge instead of seeking His will completely.

5. Sometimes Christians use the term *Sabbath* to mean the first day of the week, the Lord's Day. Is this accurate? Has the meaning of the Sabbath been transferred to the Lord's Day?

It is not accurate to call the Lord's Day the Sabbath. The Sabbath was the seventh day of the week; the Lord's Day is the first day of the week. Nowhere in the New Testament are Christians commanded to observe Sabbath regulations on the Lord's Day.

Without Honor in His Own Country

LESSON SCRIPTURE: Mark 6:1-13.

PRINTED TEXT: Mark 6:1-13.

Mark 6:1-13

1 And he went out from thence, and came into his own country; and his disciples follow him.

2 And when the sabbath day was come, he began to teach in the synagogue: and many hearing him were astonished, saying, From whence hath this man these things? and what wisdom is this which is given unto him, that even such mighty works are wrought by his hands?

3 Is not this the carpenter, the son of Mary, the brother of James, and Joses, and of Judas, and Simon? and are not his sisters here with us? And they were offended at him.

4 But Jesus said unto them, A prophet is not without honor, but in his own country, and among his own kin, and in his own house.

5 And he could there do no mighty work, save that he laid his hands upon a few sick folk, and healed them.

6 And he marveled because of their unbelief. And he went round about the villages, teaching.

7 And he called unto him the twelve, and began to send them forth by two and two; and gave them power over unclean spirits;

8 And commanded them that they should take nothing for their journey, save a staff only; no scrip, no bread, no money in their purse:

9 But be shod with sandals; and not put on two coats.

10 And he said unto them, In what place soever ye enter into a house, there abide till ye depart from that place.

11 And whosoever shall not receive you, nor hear you, when ye depart thence, shake off the dust under your feet for a testimony against them. Verily I say unto you, It shall be more tolerable for Sodom and Gomorrah in the day of judgment, than for that city.

12 And they went out, and preached that men should repent.

13 And they cast out many devils, and anointed with oil many that were sick, and healed them.

GOLDEN TEXT: Jesus said unto them, A prophet is not without honor, but in his own country, and among his own kin, and in his own house.—Mark 6:4.

The Strong Son of God

Unit 1: Mission and Message

(Lessons 1-4)

Lesson Aims

As a result of this study, the students should be able to:

1. Summarize briefly the two incidents reported in Mark 6:1-13.

2. Give a reason for Mark's linking the incident at Nazareth with the sending of the twelve apostles on their mission.

3. Accept more readily and patiently the disadvantages that may come from a daily acknowledgment of Jesus Christ as Lord.

Lesson Outline

INTRODUCTION
  A. "Then I'll Be Happy"
  B. Lesson Background
I. JESUS RECEIVED AND REJECTED (Mark 6:1-6)
  A. Misled by Familiarity (vv. 1-3)
    A Change of Career
    Similar, but Different
  B. Disbelief Astonishes Jesus (vv. 4-6)
II. APOSTLES TO BE RECEIVED AND REJECTED (Mark 6:7-13)
  A. Instructed and Empowered (vv. 7-10)
  B. Apostles Warned of Rejection (v. 11)
  C. Twofold Mission Completed (vv. 12, 13)
CONCLUSION
  A. What Happened After That?
  B. Support for Servants
  C. Prayer for Patience
  D. Thought to Remember

Visual 3 of the visuals packet states a vital truth regarding our discipleship for Jesus. Display the poster as the session begins and let it remain before your class throughout the session. The visual is shown on page 247.

Introduction

A. "Then I'll Be Happy"

An old-time love song includes these lines:"I want to go where you go, do what you do, love when you love; then I'll be happy . . . I want to sigh when you sigh, cry when you cry, smile when you smile, then I'll be happy."

If two people are to spend a great deal of time together, they need to be congenial. And if any one of us is going to be happy forever in the presence of God's glorified Son Jesus, we shall do well to practice going where He goes, loving what He loves, smiling at what pleases Him, and grieving at what breaks His heart. We'll want to be accepted where He is accepted, and we should expect rejection by those who reject Him.

The message of Mark 6:1-13, therefore, is intensely practical. It deals with circumstances in which Jesus was rejected by those who thought they knew Him best. They just didn't want to go where He went, or do the loving, helpful things He did. The same kinds of folk rejected the apostles who came doing and saying and thinking the things He did and said and thought. So the experience of the apostles forms an appropriate second half of our lesson.

B. Lesson Background

The Gospels include three accounts of Jesus' teaching in the synagogue at Nazareth, where He had lived from about age three to age thirty. The accounts are in Matthew 13:53-58; Mark 6:1-6; and Luke 4:16-30. Do they all refer to one incident, or do they tell of more than one? Opinions on that question are divided. Luke presents the visit to Nazareth as a sort of introduction to Jesus' ministry, before He chose the twelve apostles. Mark says Jesus' disciples followed Him on the visit to "his own country." Undoubtedly, the twelve were among the disciples who followed Him, for the apostles were sent on their own mission of preaching and healing soon thereafter (Mark 6:7-13).

On Jesus' several preaching tours throughout Galilee, He may have visited the scenes of His boyhood and youth on more than one occasion. If so, His experiences in the synagogue at Nazareth would naturally have been enough alike to produce a similar impression and report. It seems to us, therefore, that Luke records Jesus' first visit to Nazareth and that Matthew and Mark report another visit that occurred perhaps a year later.

Mark's Gospel includes today's text in a series of accounts relating mixed responses to Jesus in Galilee, including enthusiastic reception and stubborn rejection. High acclamation met Jesus' miraculous stilling of a storm on the Sea of Galilee (4:35-41). Citizens of Gadara rejected Jesus after He healed a demon-possessed man and in doing so destroyed a herd of swine (5:1-20). In the course of raising Jairus's young daughter from the dead, Jesus met scornful derision from unbelievers (5:22-43). These and the events before us in 6:1-13 happened in places widely scattered throughout Galilee.

I. Jesus Received and Rejected (Mark 6:1-6)

A. Misled by Familiarity (vv. 1-3)

1. And he went out from thence, and came into his own country; and his disciples followed him.

Leaving the vicinity of Capernaum, Jesus made His way into the hills to the site of His boyhood and youth. Nazareth, not named here by Mark, is located about midway between the southern tip of the Sea of Galilee and the Mediterranean coast. Concerning the disciples accompanying Jesus, Mark had reported, "He ordained twelve, that they should be with him, and that he might send them forth to preach, and to have power to heal sicknesses, and to cast out devils" (3:14, 15).

A CHANGE OF CAREER

When the thirty-year-old Jesus left home and took up preaching, there were probably some who mistakenly thought that it was simply a mid-life career change. And probably there were those who criticized Him for leaving His mother and sisters and brothers and taking up a calling the material benefits of which are often questionable.

Career changes are never easy. I have known a number of men, well launched in their careers, who have left their jobs to become ministers, and I have also known preachers who have given up their ministries to take up some secular position.

Whenever this happens, criticisms are heard: "He'd better keep his good job so he can take care of his family instead of going off half-cocked to try preaching," or, "We've got enough preachers," or "He's too old to learn enough to be a good preacher." On the other hand we hear, "What a great loss to the ministry," or, "Why did he leave the ministry? Is there something in his background we don't know?" or, "He's just interested in money."

Yes, I suppose Jesus wasn't unique in being criticized for His "career change." May we learn to give people the right to make choices that will benefit them and the kingdom.   —T. T.

2. And when the sabbath day was come, he began to teach in the synagogue: and many hearing him were astonished, saying, From whence hath this man these things? and what wisdom is this which is given unto him, that even such mighty works are wrought by his hands?

We are not told what Jesus and the twelve did between the time of their arrival at Nazareth and the coming of *the sabbath*. By well established habit Jesus went to the synagogue on that day, and according to the habit of His public ministry He used the occasion for teaching (Luke 4:16-22). Any visiting rabbi might be invited to address the assembly, and special interest would attach to this widely acclaimed Teacher.

Began to teach. This construction appears commonly to introduce any new action of Jesus. Here it may possibly suggest that Jesus did not finish His teaching that day. On the occasion described by Luke, Jesus read from Isaiah 61:1, 2 and declared His own ministry to be fulfillment of that prophecy (Luke 4:16-21).

The amazed townspeople asked, "Where did this man get all this? What is the wisdom given to Him? What mighty works are wrought by His hands!" (*Revised Standard Version*). In His teaching was a completeness of grace and truth, of humility and authority, of tenderness and judgment that they could not explain. No natural source could account for it, and they were unwilling to acknowledge a supernatural source.

Jesus' *mighty works* had been reported to them (perhaps among others the raising of Jairus's daughter in Capernaum—Luke 6:35-43), but their disbelief prevented their benefiting from any substantial miracles on this occasion (v. 5).

3. Is not this the carpenter, the son of Mary, the brother of James, and Joses, and of Judas, and Simon? and are not his sisters here with us? And they were offended at him.

Clearly, no marvelous happenings had followed Jesus in His childhood. His neighbors had seen no such things. This Teacher now before them was so different from the youth who had grown up and become a carpenter among them that they could hardly believe that He was the same person. His family were common folk like their neighbors. Mary's husband Joseph was perhaps no longer living, but was remembered. Jesus' brothers were ordinary young men, and His sisters still lived in the area. How could Jesus be so different from them?

Jesus' neighbors were so familiar with His humanity that their minds were closed to His divinity. Thus they were *offended*, or caused to stumble into error, concerning Him. The offense was also emotional resentment, so intense that earlier they tried to destroy Him (Luke 4:28-30).

How to Say It

CAPERNAUM. Kuh-*per*-nay-um.
GOMORRAH. Guh-*mor*-uh.
JAIRUS. Jay-*eye*-rus or *Jay*-ih-rus.
SODOM. *Sod*-um.

SIMILAR, BUT DIFFERENT

Having been away at Bible college I returned home for a summer vacation. Near the end of that summer, as well as I recall, the youth of the church were asked to be in charge of one of the evening services. A friend of mine was asked to make a few remarks, and because he was having trouble with his wording I suggested a helpful line that contained the scholarly-sounding expression, "by divine apostolic precedent" (which, you must admit, sounds like what a Bible college student might say!).

He didn't like that line; apparently he thought the words were too difficult to say. As I was berating him for his unwillingness to try, the preacher's wife intervened and suggested some words less difficult to utter.

I still remember the humiliation of the experience, and how I crawled back into my hole as a result of the mild rebuff I had received.

I now understand that the preacher's wife was telling me in her sweet, subtle way that I would do well to back off from what might be interpreted as an arrogant display of knowledge.

Like Jesus, I experienced a rejection, of sorts, in my home congregation. But there was a vast difference in the two incidents: I deserved my rebuke, but He didn't deserve the treatment He received.   —T. T.

B. Disbelief Astonishes Jesus (vv. 4-6)

4. But Jesus said unto them, A prophet is not without honor, but in his own country, and among his own kin, and in his own house.

We hear often that "familiarity breeds contempt." Perhaps the family and neighbors become jealous of anyone who rises from among them to prominence. Perhaps they feel put down and overshadowed by another's honor. Perhaps they have so low an estimate of their own family and community that they can't believe anyone among them to be worthy of honor.

It is not so, however, in all walks of life. Prominent athletes, actors, and statesmen today are acclaimed as heroes in their hometowns. Should it not have been so also with a *prophet.* That, however, was different. By definition a prophet was a spokesman for God. He announced, "Thus saith the Lord," and so laid claim to some special relationship with the Almighty. And, of course, Jesus' claims were even greater! The people of Nazareth could not bring themselves to believe that one from among them could have such a special relationship with God.

Jesus knew all too well the problem of acceptance in the family. Mark 3:21, 31-35, tells of an attempt made by His own mother and siblings to remove Him from the public view as being mentally unbalanced. John 7:3-5 tells of taunts by His unbelieving brothers—the same brothers who took their places among His disciples after He rose from the dead (Acts 1:14).

5. And he could there do no mighty work, save that he laid his hands upon a few sick folk, and healed them.

Matthew 13:58 says, "And he did not many mighty works there because of their unbelief." Jesus power, of course, was unlimited. But there were times when a person's faith was the condition upon which He chose to use His miraculous power (see Mark 5:34, 36; 9:23; 10:52). That seems to have been the situation on this occasion. Yet even at Nazareth Jesus found a few who welcomed His ministrations, and He *healed them.*

6. And he marveled because of their unbelief. And he went round about the villages, teaching.

Jesus' clearly did not expect great honor at Nazareth; but the stubbornness of the townsfolks' rejection went far beyond His expectation. Various translations read, He wondered, was amazed, surprised, and astonished at what He found. If we ever wonder whether God is concerned about our response to Him, this should be a sufficient answer. Our attitude makes a big difference in Heaven, as well as on earth.

Did someone say that faith is a divine gift, bestowed by God on some folk and not on others? If that were so, Jesus would not have been surprised at someone's lack of it, would He?

The Lord did not go off to sulk and lick His emotional wounds. He went out to the nearby villages to teach whoever was willing to listen.

II. Apostles to Be Received and Rejected (Mark 6:7-13)

A. Instructed and Empowered (vv. 7-10)

7. And he called unto him the twelve, and began to send them forth by two and two; and gave them power over unclean spirits.

Jesus had selected the twelve apostles from among His disciples so that He might prepare them to preach and to heal the sick (see Luke 6:12-16; Mark 3:16-19). These twelve had been taught by Jesus for about a year. Now they would be *sent out* (the meaning of the word *apostle*) to go before Him into villages where He would later come (Luke 10:1), and also to places He could not reach, to announce that God's reign was being established (Matthew 10:7). Their present mission was limited to "the lost sheep of the house of Israel" (Matthew 10:5, 6).

Began to send. This may suggest that the sending was not all done at once. But the meaning is not necessarily so limited (see verse 2). The apostles were entering a sort of internship. Afterward they would report back to Jesus for further instruction before receiving their fuller commission to all the world. They were to go now in six teams of two each—a procedure that provided for support and encouragement one to another, for safety, and for supply of varying talent in each team. It would keep their attention on the task before them, and lend credibility to their work.

How, though, could mortal men do the work of God? That question was answered when Jesus gave the apostles their assignment: they were given *power over unclean* (or evil) *spirits.* They were to "heal the sick, cleanse the lepers, raise the dead, cast out devils" (Matthew 10:8). This kind of empowerment became a mark of the apostleship (Matthew 10:1; 2 Corinthians 12:12), extending the compassion of Christ to the needy, but even more immediately certifying the message they brought as from God. No material gain was to come to these men, though, from their miracles. Jesus instructed, "Freely ye have received, freely give" (Matthew 10:8).

8, 9. And commanded them that they should take nothing for their journey, save a staff only; no scrip, no bread, no money in their purse: but be shod with sandals; and not put on two coats.

The apostles were to travel light, bringing spiritual treasures, but not material. One sturdy walking stick would help the traveler over rugged trails and test the depth of streams to be waded, and would help to ward off attacks from man or beast. Each was to wear sandals but was to take no spare provisions. He was not to carry a spare tunic, or money, or food, or *scrip* (a small bag) in which to accumulate provisions along the way. These men would learn really to pray, "Give us this day our daily bread" (Matthew 6:11). They must expect God to supply their need through the hands of His people. "The workman is worthy of his meat" (Matthew 10:10, 40-42; 1 Corinthians 9:14).

There is no record that Jesus or the apostles applied the same restrictions to traveling evangelists later, but this should be enough to rebuke any Christian worker who would suppose that godliness is to be regarded as a way of gain (1 Timothy 6:5-10).

10. And he said unto them, In what place soever ye enter into a house, there abide till ye depart from that place.

Matthew 10:11-13 records these instructions of Jesus more fully. On entering a community

visual 3

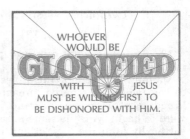

the apostles were to "inquire who in it is worthy," that is, who is willing and able to entertain guests without undue strain on the family. There they were to stay as long as they remained in that community. They were to pray God's peace on that house, but if they were refused hospitality, the peace they had requested would return to themselves. It would indeed be futile to ask God's peace on a household that rejected His message. Hospitality, graciously offered and graciously accepted, is a timeless quality of godliness.

B. Apostles Warned of Rejection (v. 11)

11. And whosoever shall not receive you, nor hear you, when ye depart thence, shake off the dust under your feet for a testimony against them. Verily I say unto you, It shall be more tolerable for Sodom and Gomorrha in the day of judgment, than for that city.

Were these Galilean apostles going to their home communities, there to be prophets without honor? Anyway, they would meet with rejection in a significant proportion of the places they visited—rejection by individuals and by whole communities. They were not to force their presence on those who did not want it, but in departing they were to leave a solemn warning about the serious finality of rejection. Jesus instructed them to *shake off the dust under your feet for a testimony against them.* To clean the feet and sandals on departure indicated that the traveler didn't want any part of this place to linger with him (compare Acts 13:51). Judgment and vengeance belong to God, and the rejected messenger cannot afford to carry the dust of lingering resentment with him as he continues his work for Christ.

God's judgment takes into account the sinners' opportunities to know the truth. Communities, therefore, that had seen the mighty works of Jesus, and still rejected Him, would be held more strictly accountable than the ancient cities of the plain that underwent fiery destruction for their wickedness in the days of Abraham (Genesis 19:1-28). Material destruction is not the final judgment!

C. Twofold Mission Completed

(vv. 12, 13)

12. And they went out, and preached that men should repent.

Matthew 10:7 reports this in Jesus' instruction to the twelve: "As ye go, preach, saying, The kingdom of heaven is at hand." The apostles were to begin with the same message presented earlier by John the Baptist and by Jesus: "The kingdom of God is at hand: repent ye, and believe the gospel" (Mark 1:15). God reigns, and people must conform themselves to His dominion. That is repentance. That preaching was the first part of the apostles' ministry.

13. And they cast out many devils, and anointed with oil many that were sick, and healed them.

The second part of their ministry was both compassionate and convincing. The miracles established the divine authority of the gospel they preached. *Devils*—demons, or evil spirits under the control of Satan—did take control of some people. Jesus cast them out, and so did His apostles, in His name and by His power. The application of oil to the sick was perhaps medicinal, though the healings were far more than what medicine could achieve. Anointing may also have been cosmetic—a preparation of the sick person to go out again into society—a dramatic announcement of the imminent healing.

In Nazareth the Lord himself could heal only a few sick folk because of hampering disbelief. In other communities His apostles healed many because of a receptive faith.

Conclusion

A. What Happened After That?

Wouldn't we like to know what happened later in Nazareth as a result of Jesus' teaching there? And what happened elsewhere in Galilee as a result of the apostles' brief visits? This much is sure. Townsfolk at Nazareth were not made whole as they might have been, and when they heard of mighty works done by Jesus in other places they were left to say, "I wouldn't know; He surely didn't do much for our town."

Receptive villages visited by the apostles, on the other hand, could rejoice in their benefits, both immediate and long term. And when the resurrection gospel came to them later, they had reason to acknowledge in its fullness the kingdom that had been announced among them.

Then there is the final judgment. If the resistant communities visited by the apostles fare worse at last than Sodom and Gomorrah, what must be the unhappy fate of Nazareth, which denied the King of glory because He grew up in their midst? Each community will, in fact, have reason to ponder Jesus' parable of seed and soils. The same good seed fell in all places, but the harvest depended on the soil.

B. Support for Servants

Even though Jesus sent the twelve on a mission without their own resources, He assured them that they would be taken care of by God's people. But He also made it clear that they were not to manipulate others in order to receive the best material things. When they entered a town and accepted an invitation to stay in someone's house, they were to remain as guests in that house while they were in that community.

Servants of God should not demand first-class service. Nor should they be above staying in the humblest of surroundings when traveling to minister to God's people.

By the same token, God's people are not to be stingy when it comes to sharing with those special workers. They are engaged in an important work, and for the good of the kingdom their physical needs must be met. The church is to be a family—a family in which each member looks out for the welfare of the others.

C. Prayer for Patience

Supply to us patience, please, God, to hear the words of men and appreciate them in their relationship to Your proven Word. Give us courage, we pray, to accept mistreatment for the sake of Him who accepted suffering and death for us. We pray in His name. Amen.

D. Thought to Remember

Whoever would be glorified with Jesus must be willing first to be dishonored with Him.

Home Daily Bible Readings

Monday, Mar. 9—He Has Borne Our Griefs (Isaiah 53:3-6)

Tuesday, Mar. 10—A True Prophet (Deuteronomy 13:1-5)

Wednesday, Mar. 11—Marvel at the Mystery of Their Unbelief (Mark 6:1-6)

Thursday, Mar. 12—The Unbelief (Hebrews 3:14-18)

Friday, Mar. 13—How Long? (Matthew 17:14-18)

Saturday, Mar. 14—Second Time Around (Mark 6:7-13)

Sunday, Mar. 15—Do Not Dismay (2 Corinthians 4:5-10)

Learning by Doing

This page contains an alternate lesson plan emphasizing learning activities. Classes desiring such student involvement will find these suggestions helpful.

Learning Goals

After this lesson a student will be able to do the following:

1. Explain why Jesus did not do many miracles in Nazareth.

2. Suggest from Jesus' example a proper response to rejection.

3. Summarize the mission of the Twelve.

Into the Lesson

On the chalkboard write, "Familiarity breeds contempt." Then label the four corners (or any four convenient areas) of the classroom with one of the following: Always True, Generally True, Seldom True, Never True.

As the class arrives, ask the students whether they agree or disagree with this statement. Ask them to move to the area of the room where the label reflects their response. As the groups form according to the different opinions, ask each group to formulate a defense of their position. Why do they believe their opinion is correct? What examples can they cite?

Allow just a few minutes and then ask each group to report. You will probably not be able to reach a conclusive judgment on the matter. Apparently the statement is true often enough to have become a truism; and it was true enough in Jesus' day for Him to say, "A prophet is not without honor except in his hometown." Yet the fact that Jesus marveled at the unbelief of the people of Nazareth, among whom He had lived and worked, leads us to conclude that in some cases familiarity ought to bring more beneficial results.

Today's lesson will focus on that incident of rejection. Perhaps we will learn something about facing rejection in our own ministries.

Into the Word

Have a class member read Mark 6:1-13 aloud. Then divide the class into an even number of small groups. Give half the groups this assignment: "Study Mark 6:1-6 and write a series of newspaper headlines that might have appeared in the Nazareth morning newspaper—if there had been one—the day after Jesus' visit. Include news headlines (which would head factual accounts of the events) as well as editorial headlines (which would head editorials that express opinions)."

Give the other half of the groups this assignment: "Study Mark 6:7-13 and write a series of newspaper headlines that might have appeared in the morning newspapers of the cities and villages visited by the apostles—if first-century cities had published newspapers. Include some from cities where the apostles were welcomed and some from cities that rejected them. Be sure also to include news headlines (which would head factual accounts of the events) as well as editorial headlines (which would head editorials that express opinions)."

After a few minutes, ask the groups to share their headlines and note how they summarize the facts recorded in the text.

Into Life

Ask the students to relate instances when they experienced some kind of rejection. How did it make them feel? What did they do about it? Call attention to Jesus' response to rejection in Nazareth: He ministered in spite of it to those who were willing to receive Him (Mark 6:5). He went on to other villages to minister (Mark 6:6b), and He sent His disciples to other cities of Israel to preach the message of repentance (Mark 6:7). Discuss how we can respond when our ministries in behalf of Christ are rejected.

Next, call attention to the mission of the apostles. Note that they were prepared to expect both acceptance and rejection. Mention also how few were their provisions (vv. 8, 9). Discuss why this was so. In the course of the discussion, suggest that this would have focused their dependence on the Lord. Discuss how that attitude would have helped them deal with rejection.

Point out that the apostles, when they were rejected, were to "shake off the dust" from their feet. Discuss what that meant. How may we express the same concept today? Are there occasions today when such an action would be appropriate? If so, when? If not, why not?

Note the results of Nazareth's rejection of Jesus. Mark tells us Jesus could not do many miracles there because of their unbelief. Ask, "When things seem to be going slowly for the church, do you think it could be that God is unable to do much with *us* because of our unbelief?" Discuss the similarity of the two situations.

Close with a prayer of repentance for unbelief and of commitment to the Lord's work.

Let's Talk It Over

The questions on this page are designed to encourage review of the lesson Scriptures and to promote discussion of the lesson by the class. The answers provided are only discussion starters. Let your class talk it over from there.

1. Is there a type of familiarity with Jesus that prevents us from seeing who He really is? What helps us to take another look at Him?

Every year at Christmas time, the attention of many people in the world is drawn once again to Jesus. This is good, of course. But for some, this yearly remembrance of Jesus goes no further than seeing Him as a tiny baby in a manger. Likewise at Easter much of the world is reminded of the resurrection of Jesus, and all rejoice at the great blessing that His victory over death brings. These great events are familiar to countless multitudes, both those who have accepted Jesus as Lord, and those who have not. Other snapshots of the Lord may give us an incomplete picture of His ministry. Many are comfortable in keeping Him within these snapshots, for they are non-threatening. It is easy to believe in Him and to like Him as long as He remains in the "picture album." We need to see Him as He intended us to see Him and to open our hearts and minds to His challenges for spiritual change and growth. That's why we need to be involved in a systematic study of God's Word. We need to challenge ourselves to read the whole Bible, not just to return to our favorite parts. We need to study authors who may challenge our understanding, and then to search the Scriptures to see if what these writers say is true. We should be growing in our understanding and love of Jesus, just as those who are married grow in the understanding and love of their mate.

2. If you were to develop a program to train members to assist in the church's ministry, how could Jesus' training of the Twelve serve as your model?

Jesus called the Twelve with a purpose in mind. To several He had issued the challenge, "Come ye after me, and I will make you to become fishers of men" (Mark 1:17). The call was also issued individually (see Mark 2:14). As He set them apart for ministry, He told them all what they were to do—preach, heal sickness, and drive out demons (3:14, 15). We note that Jesus wanted the Twelve to be with Him (3:13). By being "with Him" the Twelve were able to see how Jesus conducted himself and His ministry in varied circumstances. By being "with Him" they were able to receive special instruction

(4:10). Then, at the proper time, He sent them out. Calling people to ministry in the church should be similar. The church's leaders should have a clear purpose of the work to be done, call people individually, provide informal and formal teaching and training, and, when the trainees are prepared, send them out to do the ministry. Later in this chapter we see the important principle of evaluation, as the apostles report to Jesus all they had done and taught (6:30). We, too, must evaluate our ministries for effectiveness.

3. Jesus sent the Twelve out two by two. What were the advantages of this, and what does this practice say to us today?

The apostles who went together had different backgrounds and different personalities, and these would give a varied approach to their hearers. If they met with rejection, the two would keep one another from discouragement. As they confirmed one another, power would be given to their testimony. Also, accountability and trust would develop between the two. Instead of being competitors, they would be companions in ministry. And, of course, two traveling together would be safer than one traveling alone. Each of these points is valid in the church's ministry today. The work goes easier when it is shared. We should be looking for others and encouraging their interest and assistance. This kind of teamwork would help prevent a worker from feeling burned out by having to do it all.

4. Why is it important to preach repentance today?

Sin abounds in our society, and it may be seen in many forms. Many also are the efforts made to excuse sin, some very elaborate. In the haze of situation ethics and the darkness of compromise, the light of the gospel must shine through in an unwavering proclamation. As long as one is separated from God by a rebellious spirit, that person will experience an inner discontent and turmoil in his or her relationships. Preaching repentance challenges us to take stock of our priorities and to submit our lives to God's will. Our spiritual needs cannot be met until we repent and give God His rightful place in our hearts.

Restoration to Wholeness

Lesson Scripture: Mark 7:24-37.

Printed Text: Mark 7:24-37.

Mark 7:24-37

24 And from thence he arose, and went into the borders of Tyre and Sidon, and entered into a house, and would have no man know it: but he could not be hid.

25 For a certain woman, whose young daughter had an unclean spirit, heard of him, and came and fell at his feet:

26 The woman was a Greek, a Syrophoenician by nation; and she besought him that he would cast forth the devil out of her daughter.

27 But Jesus said unto her, Let the children first be filled: for it is not meet to take the children's bread, and to cast it unto the dogs.

28 And she answered and said unto him, Yes, Lord: yet the dogs under the table eat of the children's crumbs.

29 And he said unto her, For this saying go thy way; the devil is gone out of thy daughter.

30 And when she was come to her house, she found the devil gone out, and her daughter laid upon the bed.

31 And again, departing from the coasts of Tyre and Sidon, he came unto the sea of Galilee, through the midst of the coasts of Decapolis.

32 And they bring unto him one that was deaf, and had an impediment in his speech; and they beseech him to put his hand upon him.

33 And he took him aside from the multitude, and put his fingers into his ears, and he spit, and touched his tongue;

34 And looking up to heaven, he sighed, and saith unto him, Ephphatha, that is, Be opened.

35 And straightway his ears were opened, and the string of his tongue was loosed, and he spake plain.

36 And he charged them that they should tell no man: but the more he charged them, so much the more a great deal they published it;

37 And were beyond measure astonished, saying, He hath done all things well: he maketh both the deaf to hear, and the dumb to speak.

Golden Text: He hath done all things well: he maketh both the deaf to hear, and the dumb to speak.—Mark 7:37.

The Strong Son of God

Unit 1: Mission and Message

(Lessons 1-4)

Lesson Aims

After this study the students should be:
1. Able to tell briefly in their own words the stories found in Mark 7:24-37.
2. Able to show how these stories demonstrate Jesus' attitude toward people who were not of the nation of Israel.
3. Eager to share the gospel of Christ, which brings wholeness of life.

Lesson Outline

INTRODUCTION
  A. Complete, or Just Contented?
  B. Crowds and Conflict
I. CLEANSED WITH THE "CRUMBS" (Mark 7:24-30)
  A. Interrupting Jesus' Vacation (vv. 24-26)
  B. Understanding Jesus' Ministry (vv. 27, 28)
  C. Receiving Jesus' Mercy (vv. 29, 30)
II. RESTORED COMMUNICATION (Mark 7:31-37)
  A. Continuing in the Borderlands (v. 31)
  B. Presenting a Twofold Problem (v. 32)
  C. Communicating the Solution (vv. 33-35)
  D. Unrestrained Praise (vv. 36, 37)
    He Is Not Silent
CONCLUSION
  A. The Orders Are Reversed
  B. Prayer of One Made Whole
  C. Thought to Remember

Refer to visual 4 of the visuals packet when discussing verses 36 and 37 and the thoughts in the lesson conclusion. The visual is shown on page 255.

Introduction

A. Complete, or Just Contented?

Do you really want to be a whole person?

That, essentially, is what Jesus asked an invalid who was brought every day to a pool in Jerusalem where healings were expected (John 5:6). The man replied indirectly by complaining that he was not able to get into the pool when healing might happen. He had a real desire for usefulness in his legs and back, so he obeyed the Lord's command to pick up his mat and walk. There was more to wholeness, though, than physical strength. So Jesus warned him,

"Thou art made whole: sin no more, lest a worse thing come unto thee" (John 5:14).

There is yet more to wholeness than physical health combined with moral living. Jesus' greatest difficulties came with those religious leaders who had these qualities and were deeply offended at His suggestion that they were still not whole. When He offered them freedom in His truth, they retorted that as Abraham's descendants they were already free (John 8:33). When He spoke of His judgment as giving spiritual sight to the blind, they scoffed, "Are we blind also?" (John 9:40).

Jesus was, in fact, far ahead of those in our time who speak of wholeness in body, mind, and spirit. They received the idea from Him, who said, "I am come that they might have life, and that they might have it more abundantly" (John 10:10). His message is sorely needed by all manner of persons who are, like the Pharisees, contented with their incompleteness. Bulging muscles proclaim the pride of devotees to body building, perhaps devoid of intellectual or spiritual development. Pride of intellect is seen in a parade of degrees on the part of some who proclaim their independence of God. Pride of spiritual attainment still leads some to trust in themselves that they are righteous, and to look down on others (Luke 18:9). Do we really want to be made whole? Then let's learn from the Lord.

B. Crowds and Conflict

As we read Mark's Gospel, we feel the pressure of the crowds that sought Jesus' healing miracles in Galilee. (See Mark 3:7-9, 20; 6:31.)

Mark 6 goes on at this point to recount the futility of the Lord's efforts at securing privacy for quiet teaching of the twelve. The multitude found them and thronged them again. In His compassion Jesus taught them "many things" throughout the day, and in the late afternoon He fed the multitude with bread and fish miraculously multiplied from a boy's lunch (vv. 32-44). John 6:15 tells that the crowd would then have taken Jesus to make Him their king, but that He escaped to a mountainside to pray.

Not all in the multitude were so favorably disposed toward Jesus. Mark 7:1-23 tells of controversy stirred up by Pharisees who had come from Jerusalem, apparently for that purpose.

Besides crowd pressures and weariness and enmity from Jewish authorities, there was the watchful eye of a guilt-ridden Herod Antipas. Might Herod try again to kill John the Baptist, who, he thought, had risen from the dead in the person of Jesus? (Mark 6:14-16). It was time, and more than time, to get away for a while.

We might say that Jesus and the twelve apostles were out of the country on vacation. But even in "heathen" and semi-heathen territory Jesus responded with compassion to bring wholeness to suffering strangers.

I. Cleansed With the "Crumbs" (Mark 7:24-30)

This story is told in greater detail in Matthew 15:21-28, and from that account we shall draw some information not recorded by Mark.

A. Interrupting Jesus' Vacation (vv. 24-26)

24. And from thence he arose, and went into the borders of Tyre and Sidon, and entered into a house, and would have no man know it: but he could not be hid.

The Pharisees from Jerusalem had found Jesus in or near Capernaum, which was the center for His ministry in Galilee. From there He and the twelve journeyed some forty miles north and westward, out of Herod's realm into the independent territory of the Syrophoenicians (modern Lebanon). Tyre, though declining in importance, was still a notable seaport city. Sidon lay some twenty miles farther north on the Mediterranean coast. Modern Beirut is about twenty-five miles north of Sidon.

This journey was an occasion not for public ministry, but for quiet instruction of the apostles. He was in Gentile territory, and His earthly ministry was entirely directed to the "lost sheep of the house of Israel." Only later would the gospel be preached to all nations.

In whose *house* did He and the apostles find refuge? Was it rented for the time? Or made available by a friend? But something—perhaps the going and coming of these strangers in the community—betrayed His presence. The report of Him had preceded Him even here.

It has been said that the presence of Christ in a life, home, or community cannot be hid, even without its being reported. But that is a poor excuse for silence where Jesus has commanded proclamation (Mark 16:15).

25, 26. For a certain woman, whose young daughter had an unclean spirit, heard of him, and came and fell at his feet: the woman was a Greek, a Syrophoenician by nation; and she besought him that he would cast forth the devil out of her daughter.

The woman was a Gentile (*Greek* is the general equivalent), born in that area, of Canaanite descent (Matthew 15:22). Thus she sprang from the nation the children of Israel had been commanded to exterminate when they entered the promised land. Here she is described only as the concerned mother of a little girl (Mark's word signifies this) possessed by a demon. On learning of Jesus' presence, the woman came immediately and persistently to Him—humble, patient, and confident of His healing power.

She "cried unto him, saying, Have mercy on me, O Lord, thou Son of David; my daughter is grievously vexed with a devil" (Matthew 15:22). Was she approaching Jesus only as the miracle-working heir to Israel's great king? Or was there a deeper meaning to her saying, "Lord"? Jesus did not respond immediately to her plea, although her loud entreaties were bringing to Him the public notice He had come here to avoid.

Matthew 15:23-25 becomes significant at this point: "His disciples came and besought him, saying, Send her away; for she crieth after us. But he answered and said, I am not sent but unto the lost sheep of the house of Israel. Then came she and worshipped him, saying, Lord, help me."

The impatient disciples wanted Jesus to send the petitioner away. It is not clear whether they first wanted Him to perform the healing the woman requested. His reply reminded them of His steadfast purpose and program in ministry to the "house of Israel."

Observe the woman's plea: "Help me!" Healing to her daughter was mercy to herself. Who could understand that as well as the One who was to say, "Inasmuch as ye have done it unto one of the least of these my brethren, ye have done it unto me"? (Matthew 25:40).

B. Understanding Jesus' Ministry (vv. 27, 28)

27. But Jesus said unto her, Let the children first be filled: for it is not meet to take the children's bread, and to cast it unto the dogs.

Here Jesus addressed to the woman the problem He had laid before the apostles. The gospel ministry and message must be given first to the *children* of the covenant. After they had received as much as they would, the Gentiles would have their opportunity. Until then it would not be proper to make other distribution.

The woman remained unperturbed by Jesus' reference to *dogs*. He used a word signifying little dogs, or household pets, rather than the wild scavengers too well known in Israel. Thus He softened the common Jewish dismissal of all Gentiles as dogs. Little dogs, as well as children, belonged to the same head of the house, and would receive their bread in their turn.

28. And she answered and said unto him, Yes, Lord: yet the dogs under the table eat of the children's crumbs.

The woman accepted the puppy dog status assigned by Jesus and used it in pressing her plea. *Yes, Lord,* "You are right."

The woman seems to have understood remarkably well the dominion of God over all persons alike. Yet she conceded the prior claim of Israel to divine grace under the covenant with Abraham, and she accepted what was left in its proper order. At least she confessed the Lord to be right in His judgment, and declared her willingness to accept the leftovers as sufficient and thankworthy.

Christians can learn a great deal about prayer from this Canaanite woman. For the sake of her beloved daughter she endured difficulty and probable rebuff to press her appeal with One she knew to be able to help. She came humbly and patiently, accepting gratefully whatever the Lord might give.

C. Receiving Jesus' Mercy
(vv. 29, 30)

29, 30. And he said unto her, For this saying go thy way; the devil is gone out of thy daughter. And when she was come to her house, she found the devil gone out, and her daughter laid upon the bed.

Jesus' delay in responding to the mother's plea had gained several things: a test and exercise of her faith, and a demonstration of the Lord's plan for gospel ministry. Her response gained His approval of her and His healing of her daughter. Another Gentile—a centurion who knew that Jesus could heal his servant, even at a distance (Matthew 8:8-10)—had won a similar commendation: "I have not found so great faith, no, not in Israel." Matthew's account of the present incident says, "Jesus answered and said unto her, O woman, great is thy faith: be it unto thee even as thou wilt" (Matthew 15:28).

How to Say It

ANTIPAS. *An*-tuh-pas.
CANAANITE. *Kay*-nan-ite.
CAPERNAUM. Kuh-*per*-nay-um.
DECAPOLIS. Dee-*kap*-uh-lis.
EPHPHATHA (Aramaic). *Ef*-uh-thuh.
GAULANITIS. Gall-on-*eye*-tis.
IDUMEA. Id-you-*me*-uh.
SIDON. *Sye*-dun.
SYROPHOENICIA. *Sye*-roe-fih-*nish*-uh (strong accent on *nish*).
SYROPHOENICIAN. *Sye*-roe-fih-*nish*-un (strong accent on *nish*).
TYRE. Tire.

The mother did not wait for any further assurance. Going home immediately she found the little girl resting quietly, blessedly relieved from the tearing strains of her demon possession. It seems most significant that *tear, tore,* or *torn,* appear only five times in the New Testament, and always in reference to the violence done by evil spirits to their victims, especially as the demons were being cast out (Mark 1:26; 9:18, 20; Luke 9:39, 42). Here the tearing was over; the patient was whole.

II. Restored Communication
(Mark 7:31-37)
A. Continuing in the Borderlands
(v. 31)

31. And again, departing from the coasts of Tyre and Sidon, he came unto the sea of Galilee, through the midst of the coasts of Decapolis.

We don't know how long Jesus and His apostles stayed in Syrophoenicia, but when they departed they continued to avoid the territory controlled by Herod Antipas and dominated by leaders of the Jews. Still north of Galilee, they seem to have gone eastward through the headwaters of the Jordan River and southward through Gaulanitis and Decapolis (named for its ten cities) to the eastern shore of the Sea of Galilee. This was an area of mixed population, mostly Gentile.

On an earlier visit here Jesus had cast many demons out of an afflicted man and had permitted the demons to enter and destroy a flock of pigs. Citizens of the territory had asked Him to leave. Jesus had left, but the healed demoniac had spread the news of his healing (Mark 5:18-20). Many were by now eager to see Jesus.

Matthew 15:29-31 tells that on arriving, the Lord found a mountainside spot near the sea to rest from His journey, but soon "great multitudes came unto him, having with them those that were lame, blind, dumb, maimed, and many others, and cast them down at Jesus' feet; and he healed them . . . and they glorified the God of Israel." (Many obviously had been worshiping other gods.) Mark describes one of these healing miracles.

B. Presenting a Twofold Problem (v. 32)

32. And they bring unto him one that was deaf, and had an impediment in his speech; and they beseech him to put his hand upon him.

This incident seems to have been chosen for special treatment because it was different. The Scriptures yield no other account of the healing of one who could not speak. And the healing of this man was not done with a single touch or word.

The man's deafness may not have been life-long. He knew enough of speech to try it, but with little success. Verse 35 suggests that he may have been tongue-tied. The divine gift of verbal communication, bestowed on mankind as to no other of God's creatures, meant little to him. He couldn't hear what others said, and they couldn't understand what he tried to say.

But aren't we all somewhat afflicted with the same twofold problem? Who among us is able really to hear all that is said to us? And who is wholly able to say, and to make himself understood in saying, what God wants him to say? We, too, need to be made whole.

C. Communicating the Solution
(vv. 33-35)

33, 34. And he took him aside from the multitude, and put his fingers into his ears, and he spit, and touched his tongue; and looking up to heaven, he sighed, and saith unto him, Eph-phatha, that is, Be opened.

Why did Jesus seek privacy in healing the man? Did He know that the deaf man's efforts at speech had made him the butt of cruel jokes, so that he had become sensitive to public notice? Was Jesus refusing to embarrass the man, even in healing him? This provides an interesting balance to the occasion when Jesus called a blind man to the center of public attention from the place where he was being pushed aside (Mark 10:47-50). Loving compassion always ministered to the whole person, whom Jesus fully understood.

Perhaps also Jesus wanted the deaf man's total attention to what He would do, without distraction from the crowd. The rest of Jesus' procedure in this incident was a teaching process, communicated in a way the deaf man could perceive and understand. The fingers in the ears signaled the first point of attention. The spittle, now applied to the tongue, signaled the second area of concern. The intense look toward Heaven made clear the divine source from which healing would come—not from any idol or any human power. The deep sigh of concern showed the depth of Jesus' own involvement. Finally came the liberating word, carefully conveyed as Jesus spoke it in the Aramaic. *Eph-pha-tha* could be seen with the eyes almost as readily as it could be heard with normal ears. It commanded that the ears *be opened*, the tongue be loosed, and so the whole person be relieved of the barriers that had kept him isolated from his fellowmen.

visual 4

35. And straightway his ears were opened, and the string of his tongue was loosed, and he spake plain.

The release was immediate and complete. Whatever had prevented hearing was removed, and whatever had prevented clear and perfect speech was taken away. We must assume a double miracle: the restoration of hearing and the ability to reproduce clearly sounds and words that the man had heard only long ago, if at all.

May we not assume also that God is interested in His children's using their powers of speech in plain, clearly understandable communication? Slovenly speech does not befit a whole person!

D. Unrestrained Praise (vv. 36, 37)

36, 37. And he charged them that they should tell no man: but the more he charged them, so much the more a great deal they published it; and were beyond measure astonished, saying, He hath done all things well: he maketh both the deaf to hear, and the dumb to speak.

He charged them. Jesus gave the people clear and positive orders not to tell others about the healing. Why did He do that? Perhaps it was to show His disciples that He did not desire to win the praise of men and women by His miracles. Certainly His teaching ministry was being hampered by the vast crowds expecting miracles. And those same crowds created the danger of premature confrontation with Rome or with the Jewish leaders in Jerusalem. That confrontation must eventually come, but only in the Lord's own time. Yet His very requests for privacy seem to have excited the observers even more. His seeming modesty became a topic for conversation.

Beyond measure astonished. This phrase represents a strange sort of double superlative invented by Mark for the occasion. Boundless amazement stirred the observers. They noted not only the double miracle worked on the dear man, but "they saw the dumb to speak, the maimed to be whole, the lame to walk, and the blind to see" (Matthew 15:31).

The people were right: Jesus not only did mighty works, but He did them *well*. He used

His power always for the good of others, and He worked His miracles with a gentle touch that healed without hurting. Yet He never compromised the truth of God or His own integrity. Admiration is not sufficient for such a Lord!

HE IS NOT SILENT

The writer, Philip Yancey, asks an important question in his book, *Where Is God When It Hurts?* With different wording, many Old Testament saints asked this question. In the midst of his suffering, Job asked, "Why do you hide your face and consider me your enemy?" (Job 13:24, *New International Version*). The psalmist cried, "Awake, O Lord! Why do you sleep? Rouse yourself! Do not reject us forever. Why do you hide your face and forget our misery and oppression?" (Psalm 44:23, 24; *New International Version*).

Whether hundreds of years before Christ, or two thousand years after Him, the same questions haunt us: "Does God really care about our pain and suffering? Does He listen to and answer our prayers?"

The Gospel accounts of Jesus' earthly ministry clearly reveal the divine concern for human suffering. Today's text tells of Jesus' healing of a demon-possessed girl and of His restoring hearing and speech to a man who was deaf and had a speech impediment. And God, who is still concerned about such suffering, has given us the privilege of prayer. The Bible challenges us to ask big things in Christ's name, expecting big answers in return.

We are not promised that every physical infirmity will be removed, but we are promised His presence and grace to endure them. We are challenged to believe that God cares for us and to trust in Him for our ultimate good. That may not satisfy some, but it's completely adequate for the child of God who understands Romans 8:28!

—T. T.

Conclusion
A. The Orders Are Reversed

The kingdom of Heaven is at hand! So Jesus proclaimed, and so He demonstrated. Embodied in Him was the loving compassion of the eternal God. That compassion *restored* wholeness to uncounted numbers of sick, demon-possessed, and crippled persons, and to some who had already died. His compassion also *brought* wholeness to some blind and lame persons who had never been whole before.

The same compassion offers restoration of spiritual wholeness to sin-sick and stained people everywhere who will accept His offer of re-pentance and pardon. Beyond that is the wholeness never previously known, in life with the highest purpose and divine fellowship for time and eternity. Christ continues to ask, "Wilt thou be made whole?" and "Will you share the way to wholeness with your friends?"

Today's text tells of Jesus' bringing wholeness by relieving a little girl from demon possession and a man from deafness and speechlessness. Yet both were healed because someone else came requesting it of Jesus. These people cared about their ailing loved ones, they saw hope in Jesus, and they overcame all kinds of obstacles in pressing their petitions. In the case of the deaf man, when healing was accomplished the people were told *not* to spread the news, but they disobeyed the order. Their enthusiasm overcame the command. Were they to be blamed?

We don't have to answer that. But now there is another question we do have to answer. It concerns Jesus' later reversal of the order about publicizing His ministry. Since the completion of His gospel, He has commanded His followers to tell about it wherever they go. If we disregard that directive, we can't say we were motivated by good intentions to honor Him. What will be our excuse?

B. Prayer of One Made Whole

Thank You, our Father, for the wholeness-bringing ministry of Jesus, Your Son. Stir in us, please, the amazed enthusiasm that comes with first meeting Him, and remove the impediments from our speech that we may spread His fame wherever we go. In His name, amen.

C. Thought to Remember

"Let the redeemed of the Lord say so" (Psalm 107:2).

Home Daily Bible Readings

Monday, Mar. 16—The Sign of Jonah (Matthew 12:38-42)

Tuesday, Mar. 17—Love Has No Bounds (John 3:14-17)

Wednesday, Mar. 18—The Least Among You (Matthew 25:31-40)

Thursday, Mar. 19—Whose Children? (Mark 7:24-30)

Friday, Mar. 20—"Ephphatha" (Be opened) (Mark 7:31-37)

Saturday, Mar. 21—Living for Others (Matthew 5:13-16)

Sunday, Mar. 22—Make Disciples of All Nations (Matthew 28:16-20)

Learning by Doing

This page contains an alternate lesson plan emphasizing learning activities. Classes desiring such student involvement will find these suggestions helpful.

Learning Goals

After this lesson a student will be able to do the following:

1. List some benefits of retreat in the advance of ministry.

2. Explain Jesus' treatment of the Syrophoenician woman and its implications for modern ministry.

3. Suggest some means of ministering to people with disabling conditions.

Into the Lesson

Spend some time during the week before this lesson collecting travel brochures and travel ads from magazines. Bring these materials to class and spread them out where the students can view them as they arrive. Near the materials put up a poster that says, "Let's take a vacation!"

As the students arrive, encourage them to browse the display. Ask questions such as, "What is your idea of the ideal vacation? What do you like best about vacations? What was the best vacation you ever took?"

After a few minutes ask, "Why do we take vacations?" There will likely be general agreement that vacations offer a time of refreshment that makes us more productive when we return to work. The real value of a vacation is the getting away, and the vacation's value does not necessarily increase in direct relationship to its cost.

Point out that in our text for today Jesus was "on vacation." Use material from the lesson background ("Crowds and Conflict") to show why Jesus needed to get away for a while. Suggest that, as we observe His example, perhaps we can learn something about refreshing our own bodies *and spirits* in a way that will enhance our ministries in the church.

Into the Word

Divide the class into two groups. Assign the first group verses 24-30 of the text. Ask them to answer the following questions:

1. What seemed to be Jesus' agenda while on vacation?

2. What interruption did He experience?

3. How did He handle the interruption?

4. Why did Jesus' seem reluctant to help the woman who came to Him?

5. Who were the "children" and the "dogs" in Jesus' analogy?

6. How did the woman respond to Jesus' explanation? What does that reveal about her?

7. Why did Jesus help the woman even though He at first said it was "not meet" (not proper)?

Assign the second group verses 31-37 and ask them to answer these questions:

1. Where did Jesus go when He left the vicinity of Tyre and Sidon?

2. What interruption to His vacation did Jesus encounter here?

3. How did Jesus respond to the interruption?

4. What special treatment did Jesus give to this man?

5. After healing the man, what command did Jesus give? How did the people respond to this command?

6. What assessment of the situation did the people make after seeing this healing?

Give the groups about ten minutes. Then go through the questions and allow the groups to answer.

Into Life

We have mentioned that we take vacations to refresh ourselves physically and emotionally. Ask, "Can a vacation or a retreat refresh us spiritually and enhance our ministry for the Lord?" Discuss this as a class. Then ask, "If such a retreat is helpful, how can it be done?" "Is dropping out of ministry for several months (as some people do when they 'need a break') really the same as taking a retreat?" Discuss some means of providing retreat and refreshment to stay active in ministry.

Call attention to the ministry Jesus performed even while on vacation. Observe two points: (1) Jesus was careful to establish priorities and to follow them to maintain effective ministry. This explains His limiting His service to Israel while He was on earth in the flesh. (2) Jesus was willing to alter His plans to respond to critical human needs. Discuss how these two points are instructive for the church today.

Finally, note Jesus' care in treating the man with hearing and speech problems. (Though we do not possess Jesus' power of healing, we can possess and demonstrate His compassion and care for disabled persons today.) Discuss what your class or church can do to minister to the disabled.

Let's Talk It Over

The questions on this page are designed to encourage review of the lesson Scriptures and to promote discussion of the lesson by the class. The answers provided are only discussion starters. Let your class talk it over from there.

1. What do we learn about the focus of the gospel from the account of the Syrophoenician woman?

Jesus showed that the gospel was to be offered first to the Jews. They were the "children" of God's covenant, the people with whom God had entered into a special relationship. Jesus' use of the term *first*, however, shows the intent to include the Gentiles as well. Thus all peoples are to be challenged with the gospel today. We cannot withhold it from anyone. Instead, we must willingly make the sacrifices necessary to send the gospel, or be sent with the gospel, wherever it needs to be proclaimed.

2. From the account of the Syrophoenician woman, what are some conclusions we may draw concerning prayer?

We learn that Jesus is approachable by anyone. Regardless of the disciples' impatience with this Gentile woman (Matthew 15:23), Jesus heard her request. He made time for her, even though she was not one of the covenant people. He would help her with her need. We also learn that Jesus works in His time. He did not immediately answer her request. By delaying, He challenged her faith in Him and taught the disciples (and us) an important lesson about persistence and patience when approaching God with our requests. We also learn that we can approach the Lord openly, honestly, and without fear of rejection. Finally, we learn to accept whatever the Lord may give in answer to our prayers. The woman would accept even "crumbs." Jesus cares for us and seeks to give only good gifts. Will we accept His answers?

3. Why do you think Jesus chose the method He used to heal the man who was deaf and had an impediment of speech?

When the man's friends brought him to Jesus, a "multitude" of people were around the Master. Jesus took the man aside, perhaps seeking to avoid any embarrassment for him. Since the man could not hear, it seems that Jesus' actions were a kind of sign language by which He communicated with the man. Touching the ears and the tongue signaled the areas of the man's need, and perhaps was intended to challenge his faith in Jesus' ability to heal him. Jesus' look toward Heaven told the man that the power for healing would come from God, not man. All that Jesus did showed His sensitivity and compassion for the man, and His concern that God would be praised for the healing.

4. A most serious problem is spiritual deafness. What is spiritual deafness, and how may this disorder be corrected?

The man about whom we are studying today suffered physical deafness, and Jesus healed him by His divine power. Spiritual deafness results when a person closes his or her heart and mind to the things of God. It comes as individuals refuse to hear God's plain call through Scripture to give their lives to Him. Unlike physical deafness, spiritual deafness yields to the will of the individual. Paul wrote, "Faith cometh by hearing, and hearing by the word of God" (Romans 10:17). One who chooses to believe the word of God when it is presented chooses the way of salvation (Romans 10:9, 10). One who chooses not to believe, who turns a deaf ear to the divine invitation, rejects the life God offers through His Son (see Acts 7:51, 52). Well did Jesus say, "He that hath ears to hear, let him hear."

5. Why would Jesus not want this miracle announced?

On an earlier visit to this region, Jesus had cast many demons out of a man. He instructed that man to tell his family and friends of the compassion the Lord had had on him (Mark 5:18-20). It seems certain that the man's testimony had a great impact on the people in that area, because on Jesus' return He was met by great multitudes who brought many people for Him to heal (see Matthew 15:29-31). A very important aspect of Jesus' ministry was the teaching He did. Overwhelmed with the huge demand for physical healings, He had less time for imparting the eternal truths of the kingdom of God. The people anticipated the coming of the Messiah, one who they thought would lead them in military conquests. A short while before this, the people had attempted to take Jesus by force and make Him their king (John 6:15). Increased excitement over His miracles would only renew such improper attempts.

The Messiah and Suffering

LESSON SCRIPTURE: Mark 8:27—9:13.

PRINTED TEXT: Mark 8:27—9:1.

Mark 8:27-38

27 And Jesus went out, and his disciples, into the towns of Caesarea Philippi: and by the way he asked his disciples, saying unto them, Whom do men say that I am?

28 And they answered, John the Baptist: but some say, Elijah; and others, One of the prophets.

29 And he saith unto them, But whom say ye that I am? And Peter answereth and saith unto him, Thou art the Christ.

30 And he charged them that they should tell no man of him.

31 And he began to teach them, that the Son of man must suffer many things, and be rejected of the elders, and of the chief priests, and scribes, and be killed, and after three days rise again.

32 And he spake that saying openly. And Peter took him, and began to rebuke him.

33 But when he had turned about and looked on his disciples, he rebuked Peter, saying, Get thee behind me, Satan: for thou savorest not the things that be of God, but the things that be of men.

34 And when he had called the people unto him with his disciples also, he said unto them, Whosoever will come after me, let him deny himself, and take up his cross, and follow me.

35 For whosoever will save his life shall lose it; but whosoever shall lose his life for my sake and the gospel's, the same shall save it.

36 For what shall it profit a man, if he shall gain the whole world, and lose his own soul?

37 Or what shall a man give in exchange for his soul?

38 Whosoever therefore shall be ashamed of me and of my words, in this adulterous and sinful generation, of him also shall the Son of man be ashamed, when he cometh in the glory of his Father with the holy angels.

Mark 9:1

1 And he said unto them, Verily I say unto you, That there be some of them that stand here, which shall not taste of death, till they have seen the kingdom of God come with power.

GOLDEN TEXT: When he had called the people unto him with his disciples also, he said unto them, Whosoever will come after me, let him deny himself, and take up his cross, and follow me.—Mark 8:34.

The Strong Son of God

Unit 2: Confession and Crucifixion

(Lessons 5-8)

Lesson Aims

As a result of this lesson, students should:

1. Realize that Jesus willingly suffered and died on the cross to save humankind from sin.

2. Have a deeper appreciation for the great cost of our redemption.

Lesson Outline

INTRODUCTION

    A. Who Am I?

    B. Lesson Background

  I. TWO IMPORTANT QUESTIONS (Mark 8:27-30)

    A. The People's Opinions (vv. 27, 28)

       True Identity

    B. The Disciples' Conviction (v. 29)

    C. Jesus' Charge (v. 30)

 II. A DIRE PREDICTION (Mark 8:31-33)

    A. Words of Impending Sorrow (v. 31)

    B. Rebuke and Response (vv. 32, 33)

III. A CHALLENGING INSTRUCTION (Mark 8:34-38)

    A. Challenge to Self-denial (vv. 34, 35)

       Hold On to Your Convictions

    B. When Gain Is Loss (vv. 36-38)

IV. A GLORIOUS AFFIRMATION (Mark 9:1)

CONCLUSION

    A. Facing the Future

    B. Prayer

    C. Thought to Remember

Display visual 5 of the visuals packet throughout this session. The visual is shown on page 263.

Introduction

A. Who Am I?

The Old Testament prophecies concerning the Messiah identified this coming one as a descendant of the royal line of David, who would liberate His people and usher in a new, everlasting kingdom with himself as its ruler under the laws of God. Other prophecies, however, spoke of the Messiah as a servant of God who would suffer and die for His people. Unable to harmonize these two concepts, the people of Jesus' day preferred the former description. Thus they looked for the Messiah to be a worldly ruler, one who would lead them in throwing off the yoke of bondage to Rome.

Jesus wasn't playing games with the disciples, nor did He have a so-called "identity crisis," when He asked, "Whom do men say that I am?" At the age of twelve, He clearly understood both His origin and His mission. He said, "I must be about my Father's business," or, as some translate, ". . . in my Father's house" (Luke 2:49). With these words He plainly announced who He was and why He had come to earth.

Now He was running a check on those men upon whom grave responsibility would fall in advancing His kingdom. If God's plan for liberating humankind from the bondage of sin was to be taken to people everywhere, the disciples too must assuredly know who He was. They must be ready to proclaim His message and messiahship and to endure stern ordeals as they shared with people everywhere God's plan for human redemption.

B. Lesson Background

For the better part of two years the disciples had been with Jesus. They had seen Him heal the sick, give strength to the lame, and restore sight to the blind and hearing to the deaf. They had witnessed His power over the tempestuous sea, over demons, and over death itself. They had eaten of the multiplied loaves and fishes, along with thousands of others by Galilee's shore. They had observed Jesus' life, His works, and found them totally in harmony with His teachings.

Some of the disciples had been with John the Baptist in the wilderness, and, no doubt, had heard him say that he would be followed by One whose shoelaces John himself was not worthy to untie. And they had heard John identify Jesus as "the Lamb of God" (John 1:35-41). On the other hand, the disciples had seen the fierce opposition to Jesus by the highly respected religious authorities as they attempted to discredit Him before the people.

Now it was testing time. It was time for the disciples to consider what people were saying about Jesus. But more than that, it was time for them to decide what they thought about Him.

Jesus' question to the disciples caused them to do far more than probe into rumors about His character. It required each of the twelve to look inside himself and draw a firm answer to the question the imprisoned John had asked (Matthew 11:2, 3). What were their own conclusions about Him? Was He all He had claimed to be? Was He indeed the long-awaited Messiah? To answer His question demanded intensive soul-searching. Their answer to the question, and the consequences of it, are seen in our lesson text.

I. Two Important Questions
(Mark 8:27-30)

A. The People's Opinions (vv. 27, 28)

Jesus' healing of the deaf man with the speech impediment, which we considered in last week's lesson, took place in Decapolis, east of the Sea of Galilee. The miraculous feeding of the four thousand followed immediately afterward in the same area. Jesus and His disciples then crossed over to Magdala (Dalmanutha) on the western shore of the Sea of Galilee, where they encountered the religious authorities once more. Wearied by their perversity, He left them and went back over to the eastern side of the sea. Near the town of Bethsaida, He healed a blind man and urged him not to tell anyone in the town about it. From there Jesus and His disciples headed toward Caesarea Philippi (Mark 8:1-26).

27. And Jesus went out, and his disciples, into the towns of Caesarea Philippi: and by the way he asked his disciples, saying unto them, Whom do men say that I am?

Visible from the northern shores of the Sea of Galilee, Mount Hermon lies about thirty miles north. Caesarea Philippi was built on the southwestern slope of this mountain; about it was a cluster we would call suburbs. Somewhere in this vicinity, when Jesus was alone praying (Matthew 16:13; Luke 9:18), He asked the disciples about the people's responses to His ministry.

Jesus knew the answer to this question, of course, but it was important for the disciples to recognize the fact that conflicting ideas were circulating about Him. Jesus was not looking for flattery, and He was not trying to conceal the fact that many in the nation had rejected Him. This probing question forced the disciples to face squarely the perplexity of the people regarding His identity.

Unlike Jesus, many individuals suffer from what we term an "identity crisis." This is the situation with one who sees no purpose or objective in life, and who endures a monotonous existence that has no goal and accomplishes little of consequence. What a totally different view is to be seen through the eyes of Christian commitment. How glorious to resolve, "I want my life to count for Jesus," and to spend that life in useful service for Him!

TRUE IDENTITY

Random Harvest, written by James Hilton, is one of my favorite novels. The hero of this story was a shell-shocked veteran of World War I who suffered amnesia for several years as a result.

Since he didn't know his real identity, he chose the name Smith and tried to put together some kind of life; but he was always haunted by a past he could not recollect.

Then, as the result of an accident in which he had a blow to his head, the situation was reversed. He remembered who he really was, but he had a blackout of the Smith years. In the end, he was able to bring together the two identities and so bring harmony to his life.

Jesus asked His disciples concerning the rumors circulating about Him, as well as their own opinions as to His identity, but He was not suffering an identity crisis. He knew very well who He was. He asked because He was concerned that His followers never forget His true identity as the Christ, the Son of the living God.

At times we may suffer identity crises just as old Smithy. In fact, in a lifetime we may become confused about many things. When we do, we must hold on to two truths: (1) we know who Jesus is, and (2) we know who we are as a result of our relationship with Him.   —T. T.

28. And they answered, John the Baptist: but some say, Elijah; and others, One of the prophets.

John the Baptist. It is difficult to understand how anyone could have believed that Jesus could have been John the Baptist. The two had been contemporaries. John had baptized Jesus, and for almost a year they had carried on simultaneous ministries. Those who had heard John preach knew that he had told of one who was to come after himself, one who was far greater than he. Now, was John to succeed himself? The principal source of this rumor was the court of Herod Antipas. Perhaps to ease a guilty conscience for having beheaded John, Herod kept insisting that Jesus was John risen from the dead (Mark 6:14-28).

Elijah. The Old Testament closed with the prophecy, "Behold, I will send you Elijah the prophet before the coming of the great and dreadful day of the Lord" (Malachi 4:5). Jesus' preaching that the kingdom of Heaven was at hand, in conjunction with His mysterious greatness, led some to believe that He fulfilled that prophecy. *One of the prophets.* Others were more vague in their identification, but they too admitted Jesus' greatness.

How to Say It

CAESAREA PHILIPPI. Ses-uh-*ree*-uh Fih-*lip*-pie or *Fil*-ih-pie.
ANTIPAS. *An*-tuh-pus.

B. The Disciples' Conviction (v. 29)

29. And he saith unto them, But whom say ye that I am? And Peter answereth and saith unto him, Thou art the Christ.

Sometime before this, the disciples had declared their faith in Jesus (see Matthew 14:33; John 6:69). But in view of the opposition of the religious authorities and the falling away of many who had followed Jesus, did they still believe in Him? Peter, the self-appointed spokesman for the twelve, came right to the point as he expressed the conviction of all of the disciples: Jesus was the Messiah! To the statement in Mark's account, Matthew adds, "the Son of the living God" (Matthew 16:16).

The disciples' constant exposure to Jesus and His teachings and miraculous works brought these men to a positive, unambiguous conclusion: the long-awaited Messiah had come! Jesus was God's one and only Son.

The way to get to know someone well is to observe that person's words, actions, and responses to all kinds of circumstances. Peter gave Jesus the disciples' unqualified endorsement. He was unique, divine, the fulfillment of the prophecies of Scripture. He was God's anointed messenger and deliverer, the Messiah.

C. Jesus' Charge (v. 30)

30. And he charged them that they should tell no man of him.

If these words seem strange, we must remember that Peter and the other disciples had much yet to learn about what the title "the Christ" implied. The event immediately following (vv. 31-33) made that clear. Even on the night before His crucifixion, Jesus said there was yet more to be revealed to them by the Spirit of God (John 16:12, 13). Jesus' words were a caution that neither He nor His mission was to be misrepresented to the people. As we noted earlier, the people expected the Messiah to be a worldly, military leader. If the disciples declared plainly that Jesus was the Messiah, they would only stir up the false expectations of the people and make it more difficult for them to understand the spiritual nature of His mission.

II. A Dire Prediction
(Mark 8:31-33)

A. Words of Impending Sorrow (v. 31)

31. And he began to teach them, that the Son of man must suffer many things, and be rejected of the elders, and of the chief priests, and scribes, and be killed, and after three days rise again.

These words of Jesus changed the scene abruptly from one of elation, reverence, and triumph to impending tragedy. He was to suffer *many things*, be rejected by the nation's leaders, and finally be killed. Even the thought of His resurrection may not have dulled or removed the pall of shock and confusion that must have gripped the disciples' minds. We can see in these words a reason for His instructing them to be temporarily silent regarding Peter's glorious confession. Central to the Messiah's purpose in coming to earth was His atoning death for humankind. Not even the disciples were prepared as yet to understand that. They could not, therefore, accurately represent to others His mission in full.

B. Rebuke and Response
(vv. 32, 33)

32. And he spake that saying openly. And Peter took him, and began to rebuke him.

Earlier, Jesus had hinted at the sufferings involved in His ministry (see Matthew 9:15; 10:16, 24, 25, 38). Now He gave that message clearly so that it could not be misunderstood. At this point, Peter took Jesus aside from the other disciples *to rebuke* Him. With the very best intentions, Peter emphatically declared that such things would never happen. Later, on the night of Jesus' arrest, Peter would attempt to defend Jesus with a sword (John 18:10). But the best of intentions can never justify an inappropriate or evil deed. Jesus was the Master, and Peter His disciple; and the disciple is out of place when he attempts to give directions to or force his will on the Master.

33. But when he had turned about and looked on his disciples, he rebuked Peter, saying, Get thee behind me, Satan: for thou savorest not the things that be of God, but the things that be of men.

In the wilderness, the devil had tempted Jesus to avoid the difficulties of the course set before Him and to take the easy way out. By using His miraculous powers Jesus could provide for all His physical needs and establish a worldwide kingdom. But the kingdom Jesus came to establish was spiritual, and His death was essential to it. He had rejected the temptation of Satan while in the wilderness. Now, momentarily, Peter had become the mouthpiece of the devil in presenting the same temptation to Him: "Avoid the cross!" To alter or frustrate God's plan for mankind by eliminating the cross would be to tamper with the very redemptive plan itself. Peter was thinking in worldly terms; he did not fully comprehend God's purpose in sending His Son (see John 3:16).

III. A Challenging Instruction
(Mark 8:34-38)
A. Challenge to Self-denial
(vv. 34, 35)

34. And when he had called the people unto him with his disciples also, he said unto them, Whosoever will come after me, let him deny himself, and take up his cross, and follow me.

Jesus and the twelve had been separated briefly from the crowds that still followed Him. Now He called the larger group of followers to Him to hear an important teaching.

Whosoever will come after me, let him . . . follow me. It is most likely that all of these people were familiar with Roman crucifixions and the agonizing death they brought. The most violent, reprehensible criminals were required to carry the heavy instrument of their death to the site of crucifixion. Jesus' meaning was clear: self-denial and intense suffering lay before Him in the completion of His ministry. His followers must be committed to undergo the same.

35. For whosoever will save his life shall lose it; but whosoever shall lose his life for my sake and the gospel's, the same shall save it.

A fair paraphrase would be, "If you go through life concerned only about what you yourself want to be, to do, and to have, you gain nothing, and you will lose your soul." To be pleasing to God requires that we give up whatever might interfere with our commitment and service to Him and make His work our primary concern. Losing one's life for Christ's sake and the gospel's has in many times and places included martyrdom. Most of us, however, lose our lives for Christ by sacrificing our selfish desires, pleasures, and ambitions so that the gospel may be advanced. The committed disciple of Jesus who thus loses his life will save his life eternally.

HOLD ON TO YOUR CONVICTIONS

I have a friend named Joe who is a giant of a man; and though he is now well into his nineties, he is still physically fit and, relatively speaking, quite strong. I suppose he always was large for his age.

Joe tells that when he was about ten years old he was attacked on the playground by two fifteen-year-old bullies who got him down and "beat the tar out of him." With both of them on top of him they forced him to call their teacher a bad name. After the recess, they told the teacher what Joe had said. When he admitted his guilt (though he didn't explain the circumstances) his boil-infected bottom received a blistering.

I do not fault my friend. I'm sure that most of us, when ten years old, would have given in to such pressure to free ourselves from tormentors. But I think the story illustrates that when we give in to pressure to avoid pain or heartache on one hand, we often encounter something worse coming at us from a different direction. Jesus warned of this regarding moral and spiritual matters. If we surrender our convictions because of pressures, we can be sure that a punishment far worse awaits us.   —T. T.

B. When Gain Is Loss (vv. 36-38)

36, 37. For what shall it profit a man, if he shall gain the whole world, and lose his own soul? Or what shall a man give in exchange for his soul?

What profit, indeed! Temporal pleasure and comfort, earthly recognition, sensual gratification, and a self-centered pride in achievement are all the world has to offer. They weigh very little on the eternal scales of God, and do not even compare to a fleeting moment in the eternal bliss of God. A price may be established for one's labors and possessions in this world; but no price can be placed on one's immortal soul.

How cheaply one can sell the soul! Some sell it for filthy lucre; others, for drinks, drugs, or luxurious living; still others, for high office or intellectual pride. The devil has written many contracts like that of the tragic Dr. Faustus, in which the man's soul is sold for empty self-gratification. The devil's lure, however attractive, conceals sharp, deadly hooks.

38. Whosoever therefore shall be ashamed of me and of my words, in this adulterous and sinful generation, of him also shall the Son of man be ashamed, when he cometh in the glory of his Father with the holy angels.

Jesus depicts a fearful future for that person whose faith is superficial, exercised only when convenient. Like the one who looks back after beginning the task of plowing (Luke 9:62), and

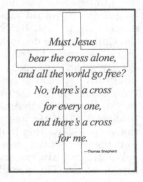

Must Jesus bear the cross alone, and all the world go free? No, there's a cross for every one, and there's a cross for me.

—Thomas Shepherd

visual 5

those who have worked iniquity instead of righteousness (Matthew 7:23), the one who is ashamed of Jesus will have no place in God's eternal kingdom.

What a glorious, triumphant day for God's faithful when Jesus comes again in the Father's glory; what a sad, tragic day for those who have mortgaged their souls to Satan!

IV. A Glorious Affirmation (Mark 9:1)

1. And he said unto them, Verily I say unto you, That there be some of them that stand here, which shall not taste of death, till they have seen the kingdom of God come with power.

In the preceding verse, Jesus made reference to His coming in judgment. This will bring to an end the kingdom on earth over which He, as the Son of man, rules, and in which He is the head of the church. In the verse before us, He speaks of the beginning of that kingdom. About one year from when Jesus spoke these words, the kingdom of God would come with power in the outpouring of the Holy Spirit on the Day of Pentecost. The descent of the Holy Spirit on that occasion, and the consequent message of salvation to be proclaimed, would fulfill Jesus' promise. The kingdom of God, the body of Jesus Christ—the church —would be ushered in with power and glory and truth for all time, and there were those in Jesus' audience that day who would witness it.

Conclusion

A. Facing the Future

Facing the future may be one of the most difficult of all human experiences. If we dwell on all the potential trials, pains, frustrations, sorrows, and other gloomy elements that enter into life, we soon are reduced to a state of helpless worry. An eminent psychologist has said that if any of us could foresee at one time all the pains and tragedies we would face in life, we would go completely insane. But he was not speaking of the Christian. We could hardly imagine a longer, more disturbing list of such trials than those of Paul in 2 Corinthians 11:22-33. Yet he most emphatically stated that he had learned to be content, whatever the circumstances, relying upon the inexhaustible strength God provided (Philippians 4:11-13). He had captured the genius of the gospel in writing that "to live is Christ, and to die is gain (Philippians 1:21).

We are not always given to know what lies ahead of us. The possibilities include those things for which we can make plans, and those that come upon us without our foreknowledge or wish. We are not long on this earth until we confront the fact that our most carefully planned events may be derailed by unexpected circumstances over which we have little or no control. James 4:13-15 warns us against letting such an eventuality upset us unduly. Whatever lies ahead, planned or not, is to be faced upon the contingency of the will of God and the actions of others. Nothing should ever be permitted to disrupt the saints' innermost tranquillity. To our shame, we sometimes let even trivial matters cause anger, resentment, or moroseness of spirit, which gnaws at this vital element of Christian character.

The Christian may face the future with confidence solidly grounded upon the past's certainties: Jesus Christ, the Son of God, has preceded us through death into everlasting life, and we all may share this triumphant, everlasting life in Him. We know who we are, why we are here, and where we are going!

B. Prayer

O holy Father, we bow before You in reverence for the promise of eternal life. Help us to be obedient followers of Jesus. Purge our hearts of all selfishness and sin. Strengthen us to our tasks and in our trials, that we may glorify the Savior. In His name we pray. Amen.

C. Thought to Remember

"What is more, I consider everything a loss compared to the surpassing greatness of knowing Christ Jesus my Lord, for whose sake I have lost all things. I consider them rubbish, that I may gain Christ" (Philippians 3:8, *New International Version*).

Home Daily Bible Readings

Monday, Mar. 23—"I Am That I Am" (Exodus 3:13-15)
Tuesday, Mar. 24—What's in a Name? (Exodus 20:1-7)
Wednesday, Mar. 25—Recognition and Response (Mark 8:27-30)
Thursday, Mar. 26—Heavenly Reward (Matthew 5:10-12)
Friday, Mar. 27—Prophecy Being Fulfilled (Mark 8:31-33)
Saturday, Mar. 28—Temporal or Eternal (Mark 8:34-37)
Sunday, Mar. 29—Love of Christ at Any Price (Romans 8:35-39)

Learning by Doing

This page contains an alternate lesson plan emphasizing learning activities. Classes desiring such student involvement will find these suggestions helpful.

Learning Goals

After this lesson a student will be able to:

1. Define the person and mission of Jesus Christ.

2. Explain what demands Jesus makes of His disciples.

3. Express commitment to Jesus and His mission.

Into the Lesson

Before class, write this question on the chalkboard: "Who do people *today* say Jesus is?" As class begins, let the students give their suggestions. Write their answers on the chalkboard. Briefly discuss why these suggestions are inadequate to explain Jesus' identity.

Most of your students will be aware that Jesus posed this same question to His apostles. Point out that Mark's record of that event is part of the text for today. Explain that Jesus wanted the disciples to evaluate the beliefs about Him so that they would see their inadequacy and come to a firm conviction of His true identity. We need to have a similar conviction about who Jesus is.

Into the Word

Divide the class into three groups. Ask each group to listen as the text is read aloud. Then give each of the groups a different one of the following assignments:

Group 1: List the wrong ideas about Jesus' identity and mission reported in this text. Explain why the views are faulty. Suggest some modern views that follow the same error and what the church can do to correct such views.

Group 2: Summarize the true identity and mission of Christ and explain what demands Jesus places on His followers. Explain how a disciple today can "take up his cross" and follow Jesus and how one may "lose his life" for the sake of Jesus and the gospel. Is the issue literal martyrdom or something else?

Group 3: Focus on Peter in this text and in Mark 9:2-13. What positive and negative discipleship qualities do you see in Peter? What do you like most about Peter, and what disappoints you the most about him? How can both qualities be present in the same person?

Appoint a reporter for each group. Allow about ten minutes for discussion before calling for the reports.

While the groups are working, write the following outline on the chalkboard, leaving space below each point to write additional remarks based on class discussion. (If you use an overhead projector in your class, prepare four transparencies before class, writing one point on each transparency.)

1. Errors exposed (Mark 8:27, 28, 33)
2. The truth expressed (Mark 8:29-32)
3. The implications explained (Mark 8:34-38)
4. Assurance given (Mark 9:1)

When time is up, discuss the groups' findings. Then call attention to the outline, noting that it summarizes the text. (If you are using the overhead projector, put all four transparencies on the platen, overlapping them so the outline reads consecutively. Then remove all but the first to begin discussing each point.) Ask the students to suggest words or phrases to put under each heading. The first two points should be fairly easy to complete. The implications will be a bit more challenging. For this point, draw on the earlier discussion. Note that the assurance of Mark 9:1 is a reference to Pentecost, when the kingdom (the church) came with the power of the Holy Spirit. This also links us today with the mission of Jesus discussed here.

Into Life

Work together to formulate a concise statement of mission for the church today, based on this text. Call special attention to verses 34-38. Then discuss the following questions: What specific demands does this mission make of us? Do you believe disciples today have generally recognized the true nature of the mission of Christ and the church? Explain. What rivals lure us away from devotion to the Lord? In view of the demands that Jesus makes of His followers, how can we overcome the temptations to stop following Him? (Emphasize the thoughts in verses 36 and 37.)

Finally, ask the students to take a minute for self-examination. They should ask themselves, What have I sacrificed for the sake of the gospel? Am I losing my life for the sake of Jesus and the gospel?

Distribute small index cards and ask the students to write one or two specific sacrifices they will make this week for the sake of Jesus and His gospel.

Let's Talk It Over

The questions on this page are designed to encourage review of the lesson Scriptures and to promote discussion of the lesson by the class. The answers provided are only discussion starters. Let your class talk it over from there.

1. As we share the gospel with someone who is outside of Christ, why is it valid to ask, "Who do you think Jesus is?"

The person and work of Jesus Christ lie at the very heart of the gospel we proclaim. People today hold various views regarding Jesus. Some think He was merely a prophet, or an exceptional teacher, or a good moral man. Knowing what a person believes about Jesus helps us as we share the New Testament revelation concerning Him. Religious discussions often center around one's view of certain religious doctrines or practices. Each of these issues, however, must be considered in light of Jesus' claim to be the Christ, the Son of God. Once Jesus' lordship is established, the place of all other matters can be more easily understood.

2. What risk did Peter take, and what risk do we take, in proclaiming that Jesus is the Christ?

Peter identified Jesus as the Messiah of the Jews and the Savior of the world. In doing this, Peter was stating his intention to follow Jesus, to put his hopes entirely in Him. From the rest of the text, we can see that Peter did not have a clear understanding of what all was involved in taking this stand. He, and many others who proclaimed Jesus as the Christ, would suffer ridicule, ostracism, physical abuse, and even death. We too "risk" our whole lives when proclaiming Jesus as the Christ. We are saying that He is Lord of life and that we will follow where He leads. Like Peter, we may not fully understand the implications of our confession. Although few of us are called on to suffer physical abuse or death for our faith in Jesus, we may experience ridicule, accusations, and ostracism. In spite of the difficulties, may we resolve daily to follow Christ, assured that only in Him will we save our lives for eternity.

3. Why did Jesus speak of His death so soon after Peter's confession? What are the implications for us?

It is natural to assume that the disciples were elated over Jesus' acknowledgment that He was the long-awaited Messiah. Jesus wanted to make certain that the disciples understood the true nature of His messiahship. They must not assume, as the people in general did, that the Messiah would be a conquering general, who would free the nation from Roman oppression and reestablish David's throne. It was necessary for them to understand that He was to be the suffering servant spoken of by Isaiah, the One who would be mistreated and finally would give His life for sinful mankind (Isaiah 53). Jesus suffered, and His followers are called to walk in His way. Let us be certain that we do not present Him as One who gives us only material wealth, excellent health, and a life with no disturbance or difficulty.

4. Why did Jesus rebuke Peter so harshly? What lesson can we learn from this?

Jesus, the Master, had just described the sufferings that were to befall Him; but Peter, the disciple, proceeded to tell Him that this could never be (compare Matthew 16:22). In fact, later, in Gethsemane, Peter would use a sword to defend Jesus from physical harm. His words here and his actions later actually were attempts to thwart the will of God. Though his intentions were well meaning, clearly he was out of place. We too must be careful not to attempt to redefine God's plans. Do we want Jesus to act in our lives in ways of our choosing only? If so, are we any different from Peter? Do we feel that we are defending Him by bashing all challengers to His kingdom, or do we instead try to win those persons to His kingdom through the power of love as He has taught us?

5. What did Jesus mean when He said that His followers must deny themselves?

The first step in denying ourselves is to acknowledge that Jesus is Lord over every aspect of our lives. Thus we no longer live to satisfy our desires but to accomplish His will through our lives. Has our goal been to amass as much money as possible for our own prestige and pleasure? If so, Jesus would have us learn the blessedness of giving of our substance to those who are in need. Have we been brought up in the competitive spirit of our day that says we must be number one? Jesus says we are to put ourselves last of all. If we have sought power over others, we are to become humble servants. Although the world does not understand, those who deny themselves for Christ now will gain much more in His eternal kingdom.

Love Says It All

April 5
Lesson 6

LESSON SCRIPTURE: Deuteronomy 6:4-9; Mark 12:28-37.

PRINTED TEXT: Mark 12:28-37.

Apr
5

Mark 12:28-37

28 And one of the scribes came, and having heard them reasoning together, and perceiving that he had answered them well, asked him, Which is the first commandment of all?

29 And Jesus answered him, The first of all the commandments is, Hear, O Israel; The Lord our God is one Lord:

30 And thou shalt love the Lord thy God with all thy heart, and with all thy soul, and with all thy mind, and with all thy strength: this is the first commandment.

31 And the second is like, namely this, Thou shalt love thy neighbor as thyself. There is none other commandment greater than these.

32 And the scribe said unto him, Well, Master, thou hast said the truth: for there is one God; and there is none other but he:

33 And to love him with all the heart, and with all the understanding, and with all the soul, and with all the strength, and to love his neighbor as himself, is more than all whole burnt offerings and sacrifices.

34 And when Jesus saw that he answered discreetly, he said unto him, Thou art not far from the kingdom of God. And no man after that durst ask him any question.

35 And Jesus answered and said, while he taught in the temple, How say the scribes that Christ is the son of David?

36 For David himself said by the Holy Ghost, The Lord said to my Lord, Sit thou on my right hand, till I make thine enemies thy footstool.

37 David therefore himself calleth him Lord; and whence is he then his son? And the common people heard him gladly.

GOLDEN TEXT: Thou shalt love the Lord thy God with all thy heart, and with all thy soul, and with all thy mind, and with all thy strength . . . Thou shalt love thy neighbor as thyself. There is none other commandment greater than these.
—Mark 12:30, 31.

The Strong Son of God

Unit 2: Confession and Crucifixion

(Lessons 5-8)

Lesson Aims

As a result of this lesson, students should:
1. Realize that loving God and loving one's neighbor require an act of the will.
2. Act in ways that demonstrate love for God and other persons.

Lesson Outline

INTRODUCTION
    A. A Relationship of Love
    B. Lesson Background
I. AN INTELLIGENT QUESTION (Mark 12:28)
    In Search of Priorities
II. A PERFECT ANSWER (Mark 12:29-31)
    A. Central Declaration (v. 29)
    B. Love, an Act of the Will (v. 30)
        The Most Important
    C. Love in Practical Extension (v. 31)
        Love of the Highest Degree
III. RESPONSE AND COMMENDATION (Mark 12:32-34)
    A. Friendly Exchange (vv. 32, 33)
    B. "Not Far From the Kingdom" (v. 34)
IV. A TOUGH QUESTION (Mark 12:35-37)
CONCLUSION
    A. Love—the Indispensable Element
    B. Prayer
    C. Thought to Remember

Display visual 6 of the visuals packet throughout this class session. The visual is shown on page 270.

Introduction

A. A Relationship of Love

In many pagan religions, the relationship between a person and the deity that is worshiped is based on fear. The individual lives under a constant threat of punishment for disobedience. And many of these gods are characterized by caprice. At times there is no apparent connection between the conduct of the person and the alleged punishment or reward of the deity.

During Jesus' ministry, the interpretations of the law of Moses, which had developed through the years and were taught by the rabbis as equal to the law, included far more negative prohibitions ("Thou shalt nots") than positive commands. The result was that God was often depicted in terms of what He forbade, condemned, and punished. He was seen as one to be feared, if the individual veered ever so slightly from the path of orthodoxy.

Jesus taught that the relationship between God and humankind is based on love. God's love for us led Him to establish the New Covenant through His Son (John 3:16), and His love for us prompts our love for Him in return (1 John 4:19). Furthermore, we can be confident that His attitude toward us is constant and unwavering (James 1:17).

In this relationship between God and humankind, love is far more than a verbal expression. It is commitment to a course of action: God's action was seen in the giving of His Son to make our salvation possible; our action is seen in our proper response to this gracious gift.

B. Lesson Background

Perhaps nine or ten months elapsed between the time of the events of last week's lesson and this lesson. Jesus was in Jerusalem in the final week of His ministry when the events recorded in our lesson text took place. It was Tuesday of that week, the day that has been called "the great day of questions."

Immediately before His conversation with the scribe, which is recorded in the first part of today's text, Jesus had been engaged in discussion with the Sadducees, who denied that there is a resurrection of the dead. He easily foiled their attempt to trap and embarrass Him regarding a technical point of law, and He did it in such a manner as to impress one of the masters of the law itself (see Mark 12:18-27). Our lesson text begins at this point.

I. An Intelligent Question
(Mark 12:28)

28. And one of the scribes came, and having heard them reasoning together, and perceiving that he had answered them well, asked him, Which is the first commandment of all?

Observing that Jesus answered the Sadducees with great skill, *one of the scribes*, those who were scholars and teachers of the law, asked Jesus a different kind of question, this one most serious: Which commandment was the greatest? Here was a matter often discussed by the scholars themselves. Although they were not in total accord, they did allow that some commandments were "greater" and some were "lesser."

Matthew records that this man was one of the Pharisees and a lawyer, and that he asked Jesus this question tempting, or testing, Him.

Some have thought, therefore, that he was not

sincere in asking this question, that he was simply laying a trap for Jesus, waiting for Him to make His pronouncement in hopes of finding the answer out of harmony with the rabbis' teachings. But it seems from the manner in which Jesus answered that this was not the case. Furthermore, after Jesus gave His answer, the scribe showed a remarkable degree of fairness and desire to know the truth.

Often persons have questions about the deeper issues and meanings of life, but they are reluctant to ask them for fear of appearing foolish before their peers. If the truth were known, in many instances other persons have the same questions, but they too are afraid to ask them. One should not be hesitant to ask questions that relate to the truly important issues of life. Someone has said that the only foolish question is the question that is not asked. This is true; but care should be taken in selecting the source for the information one seeks. The scribe in today's text came to the correct source.

IN SEARCH OF PRIORITIES

Occasionally we read a statement that not only catches our attention, but also helps shape our lives. In Charles E. Hummel's little book, *The Tyranny of the Urgent*, there is just such a statement. Written twenty-five years ago, it is pertinent to us yet today. Hummel warns, "Don't let the urgent take the place of the important in your life." What great advice! How easy it is for us, in our hectic world, to spend so much time dealing with pressing matters that we never take time for what is eternally important!

We are impressed with the scribe who asked Jesus, "Of all the commandments, which is the most important?" Unlike many of his associates, this man obviously asked his question to learn the truth. His motive wasn't to trick Jesus, but to discover what He valued most.

We all need to establish priorities. Our world has a mixed-up value system, and it seeks to press us into its mold. May we be wise like this scribe and seek for answers in the proper place—the Word of God. —T. T.

II. A Perfect Answer
(Mark 12:29-31)

A. Central Declaration (v. 29)

29. And Jesus answered him, The first of all the commandments is, Hear, O Israel; The Lord our God is one Lord.

Jesus quoted Deuteronomy 6:4, a verse of Scripture well known among the Jews. It is called the *Shema*, which is the Hebrew word for *Hear* and is the first word in the verse. The phy-

---

How to Say It

PHARISEES. *Fair*-ih-seez.
SADDUCEES. *Sad*-you-seez.
SHEMA (HEBREW). She-*mah*.

---

lactery, a small leather box that the scribes wore fastened to the head or arm, contained a slip on which the *Shema* was written. The statement that God is one was learned in earliest childhood, and conscientious believers repeated it several times every day. The concept of one God, Creator of heaven and earth, man, and all else in the universe, lay at the heart of the religion of the children of Abraham.

This central doctrine was the notable distinction between the people of Israel and the pagan world. Anyone who allowed a plurality of gods instantly and automatically set oneself apart from the people of God. Nobody, whether scribe, Pharisee, Sadducee, or ordinary child of Abraham, would have quarreled with the first segment of Jesus' answer or with what He said next.

B. Love, an Act of the Will (v. 30)

30. And thou shalt love the Lord thy God with all thy heart, and with all thy soul, and with all thy mind, and with all thy strength: this is the first commandment.

Thou shalt love the Lord thy God. It is one thing to ask for and seek the love of another; it is quite another to command it. Is this possible? Is it reasonable? Is love not an "affair of the heart," beyond the control of the mind and will? This is the current concept, the way of the world and the way of the flesh. We have managed to convince ourselves that we "fall" in love, as accidentally as one might trip over loose carpet. It is perceived to be sudden, usually unexpected, and beyond prevention or control. The devil and our human frailties have set us up to accept this notion.

We must never forget that love is defined and shaped by the object toward which it is directed; and it would be impossible to find one more worthy of our love than God himself. Loving God is to be a conscious, deliberate choice on our part. To love God is a totally valid, reasonable element of our lives, ideally to be found in the heart of all mankind.

Every aspect of the human being and personality is included in Jesus' statement in this verse. The terms *heart*, *soul*, *mind*, and *strength* overlap and emphasize this. *With all thy heart.* Most persons today associate the heart especially with emotions and sentiment; in the Bible, the heart was associated with the intellect, the emotions, and the will. *With all thy soul.* The *soul* is one's spiritual essence, the Godlikeness in a human being. It is the part of one that is immortal—the I, the person who controls what one thinks and says and does. *With all thy mind.* The *mind* is the seat of our reason, knowledge, and wisdom. It is our collective intellectual faculties. The word *mind* is not included in the passage in Deuteronomy 6:5. Its addition emphasizes the place of the intellect in conversion and maturity in faith and life. On this basis, God has invited His people, "Come now, and let us reason together" (Isaiah 1:18). *With all thy strength.* The *strength* is both physical ability and strength of conscience and character: the whole person, with all of his or her strength and ability, is to be dedicated to the service of the Creator. Altogether, these components encompass all of our complex nature, our total being. And this is precisely what we are to commit to God through our love for Him.

THE MOST IMPORTANT

The young man proposed to his sweetheart as they sat overlooking a beautiful lake. "Darling," he said, "I love you more than anything else in the world. I want you to marry me. I'm not wealthy; I don't have a yacht or a Rolls Royce like Johnny Green; but I do love you with all my heart."

His sweetheart thought for a moment and then replied, "I love you with all my heart, too, but tell me more about Johnny Green."

In regard to our Christian commitment, how many of us are like this fickle young lady? Do we tell God we love Him and want to serve Him, and then carry on a flirtation with the world? We need to remember that we serve a jealous God, who commands us to give Him our complete devotion. That is the kernel of Jesus' statement in this verse. "Love the Lord your God with all your heart and with all your soul and with all your mind and with all your strength." Nothing is as important as this.

Let us not be fickle disciples. Let us not say, "Tell me more about the world," but, "Tell me more about God."   —T. T.

C. Love in Practical Extension (v. 31)

31. And the second is like, namely this, Thou shalt love thy neighbor as thyself. There is none other commandment greater than these.

Some in Jesus' day taught that the law could be summarized with this axiom: "What you would not have done to yourself, do not do to your neighbor: that is the whole Torah [law]." Jesus extended this concept immeasurably in

what we call the "Golden Rule," showing that the proper emphasis is what we *do* for others, not what we do *not* do to them (Matthew 7:12). The command to love one's neighbor is found in Leviticus 19:18: "Thou shalt not avenge, nor bear any grudge against the children of thy people, but thou shalt love thy neighbor as thyself." In its setting, the command accompanied instructions for maintaining a proper relationship with one's neighbor, and most of these were prohibitions of improper behavior. One was neither to defraud nor rob one's neighbor (Leviticus 19:13), nor bear tales, nor endanger the life of another (v. 16). And one was not to hate one's neighbor, although the neighbor might be rebuked wisely for his own sake (v. 17). Other instructions related to such a relationship, but the statement of verse 18 was notable because of its positive nature: "Thou shalt love thy neighbor as thyself."

Just as our love for God is to be an act of our wills, so too should be our love for others. The love of which Jesus speaks is not to be based on emotional or physical attraction or preference. Many individuals are, of themselves, unlovely. For whatever reason, their appearance, personality, character, or habits may be objectionable or even repulsive to us. Yet these factors should not prevent our concern for their physical, emotional, and spiritual well-being. The Greek word for love in verses 30 and 31 is *agape*. It means a generous, kindly attitude such as we may maintain to people we have never seen and do not know, or to people we know to our sorrow. This is the kind of love that God has for sinful, rebellious humankind and that led Him to send His Son into the world to save us (John 3:16). It is such love that we are to extend to our neighbors.

LOVE OF THE HIGHEST DEGREE

When five American missionaries, headed by Jim Elliot, were brutally murdered in Ecuador by Auca Indians, whom they had hoped to evangelize, much was written about it by the Ameri-

visual 6

can press. Not much mention was made, however, of a prayer offered soon thereafter by T. E. McCully, father of Ed McCully, another of the slain missionaries. Mr. McCully prayed, "Lord, let me live long enough to see those fellows saved who killed our boy, that I may throw my arms around them and tell them I love them because they love Christ."

That is love of the highest form. It was that type of love Jesus had in mind when he commanded, "Love thy neighbor as thyself." Earlier, in His parable of the good Samaritan, Jesus showed that a person's neighbor may be anyone, even a person of another, hated group (Luke 10:30-37). That's what makes this command of Jesus so difficult. To love one's neighbor as oneself can occur only when a person first loves God supremely and allows Him to transform one's life.

T. E. McCully's prayer was answered. The widows of the five slain missionaries returned to Ecuador and won the Auca Indians to Christ.

—T. T.

III. Response and Commendation (Mark 12:32-34)

A. Friendly Exchange (vv. 32, 33)

32, 33. And the scribe said unto him, Well, Master, thou hast said the truth: for there is one God; and there is none other but he: and to love him with all the heart, and with all the understanding, and with all the soul, and with all the strength, and to love his neighbor as himself, is more than all whole burnt offerings and sacrifices.

This lawyer proved to be a man of surprisingly open mind for a Pharisee. Whereas the questions of these religious leaders usually were designed to trap Jesus in what they considered to be erroneous and even blasphemous statements, this man came with a sincere desire to learn from the Master. He showed a superior character and spirit and responded with intelligence and honesty to Jesus' discussion. It was the final week before Calvary, and the enemies of Jesus were engaging Him in debate that had His murder as its objective. Coming when it did, this friendly exchange between Jesus and this Pharisee, who was able to rise above the prejudice of His fellows, was most delightful and refreshing.

The relationship between human beings and God is pure and complex. The creature will always be the creature, and as such, subject to all limitations and obligations of his state. The scribe put it well: a person's duties begin with an unqualified love for God—love that involves the totality of one's being. But he also understood that the first commandment as given by Jesus cannot be separated from the second. Love for God must produce love for one's fellow human beings. If one does not manifest kindly, generous, and forgiving attitudes and actions toward others, love for God is non-existent in that person.

Furthermore, this scribe understood that to love God and to love one's neighbor, as described in the verses of the law that Jesus quoted, *is more than all whole burnt offerings and sacrifices.* God commanded His people to make such offerings and sacrifices, and the devout believers would surely do so. But the scribe was quick to see that the observance of religious ceremony, devoid of a sincere, loving, and generous spirit, would not be well pleasing to God.

B. "Not Far From the Kingdom" (v. 34)

34a. And when Jesus saw that he answered discreetly, he said unto him, Thou art not far from the kingdom of God.

The scribe had a clear understanding of the essential and eternal truths of God, and of man's proper relationship to Him and to all other human beings. *The kingdom of God,* which was about to be established, would be made up of persons who, like this scribe, held to and practiced these truths. He received a most significant commendation for his wisdom and insight in spiritual matters.

34b. And no man after that durst ask him any question.

Those whose object had been to enmesh Jesus in tricky questions saw themselves frustrated by the answers He had given. They recognized the depth and the self-evident truths in His words. The questions had, as a matter of fact, given Him an opportunity to press home some solid, vital instruction. His answers put His critics to silence.

IV. A Tough Question (Mark 12:35-37)

35. And Jesus answered and said, while he taught in the temple, How say the scribes that Christ is the son of David?

Had Jesus ended His question here, the answer would have been simple: that the Messiah would be a descendant of David was a fact well established in Scripture and understood by all (2 Samuel 7:11-16, 25-29; Psalm 89:3, 4, 34-37). Jesus was not casting doubt on this truth; rather, He was trying to get the Pharisees to come to a greater understanding of the Messiah's nature.

36. For David himself said by the Holy Ghost, The Lord said to my Lord, Sit thou on my right hand, till I make thine enemies thy footstool.

Jesus quoted Psalm 110:1 and affirmed that David was inspired by the Holy Spirit when he said these words. The word "Lord" in this verse of the psalm is the Hebrew word for "Jehovah." God is pictured in this psalm as speaking to Christ.

37. David therefore himself calleth him Lord; and whence is he then his son? And the common people heard him gladly.

In Hebrew custom, a father would not address his son as "my Lord." The people knew the Scriptural teaching that the Christ would be David's son. Yet here, in this psalm, David addressed the Christ as "my Lord." The point of Jesus' question was, why did David do that? Jesus didn't give an answer; He simply let his hearers ponder the question. The answer, of course, is that Christ was God's Son as well as David's son. It was altogether fitting, therefore, for even the great King David to address Him as Lord.

It is not uncommon to meet those who admit that Jesus was an outstanding teacher, that His life was one of exemplary service, and even that He was a prophet of God; but they balk at confessing Him as the Son of God. Such a position is untenable. If Jesus was not divine, as He claimed, He lied consistently and repeatedly and is not to be trusted. The heart of His message and mission was based upon His uniqueness in character and power. Remove this, and He becomes little more than an intelligent social worker; furthermore, we have no Savior, no hope of Heaven, and no unique message for the salvation of mankind.

Home Daily Bible Readings

Monday, Mar. 30—The First Commandment (Deuteronomy 6:4-9)
Tuesday, Mar. 31—Mind Included (Mark 12:28-30)
Wednesday, Apr. 1—The Commandments (Leviticus 19:11-18)
Thursday, Apr. 2—Closer to God (Mark 12:31-33)
Friday, Apr. 3—Question of Lineage (Mark 12:35-37)
Saturday, Apr. 4—Holy Spirit and Genealogy (Matthew 1:17-25)
Sunday, Apr. 5—God's Revelation (John 1:14-18)

Conclusion

A. Love—the Indispensable Element

God has every ground upon which to demand our love. In making such a demand, the Creator is seeking due regard, affection, and service from the creature. It is to be a love expressing devotion, respect, submission, gratitude, awe, and worship—all fully due to a loving Father.

In affirming that love is the indispensable element in the Christian faith, we must remember that we cannot truthfully profess to love God if we hate our brothers (1 John 4:20, 21); and it is clear from the context that John is including all humankind in his use of the term *brother.* Christians often make themselves repulsive to those who are not in Christ by treating them with disdain, or by simply ignoring them. Such behavior indicates that a person's faith has not been refined by the purging power of the love of God, who has a special concern for the lost. That person has forgotten the truth, "While we were yet sinners, Christ died for us" (Romans 5:8). One of the supreme expressions of our love for God is the extension of warmth, friendship, love, and our Christian faith with those outside of the Savior.

Christians should find many ways to spread the love of Jesus Christ among the needy, the widowed, orphaned, friendless, destitute, and the sorrowing. Sometimes, such ones desperately need someone who genuinely cares and shares willingly of love and friendship. And some food, clothing, and shelter may help! James noted that "pure religion and undefiled before God and the Father is this, To visit the fatherless and widows in their affliction, and to keep himself unspotted from the world" (1:27).

If we are to excel in this world in any respects, let it be in our love for the lost, our concern for the needy, and our efforts to be a blessing to all. Only when we truly love others—all others—from the heart, will they believe our professed love of God is genuine.

B. Prayer

Our Father, guide Your children into a deeper, broader love like that which You have manifested unto us. May we be the means by which Your universal love is made known to all, to Your greatest glory. In Jesus' name we pray. Amen.

C. Thought to Remember

"Love is the greatest thing that God can give us, for himself is love; and it is the greatest thing we can give to God, for it will also give ourselves, and carry with it all that is ours."

—Jeremy Taylor

Learning by Doing

This page contains an alternate lesson plan emphasizing learning activities. Classes desiring such student involvement will find these suggestions helpful.

Learning Goals

This lesson should enable the students to:

1. State the "greatest commandment."
2. Explain that love is more an act of the will than an accident of emotions.
3. Decide on one way they will show to another person God's kind of love in the coming week.

Into the Lesson

Write the following conversation on a piece of paper, make copies, and distribute them to the class. Ask the students to read it and respond. Why do they believe this is not accurate?

An angel approached the Lord and asked, "Why do You love these humans so?"

And the Lord replied, "I don't know. It's not something I can explain with My head—it's more a matter of the heart. My head keeps telling Me, 'Forget them. They're sinful, rebellious, and ungrateful.' But My heart just can't give them up. I know it doesn't make sense. But, after all, this is love!"

Discuss God's love for man. Obviously, it is not mindless, but intelligent and active. Remark that the love we are required to have for God and for all people is to have these same characteristics. It is not based on emotion alone.

After some discussion, indicate that today's lesson deals with love—loving God and loving our neighbors. We will see how important love is to God and how to put love into practice toward our fellow human beings.

Into the Word

Assign three readers to read today's text aloud to the class: One is to read the words of the scribe who asked Jesus about the greatest commandment and who commented on Jesus' response; another is to read the words of Jesus; the third is to be the narrator, reading all the words not read by the other two readers.

After the text is read, divide the class into groups of four to six students each. Have a third of the groups consider the scribe and report on what we learn from his example about following Jesus. Ask another third of the groups to study the question the scribe asked and also Jesus' answer to it. What do we learn from this exchange about following the Lord? The remaining groups are to consider Jesus' question after the exchange with the scribe (vv. 35-37). What do we learn about Jesus and about following Him from this passage?

Give the groups about ten minutes for discussion before calling for their reports.

Into Life

Call attention to the "Shema," with which Jesus introduced the greatest commandment. (See the comments of explanation under Mark 12:29.) This is how the Old Testament introduces this command (Deuteronomy 6:4, 5), and the scribe referred to it in His summary of Jesus' answer. Discuss why the oneness of God is so important to the command to love God with all one's being. What does this say about Jesus? If God is "one," how can Jesus be God? Call attention to verses 35-37 of the text. Here Jesus affirmed His humanity and divinity. He showed that the Christ was human (the son of David) and also divine (for David called Him "Lord"). The scribes and Pharisees had not understood this connection.

Ask the class, "What does it mean to love God 'with all thy heart, and with all thy soul, and with all thy mind, and with all thy strength'?" List each of these categories on the chalkboard: heart, soul, mind, strength. List ideas under each for how we can love God. Discuss what this means about the nature of love: does this sound like something one "falls into" or a commitment made deliberately and carefully?

Then discuss how loving one's neighbor is related to loving God. Consider 1 John 4:20, 21 in this connection. What kind of commitment is required? Can you "love" someone with whom you do not get along well?

Note Jesus' evaluation of the scribe: he was "not far from the kingdom of God." Discuss what that means. (Those in God's kingdom would share this man's attitude of seeking and hearing Jesus' teaching. The following step would naturally be to obey that teaching.)

Write these column headings on the chalkboard: family members, neighbors, the elderly, and any other groups that are relevant to your class. Ask for suggestions of acts that would show God's kind of love for each group, and write their suggestions in the appropriate column. Suggest that each student choose one of these ideas to put into practice this week.

Let's Talk It Over

The questions on this page are designed to encourage review of the lesson Scriptures and to promote discussion of the lesson by the class. The answers provided are only discussion starters. Let your class talk it over from there.

1. How does Jesus' statement in verses 29-31, given in response to the scribe's question, show Jesus to be a great moral teacher?

The question asked by the scribe was one that had been discussed for years by the teachers of the law. They were concerned about how to best live a life for God. Jesus cut to the heart of the matter by showing that God's followers have a moral responsibility to God and a moral responsibility to their fellowman. The commandment He gave is positive ("Love your neighbor") rather than negative ("Do not hate your neighbor"). This is a life of benevolence and concern rather than one of simply avoiding conflict. He showed that one's neighbors were not limited to members of one's nation or race, but included all peoples (see Leviticus 19:18; Luke 10:30-37). Finally, we see that a proper view of ourselves is the gauge by which we measure our love for others. Following Jesus' teaching here demands responsible, moral living.

2. What is involved in our loving God as Jesus indicated?

Jesus calls us to love God with our whole heart, our emotions and our will. He challenges us to love Him with our soul, our spiritual essence. Our love for God involves our intellect, our mind. We don't leave our intellectual bags packed when we worship and serve God. Jesus exhorts us to love God with all our strength. Our love is rooted in the fact that God loves us unconditionally. He already knows our heart, soul, mind, and strength, and He accepts us for who we are. One's love for God does not exist in isolation. It involves our relationship with other people. Because of God's unconditional love, we are free to love others unconditionally. We can look out for their needs, because God has met our need to be loved. Our love, then, is active toward others and is seen as we seek what is best for them.

3. What steps can we take to increase our love for God and for our neighbors?

Regarding love for God, we simply need to stop, open our eyes, and look around us to consider all that He has done for us. The very fact that we can do this suggests the first reason why love for God should be uppermost in our lives,

and that is, He has given us life. Not only so, but He has made provision for us to live eternally! Contemplation of Christ's death for our sins will help us to see what a high value God places on each of us. How can we help but respond to Him in love for what He has done and continues to do in our lives? Concerning others, we need to look for admirable qualities in them. Looking beyond others' faults will help us to see those persons as God sees them. We can pray for specific persons. Praying for another person tends to modify our attitudes toward that person. We develop a certain kinship with those persons whom we lift up to God in prayer. Finally, we need to become involved in a project that will allow us to express our concern for others in a positive way. Perhaps participation in a short-term mission trip, a building project, or meals-on-wheels program would be in order.

4. How can we use the Bible to bring about personal growth in love?

This is a question involving the practical use of the Bible, a way of demonstrating the Bible's relevance for today. Here are some suggested steps: First, we need to use the Bible as a mirror to see just how unlovable we are. It will reveal to us our sins, our pettiness, even our ugliness. Second, we can immerse ourselves in those passages that testify to God's love for us despite our unloveliness. Third, we should return to the "mirror" and observe how the same imperfections God overlooked in loving us are the blemishes in our fellow human beings that we find so unlovable. This should break down the inner barriers of prejudice, bitterness, jealousy, etc. and allow God's love to flow through us.

5. What does it mean to call Jesus "Lord"?

The Greek word for *Lord* had several meanings. It could mean the owner of a thing; it could also mean master, one who controls another; it also was used to designate a sovereign ruler. To call Jesus "Lord" is to recognize His right to rule over our lives. It is to admit that we are subject to Him in His kingdom and that we will live as He directs. Those who have made Jesus Lord of their lives have surrendered control of their lives to Him. They do not argue about His commands; they simply obey them.

The Crucified Son of God

LESSON SCRIPTURE: Mark 15:1-41.

PRINTED TEXT: Mark 15:22-39.

Mark 15:22-39

22 And they bring him unto the place Golgotha, which is, being interpreted, The place of a skull.

23 And they gave him to drink wine mingled with myrrh: but he received it not.

24 And when they had crucified him, they parted his garments, casting lots upon them, what every man should take.

25 And it was the third hour, and they crucified him.

26 And the superscription of his accusation was written over, THE KING OF THE JEWS.

27 And with him they crucify two thieves; the one on his right hand, and the other on his left.

28 And the Scripture was fulfilled, which saith, And he was numbered with the transgressors.

29 And they that passed by railed on him, wagging their heads, and saying, Ah, thou that destroyest the temple, and buildest it in three days,

30 Save thyself, and come down from the cross.

31 Likewise also the chief priests mocking said among themselves with the scribes, He saved others; himself he cannot save.

32 Let Christ the King of Israel descend now from the cross, that we may see and believe. And they that were crucified with him reviled him.

33 And when the sixth hour was come, there was darkness over the whole land until the ninth hour.

34 And at the ninth hour Jesus cried with a loud voice, saying, Eloi, Eloi, lama sabachthani? which is, being interpreted, My God, my God, why hast thou forsaken me?

35 And some of them that stood by, when they heard it, said, Behold, he calleth Elijah.

36 And one ran and filled a sponge full of vinegar, and put it on a reed, and gave him to drink, saying, Let alone; let us see whether Elijah will come to take him down.

37 And Jesus cried with a loud voice, and gave up the ghost.

38 And the veil of the temple was rent in twain from the top to the bottom.

39 And when the centurion, which stood over against him, saw that he so cried out, and gave up the ghost, he said, Truly this man was the Son of God.

GOLDEN TEXT: When the centurion, which stood over against him, saw that he so cried out, and gave up the ghost, he said, Truly this man was the Son of God.
—Mark 15:39.

The Strong Son of God

Unit 2: Confession and Crucifixion

(Lessons 5-8)

Lesson Aims

After this lesson the students should:

1. Feel a deeper sense of gratitude for Jesus' willingness to endure the agony of the cross to save us from punishment for our sins.

2. Look upon death as a necessary step in the transition from time to eternity, made possible by Jesus' own death and resurrection.

Lesson Outline

INTRODUCTION
  A. Facing the Cross
  B. Agonizing Death
  C. Lesson Background
 I. THE CRUCIFIXION (Mark 15:22-32)
  A. The Place of a Skull (v. 22)
  B. A Drink Refused (v. 23)
  C. Prophecy Fulfilled (v. 24)
  D. Time and Title (vv. 25, 26)
  E. In the Company of Thieves (vv. 27, 28)
    The Guilty and the Innocent
  F. Taunts (vv. 29-32)
    Life Isn't a Bowl of Cherries
 II. MERCIFUL DEATH (Mark 15:33-37)
  A. Anguished Cry (vv. 33, 34)
  B. Derision Until Death (vv. 35-37)
III. RESPONSES (Mark 15:38, 39)
  A. Response From the Natural Realm (v. 38)
  B. Response of the Centurion (v. 39)
CONCLUSION
  A. Death: Tragedy or Triumph?
  B. Prayer
  C. Thought to Remember

Visual 7 of the visuals packet lists the prophecies that Mark mentions as being fulfilled when Jesus was crucified. The visual is shown on page 279.

Introduction

A. Facing the Cross

The specter of death faced Jesus throughout His earthly life. At the beginning of Jesus' ministry, John had directed his own disciples' attention to Jesus and said, "Behold the Lamb of God, which taketh away the sin of the world" (John 1:29). Fully aware of His mission, Jesus later stated, "The Son of man can . . . to give his life a

ransom for many" (Mark 10:45). After Peter made the great declaration that Jesus was "the Christ, the Son of the living God" (Matthew 16:16), Jesus broke the news to them that He must suffer many things, including death (see lesson five).

Calvary was both an ugly and a beautiful scene; ugly in that the only totally innocent Man who has ever walked on the earth was sent to an undeserved and cruel death; beautiful in that through His death we have forgiveness of sins, and thus our reconciliation with God is made possible (Ephesians 1:7; 2:16). Jesus resolutely faced the anguish of the cross because of the "joy that was set before him" (Hebrews 12:2). We gain a single, consistent impression in studying the life of Jesus Christ: death held no fear for Him. He was as certain of His resurrection as He was of the crucifixion.

B. Agonizing Death

We cannot imagine the pain and disgrace of the mode of death Jesus faced. A form of capital punishment practiced by many ancient nations, crucifixion was intended as a torturous death, imposed only on the most despicable criminals. The Romans tied their victims' arms to a cross-beam, or, as in Jesus' case, nailed them with long spikes, sometimes at the base of the hand rather than through the palm. The victim was intentionally fixed to prevent any kind of relief from suspension. Sometimes the feet were crossed over one another, and a single spike was driven through both. With the feet in such a position, the misery compounded.

According to historians, some individuals were able to survive the horror for as long as three days! Jesus died after six hours. His more rapid death was due perhaps to the effects of the scourging He received, the severity of which was indicated by His falling under the weight of the cross on the way to Calvary.

Added to the physical agony Jesus suffered was the gnawing thought that His mission would be futile and wasted on so many to whom He offered the peace of God and full pardon from sin.

C. Lesson Background

Soon after the events we studied in last week's lesson, Jesus' public ministry came to a close. He spent the next couple of days with His disciples. Then came the final Passover meal shared with His disciples, at which time He instituted the Lord's Supper and gave them further private instruction. During this time also, Judas Iscariot plotted with the religious leaders to betray Jesus unto them.

After the Passover meal, events moved swiftly. Jesus and the eleven made their way to Gethsemane, and to that spot Judas led the henchmen of the chief priests, scribes, and elders. The betrayal and arrest of Jesus were followed by nighttime trials before the Jewish authorities and an early morning trial before the Roman governor, Pilate.

Failing in his attempt to gain Jesus' release, Pilate finally caved in to the relentless pressure of the nation's religious leaders and delivered Jesus to be scourged and crucified.

I. The Crucifixion
(Mark 15:22-32)

A. The Place of a Skull (v. 22)

22. And they bring him unto the place Golgotha, which is, being interpreted, The place of a skull.

Golgotha. The word means "skull" in the language of the Jews; "Calvary," which comes from Latin, has the same meaning. The reason why the place of Jesus' crucifixion was called *the place of a skull* is not known. There are two principal views regarding its location. The traditional view is that the Church of the Holy Sepulchre, which is located inside of present-day Jerusalem, stands on the place of both Jesus' crucifixion and burial. Since the latter part of the nineteenth century, many have held the site to be a hill just north of Jerusalem, on the side of which are rock formations and small caves that give the appearance of a skull. This hill matches all the details given in Scripture regarding the location of the place, but it cannot be known for certain if the hill had the same appearance two thousand years ago. Only God knows the actual location of Golgotha.

Far more important than the location are the events that occurred here—events that have eternal consequences: the Son of God gave His life, and took it up again, to bring all the world hope beyond the grave.

B. A Drink Refused (v. 23)

23. And they gave him to drink wine mingled with myrrh: but he received it not.

The *wine* was a diluted sour wine commonly used by soldiers. *Myrrh* was a bitter narcotic. This mixture was given to dull the senses and reduce the pain of crucifixion. When this liquid was offered to Jesus, He tasted it and promptly refused it (Matthew 27:34). Jesus' refusal can be explained as an action that committed Him to the total, unrelieved misery of the death He faced. He would totally fulfill the role of the "Suffering Servant."

C. Prophecy Fulfilled (v. 24)

24. And when they had crucified him, they parted his garments, casting lots upon them, what every man should take.

Having nailed their victim's hands and feet to the rough wooden cross and raised the cross to its fixed upright position, the soldiers set about to lay claim to the spoils: the division of the clothing of the crucified One. John indicates that four soldiers had charge of Jesus' execution (John 19:23). The division was made by means of *casting lots*. This can refer to any method of reaching a decision by chance, such as flipping a coin, throwing dice, etc. John also makes mention of Jesus' tunic. Since it had no seams, it would have been ruined had the soldiers torn it into two or more parts. So they cast lots and let the winner have the whole tunic (v. 24). Totally unaware of the significance of their actions, the soldiers fulfilled the prophecy of Psalm 22:18 given one thousand years earlier.

D. Time and Title (vv. 25, 26)

25, 26. And it was the third hour, and they crucified him. And the superscription of his accusation was written over, THE KING OF THE JEWS.

The third hour, according to the Jewish method of counting time, was 9:00 A.M. The *superscription* nailed above Jesus' head was written by Pilate (John 19:19) and displayed in three languages (Luke 23:38). Mark quotes the shortest superscription, probably the Latin version. Having been pressured by the Jewish leaders to crucify Jesus, Pilate, it seems, took pleasure in making this sarcastic jab at them. He refused the request of the chief priests to change the wording (see John 19:21, 22).

E. In the Company of Thieves
(vv. 27, 28)

27, 28. And with him they crucify two thieves; the one on his right hand, and the other on his left. And the Scripture was fulfilled, which saith, And he was numbered with the transgressors.

The *two thieves* who were crucified on either side of Jesus undoubtedly were not just petty thieves. They were robbers, men who stole with violence. It is possible that they were comrades of Barabbas (see Mark 15:7). The religious leaders pressed for the immediate execution of Jesus, and they must have rejoiced over the fact that these two robbers were crucified with Him. To have Jesus put to death in such company would suggest that He was a criminal worthy of death. Once again, an ancient Old Testament prophecy was fulfilled unknowingly by the people who arranged for Jesus to die in this way (see Isaiah 53:12).

THE GUILTY AND THE INNOCENT

Both of them were thieves, robbers, the two men who were crucified with Jesus. There is nothing in the Scriptures to mitigate the charge. The Bible labels them for what they were— thieves. Exactly what they stole, and under what circumstances, we are not told. One wonders if they might have been comrades of the notorious Barabbas.

Criminals such as they were, they deserved punishment. By Roman standards, they deserved crucifixion. Probably they complained; perhaps they exhausted every form of appeal in an effort to be spared. But the fact remains that they were criminals, and as such they were punished for their crimes.

The only innocent person to die on Calvary that day was Jesus. He had committed no crime, violated no law, neglected no duty. Yet, without resistance, He allowed himself to be taken, mistreated, and finally killed in a horribly painful manner. He gave His life to pay the price for the sins of us all.

How to Say It

BARABBAS.   Buh-*rab*-us.
ELOI, ELOI, LAMA SABACHTHANI.   Ee-lo-eye-*lay*-muh or *lah*-mah suh-*back*-thuh-nee (or nie).
GETHSEMANE.   Geth-*sem*-uh-nee.
GOLGOTHA.   *Gahl*-guh-thuh.
ISCARIOT.   Iss-*care*-e-ut.

Our sins may not be as flagrant as those of the two men crucified with Jesus. But rebels we are in the sight of God nonetheless. How blessed we are that God gave His Son, the innocent for the guilty, that all who accept Him might be pardoned from their due punishment!   —T. T.

F. Taunts (vv. 29-32)

29, 30. And they that passed by railed on him, wagging their heads, and saying, Ah, thou that destroyest the temple, and buildest it in three days, save thyself, and come down from the cross.

Golgotha was located near a highway, and the crucified victims were conspicuous to the people who passed by. They *railed on him:* that is, they used language that was reproachful. Their scoffing served as a means of torturing the dying Jesus. *Thou that destroyest the temple, and buildest it in three days.* This is a garbled version of what Jesus had said three years earlier (see John 2:19). The people did not understand Jesus' statement, but it implied His possession of miraculous power. "If indeed You have miraculous power," they taunted, "come down from the cross."

31. Likewise also the chief priests mocking said among themselves with the scribes, He save others; himself he cannot save.

The religious rulers were there, adding their insults and continuing their efforts to convince all that Jesus was a fraud. Sarcasm drips from their words. Jesus *had* saved many persons from sickness, crippling conditions, and even death; but, of course, these rulers didn't believe those reports. In their thinking, the fact that Jesus could not save himself now gave the lie to all those claims of miraculous deeds.

We are brought to wonder: Where were those who had witnessed Jesus' mighty works of raising the dead, healing the sick, or multiplying bread and fish? Where, for that matter, were His own disciples? Were they afraid? disillusioned? confused? His mother and John were at the cross, and He committed her to John's care. But no voice had been raised in His defense at any of the trials. Quite the contrary. His staunchest defender, Peter, denied with an oath that he had ever associated with Jesus.

Although it is most unlikely that Christians in our society today will face the agonies of crucifixion or any form of martyrdom, we may certainly be asked to endure the taunts and derision of non-Christian forces. The voices of many atheistic scientists, humanistic teachers and philosophers, amoral entertainers, and others are often raised in ridicule of Christian teaching and values. Will Christ's followers today "stand up and be counted" for Him?

32. Let Christ the King of Israel descend now from the cross, that we may see and believe. And they that were crucified with him reviled him.

The leaders spoke these words sarcastically, without the remotest expectation that Jesus would come down from the cross. Even had He done so, we cannot believe it would have changed their attitudes. He was a target for ridicule and contempt, to the extent that even the two robbers who were crucified on either side of Him added their cruel insults. One of these, however soon repented and received Jesus' promise of a place in Paradise (see Luke 23:39-43). We too may be falsely accused by others who resent or misunderstand us. The wrong response is to retaliate in kind, thus inviting a continuation of an unprofitable feud, or to live in unspoken, seething hatred, wishing for vengeance. Either course results in the eroding of the soul. Instead, like Jesus, we should consider the sources of such accusations and pray for God to forgive the false accusers (see Luke 23:34). The words of Paul are appropriate in this regard: "If it is possible, as far as it depends on you, live at peace with everyone" (Romans 12:18, *New International Version*).

LIFE ISN'T A BOWL OF CHERRIES

Erma Bombeck is surely one of the great humorists of the contemporary scene. She has a syndicated newspaper column, speaks widely, and has authored a number of books. A taste of her humor can be savored in the titles of her books. One of them is called, *The Grass Is Always Greener Over the Septic Tank;* another is, *I Lost Everything in the Post-Natal Depression;* and still another, *If Life Is a Bowl of Cherries, What Am I Doing in the Pits?*

I don't know Erma Bombeck personally, but I would like to count her among my friends. In titling the last book named above, she has humorously picked up on an expression familiar to most people. I'm certain that she is as well aware as anyone that we have no reason to believe that life is going to be a bowl of cherries. Nothing in this life supports such a philosophy, and certainly nothing in the Bible teaches it. It's the philosophy of naive idealists, not of Christian realists.

The Bible declares that the sun and the rain come upon the just and the unjust (which, as I see it, includes us all). Furthermore, the life of Jesus, the best man who ever lived, the only one ever to live without sin, shows us that sometimes, temporarily, evil prevails over good. Since that was true for Jesus, how can we expect anything better?   —T. T.

II. Merciful Death
(Mark 15:33-37)

A. Anguished Cry (vv. 33, 34)

33, 34. And when the sixth hour was come, there was darkness over the whole land until the ninth hour. And at the ninth hour Jesus cried with a loud voice, saying, Eloi, Eloi, lama sabachthani? which is, being interpreted, My God, my God, why hast thou forsaken me?

From about noon till 3:00 P.M. darkness prevailed as Jesus' death neared. The widespread coverage and duration of the darkness suggest that it was no natural event. God was, in this manner, calling earthlings' attention to a divine spectacle, the imminent death of His Son.

Jesus words are a quotation of Psalm 22:1. He spoke the words in Aramaic, the language commonly spoken in Palestine. Mark, who was writing in Greek, translated them for his readers.

Jesus' great cry has been the subject of much discussion by scholars. Some state that it was necessary for Jesus to be completely separated from God to bear the full weight of the sin of humankind. Others question whether it was possible for such separation to occur, since the Father and Son are one (John 10:30). Needless to say, the nature of the relationship between the divine Father and the divine Son is beyond our ability as humans to understand. But Jesus was also a man, and He was dying for the sins of the world, the innocent for the guilty. It was a bitter cup that He, and He alone, must drink (Matthew 26:39, 42). His death was coming in agony, in darkness, and in the face of the jeering derision of the milling mob. We can understand His feeling utterly forsaken in such circumstances.

B. Derision Until Death (vv. 35-37)

35. And some of them that stood by, when they heard it, said, Behold, he calleth Elijah.

The people of Israel looked for Elijah to come and make things right. Some of the bystanders at the cross either misunderstood or pretended to misunderstand Jesus' words and said that He was calling Elijah.

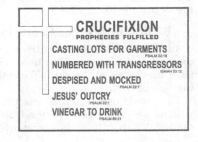

CRUCIFIXION
PROPHECIES FULFILLED
CASTING LOTS FOR GARMENTS
PSALM 22:18
NUMBERED WITH TRANSGRESSORS
ISAIAH 53:12
DESPISED AND MOCKED
PSALM 22:7
JESUS' OUTCRY
PSALM 22:1
VINEGAR TO DRINK
PSALM 69:21

visual 7

36, 37. And one ran and filled a sponge full of vinegar, and put it on a reed, and gave him to drink, saying, Let alone; let us see whether Elijah will come to take him down. And Jesus cried with a loud voice, and gave up the ghost.

John 19:28, 29 indicates that the sponge with vinegar was offered to Jesus after He said, "I thirst." These were His next words spoken after His cry to God. The vinegar was the same wine that soldiers drank. Earlier, Jesus had refused wine mingled with myrrh when offered as an anesthetic. Now He received the plain sour wine, probably offered by one of the soldiers, to assuage His thirst. Some believe He did so in order to be able to cry with a loud voice the words recorded in Luke 23:46. Even as this act of kindness was being done, some continued their derision and would have withheld the liquid from Him.

With one final anguished outburst, Jesus gave up the ghost. Amidst a throng of jeering, bloodthirsty witnesses, He breathed His last.

III. Responses
(Mark 15:38, 39)
A. Response From the Natural Realm
(v. 38)

38. And the veil of the temple was rent in twain from the top to the bottom.

At the moment of His death, a tremendous earthquake occurred, opening many graves (Matthew 27:51, 52). Simultaneously, another marvelous, mysterious, and symbolic event occurred: the veil, which separated the Holy Place from the Holy of Holies in the temple, was split from the top to the bottom! The veil was made up of many layers of fine linen and blue, purple, and scarlet yarn. Tearing such a curtain required tremendous force. The curtain was torn from the top, as God would tear it.

Symbolically, this action signified that the Holy of Holies, which was separated from all other areas of the temple and symbolized God's presence, had served its purpose. Now, by the death of Jesus Christ, the way was opened for all His people to come into the very presence of God, being cleansed from their sins. See Hebrews 9:1-15; 10:12-22.

B. Response of the Centurion (v. 39)

39. And when the centurion, which stood over against him, saw that he so cried out, and gave up the ghost, he said, Truly this man was the Son of God.

The words of the Roman centurion are strong witness to the person crucified under his command. As an officer in the world's strongest army, he must have seen more than his share of people die. Some, no doubt, died in anger, cursing their tormentors. Some may have died like Spartans, displaying no emotion and resigned to fate. Jesus, however, reacted in none of these ways. He called on God to forgive those who taunted and tortured Him!

The centurion was aware that Jesus had claimed to be the Son of God (Matthew 27:43). The elements of the entire event—Jesus' demeanor in dying, the darkness at noon, the terrifying earthquake at the moment of Jesus' death—all combined to penetrate this tough soldier's heart and cause him to reach this conclusion: Jesus was exactly who He claimed to be, the Son of God.

Conclusion
A. Death: Tragedy or Triumph?

Attitudes toward death vary, from stark terror in many who have no hope of life beyond the grave, to joyous anticipation found in those who have firm faith in the Lord Jesus Christ.

Views toward death reflect our attitudes toward life. The Greeks viewed death as the one great and final tragedy, ending all. Atheistic communists say man reverts to dust and is fertilizer for the fields. All thoughts, plans, achievements, and joys end at the grave. Others who do not believe in an afterlife can only hope to be remembered by their children and others for any respect they may have earned in this life.

How different the Christian view! Death is not only the inevitable end of physical life, but the glorious beginning of eternity in the "many mansions" prepared for those who love God. For those faithful unto death, it is a transition from trial to triumph, from grace to glory, a transition made possible when Jesus died at Calvary. We weep when we consider the agony He endured as He bore the punishment for our sins. We shall praise Him eternally, for in His death and subsequent resurrection, He "abolished death, and hath brought life and immortality to light" (2 Timothy 1:10).

B. Prayer

Dear Father, we come before the cross in prayer and penitence. In the light of Your love and goodness, we confess our sinfulness and failure. Give us the wisdom and strength to live in such a way that we will bring only glory and honor to Christ Jesus our Lord. We ask it in His name. Amen.

C. Thought to Remember

We live because Jesus died for us.

Learning by Doing

This page contains an alternate lesson plan emphasizing learning activities. Classes desiring such student involvement will find these suggestions helpful.

Learning Goals

After this lesson, a student will be able to:

1. Explain the significance of Jesus' crucifixion.

2. Suggest how the crucifixion offers a model for Christians who suffer persecution today.

3. Make a commitment to take up his or her cross and follow Jesus.

Into the Lesson

Lead the class in singing the hymn, "The Old Rugged Cross." Then have students work in pairs to discuss these two questions: "What aspect of the cross—or the crucifixion—is most troubling to you?" and, "What aspect is the most comforting to you?" After each person has shared answers with his or her partner, ask for volunteers to share their answers with the class.

Sum up the discussion by noting that the cross is a powerful symbol for Christians. It recalls the terrible suffering of Jesus and, at the same time, is a symbol of victory. It assures us that payment for our sins has been made. But it also challenges us. We cannot think of the cross of Jesus without remembering His words, "If anyone would come after me, he must deny himself and take up his cross daily and follow me" (Luke 9:23, *New International Version*). Today we will examine the suffering, the victory, and the challenge of the cross.

Into the Word

Ask two readers to read today's text aloud, one reading Mark 15:22-32 and the other reading Mark 15:33-39. Point out that the text does not say much about the physical suffering of Jesus; it merely states that "they crucified him." Use the section entitled "Agonizing Death" in the introduction of the lesson to provide background information on the Roman practice of crucifixion and the physical suffering involved.

Then give each student a sheet on which the following references are listed: 24, 26, 27, 29, 30, 31, 32, 34, 36. Have the students work in pairs and examine these verses to see what kinds of mental, emotional, and spiritual suffering are indicated. After a few minutes, ask for reports and list the various types of suffering on the chalkboard. Ask the students why they think the Gospel writers focused on the non-physical aspects of Jesus' suffering. If no one mentions it,

suggest that it may have been to prepare the followers of Christ for the non-physical suffering they would have to endure. Though there have been numerous martyrs over the years, Christians more commonly have had to deal with insult and ridicule rather than physical violence because of their faith. The example of Jesus helps us in this respect.

Finally, note the responses to Jesus' death. Ask the students to examine verses 33, 38, and 39 to discover God's response and the response of the centurion. What do these responses teach us? How do they give us assurance?

Into Life

The concept of assurance is the first application of this lesson. Because Jesus died—and then rose again—we have redemption and forgiveness of sins. Ask students to work in pairs again to affirm this assurance. Have them role play an event in which encouragement and assurance are shared. One student will play a Christian lacking assurance; have this one express his "doubt" to the other, who will use Mark's account of the crucifixion to offer words of assurance. After a few minutes, ask volunteers to share some of the assuring thoughts with the class.

The second aspect of application is Jesus' example for us. First Peter 2:21 says, "To this you were called, because Christ suffered for you, leaving you an example, that you should follow in his steps" (*New International Version*). Jesus said His followers were to take up their crosses and follow Him. (See Luke 9:23.) Ask, "In what situations are we called on to follow Jesus in suffering? What does it mean to take up your cross to follow Jesus?" List the situations your class suggests. Then discuss suggestions for bearing one's cross in these cases.

In the course of your discussion, ask how we can tell when we are suffering for our faith and when we are suffering for some other reason—perhaps justifiably. Is it possible that we sometimes bring trouble on ourselves and excuse it as suffering for our faith? Peter mentions this possibility in the verses just prior to the passage cited earlier—1 Peter 2:19, 20.

Close with a prayer of commitment to follow the Lord in suffering, thanking Him for the victory His death has won for us.

Let's Talk It Over

The questions on this page are designed to encourage review of the lesson Scriptures and to promote discussion of the lesson by the class. The answers provided are only discussion starters. Let your class talk it over from there.

1. The superscription placed above Jesus' head while He hung on the cross (v. 26) and the statement of the chief priests and scribes (v. 31) were ironic in nature, containing truths not intended by those who uttered them. What do these true statements mean to us?

By Pilate's order, the superscription "The King of the Jews" was attached to Jesus' cross. It was a humiliating statement, probably intended to aggravate the crowd. The chief priests and teachers of the law stated, "He saved others; himself he cannot save." Both of these statements are true, although those who made them did not know it. Jesus was the King of the Jews. He was Messiah, the Christ, foretold in prophecy. He is our Lord, too, the King of the whole world. His title was rightly given. The priests and scribes also were correct; Jesus had saved others, and He could not save himself and still be the Savior of humankind. By remaining on the cross, He made the atoning sacrifice for our sins and opened the way to Heaven for us.

2. What did the conduct of the chief priests and teachers of the law at the crucifixion of Jesus reveal regarding them? What are some demands people put on God before they will believe?

The conduct of these men revealed their perversity and hardness of heart. In heaping scorn upon Jesus, they attempted to convince the people that Jesus was not the Christ. Sarcastically, they demanded a miraculous sign from Him. They had already had firsthand knowledge of many of His miracles (see, for example, Mark 2:1-12; 3:1-6; John 9:1-34; 11:38-47). They had also heard His teaching and had found it irrefutable. In order to protect their own position of power and influence over the people, these leaders simply refused to accept the evidence regarding Jesus' divinity when it was presented to them (see John 11:47, 48). Today, many persons demand a sign so that they will have reason to believe in God. "Rid the world of evil," they say. "Heal all diseases." "Alleviate all poverty." "Bring peace to the world." "Grant me health, wealth, and peace of mind." The list goes on and on. One wonders if, as in the case of the Pharisees and teachers of the law, any sign would ever be enough to cause such persons to accept the testimony already given in Scripture and yield their hearts to God.

3. In what way is the centurion's confession a climax to the whole of Mark's Gospel? How should we respond to Jesus' death?

Mark begins his Gospel account by introducing Jesus Christ as the Son of God. At various points in his record, he includes testimony from different sources to show the validity of this opening assertion (see 1:10, 11; 5:6, 7; 8:29; 9:2-7). Then, at the time of Jesus' death, the statement of the centurion is added as a concluding witness. In His death, as in His life, Jesus exhibited divine majesty, and even the forces of nature acknowledged it. The centurion's summary statement is correct: "Truly this man was the Son of God." We should respond with worship, thanksgiving, and service. Worship, for "God was in Christ, reconciling the world unto himself" (2 Corinthians 5:19). Thanksgiving, because Jesus died for each of us. As a result of His suffering and death, our sins are no longer counted against us. Service, so that all of humankind may know the blessedness of forgiveness of sin and eternal life with God.

4. We who are Christians share the conviction of the centurion who said, "Truly this man was the Son of God." What are some ways in which we can make our conviction known to others?

By our conduct we can give strong testimony to our belief that Jesus is God's Son. For some, accepting Jesus as Savior involves a drastic change in life-style, and that change can have a powerful impact on friends and acquaintances. Feet that once took one in search of pleasure, personal gain, and power over others now direct one to God's house—a place of praise and prayer. Hands that once grabbed all they could find for self are now opened generously to those in need. Lips that may have been given to lying are now devoted to speaking only the truth. Unkind and unclean speech is replaced by words that comfort and promote holiness. And when others speak derisively of Jesus, we can speak clearly in His defense. By allowing Jesus thus to control our lives, we proclaim our conviction that He is the Son of God.

An Empty Tomb

LESSON SCRIPTURE: Mark 15:42—16:8.

PRINTED TEXT: Mark 15:42—16:8.

Mark 15:42-47

42 And now when the even was come, because it was the preparation, that is, the day before the sabbath,

43 Joseph of Arimathea, an honorable counselor, which also waited for the kingdom of God, came, and went in boldly unto Pilate, and craved the body of Jesus.

44 And Pilate marveled if he were already dead: and calling unto him the centurion, he asked him whether he had been any while dead.

45 And when he knew it of the centurion, he gave the body to Joseph.

46 And he bought fine linen, and took him down, and wrapped him in the linen, and laid him in a sepulchre which was hewn out of a rock, and rolled a stone unto the door of the sepulchre.

47 And Mary Magdalene and Mary the mother of Joses beheld where he was laid.

Mark 16:1-8

1 And when the sabbath was past, Mary Magdalene, and Mary the mother of James, and Salome, had bought sweet spices, that they might come and anoint him.

2 And very early in the morning, the first day of the week, they came unto the sepulchre at the rising of the sun.

3 And they said among themselves, Who shall roll us away the stone from the door of the sepulchre?

4 And when they looked, they saw that the stone was rolled away: for it was very great.

5 And entering into the sepulchre, they saw a young man sitting on the right side, clothed in a long white garment; and they were affrighted.

6 And he saith unto them, Be not affrighted: ye seek Jesus of Nazareth, which was crucified: he is risen; he is not here: behold the place where they laid him.

7 But go your way, tell his disciples and Peter that he goeth before you into Galilee: there shall ye see him, as he said unto you.

8 And they went out quickly, and fled from the sepulchre; for they trembled and were amazed: neither said they any thing to any man; for they were afraid.

Apr 19

GOLDEN TEXT: Be not affrighted: ye seek Jesus of Nazareth, which was crucified: he is risen; he is not here: behold the place where they laid him.—Mark 16:6.

The Strong Son of God
Unit 2: Confession and Crucifixion
(Lessons 5-8)

Lesson Aims

This lesson will challenge the students to:
1. View the resurrection of Jesus Christ as the basis for their hope of eternal life.
2. Tell others the joyous news of Jesus' victory over the grave.

Lesson Outline

INTRODUCTION
  A. Out of the Shadows
  B. The Final Week
I. THE HASTY BURIAL (Mark 15:42-47)
  A. Joseph's Request (vv. 42, 43)
  B. Mercifully Quick Death (vv. 44, 45)
  C. Hasty Burial (v. 46)
  D. Burial Site Observed (v. 47)
    Victory in Jesus
II. AT THE TOMB (Mark 16:1-4)
  A. Thoughtful Women (v. 1)
  B. Time of the Resurrection (v. 2)
  C. A Major Problem (v. 3)
  D. An Open Tomb (v. 4)
III. HE IS RISEN! (Mark 16:5-8)
  A. The Divine Messenger (v. 5)
  B. An Indisputable Fact (v. 6)
    A Joyful Sound
  C. Tell the Good News (v. 7)
  D. Mixed Emotions (v. 8)
    Resurrection Confidence
CONCLUSION
  A. Certainty of the Resurrection
  B. Prayer
  C. Thought to Remember

Visual 8 of the visuals packet illustrates a truth mentioned in the introduction of this lesson. The visual is shown on page 287.

Introduction

A. Out of the Shadows

The writer of the epistle to the Hebrews stated that "it is appointed unto men once to die" (Hebrews 9:27). This statement assuredly meets with universal agreement. Life in this world is lived under the shadow of physical death. Furthermore, we are not long on the earth until we learn firsthand that life in the flesh can be both

disappointing and tragic. Disease, injury, the failure of vital organs—the list of sources of premature disablement is long and distressing. But whether or not one falls victim to such serious misfortune during one's time on earth, death remains the lot of us all. If all of one's efforts, hopes, and goals are directed to this physical life, the approach of life's end must bring an ever-increasing sense of emptiness and loss.

Death is no tragedy, however, for those in Christ Jesus; indeed, it is the welcome end to sufferings, anguish, trials, temptations, frustration, and other obstacles to a happy life.

Death is also a transition. The change that occurs then may be illustrated by the planting of a flower seed in the ground. The seed dies, but issuing forth from it is a flower, whose beauty exceeds that of the body from which it came. So it will be for those persons who place their trust and hope in Jesus Christ. When this life ends, they will cast off this fleshly body and begin a new, more glorious form of existence. They will step out of the shadows into the realm of eternal light and life.

B. The Final Week

The week preceding the crucifixion of Jesus was filled with numerous and diverse activities. The four Gospels include far more details regarding this one week of Jesus' ministry than they do of any other period of His life. Each of them relates at least some details of the events in the upper room, and Jesus' betrayal, trials, crucifixion, and resurrection.

Jesus regularly spent the nights of that week in the home of Mary, Martha, and Lazarus at Bethany, a scenic two-mile walk from Jerusalem over and around the southern end of the Mount of Olives, to its eastern slope. Returning to the city each morning, He went to the temple and taught the people. There He encountered much opposition by the religious leaders, as their efforts to discredit Him before the people intensified. His disciples followed Him about constantly. If they had understood all He had said then and in the weeks immediately preceding, they should not have been surprised when He was betrayed, placed on trial, and crucified; nor would they have been amazed at His resurrection.

I. The Hasty Burial
(Mark 15:42-47)

A. Joseph's Request (vv. 42, 43)

42, 43. And now when the even was come, because it was the preparation, that is, the day before the sabbath, Joseph of Arimathea, an

honorable counselor, which also waited for the kingdom of God, came, and went in boldly unto Pilate, and craved the body of Jesus.

Jewish custom required the dead to be buried before sunset on any day. Jesus died about 3:00 P.M., and darkness fell about 6:00 P.M. Sometime during that three-hour interval Joseph went to Pilate and asked for Jesus' body so he could give it a suitable burial.

Joseph is described as being *of Arimathea.* Arimathea was "a city of the Jews" (Luke 23:51), but its location is not known for certain. This man was *an honorable counselor,* which means that he was a member of the Sanhedrin, the high council of the Jews. Thus he was held in high esteem in the Jewish community and explains, perhaps, why he could gain access to Pilate, the Roman governor. Joseph *also waited for the kingdom of God.* At some point he had come in contact with Jesus and had become His disciple (John 19:38). He, along with the others, had waited for Jesus to make clear His divine mission.

B. Mercifully Quick Death (vv. 44, 45)

44, 45. And Pilate marveled if he were already dead: and calling unto him the centurion, he asked him whether he had been any while dead. And when he knew it of the centurion, he gave the body to Joseph.

Weakened by the rush of events and harsh mistreatment prior to being nailed to the cross, Jesus died in the relatively short time of six hours. Victims sometimes survived much longer than this, hence Pilate's amazement is understandable. A check with the centurion in charge of the crucifixions assured Pilate that Jesus was most assuredly dead. John adds details concerning the deaths of the two thieves. Death came more slowly to them, and to hasten it, the soldiers broke their legs (John 19:31, 32). Because Jesus was already dead, they did not break His legs (v. 33), fulfilling the Scripture concerning the Passover lamb (John 19:36; Exodus 12:46). Jesus was the "Lamb of God, which taketh away the sin of the world" (John 1:29).

C. Hasty Burial (v. 46)

46. And he bought fine linen, and took him down, and wrapped him in the linen, and laid him in a sepulchre which was hewn out of a rock, and rolled a stone unto the door of the sepulchre.

It was still Friday afternoon, so there was time for Joseph to purchase the *fine linen* in which to wrap the body of Jesus. Joseph was "a rich man" (Matthew 27:57), so it may be that he sent a servant to purchase this expensive material. Nicodemus, another disciple, provided spices

---

How to Say It

ARIMATHEA. Air-uh-muh-*thee*-uh.
MAGDALENE. *Mag*-duh-leen or Mag-duh-*lee*-nee.
SALOME. Suh-*lo*-me.
SANHEDRIN. *San*-huh-drun or San-*heed*-run.

---

for the burial. With the help of attendants, they removed Jesus' body from the cross and wrapped it in the linen with the spices (John 19:39, 40). Joseph had a tomb, which recently had been cut out of the rock in a garden near the crucifixion site (Matthew 27:60; John 19:41). Placing Jesus' body inside, they then rolled a huge stone, shaped like a wheel, in front of the door to close the tomb.

D. Burial Site Observed (v. 47)

47. And Mary Magdalene and Mary the mother of Joses beheld where he was laid.

Matthew reports that a number of women who had followed Jesus from Galilee observed His crucifixion "afar off" (Matthew 27:55). Of these, at least the two Marys mentioned by Mark remained to observe the burial of Jesus. Luke tells us that a larger group of these Galilean women watched the burial (Luke 23:55).

VICTORY IN JESUS

Winston Churchill was one of those rare individuals who was a legend in his own time. His wide interests, masterful leadership qualities, and brilliant oratorical ability all contributed to his legendary status. The fact that his father was British, and his mother, American, endeared him to people on both sides of the Atlantic.

He was famous for a number of great statements, some humorous, some earnest. Early in his military career he wrote, "Nothing in life is so exhilarating as to be shot at without result." Upon becoming prime minister of Great Britain early in World War II, he stated, "I have nothing to offer but blood, toil, tears, and sweat." Another of his famous wartime statements was his tribute to the British airmen for their victory in the "Battle of Britain": "Never in the field of human conflict was so much owed by so many to so few."

As one considers the empty tomb of Jesus and views it in the shadow of the cross, a similar thought enters the mind: Never in the history of humankind has so much been owed by so many to just One! Jesus stood bravely against the devil, and in doing so, He turned what seemed to be certain defeat for us all into glorious victory.   —T. T.

II. At the Tomb
(Mark 16:1-4)

A. Thoughtful Women (v. 1)

1. And when the sabbath was past, Mary Magdalene, and Mary the mother of James, and Salome, had bought sweet spices, that they might come and anoint him.

The women who observed Jesus' burial prepared spices and ointments late Friday afternoon with which to anoint His body when the Sabbath was past (Luke 23:55, 56). In addition, the three women whom Mark mentions here purchased more spices on the way to the tomb on the first day of the week. They came to the tomb to pay their respects and to add their spices to those already placed among the cloths in which Jesus' body was wrapped. Luke mentions that other women were now in the group coming to the tomb (Luke 24:1, 10).

B. Time of the Resurrection (v. 2)

2. And very early in the morning, the first day of the week, they came unto the sepulchre at the rising of the sun.

The women began their walk to the tomb on *the first day of the week* while it was yet dark (John 20:1), and they arrived at the tomb when the sun had risen. This indicates the resurrection occurred in the early dawn of that day.

C. A Major Problem (v. 3)

3. And they said among themselves, Who shall roll us away the stone from the door of the sepulchre?

Overcome by grief as they were, the women had not considered how they would remove the huge stone from the door of the tomb. Only now the thought occurred to them.

D. An Open Tomb (v. 4)

4. And when they looked, they saw that the stone was rolled away: for it was very great.

The stone could be seen from some distance because of its great size. As the women looked in the direction of the tomb, they could see that *the stone was rolled away.*

III. He Is Risen!
(Mark 16:5-8)

A. The Divine Messenger (v. 5)

5. And entering into the sepulchre, they saw a young man sitting on the right side, clothed in a long white garment; and they were affrighted.

We can only imagine the women's awed reaction at the sight of the *young man* (an angel, as

Matthew 28:5 affirms) soon to be joined by another angel (Luke 24:4). Understandably, the women experienced the fright common to humans in such supernatural appearances.

B. An Indisputable Fact (v. 6)

6. And he saith unto them, Be not affrighted: ye seek Jesus of Nazareth, which was crucified: he is risen; he is not here: behold the place where they laid him.

On the right hand side, as one entered the tomb, was a hollowed-out area where Jesus' body had lain. The women noticed immediately that the place was empty. Their fright was twofold: the shock at the circumstances of the stone and the empty tomb, and the angel who spoke to allay their fears.

It was the message of the angel that gained the focus of their attention: Jesus had risen! They were reminded that He had fulfilled His own prediction of His resurrection, and they remembered His words (Luke 24:6-8).

What a blessed assurance to know that death is not the end, but is, in reality, the avenue to life everlasting! Humankind was not created to live for a few brief moments and then to melt back into the earth from which they came. Made in the very image of God, and endowed with qualities that extend far beyond the physical, human beings are designed for eternity. The Christian, then, cannot view the death of the flesh-body as a tragedy, but a prelude to the greatest of all triumphs—life everlasting in the presence of God. Jesus' own resurrection has made it so!

A Joyful Sound

For most people, death is a somber subject, and funerals are cold, silent reminders that life is fleeting. But my son, David, who is also a preacher, told me about an exception, a funeral that he performed early in his ministry. The service was for a woman named Barbara, a member of the church he served, who had died at the age of fifty.

The funeral was held in Barbara's hometown, some two hundred miles from where she had resided. At the service, the folk were highly emotional, and David, like preachers often at funerals, felt that his words had provided little real comfort for the mourners.

Following the sermon came an uplifting message from an unexpected source. Barbara, who had been a strong believer, had requested that her funeral close with a taped song that had been her favorite. It was a joyful song that spoke about flying off to be with the Lord, and the funeral parlor reverberated with the sound of exhilarating music. Astonished faces changed from tear-filled to cheerful as Barbara's message rang forth: she was not dead, but alive!

The message of the empty tomb is one of joy and victory, and it has no limits. It is for everyone who, like Barbara, will accept it in faith.

—T. T.

C. Tell the Good News (v. 7)

7. But go your way, tell his disciples and Peter that he goeth before you into Galilee: there shall ye see him, as he said unto you.

Jesus' appearances during the forty days between the resurrection and ascension occurred at different places and times. It was natural that He should appear to His disciples in Galilee, where He had done much teaching and, as a matter of fact, had lived most of His earthly life. He did appear to them later in Galilee (John 21; Matthew 28:16, 17), but first, on this very day, they had the happy surprise of seeing Him in Jerusalem (John 20:19-23). The mention of Peter by name indicates that he had been forgiven for his denials of Jesus and that he was still regarded as one of Jesus' disciples.

We sing the familiar hymn, "We've a Story to Tell to the Nations," which is simply the present extension of the mission assigned to the women at the empty tomb. Our story does not vary in any respect: Jesus Christ is risen! His conquest of death is the greatest triumph in all history, overcoming Satan's sharpest weapon and bringing solid hope to us all. "Because He lives, we too shall live!" The entire message of Jesus Christ rests directly on this point, today as well as ever. The simple facts of the gospel we know: Jesus Christ died for our sins. Salvation is offered in no other name. The gospel is to be proclaimed to every nation, tongue, and tribe. Those who turn from sin and yield their hearts, souls, and lives to Jesus, accepting Him as Savior and Lord, are resurrected to a new life—a glorious life that has no end! No words are more consoling at the death of a loved one than the reassurance that the dead in Christ shall rise in

triumph, and that all who share this blessed hope will be united for eternity. What otherwise would be a scene of unmixed sorrow and mourning becomes an occasion of genuine joy and victory.

This is our message to a confused, lost, and dying world. Whatever seems to be gain in our present world is lost at death; whatever is lost in this world for the sake of Jesus Christ results in eternal gain.

D. Mixed Emotions (v. 8)

8. And they went out quickly, and fled from the sepulchre; for they trembled and were amazed: neither said they any thing to any man; for they were afraid.

Seized by the very eeriness of the events, the women left the scene immediately, trembling with amazement and fear. They had gone to the tomb expecting to find the dead body of their beloved Lord. What they found instead was first one then two angels in shining garments who spoke to them, announcing that Jesus was alive! The women were told not to be afraid, but who can blame them for not obeying the order?

Neither said they any thing to any man. Matthew 28:8 says that the women did as they were told and ran to tell the disciples of what they had seen. Mark's comment here means that they did not stop along the way to tell anyone else. As they went, Jesus himself appeared to them and confirmed what the angel had said. Recognizing Him, the women "held him by the feet, and worshipped him" (Matthew 28:9). Thus, when the women arrived at the place where the disciples were, they could report not only that they had seen an angel, but also that they had seen, talked with, and touched the risen Jesus himself.

RESURRECTION CONFIDENCE

In his book, *Say Hello to Life*, Rod Huron suggests that if a person in the first century had had any doubt as to whether Jesus had been raised from the dead, he could have resolved his difficulty by journeying to Palestine, seeking out those who claimed to have seen the resurrected Christ, and hearing their testimony.

During the forty days between His resurrection and ascension, Jesus made a number of appearances, in various places, and to an assortment of persons. He had been seen by Mary Magdalene, by a group of women, by two disciples, by Peter, by the other apostles, by more than five hundred persons at one time, by James, and by Paul. He had been seen in a garden, on a roadway, in an upper room, by a sea, and on a mountain. He had appeared to believers and to doubters.

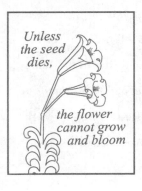

Unless the seed dies, *the flower cannot grow and bloom*

visual 8

The point is that an earnest seeker for truth could have found one or more of these eyewitnesses, heard their testimony, and then come to a decision.

We do not have the same opportunity as did the folk of the first century. But, thank God, we have the testimony of a number of first-century persons who testified that they saw the risen Christ, and who sealed their testimony with their blood. That is very convincing, too!

—T. T.

Conclusion

A. Certainty of the Resurrection

We no longer need be overwhelmed by fear and confusion because of the certainty of death. Jesus' resurrection provides a firm, unshakable certainty: there is life beyond the grave. And all those persons who are united with Christ will share in His victory over death. In 1 Corinthians 15 the apostle Paul set forth many truths regarding Christ's resurrection, among which are these: the saving gospel of Christ is established through His conquest of death (vv. 1-4); His numerous appearances to those who knew Him left no doubt of His victory over the grave (vv. 5-8); our hope of being raised from the dead is securely based upon Christ's resurrection (vv. 12-23); the ultimate destruction of death is certain, and all things are now under Christ's rule (vv. 26-28); we shall be resurrected in a newer, more splendid spiritual form (vv. 35-54); no person need fear death any longer (vv. 55-57); and our labors in the Lord are not in vain (vv. 58, 59).

The testimony presented in the New Testament is more than adequate to establish the fact of Jesus' resurrection. We note first that Jesus had predicted on a number of occasions that He would be raised from the dead (John 2:19-22; Luke 9:22; Mark 9:30-32; Matthew 20:17-19). The testimony of those who knew Him continually and intimately before His crucifixion, and under the various circumstances of the resurrection, is the strongest possible proof that the crucified Jesus had in truth been raised from the dead. These witnesses had nothing to gain and everything to lose by lying. And yet they bore harmonious witness to having seen Jesus alive again.

Had Jesus not risen from the dead, His enemies had only to produce His dead body to refute the claims of the disciples. The fact that Jesus' disciples were only slowly convinced of His resurrection, and with no little reluctance, removes the argument of some that they were so eager to believe that they readily accepted even the flimsiest evidence in order to support their belief. Furthermore, the willingness of His witnesses to endure innumerable hardships, and even death itself, in proclaiming their message, speaks of their absolute commitment to the truths they preached. The lengthening, growing spiritual kingdom Jesus founded, and the superior caliber of His message for all persons, testify to the truth of His words spoken both before and after His conquest of death and the grave.

Christ has conquered death! His empty tomb testifies to it. In our world today we have the privilege and obligation to share this glorious news with all people. Outside of Jesus Christ, no basis is found upon which to build one's hopes beyond the grave; in Him, a glorious eternity awaits.

B. Prayer

Holy Father, we rejoice in the triumph of Jesus Christ Your Son over sin, death, and Hell. We are made humble in realizing that all this was done for sinners like ourselves. We would commit our lives, our very souls to Him, now and ever. May we have courage to give expression to our commitment by sharing with everyone we meet the news of Jesus' victory. In His name we pray. Amen.

C. Thought to Remember

Death be not proud, though some have called thee
Mighty and dreadful, for, thou art not so,
For, those, whom thou think'st, thou dost overthrow,
Die not, poor death, nor yet canst thou kill me . . .
One short sleep past, we wake eternally,
And death shall be no more; death, thou shalt die.

—John Donne

Home Daily Bible Readings

Monday, Apr. 13—Reconciliation in Death (John 12:20-33)
Tuesday, Apr. 14—The Day of Preparation (Mark 15:42-45)
Wednesday, Apr. 15—Facing the Grave (Isaiah 53:8-11)
Thursday, Apr. 16—Laid Him in the Tomb (Mark 15:46,47)
Friday, Apr. 17—Belief and Fear (Matthew 27:62-66)
Saturday, Apr. 18—"He Has Risen" (Mark 16:1-6)
Sunday, Apr. 19—Alive in Christ (Romans 6:5-11)

Learning by Doing

This page contains an alternate lesson plan emphasizing learning activities. Classes desiring such student involvement will find these suggestions helpful.

Learning Goals

After this lesson students will be able to do the following:

1. Identify Joseph of Arimathea as a secret disciple who found the courage to take a stand for Jesus.

2. Cite evidence for believing in the resurrection.

3. Recognize their own fears about telling people of Jesus and the resurrection, and suggest some ways to overcome those fears.

Into the Lesson

Write the word *fear* vertically on the chalkboard. Then say, "What makes you reluctant, or perhaps afraid, to share your faith in Christ? Take each letter of the word *fear* to suggest another word or phrase that describes what makes us afraid to tell others about Christ." Have the students work in pairs or small groups to come up with suggestions. After a few minutes, ask the students to report on their results. You may get answers such as the following:

F—friends, family

E—embarrassment, expressions of disapproval

A—alienation, attack on personal integrity

R—ridicule, rejection.

Write several of the ideas on the chalkboard. Observe that, while we have concern for these matters, none of them is life threatening. Disciples in the first century could add threat of death to their list. Point out that today's lesson will examine some of the fears shared by Jesus' early disciples and by disciples today. We will seek courage in the Lord's resurrection.

Into the Word

Have a student read the lesson text aloud: Mark 15:42—16:8. Then divide the class into small groups to research the following ideas.

Group One: Study Mark 15:42-47 as well as Matthew 27:57-60; Luke 23:50-54; and John 19:38. Who was Joseph of Arimathea, and why don't we hear about him before this event? What was he afraid of? How do we know he overcame that fear?

Group Two: Study today's lesson text and any parallel passages you choose (Matthew 28, Luke 24, John 20 and 21, and 1 Corinthians 15). List as many points for believing in the resurrection as you can find, including the following: certification that Jesus was really dead, eyewitnesses to His appearances after He had died and risen, and evidence that the women went to the right tomb to find Jesus.

Group Three: Notice especially Mark 16:7, where the angel told the women specifically to tell Peter that Jesus would meet with the disciples in Galilee. Compare this with Luke 24:34, 1 Corinthians 15:5, and John 21. Why the special emphasis on Peter? What special assurance does this provide for believers today?

Provide each group with a poster or large sheet of newsprint and appoint a reporter. The reporter can record the group's findings on the poster and then use that for reporting later. After about ten minutes, ask the groups to report their findings to the class.

Into Life

Point out that the resurrection is the cornerstone of our faith in Jesus. (Use 1 Corinthians 15 if you feel you need to support that statement.) Thus, we need to be fully assured of the resurrection in order to communicate our faith.

Note, however, that sharing one's faith is not just a matter of explaining facts; it is sharing one's life. It includes feelings, motives, and attitudes as well as facts. Persons will often use facts as an argument—that is, they will claim they cannot accept the evidence—when the real problem is emotional. Many persons just don't *want* to believe, because they are afraid of what they will have to give up to be a Christian. How do we deal with that?

After this discussion, write the following headings on the chalkboard: "Joseph of Arimathea" and "The Apostles (after Pentecost)." Ask the class to consider them and decide which they are most like. Are they like Joseph, secret disciples until some event of major significance moves them to action? Or are they like the apostles after Pentecost, bold proclaimers of their faith? Refer again to the list of fears that the students suggested in the activity at the beginning of the class. Discuss some specific actions Christians can take to overcome these fears that prevent our sharing our faith.

As you close the class session, ask the students to think of someone they know who is not a Christian. Pray for boldness for the students to be able to share their faith with those persons.

Let's Talk It Over

The questions on this page are designed to encourage review of the lesson Scriptures and to promote discussion of the lesson by the class. The answers provided are only discussion starters. Let your class talk it over from there.

1. What risk did Joseph of Arimathea take in asking for and burying the body of Jesus? What risk do we take when we identify with Christ?

Jesus had been tried and convicted as a blasphemer by the Jews, and He had been crucified by the Romans, the legal authorities in Palestine. For Joseph to ask for the body was to admit an allegiance to Jesus. As a member of the Jewish council, Joseph risked his position of power, his wealth, and his community standing by so doing. His action would have set him against his fellow rulers who contrived Jesus' death, and their ability to turn the community against him would have been considerable. In truth, Joseph stood to lose all that the world considers valuable by taking this action. In identifying with Jesus we may lose certain friendships. Some persons may become openly hostile toward us. Opportunities for material gain may be denied us. Our popularity and status can be threatened. Like Joseph, however, we must stand for Christ.

2. When the angel commanded the women to go and tell Jesus' disciples of the resurrection, he mentioned Peter by name. Why was this significant, and what does this say to us today?

What guilt and alienation Peter must have been feeling because of his personal denial of Jesus! He was defeated and full of despair. If there was ever one needing special encouragement, it was Peter. And that encouragement wasn't long in coming. This word from the angel was meant to reassure Peter that he had been forgiven and that he was to consider himself still among the Lord's disciples.

There may be times when we, like Peter, are in turmoil, suffering mental and spiritual anguish from a wrong we have committed. Feelings of isolation from the community of God's people may overwhelm us. At just such a time we need to be assured of the love and forgiveness of Jesus Christ! This incident tells us that the penitent find forgiveness in the Lord and are restored to fellowship with Him. It also speaks a word concerning our responsibility to our brothers and sisters in Christ. We should not push them away when they are hurting and ashamed. We should seek them out and give them help in their time of need. To do so builds up a brother or sister (Galatians 6:1, 2). Like Peter, we may go on from

that moment of deepest agony to scale the highest heights because of Christ's unfailing love.

3. How would you complete the following: "Christ's death and resurrection mean . . ."?

Christ died for the sins of the world and for my sins. Had He not offered himself as the atoning sacrifice for sin, I would be destined for Hell, separated from God eternally. Now, though, I have eternal life through Him. His death and resurrection assure me of His deity, so I can worship Him without reservation. I also realize I have nothing to fear from those who might harm me in any way for believing in Christ. Were they to succeed, that would be only a temporary setback, for I am assured of ultimate victory in Him. Because He was raised from the dead, I too shall be victorious over death. Finally, the death, burial, and resurrection of Jesus is "good news" for all mankind. I am compelled to tell it!

4. How should a Christian view death?

Death is very serious, both for the one involved and for the loved ones and friends. All are faced with very strong emotional forces, such as shock and the reality of permanent separation, as far as this life is concerned. In looking at death from the point of view of the deceased, however, one must only feel overwhelming joy. A Christian brother or sister who has died has left this life, but has inherited a greater, more glorious, eternal life with the Father. Truly, to die is gain (Philippians 1:21).

5. A quick reading of the four Gospel accounts of the resurrection can lead to confusion. Why should God have permitted this in the Bible?

Of course, those accounts can be easily harmonized; and our faith is strengthened when we see how remarkably four independent accounts dovetail into one another. The day of Jesus' resurrection and the following weeks were no doubt times of confusion, but they were also times of excitement as the one clear fact was made known to all the disciples: Jesus had indeed risen! The manner in which the four Gospels describe those days enables us not only to ascertain the fact of Jesus' resurrection, but to share also in that excitement.

The Gift of Living Hope

LESSON SCRIPTURE: 1 Peter 1:1-25.

PRINTED TEXT: 1 Peter 1:3-9, 13-21.

1 Peter 1:3-9, 13-21

3 Blessed be the God and Father of our Lord Jesus Christ, which according to his abundant mercy hath begotten us again unto a lively hope by the resurrection of Jesus Christ from the dead,

4 To an inheritance incorruptible, and undefiled, and that fadeth not away, reserved in heaven for you,

5 Who are kept by the power of God through faith unto salvation ready to be revealed in the last time.

6 Wherein ye greatly rejoice, though now for a season, if need be, ye are in heaviness through manifold temptations:

7 That the trial of your faith, being much more precious than of gold that perisheth, though it be tried with fire, might be found unto praise and honor and glory at the appearing of Jesus Christ:

8 Whom having not seen, ye love; in whom, though now ye see him not, yet believing, ye rejoice with joy unspeakable and full of glory:

9 Receiving the end of your faith, even the salvation of your souls.

. . . .

13 Wherefore gird up the loins of your mind, be sober, and hope to the end for the grace that is to be brought unto you at the revelation of Jesus Christ;

14 As obedient children, not fashioning yourselves according to the former lusts in your ignorance:

15 But as he which hath called you is holy, so be ye holy in all manner of conversation;

16 Because it is written, Be ye holy; for I am holy.

17 And if ye call on the Father, who without respect of persons judgeth according to every man's work, pass the time of your sojourning here in fear:

18 Forasmuch as ye know that ye were not redeemed with corruptible things, as silver and gold, from your vain conversation received by tradition from your fathers;

19 But with the precious blood of Christ, as of a lamb without blemish and without spot:

20 Who verily was foreordained before the foundation of the world, but was manifest in these last times for you,

21 Who by him do believe in God, that raised him up from the dead, and gave him glory; that your faith and hope might be in God.

Apr
26

GOLDEN TEXT: Blessed be the God and Father of our Lord Jesus Christ, which according to his abundant mercy hath begotten us again unto a lively hope by the resurrection of Jesus Christ from the dead.—1 Peter 1:3.

God's People in the World

(Lessons 9-14)

Lesson Aims

This study, which focuses on our hope in Christ, should help the students:

1. Face the trials of life, knowing that they will ultimately triumph over them.

2. Exemplify holiness in all aspects of their lives.

3. Express a greater appreciation for God's plan of salvation.

Lesson Outline

INTRODUCTION
    A. The Least of These
    B. The Appeal of Peter
I. THE LIVING HOPE (1 PETER 1:3-9)
    A. The Praise of the Giver (v. 3)
       The Need for Hope
    B. The Promised Gift (v. 4)
    C. The Power of God (v. 5)
    D. The Present Grief (v. 6)
    E. From Proving to Glory (v. 7)
       Nothing to Fear
    F. The Presence of Glorious Joy (vv. 8, 9)
II. LIVING THE HOPE (1 PETER 1:13-21)
    A. The Preliminary Conditions (vv. 13, 14)
    B. The Primary Command (vv. 15, 16)
    C. The Practice of Fear (v. 17)
    D. The Purchase by Christ (vv. 18, 19)
    E. The Plan Fulfilled (vv. 20, 21)
CONCLUSION
    A. Hope and Holiness
    B. Prayer
    C. Thought to Remember

Visual 9 of the visuals packet highlights the bases of our hope in Christ, which are mentioned in the lesson text. The visual is shown on page 295.

Introduction

A. The Least of These

"But now abide faith, hope, love, these three; but the greatest of these is love" (1 Corinthians 13:13, *New American Standard Bible*). If love is the greatest, which is the least? Most would concur that hope ranks after love and faith. This, however, does not diminish the quality of hope.

Hope defined. The dictionary defines hope as "desire with expectation of obtaining what is desired." Hope, therefore, is more than desire; it adds the ingredient of expectation of fulfillment. Either desire or hope may motivate an individual's efforts, but hope is greater than desire.

Florence Chadwick, the great swimmer, failed in her first attempt to swim the Catalina Channel in 1952. She quit after she had been in the water sixteen hours, and her goal was only one mile away. The fog prevented her from seeing land. She said, "If I could have seen the land, I might have made it." Genuine hope demands a reasonable expectation of obtaining the goal.

Hope distinguished. The Gentiles were described as "having no hope, and without God in the world" (Ephesians 2:12). The Gentile world had the word *hope* in their languages, but it could mean an expectation of either good or evil. For the Christian it meant only good.

The hope of Israel lay in keeping the law. But James points out that "whosoever shall keep the whole law, and yet offend in one point, he is guilty of all" (2:10). Clearly, no one could keep the law perfectly, and so those who lived under the law were condemned by it.

That Christ is superior to the law is the central theme of the book of Hebrews. At one point the writer states that those who are in Christ have "a better hope" than those who are under the law (Hebrews 7:19). This is so because they trust Christ's perfect righteousness and do not rely on their own imperfect ability to keep the law. *Certainty,* therefore, is a key word describing a Christian's hope.

B. The Appeal of Peter

Peter personally. It is easy to identify with Simon Peter. He possessed the very human trait of sometimes acting or speaking before he thought a situation through. The class should be able to cite several instances in which Peter's words or works were embarrassing. Here are some examples: his being rebuked by the Lord at Caesarea Philippi (Matthew 16:21-23); his rejecting Jesus' offer to wash his feet (John 13:6-9); his pledging to go to prison or death with Jesus, and then being told that he would deny Jesus that very night (Luke 22:33, 34); his practicing segregation at Antioch (Galatians 2:11-14).

Peter had many positive traits, too. Following his denial of Jesus, Peter wept when the rooster crowed; and he repented completely in the footwashing incident. He was given the keys of the kingdom—the privilege of proclaiming the gospel first to the Jews (Acts 2) and to the Gentiles (Acts 10). And after being rebuked by Paul at Antioch, he did not harbor a grudge against Paul. Peter's affection and respect for him are seen as he commends Paul's epistles to his readers (2 Peter 3:15, 16).

Peter's epistle. First Peter has been called "the epistle of the living hope" because of its frequent mention of this subject. Peter's purpose was not simply to write about hope, but to show that it is to produce a positive effect in the lives of Christians—especially those whose faith is challenged by trials and suffering. His epistle has contemporary appeal to any believer whose hope is being tested by the events of life.

Peter addressed his epistle to believers who were scattered through central and northern Asia Minor. He wrote from "Babylon" (1 Peter 5:13). Some understand this to be the literal city of Babylon on the Euphrates, but most Bible students consider it to be a veiled reference to Rome. Nero's persecution of Christians began in A.D. 64. It is thought that this epistle may have been written at about that time.

I. The Living Hope
(1 Peter 1:3-9)

A. The Praise of the Giver (v. 3)

3. Blessed be the God and Father of our Lord Jesus Christ, which according to his abundant mercy hath begotten us again unto a lively hope by the resurrection of Jesus Christ from the dead.

Peter's salutation (vv. 1, 2) is followed by a doxology of praise. *God* is declared to be *blessed*—worthy of praise because of who He is, what He has done, and what He will do. It was important that Peter place things in the proper order. Later he would develop the themes of steadfastness and victory over suffering, but that superstructure needed this foundation of praise to God for all His provisions for the redeemed.

The relationship of God to Jesus is stated in a twofold sense: He is both *the God and Father of our Lord Jesus Christ.* It is unusual to say that God is the God of Christ, but it is found in other places (see Matthew 27:46; John 20:17; Ephesians 1:17).

Peter first looked to the past and stated that it was God's *abundant mercy* that caused Him to beget us again. The Christian life is described in other passages as a new birth (John 3:5; James 1:18), a new creation (Galatians 6:15, *New American Standard Bible*), and regeneration (Titus 3:5).

How to Say It

ANTIOCH.   *An-tee-ock.*
CAESAREA PHILIPPI.   Ses-uh-*ree*-uh Fih-*lip*-pie or *Fil*-ih-pie.
EUPHRATES.   U-*fray*-teez.

As we examine our own lives, we who are Christians must surely be aware of the abundance of God's mercy in forgiving our sins and granting us new life

Christians are begotten to a *lively* (living) *hope.* Believers do not have a false expectation. This hope is the "anchor of the soul" that enables us to weather the storms of life (Hebrews 6:18, 19). This is a living "hope of eternal life, which God, that cannot lie, promised before the world began" (Titus 1:2).

The resurrection of Jesus Christ from the dead made this hope possible. We have a living hope because of the living Lord! The resurrection is the foundation of the entire Christian system. If Christ did not come out of the tomb, we may as well close the Bible and the doors of the church building. "If Christ be not risen, then is our preaching vain, and your faith is also vain" (1 Corinthians 15:14). If, however, Jesus came from the tomb bodily (and He did!), then Christ is entitled to first place in our lives.

It is very fitting that this lesson follows immediately after the Lord's Day on which the resurrection was celebrated. That historical event has changed the history of the world and has produced a living hope for all who are in Christ.

THE NEED FOR HOPE

A close relative of mine has been struggling with cancer. When the chemo treatments she was taking had apparently failed to put her lymphoma in remission, she decided to go to the Mayo Clinic in Rochester, Minnesota, for a second opinion regarding her condition.

Her local oncologist, informed of this decision, replied, "You're looking for magic, and there is none." By way of contrast, a representative of Mayo's said, "We never give up; we've seen unusual things happen."

Whereas the local oncologist suggested that my relative's efforts to find a cure were futile, the Mayo specialist had given a great deal of hope. Assurance was given that there was still a chance, and that that chance should be pursued.

The people of northern Asia Minor suffered from the futility of life. They had been trapped in the vain, idolatrous life-styles handed down to them by their fathers. But then they were introduced to Jesus, and now they possessed a living hope, a hope that brought power for daily living and the promise of eternal life in Him.

Christians are aware that apart from Jesus and the hope we have in Him, life, in reality, is futile. But in Him we have a *living* hope, and that hope changes everything. It gives meaning to life now, and the certain expectation of a joyous, eternal future with God.   —T. T.

B. The Promised Gift (v. 4)

4. To an inheritance incorruptible, and undefiled, and that fadeth not away, reserved in heaven for you.

God has also begotten us *to an inheritance*. This inheritance is described with three terms that are in marked contrast with any earthly legacy. First, our inheritance from God is *incorruptible*: it will not decay. The same word is used in 1 Corinthians 9:25 to describe the crown that Christians receive.

The inheritance is *undefiled*: it will remain pure. This term also depicts the character of our great high priest (Hebrews 7:26).

Finally, this inheritance *fadeth not away*. It is like a flower that is always fresh. The qualities of our spiritual inheritance are vastly different from any of our earthly experiences.

C. The Power of God (v. 5)

5. Who are kept by the power of God through faith unto salvation ready to be revealed in the last time.

Now the subject changes from the inheritance to the heirs. God's power will also guard them. The word *kept* is a military term. It indicates that the goal of the guarding is to insure that God's children will receive their inheritance, the *salvation ready to be revealed in the last time*. We *are kept by the power of God*, but there is a condition. Our *faith* must not falter. (See Hebrews 3:12; 1 Timothy 1:19; 4:1.)

D. The Present Grief (v. 6)

6. Wherein ye greatly rejoice, though now for a season, if need be, ye are in heaviness through manifold temptations.

Knowing that our salvation is all ready and that it will be revealed when Jesus returns, we who are Christians *greatly rejoice*. This joyous expectation ought to sustain us in all of life's circumstances. It is true that in this life *temptations* (tribulations) may come to us. It seems certain that the people to whom Peter was writing were being called on to suffer for their faith in Christ. Peter's words were a reminder to them (and to us) that such trials are only *for a season*. The expression *if need be* may indicate that the trials are intended to produce a disciplinary blessing. See Hebrews 12:11.

E. From Proving to Glory (v. 7)

7. That the trial of your faith, being much more precious than of gold that perisheth, though it be tried with fire, might be found unto praise and honor and glory at the appearing of Jesus Christ.

Here Peter gives one answer to the problem of suffering: it is a *trial* (or proof) of our faith. Just as *gold* is refined by *fire*, so the faith that stands the test is shown to be genuine. Such faith will receive *praise and honor and glory* when the Lord returns.

Our faith means more to us if it has been tested, and if we have passed the test through determined effort. James 1:2, 3 states that such trials produce patience or steadfastness, and for this reason we may rejoice in them.

Triumphant faith is *more precious than gold*. Gold, desired by so many in this life, will one day perish. But faith that has been tested and has stood the test will secure an inheritance from the Father that is incorruptible (v. 4).

NOTHING TO FEAR

Franklin Delano Roosevelt—FDR as he has come to be called—was a very popular president. He came into power at the height of a great depression and played an important role in leading the nation to recovery. He was in office during most of World War II and provided excellent leadership for the war effort. One of his most famous statements, made during the dark days of the depression, was, "The only thing we have to fear is fear itself."

There were other things to fear: the possibility of not having a job, the uncertainty of having money to buy food and clothing, the likelihood of losing house or farm. But still, FDR was correct in that, in the ultimate sense, all that had to be feared was fear itself. If that could be conquered, all other fears would vanish.

One of the great blessings we as Christians enjoy is that we have nothing to fear. Nothing, absolutely nothing, can separate us from God's love (Romans 8:31-39). Fiery trials may come, as they did to those whom Peter addressed, but our faith in Jesus will sustain our spirits; our hope of salvation will stabilize our souls. With the writer of Hebrews we may confidently say, "The Lord is my helper, and I will not fear what man shall do unto me" (13:6). —T. T.

F. The Presence of Glorious Joy (vv. 8, 9)

8, 9. Whom having not seen, ye love; in whom, though now ye see him not, yet believing, ye rejoice with joy unspeakable and full of glory: receiving the end of your faith, even the salvation of your souls.

Redemption in Christ is not limited to people of the first century who actually saw the Lord. During one of His appearances after His resurrection, Jesus promised that those persons are "blessed . . . that have not seen, and yet have believed" (John 20:29).

The tested faith in an unseen Christ results in *love* for Christ, and this produces an unutterable, glorious *joy*. The word *rejoice* is the same as in verse 6, and the cause of the joy is the same in both instances: *the salvation of your souls.* Having received the forgiveness of our past sins, we who are Christians are saved even now. In another sense, however, we must await Christ's return for the final consummation of our salvation and the receiving of our eternal inheritance. It is uncertain whether Peter is referring to the present or the future; but as we consider either aspect of our salvation, we are filled with inexpressible joy.

II. Living the Hope
(I Peter 1:13-21)

In verses 10-12 Peter states that the prophets of old, who prophesied of this salvation, desired to know the time and circumstances concerning it. Even the angels longed to look into these things. That grace, Peter says, was bestowed through Christ. We who have received salvation through Him have certain responsibilities, and Peter discusses some of them beginning with verse 13.

A. The Preliminary Conditions (vv. 13, 14)

13, 14. Wherefore gird up the loins of your mind, be sober, and hope to the end for the grace that is to be brought unto you at the revelation of Jesus Christ; as obedient children, not fashioning yourselves according to the former lusts in your ignorance.

The word *wherefore* is rendered "therefore" in most modern versions. Peter has laid his doctrinal foundation, and now he is ready to give a variety of practical exhortations for God's *obedient children* (see v. 2). Good doctrine should result in a good life!

Gird up the loins of your mind. In ancient times, people wore long robes. As part of their preparation for a strenuous physical activity, they would gather up the long folds of their garments and tuck them securely under their belts. Then they were ready for action! By using this figure, Peter urges Christians to be mentally prepared for what is involved in living the Christian life.

The command to *be sober* has a double meaning: to be unintoxicated, or to be levelheaded. Perhaps Peter had both concepts in mind. We are not to be controlled by the evil desires that characterize the life lived in *ignorance* of spiritual matters. Instead, our lives should befit those who have set their *hope* on the *grace* that God will give when Jesus Christ is revealed.

visual 9

B. The Primary Command (vv. 15, 16)

15, 16. But as he which hath called you is holy, so be ye holy in all manner of conversation; because it is written, Be ye holy; for I am holy.

As he which hath called you is holy. The one true God was exactly the opposite of the immoral gods of Canaan, Greece, and Rome. A fundamental teaching in both the Old Testament and the New is that God is holy. The ordinary Hebrew word for "holy" means separated, consecrated. God is holy, for He is separated from all other beings by His perfection. In Him alone is perfect wisdom, power, goodness, truth, and justice. Peter cites Leviticus 11:44, 45, showing that Israel of old was called to be holy, because God who called them is holy. They were to be consecrated to God. They were to separate themselves from the pagan peoples among whom they lived, and were to keep themselves from idolatry and immorality.

In verse 14 Peter referred to "the former lusts" in which Christians lived before they knew Christ. The holy God has called us to new life, a life that is to be lived separated from sin and consecrated to Him. God expects those who follow Him to be like Him—not occasionally, not just on Sunday, but *in all manner of conversation* (in every aspect of life).

C. The Practice of Fear (v. 17)

17. And if ye call on the Father, who without respect of persons judgeth according to every man's work, pass the time of your sojourning here in fear.

Each of the phrases in this verse is packed with meaning. *If ye call on the Father.* This is a reminder of a great blessing that is ours, namely that the One to whom we pray is our Heavenly Father. The word *if* in this clause does not imply doubt. It is to be understood as follows: "If you pray . . . and you do!"

Who without respect of persons judgeth according to every man's work. When preaching the gospel to the Gentile Cornelius, his family, and his friends, Peter had said, "Of a truth I perceive that God is no respecter of persons" (Acts 10:34).

God is impartial regarding admission to His kingdom, and He will be impartial when He administers judgment. His judgment will not be swayed by one's nationality, social standing, or economic status. Each will be judged on the character of his or her work.

Pass the time of your sojourning. With these words Peter reminds us that life on earth is only temporary. It is a brief journey from point to point. Life on earth is only the beginning, not the totality of our existence.

The last word of this verse, *fear*, is intended to provide the controlling factor that will prompt a life of holiness. This fear is a reverence that produces an awareness of God's presence in every situation. It is "the beginning of wisdom" (Psalm 111:10) that will stimulate correct decisions when facing the issues of life—if those decisions are made in prayer (James 1:5).

D. The Purchase by Christ (vv. 18, 19)

18, 19. Forasmuch as ye know that ye were not redeemed with corruptible things, as silver and gold, from your vain conversation received by tradition from your fathers; but with the precious blood of Christ, as of a lamb without blemish and without spot.

Peter has been giving reasons why Christians should live holy lives. The first of these is that God who has called us is holy, and He commands it. Second, we know that a time is coming when we shall be judged according to our works. Now he adds another reason: the great value of the price of our redemption from the bondage of sin.

In the ancient world, a slave's freedom might be purchased with *silver and gold*. But the Gentile Christians, to whom Peter was writing, had been held in a greater bondage, the *vain conversation* (conduct) that had been passed on to them by their fathers. In Acts 14:15, the word *vain* is used of idolatry and the evils accompanying it. It took a far greater price than silver or gold to redeem them (and all persons) from slavery to sin. The price was death—not just the death of anyone, but that of the pure, holy, and blameless Son of God! He was the perfect sacrifice—the Lamb of God (John 1:29, 36).

E. The Plan Fulfilled (vv. 20, 21)

20, 21. Who verily was foreordained before the foundation of the world, but was manifest in these last times for you, who by him do believe in God, that raised him up from the dead, and gave him glory; that your faith and hope might be in God.

Before the foundation of the world, God knew that man would sin. This expression is frequently associated with God's plan (Matthew 13:35; 25:34; Hebrews 4:3; Revelation 13:8; 17:8). God's mercy and love compelled Him to put into operation the only plan that would save humankind and satisfy His holiness. That plan culminated in the incarnation, death, and resurrection of Christ. Together they yield an absolute confidence that our love, living hope, and abiding faith may *be in God.*

Conclusion

A. Hope and Holiness

The final reference in the New Testament to our hope in Christ is an appropriate admonition: "And every man that hath this hope in him purifieth himself, even as he is pure" (1 John 3:3). That is a perfect blending of the thoughts of hope and holiness.

No matter what may come to us in life, our hope in Christ sustains us as we keep our hearts and minds focused on the glorious, eternal inheritance that awaits us. May that hope strengthen our resolve day by day to honor in our lives the One who redeems us.

B. Prayer

Thank You, Heavenly Father, for Your love and mercy manifest in Your only Son! Today we reaffirm our faith that Jesus is the Christ, and that our lives will exemplify our faith, our hope, and our love. In the name of the Redeemer Lamb, amen.

C. Thought to Remember

"For whatsoever things were written aforetime were written for our learning, that we through patience and comfort of the Scriptures might have hope" (Romans 15:4).

Home Daily Bible Readings

Monday, Apr. 20—Rejoice in Hope (Romans 5:1-5)
Tuesday, Apr. 21—Hope Through the Christ (1 Peter 1:1-5)
Wednesday, Apr. 22—Faith Is Tested (1 Peter 1:6-9)
Thursday, Apr. 23—The Living Bread (John 6:47-51)
Friday, Apr. 24—The Gift From God (Ephesians 2:4-10)
Saturday, Apr. 25—A Living Response (1 Peter 1:13-16)
Sunday, Apr. 26—Toward Godliness (1 Peter 1:17-21)

Learning by Doing

This page contains an alternate lesson plan emphasizing learning activities. Classes desiring such student involvement will find these suggestions helpful.

Learning Goals

After this lesson a student will be able to do the following:

1. Define the concept of hope as it is expressed in Scripture.

2. Explain how hope helps a Christian affirm his faith in the midst of trials.

3. Describe the relationship between hope and holiness.

Into the Lesson

As the students arrive, give each one a copy of the following statements (or refer them to the student book). Ask them to complete each statement that is applicable to them:

1. At work this year, I hope to—

2. Considering this fall's elections, I hope—

3. With the economy the way it is, I hope—

4. When I think of Heaven, I hope—

After the class has had a few minutes to consider these statements, ask for a few volunteers to share some of their hopes. Note in how many different contexts we use this word *hope*.

Then ask, "How confident are you of realizing these hopes?" For most of them, we have little or no confidence of attaining what we hope for. Yet Paul said, "Hope does not disappoint us" (Romans 5:5, *New International Version*). This is the difference between what we generally call "hope" and what the Scriptures call "hope." In Scripture, *hope* is more than mere desire or wishing something to be so. It is a confident expectation based on the promises of Him who cannot lie. It is "living hope," guaranteed by the living Lord who rose from the dead.

Lead the class in singing the first verse of "The Solid Rock" ("My hope is built on nothing less . . ."). Then pause for prayer before going into the Scripture study for today.

Into the Word

Have someone read the lesson text aloud. Then divide the class into three groups, one to examine hope's past, another for hope's present, and a third to examine hope's future. Ask group one to examine the text and describe the source of hope: what facts or events from the past provide the foundation for Christian hope? How do these facts or events provide assurance for Christian hope? Group two is to list the goals of hope: what can the person of hope expect?

Group three is to describe the present expression of hope: what activities are characteristic of a person of hope, and in what situations is hope most vital or active? (The present is assigned to the third group so that discussion of the group's findings can lead into a discussion of how we are to live in view of hope.)

Allow the groups five or ten minutes for discussion; ask one person in each group to report on the group's findings. List the items from each report on the chalkboard or on an overhead transparency. Discuss the significance of each item, using information from this commentary for supplemental insights.

Of course, it is important to view hope's past for the assurance it provides, and it is important to view the future to know our goal. But focusing on the present brings out hope's practical value. With this in mind, ask the class to consider verses 13 through 16. Discuss these two questions: (1) For what specific "action" should we prepare? (See verse 13.) This will likely be an expansion of group three's findings. (2) What is the connection between hope and holiness? (See verses 15 and 16, and note also 1 John 3:3.) As you discuss this, note the role of "fear" as well (v. 17). How can fear and hope be compatible?

Into Life

After a time of discussion, say, "So where does all this leave us? How can we put this into practice and be people of hope?" Recall that group three (above) was asked to consider in what situations hope is most vital or active. From verse 7, they should have noted the importance of hope in trials. Ask, "What trials do Christians today experience in which hope is most vitally needed? How do we maintain hope in the face of opposition?" Have class members share some of their experiences in which they have had trials of various sorts and note how hope did, or could have, helped them through it. Discuss how enduring the trials has made them appreciate their faith more than before.

In conclusion, say, "We have noted several trials that Christians face or have faced. What do you think the future holds for us: will it be easier or harder to be a Christian?" Discuss how hope will be crucial to dealing with whatever comes.

Let's Talk It Over

The questions on this page are designed to encourage review of the lesson Scriptures and to promote discussion of the lesson by the class. The answers provided are only discussion starters. Let your class talk it over from there.

1. Peter notes our unique identity in Christ and describes the transforming power of the living hope that the community of the redeemed possesses. How should this identity in Christ and this living hope affect our attitudes and behavior?

The anticipation of God's blessings for daily Christian living because we are His elect should create in us a confidence that God's best awaits us in every circumstance and situation. Our attitude, therefore, should be one of joy in which we are free from the anxiety and fear of what the future holds. Since each of us belongs to Jesus Christ and to the significant community called the church, we have been set apart wholly for God's use. As a result, the way we relate with people, the priorities we have, and the work that we do should honor God. "And whatsoever ye do in word or deed, do all in the name of the Lord Jesus, giving thanks to God and the Father by him" (Colossians 3:17).

2. Since struggles with the demands of life face us daily, how does "a living hope because of the living Lord" become increasingly important to us?

Often the struggles and problems of daily life appear as insurmountable obstacles. How desperately we need the certainty that God is on our side, that we can overcome with His strength, and that God's ultimate good for us will triumph! We are inclined to focus on the things of this life that rob us of our joy and bring us failure. Our living hope helps us instead to keep our eyes fixed on the resurrected, triumphant Lord, who has the power to assist us in living life victoriously. Because of this living hope, we truly can "have life, and . . . have it more abundantly" (John 10:10).

3. Society today has little tolerance for individuals who hold unwaveringly to convictions. Consequently, we may be ridiculed and rejected for our faith, which is based on Biblical revelation. How may our living hope help us when our convictions are being tested by the events of life, and how may this testing deepen our convictions and our faith?

The Christian's hope is rooted in an expectation that the future will bring the blessings and goodness of God. Realizing that the rewards of God are not of this world and that they await us in the future, we gain strength to deal with unpleasant circumstances in the present. The challenges to our convictions and our faith often will cause us to reevaluate our relationship with God, to search the Scriptures, and to reaffirm our commitment to the Lord. Affliction thus can result in the strengthening of our resolve to follow Him and the deepening of our trust in His promises.

4. Peter describes Christians as those who "are filled with an inexpressible and glorious joy" (v. 8, *New International Version*). What is the link between a living hope and an inexpressible joy in our lives as Christians, and how can we be joyful even though we are facing stressful situations?

Our joy flows from a confidence that our deepest needs are met fully and permanently in God. We know that we are loved unconditionally, and we are secure in our knowledge that God's purpose is being done in our lives. Therefore, our sense of well-being and joy does not depend upon current circumstances but upon a future hope that is anchored in God's promises. Since our faith is refined and developed in the midst of adversity (1 Peter 1:7; Hebrews 12:11; James 1:2-4), we can see the growth in character that trials produce. The grief from trials lasts only for a little while, but the transformation of our lives into the likeness of Christ that results from these trials brings eternal blessings. This is a cause for rejoicing.

5. The pressures for Christians to fit into the world's mold are enormous. How is it possible to stop conforming to the world's standards and to practice holiness in our daily lives?

We need to recognize that what the world considers important simply will not last into eternity, and to begin investing our time, money, and energies to produce lasting fruit for God's kingdom. We need to shape our desires, mold our lives, and set our priorities on the enduring, eternal realities of God as revealed in Scripture. We must learn to recognize the subtlety and deceitfulness of sin, and to learn to say "no" to ungodliness in all its forms in our lives.

Called to Be God's People

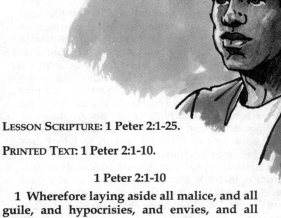

LESSON SCRIPTURE: 1 Peter 2:1-25.

PRINTED TEXT: 1 Peter 2:1-10.

1 Peter 2:1-10

1 Wherefore laying aside all malice, and all guile, and hypocrisies, and envies, and all evil speakings,

2 As newborn babes, desire the sincere milk of the word, that ye may grow thereby:

3 If so be ye have tasted that the Lord is gracious.

4 To whom coming, as unto a living stone, disallowed indeed of men, but chosen of God, and precious,

5 Ye also, as lively stones, are built up a spiritual house, a holy priesthood, to offer up spiritual sacrifices, acceptable to God by Jesus Christ.

6 Wherefore also it is contained in the Scripture, Behold, I lay in Zion a chief corner stone, elect, precious: and he that believeth on him shall not be confounded.

7 Unto you therefore which believe he is precious: but unto them which be disobedient, the stone which the builders disallowed, the same is made the head of the corner,

8 And a stone of stumbling, and a rock of offense, even to them which stumble at the word, being disobedient: whereunto also they were appointed.

9 But ye are a chosen generation, a royal priesthood, a holy nation, a peculiar people; that ye should show forth the praises of him who hath called you out of darkness into his marvelous light:

10 Which in time past were not a people, but are now the people of God: which had not obtained mercy, but now have obtained mercy.

GOLDEN TEXT: Ye are a chosen generation, a royal priesthood, a holy nation, a peculiar people; that ye should show forth the praises of him who hath called you out of darkness into his marvelous light.—1 Peter 2:9.

God's People in the World
(Lessons 9-14)

Lesson Aims

This lesson should help the student to do the following:
1. Determine to grow spiritually by spending more time in the Word and in prayer.
2. Resolve to "show forth the praises" of God to others so that they may be God's people.

Lesson Outline

Visual 10 of the visuals packet highlights three principles that should guide God's people. The visual is shown on page 303.

Introduction

A. Grow, Christian! Grow!

The doctor decided to admit the newborn boy to the hospital, even though it had been only a few days since he had gone home with his mother. The doctor was concerned because the baby was barely maintaining his birth weight, and it is normal for infants to gain approximately an ounce a day, or almost a half pound a week. (It was determined that the baby had an allergy to milk. He was placed on a soybean formula, and he thrived on it.)

The necessity of growth. We understand that growth is normal in the physical world, and it must be recognized that the same principle applies spiritually! The New Testament abounds in references to the fact that God expects His people to grow: in the fruits of righteousness (2 Corinthians 9:10); in grace and in the knowledge of Jesus Christ (2 Peter 3:18); unto perfection, or maturity (Hebrews 6:1); in love to one another and to all persons (1 Thessalonians 3:12); and into Christ in every way (Ephesians 4:15).

Cautions about growth. A slowdown in the rate of a person's growth is normal in the physical realm. If the baby spoken of earlier gained one-half pound per week for thirty years, he would weigh 780 pounds! Even so, growth in Christ is not an inclined plane of steady ascent. There are times of great increase, other times when the rate of growth may be only moderate, and perhaps times when a plateau is reached and no growth occurs. Christians must not become discouraged because they do not always experience the same rate of spiritual growth as when they first became Christians.

Christian growth is not automatic. It results from communing with God regularly in prayer and in making the effort to understand the truths His Word holds for us. Consistent fellowship with God's people and conscientious application of Christian principles to life combine to verify the goodness of God and the correctness of His ways. Our Christian convictions are thus confirmed and we are motivated to accept greater challenges in Christ's service.

The conclusion of growth. Christianity has no retirement plan; instead, the person who is "faithful unto death" will receive "a crown of life" (Revelation 2:10). The death experience itself may provide opportunities for one to demonstrate to others that "to live is Christ, and to die is gain" (Philippians 1:21).

B. Lesson Background

Peter concludes chapter 1 by referring to the spiritual cleansing we receive when we are born again through the living word of God that is preached to us. Briefly he mentions that the community of which we are now a part is to be characterized by sincere love for one another (vv. 22-25). He expands on this thought in chapter 2, as we see in today's lesson text.

How to Say It

LOGOS (Greek). *lah*-goss.
SEPTUAGINT. Sep-*tyoo*-uh-jint.

I. Called to Grow

(1 Peter 2:1-3)

A. By Discarding Sin (v. 1)

1. Wherefore laying aside all malice, and all guile, and hypocrisies, and envies, and all evil speakings.

Peter begins chapter 2 with the word *wherefore*. Recent translations give this as "therefore." Having been "purified" (1:22), we who are in Christ are to live in keeping with our new spiritual status. We are to lay aside, that is, put from us, that which is bad or sinful (Colossians 3:8; James 1:21).

The word *all* occurs three times in this verse. It is interesting that Peter does not say "most" of our *malice*, "some" of our *guile*, and "selected" *evil speakings*. He says to remove *all* these sinful attitudes or actions.

The sins that Peter mentions are all disruptive of brotherly love, which, a few verses earlier, he has strongly urged his readers to develop (1:22). This same brotherly love is a part of Peter's famous list of graces (see 2 Peter 1:7). Lack of love for one another was evidently a problem among some in the church of the first century. The apostles themselves experienced some internal strife, and that may have made a strong impression on Peter's mind (Luke 22:24).

The first *all* that Peter mentions is *malice*. The word in the Greek language can be a general term for evil, or it can refer to ill will or harm to others. The latter meaning seems to fit the context here, for the desire to injure others is the opposite of "unfeigned love of the brethren" (1:22).

The second *all* applies to the word *guile*, and it probably includes *hypocrisies* and *envies*. The person with guile intends to deceive others, and to do so for personal gain or advantage. Such a person may resort to hypocrisy, feigning to be what he or she is not, in order to achieve the desired goal.

Some persons find it difficult to rejoice when another is blessed with treasure or talent. There is a tendency to defame, to speak evil of God's people. Christians are expected to rise above such behavior.

B. By Desiring the Word (v. 2)

2. As newborn babes, desire the sincere milk of the word, that ye may grow thereby.

As everyone knows, *newborn babes* cannot speak to express their desires. If they are hungry, they can make this known only by crying; and the crying intensifies until they are fed. With the same intensity, Christians are to *desire the sincere*

milk of the word. The word *desire* is the major verb of the thought that began in verse 1. The desire for spiritual nourishment is to be possessed by all Christians at all times.

In the verses immediately preceding our lesson text, Peter made reference to the word of God, by which we are saved (1 Peter 1:23-25). He is referring to that word in the expression *the sincere milk of the word*. In this instance, *word* is an adjective form of the Greek *logos* (word), and it means rational, that which is agreeable to reason. This adjective is used in the same sense in Romans 12:1: "your reasonable service." Some versions give is as "spiritual." Peter is saying that we are to desire the milk (that is, the teaching) that is conveyed in and by the Word of God. It is rational and reasonable for Christians to do so, for by it our minds and spirits receive proper nourishment. In the final analysis, this spiritual milk refers to the gospel, which is "the power of God unto salvation" (Romans 1:16).

The milk is further described as *sincere* (or pure). This word is a negative form of the word given as "guile" in verse 1. The reasonable, spiritual diet of the Christian should not include the impure items on the menu of the world. God's people are told to think instead on the things that are true, honest, just, pure, lovely, and of good report (see Philippians 4:8).

The translators of the *King James Version* worked from a text that omitted the last two words of the verse. They are "unto salvation." These words are in most of the modern translations. Peter asserts that salvation is the goal of a Christian's growth. The implication is that salvation may be jeopardized if there is no growth.

C. By Delighting in the Lord (v. 3)

3. If so be ye have tasted that the Lord is gracious.

Peter gives another reason for God's people to desire the spiritual nourishment that God provides: they have already experienced the Lord's goodness in their redemption from sin. The word *if* here does not express doubt. The meaning is, "Since you have tasted that the Lord is good, continue to feed on His Word!"

THE "PETER PAN" SYNDROME

The children's classic, *Peter Pan*, has long been a favorite of adults and youngsters alike. The fantasy centers on a boy who desires to remain a child forever, and refuses to grow up. The story makes for a charming stage play. In real life, however, it is tragic if a person does not mature. In fact, true joy in living comes from constant growth, as we progress from one stage of understanding to the next.

The Christian life, more than anything else, is a steady progression into maturity. Peter encouraged his readers to crave spiritual milk so that they might grow. The author of Hebrews went a step further, exhorting his readers to leave the milk and dig into solid food (5:11-14). And Paul stated that his preaching was for the purpose of presenting his hearers "perfect in Christ" (Colossians 1:28).

The New Testament teaching is clear: we are to grow in our spirituality and our relationship with the Lord. Constantly we are to be learning more, giving more, and committing ourselves more fully to the kingdom. For when we reach that comfortable plateau in our faith that tells us we are good enough, we are then in serious trouble. Realizing this, may we grow into the mature Christians that God wants us to be.   —T. T.

II. Called to Be a Building
(1 Peter 2:4-8)

A. The Living Stone (v. 4)

4. To whom coming, as unto a living stone, disallowed indeed of men, but chosen of God, and precious.

At this point Peter changes his choice of metaphors (from food to stones). The word *stone* appears five times in verses 4-8. He begins by stating that the persons who come to Jesus, a living stone, are siding with *God* instead of with men.

Disallowed (rejected) *of men.* Peter's sermons in Acts developed the same theme. By His miracles and wonders and signs, Jesus was shown to be approved by God. Even so, he was rejected by men (see Acts 2:22-24; 4:10, 11; 5:30, 31). Jesus fulfilled God's prophecies and plan, but He did not meet the expectations of the Jewish leaders. They therefore crucified Him and later persecuted the apostles, who preached His gospel.

The concept of Jesus' being a stone was not original with Peter. Jesus had applied this same terminology to himself (Matthew 21:42-44). Paul said that Jesus is a spiritual Rock (1 Corinthians 10:4), a corner stone (Ephesians 2:20), and a stone of stumbling (Romans 9:32, 33; 1 Corinthians 1:23). Peter does add new dimensions to this figure of speech. Jesus was a *living, chosen,* and *precious stone.*

B. The Living Stones (v. 5)

5. Ye also, as lively stones, are built up a spiritual house, a holy priesthood, to offer up spiritual sacrifices, acceptable to God by Jesus Christ.

If Christ may be described with the paradoxical language of being a stone that lives, what about His followers? The first two words of verse 5 answer the question when they say, *Ye also.* Five phrases follow, and each helps to provide an answer, or adds new perspectives.

(1) *Lively stones.* Believers have the same description applied to them as did Jesus. They are stones that are alive!

(2) *A spiritual house.* Collectively the saints are *built up* into a *spiritual house.* The spiritual quality implies that it is a temple. This reaffirms Paul's teaching found in 1 Corinthians 3:16, 17. God's temple is not made with hands, nor is it confined to one location.

Each stone must be a part of the building—not off by itself. This demonstrates unity, and it shows the error of a popular motto from a recent decade that stated, "Jesus, yes! The church, no!"

(3) *A holy priesthood.* Peter now changes his imagery. Christians are both the temple and its priests! This verse combines with verse 9 to proclaim the priesthood of all believers.

(4) *Spiritual sacrifices.* Christ, our great high priest, has already offered himself as the atoning sacrifice for our sins. Still, there are sacrifices that we as priests must make. They include the following: acts of service (Philippians 2:17), benevolent gifts (Philippians 4:18), the expression of praise and thanks to God (Hebrews 13:15), and doing good and sharing with others (Hebrews 13:16). All of these flow from the giving of our bodies, our very selves, as "living" sacrifices (Romans 12:1).

(5) *By Jesus Christ.* Two interpretations are possible here: the sacrifices are *acceptable* because they are offered through Christ, or simply that they are offered *by Jesus Christ.* The result is the same either way.

THE WALLS OF THE CHURCH

A famous story comes to us from the ancient city of Sparta. It seems that a Spartan king once boasted about the walls of his city to a visiting monarch. The visiting dignitary looked around and could see no walls. He said, "Where are these walls about which you boast so much?" His host pointed to his bodyguard of magnificent troops. "Those," he said, "are the walls of Sparta, every man a brick."

Peter makes a similar point in regard to the kingdom of God, telling us that like "living stones" we are erected into a spiritual house. While this certainly teaches the importance of unity (every brick by itself is useless and gains strength only as it is incorporated into the building), it also stresses the fact that each individual is vital to the church. Every brick that is removed from a house leaves a gaping hole, which lets in cold air, dust, and other undesirable elements. So each "living stone" that fails in its purpose in God's spiritual house leaves a space no one can fill and brings hardship on the church.

The moral of Peter's teaching is quite clear. Every member has value to the kingdom, regardless of age, financial capability, or number of talents. You see, the church of Jesus Christ is dependent on us all. If we are simply willing, the Master Architect will incorporate us into His marvelous structure.   —T. T.

C. The Cornerstone (v. 6)

6. Wherefore also it is contained in the Scripture, Behold, I lay in Zion a chief corner stone, elect, precious: and he that believeth on him shall not be confounded.

Peter documents the description of Christ in verse 4 by citing Isaiah 28:16. Two new features are added. (1) The *corner stone* was laid *in Zion*. One of the hills of Jerusalem was "Zion," and this term was used by the prophets for the city itself. Here Jesus gave His life and was raised from the dead, and here the church had its beginning.

(2) *He that believeth on him shall not be confounded.* Peter bases his quotation on the Septuagint, which is a Greek translation of the Hebrew Old Testament. The Hebrew words in Isaiah 28:16 literally mean "shall not be in haste." The English word *confounded* means shamed or confused. The person who trusts in Christ shall not be ashamed or confused, but shall know inner calm.

D. The Stumbling Stone (vv. 7, 8)

7. Unto you therefore which believe he is precious: but unto them which be disobedient, the stone which the builders disallowed, the same is made the head of the corner.

The first part of the verse describes the believers' regard for Jesus: *he is precious.* This word can mean prized, dear, honored, or revered.

What about the unbelievers? Peter answered that question with a quotation from Psalm 118:22. Jesus had quoted the same passage during his earthly ministry (Luke 20:17), and Peter cited it when he and John were questioned by the Jewish council (Acts 4:11). The unbelievers are the *disobedient*, those who do not consider Jesus precious at all. The *builders*, the religious leaders and teachers of the Jews who should have gladly worked with God in the building of His temple, rejected the Stone He had provided for its foundation. Their rejection did not stop His building, however; it merely kept them, and those who followed in their disobedience, out of God's temple.

8. And a stone of stumbling, and a rock of offense, even to them which stumble at the word, being disobedient: whereunto also they were appointed.

Peter now quotes Isaiah 8:14. Isaiah called for Israel to sanctify the Lord in their hearts, to trust in Him. If they would do that, He would be their sanctuary, their refuge, from their enemies. Those who refused to obey would find Him to be a rock over which they would stumble and fall, and thus become prey to their enemies. Jesus is an obstacle in the way of those who are disobedient. When they hear His word preached or taught, they stumble. Instead of being led into His kingdom, they fall to their destruction.

Whereunto also they were appointed. They were not appointed to be disobedient. But those who choose to disobey and reject Christ are *appointed* to stumble over Him, and to be defeated.

III. Called to Be a People (1 Peter 2:9, 10)

A. A Chosen People (v. 9a)

9a. But ye are a chosen generation, a royal priesthood, a holy nation, a peculiar people.

The emphasis changes from the disobedient to the obedient. Four descriptive phrases are used to show the blessings and responsibilities that are ours as Christians.

A chosen generation, "chosen race," or "an elect race." The word *chosen* was translated as "elect" in verse 6. We are among the chosen of God because we have elected to become obedient children of the Heavenly Father.

The word *generation* is often given as "family," or people who are related physically. Christ is our older brother, and we have a common Father. It is imperative that we work to maintain the unity of the family (Ephesians 4:3, 4).

Royal priesthood. In verse 5 we are called "a holy priesthood." Here we are further described as *royal.* This word means kingly, or pertaining to the king. We see this same combination of

PRIORITIES
FOR GOD'S PEOPLE

1 DISCARD SIN..

2 DESIRE THE WORD..

3 DELIGHT IN THE LORD..

visual 10

roles in Revelation 1:6 and 5:10. As God's children we are members of the royal family. The priestly duties of offering sacrifices has been mentioned in verse 5.

Holy nation. Just as Israel was to be separated from the heathen to serve God (see Exodus 19:6), Christians, who come from many nations, are one nation under one King and are His obedient servants.

Peculiar people. The word *peculiar* has had a drastic change in meaning since the *King James Version* was written. Literally this says "a people for possession"; therefore, it means that which belongs to God in a special way.

B. A Challenged People (v. 9b)

9b. That ye should show forth the praises of him who hath called you out of darkness into his marvelous light.

The role of the believer is not to bask in the *marvelous light*, but to *show forth the praises* of God at every opportunity. Offering praise to God is one of the spiritual sacrifices we make to God (v. 5). Indeed, how can we not praise Him? We were in the darkness of sin and death, and He has brought us to salvation and eternal life!

C. A Changed People (v. 10)

10. Which in time past were not a people, but are now the people of God: which had not obtained mercy, but now have obtained mercy.

The people to whom Peter first wrote, and Christians of every generation since, were from scattered and distinct tribes and nations, having no bond of unity. We were *not a people.* But now, all who are in Christ are *the people of God*, a distinct group, a separated, holy nation. When we were lost in sin, we received God's mercy, and now we have the promise of eternal life.

Home Daily Bible Readings

Monday, Apr. 27—The Corner Stone (Psalm 118:19-23)
Tuesday, Apr. 28—Grow Up to Salvation (1 Peter 2:1-5)
Wednesday, Apr. 29—A Holy People (Deuteronomy 7:6-11)
Thursday, Apr. 30—Love and Bear Fruit (John 15:12-17)
Friday, May 1—Consider Your Call (1 Corinthians 1:26-31)
Saturday, May 2—God Chose Us (Ephesians 1:3-10)
Sunday, May 3—A Royal Priesthood (1 Peter 2:9-12)

FROM DARKNESS TO LIGHT

Phillip Bliss, the marvelous nineteenth-century hymnist, died before he reached the age of forty. He penned such favorites as, "Wonderful Words of Life," "I Will Sing of My Redeemer," "Let the Lower Lights Be Burning," "More Holiness Give Me," and, "Almost Persuaded." He also wrote the hymn, "The Light of the World Is Jesus." Its message of the power of conversion is especially moving to the believer. The first stanza proclaims,

> The whole world was lost in the darkness of sin;
> The Light of the world is Jesus;
> Like sunshine at noonday His glory shone in,
> The Light of the world is Jesus.
> Come to the Light, 'tis shining for thee;
> Sweetly the Light has dawned upon me;
> Once I was blind, but now I can see;
> The Light of the world is Jesus.

Peter makes a striking analysis in today's lesson text. He says that we have been called "out of darkness into [God's] marvelous light." Blinded by the pitch blackness of sin, we who were helpless were illuminated with glory through the power of Christ. May we ever remember that, save for God's marvelous grace, we are nothing at all. But may we never forget that through Christ, we are God's chosen people and heirs of His kingdom.　　　　　　　—T. T.

Conclusion

A. People With a Purpose

God has called us to be His people—a people whose purpose is to serve Him and to show forth His praises to all persons. There is a work to be done, a message to be proclaimed, a church to be built. In response to God's mercy, which we have received, let us give our lives in daily service to Him. In that way, we will show ourselves to be "living stones" in His spiritual house.

B. Prayer

Thank You, Father, for the privilege of being adopted by You as Your special people! We desire to show our gratitude by the way we live—by growing in our commitment and service to You every day. Please help us to do this. We pray in Jesus' name. Amen.

C. Thought to Remember

Our purpose must agree with God's purpose for us: to be "a people that are his very own, eager to do what is good" (Titus 2:14, *New International Version*).

Learning by Doing

This page contains an alternate lesson plan emphasizing learning activities. Classes desiring such student involvement will find these suggestions helpful.

Learning Goals

This lesson should help students:

1. State a plan for spending more time studying the Bible.

2. List some of the "spiritual sacrifices" that Christians are to offer to God.

3. Express a commitment to share the good news of Christ with one other person in this week.

Into the Lesson

As students arrive, ask them to think of activities that require special clothing. For example, those running a race need light, loose-fitting clothes and shoes with a cushioned sole and good arch support. Ask them to list as many activities as they can think of.

When everyone has had a chance to think about the assignment, ask for volunteers to share some of their ideas. As they do, make a list on the chalkboard. Point out that those persons engaging in any of these activities would need to rid themselves (even if just temporarily) of the clothes they were wearing and put on the clothing noted on your list. This is exactly the metaphor Peter uses in the opening verse of the text when he says, "Rid yourselves of all malice and all deceit, hypocrisy, envy, and slander" (1 Peter 2:1, *New International Version*). Just as our dress clothing is inappropriate for a footrace, so these attitudes are inappropriate for the Christian life.

Into the Word

Read the Scripture text aloud. Then provide dictionaries and ask several students to look up the definitions of the following terms: *malice, guile, hypocrisy, envy,* and *slander.* Write the definitions on the chalkboard. Add to these the comments from this commentary.

Note the change of metaphor—from clothing to nutrition. Ask the students to compare verses 2 and 3 with 1 Corinthians 3:1, 2 and to suggest some reasons for the difference in Peter's and Paul's use of the metaphor "milk." Note that Paul is criticizing the Corinthians for their lack of *development* in Christian attitudes and conduct. But Peter is emphasizing our *desire* for the Word. He is saying that our desire for spiritual nourishment should be as strong as a baby's desire for milk.

Observe that the major portion of the text is a development of a third metaphor: that of a building. Even so, the metaphor is mixed, alternating between the picture of the building (a temple) and its occupants (the priests) and their duties (offering sacrifices). Ask the class to consider the following questions:

1. Who is the living stone and who are the living stones? What is the significance of the similarity of these designations?

2. What is the "spiritual house" described here, and how is it "built up"? What does this concept suggest in terms of Christian unity?

3. How should Christians uphold the duties of a "holy priesthood"? What "spiritual sacrifices" should we be offering, and how? (See Romans 12:1; Philippians 4:18; Hebrews 13:15, 16.)

4. What is the significance of describing Jesus as the "cornerstone," and a "stumbling stone"?

5. What is the significance of describing Christians as a "chosen generation," a "royal priesthood," a "holy nation," and a "peculiar people"?

Into Life

Question 5 suggests that Christians have a purpose, and therefore a responsibility to act. Three areas of responsibility are suggested by the text: Bible study (desiring spiritual milk), Christian worship and service (the offering of "spiritual sacrifices"), and sharing our faith (declaring the praises of Him who called us). The sacrifices were noted earlier, so spend your remaining time on Bible study and sharing the gospel.

Ask several people who are known for their familiarity with the Bible to come to class and share how they find or make the time to study the Bible. Encourage your students to write down any suggestions given that would help them to implement a daily Bible study program.

Ask the class to think of people they know who need the Lord. Then, instead of focusing on the differences between these people's values and Christian values, ask the students to focus on things they have in common with these persons that might open a door to sharing their faith with them. Ask each student to think of one person with whom he can share his faith in the coming week.

Let's Talk It Over

The questions on this page are designed to encourage review of the lesson Scriptures and to promote discussion of the lesson by the class. The answers provided are only discussion starters. Let your class talk it over from there.

1. Since an eager desire for the nourishment of God's Word is essential for a Christian's spiritual growth, how can we grow in God's Word, and in what ways can we encourage one another daily to long for "the sincere milk of the word"?

Cultivating a daily Bible reading program, undertaking a Scripture memory cycle, developing a habit of Scripture meditation, and engaging in a regular personal Bible study time will contribute to feeding our spirits with the Word of God. Apart from regular, systematic Bible reading, meditation, and study, it is unlikely that much spiritual growth will occur in our lives. By sharing with other Christians the truths we are learning from God's Word, we can exhort them in their daily walk with God through His Word. Moreover, we can incorporate teachings of the Scriptures into all areas of our lives, using God's Word as the basis of our discussions, counsel, and teaching in both formal and informal times with members of God's family (Deuteronomy 6:6-9).

2. No one in Christ is in isolation because, as living stones, we are all being built collectively into the spiritual house of God. What does this image of a "spiritual house" suggest about how we should see ourselves, other Christians, and the church?

Each of us is an important part in God's design for His church, and each has a role that contributes to the accomplishment of God's purpose for the church. We dare not minimize the part that we and others play in the functioning of God's work on earth. Moreover, we must be careful to avoid thinking that we can get along without the contribution of others, because God's Spirit has empowered their lives and ministries, as well as ours. The church, therefore, is a unit that is built by God's Spirit from the many who have been saved by God's grace. (See 1 Corinthians 12:12-27 and Romans 12:3-8.)

3. We who believe that Jesus is the cornerstone for our lives have the promise that our faith shall not bring us shame, disappointment, or disquiet. How does the trustworthiness of our "Cornerstone" help us face the struggles

and issues that come at different stages in our lives?

At different times in our lives, many of us will wrestle with low self-esteem or with feelings of rejection and hurt. How comforting it is to know that we can trust God to always see us with eyes of compassion, unconditional love, and acceptance! At other times, we will face uncertainty and the unfamiliar. The reassurance of the promises of a God who can be trusted to keep His word provides for us the stability and strength to persevere in those moments of testing.

4. Peter states that we who are in Christ are "a chosen people, a royal priesthood, a holy nation, a people belonging to God" (1 Peter 2:9, *New International Version*). What do these unique designations suggest about our relationship with God and with other Christians?

They indicate that Christians are a people set apart for God's own glory and service. We belong to Him, which means that all other allegiances to self, family, friends, job, and country must be submitted to God's sovereign lordship. As a result, His honor and holiness must be our top priority. Moreover, other Christians should be viewed as sharing the same calling, purpose, and allegiance. We should treat each other as royalty, showing love for one another and maintaining the unity of Christ's church.

5. Each disciple is to use every opportunity to proclaim the message of salvation to an unbelieving world. What are some specific ways that we can declare God's praises to our generation?

God is most highly honored when we live changed lives before everyone. The sincerity of a transformed life is a convincing testimony to the power of the gospel. In addition, God's goodness and love for humankind are magnified when others who are lost in sin see the transformation that the gospel can make in a person's life. Moreover, we should actively share the gospel of Christ with those we meet so that they too may become God's people and join in praising Him. Many persons around us are open to hearing the message of the Savior if we will only approach them sensitively and intelligently.

Witness in the Midst of Suffering

LESSON SCRIPTURE: 1 Peter 3:13—4:11.

PRINTED TEXT: 1 Peter 3:13-18; 4:1, 2, 7-11.

1 Peter 3:13-18

13 And who is he that will harm you, if ye be followers of that which is good?

14 But and if ye suffer for righteousness' sake, happy are ye: and be not afraid of their terror, neither be troubled;

15 But sanctify the Lord God in your hearts: and be ready always to give an answer to every man that asketh you a reason of the hope that is in you, with meekness and fear:

16 Having a good conscience; that, whereas they speak evil of you, as of evildoers, they may be ashamed that falsely accuse your good conversation in Christ.

17 For it is better, if the will of God be so, that ye suffer for well doing, than for evil doing.

18 For Christ also hath once suffered for sins, the just for the unjust, that he might bring us to God, being put to death in the flesh, but quickened by the Spirit.

1 Peter 4:1, 2, 7-11

1 Forasmuch then as Christ hath suffered for us in the flesh, arm yourselves likewise with the same mind: for he that hath suffered in the flesh hath ceased from sin;

2 That he no longer should live the rest of his time in the flesh to the lusts of men, but to the will of God.

. . . .

7 But the end of all things is at hand: be ye therefore sober, and watch unto prayer.

8 And above all things have fervent charity among yourselves: for charity shall cover the multitude of sins.

9 Use hospitality one to another without grudging.

10 As every man hath received the gift, even so minister the same one to another, as good stewards of the manifold grace of God.

11 If any man speak, let him speak as the oracles of God; if any man minister, let him do it as of the ability which God giveth; that God in all things may be glorified through Jesus Christ: to whom be praise and dominion for ever and ever. Amen.

GOLDEN TEXT: It is better, if the will of God be so, that ye suffer for well doing, than for evildoing.—1 Peter 3:17.

God's People in the World
(Lessons 9-14)

Lesson Aims

As a result of studying this lesson the students should be able to:

1. Understand the place of suffering in the Christian life.

2. Give an answer to those who ask for an account of the hope that is within them.

3. Bear witness not only by what they give up but also by how they live.

Lesson Outline

Visual 11 of the visuals packet highlights an important teaching in the lesson text. The visual is shown on page 311.

Introduction

A. Through Much Tribulation

A fellow traveler on a Holy Lands tour spent much time rehearsing the many "crosses" she had to bear—declining health, an ungrateful child, nasty neighbors. The pilgrimage we were on somehow added significance to what she saw as her suffering for the Lord. But not all of our suffering is a result of our righteousness. Some suffering may result from our bad temper or our uncooperativeness or our judgmental spirit.

Another acquaintance was fond of thanking God that we, unlike believers in some places, did not have to suffer because of our faith. It always made me wonder if our lack of suffering was due to the blessing of God or to our failure to live authentic, active Christian lives.

The fact is that many Christians are persecuted for righteousness' sake even today. The persecution may range from imprisonment and death in a totalitarian country that refuses the free expression of religion, to the mockery and ostracism directed at a child who refuses to participate in some ungodly activity. Suffering for the faith is more a part of the modern Christian experience than we know, or care to admit.

It always has been. When, on his first journey, Paul revisited the churches he had founded earlier, he not only encouraged them to remain firm in faith, but he also warned them "that we must through much tribulation enter into the kingdom of God" (Acts 14:22). Suffering is an almost inevitable part of the Christian witness. Our task is to understand its place in our lives.

B. Lesson Background

As our lesson text implies, the Christians of Asia Minor, who first received Peter's letter, were facing persecution. Peter himself was no stranger to persecution, and he gave them and Christians of all generations instructions for facing it. Only a tree with a good root system and mature growth can withstand a storm. Our root system is the Lord Jesus Christ, the firm foundation on which our lives must be built. And the mature growth is the life of sanctification to which we have been called: "Be ye holy; for I am holy" (1:16). After advising specific groups within the church, Peter returns to these topics—the suffering Christians must face, the Lord they must serve, and the life they must lead.

I. Ready With A Reason
(1 Peter 3:13-18)
A. Suffering for Righteousness
(vv. 13, 14)

Our lesson title, "Witness in the Midst of Suffering," suggests that tribulations may come to Christians. If it does, we are to view it as an opportunity to bear witness of our faith and hope in Christ. The key word of our title is *witness* even more than *suffering*.

13. And who is he that will harm you, if ye be followers of that which is good?

We who are Christians should not assume that persecution is constant or inevitable. If we are *followers of that which is good*, that is, if we are zealous to live morally upright lives, people, especially authorities, are not likely to harm us. After Pentecost the church in Jerusalem had "favor with all the people" (Acts 2:47). This very letter asserts that God has ordained governing authorities "for the punishment of evildoers, and for the praise of them that do well" (1 Peter 2:14). On the other hand, persecution is always possible. The more the early church witnessed the more it was persecuted. Peter may also be reminding us that if we are right with God no *ultimate* harm will come to us. "If God be for us, who can be against us?" (Romans 8:31).

14. But and if ye suffer for righteousness' sake, happy are ye: and be not afraid of their terror, neither be troubled.

Zeal for what is right usually brings favor not harm. But suffering does come to Christians, and when it does it has a unique cause and a unique outcome. Much suffering in the world is due to unrighteousness, but the Christian often suffers precisely for doing what is right and saying what is true. Most suffering in the world results in sorrow, but suffering for righteousness' sake results in happiness, just as Jesus promised (Matthew 5:10-12). This happiness is not giddiness or silliness, but a serious yet joyful blessedness based on trust in God. *Be not afraid* does not imply that no harm will ever come, but that the Christian's focus is on the victory of God, not any human threat (see Isaiah 8:12, 13). *Neither be troubled* suggests that the Christian possesses a confidence that produces calm even in the midst of crisis.

B. Sanctifying Christ as Lord (v. 15)

15. But sanctify the Lord God in your hearts: and be ready always to give an answer to every man that asketh you a reason of the hope that is in you, with meekness and fear.

According to the oldest and most accurate manuscripts, this verse begins, "Sanctify Christ as Lord in your hearts." This is the confidence that casts out fear: Christ is the Lord, the almighty one who has all authority and is over all other authorities. By setting Him apart in their hearts, by giving Him first place, Christians set aside their fear. This also is the basis of the confidence that allows them to speak out boldly when their faith is challenged. Thus persecution provides the Christian the opportunity to testify for Christ, to give a testimony of hope to a hopeless world. The Christian's hope is meaningful life in the present as well as eternal life in the future. Christians should be ready and willing to explain the reasons for their hope. As they do, however, their attitude must be that of *meekness* (gentleness, strength under control) and *fear* (respect both for God and for their accusers).

A REASON

One of the strongest reasons for my belief in God is that I find it much more preferable than its alternative. Even apart from God's revelation of himself, which He has given us in His Word, it seems to me that His revelation in nature—in the world's existence— is adequate to convince a reasonable person that He must exist.

If there is no God, then how did all of this happen? And beyond that question looms the monumental one, Why did it occur at all? If there is no God to give ears, why did hearing come to be? If there is no God to give eyes, why did sight ever develop? And if there is no God, and life forms began developing and multiplying because of the separation of cells, why did sexuality develop? And why did reproduction begin to depend on sexual contact? Isn't such a development a regression instead of a progression, complicating rather than simplifying the continuance of a species?

If God did not create matter, then matter itself is eternal, and for some unexplained reason it acts as though it is being controlled by intelligence.

Yes, I believe in God because it is impossible for me not to believe. The alternative stretches faith all out of shape and turns it into a grotesque credulity.   —T. T.

C. Keeping a Clear Conscience (vv. 16, 17)

16. Having a good conscience; that, whereas they speak evil of you, as of evildoers, they may be ashamed that falsely accuse your good conversation in Christ.

When Christians are persecuted and falsely spoken against, their response to their persecutors must come from *a good conscience*. Their motive must not be to vindicate themselves. Rather, it must be to honor Christ and uphold that which is good; to share the truth, not to shame the accuser. The accuser's shame will be the natural result of a false, baseless accusation. And the accusation will be shown to be baseless when it is known that the Christian's behavior is above reproach. As Peter will emphasize in the verses below, the clearest testimony to the truth that a Christian speaks is the consistency of his or her life. When Peter says *good conversation*, he means not only the way we talk but our whole way of life, our life-style, oriented around the lordship of Christ.

17. For it is better, if the will of God be so, that ye suffer for well doing, than for evil doing.

Once again Peter suggests that persecution is not the lot of all Christians—"if perchance God wills it." But again Peter makes it clear that Christians may indeed suffer in this life. If suffering comes, he says, let it be for good deeds that can be justified with a good conscience, and not for evil deeds that merit punishment. Some people take this and others passages to mean that God specifically wills suffering and persecution for some people. It seems more consistent with the nature of God revealed in Christ to say that God *permits* suffering to come. To ask why He does is to raise a question that He alone can answer. Earlier, however, Peter indicated that if a person endures unjust suffering for conscience toward God, it is acceptable with God (1 Peter 2:19, 20).

D. Sanctified by Christ (v. 18)

18. For Christ also hath once suffered for sins, the just for the unjust, that he might bring us to God, being put to death in the flesh, but quickened by the Spirit.

The confidence of the Christian under persecution is based not only on the lordship of Christ but on the example of Christ. He too suffered. He too suffered for wrongs not His own. He too suffered for righteousness' sake. He too suffered death, as Peter and some Christians from Asia Minor would, and as some Christians do even today. But Christ was *quickened by the Spirit*, raised from the dead, vindicated by God. The victory of God in Christ is the victory of each Christian. If we share in Christ's sufferings, we will share in His glory (1 Peter 4:13). Christ who is our Lord and example is also our Savior. By His suffering, we have access to the very presence of God.

ALREADY DONE

Stephen Travis, in his book *The Jesus Hope*, gives an interesting twist to the Judgment Day. He pictures billions of people on a great plain before God's throne. Most of the people cringe in fear, but a few are belligerent, denying that God is qualified to judge them, inasmuch as He has not had the awful experiences that they had in life. Groups of such complainers can be seen all across the plain.

Representatives of the complaining groups then meet to prepare their case so they can present it to God. They come to the conclusion that the only way God can qualify to judge them is by becoming a man and enduring the same sort of things they endured. After that decision is spoken, there is a long silence; for at that moment the people realize that God has already met the requirement!

And indeed He has! God came into this world in the person of Christ, and in this world suffered all forms of injustice. Since Christ, the Just, suffered for us, the unjust, we can never complain that He doesn't understand.   —T. T.

II. Ceasing From Sin
(1 Peter 4:1, 2)

The manner in which Christians accept suffering on behalf of Christ bears witness to the Lord. Another powerful testimony for Christ is the life of the person who, though suffering persecution, has ceased from sin.

A. Armed in Your Mind (v. 1)

1. Forasmuch then as Christ hath suffered for us in the flesh, arm yourselves likewise with the same mind: for he that hath suffered in the flesh hath ceased from sin.

Peter exhorts his readers to arm themselves like soldiers of the faith. The Christian's armor is to be the attitude that Christ had in His suffering. He suffered, but not for His own sin. He was reviled, but did not revile in return. Through it all He resolved to do God's will. *He that hath suffered in the flesh* refers to the Christian who by suffering for righteousness' sake shows that he or she has *ceased from sin*, that is, has rejected a life of sin. Peter does not mean that suffering Christians never do and never will sin. Rather, the believers' incorporation into Christ means they are no longer slaves to sin (Romans 6:6, 7).

B. Living in God's Will (v. 2)

2. That he no longer should live the rest of his time in the flesh to the lusts of men, but to the will of God.

As beneficiaries of and sharers in the sufferings of Christ, Christians have a new purpose for their lives. Human desires are no longer the focus; doing the will of God is.

Bold testimony for Christ in times of persecution is powerful testimony. So too is the changed life. The world notices when a person has ceased from sin, for there is an obvious change in one's habits, attitudes, and relationships. More is involved in a Christian's testimony for Christ, but an important part of that testimony is the Christian's refusal to use the time allotted to him or her in gratifying the lusts of the flesh.

A CALL TO SENIOR CITIZENS

Peter says that a Christian is done with sin, and adds, "As a result, he does not live the rest of his earthly life for evil human desires, but rather for the will of God" (1 Peter 4:2, *New International Version*).

There seems to be a growing feeling that when one reaches the age of retirement, one's obligations to the Lord have all been fulfilled, that the latter days of life are exempt from the requirement of being lived "for the will of God."

How unfortunate that such an attitude should prevail among Christians at a time when a bumper crop has developed in the Lord's vineyard! And if you doubt that, just ask one of your church's leaders for a list of service opportunities. You will be amazed!

One area in which retirees could have a significant impact in the work of the Lord is on the mission field. Service there could turn one's sunset years into high-noon years of productivity. Two of the more serious concerns of young mission families as they leave the home shores are the lack of funds and the well-being of their children. Many senior citizens are not troubled by either of these concerns. Retirement checks can be sent anywhere in the world, and the children of most retirees are grown and live independent lives.

Christian senior, think about it. God may be calling you to new service through this Sunday-school lesson.   —T. T.

III. Living in Love
(1 Peter 4:7-11)

Witnessing to the world is perhaps never more powerful than during persecution. And "ceasing from sin" is a dramatic demonstration of the effect of the saving death and victorious resurrection of Christ. Peter now emphasizes three traits that should characterize the lives of Christians, especially in difficult times.

A. Sober in Prayer (v. 7)

7. But the end of all things is at hand: be ye therefore sober, and watch unto prayer.

The Christians of Asia Minor were very aware of the threat of persecution, but Peter, in the most serious of tones, urged them to be faithful to Christ. Why? Because the *end of all things is at hand,* or, is near. This is a reference to the return of Christ, the day that will usher in eternity. Peter was not speaking in chronological terms, as if Christ would surely return in the next year or two from the time when this letter was written. He meant that the last days, the final dispensation of God's dealing with mankind, had begun. In God's plan, nothing stands between us and Christ's return. In a sense, this final dispensation began when Jesus came preaching the kingdom of God; it had certainly begun by Pentecost. All Christians live in the last days, under the motivation and assurance of Christ's return.

In difficult situations, Christians should be characterized by prayer, constant, conscientious communication with God. To face a fearful present and an unseen future with prayer, Christians must be sober and watchful. The word translated *sober* means sound-minded, having their wits about them. The word *watch* literally means *sober,* but here refers to self-control. A mind settled and certain and a life under control are essential for prayer during unsettling times of trial.

B. Loving Towards Others (vv. 8, 9)

8. And above all things have fervent charity among yourselves: for charity shall cover the multitude of sins.

A life that witnesses to Christ and stays stable in crisis is characterized not only by a close relationship with God but also with others. When our lesson text speaks of *fervent charity* it means unfailing love, the self-sacrificing love that God demonstrated in Christ, the earnest love that Christ showed to foe and friend alike. Christians are to love each other in this manner. Peter's statement that *charity shall cover the multitude of sins,* or better, "love covers a multitude of sins," does not mean that our acts of love atone for our sins. Only the love of God in Christ does that. It means that our love for others allows us to look upon the offenses of others, even our persecutors, as God looks upon our offenses—with grace and forgiveness.

9. Use hospitality one to another without grudging.

One evidence of self-sacrificing love is hospitality, literally, love for strangers. Love is at its best when shown to others who are truly "other," with other perspectives, other backgrounds, from other places, and of other races. Hospitality is an action that can include shared homes, shared food, or shared time. But it is also an attitude. *Grudging* means murmuring or grumbling. Like love, hospitality is based not on compulsion, but on consent.

THE FOCUS OF FAITH IS NOT ON TROUBLE BUT ON **TRIUMPH**

visual 11

C. Serving to God's Glory (vv. 10, 11)

10. As every man hath received the gift, even so minister the same one to another, as good stewards of the manifold grace of God.
The third characteristic of Christians, which sees them through suffering all the way to the second coming, is service. Each Christian is gifted. But spiritual gifts are not ends in themselves, ornaments to be placed on our walls and admired. They are to be used in service to others. The analogy of a steward is helpful. A steward oversaw his master's household or fields or business. The master was the owner, but the steward was responsible for the wise and productive use of all that the master had entrusted to him. So Christians have been entrusted with the multifaceted expressions of God's grace, and we are to use these gifts for the benefit of others.

11. If any man speak, let him speak as the oracles of God; if any man minister, let him do it as of the ability which God giveth; that God in all things may be glorified through Jesus Christ: to whom be praise and dominion for ever and ever. Amen.
If any man speak, let him speak as the oracles of God. Peter has in mind Christian teaching, whether done publicly or in private. The Christian teacher is to speak as one completely yielded to God's Spirit, delivering God's message. The teacher is not to seek praise for himself, but is to glorify God. Likewise, a person who has received a gift must recognize God as its source and use it for the good of others as God intended. Sacrificial service to others is yet another way in which devoted Christians bear witness to the glory of their God and His Christ.

Conclusion

A. Living Martyrs

When the early Christian leader Ignatius was on his way to Rome to be martyred, he wrote several letters to fellow Christians. One of these letters begs the believers not to attempt to rescue him or otherwise thwart his execution. Ignatius believed that his martyrdom was the best way to proclaim his Lord and to assure his salvation. Indeed, the brave men and women of the church's early years, who died rather than renounce their faith, are stirring testimony to the gospel. It was not uncommon for the guards of condemned Christians to confess Christ and join them in the arena when they observed the depth of commitment in their suffering for righteousness' sake. And the notion that martyrdom assured one's salvation was so widespread that Christians were known to seek out their ac-

cusers in hopes of this glorious end. But what Ignatius and other early Christians may not have realized in their zeal for martyrdom is that a life given over to God may be as effective as a life given up for God. The Greek word from which the English *martyr* is derived means simply a witness, one who testifies from what he or she has seen or experienced. The testimony those early Christians bore was seen in their changed lives and loyalties. They no longer lived to satisfy the lusts of the flesh, but to fulfill the will of God; and this is what led to their deaths. The pages of church history are illuminated by the red ink of those who died for their faith, but they are written in the bold, black ink of those who lived for their faith.

Our witness may include suffering; it certainly does for many committed Christians in many parts of the world even today. But each one of us has the ever-present opportunity to witness through our changed lives—the putting on of the robes of righteousness in prayer and love and service.

B. Let Us Pray

Sovereign God, we know that nothing—neither life, nor death, nor angels, nor principalities, nor things present, nor things to come, nor powers, nor height, nor depth, nor anything else in all creation, will be able to separate us from Your love in Christ Jesus our Lord. Help us to live and witness in the confidence and conviction of Your love. We ask in Jesus' name. Amen.

C. Thought to Remember

"But rejoice, inasmuch as ye are partakers of Christ's sufferings; that, when his glory shall be revealed, ye may be glad also with exceeding joy" (1 Peter 4:13).

Home Daily Bible Readings

Monday, May 4—To Live Is Christ (Philippians 1:15-21)
Tuesday, May 5—Be Prepared (1 Peter 3:13-18)
Wednesday, May 6—Witness by Abstaining From Evil (1 Peter 4:1-6)
Thursday, May 7—In Everything Glorify God (1 Peter 4:7-11)
Friday, May 8—Judgment to Begin (1 Peter 4:12-19)
Saturday, May 9—The Spirit Strengthens Us (Romans 8:18-25)
Sunday, May 10—God Comforts Us in Our Afflictions (2 Corinthians 2:1-11)

Learning by Doing

This page contains an alternate lesson plan emphasizing learning activities. Classes desiring such student involvement will find these suggestions helpful.

Learning Goals

After this lesson the students should:

1. Be able to explain how suffering can have a positive effect in the life of a Christian.

2. Express a commitment to use their spiritual gift(s) to serve others and to glorify God.

Into the Lesson

Write these statements on the chalkboard:

1. All Christians will suffer for their faith.

2. Some, perhaps even most, Christians will suffer for their faith.

3. Few Christians today should ever have to suffer for their faith.

As the students arrive, give each a slip of paper. Ask each to choose which statement best expresses his or her opinion and to write the corresponding number on the paper. Encourage them to discuss their ideas with other students as the class assembles.

After a while, read 1 Peter 4:12-19 aloud. Point out that Peter tells us suffering is not something strange for the Christian—at least in his day. We may feel that things are different today. Certainly, we who live in a free country do not experience the kinds of suffering the early Christians did. Perhaps our suffering is more subtle than outright persecution. And what of the world as a whole—what do Christians in oppressive countries face? Suffering remains nothing strange for the Christian.

Into the Word

Read 1 Peter 3:13-18 aloud. Focus on verse 15 and observe that this was written to Christians, people who had already accepted and confessed Jesus as Lord. Discuss what Peter meant when he said, "In your hearts set apart Christ as Lord" (v. 15, *New International Version*). Is this a one-time action or something that must be done continually?

After brief discussion, ask, "What evidence can be seen in one's life that indicates that Christ is set apart in that person's heart?" List these characteristics on the chalkboard.

Divide the class into three sections. Ask each section to examine one of the following parts of the text for today and list positive results of suffering for the faith: 1 Peter 3:13-18; 4:1, 2; 4:7-11. Have the students work in small groups (by section). Allow five or ten minutes for this and then ask the groups to share their results. Take the first section first; then ask for a reader to read aloud each of the two remaining sections of the text before hearing reports on them. List on the chalkboard these positive results of suffering for the faith. Add clarification as necessary.

Observe that chapter 4 has a strong emphasis on action. Ask the class to note the things Peter says we should do in order to "live . . . for the will of God" (1 Peter 4:2, *New International Version*). List them on the chalkboard. As the list is completed, note verse 10 and its insistence on using one's "gift" for ministry. Discuss the concept of spiritual gifts: Does everyone have one or more? What is the purpose of these gifts? How does one determine what gift or gifts he has? (See Romans 12:1-8; 1 Corinthians 12:1-12; and Ephesians 4:7-16.)

Into Life

By this time, you will have several lists on your chalkboard: one list of characteristics of a "set apart" life, three lists of beneficial results of suffering, and a list of actions or ministries that typify living for the will of God. Review these lists and ask, "How can Christians make these realities in their lives?"

Have a poster prepared before class for display at this time. Under the heading "Christians should," have these statements listed:

1. Set apart Christ as Lord of their lives.

2. Determine to live for the will of God and use their spiritual gifts to serve others.

3. Endure suffering as it comes, knowing it is temporary and can even be beneficial.

Give each student a piece of paper and ask them to do the following:

1. Write your confession of Jesus as Lord. Include in this a commitment of one area of your life that seems most rebellious against His lordship (for example, some habit you want to break but still have problems with).

2. Identify a spiritual gift that you believe you possess. Write one or two ways you can express this gift in a ministry that will glorify God and meet the needs of people around you.

3. Specify the type of "suffering" you most often encounter. Write a plan for dealing with this suffering so you can demonstrate Christian endurance and grow spiritually from the experience.

Let's Talk It Over

The questions on this page are designed to encourage review of the lesson Scriptures and to promote discussion of the lesson by the class. The answers provided are only discussion starters. Let your class talk it over from there.

1. Although people usually are not harmed for doing good, suffering for righteousness is, as the lesson writer notes, "an almost inevitable part of the Christian witness." When we are faced with stresses in life for what we believe is right, how can we maintain attitudes and behaviors that honor God?

Too many Christians succumb to people-pleasing when stresses mount because they judge situations in a worldly manner and fear those who are opposed to God. Instead, we need to respond to suffering with a commitment to please God and to fear Him more than men. God will be honored through us if we show kindness to our enemies, guard our words, fight feelings of revenge, and withhold any retaliation (see Romans 12:17-21).

2. In the midst of suffering for our witness for God, we are to set apart Christ as Lord in our hearts. What does that mean and how can we do it?

By accepting Christ's authority in all areas of our lives, trusting His sovereignty over any situation, and worshiping Him alone, we live in daily communion with Christ as Lord and maintain a reverence for Him. His lordship over our lives will be evident as our thoughts dwell on that which is true, honorable, just, pure, lovely, and of good report (Philippians 4:8), as our values and priorities reflect those of Christ (John 4:34), and as our activities and work bring glory to God (Colossians 3:17).

3. Christians are always to be prepared to give a testimony of their faith. What can we do to be ready in the ordinary conversations of life to explain our faith in an informal and spontaneous manner?

Many Christians feel ill-prepared to share their faith in Christ because (1) they do not know what they believe, or (2) they feel that a theological defense of the gospel is necessary, or (3) they think religious beliefs can be kept separate from secular life. In response to the first of these, we should prepare ourselves by regular study of God's Word, especially the life of Jesus, so that we do know what we believe. Regarding the second, we should understand that we do not need to be Biblical scholars to witness to the

changes that the gospel of Christ has brought about in our lives. A transformed life, which includes new motives, new goals, and new sources of satisfaction and joy, speaks volumes to an unbeliever who is searching for meaning and purpose in life. Finally, we need to recognize that our faith in Christ was meant to be an integral part of our everyday lives, having a direct bearing on our attitudes, speech, and conduct. A sensitivity to those around us will open up many doors for the sharing of our faith.

4. What can we do to keep a clear conscience in our witness for Christ?

God judges a person's motives, so we need to regularly evaluate our reasons for what we say and do as we witness for Christ. Christians cannot be justified if they "preach" at people, insult them, or attack their values and beliefs. Instead, a clear conscience is maintained by having a humble spirit when speaking for Christ and by showing due respect and deference toward others whose beliefs differ from ours. The spirit in which our witness is made may have a greater effect on some people than what we say. A proper spirit will insure a clear conscience in ourselves and will attract a more receptive audience to our message.

5. How does the example of Christ's life give us encouragement in times of trials and suffering?

What an encouragement it is to know that "we do not have a high priest who is unable to sympathize with our weaknesses, but we have one who has been tempted in every way, just as we are—yet was without sin"! (Hebrews 4:15, *New International Version*). All of the sufferings and pain that Jesus endured were undeserved, yet He never demanded that justice be served or that His rights be granted. His attitude was one of wholehearted devotion to God and submission to His will in any and every circumstance. Jesus placed himself in God's hands, trusting the Father to work everything out for the accomplishing of His eternal purpose (1 Peter 2:23). Moreover, Christ's example shows us the hope of receiving the blessings of God and final victory if we faithfully persevere through any unjust hardship.

Humble, Steadfast, Vigilant

LESSON SCRIPTURE: 1 Peter 5:1-11.

PRINTED TEXT: 1 Peter 5:1-11.

1 Peter 5:1-11

1 The elders which are among you I exhort, who am also an elder, and a witness of the sufferings of Christ, and also a partaker of the glory that shall be revealed:

2 Feed the flock of God which is among you, taking the oversight thereof, not by constraint, but willingly; not for filthy lucre, but of a ready mind;

3 Neither as being lords over God's heritage, but being ensamples to the flock.

4 And when the chief Shepherd shall appear, ye shall receive a crown of glory that fadeth not away.

5 Likewise, ye younger, submit yourselves unto the elder. Yea, all of you be subject one to another, and be clothed with humility: for God resisteth the proud, and giveth grace to the humble.

6 Humble yourselves therefore under the mighty hand of God, that he may exalt you in due time:

7 Casting all your care upon him; for he careth for you.

8 Be sober, be vigilant; because your adversary the devil, as a roaring lion, walketh about, seeking whom he may devour:

9 Whom resist steadfast in the faith, knowing that the same afflictions are accomplished in your brethren that are in the world.

10 But the God of all grace, who hath called us unto his eternal glory by Christ Jesus, after that ye have suffered a while, make you perfect, stablish, strengthen, settle you.

11 To him be glory and dominion for ever and ever. Amen.

GOLDEN TEXT: Humble yourselves therefore under the mighty hand of God, that he may exalt you in due time: casting all your care upon him; for he careth for you.
—1 Peter 5:6, 7.

God's People in the World
(Lessons 9-14)

Lesson Aims

As a result of studying this lesson the students should:

1. Have a better understanding of the type of leaders God intends the church to have.

2. Continue to develop the attributes of humility and watchfulness.

3. Understand their leading and following better in the light of trust in God.

Lesson Outline

INTRODUCTION
 A. Leading and Following
 B. Lesson Background
 I. THE WILLING SHEPHERDS (1 Peter 5:1-4)
 A. Peter, the Fellow Shepherd (v. 1)
 B. Plea for Shepherds (vv. 2, 3)
   Follow the Leader
 C. Promise for Shepherds (v. 4)
 II. THE HUMBLE FLOCK (1 Peter 5:5-9)
 A. Humble Toward One Another (v. 5)
 B. Humble Before God (vv. 6, 7)
 C. Sober and Watchful (v. 8)
 D. Standing Firm (v. 9)
 III. OUR MIGHTY GOD (1 Peter 5:10, 11)
 A. The Outcome of Our Trust (v. 10)
   Soft Eyes
 B. The Basis of Our Trust (v. 11)
CONCLUSION
 A. Cattle or Sheep
 B. Let Us Pray
 C. Thought to Remember

Display visual 12 of the visuals packet and refer to it in your discussion of humility. The visual is shown on page 319.

Introduction

A. Leading and Following

One day at recess Miss Marzulla insisted that the whole fourth-grade class, all thirty-two of us, play follow-the-leader. At first we all tried to keep an eye on the leader. But as the line stretched and snaked its way across the playground we soon realized that we needed to keep an eye on the person directly in front of us. We had to trust that when they hopped, they were following the person in front of them, and so on. I also realized something else: I was as much a

leader as a follower. Someone, everyone, behind me was depending on me to hop or skip or jump at the right time, just as I was depending on all those in front of me. In a sense, the game could be called lead-the-followers just as well as follow-the-leader.

In several ways, the Christian life is similar to the game of follow-the-leader/lead-the-followers. The participants stretch across the centuries and around the world. They must have humility—the willingness to follow their leaders—trusting that the leaders are following the Leader. Steadfastness is necessary also. The effort is weakened if anyone breaks the process of following/leading. And vigilance is required, too. By carefully watching the faithful example of those who go before, a person is better prepared to lead those who follow. Our lesson today calls us to develop and maintain those very virtues—humility, steadfastness, and vigilance. And it calls us to get in the line.

B. Lesson Background

In the verses that come between the text for last week's lesson and the text we are studying in this lesson, Peter reemphasizes several points. Christians are not to think it unnatural when they suffer for their faith in Christ, but are to rejoice instead, knowing that when Christ is revealed in all His glory they will share in His triumph. Peter cautions Christians, however, not to commit the kinds of offenses that rightfully bring punishment. Then he warns of the unspeakably terrible punishment that will come with God's final judgment. He urges all who suffer for Christ to commit their souls to God, to trust in His faithfulness, and to continue in well doing (1 Peter 4:12-19). Help in doing this is found in the verses that follow, as Peter gives instruction to church leaders.

I. The Willing Shepherds
(1 Peter 5:1-4)

Peter begins this passage with exhortations to the elders of the church. These men are spiritual leaders by virtue of maturity more than age, function more than office. In the early church each congregation included a number of spiritual leaders whose responsibility was to guide their fellow Christians. These verses are Peter's instructions to these leaders.

A. Peter, the Fellow Shepherd (v. 1)

1. The elders which are among you I exhort, who am also an elder, and a witness of the sufferings of Christ, and also a partaker of the glory that shall be revealed.

Peter first establishes his relationship with the elders he addresses. He is a fellow elder. He can call himself an apostle, but his own authority is not the issue. Peter sees himself in the crucial role of a fellow spiritual leader who also leads by following the Lord. He is a witness. Our text says *witness of the sufferings of Christ*. He observed what Jesus suffered, and he knows better than most the hostility the world can harbor for those who seek to do God's will. Peter also is a witness *to* the sufferings of Christ. His responsibility to bear witness to the saving death of Jesus is always uppermost in his mind. And he is *a partaker of the glory that shall be revealed* at the return of Christ. Peter has already suffered for his faith in Christ, and he knows that he may be called to further suffering; but he also knows that the flipside of suffering is eternal, indescribable glory.

B. Plea for Shepherds (vv. 2, 3)

2. Feed the flock of God which is among you, taking the oversight thereof, not by constraint, but willingly; not for filthy lucre, but of a ready mind.

Peter's exhortation here speaks to action and motive. The word translated *feed* actually refers to the broader activity of shepherding, tending a flock of sheep. It includes giving guidance and protection as well as nourishment. We are not surprised that Peter uses this imagery. In one of his last encounters with Jesus, Peter was admonished again and again to tend the Lord's sheep, to feed His flock (see John 21:15-17). Now he passes the mandate on to his fellow elders. *Taking the oversight thereof.* Overseeing God's flock is another responsibility of the elders of the church (see Acts 20:17, 28). The actions of tending and overseeing must be accompanied by proper attitudes. No one should be forced to be an elder, either by well-intentioned pressure from others or by the person's own guilt. Leadership must be based on one's willingness to lead, a willingness that flows from a sense of responsibility and an honest appraisal of one's own gifts. It must arise from free will, not force; from gifts, not guilt. Furthermore, no one should serve as an elder for monetary gain. *Filthy lucre* is better translated "shameful gain." The focus of the phrase is on the motive of the person, not the money itself. Elders in the early church evidently received some financial support in consideration of their leadership responsibilities, but it was not to be their motive for serving. *Of a ready mind.* This phrase is emphatic, having a stronger meaning than the word *willingly*. It means "earnest desire." An eagerness to serve by leading should characterize those who tend God's flock.

3. Neither as being lords over God's heritage, but being ensamples to the flock.

This verse continues the list of attitudes that the church's spiritual shepherds should possess, and it is based on the obvious but often overlooked fact that the flock belongs to the Owner, not the overseer. The warning against lording it over the flock also reechoes words Peter heard from the lips of Jesus himself. When the disciples James and John sought positions of authority in His kingdom, Jesus told the twelve that pagan rulers lorded it over their subjects, "but it shall not be so among you" (Matthew 20:20-28). The flock is *God's heritage*, which implies that the congregation has been entrusted by God into the care of their spiritual leaders. Thus the elders are not to be rulers but role models, *ensamples,* or examples, of Christian maturity. They are to be the kind of caring leaders who are carefully following Christ and conscious of being followed.

FOLLOW THE LEADER

At one point while advancing across Europe, General Patton's tired men came to a deep, icy river. They began to grumble that they weren't about to swim across the stiff, cold stream wearing backpacks. Patton didn't say a word. Wading into the water with his backpack, he swam across to the other side, turned around, looked at the men, and swam back. He then asked, "Men, are you ready to go?" Without another word of complaint every one of them jumped into the water and swam across.

The church needs such leaders. Peter exhorts the church's spiritual leaders to oversee the flock of God, not by lording their authority over them, but by directing them through example. Peter could testify to the example of the chief Shepherd himself, Jesus Christ, in this regard. For it was He who took a towel and basin and washed His disciples' feet.

Put bluntly, the church does not need dictators who rule with iron fists. It needs leaders who show the way by loving and humble service. Such leaders will not need to insist that others follow them; they will do so naturally.

—T. T.

C. Promise for Shepherds (v. 4)

4. And when the chief Shepherd shall appear, ye shall receive a crown of glory that fadeth not away.

In the game of follow-the-leader there is ultimately one leader, the one whom all the other leaders follow. Peter reminds his readers that there is a *chief Shepherd,* Jesus himself, the true leader, the pioneer on our journey of faith. Peter also borrows this insight from Jesus. Jesus spoke eloquently of himself as the "good shepherd," who exercised His power by protecting the flock and demonstrated His sovereignty by sacrificing himself for the flock (John 10:11-15). The *chief Shepherd* thus is the ultimate leader and the ultimate example of leadership. He has gone on before us and is waiting to give something to faithful leaders when they reach the end of their journey. It is a crown—a glorious crown because it shares His glory, an unfading crown because it partakes of eternity. The Greek word that is used here for *crown* is not the word for a king's crown. Rather, it is the word for a laurel wreath, such as was given to victors in public games and to military conquerors. Christian leaders who faithfully guide and guard the Lord's flock will be given a crown, not because they share Christ's reign but because they share His victory.

II. The Humble Flock
(1 Peter 5:5-9)

Peter now moves from specific instructions directed to the spiritual leaders to those pertaining to others in the church. The first word in verse 5, "Likewise," reminds us that like the teachings to the elders, these instructions come in the light of the persecution that the church was suffering and the hope of Christ's return in the future.

A. Humble Toward One Another (v. 5)

5. Likewise, ye younger, submit yourselves unto the elder. Yea, all of you be subject one to another, and be clothed with humility: for God resisteth the proud, and giveth grace to the humble.

Younger. It is uncertain who is meant by this term. Some would limit it to young men or to young male officers in the church, assistant ministers who helped the elders and apostles. Others feel that Peter was referring to all in the church who were not elders. Certainly the following admonitions are appropriate for all those under the lordship of Christ and the guidance of the elders, male or female, officers or not. Respect for spiritual leaders is the first admonition. It comes soon after Peter's warnings to the elders against tyrannical leadership (v. 3). Respect begets respect. When the *Authorized Version* says, *submit yourselves unto the elder,* it may give the false impression that one elder, a kind of ruling bishop, led early Christian congregations. But this practice was a later development in the history of the church. The Greek text actually has, "submit to the elders."

All of you be subject one to another. This thought is certainly consistent with Scriptural teaching.

Mutual submission is urged elsewhere (see Ephesians 5:21). But the word rendered *be subject* is omitted in the oldest manuscripts. If their reading is followed, the words *to one another* may be connected with the preceding clause, "submit yourselves unto the elder; yea, all of you, one to another" or with what follows, "Yea, all of you be clothed with humility one to another." *Be clothed* suggests the action of a slave putting on an apron for service and is reminiscent of Jesus' actions at the washing of the disciples' feet (see John 13). In pagan culture, such acts were considered repugnant. The early Christians' willingness to humble themselves in the manner of slaves is further evidence of the revolutionary changes brought about by the gospel. Jesus said that the greatest among you is the servant of all (see Mark 10:44). The goal of Christian humility is grateful service that seeks what is in the best interest of those served (see Philippians 2:1-4). The quotation at the close of the verse is from Proverbs 3:34 and reaffirms God's timeless concern for the lowly and His distaste for the arrogant and self-centered.

B. Humble Before God (vv. 6, 7)

6. Humble yourselves therefore under the mighty hand of God, that he may exalt you in due time.

Therefore, in the light of God's priorities, in the light of God's graciousness toward the humble, humble yourselves before God. There is a threefold call to humility and submission in verses 5 and 6. Submission to the caring guidance of our spiritual leaders is encouraged in verse 5. This falls within the broader framework of humility toward all fellow followers, an eagerness to uplift not ourselves but one another. These are founded on the most basic, most obvious, most essential reason for humility—the awareness of the presence and power of God. The *mighty hand of God* is a reference to God's power and activity. This expression is used on a number of occasions in the Old Testament in connection with God's deliverance of His people from difficult circumstances. The people to whom Peter wrote were suffering persecution for their faith in Christ. His words are a reminder to them not to rely on the world or on themselves but on the proven power of God for strength and deliverance. *That he may exalt you.* This promise of exaltation must not be misunderstood. It must never become the motive for humblemindedness toward God or others. In fact, being humble so as to be exalted amounts to a selfishness that automatically crowds out humility and prevents exaltation. *In due time.* Exaltation is not necessarily experienced in this life. It will come in God's own time, not ours. Peter probably refers to the time of Christ's return when His people will share in His glory.

7. Casting all your care upon him; for he careth for you.

One of the marks of humility is the recognition that we cannot always rescue ourselves, that we are not self-sufficient, that we are weak and helpless in many situations of life. The assumption that we do not need God is the height of arrogance. Peter urges instead that we throw all our *care*, that is, our anxiety upon God. We are to let Him carry our cares and concerns. Jesus referred to such anxiety in the Sermon on the Mount (Matthew 6:25-34), and that may be included in Peter's thought here. He may also have in mind the suffering Christians must endure because of persecution, or the pressures of everyday life, of the stress of trying to live godly lives in an ungodly world. With confidence we may cast all our anxiety upon God because we have the assurance that He cares for us. Pagans thought that the gods cared nothing for their daily lives. Some Jews and even some Christians thought of God more as critic than caretaker. But He cares for us. Frequently in His letters to the churches in Revelation, Jesus states, "I know" (see 2:2, 9, 13, 19; 3:1, 8, 15). He knows His people as well as if He were visible in their midst. Because our Lord knows of our life situations and cares about us, we can cast all our worries on Him.

C. Sober and Watchful (v. 8)

8. Be sober, be vigilant; because your adversary the devil, as a roaring lion, walketh about, seeking whom he may devour.

We are encouraged to cast all of our anxieties upon God and to lean on His strength, but this does not mean that we are to be careless and unconcerned in our attitudes and behavior. We are to *be sober*, to cultivate serious-minded self-control, to face the challenges of life with self-discipline. We are also to *be vigilant*, watchful, wide awake. We must ever be alert to our spiritual enemy who would prey upon the unsuspecting. He is described as the *adversary*, the opponent, of godly people. The term *devil* means "false accuser." He was at work when the Christians to whom Peter wrote faced the false accusations of their pagan neighbors and the Roman judicial system, and he is no less active today. The evil one is pictured as a lion walking about, looking for those whom he may devour. He cannot touch those "who are kept by the power of God through faith unto salvation" (1 Peter 1:5), but the wanderer from the fold would be in immediate danger. In this striking manner Peter de-

visual 12

They that know GOD will be humble; they that know themselves cannot be proud.
—FLAVEL

scribes the temptations that come to Christians. We should not forget that the image of Satan as an all-consuming lion would have been very real to those whose fellow Christians were facing real wild beasts in Roman arenas.

D. Standing Firm (v. 9)

9. Whom resist steadfast in the faith, knowing that the same afflictions are accomplished in your brethren that are in the world.

In the face of bitter persecution, Christians are to *resist steadfast in the faith*. Christians are to resist, not retreat. But by the same token they are to resist, not retaliate. Neither running from their accusers nor attacking them will accomplish the purpose of humble testimony to the truth of Christ. Christians are to stand *steadfast*, that is, with solid, rocklike firmness in their faith in God. With an unfaltering confidence in Him, they will be able to stand firm in the profession of their faith even in the face of persecution. Revelation 12:10, 11 speaks of those in Heaven who suffered persecution and overcame Satan "by the word of their testimony." Persecution, which had begun in Jerusalem and had stretched with the gospel to Rome, was being felt by the Christians in Asia Minor. The encouragement to stand firm came in part from knowing that they were in solidarity with other suffering Christians around the Roman empire (*the world*). The word *brethren* is actually "brotherhood," emphasizing not only their oneness in suffering but their oneness in Christ.

III. Our Mighty God
(1 Peter 5:10-11)

A. The Outcome of Our Trust (v. 10)

10. But the God of all grace, who hath called us unto his eternal glory by Christ Jesus, after that ye have suffered a while, make you perfect, stablish, strengthen, settle you.

The little word *But* is not without significance. God's grace, which forgives and reconciles, stands in stark contrast to the work of the enemy, who accuses and attacks. The *God of all grace* has the resources to overcome all the effects of sin and all the influences of Satan. His grace is demonstrated not only in what He has called us to, but that He has called us at all! The call is *unto his eternal glory*, to eternal life in His glorious presence. Beyond suffering is glory. Beyond this present, temporary persecution is eternity. God's grace, His call, and His glory, are extended to us through Christ Jesus. This same God who has called us to a life beyond suffering will enable us to live in the midst of suffering, which, relative to eternity, lasts but *a while.*

The *Authorized Version* follows some manuscripts that make this verse sound like a wish: *the God of all grace . . . make you perfect. . . .* But the weight of manuscript evidence suggests the reading, "the God of all grace *will* make you perfect." This is not merely a petition; it is a statement of faith.

Make you perfect, stablish, strengthen, settle you. These words are very similar in meaning. The effect of the repetition is to build up the confidence of Peter's readers in the sustaining power of God. *Perfect* implies good order in the midst of great chaos. *Stablish* and *strengthen* suggest strength in the midst of powerlessness. *Settle* speaks of a firm foundation in the midst of the instability of troubled circumstances.

SOFT EYES

James Barrie tells of his mother's total devastation when she lost her favorite son. He goes on to say, "That is where my mother got her soft eyes, and that is why other mothers ran to her when they had lost a child."

None of us fully understands the ways of the Lord. Calamity, suffering, and sorrow are not strangers to the child of God. Peter does not attempt to account for all of the injustices of life, but he does offer encouragement and hope. He reminds us that if suffering is our lot, we can take some comfort in knowing that we are not alone in our struggles. Better yet, he promises us that after we have suffered a little while, God will restore us, make us strong, firm, and steadfast.

How encouraging to realize that God can use even our suffering for a good purpose! Though we are broken down, He can build us back in a sturdier form so that we can more effectively minister to those around us who are hurting. Someone has said, "It is doubtful if God uses anybody greatly before that person has been hurt deeply." Even our worst pain, placed in the loving hands of our powerful God, can produce good results. Through it we can develop those "soft eyes" by which we can reach the sin-hardened folk of this world.   —T. T.

B. The Basis of Our Trust (v. 11)

11. To him be glory and dominion for ever and ever. Amen.

The final verse moves from a statement of faith to a statement of praise. This doxology ascribes "might" to God. (The word *glory* does not appear in the best manuscripts.) God can provide us with strength precisely because strength resides within Him. These words of doxology are a benediction concluding this section on humble leadership and humble following. But they also draw to a close the whole letter. Both the holiness we are called to and the suffering we are called through are based on the power of our gracious God.

Conclusion

A. Cattle or Sheep

I was raised on a dairy farm where herding cattle meant standing behind the last cow and prodding her with a stick. Since then I have observed shepherds who guided their flock by leading, not by forcing. The Christian congregation is a flock, not a herd. The Christian elder is a leader, not a lord.

B. Let Us Pray

Sovereign God, if we may not be spared suffering in this life, see us through our suffering by Your strength. In Jesus' name we pray. Amen.

C. Thought to Remember

"My grace is sufficient for thee: for my strength is made perfect in weakness" (2 Corinthians 12:9).

Home Daily Bible Readings

Monday, May 11—Greatness in Lowliness (Matthew 18:1-5)
Tuesday, May 12—Justified in Humility (Luke 14:7-11)
Wednesday, May 13—Grace Is the Reward (1 Peter 5:1-5)
Thursday, May 14—Exaltation Comes From God (1 Peter 5:6-11)
Friday, May 15—God Takes Care of You (Hebrews 13:1-8)
Saturday, May 16—The Gentle Yoke (Matthew 11:25-30)
Sunday, May 17—Boast Only in the Lord (2 Corinthians 11:16-30)

Learning by Doing

This page contains an alternate lesson plan emphasizing learning activities. Classes desiring such student involvement will find these suggestions helpful.

Learning Goals

After this lesson a student will be able to:

1. Explain how the description of elders as shepherds applies to the elders themselves and to the rest of God's people.

2. Describe the characteristics of one who resists the devil and stands firm in the faith.

3. Commit one item of worry into God's hands.

Into the Lesson

Write the word *elders* vertically on the chalkboard before the class arrives. As students begin to come into your classroom, give each one a piece of paper and ask them to write some words beginning with each letter of this word that describe the role of elders.

When it is time for the class to begin, ask for volunteers to share their ideas and write them on the board. Some suggestions follow:

Example, **E**ducator
Leader, **L**istener
Defender, **D**irector
Experienced, **E**ncourager
Reconciler, **R**estorer
Shepherd, **S**ervant

Comment on each item suggested as it relates to the role of elders. Note that many of them are character traits all Christians should have. However, these traits should be more highly developed in those who lead God's people. This maturity, added to the responsibility elders bear for others, is what distinguishes these spiritual leaders from others in the church. Both the character traits and the responsibility are noted by Peter in our text.

Into the Word

Read the text, 1 Peter 5:1-11, aloud. Then divide the class into three groups. Assign each one a section of the text as divided in the lesson outline: group one, "The Willing Shepherds" (vv. 1-4); group two, "The Humble Flock" (vv. 5-9); group three, "Our Mighty God" (vv. 10, 11). Have one person in each group serve as recorder and reporter. Group one is to examine the first portion of the text and list the elders' duties and attitudes mentioned in these verses. Have this group discuss why a shepherd is an apt figure for describing elders.

Group two is to examine the next section of the text and list the attitudes and responsibilities mentioned there for Christians in general. How is the figure of "sheep" appropriate for Christians? How do these thoughts apply to church leaders? (After all, elders are both "shepherds" and "sheep.")

Group three is to look at the last two verses. What do we learn of God here? What does He promise? Do these promises apply more to elders, Christians in general, or both equally?

After about ten minutes, ask the reporters to share the results of their groups' discussion. As each one reports, expand on the findings with observations from the commentary section of this lesson. Discuss the importance of the attitudes mentioned in the text. Why is having the proper attitude so important for church leaders? What about persons who are not in leadership—how important is attitude for them?

Into Life

Call attention to verse 7. Discuss the difficulty of casting *all* our cares on the Lord. Does this difficulty betray a lack of trust in God, or is it merely a human weakness? Does the connection of the directive in verse 7 to the command to "humble yourselves . . . under the mighty hand of God" indicate that *pride* is one reason we worry? Why or why not?

Note Peter's call to vigilance (verse 8). Ask the students to describe the characteristics of one who is alert to the devil's tactics and list these on the chalkboard. Is there any connection between these characteristics (or the lack of them) and whether or not one worries? Note the contrast between faith and worry. Does the presence of worry reveal a lack of faith in a person's life? Ask the class to choose one or two of the characteristics on your list and make it a point to begin developing them in their lives.

Distribute three-by-five cards. Ask the students to write on one side the characteristics of vigilance they intend to work on. On the other side, each student should write one anxiety or worry he or she has difficulty in releasing to the Lord. Ask them to take the cards home and put them in a place where they will see them frequently. Ask them to pray each time they see their cards that God will take away their anxieties.

Let's Talk It Over

The questions on this page are designed to encourage review of the lesson Scriptures and to promote discussion of the lesson by the class. The answers provided are only discussion starters. Let your class talk it over from there.

1. Why is it especially important in this day for the church's spiritual leaders to have the attitudes and motives that Peter mentions in today's text?

In our age, when the integrity of religious leaders is questioned and when the challenge of other religions confronts the church on all sides, a spiritual leadership that serves humbly and willingly is especially important for the spiritual health and welfare of the "flock of God." God's people are reluctant to follow leaders who are insensitive to the needs of others, who are out for their own personal gain, or who demonstrate an unwillingness to follow Christ's example and teaching. Thus the work of the church is impaired. Moreover, even the unbelievers in our society expect religious leaders to adhere to the highest standard of conduct. When the church's leadership fails in this regard, the church, indeed Christ himself, is held up to ridicule, and those who are lost in sin may be turned away from Him who alone can save them.

2. Peter states that, along with willing, humble leaders, the church needs willing, humble followers. How can we as members of the church make it easier for our leaders to do their jobs?

In an age of rebellion and rejection of authority, Christians need to display attitudes and actions that reflect respect and deference for their church leaders. Instead of grumbling and complaining against our spiritual leaders, which seems to be the natural tendency of some in the church, we need to be willing to be led, to be eager learners at the feet of our teaching elders, and to trust their decisions and guidance. An eagerness to serve, to encourage, and to express appreciation for our elders and for one another will propel our congregation in positive ministry toward one another and the surrounding community.

3. How are our homes, our job environments, our communities, and our church affected when we follow Peter's exhortation to live in "humility toward one another"? (1 Peter 5:5, *New International Version*).

Humility in our daily lives makes us much slower to judge others, or to insist on our rights, or to demand our ways. It enables us to assist in the work of others who may not be on our same educational, economic, or social level. Prejudice, pride, and conceit disappear from our relationships, and harmony is restored as we willingly associate with all people. Our desires and wants take a back seat to the needs of those around us as we seek to serve and honor them.

4. The lesson writer notes that the fact that we matter to God should be the basis of our humility. Nevertheless, many of us have trouble risking humility and casting all our anxieties on God. Why is it often difficult for us to humbly place our cares in God's hands, and how can we overcome our fears and begin to trust ourselves to God's care?

Many of us have bad memories of experiences with our fathers or other key care-givers in our lives, and as a result do not feel safe trusting God. We need to ask God to free us from the shackles of the past, to help us extend forgiveness to those who have offended us, and to aid us in seeing Him as One who will never betray our confidence and trust. Others of us have allowed our anxieties to get us down, disturb our peace, and distract our minds for so long that we are unable to give wholehearted devotion to God. We need to break these old habits that bind us, to turn to God, and to find relief in pouring out our cares upon Him. Still others of us have carried our burdens alone, never attempting to surrender them to God. We need to decide to commit our cares to God, to act on that decision, and in faith to allow Him to free us from our anxieties.

5. Casting all our anxieties on God does not allow us to be lazy or careless. Our adversary, the devil, is always looking for a chance to destroy us. How can we recognize the devil's work in our midst and then combat it?

The devil wants to sow discord, break fellowship, make accusations, undermine confidence, silence our testimony, and get us to stop believing in Christ. We must combat our enemy by seeking harmony, peace, and love in our relationships and by standing with conviction and faith in God's love for us, even when we are facing difficulties.

Growing in Grace

LESSON SCRIPTURE: 2 Peter 1:1-14.

PRINTED TEXT: 2 Peter 1:1-14.

2 Peter 1:1-14

1 Simon Peter, a servant and an apostle of Jesus Christ, To them that have obtained like precious faith with us through the righteousness of God and our Saviour Jesus Christ:

2 Grace and peace be multiplied unto you through the knowledge of God, and of Jesus our Lord.

3 According as his divine power hath given unto us all things that pertain unto life and godliness, through the knowledge of him that hath called us to glory and virtue:

4 Whereby are given unto us exceeding great and precious promises; that by these ye might be partakers of the divine nature, having escaped the corruption that is in the world through lust.

5 And besides this, giving all diligence, add to your faith virtue; and to virtue, knowledge;

6 And to knowledge, temperance; and to temperance, patience; and to patience, godliness;

7 And to godliness, brotherly kindness; and to brotherly kindness ,charity.

8 For if these things be in you, and abound, they make you that ye shall neither be barren nor unfruitful in the knowledge of our Lord Jesus Christ.

9 But he that lacketh these things is blind, and cannot see afar off, and hath forgotten that he was purged from his old sins.

10 Wherefore the rather, brethren, give diligence to make your calling and election

sure: for if ye do these things, ye shall never fall:

11 For so an entrance shall be ministered unto you abundantly into the everlasting kingdom of our Lord and Saviour Jesus Christ.

12 Wherefore I will not be negligent to put you always in remembrance of these things, though ye know them, and be established in the present truth.

13 Yea, I think it meet, as long as I am in this tabernacle, to stir you up by putting you in remembrance;

14 Knowing that shortly I must put off this my tabernacle, even as our Lord Jesus Christ hath showed me.

GOLDEN TEXT: His divine power hath given unto us all things that pertain unto life and godliness, through the knowledge of him that hath called us to glory and virtue.—2 Peter 1:3.

Lesson Aims

This lesson should produce within each student:

1. A better understanding of the nature of godliness.

2. A renewed commitment to Christian growth.

3. A greater appreciation for those who encourage their growth.

Lesson Outline

Display visual 13 of the visuals packet and let it remain before your class. The visual is shown on page 325.

Introduction

A. Experienced Counsel

Would you hire a preacher who had a reputation for speaking before he thinks, talking back to superiors, assaulting with a deadly weapon, even lying and denying his faith? Surely not—unless that preacher were Simon Peter.

Perhaps this is not a fair question, since Peter did all of these things as a young disciple. A better question would be, Would you trust a preacher who had experienced as much growth as Peter had to tell you what changes you needed to make in your life? If so, then pay close attention to this lesson from Peter.

B. Lesson Background

Peter wrote his second epistle to Christians in Asia Minor (see 1 Peter 1:1 and 2 Peter 3:1) shortly before his martyrdom believed to have taken place about A.D. 68. The prospect of dying was before him (see 2 Peter 1:13, 14). Thus his choice of themes for what would be his final written message may give some clue to what he felt were important matters for his readers to consider. In chapter 2 he warned of the heresy of false teaching in the church, and in chapter 3 he countered arguments against the doctrine of the second coming. But he began with what may have been the more significant theme to him (judging by the similar beginning in 1 Peter 1:13-25)—the duty of Christians to pursue godliness.

I. Our Precious Faith
(2 Peter 1:1-4)

A. Obtained Through God and Christ
(vv. 1, 2)

1. Simon Peter, a servant and an apostle of Jesus Christ, To them that have obtained like precious faith with us through the righteousness of God and our Saviour Jesus Christ.

Considering Peter's prominent role in the early church, the Christians in Asia Minor would have given respectful attention to the words he addressed to them. He first identifies himself as a *servant*, that is, a slave, of Jesus Christ. By this he implies his entire devotion to Christ. In referring to himself as *an apostle* of Christ, he refers to his service for Christ, by which he expressed his devotion. Then he tells his readers that they share a *like precious faith with us*, or as the *Revised Standard Version* expresses it, "a faith of equal standing with ours." Peter quickly establishes with his readers a common ground, lest they assume that his message has no relevance for "lesser" levels of spirituality. All Christians, from the greatest to the least, have equal privileges through faith, and all have equal responsibility to grow spiritually.

2. Grace and peace be multiplied unto you through the knowledge of God, and of Jesus our Lord.

Peter begins his discussion of Christian growth by grounding our faith in both God the Father and Jesus Christ (vv. 1, 2). Some might discount all talk of godliness or behaving like God as merely theoretical niceties, since an invisible and exalted God does not display an easy pattern for human beings to follow. But when godliness is grounded in Jesus, we have a practical example of what we are to strive toward.

B. Offering Life and Godliness

(vv. 3, 4)

3. According as his divine power hath given unto us all things that pertain unto life and godliness, through the knowledge of him that hath called us to glory and virtue.

All things that pertain unto life and godliness. Through Christ, God has given us all things that are necessary for the spiritual life of the soul. While Peter's reference to the divine gift of *life* may be intended to focus upon our hope of living forever in Heaven, his reference to *godliness* points to the distinctive character Christians should be developing now. Godliness means reverence, true piety toward God. This attitude of heart and mind is to shape and direct all of our actions. As we live with reverence for God, displaying such qualities as holiness, kindness, and fairness, we display on a lesser scale the *glory and virtue* of God, a challenge to which He *hath called us.*

4. Whereby are given unto us exceeding great and precious promises; that by these ye might be partakers of the divine nature, having escaped the corruption that is in the world through lust.

Exceeding great and precious promises. This refers to all that is promised us through Christ, such as the forgiveness of sins and the gift of the Holy Spirit. But these actually serve as steppingstones for achieving an even greater blessing—to become *partakers of the divine nature.* Many cults have taken this phrase to mean that man can become a god, eventually possessing even the power and knowledge of God. This view is discredited by the general teaching of Scripture, which makes a sharp distinction between Creator and creature (see, for example, Romans 1:22-25), as well as by the context of 2 Peter 1. There is no hint in 2 Peter or the rest of Scripture that man can actually acquire the special powers of deity, such as eternal existence in *both* past and future, unlimited strength (omnipotence), unlimited

knowledge (omniscience), or unlimited presence (omnipresence). To "participate in the divine nature" (*New International Version*) is to practice the moral qualities of God taught in Scripture. By God's power through Christ we escape *the corruption that is in the world*, and by the strength He supplies we are enabled to grow into "the stature of the fulness of Christ" (Ephesians 4:13).

II. Our Godly Nature
(2 Peter 1:5-9)

A. Godly Qualities (vv. 5-8)

5. And besides this, giving all diligence, add to your faith virtue; and to virtue, knowledge.

And besides this. Rather, "for this very reason." Because God has so blessed us in Christ, certain responsibilities are ours. Peter lists seven godly qualities Christians should seek after. And while each one provides an instructive lesson, the significance of this passage is not to be found in which qualities Peter chose to list, but in the idea that faith is only the beginning of the Christian experience. One is to give *all diligence* to add moral qualities to one's faith, that is, to grow in godliness.

Peter's list of godly qualities begins with *virtue*. This is a special Greek term virtually untranslatable in English. (Some have suggested "goodness" or "moral excellence" or "moral strength.") The idea seems to be moral strength or courage to put our faith into action, to do the right thing.

Peter commends the pursuit of *knowledge*, which in this case may particularly refer to the development of the thinking processes so that one learns to think carefully before acting and speaking.

6. And to knowledge, temperance; and to temperance, patience; and to patience, godliness.

Temperance is self-control that extends over all of one's life. It consists in the governing of one's appetites, longings, and passions. Those who are self-controlled will not allow themselves to be pushed to extremes but will have rule over themselves. Self-control is the natural result of true knowledge as described above.

Patience is more than passive endurance of whatever comes along. It means determined loyalty to one's faith and ideals, regardless of the misfortunes of life and the aggravations of others. The one who is patient perseveres in his or her loyalty to Christ no matter what happens.

Godliness has already been described (see verse 3). This is a general principle that encompasses the other qualities in this list as well as a host of others.

visual 13

7. And to godliness, brotherly kindness; and to brotherly kindness, charity.

Brotherly kindness refers to a care and concern for other members of the church, much like the unfailing devotion that is found within strong families. And while *charity* is used in the New Testament in different ways, it is perhaps best understood here to refer to a spirit of benevolence or goodwill toward those for whom one has little attraction.

8. For if these things be in you, and abound, they make you that ye shall neither be barren nor unfruitful in the knowledge of our Lord Jesus Christ.

Peter well understands that none of these godly qualities is bestowed upon a person in full measure in a moment of time. A person may possess these qualities to a certain extent and still have room for them to *abound,* that is, to increase. The *New International Version* emphasizes the process of growth with the translation, "If you possess these qualities in increasing measure." Godliness is attained by degrees depending upon how much we apply ourselves to the task of growing. To fail to pursue growth is to limit one's potential service for the Lord and risk becoming unproductive (*barren* and *unfruitful*).

CHRISTIANS NEED TO GROW

One day early last spring, as I walked about my yard, I noticed a row of tulips, each two or three inches tall. In the midst of the row stood a large flower pot where I had put it the previous summer. Since there were tulips on each side of the pot, I concluded that I had put the pot in a bad place and that, undoubtedly, there were other tulip bulbs in the ground under it. I rolled the pot to one side, and there, to my amazement, were several spindly tulip plants.

What a testimony to the power of new life! Those bulbs had a built-in desire to grow, to become what they were designed to be. True, they were white and sickly looking, having been deprived of sunlight, but still they were there and doing the best they could under very adverse circumstances. I was sure that they would not be able to recover and produce flowers that spring, but I was wrong. In only a few days they greened up, promising to bud and bloom.

We who are Christians have been given new life in Christ. Like those tulips, we are to strive to become what the Giver of that life intends us to be. The spiritual graces Peter mentions are to be seen in us. Their presence in our lives at once glorifies God and gives evidence of our spiritual health.   —T. T.

B. Spiritual Blindness (v. 9)

9. But he that lacketh these things is blind, and cannot see afar off, and hath forgotten that he was purged from his old sins.

An apt analogy of a Christian who is not actively pursuing spiritual growth is that of a nearsighted person who *cannot see afar off.* Peter does not mean to suggest that such a Christian is totally off base, for there will be some things that he understands and does well. And yet, just as the nearsighted person cannot clearly see things at a distance, the Christian who ignores his spiritual growth is *blind* to a key aspect of the Christian life. Such a person has *forgotten that he was purged from his old sins,* that is, he is failing to see the inconsistency of claiming to be freed from sin through Christ while continuing to practice old habits that Scripture identifies as sinful.

III. Our Constant Challenge (2 Peter 1:10-14)

A. Salvation Requires Growth (vv. 10, 11)

10. Wherefore the rather, brethren, give diligence to make your calling and election sure: for if ye do these things, ye shall never fall.

In verses 5-7 Peter has listed some of the qualities that Christians must strive for if they would grow in grace. In verse 10 he again stresses that Christians must assume responsibility for their spiritual welfare. He begins by repeating the command, *Give diligence,* which means, "earnestly endeavor." *To make your calling and election sure.* The call of God comes through the preaching of the gospel, and those who respond to that call are God's elect (Colossians 3:12), "a chosen people" (1 Peter 2:9, *New International Version*). Throughout this section of his letter, Peter is striving to show that one must not be content merely to answer God's initial call. The Christian life is not static. It involves growth and development as one strives to become more and more like Christ. Those persons who pursue godliness as outlined by Peter in these verses (and by the other New Testament writers) are ensuring against a *fall* from which they would not rise.

11. For so an entrance shall be ministered unto you abundantly into the everlasting kingdom of our Lord and Saviour Jesus Christ.

God is not stingy in His dealings with us. Heeding His command to draw near to Him and to become more and more like Him, we are richly rewarded, now and hereafter. Then we shall be granted entrance into the kingdom of glory in Heaven, and our entrance shall be abundantly supplied.

B. Growth Requires Encouragement
(vv. 12-14)

12. Wherefore I will not be negligent to put you always in remembrance of these things, though ye know them, and be established in the present truth.

Peter presents himself not as one proclaiming new truths, but as one who encourages the Lord's people to practice what they already know. So it is with most sermons and lessons. Their effectiveness often lies not in catchy, new ideas, but in the persistent reminder of what yet remains to be done.

Thus we see how our spiritual growth is aided by those who remind us of our goal of godliness, whether it be through sermons, Bible-study lessons, counseling, or informal conversation. Rather than being annoyed and regarding such efforts as "meddling," we should appreciate the instruction and encouragement given, for our growth depends upon it. And as we grow in godliness, we should, in true love and concern, serve others by providing them similar encouragement toward spiritual growth.

13, 14. Yea, I think it meet, as long as I am in this tabernacle, to stir you up by putting you in remembrance; knowing that shortly I must put off this my tabernacle, even as our Lord Jesus Christ hath showed me.

Peter referred to his body as a *tabernacle*, calling to mind the image of a person setting up a tent temporarily, knowing that he will soon have to take it down. Peter was advanced in age, and he knew that Jesus' prophecy concerning his death (see John 21: 18, 19) must soon come to pass. But whatever time remained to him in this life, Peter would use it to emphasize the theme that was dear to his heart—God expects His people to actively pursue godliness.

Conclusion
A. Room to Grow

It is stirring to hear the testimony of those whose lives have been dramatically changed by Christ—former drug addicts, prostitutes, gang members, thieves, and murderers. And while we rejoice in the accounts of God's mighty power at work, these great conversions can seem somewhat irrelevant to those of us who do not share such scandalous pasts. Thus it is good to be reminded by Peter that, despite our differences, all of us who share a precious faith need to strive constantly for spiritual growth.

How can we do this? To begin, we should examine our lives to find areas needing improvement. The Scriptures mention a number of problem areas, and perhaps this is where we should start. Among them are speech, temper, impatience, pride, and lust.

When we have identified our areas of weakness, it is best to concentrate on them one at a time. We can ask ourselves, "Under what circumstances has this weakness manifested itself?" This will help us anticipate a recurrence in the future and perhaps allow us to recognize and avoid those settings in which we are most vulnerable.

In keeping with Peter's advice in verses 12-14, it is wise to take advantage of the encouragement for spiritual growth offered by our fellow Christians. By being consistent in attendance at worship services and Bible studies, we will receive practical guidance in Christian living.

It may help to tell a trustworthy friend of our desire to more actively pursue godliness and to ask this friend, "Where do you see that I need to improve?" Then periodically we should seek out our friend's assessment of how well we are progressing.

And let us not overlook a method Peter himself found of great advantage—that of focusing on Jesus, the perfect model of godliness in the flesh. We can observe the Master as we spend time reading the Gospel accounts of His life.

All of this will require some time and effort, but the rewards will be eternally gratifying.

B. Let Us Pray

Father, help us to take seriously our need to actively pursue godliness. May we see progress each day as we join with our brothers and sisters in a mutual ministry of encouragement. In Jesus' name, amen.

C. Thought to Remember

"Grow in grace, and in the knowledge of our Lord and Saviour Jesus Christ" (2 Peter 3:18).

Learning by Doing

This page contains an alternate lesson plan emphasizing learning activities. Classes desiring such student involvement will find these suggestions helpful.

Learning Goals

After this lesson students will be able to:

1. List some of the provisions God has made to help us live the Christian life.

2. Suggest some standards by which to measure their growth in the "knowledge of our Lord Jesus Christ" (2 Peter 1:8).

3. Identify at least one area of weakness in their lives and make specific plans to improve.

Into the Lesson

As the students arrive, give each one a copy of the following "letter." Tell them you would like their help in answering it, for it raises a difficult question. Have the students work on this project in small groups.

Dear friends at (add the name of your church or class),

I need help! I don't think I can go on. I know Jesus died for me, and I want to live for Him. But I just can't. I don't have what it takes to live the Christian life. I know I am supposed to be "godly," but I am still "worldly"; and I don't seem to be able to do anything about it.

Can you help me? What has God done to help me live the Christian life and be godly? And how do I make it work for me? How does He help you—and can He help me that way, too? If I don't get some answers, I think I'll just quit trying and go back to living as I please.

Signed,
A Struggling Christian (I think)

Give the students a few minutes to work on their responses. Then ask, "What can we tell our friend? What has God done to help us live the Christian life?" List on the chalkboard the students' suggestions. Then note that Peter deals with this very issue in today's text. He states that God "has given us everything we need for life and godliness" (2 Peter 1:3, *New International Version*).

Into the Word

Read the lesson text, 2 Peter 1:1-14, aloud. If visitors or new Christians are in your class, it may be helpful to read the text from a modern translation.

Write the headings *Knowledge, Calling,* and *Growth* on three posters and display them at this time (but do not mount them on the wall). Note the significance Peter attaches to these concepts. Then divide the class into thirds to explore them in depth, each group considering one of the concepts.

The first group is to list all of Peter's references to *know* or *knowledge* in this text. Ask them to report on what Peter says we should know and the benefits we will receive if we know these things.

The second group is to consider our "calling." By what and to what does Peter say we have been called? What response does this calling demand of us?

The third group is to examine Peter's references to growth. Although that term is not used, he does speak of the developing characteristics that should "abound" in us. Ask this group to report on the source of growth, the results of growth, and the consequences of the lack of growth.

Give each group the poster with the appropriate heading written on it. As they discuss their assignments, they can list their findings on the posters. Give them about ten minutes to work; then call for reports.

Into Life

Point out that we have been called for a purpose. We are expected to grow in our knowledge of the Lord. But how do we know whether or not we are doing this? Ask the class to suggest some standards by which we can measure our effectiveness and productivity in the knowledge of Christ. (These should be actions that correspond to the qualities Peter lists in verses 5-7.)

Then ask, "What if one doesn't possess these qualities? How can that person develop them?" After a brief discussion, call attention to the lesson writer's suggestions in the conclusion of the commentary section. (Briefly, one should concentrate on one problem area at a time, take advantage of opportunities afforded by the local congregation, confide in a trustworthy friend, and spend more time focusing on Jesus.)

Discuss these ideas briefly; then say, "Each of us needs to identify an area of his or her spiritual life that needs attention. Think of one now. Write it down. Now list two or three things you can do this week to improve that area."

After a couple of minutes, close with prayer.

Let's Talk It Over

The questions on this page are designed to encourage review of the lesson Scriptures and to promote discussion of the lesson by the class. The answers provided are only discussion starters. Let your class talk it over from there.

1. God may not give us all that we might like, but Peter states that God's divine power has provided everything we need for life and godliness (2 Peter 1:3). How does this truth help us face the daily challenges of Christlike living?

Many of us today wrestle with being content with what God has given us. We secretly desire more from God, and envy what He has given to others in terms of talents, gifts, circumstances, relationships, and the like. This can create ungratefulness in our hearts toward God. Recognizing that God has empowered us with His Spirit to live abundantly should produce an attitude of thankfulness to God for what we have. It should also motivate us to serve Christ boldly and faithfully in the day-in and day-out routine of life.

2. How can we practice godliness in our daily lives—in our homes, on our jobs, with our neighbors?

Colossians 3:12 says, "As God's chosen people, holy and dearly loved, clothe yourselves with compassion, kindness, humility, gentleness and patience" (*New International Version*). These virtues, as well as others described in Scripture, will be seen in the life of a godly person, one who truly holds God in reverence. No room exists in a godly life for unkindness towards one's spouse, harshness towards one's co-worker, or impatience with one's neighbors. Godliness is the mark of the person who seeks to do God's will and who, by his or her actions, draws people to Him (see John 17:4; Matthew 5:16).

3. God, by His power, has given us what we need to live a godly life. What can we do to combat the tendency to compromise our morality and godliness in today's society and, instead, to "participate in the divine nature and escape the corruption in the world"? (2 Peter 1:4, *New International Version*).

A universal human tendency is to make excuses for our sin, to shift the blame for our failures, and to refuse to take personal responsibility for our situation in life. All of these attitudes can cause us to compromise our walk with God and to fail to see the opportunities God allows for growth in our lives. We need to look to God and His power for personal victories, instead of making excuses for our defeats.

Confession of sins to one another (James 5:16) and life-changing repentance (2 Corinthians 7:10, 11) will combat any compromising attitudes concerning the moral qualities of God and will contribute to a dynamic relationship with Him.

4. All of us should make an effort to grow in faith, virtue, knowledge, self-control, steadfastness, godliness, brotherly affection, and love. Why is this spiritual growth so desirable?

As the lesson writer notes, faith is only the beginning of our Christian experience. Change that can be seen in these qualities of character will be evidence that we are making an effort to become like Christ in every area of our lives. James 2:20-26 makes it clear that faith without actions is useless. Therefore, our growth in these virtues is proof of the genuineness of our faith in Christ and will produce a well-rounded, fruitful Christian life.

5. Failure to develop the qualities Peter lists is a sign of spiritual illness and will result in an unproductive and ineffective life. How may we take our "spiritual temperature," and what "spiritual prescription" may we need in order to put us on the road to recovery in our spiritual growth?

An honest look at our character, in light of God's Word and with the assistance of a committed Christian friend, can help us see where we need to change, what we need to work on, and how we need to grow. God made us new when we became Christians (2 Corinthians 5:17), and we need to allow Him daily to transform us into His likeness (Romans 12:2, 2 Corinthians 3:18). Daily Bible reading and study, accountability to godly Christians, and an openness and willingness to change will produce growth.

6. How may development of godliness in our lives increase our confidence as Christians?

Most often when we experience some measure of victory in our battle with Satan, we have a greater zeal, desire, and commitment to persevere in our walk with Christ. We are reassured that He is with us and we gain renewed confidence that He will strengthen us to face the problems that may lie ahead.

Focused on the Future

LESSON SCRIPTURE: 2 Peter 3:3-14.

PRINTED TEXT: 2 Peter 3:3-14.

2 Peter 3:3-14

3 Knowing this first, that there shall come in the last days scoffers, walking after their own lusts,

4 And saying, Where is the promise of his coming? for since the fathers fell asleep, all things continue as they were from the beginning of the creation.

5 For this they willingly are ignorant of, that by the word of God the heavens were of old, and the earth standing out of the water and in the water:

6 Whereby the world that then was, being overflowed with water, perished:

7 But the heavens and the earth, which are now, by the same word are kept in store, reserved unto fire against the day of judgment and perdition of ungodly men.

8 But, beloved, be not ignorant of this one thing, that one day is with the Lord as a thousand years, and a thousand years as one day.

9 The Lord is not slack concerning his promise, as some men count slackness; but is long-suffering to us-ward, not willing that any should perish, but that all should come to repentance.

10 But the day of the Lord will come as a thief in the night; in the which the heavens shall pass away with a great noise, and the elements shall melt with fervent heat, the earth also and the works that are therein shall be burned up.

11 Seeing then that all these things shall be dissolved, what manner of persons ought ye to be in all holy conversation and godliness,

12 Looking for and hasting unto the coming of the day of God, wherein the heavens being on fire shall be dissolved, and the elements shall melt with fervent heat?

13 Nevertheless we, according to his promise, look for new heavens and a new earth, wherein dwelleth righteousness.

14 Wherefore, beloved, seeing that ye look for such things, be diligent that ye may be found of him in peace, without spot, and blameless.

GOLDEN TEXT: We, according to his promise, look for new heavens and a new earth, wherein dwelleth righteousness.—2 Peter 3:13.

God's People in the World (Lessons 9-14)	

Lesson Aims

As a result of studying this lesson each student should:

1. Be able to give two reasons for the seeming delay in Christ's return.

2. Recognize the temporal nature of worldly achievements.

3. Be further motivated to godly living.

Lesson Outline

Visual 14 of the visuals packet expresses the Christian's hope for eternity. The visual is shown on page 333.

Introduction

A. Two Extremes

Throughout church history many have attempted, and failed, to predict the date of Christ's return. Yet this fact has not deterred people in modern times from trying to prove through Biblical texts that we are living in the final days of the world's history.

In 1988 hundreds of churches across America received complimentary copies of a book predicting that the rapture would occur in 1988. By January 1, 1989, it was apparent that the book was in error. Not long after, the author said he had miscalculated by one year. It came as little surprise, therefore, to hear reports that he was producing a new book, which predicted that the rapture would occur in 1989. He has since decided to make no further predictions of the event.

Just as some persons are caught up in excessive concern over when the Lord will return, there are those who reject the reality of His return and regard this Biblical teaching as a superstitious idea. Peter confronts the latter position in the third chapter of his second epistle.

B. Lesson Background

Peter was highly qualified to address the issue of the second coming, not only because he was inspired by the Holy Spirit, but also because he was present on the Mount of Olives when Jesus gave His famous discourse on the fall of Jerusalem and the return of Christ (Matthew 24, 25). Second Peter does provide some interesting data related to the day of Christ's return. But what makes Peter's account of the second coming so interesting is his use of this doctrine to impart teaching on some very important themes—God's mercy and long-suffering, and man's response.

I. A Challenge to the Church (2 Peter 3:3, 4)

A. Why the Delay? (vv. 3, 4a)

3, 4a. Knowing this first, that there shall come in the last days scoffers, walking after their own lusts, and saying, Where is the promise of his coming?

Peter warns the church to be prepared to face the *scoffers* who will ridicule the doctrine of the second coming. When they ask, *Where is the promise of his coming?* they are not asking for a list of Scripture passages that teach this doctrine. They know that Jesus spoke of returning and they are aware of the assumption of many Christians that Christ would return within only a few years of His departure. Statements such as "the Lord's coming is near" (James 5:8, *New International Version*) lead to this mistaken opinion. Thus the scoffers will try to put the Lord's people on the spot by demanding that they account for the unexpected delay. What they are really asking is, "Where is this coming that was promised?"

This scoffing is to occur *in the last days*. While this expression is often understood today as a reference to the final years before the second coming, the New Testament uses this and similar phrases to refer to the entire period from Christ's ascension to His return. Peter himself announced on the Day of Pentecost that the "last days" were inaugurated by the outpouring of the Holy Spirit that occurred on that day (Acts 2:16,

17). Thus Peter is not addressing a problem relating to the distant future, but a challenge to the church of his day and every period down to the present.

B. How Could It Be Possible? (v. 4b)

4b. For since the fathers fell asleep, all things continue as they were from the beginning of the creation.

Since the fathers fell asleep. When Peter wrote this letter, more than thirty years had passed since the ascension. Christ had promised to return, but He had not done it. Now the first generation of Christians was rapidly passing away. "It is foolish for us to look for Him," the scoffers said, "when the fathers looked in vain for His return."

All things continue as they were from the beginning of the creation. In addition to ridiculing the delay in Christ's return, the scoffers propose a "scientific" argument. Spectacular signs were promised in connection with Jesus' coming (Matthew 24:29, 30), but the scoffers imply that such a cataclysmic occurrence will not occur because nothing so radical has ever occurred in history. They assume that the forces that are observable now are the same as those that have always been, and always will be, at work in the universe.

II. A Response to the Skeptics
(2 Peter 3:5-9)

A. Precedent for Radical Events
(vv. 5-7)

5. For this they willingly are ignorant of, that by the word of God the heavens were of old, and the earth standing out of the water and in the water.

By pointing to the creation of the world, Peter responds to the argument that no radical event comparable to the coming destruction of the earth has ever occurred. While every act of God during the creation was stupendous, Peter particularly emphasizes the power of God's word that caused the earth to stand *out of the water and in the water.* This is a reference to the separating of the seas from the land masses, which is recorded in Genesis 1:9, 10, truly a radical event.

Peter accuses the scoffers of not being wholly sincere in debating this issue when he says that they *willingly are ignorant* of the implications of creation upon their argument. They introduced the concept of creation in their challenge in verse 4, and yet they pretend not to see how it weakens their case.

6. Whereby the world that then was, being overflowed with water, perished.

As a second example of a radical event comparable to the destruction of the world by fire, Peter cites the flood of Noah's day. This was certainly a unique episode in earth's history, demonstrating that God can intervene into the normal operations of nature.

7. But the heavens and the earth, which are now, by the same word are kept in store, reserved unto fire against the day of judgment and perdition of ungodly men.

Having spoken of the state of the earth during creation and the flood, Peter turns his attention to *the heavens and the earth, which are now.* The universe remains under God's control. The reference to *the same word* goes back to verse 5, where the dividing of the waters was produced "by the word of God." God preserves the universe by His power: it is "reserved for fire, being kept for the day of judgment and destruction of ungodly men" (*New International Version*). The end of the world will come in a great conflagration, which is presented more vividly in verse 10.

Thus Peter contends that the destruction of the universe by fire is believable because there is sufficient precedent for such a radical event.

THE RISE OF RIDICULE

An eight-year-old returned home after Sunday school and found his dad reading the paper.

"What did you learn today?" asked the father, his eyes never leaving the sports section.

"Well, Dad," responded the boy, "we learned how Moses led the Israelites across the Red Sea, and it was great! The Israelites got out of Egypt, but Pharaoh and his army chased them. When the Israelites got to the Red Sea they were trapped. So Moses got on his walkie-talkie and told the corp of engineers to build a pontoon bridge. Then the Israelites crossed over the bridge. Then he called up the air force, and they came and bombed the bridge just as the Egyptians were beginning to pass over it. After that, Moses and the children of Israel headed off to the promised land."

Dad, who by now had dropped the newspaper, asked, "Is that what your teacher taught you?"

"Well, not exactly," the boy replied, "but if I told you the way she taught it, you'd never believe it!"

Many of the events recorded in Scripture are passed off by some as fairy tales. Such persons scoff at the teaching of the second coming as well. Doubtless, people scoffed at Noah, but they could not hold back the waters when the flood came. Christ has promised that He will return, and we who believe in Him trust His word. When He appears, He will end all doubt for eternity.

—T. T.

B. God's Timing (v. 8)

8. But, beloved, be not ignorant of this one thing, that one day is with the Lord as a thousand years, and a thousand years as one day.

The scoffers' used the delay in Christ's return to ridicule the promise of it. Peter gives two responses in verses 8 and 9. First he notes that the eternal God does not reckon time on the same scale as humankind. *Be not ignorant of this one thing.* Don't overlook this fact. The scoffers in Peter's day had the mistaken idea that God views time the same as we humans do. But God is infinite, and we are finite. God does not have to think in terms of minutes or hours or days as we do. For the eternal God, time does not exist. How then can we attempt to subject Him to this human standard? *A thousand years as one day.* Peter alludes to Psalm 90:4. This statement is a very expressive way of saying that time means little or nothing to God.

A caution, therefore, is in order for this verse. It is dangerous to assume that Peter is giving a secret formula for deducing the date of Christ's return. Many of the failed attempts referred to earlier have used the "one thousand years equals one day" scheme unconvincingly. It would seem appropriate to encourage less interest in date guessing and more emphasis upon Peter's lesson in this passage—that of staying ready for Christ's return at all times as if He might return at any time.

C. God's Patience (v. 9)

9. The Lord is not slack concerning his promise, as some men count slackness; but is long-suffering to us-ward, not willing that any should perish, but that all should come to repentance.

The second insight Peter gives concerning the seeming delay in Christ's return is that God is long-suffering toward us. Every day that God holds back the destruction of the world the church gains a little more time to rescue sinners

visual 14

who are destined for Hell. Thus God is not *slack* as if He were "dragging His feet" or being tardy, but is considering what is in the best interest of humankind.

God is *not willing that any should perish, but that all should come to repentance.* In 1 Timothy 2:4 Paul expressed the same thought when he said that God "will have all men to be saved, and to come unto the knowledge of the truth." Eternal life is God's gift to fallen humanity, but the lost must accept the gift when it is offered. God does all He can, short of destroying our wills, to bring us to love and serve Him. He longingly waits for men and women to repent.

III. A Lesson for the Prudent (2 Peter 3:10-14)

A. Prepare for God's Judgment (vv. 10-12)

10. But the day of the Lord will come as a thief in the night; in the which the heavens shall pass away with a great noise, and the elements shall melt with fervent heat, the earth also and the works that are therein shall be burned up.

Christ's return will resemble the coming of *a thief in the night* in one respect: there will be no advance warning. Undoubtedly Peter remembered Jesus' use of this comparison when He spoke of His return (see Matthew 24:43).

The day of the Lord will signal the destruction of the material universe. In a terrible blast the heavens will disappear, and in tremendous heat the elements will disintegrate. The earth and everything in it will be *burned up.* All of humankind's creations and everything human beings have done are included in the expression *the works that are therein.* Since these will be destroyed, Peter recommends in the following verse that Christians concentrate upon building that which can survive the fire.

11. Seeing then that all these things shall be dissolved, what manner of persons ought ye to be in all holy conversation and godliness.

Here Peter relates the doctrine of the second coming to his theme of godliness. All things related to this physical world *shall be dissolved* by the fire. All earthly accomplishments will be stripped away. The things of this world that many believe give life meaning and value will be worthless at the judgment. Only those treasures that we have laid up in Heaven will withstand the devastation of that day (Matthew 6:19, 20). By our *holy conversation* (conduct) *and godliness* we show that we have separated ourselves from the value system of this world and that our citizenship is in Heaven.

12. Looking for and hasting unto the coming of the day of God, wherein the heavens being on fire shall be dissolved, and the elements shall melt with fervent heat?

God's people who live holy and godly lives need not fear *the coming of the day of God* for their character will withstand the fires of judgment. They can be eagerly anticipating Christ's return and *hasting* it, that is, speeding it up. Peter probably means that we can make the delay seem shorter by an attitude of anticipation.

B. Prepare for the New Creation
(vv. 13, 14)

13. Nevertheless we, according to his promise, look for new heavens and a new earth, wherein dwelleth righteousness.

Although the present physical order will be destroyed, God has promised that there will be *new heavens and a new earth.* The traditional view has been that the fire associated with the day of the Lord will annihilate the present physical universe so that God can then replace it with a "heaven and earth" created totally from scratch. This concept fits well with passages of Scripture such as Isaiah 65:17 and 66:22 and may in fact be what literally will happen.

An alternate view, however, is that God will use the fire to refine the earth and put it into a state comparable to its original goodness. The heavens and earth would be *new* in the sense of being renewed or restored to perfection once again. This theory makes use of the obvious parallel in this passage between the end of the world and the great flood (v. 6). The world is said to have *perished* in the flood, and yet rather than having been wiped out of existence, the sinful element of humanity was purged by the water.

Regardless of how God chooses to create the *new heavens and a new earth,* one fact is certain: there will be no unworthy element in them. In the new order, only *righteousness* will be found.

14. Wherefore, beloved, seeing that ye look for such things, be diligent that ye may be found of him in peace, without spot, and blameless.

Seeing that ye look for such things. That is, the return of Christ and the promise of the new heavens and earth. Since only righteousness will survive in the new order, Peter urges us to diligently practice now the type of behavior that is fitting for the new creation. Trusting in Christ and trying to imitate Him in our daily lives, we can know the *peace* that He alone can give, and we need not fear the judgment.

Conclusion
A. Two Reactions

The sounds of a fire engine racing by instinctively fill us with emotions of terror and excitement. We shudder to think of what damage and injuries may have occurred, and yet we are stimulated by the intense activity. These contrasting emotions will likewise be experienced on the day Christ returns, though not by the same persons. For sinners there will be terror in their hearts as they face the onslaught of the fires of judgment, but not so for the saints. Those who have faithfully pursued a holy and godly life will be thrilled with excitement at the sight of the fire that marks the final act of refining toward their goal of righteousness.

The good news is that we get to choose in advance which emotion we will experience when Christ returns. This passage from 2 Peter gives ample warning of what is to come and good advice on how we can put ourselves in a position to reap blessings rather than condemnation on that day. But the lesson drawn from this chapter will prove effective only if it instills within us a sense of urgency. Let us act now to get our lives in order so as not to be found unprepared on the day of accounting.

B. Let Us Pray

Father, Your word reminds us that Christ will surely return to usher in the Day of Judgment. Help us to see the importance of making preparation now to face that day. In Jesus' name we pray. Amen.

C. Thought to Remember

"He which testifieth these things saith, Surely I come quickly: Amen. Even so, come, Lord Jesus" (Revelation 22:20).

Home Daily Bible Readings

Monday, May 25—Signs of the End (Matthew 24:3-14)

Tuesday, May 26—Watch at All Times (Luke 21:29-36)

Wednesday, May 27—Under Perditions (2 Peter 3:1-7)

Thursday, May 28—Trust in the Promise (2 Peter 3:8-13)

Friday, May 29—Grow in Grace (2 Peter 3:14-18)

Saturday, May 30—Live for the Promise (Hebrews 11:8-16)

Sunday, May 31—Rejoice in the Promise (Isaiah 65:17-25)

Learning by Doing

This page contains an alternate lesson plan emphasizing learning activities. Classes desiring such student involvement will find these suggestions helpful.

Learning Goals

After this lesson a student will be able to do the following:

1. Compare the destruction of the earth by water in the days of Noah with the final destruction of the earth with fire.

2. Contrast the value of temporal and eternal things.

3. Suggest some activities appropriate for one who anticipates the coming of the Lord.

Into the Lesson

Write "Items of Value" on the chalkboard before class begins. As the students arrive, ask them to write under this heading on the chalkboard things they consider valuable.

When the class has assembled and there are several items listed, ask the class to note which ones have eternal value. Mark an "E" next to each of these. Among the items listed should be salvation, one's children, the church, and the souls of the lost.

Discuss the relative value of the eternal and the temporal items listed. Note the irony of our devoting so much time and effort to attaining or maintaining temporal things while we spend relatively little time providing for that which is eternal.

Into the Word

Ask a student to read the text, 2 Peter 3:3-14, aloud. Then divide the class into groups of three or four students and give each group one of the arguments from the following list of "Arguments Against the Second Coming of Christ and the End of the Present World." Ask each group to use this text to refute the argument it has been given. After five minutes, call for reports and list on the chalkboard arguments *for* the second coming and the Biblical doctrine of the end of the world.

Arguments Against the Second Coming of Christ and the End of the Present World

The Scientific Argument: Everything happens just as it has always happened.

The Time Argument: If Christ hasn't come by now, He must not be coming.

The Good Earth Argument: We make our own Heaven or Hell right here on earth.

The Conservation Argument: God wouldn't destroy His own creation.

After briefly discussing Peter's description of the final destruction of the physical universe, call attention to the fact that God "destroyed" the world once before (see verse 6). Make two columns on the chalkboard, one headed "Flood" and the other "Final." Ask the class to compare and contrast the two events. Then ask, "What do God's actions in relation to the great flood suggest concerning the end of the world?" (Examples: God keeps His promises, God judges the wicked and saves the righteous, the Lord is patient and willing to save all who repent of sin.)

Into Life

Ask the class, "What do you think is the proper response to what we know about the Lord's return?" After a few minutes, note that some people think the information we are given is designed to help us determine when the Lord will return. Point out that these unsuccessful efforts add fuel to modern "scoffers" who ridicule Christians for believing in the second coming. Mention Peter's own application: "What kind of people ought you to be? You ought to live holy and godly lives as you look forward to the day of God. . . . So then, . . . make every effort to be found spotless, blameless and at peace with him" (2 Peter 3:11, 12, 14, *New International Version*).

Ask the class to suggest some characteristics of one who is looking forward to the Lord's return. Make a list on the chalkboard. As you conclude this discussion, note that God is as much or more concerned with what kind of persons we *are* as what we *do*. Peter says we should "make every effort to be found spotless, blameless and at peace with him [God]." Discuss these three concepts and consider how one can be what they describe.

As you conclude the session, ask the students to think about what we should do and be as we look forward to Christ's return. Ask each student to choose one or two of these and make a special effort this week to develop that characteristic. Also, have each one choose another student (not related to himself or herself) and pray for that person during the week. Students do not need to tell what characteristics they are trying to improve (unless they feel comfortable sharing such information). Simply assign "prayer partners" and ask them to pray for each other, that they will live holy and godly lives.

Let's Talk It Over

The questions on this page are designed to encourage review of the lesson Scriptures and to promote discussion of the lesson by the class. The answers provided are only discussion starters. Let your class talk it over from there.

1. Peter asserts that a time of moral accountability and judgment before God is coming when He will destroy the heavens, the earth, and ungodly persons. Why do some people today find that difficult to believe, and what does all this tell us about their perception of God?

Many people think God is impotent because evil persons appear to go unpunished and those who do good seem to suffer. Others insist that God is a God of love and would never bring such punishment on humankind. Still others believe that because so many years have passed, Christ's coming will not happen. These false ideas, along with others, contribute to the belief of some that Christ will not return and God's judgment will not come. Such persons ignore the truth of God's holiness and righteousness, which require the punishment of sin. They also mistake God's love and patience toward sinful humanity as impotence. Basically they err in lowering God to their human level of understanding.

2. Peter says that God is long-suffering to us, that is, He is patient (3:9). How does God's patience produce frustration in us, and how is God's patience a blessing to us?

Most of us tend to become impatient when difficulty and distress mount, situations grow worse, and no relief appears. We are angered at the injustices we observe in life. We cry for justice and fairness, and when none comes we grow frustrated. Our world goes from bad to worse, and in our frustration, we question God's wisdom in allowing these conditions to continue. However, as Peter points out, God's patience is a blessing to us because it has allowed time for us to repent and escape the punishment for our sins. God's patience is allowing time for others to be given the opportunity to be reconciled to Him. If we look honestly at our lives, how grateful we should be that God is patient in extending His love and withholding His judgment, so that we can get right with Him!

3. Christ's coming is certain; yet, many of us remain somewhat apathetic about it. In what ways should the certainty of Christ's return affect our thinking and behavior?

The certainty of Christ's return should cause us to bring into focus that which is eternal and that which is only temporal. A conviction about the coming of Christ should make us question such life goals as keeping up with the Joneses or accumulating possessions simply for pride or personal enjoyment. We should begin to sort through our values, goals, life-styles and the like to determine the things of eternal consequence that are worthy of presenting to the victorious Lord upon His return. We should cease our halfhearted commitment to God and begin to make the pursuit of holiness and godliness the top priority in our lives.

4. Christ's return may occur at any time, and some in their enthusiasm attempt to determine the date for the end. How may the fixing of dates for Christ's return distract us in our Christian discipleship?

An excessive enthusiasm for attempting to determine the time of Christ's return may lead us to focus energies away from the important issue of being prepared for a sudden and unexpected return. It is crucial for us to be ready at any moment for Christ to appear. We need to heed Peter's exhortations to godly living. Moreover, Jesus told His followers not to speculate about the dates that the Father alone knows (Acts 1:7), and an excessive preoccupation with fixing a date for the second coming ignores Christ's word regarding this matter.

5. When Jesus comes again in judgment, everything will be stripped away, and He will be looking for holiness and godliness in our lives. How can we cultivate these attitudes and actions that will prepare us for the Lord's return?

Knowing the high value that God places on godly character should motivate us to search the Scriptures daily to see what God wants us to do and to be. We should be open to the Spirit's convicting, and we should pray for God's Spirit to help us make our lives pleasing to Him. Repentance of sin should naturally occur and be followed by the life changes that God commands in His Word. Devotion to God and humble service toward others need to be permanently present in our lives.

Summer Quarter, 1992

Theme: God's Judgment and Mercy

Special Features

Lessons

Unit 1: Warnings and Promises From God

Unit 2: A Remnant Is Saved

Theme: Guidelines for Ministry

Unit 1: Guidelines for Leading

Unit 2: Guidelines for Serving

Related Resources

The following publications give additional help for the lessons in the Summer Quarter. They may be purchased from your supplier. Prices are subject to change.

Old Testament Maps and Charts. This packet contains eight maps and four charts. Order #14-02607, $9.95.

Teach With Success, by Guy P. Leavitt; revised by Eleanor Daniel. Offers ideas for successful teaching and includes an update on terms and trends. Order #18-03232, $9.95.

Timothy—Philemon (Standard Bible Studies), by Knofel Staton. Practical help for all who serve Christ. Order #11-40112, $9.95.

Jun 7

Jun 14

Jun 21

Jun 28

Jul 5

Jul 12

Jul 19

Jul 26

Aug 2

Aug 9

Aug 16

Aug 23

Aug 30

Continuing Concern

by Knofel Staton

THE LESSONS of the Summer 1992 quarter are based on two distinct sections of the Bible. Lessons 1-7 come from the minor prophets in the Old Testament, and lessons 8-13 from the pastoral letters in the New Testament. While hundreds of years separate the historical periods dealt with by these sections of the Bible, a natural bridge with several common planks connects the two time zones.

One plank on the bridge is the plank of inspiration—the Holy Spirit inspired the writing of both sections. Another plank is that both sections deal with the application of God's truth to the life-styles of the readers. A third plank is that both sections are pastoral in nature; they are written to God's people for their benefit.

Some of the instructions, principles, guidelines, and commands are not easy reading, because they call for changes of life. Nevertheless, they are essential reading, for they contain vital elements for character building.

Major Principles From Minor Prophets

Below is a snapshot of some of the major principles coming from the minor prophets:

Lesson 1 (June 7). This lesson is based on Obadiah, a little book with a big message. It is about the fall of a pagan nation on the one hand, and about God's protection of a part of His people on the other hand. Both peoples had done wrong, but their destiny rested in what they did with that wrong. Edom (the nation that would fall) refused to repent, while some of Judah (the nation that would stand) repented. Repentance *does* make a difference in our destinies.

Although life may be falling apart all around us, we who are God's people do not have to fall apart with it.

Lesson 2 (June 14). This lesson is taken from the first chapter of Jonah and shows us what happened when a prophet clearly heard God's command but refused to heed it. God said, "Go," but Jonah said, "No."

This lesson also shows a significant difference between nature and human beings. Nature does not have the freedom to choose to obey or disobey when God gives any element of it a command (such as a command to the wind or the fish), but God has given human beings that freedom. Thus, our response to God comes out of our own desires. It can be a response of love toward Him or love toward self.

This lesson also reaffirms the fact that there is no place on earth where a person can run and get away from God's awareness.

Lesson 3 (June 21). This lesson comes from the last portion of the book of Jonah. It shows God's response when people repent of sin and turn to Him. It shows also that the mercy of God is above the rationality of man. The amazing power of God's word to change human lives is demonstrated in the actions of the Ninevites after Jonah brought God's message to them.

This lesson also pinpoints the barrier of prejudice as it relates to the advancement of God's kingdom. Jonah's prejudice against Nineveh originally kept him from taking God's word to its citizens; and when they did turn to God, he could not rejoice in their salvation.

Lesson 4 (June 28). This lesson comes from the pen of Nahum. Evil was all around God's people, and they were getting the brunt of it. It sometimes seems odd that evil can increase, while the hurt and pain against Christians continue. This lesson addresses this issue.

God knows what is going on, but He is patient and gives the enemies of His people time to change. God is not quick to destroy the rebellious. We should be grateful for the patience of God, because it affects us positively, too. God's slowness to punish does not reflect a weakness; rather, His patience is another demonstration of divine power.

The wicked can go only so far, however; God will intervene if repentance does not occur.

Lesson 5 (July 5). This lesson addresses the issue of the mounting evil of Judah and how God was going to deal with it. God's sovereignty over the nations is seen in His use of the Chaldeans to bring His judgment to bear on His rebellious people. This lesson is organized around Habakkuk's complaint to God and God's answer to him.

Lesson 6 (July 12). This lesson, based on the first two chapters of Zephaniah, deals with one of the darkest periods in the history of God's people. The prophet warned of the terrible punishment that was coming and pled for the people to repent.

Lesson 7 (July 19). This lesson comes from the last chapter of Zephaniah and emphasizes God's act of restoring, reconciling, and recycling His people who had previously turned their backs on Him.

This unit begins with the rebellion of people who wouldn't repent and ends with the restoration of those who did repent. God's extensive love for all people is obvious.

Guidelines for Ministry

Lessons 8-13 are based on 1 and 2 Timothy and Titus. These letters are called "pastoral" because Paul was writing to those who were pastors, or shepherds, of God's flock, the church. Lest we think, however, that these letters do not apply to us, we must remember that all of us have been called to be ministers of reconciliation (2 Corinthians 5:19, 20). All of us are leaders to someone, whether we realize it or not. We are either good leaders or bad leaders. This section of lessons gives us guidelines for being good leaders.

Below is a summary of the lessons in this section:

Lesson 8 (July 26). People today are exposed to many philosophies, and it is obvious that there is disagreement in both content and emphasis in what is taught. What is a person to listen to, believe, and apply? This is not a new problem, nor are these new questions. That was the same situation that faced the church at Ephesus when Paul wrote 1 Timothy.

This lesson teaches us to avoid majoring in minors and minoring in majors. The purpose of Christian teaching is to help us to express love from a pure heart, to possess a sincere faith, and to live with a good conscience. It should help us to recognize and avoid those philosophies that are merely human speculation, which generate fruitless discussion and division in the body of Christ.

We must be good listeners of apostolic truth, good lovers with a godly spirit, and good warriors in the correct fight—not in fighting one another.

Lesson 9 (August 2). Since all of us are leaders of some, it is not enough just to know the right things; we must also become the right kind of people.

Being the right kind of person involves the right kind of teaching and the right practices. Right practice is summarized in the word "godliness." To be godly is to be Christlike. God's goal for us is to mature into the image of His Son.

Lesson 10 (August 9). A leader who rightly leads others is not only the one who has the right content in teaching and the right kind of character, but also one who models the right kind of contentment. Our attitude toward material possessions will strongly determine the strength of our godliness. A person filled with greed will do little to serve another unselfishly.

This lesson teaches that a person's value is not determined by what he owns, but by what owns him. A Christian who is wealthy in doctrine but stingy in dollars is out of balance.

Lesson 11 (August 16). We have seen thus far several aspects of a good leader, and God wants all of us to be good leaders. Indeed, we are all leaders of one kind or another, for someone is watching us and following us whether we know it or not. Good leaders are not just busy doing things, but are also busy studying truth. Our behavior comes out of our beliefs; our beliefs come out of how we understand God's Word. In this lesson we find many metaphors to describe the well-rounded Christian—a soldier, an athlete, and a farmer.

Lesson 12 (August 23). This lesson comes from Paul's second letter to Timothy and emphasizes the following three truths about leadership:

1. It is lonely at the top. Leaders will often get criticized and/or persecuted.

2. All Scripture is inspired by God; it is flawless and is God's primary source for training us toward maturity of Christlikeness.

3. Christian leaders are to be on twenty-four hour alert. They are to be ready for service in the name of Christ at any time—in season or out of season.

Lesson 13 (August 30). This lesson is based on Paul's letter to Titus and emphasizes three major truths:

1. Christianity is a religion in which every member has concern for every other member, and that concern is seen as each sets a good example for others in word and deed.

2. God's grace is always greater than man's disgrace. God's grace does not give us the "green light" to continue to sin, but rather deepens our respect and reverence for Him and helps us say "no" to ungodliness.

3. Our salvation does not rest upon a work ethic—that we have done everything right—but upon God's mercy—that He has done right things for us and to us. Because of Jesus, we can experience two big "R" words—rebirth into the family of God and the renewal of the Holy Spirit in the life of the individual.

These lessons from the pastoral epistles remind us that we are all like sheep who have gone astray. We need not only the Chief Shepherd who is the Lord Jesus, but we also need some under-shepherds—pastors—to help us stay in the flock, to search for us when we stray, to rescue us when we get lost in our detours, and to keep reminding us that the Chief Shepherd has died for us, that He loves us, and that one day He will return for us.

Wait on the Lord

by S. Edward Tesh

SHALL NOT THE JUDGE of all the earth do right?" (Genesis 18:25). This simple question from the lips of Abraham was so phrased as to evoke an affirmative answer. Most assuredly God will never deviate from the path of rectitude. The very thought that He could ever be guilty of injustice is abhorrent to a devout soul. Yet, in view of events continually transpiring all about us, are there not times when we would question God's governance of the world? We struggle with life's injustices. We see evil rampant in the world, and we ask, "Why doesn't God act? Is He not all-powerful? Is He not good? Why, then, does evil persist? Why do we seem to find 'truth forever on the scaffold, wrong forever on the throne'?" (James Russell Lowell).

The Circumstances

This matter deeply concerned the prophet Habakkuk. A contemporary of Jeremiah, he witnessed in his land those circumstances that brought tears to Jeremiah and caused him to become known as "the weeping prophet." The nation of Judah was torn within by strife, as the righteous suffered at the hands of the wicked. And great danger threatened from without also, for Babylon was rising to the status of a world power under Nebuchadnezzar.

Why did God permit this? All around, Habakkuk saw the unrighteous pursuing wickedness, deliberately and audaciously. Why should these wicked ones prosper? Why would a righteous God continue to permit this sin to go unpunished?

Why Doesn't God Do Something?

God apparently had kept silent in the matter. Could it be that He had forgotten the world and its problems? Did He set the universe in motion only to go off and abandon it to itself? Or, had He established the seed of Abraham as a nation as He had promised (Genesis 12:2), only to see it perish in sin? This fate had come to the northern kingdom, Israel. So set had they become in their evil ways that God permitted the land to be overrun by the Assyrians, and Israel was no more.

Now the unrestrained evil in Judah threatened the existence of this nation also. Habakkuk had prayed earnestly to God, but still the evil persisted. The law was ineffective. The wicked prevailed. Why didn't God do something?

God Is Doing Something

The apostle Peter reminds us that God is patient and long-suffering toward sinful humanity. This we should remember when we see the triumph of evil persons, and when we feel that God is slow to administer justice (2 Peter 3:9). Be assured that God is aware of what is going on in the world and that His judgment will certainly come. In the case of Judah, that judgment was about to fall. "I am bringing the Chaldeans to power," God said, "a fierce, dreadful, restless people. Their army is ruthless, violent, and invincible. With no regard for king or prince, they will sweep over the land."

Does this mean that God deliberately raised up such a barbarous nation for this one purpose—to punish Judah for her wickedness? We think not. In similar fashion the Lord had spoken of Assyria as "the rod of mine anger" that would chastise Jerusalem for her sins (Isaiah 10:5). Yet God made clear that the Assyrians were not motivated by any desire to accomplish His will (see Isaiah 10:7). They were motivated rather by a lust to conquer, to pillage, and to destroy. Consequently, after they had served God's purpose of disciplining Jerusalem, the Lord would hold them accountable for their terrible deeds (see Isaiah 10:12-19).

So with the Chaldeans. They were barbarous, ruthless, cruel, because they chose to be. But even in a world where humankind exercises its will to do evil, ultimate control is in the hands of God, and even "the wrath of man" may serve to accomplish God's purpose and to bring praise to Him (Psalm 76:10).

Yet Another Problem

The wickedness and violence in Judah that caused Habakkuk such distress would be dealt with. God had heard his prayer and assured him of this. But the Chaldeans were a brutal and idolatrous people, much more wicked even than Judah. "O Lord," Habakkuk acknowledged, "you have appointed them to execute judgment . . . you have ordained them to punish. . . . [But] why then do you tolerate the treacherous? Why are you silent while the wicked [Chaldeans] swallow up those more righteous than themselves?" (1:12, 13, *New International Version*). Judah was sinful, but was it right that she suffer abuse from a people more wicked?

This question of theodicy (the presence of evil in a God-ordered world) has broader ramifications as presented in the book of Job. "Wherefore," Job asked, "do the wicked live, become old, yea, are mighty in power? . . . Their houses are safe from fear." The "rod of God" does not fall upon them.

In perfect health they enjoy a luxurious life with their children and with their children's children, and at death they slip peacefully away—"in a moment [they] go down to the grave"—with no lingering illness, no suffering. (See Job 21:7-15.) On the other hand, Job, whom God himself had declared to be "perfect" and "upright" (Job 1:8), was bereaved of all his children, had lost all his possessions, and was suffering from a dreadful and painful disease. Why?

Throughout his ordeal, the most distressing thing for Job was the belief that God had abandoned him. In fellowship with God, Job had enjoyed good health and a good life with his family. Now all of this was gone! Why? Why had God abandoned him? These were his thoughts. He was to learn that God had not forsaken him, and this knowledge would be enough to quiet his troubled heart (Job 42:5, 6). But the answer to the why of his suffering was never disclosed to him.

A Partial Answer

Is a complete answer granted us? I think not. So much is involved—the sovereignty of God, the free will of man, the interaction of the laws of nature (cause and effect), the exercise of God's mercy toward the sinner, etc. It is evident that God allows humankind, even the wicked, considerable freedom to do as they please, even when they please to do evil to others. (See John 19:10, 11.) God would not deprive even the wicked the power of choice, for without this there would be no basis for moral judgment. Or, put another way, if a person did not have the choice of saying "no" to God, then his "yes" would be wholly without significance. Sadly, many choose all the while—and others, part of the time!—to disobey God (the Ten Commandments, for example), even as they reject the admonition of Christ to love one another. And evil is the result. Here is a very obvious answer to the why of evil. Much of it, even much of sickness and disease, is the result of choosing by humankind to do evil. In such cases it is not our prerogative to ask God, "Why?" but to repent. If we depart from the way of God and reap the consequences, let us not seek to lay the blame for our condition upon Him, but return to Him to receive His mercy and forgiveness.

But why should the righteous have to bear suffering at the hands of the wicked? Or, why should the homes of the godly be swept away by the cyclone while others remain untouched?

The Scriptures give some insights relative to the matter. To Habakkuk it was revealed that the evil of the Chaldeans would serve as a chastisement of Judah for the sins of the nation. But lest one who suffers feels that he must entertain a guilt complex, let it be remembered that there is much undeserved suffering in the world. The innocent do suffer at the hands of others. Why?

Sometimes it appears that the evil are permitted to prevail in order to temper the character of the righteous. No one may know the true strength of his or her character until it is put to the test. Surely, no one would invite mistreatment at the hands of the wicked. But just as surely, only those who have experienced such a test can know their true mettle.

Others who undergo the abuse of those around them develop the virtues of patience, courage, and endurance, and they learn the grace of returning good for evil. Above all, they are enabled to grow stronger in faith. However, the time comes when even the most patient soul may cry out with Habakkuk, "How long, O Lord!"

What to Do

The answer to Habakkuk was concise, but clear. "Those who are evil will not survive, but those who are righteous will live because they are faithful to God" (Habakkuk 2:4, *Today's English Version*). This message was to be written by the prophet on tablets—clearly, so as to be easily read (2:2), and written because it was not yet time for it to come to pass. It was "for an appointed time." However, it would surely come, so "wait for it" (2:3).

This assurance was enough for Habakkuk. See his great expression of faith: "I will wait patiently for the day of calamity to come on the nation invading us. Though the fig tree does not bud and there are no grapes on the vines, though the olive crop fails and the fields produce no food, though there are no sheep in the pen and no cattle in the stalls, yet I will rejoice in the Lord, I will be joyful in God my Savior" (3:16-18, *New International Version*).

"The Lord is a God of justice. Blessed are all who wait for him!" (Isaiah 30:18, *New International Version*). Where the heart is completely devoid of hope, waiting is torture. But one waits for the Lord as he may wait for the sunrise—expectantly, knowing that what he anticipates will be realized. "Weeping may endure for a night, but joy cometh in the morning" (Psalm 30:5). Wait on the Lord!

Make Your Life Count

by James B. North

THE LETTERS TO TIMOTHY AND TITUS are often referred to as "the Pastoral Letters." While this is a valid title (the letters are full of advice to preachers or anyone else who is involved in a caring for God's flock), some people perceive these letters to have value only to ministers. This is unfortunate, because the letters are full of advice on how Christians ought to act toward each other. A person doesn't have to be a preacher to find these letters worth studying. Everyone can profit from them.

It may also be helpful to keep in mind the great principle that Martin Luther brought out in the Protestant Reformation—the priesthood of all believers. The apostle Peter tells us that all Christians are a royal priesthood (1 Peter 2:9). If that is true, then we all have a ministry to perform as priests—perhaps even as pastors. Therefore, we ought to give even more attention to the lessons and principles covered in the Pastoral Letters.

A thorough study of these letters will indicate that there is much here that all Christians can learn. If we simply remember that we can all minister to each other, each of us will find areas of ministry where we can serve. In so doing, we can make our lives count.

General Service

There are some general areas of ministry that virtually all Christians can fill.

(1) Calling people on the telephone can be a very vital ministry for people who are shut-in, ill, recovering from illness, or just plain lonely. Some churches set up a phone chain of callers to contact people in these categories every day just to check on them to see that they are all right, or just to spend a few minutes of time with them over the telephone.

(2) Beyond telephoning is the matter of making personal visits. Some persons in the categories mentioned above appreciate having someone drop by for a brief visit. A personal visit takes more time than a telephone call, but the added investment of time also brings forth added appreciation from those being visited. Some churches have a few retired persons who are willing to devote a day or two per month to such home visitation. It provides a meaningful ministry for those being visited; it may also provide a meaningful ministry for those doing the visiting.

(3) All Christians can pray for others. A few churches have organized prayer groups that meet at the church building one day or more per week to pray for special needs within the congregational life. They pray both for group and individual concerns. One particular church has a widow's prayer circle. These women unite their prayer efforts on a regular basis. It provides a meaningful outlet of service for them, and various individuals within the congregation can also testify to its usefulness.

Concerted prayer efforts can be made even when Christians cannot meet together. One church has an organized prayer group that receives updates weekly through a telephone call. This way those who pray do not even leave their homes, but they all pray regularly for the needs they are informed of. Prayer is a mighty spiritual weapon, and it can be wielded in a variety of innovative ways.

Special Service

There are numerous areas of ministry that most people can do without special training—without being "the minister" of a local congregation. But there are also specialized tasks that need to be done that can be considered ministries.

(1) Many persons have craft skills in plumbing, carpentry, masonry, etc. Some use these skills to build new cabinets in the nursery departments of the church building. Others use their skills to provide repairs to the church plumbing or the roof. Others have used their skills as electricians to provide power outlets for window air conditioners. Both men and women who have approved chauffeurs' licenses have given their time and abilities to drive church buses. Those who are skilled in the use of computers have set up church offices with this type of equipment, trained the secretaries in how to use it, and have remained as a resource to advise on how to use computer technology in the church setting. All those persons who possess such specialized skills and training and have used them to advance the church's work have rendered ministry.

(2) Not everybody is comfortable speaking in front of an audience. But some persons have natural speaking skills that befit them to be good teachers. Sunday-school classes, youth groups, and numerous other areas of church life need

good teachers. Many persons have given of their time and efforts to serve in this way. Some persons have compiled Bible knowledge through the years and are willing to share it. Others have to study harder to feel prepared to stand before a class, but they devote themselves to this preparation in order to be equipped to teach.

(3) Musical abilities may not always be acquired simply through study. They involve a special, inherent talent. Some persons have this; others don't. However, those who are blessed with musical talent can always provide ministry in the life of the church. Congregational singing is a joyful time of praise, but for this part of the corporate worship service to be most effective, a qualified leader is needed. Any church that desires special music will need persons with musical talents. Churches large enough to have a choir must have someone who possesses the abilities of musical leadership to direct such a choir. All of these positions are music ministries.

This writer knows of a woman who is talented musically and has organizational skills. The church she was attending did not have a music program for children. Because of the age of her own children, she decided that a children's choir could be organized and could be a ministry within that congregation. The need had been there for some time, but no one had ever seen the opportunity or taken the initiative. So she organized a children's choir. Several years later her family moved out of town, but she encouraged another woman in the church to take over the children's choir. It is still functioning in that church.

In the new location, this woman saw a similar need. She organized another children's choir. After a few years, her children were in the junior high age bracket, and this church had no choir for that age group. She encouraged another woman to take over the children's choir, and she organized a junior and high school youth choir. After several successful years, this woman felt the need to go on to a different form of ministry, and she left the youth choir in the hands of another qualified person whom she had encouraged to take the position. The result of all this? There now exist three choirs that are still providing a musical ministry to children, youth, and the general life of the two congregations involved—all because of one woman who saw possibilities for ministry. She has never been paid for any of this—she simply saw these as opportunities for using her talents within the local congregation.

(4) Some people have professional skills that can be very useful in ministry. A certain medical doctor lives about a hundred miles away from a Bible college, but twice a month or so he takes a day and goes to the college where he provides a free medical clinic for the students, staff, and faculty. He provides excellent medical care while saving them a good deal of money. Also he is able to dispense without cost sample medications that he receives free from pharmaceutical suppliers. Indeed, his is a very much appreciated ministry.

This doctor is also active with the local high school athletic teams. Because the young people know him, they often come to his office for medical needs. There he is able to talk to them about spiritual matters and invite them to church. Many have come and there accepted Christ. More than once he has been chosen as the grand marshal of the town parade for the homecoming football game. Here is a man who is making his life count by providing a ministry through his special abilities.

Ministry

All Christians are called upon to serve the body of Christ, to perform a useful ministry. In the "Pastoral Letters," Paul gives advice to Timothy and Titus about how to conduct their own lives in light of some significant principles of Christian servanthood. Therefore, the content of these letters is beneficial beyond the circle of professional "pastors." These guidelines for ministry apply to all who wear the name of Christ—for we are all servants, we are all priests, we are all ministers. We are to look out for and promote the welfare of each other, and these three letters help us do that.

Answers to Quarterly Quiz
on page 344

Lesson 1—1. Edom. 2. violence. **Lesson 2**—1. Nineveh. 2. Tarshish. 3. three days and three nights. **Lesson 3**—1. believed God, proclaimed a fast, and put on sackcloth. 2. he was very angry. **Lesson 4**—1. Nineveh. 2. anger, power. **Lesson 5**—1. the Chaldeans. 2. faith. **Lesson 6**—1. Josiah. 2. good, evil. **Lesson 7**—1. enemy. 2. praise, fame. **Lesson 8**—1. heart, conscience, faith. 2. Hymeneus and Alexander. **Lesson 9**—1. godliness. 2. his youth. **Lesson 10**—1. great gain. 2. the love of money. 3. uncertain riches. **Lesson 11**—1. hardness. 2. the affairs of this life. 3. the word of truth. **Lesson 12**—1. salvation. 2. fables. **Lesson 13**—1. pattern. 2. good works.

Quarterly Quiz

The questions on this page may be used in several ways: as a pretest at the beginning of the quarter; as a review at the end of the quarter; or as a review after each lesson. The questions are based on the Scripture text of each lesson (King James Version). **The answers are on page 343.**

Lesson 1

1. Obadiah's prophecy concerned the punishment that God was bringing upon what nation? *Obadiah 1*

2. This nation would be covered with shame and cut off forever for their_____against their brother Jacob. *Obadiah 10*

Lesson 2

1. God told Jonah to go to what city and preach against their wickedness? *Jonah 1:2*

2. Jonah tried to escape God's presence by fleeing to what place? *Jonah 1:3*

3. How long was Jonah in the belly of a great fish? *Jonah 1:17*

Lesson 3

1. When Jonah finally did as God commanded and warned the wicked city of its impending doom, what three things did the people of the city do? *Jonah 3:5*

2. What was Jonah's response when God withheld His judgment of the city? *Jonah 4:1*

Lesson 4

1. Nahum foretold the utter ruin of what great city? *Nahum 1:1*

2. Nahum said, "The Lord is slow to _____, and great in _____, and will not at all acquit the wicked." *Nahum 1:3*

Lesson 5

1. What people, described by Habakkuk as "that bitter and hasty nation," was God raising up to punish Judah? *Habakkuk 1:6*

2. Habakkuk said, "The just shall live by his _____." *Habakkuk 2:4*

Lesson 6

1. Zephaniah prophesied during the reign of what king of Judah? *Zephaniah 1:1*

2. Zephaniah spoke of some in Jerusalem who did not fear the day of God's wrath, and who smugly thought, "The Lord will not do _____, neither will he do _____." *Zephaniah 1:12*

Lesson 7

1. In exulting over the restoration of Judah following her captivity, Zephaniah states that God has cast out her _____. *Zephaniah 3:15*

2. God said that in every land where His people had been put to shame, He would get them_____and _____. *Zephaniah 3:19*

Lesson 8

1. Paul said, "The end of the commandment is charity out of a pure _____, and of a good _____, and of _____unfeigned." *1 Timothy 1:5*

2. What two persons did Paul deliver unto Satan, that they might learn not to blaspheme? *1 Timothy 1:20*

Lesson 9

1. Paul told Timothy that bodily exercise profits little, but what is profitable unto all things, in this life and the life that is to come? *1 Timothy 4:8*

2. What was Timothy not to let anyone despise? *1 Timothy 4:12*

Lesson 10

1. Paul describes "godliness with contentment" as being what? *1 Timothy 6:6*

2. What does Paul say is the root of all evil? *1 Timothy 6:10*

3. Timothy was to instruct the wealthy that they were not to trust in what? *1 Timothy 6:17*

Lesson 11

1. As a good soldier of Jesus Christ, what was Timothy to endure? *2 Timothy 2:3*

2. A person who goes to war does not entangle himself with what? *2 Timothy 2:4*

3. What is God's workman to rightly divide? *2 Timothy 2:15*

Lesson 12

1. The holy Scriptures are able to make a person wise unto _____through faith which is in Christ Jesus. *2 Timothy 3:15*

2. Paul told Timothy that the time would come when people would turn away from the truth and be turned unto what? *2 Timothy 4:4*

Lesson 13

1. In all things, Titus was to be a _____of good works. *Titus 2:7*

2. Jesus Christ gave himself for us to redeem us from all iniquity and purify to himself a people zealous of what? *Titus 2:14*

The Lord Will Restore Judah

June 7
Lesson 1

LESSON SCRIPTURE: Obadiah.

PRINTED TEXT: Obadiah 1-4, 10, 11, 15, 17, 21.

Obadiah 1-4, 10, 11, 15, 17, 21

1 The vision of Obadiah. Thus saith the Lord GOD concerning Edom; We have heard a rumor from the LORD, and an ambassador is sent among the heathen, Arise ye, and let us rise up against her in battle.

2 Behold, I have made thee small among the heathen: thou art greatly despised.

3 The pride of thine heart hath deceived thee, thou that dwellest in the clefts of the rock, whose habitation is high; that saith in his heart, Who shall bring me down to the ground?

4 Though thou exalt thyself as the eagle, and though thou set thy nest among the stars, thence will I bring thee down, saith the LORD.

. . . .

10 For thy violence against thy brother Jacob shame shall cover thee, and thou shalt be cut off for ever.

11 In the day that thou stoodest on the other side, in the day that the strangers carried away captive his forces, and foreigners entered into his gates, and cast lots upon Jerusalem, even thou wast as one of them.

. . . .

15 For the day of the LORD is near upon all the heathen: as thou hast done, it shall be done unto thee: thy reward shall return upon thine own head.

. . . .

17 But upon mount Zion shall be deliverance, and there shall be holiness; and the house of Jacob shall possess their possessions.

. . . .

21 And saviours shall come up on mount Zion to judge the mount of Esau; and the kingdom shall be the LORD's.

GOLDEN TEXT: For the day of the LORD is near upon all the heathen: as thou hast done, it shall be done unto thee: thy reward shall return upon thine own head.
—Obadiah 15.

God's Judgment and Mercy
Unit 1: Warnings and Promises From God (Lessons 1-5)

Lesson Aims

This lesson is designed to help students:
1. Identify negative attitudes and actions that can destroy others and self.
2. Search their own experiences and identify any past grudges that they are keeping alive.
3. Take positive steps toward reconciliation rather than negative steps of retaliation.

Lesson Outline

INTRODUCTION
    A. Let It Go and Grow
    B. Lesson Background
I. RUIN OF EDOM FORETOLD (Obadiah 1-4)
    A. Obadiah's Vision (v. 1)
    B. Edom Brought Low (v. 2)
    C. Deceptive Pride (vv. 3, 4)
    Endangered Species
II. REASONS FOR PUNISHMENT (Obadiah 10, 11)
    A. Violence Against Judah (v. 10)
    B. Indifference Turned Into Involvement (v. 11)
    Passive Sinners
III. RETRIBUTION BY THE LORD (Obadiah 15)
    Repayment
IV. RESTORATION OF JUDAH (Obadiah 17, 21)
    A. God's Deliverance (v. 17)
    B. God's Reign (v. 21)
CONCLUSION
    A. Re-cancellation as Reconciliation
    B. Prayer
    C. Thought to Remember

Visual 1 of the visuals packet illustrates an important truth concerning human relationships. The visual is shown on page 348.

Introduction

A. Let It Go and Grow

When she was seventeen years old, she was wrongly locked up in a mental hospital where she stayed for twenty years. She was misdiagnosed, given the wrong drugs, locked away, and written off as a hopeless case. At one time she weighed only eighty-eight pounds.

A doctor at the hospital saw some potential in her and would not give up. She gradually began to recover, a step at a time. Twenty years later she was released.

Did she hold a grudge or sue the hospital for misdiagnosing her problem? No, at the age of thirty-seven, she entered college as a freshman and earned a degree in psychology. Then she went to Harvard University where she graduated with a master's degree. She returned to the hospital where she had been a patient all those years and worked as a social worker. She now is head of her own mental health institute—the Balter Institute.

Marie Balter let go of the negative past without a retaliatory spirit. She let it go and was able to grow from being "Nobody's Child" (the name of a television special about her) to becoming everybody's helper.

Sometimes, however, an individual, or a group of people, or even a whole nation will refuse to let go of a negative past and will not grow beyond it. Our lesson study for today describes the fall of what could have been the great nation of Edom had the people learned to "let it go and grow."

B. Lesson Background

Little is known of the prophet Obadiah. Several persons in the Old Testament have that name, but the prophet cannot be identified with any of them. Nor is the date of Obadiah's prophecy known for certain. Some regard him as among the earliest of the minor prophets (about 845 B. C.), whereas others place him after the destruction of Jerusalem (586 B. C.).

The book of Obadiah is small, but it has a big message. It concerns a historical situation that has a timeless application. It deals with the fall of the nation of Edom, and God's protection of a remnant of His people, Israel.

Edom and Judah had a common ancestry in Isaac. Isaac had twin sons, Esau and Jacob. The Edomites were descendants of Esau, and the Israelites were descendants of Jacob.

We recall the animosity that developed between the two brothers. On one occasion, Jacob took advantage of his brother and traded some food for Esau's birthright (Genesis 25:27-34). Later, when the father was old and wanted to bless Esau, the eldest son, Jacob disguised himself and pretended to be Esau so he could receive the blessing instead (Genesis 27).

Esau vowed to kill his brother after his father died. Learning of Esau's plan, Jacob ran away to escape his angry brother. Years later, when Jacob returned, they were reconciled. It seems however, that Esau's descendants continued to remember how their forefather had been mistreated, and thus they kept the feud alive.

Hundreds of years later the Edomites, who lived in the area south of the Dead Sea, refused to allow the Israelites to pass through their land while enroute to the promised land (Numbers 20:14-21).

God told the Israelites not to hate the Edomites, "for he is thy brother" (Deuteronomy 23:7). God is patient, but by the time of Obadiah, He had had enough of the unbrotherliness of the Edomites. Since they would not let go of the past, God let go of them.

This stands as a warning to us today. God commands us not to let the sun go down on our anger, nor allow the anger to cause us to sin against others (Ephesians 4:26). Instead, we are to forgive others as Christ has forgiven us.

The book of Obadiah has a vital message for every person who is holding a grudge, who refuses to let the past be past.

I. Ruin of Edom Foretold (Obadiah 1-4)

A. Obadiah's Vision (v. 1)

1. The vision of Obadiah. Thus saith the Lord God concerning Edom; We have heard a rumor from the Lord, and an ambassador is sent among the heathen, Arise ye, and let us rise up against her in battle.

The name *Obadiah* literally means "a servant" or "a worshiper of Jehovah." Here Obadiah served God by communicating the vision he received from Him. The exact manner in which the vision was given to the prophet is not stated.

It is clear that the revelation Obadiah received came directly from *the Lord God*. So what we read in this book are not the wishes of Obadiah, but the words that God commanded him to speak. Peter wrote centuries later, "For the prophecy came not in old time by the will of man: but holy men of God spake as they were moved by the Holy Ghost" (2 Peter 1:21).

The revelation concerned Edom, the nation that carried a grudge against Israel for centuries (see Lesson Background above). The message from God was not pleasant. An ambassador was sent to the heathen nations to stir them up to make war against Edom. God would use these nations to accomplish His purposes of judgment. In a similar way, God worked through nations to bring about the return of Judah after the Babylonian captivity (see Ezra 1:1-4).

Edom would have been surprised by this message from God, because she had gotten by with her grudge-bearing for so long. We may get by with carrying a grudge for years, but we do not know when God's patience with us will wear out. God will not stand idly by while His children are mistreated or slandered forever. God forgives, and He expects us to do the same.

B. Edom Brought Low (v. 2)

2. Behold, I have made thee small among the heathen: thou art greatly despised.

I have made thee small. Two interpretations have been suggested for this statement. Some point out that God regards the future as if it were past. When He has determined something, it is as good as accomplished. So, even though Edom's fall may have been in the future, it was as certain as if it had already happened. Others believe that this statement refers to the attitude of the nations toward Edom. God's "messenger" who had been sent among them had succeeded in his mission. Whereas they once regarded Edom as a strong nation, now they considered her *small. Thou art greatly despised.* No longer respected or feared by the nations, Edom was despised by them. She now appeared insignificant in their eyes.

C. Deceptive Pride (vv. 3, 4)

3. The pride of thine heart hath deceived thee, thou that dwellest in the clefts of the rock, whose habitation is high; that saith in his heart, Who shall bring me down to the ground?

The Edomites lived in a mountainous area, which afforded them much protection. The capital was built within a natural fortress that could be approached from only one direction. The ancient city of Petra—the rock city that is visited by thousands today—is an example of the Edomite habitation. Their city was inaccessible. A dozen guards at the entrance of a rock tunnel leading into Petra could keep out the largest army. People lived in caverns cut out of rock on the hillsides. If invaders were able to get in, the people could hide in their indestructible houses. Feeling certain that they were safe from attack by other nations, the Edomites became a proud and haughty people.

An eternal truth is clearly stated in God's Word: "Pride goeth before destruction, and a haughty spirit before a fall" (Proverbs 16:18).

How to Say It

EDOM. *Ee*-dum.
EDOMITES. *Ee*-dum-ites.
ESAU. *Ee*-saw.
NEBUCHADNEZZAR. *Neb*-you-kad-*nezz*-er (strong accent on *nezz*).
OBADIAH. O-buh-*die*-uh.
PETRA (Greek). *Pet*-ruh.

Pride brought Satan down, pride brought the Edomites down, and pride will bring us down.

We must be careful lest we take too much pride in such things as our IQ, education, accomplishments, wealth, position, etc. All of these are temporary. They are tools for us to use, but not to abuse. The church must guard against feelings of pride in its facilities, the status of the members who attend, etc. God will allow us to succeed. He is not against success, for no one is better at that than God is. When our heads get bigger than our hearts, however, God can bring us down.

4. Though thou exalt thyself as the eagle, and though thou set thy nest among the stars, thence will I bring thee down, saith the Lord.

Obadiah described Edom's pride in picturesque terms. As the eagle flies high above its prey, so Edom looked down on other people. The Edomites' homes, situated high in the rocky cliffs, were like the eagle's nest, seeming to be among the stars and out of reach of all enemies.

The higher the pride, the deeper the fall. God did not just say that He would discipline Edom or that He would bring balance to their lives. He said He would bring them down. No more would they fly like an eagle. No more would they look down upon people.

Do we ever look down on those who may be less fortunate than we are? Do we ever think we are God's "stars"—that others should look at us and marvel at us? Remember, the higher the pride, the deeper the fall.

ENDANGERED SPECIES

The Philippine Eagle, formerly called the "monkey-eating eagle," is nearly extinct. The second-largest eagle in the world, it nests high in the trees of the rain forests of Mindanao and a few others of the Philippine Islands. Commercial logging operations, as well as slash-and-burn farmers, have threatened the natural habitat of this rare bird. Conservationists have made efforts to preserve the forests and the

species. Without such environment-conscious crusaders to champion the cause, the Philippine Eagle could disappear from the face of the earth, forever brought down from their nests "among the stars."

Birds are endangered through no fault of their own. Edom, that proud nation that soared like an eagle, became endangered, and finally extinct, because of the course they chose. The Edomites hated the Jews, who were their brothers, and oppressed them violently. Divine judgment fell on this nation for its mistreatment of God's people and for its proud and haughty spirit in so doing.

Indeed, pride goes before destruction, and every nation should learn from Edom's example. Beware the arrogance that divorces a nation from God. It can put that nation on the endangered species list.   —R. W. B.

II. Reasons for Punishment (Obadiah 10, 11)

A. Violence Against Judah (v. 10)

10. For thy violence against thy brother Jacob shame shall cover thee, and thou shalt be cut off for ever.

For thy violence against thy brother Jacob. As we have already mentioned (see Lesson Background), the harm that Esau had intended against his brother Jacob was never carried out. When Jacob returned to Canaan after many years' absence, the two brothers made up, and their reconciliation was permanent. In later years, however, there was continuing animosity between their descendants. Judah is here referred to as Jacob, suggesting the bonds of brotherliness that should have existed between these two peoples.

Thou shalt be cut off for ever. No hope was held out to Edom for a future restoration. Her fall would be complete (v. 4).

B. Indifference Turned Into Involvement (v. 11)

11. In the day that thou stoodest on the other side, in the day that the strangers carried away captive his forces, and foreigners entered into his gates, and cast lots upon Jerusalem, even thou wast as one of them.

In the day. It is not known for certain what *day*, or time of calamity in the life of Judah, the prophet refers to. If Obadiah was one of the early prophets, as many Bible students think, he probably had in mind the invasion of Judah by the Philistines and Arabians in the middle of the ninth century B.C. (2 Chronicles 21:16, 17). If Obadiah lived at a later time, he probably re-

GOD WANTS US TO TURN OUR GRUDGES INTO GRACE OUR FEUDS INTO FRIENDSHIP

visual 1

ferred to the overthrow of Jerusalem by Nebuchadnezzar in 586 B.C.

Thou stoodest on the other side. Judah was in dire need, and the Edomites were in a position to help their brother. Instead of coming to Judah's defense, however, Edom simply stood by as a curious observer.

Jesus' parable of the good Samaritan addresses the subject of indifference to the needs of others (Luke 10:30-37). A man who had been beaten half to death was lying in the roadway, but his brothers went by on the other side and ignored him. In some situations, doing nothing may be as bad as doing something harmful to another. If you want to know how God will judge those who stand on the other side, read carefully Matthew 25:41-46.

Indifference, standing on the other side, may even turn into active opposition, as we see in the case of the Edomites. At first, they stood aloof and watched the mistreatment of God's people. Before it was completed, they were standing on the same side as the enemies. When the foreigners entered Jerusalem to destroy it, the Edomite nation was *as one of them,* actively joining them in spoiling the city and its people (see verses 12-14).

At Jesus' trial before Pilate, no doubt some in the crowd were just standing on the other side saying nothing to support Jesus. Before that morning was far spent, however, those who were "neutral" undoubtedly lent their voices to the swelling chant, "Crucify Him, crucify Him!" We can't stand by without being on someone's side. If we don't stand up for our brothers and sisters in the family of God, we may find ourselves standing against them.

PASSIVE SINNERS

"Some say that ignorance and apathy are the two worst afflictions of contemporary society. What do you think?"

"I don't know, and I don't care!"

That's a very old joke; but when you think about it, it's really no joke. Current culture suffers because millions are uninformed, unconcerned, and uncommitted. The attitude that so often prevails is, "I don't want to get involved." Most of us excel in keeping the "thou shalt nots"

among God's absolutes, but we frequently fail to obey the "thou shalts."

Edom stood by and watched the enemies of Judah pillage and spoil Jerusalem. At a distance, they condoned and actually assisted the attacks on Jacob's descendants by simply not interfering. They became accomplices in the crimes of war when they withheld aid and reinforcements from their neighbors in need.

Christians dare not be uninvolved as long as people need help, as long as souls are lost. Uninvolvement is passive sin.   —R. W. B.

III. Retribution by the Lord (Obadiah 15)

15. For the day of the Lord is near upon all the heathen: as thou hast done, it shall be done unto thee: thy reward shall return upon thine own head.

The day of the Lord is a phrase in the Bible used consistently to refer to a time of judgment. Usually it refers to the Day of Judgment, the final judgment of all persons. Sometimes, however, it indicates a time of God's judgment whose execution takes place in this life. The prophet has in mind God's judgment of Edom. It is called *the day of the Lord* to make it clear that God is still on His throne.

The day of Edom's judgment was near as God calculates nearness, not necessarily as humans do. In saying Edom's judgment was near, the prophet indicated that it was certain.

The fairness of God's judgment is seen in the words, *As thou hast done, it shall be done unto thee: thy reward shall return upon thine own head.* That means God would do to Edom as she had done to others. The *New International Version* translates it this way: "As you have done, it will be done to you; your deeds will return upon your own head." God's judgment would be like a boomerang, returning to them what they had done to others. It is the principle of the harvest—which was stated by the apostle Paul in Galatians 6:7, 8: "Whatsoever a man soweth, that shall he also reap."

If you are prone to be less than merciful to another, don't forget this principle. James reminds us that those persons who have shown no mercy upon others will themselves have judgment without mercy (James 2:13).

REPAYMENT

God's law of retribution was stated clearly by Obadiah: "As you have done, it will be done to you" (v. 15, *New International Version*). Mercilessly the Edomites had treated their brothers, the Jews. Without mercy, God's judgment would fall on Edom.

Sometimes it is called poetic justice when a thief is robbed, when a liar is lied to, when a bully is intimidated, when a gossip is slandered. We say they "got their just deserts." It is neither the duty nor privilege of a Christian, however, to avenge wrongdoing. Prescribing for wrongdoers tastes of their own medicine is God's prerogative. " 'It is mine to avenge; I will repay,' says the Lord" (Romans 12:19, *New International Version*).

Our concern should be not so much getting even with God's enemies, as concentrating on remaining God's friends. That will keep most of us busy enough!   —R. W. B.

IV. Restoration of Judah (Obadiah 17, 21)

A. God's Deliverance (v. 17)

17. But upon Mount Zion shall be deliverance, and there shall be holiness; and the house of Jacob shall possess their possessions.

Upon Mount Zion shall be deliverance. While the Edomites thought they were indestructible, it was God's people who would be delivered from destruction. Lives were lost at the hands of the heathen nations, but God would preserve a remnant of His people. Even after they were deported from their land, God saw to it that they returned to "possess their possessions."

There shall be holiness. The Edomites and the other nations had desecrated God's holy place by their revelry (see verse 16). With the restoration of Judah, Mount Zion would be a holy sanctuary once again.

Do you ever get in the pits and wonder if you will ever get out? Though we walk through the valley of the shadow of death, God is with us.

When David felt down, he waited patiently for the Lord, and God heard his cry. He lifted David out of the slimy pit, set his feet on a rock, and gave him a firm place to stand. He also gave him a new song to sing (Psalm 40:1-3).

We will have setbacks and suffering. People may turn against us. But God can turn our scars into stars if we don't give up on Him.

B. God's Reign (v. 21)

21. And saviours shall come up on mount Zion to judge the mount of Esau; and the kingdom shall be the Lord's.

Here, Obadiah combines both literal and spiritual concepts. *Saviours* were human deliverers, as were the judges (in the book of Judges). Leaders arose in Israel, severely punishing the Edomites and, in time, incorporating them into the Jewish nation. Finally, after the capture of Jerusalem by the Romans, the name of the Edomites perished, thus bringing to fulfillment this prophecy. These *saviours* were also types and forerunners of the Messiah. Obadiah expands his focus from the primary subject of his prophecy—the judgment of Edom—to include God's final judgment on all evil. He identifies the seat of God's kingdom as *mount Zion* and the enemies of God as *the mount of Esau*. Ultimately, righteousness, through Christ the Savior, will *judge* the forces of evil, and eternally the Lord's victorious kingdom will be established.

Conclusion

A. Re-cancellation as Reconciliation

This destruction could have been avoided had Edom repented and turned their grudges into grace and their feud into friendship. But they would not cancel the past.

A married couple having difficulties came to a counselor and announced, "We need some re-cancellation." That's the way they pronounced the word *reconciliation*. If we are going to be reconciled with those who have hurt us in the past, we need to do some re-cancellation. May we let go of the negative past so we can grow.

B. Prayer

Father, thank You for putting us into Your family with so many brothers and sisters who differ from us in so many ways. Fill us with Your Spirit so we may understand that our differences are to be a supply of strength for us and not a source of conflict. In Jesus' name, amen.

C. Thought to Remember

Are you holding a grudge? Let it go before it consumes you.

Learning by Doing

This page contains an alternate lesson plan emphasizing learning activities. Classes desiring such student involvement will find these suggestions helpful.

Learning Goals

After studying the prophecy of Obadiah, the pupils will be able to:

1. Identify the historical source of enmity between Edom and the people of God.

2. Identify the specific attitudes and actions that brought destruction to Edom.

3. Identify personal grudges that they are keeping alive.

4. Choose a step of reconciliation they will take this week to resolve a grudge.

Into the Lesson

As the class members arrive, give each a half sheet of paper with the word grudge written vertically down the side. Ask them to take a few minutes to write down words associated with the word grudge that begin with each of the letters. Allot four or five minutes for them to do their work. Then make a master acrostic (on a sheet of newsprint, the chalkboard, or an overhead transparency).

Make the transition into the Bible study portion of the lesson by observing that the culmination of a grudge held between two peoples for generations is the subject of today's Bible lesson. Our session will focus on finding out why the grudge existed and what the outcomes were.

Into the Word

Divide the class into work groups of four or five people. Each group will examine the historical background that gave rise to the prophecy that is the text for this lesson. The assignments for the groups are as follows:

Group One: Read Genesis 27:1-41. Identify the factors in this passage that caused Esau to hold a grudge against Jacob. Check in a Bible dictionary to find the relationship between Esau and the Edomites.

Group Two: Read Numbers 20:14-21. Identify any evidence of or reason for a continuing grudge between the Israelites and the Edomites. Check in a Bible dictionary to find out from whom the Edomites were descended. Identify additional reasons for this grudge. How does this relate to Deuteronomy 23:7?

If you have more than eight or ten pupils in the class, assign each task to more than one group. Allot approximately ten minutes for the class members to prepare this information.

At the end of the preparation time, let the groups make their presentations. Fill in any relevant details that may be overlooked.

Now read the entire prophecy of Obadiah. Develop a discussion by using these questions:

1. What attitudes among the Edomites were unacceptable to God? (Their enmity toward Judah; pride; a sense of indestructibility.)

2. What did God say would happen to Edom? Why? (Edom would be totally destroyed because of their violence against their brother Jacob—the people of Judah.)

3. What would happen to the house of Jacob as a result of God's action? (After their captivity they would repossess their land.)

4. Why would God have allowed this grudge to go on for generations before bringing judgment on Edom? (Let the pupils suggest reasons. Be sure to note that God is patient and that He gives mankind every opportunity to turn from evil and do right before He brings judgment (read 2 Peter 3:9). Emphasize, however, that there are limits to His patience.

Summarize the discussion before you go to the next section.

Into Life

Display the following statement on a sheet of newsprint, the chalkboard, or an overhead transparency: "It doesn't really hurt a person to hold a grudge against another." Ask the students to decide whether they strongly agree, agree, disagree, or strongly disagree. Let those who hold a similar view work together for two minutes to state a rationale for their answer. Then let the groups present their views.

Let this be a springboard for discussion enhanced by the following questions:

1. What are the personal effects of holding a grudge?

2. How does Ephesians 4:26 speak to this issue?

3. What spiritual effects can holding a grudge have on us?

4. How can we overcome the tendency to hold a grudge when we are hurt by someone?

Summarize the discussion. Then give each person a small index card. It any are holding grudges against another person, ask them to write a memo to God stating a step of reconciliation they will take toward that person this week.

Let's Talk It Over

The questions on this page are designed to encourage review of the lesson Scriptures and to promote discussion of the lesson by the class. The answers provided are only discussion starters. Let your class talk it over from there.

1. People who manifest a hateful, bitter spirit are generally disliked. Why is this so?

Perhaps most of us feel that we have as many problems as the persons around us, and we conclude that if we can endure our problems with a measure of cheerfulness and forbearance, then others should be able to do the same. Therefore, we tend to resent people who give the impression by their attitude of complaining and spitefulness that their problems are worse than ours. Also, we may be personally sensitive to criticism, and so we shun persons who are prone to voicing bitter criticism. Jesus would not have us disliking or avoiding such persons. They were among the people He had in mind when He said, "Love your enemies, bless them that curse you, do good to them that hate you, and pray for them which despitefully use you, and persecute you" (Matthew 5:44).

2. The Edomites derived a sense of false security from the mountainous area in which they lived. What kind of false security do people cling to in our time?

The most obvious answer is money and material possessions. It is easy to believe that we are safe and secure when we have a sturdy house, comfortable furnishings, an abundant supply of food and clothing, and money in the bank. But Jesus' parable of the rich fool illustrates how that is false security (Luke 12:13-21). On a national basis, one point to military might as a source of security. But with the unimaginably destructive weapons of today, that is a very uncertain kind of security, to say the least. We would do well to view our military might in the same way David did his: "Some trust in chariots, and some in horses: but we will remember the name of the Lord our God" (Psalm 20:7).

3. Why should we be wary of the tendency to take pride in our possessions or accomplishments?

Pride may be accompanied by a sense of self-satisfaction. We may be tempted to feel that we have become as good a person as we need to be or that we have done all that we need to do. Growth in character and in accomplishments, however, must be an ongoing task throughout life. Pride may be accompanied also by an attitude of self-sufficiency. Jesus said, "Without me ye can do nothing" (John 15:5), but we may reach the conclusion that we can handle life's challenges all by ourselves. Further, pride may be accompanied by a tendency to look down on others. It is easy to develop contempt toward those who are not as intelligent or talented or dedicated as we are. The Bible is filled with warnings about the peril of exalting ourselves above our fellow human beings.

4. How is aloofness toward someone against whom we hold a grudge as bad as speaking angry, bitter words to that person?

As the lesson writer points out, we tend to think that this deliberately indifferent approach is not so bad as an outward show of hostility. But it produces similar results. Unlike the "soft answer [that] turneth away wrath" (Proverbs 15:1), this approach can intensify anger. Instead of promoting a mutual understanding that could eliminate the ill-will, it widens the chasm between us and another human being. Rather than bringing healing into the relationship, it serves as a form of revenge; and God has forbidden us that (Romans 12:19). No doubt it can be very satisfying to "punish" someone by the silent treatment, but it is far better to use our tongue to work out the problem and be reconciled to our brother or sister.

5. How can we cancel old grudges?

It is always a temptation to expect the other person to take the first step, and that expectation can prolong the ill-will. God took the initiative in reconciling us to himself (2 Corinthians 5:19), and we should make up our minds to take the initiative in resolving our grudges. Then we should proceed with the idea of "cancellation" firmly in mind. We are familiar with the vow, "I'll forgive, but I won't forget." To take such a position suggests one's unwillingness to let go of one's feelings of hostility. We may indeed be unable to forget what another person has said or done to us, but through God's grace we should be able to remember it in a transformed way, with the bitterness canceled. If we meditate on God's forgiveness extended to us through Christ (Ephesians 4:31—5:2), we should be able to accomplish such a step of cancellation.

Fleeing From God

LESSON SCRIPTURE: Jonah 1, 2.

PRINTED TEXT: Jonah 1:1-9, 15-17.

Jonah 1:1-9, 15-17

1 Now the word of the LORD came unto Jonah the son of Amittai, saying,

2 Arise, go to Nineveh, that great city, and cry against it; for their wickedness is come up before me.

3 But Jonah rose up to flee unto Tarshish from the presence of the LORD, and went down to Joppa; and he found a ship going to Tarshish: so he paid the fare thereof, and went down into it, to go with them unto Tarshish from the presence of the LORD.

4 But the LORD sent out a great wind into the sea, and there was a mighty tempest in the sea, so that the ship was like to be broken.

5 Then the mariners were afraid, and cried every man unto his god, and cast forth the wares that were in the ship into the sea, to lighten it of them. But Jonah was gone down into the sides of the ship; and he lay, and was fast asleep.

6 So the shipmaster came to him, and said unto him, What meanest thou, O sleeper? arise, call upon thy God, if so be that God will think upon us, that we perish not.

7 And they said every one to his fellow, Come, and let us cast lots, that we may know for whose cause this evil is upon us. So they cast lots, and the lot fell upon Jonah.

8 Then said they unto him, Tell us, we pray thee, for whose cause this evil is upon us; What is thine occupation? and whence comest thou? what is thy country? and of what people art thou?

9 And he said unto them, I am a Hebrew; and I fear the LORD, the God of heaven, which hath made the sea and the dry land.

. . . .

15 So they took up Jonah, and cast him forth into the sea: and the sea ceased from her raging.

16 Then the men feared the LORD exceedingly, and offered a sacrifice unto the LORD, and made vows.

17 Now the LORD had prepared a great fish to swallow up Jonah. And Jonah was in the belly of the fish three days and three nights.

GOLDEN TEXT: Jonah rose up to flee unto Tarshish from the presence of the LORD.
—Jonah 1:3.

God's Judgment and Mercy

Unit 1: Warnings and Promises From God (Lessons 1-5)

Lesson Aims

This lesson is to encourage students to:
1. Identify responsibilities for God that they may have evaded.
2. Fulfill their responsibilities to God instead of fleeing from them.

Lesson Outline

INTRODUCTION
    A. The Greater Beauty
    B. Lesson Background
I. COMMAND AND RESPONSE (Jonah 1:1-3)
    A. God's Approach to Jonah (vv. 1, 2)
    B. Jonah's Flight From God (v. 3)
        Running
II. A FUGITIVE FOILED (Jonah 1:4-9)
    A. Divine Intervention (v. 4)
    B. Feeble Efforts (v. 5)
        Psycholepsy
    C. Frantic Request (v. 6)
    D. Discovery (vv. 7, 8)
    E. Confession (v. 9)
III. MAN OVERBOARD (Jonah 1:15-17)
    A. Result (v. 15)
    B. Reverence (v. 16)
    C. Rescue (v. 17)
        Icthus
CONCLUSION
    A. Nothing Is Impossible With God
    B. Prayer
    C. Thought to Remember

Display visual 2 of the visuals packet and let it remain before the class. The visual is shown on page 356.

Introduction

A. The Greater Beauty

Which has more beauty—the Pacific Ocean or Philadelphia? Yellowstone National Park or New York City? The Grand Canyon or Los Angeles?

When God created those elements that we refer to as naturally beautiful, He judged them to be "good." But His entire creation was seen to be "very good" only after He created man (male and female). Only human beings are made in the image of God. Jesus did not die for the Pacific Ocean or the Grand Canyon. He died for people.

Jesus looked over the city of Jerusalem, and probably with misty eyes declared, "O Jerusalem, Jerusalem, . . . how often would I have gathered thy children together, even as a hen gathereth her chickens under her wings" (Matthew 23:37). God loves the cities, because they are populated by people who are created in His image and for whom He has never diminished His compassion. May we learn to love as God loves, and see the beauty that He sees.

B. Lesson Background

Jonah was a prophet of the northern kingdom of Israel, who was born at Gath-hepher, about three miles northeast of Nazareth. He preached at about 790-780 B. C., before or during the early part of the reign of Jeroboam II of Israel (2 Kings 14:23-25).

Jonah means "dove." In our modern world, a dove symbolizes one who does not want to participate in violence. Jonah's attitude, however, was not one of peace. He was upset when God commissioned him to warn the city of Nineveh of their impending doom. As we shall see in next week's lesson, Jonah became very angry when God did, in fact, spare the city following their repentance.

Some scholars teach that the book of Jonah does not record actual historical events. They think the contents are a myth, a legend, or an allegory to be taken symbolically. Standing in direct contradiction to such views is the testimony of Jesus himself (see Matthew 12:39-41). It is obvious that He regarded Jonah as a historical character. Are we to believe that the men of Nineveh, who Jesus said would rise up in the judgment and condemn the people of Jesus' generation, were merely fictitious characters? If the account of Jonah were nothing more than an allegory, could Jesus have referred to Jonah's imprisonment in the fish's belly as a sign of His own three-day stay in the grave? No, Jesus spoke those words to an audience of people who also knew that the facts in Jonah were historical, for they had not read the views of modern-day theologians—and we should not take those views seriously either.

How to Say It

AMITTAI.   Uh-*mit*-eye.
GATH-HEPHER.   Gath-*he*-fer.
JEROBOAM.   Jair-o-*bo*-um.
NINEVEH.   *Nin*-uh-vuh.
TARSHISH.   *Tar*-shish.
TARTESSUS.   Tar-*tess*-us.

I. Command and Response
(Jonah 1:1-3)

A. God's Approach to Jonah (vv. 1, 2)

1. Now the word of the Lord came unto Jonah the son of Amittai, saying.

We do not know if God's word came to Jonah through a dream, a vision, or if it was spoken audibly. The method does not matter. The fact is Jonah received a commission from God. He was not given the counsel of his peers, neither the wishes nor the directives of his countrymen.

2. Arise, go to Nineveh, that great city, and cry against it; for their wickedness is come up before me.

Jonah was to take a long trip to Nineveh, the capital city of Assyria about 750 miles east of Israel. In the years prior to and during Jonah's time, the Assyrians were the leading power in the regions east of Israel. They were a warlike people who, fifty years earlier, had invaded the west and had forced Jehu, king of Israel, to pay tribute to them. The Assyrians were known for being extremely cruel to their prisoners.

God called Nineveh a great city, not because of its morals but because of its size and potential. At the time God spoke to Jonah, one hundred twenty thousand young children lived in Nineveh (Jonah 4:11). It is estimated that the entire population of the city was about six hundred thousand.

Jonah was to cry *against* Nineveh—to preach against the life-style of that city, *for their wickedness is come up before me*.

When God has a warning that people need to hear, He expects His servants to communicate it as His representatives. Sometimes we shy away from speaking negatively for fear we may offend someone. But is warning people against danger worth the risk of offending them?

The cry against Nineveh was to be for the city's good. It was to help the people change. It was a negative message with a positive goal.

B. Jonah's Flight From God (v. 3)

3. But Jonah rose up to flee unto Tarshish from the presence of the Lord, and went down to Joppa; and he found a ship going to Tarshish: so he paid the fare thereof, and went down into it, to go with them unto Tarshish from the presence of the Lord.

God said, "Arise," and Jonah rose up, but that was the one and only part of God's command that Jonah obeyed.

Tarshish is probably Tartessus in Spain, which is two thousand miles west of Palestine. Jonah decided to get nearly three thousand miles away

from Nineveh. That is a long distance even by today's standards—just think of what a long distance it was in Jonah's day!

Jonah decided to go in the opposite direction from what God wished. God wanted him to go east, and Jonah went west. Do we ever do that? God instructs us to let no unwholesome word proceed out of our mouths and to speak only what will benefit others (Ephesians 4:29). Are there times when we do just the opposite? God says, "Lay up for yourselves treasures in heaven" (Matthew 6:20), but do we do the opposite and devote most of our energies to laying up treasures on earth just for ourselves? Do we speak up when we should be silent, and clam up when we should speak out?

Joppa was a seaport on the Mediterranean, and that's where Jonah found a ship that would take him in the direction opposite to where God wanted him to go. There always are people who will help us do just that. Have you ever had your peers counsel you to walk in a way contrary to God's direction, and who were willing to help you?

What Jonah really wanted to do was to get away *from the presence of the Lord*. Evidently he figured that getting thousands of miles away from the "holy land" would do it. But God is not localized. We may be able to get away from people we don't like (as Jonah tried to distance himself from the Ninevites, whom he disliked), but we cannot get away from God who loves and cares for us.

RUNNING

The Fugitive was a popular, long-running TV series, starring David Jansen. Jansen played the role of a man wrongly convicted of his wife's murder. He had escaped prison to search for the real killer, a one-armed homicidal maniac. Each week, the fugitive would come very close, either to being discovered by authorities, or to capturing his wife's killer, or to being murdered himself. Millions of us rooted for Jansen week after week, hoping he would catch the killer and be exonerated.

The man portrayed by Jansen could be called a "fugitive from injustice." He was running from authority, but he was innocent. Jonah was a runner, too, but he was guilty—guilty of disobeying a direct commission from God. He was running from responsibility and opportunity. Full of selfish pride and prejudice, he tried to escape the presence and authority of God.

Many Christians have responded in a similar manner to the Lord's directives. His command to preach against wickedness has rarely been well-received. Even otherwise-faithful followers often run from His divine call to share the good news of salvation. Let us learn from Jonah that we may run from responsibility, but we cannot hide from God.

—R. W. B.

II. A Fugitive Foiled
(Jonah 1:4-9)

A. Divine Intervention (v. 4)

4. But the Lord sent out a great wind into the sea, and there was a mighty tempest in the sea, so that the ship was like to be broken.

God gives us the freedom to choose, but that does not mean that He always approves our choices or that He will stand on the sidelines and never intervene. God is patient, but His patience is not always passive. Even in the midst of His patience, He may act to intervene in human affairs. In Jonah's case, *the Lord sent out a great wind* that changed the prophet's plans.

In this event, we are reminded that the Lord is God Almighty. There is really no such thing as natural laws, as if the laws were owned by nature. They are all supernatural laws, created by God and belonging to Him. God can intervene in the laws that He has established anytime He wants to. The Bible affirms that in different ways: (a) what is impossible with man is possible with God; (b) "The Lord does whatever pleases him, in the heavens and on the earth, in the seas and all their depths. He makes clouds rise from the ends of the earth; he sends lightning with the rain and brings out the wind from his storehouses" (Psalm 135:6, 7, *New International Version*); (c) when God gives a command to the elements of nature—the wind, the mountains, the trees—they cannot disobey Him. Here the obedient wind caused *a mighty tempest in the sea* that threatened the ship in which Jonah placed his trust.

B. Feeble Efforts (v. 5)

5. Then the mariners were afraid, and cried every man unto his god, and cast forth the wares that were in the ship into the sea, to lighten it of them. But Jonah was gone down into the sides of the ship; and he lay, and was fast asleep.

The storm was so fierce that the ship was about to break apart. The sailors, who were accustomed to storms, were terrified, and *every man* cried unto his god. These men were pagans, who doubtless believed in many "gods of nature." Some believed in a god of the sea, some in a god of the rain, some in a god of the wind, etc. They believed that when such a god was angry, he would show it in a rampage. But their lifeless idols had ears that could not hear.

The seamen coupled their spiritual efforts with shipping skills and physical strength and threw the cargo overboard. A heavy ship in the midst of a fierce storm would more easily capsize. Neither the cries to their gods nor their professional skills were helping them.

Meanwhile, Jonah, who had earlier gone down into the sides of the ship (that is, inside, into the innermost part—see verse 3), lay there fast asleep. Apparently he was exhausted from the physical exertion of his flight and the mental anxiety that attended it.

PSYCHOLEPSY

I can't find the word in my dictionary, but I didn't invent it. Apparently, someone coined the term to describe a disorder that causes one to sleep, sometimes trance-like, to escape pain, anxiety, or other discomforts. When I drove my car into the back of a milk truck in 1961, I blacked out to escape the pain—even before it happened. I saw it coming, but I have no recollection of the impact. Psycholepsy.

Do you get drowsy in nervous situations? Do anxiety and tension sometimes give you the yawns? Jonah tried to sleep away his guilt. While everyone else on board was fighting for his life in the killer storm, Jonah slept as if in a psychosomatic coma. The only escape from the conviction of his sin may have been lepsy—stress-induced sleep. Jonah didn't want to think about it, so he tried to sleep it off, as it were.

"All have sinned and fall short of the glory of God" (Romans 3:23, *New International Version*). And what can take away our sin? Not sleep, not wakefulness; nothing but the blood of Jesus.

—R. W. B.

C. Frantic Request (v. 6)

6. So the shipmaster came to him, and said unto him, What meanest thou, O sleeper? arise, call upon thy God, if so be that God will think upon us, that we perish not.

Only one person had not called upon his God to save the ship, and that was Jonah. He seemed to be insensitive to the danger he and the others were in. He was sleeping through the crisis, not

WE MAY RUN FROM RESPONSIBILITY, BUT WE CAN'T HIDE FROM GOD

visual 2

because he had a good conscience and was unworried, but because he was running away from God. A person who is running away from God certainly does not want to talk with Him. Isn't it interesting that pagans and a person of God were on the same journey, and the person of God had the answer for their safety—but he was silent and asleep?

In a similar way, pagans and Christians are traveling together through life. This earth is headed toward destruction, and all who cry to the pagan gods (substitutes for the real God) and put their security only in human abilities will perish. What are Christians doing about that? Are we sleeping through the crisis and remaining silent? Are we keeping the means of escape to ourselves?

The shipmaster asked Jonah to cry unto his God, not because he believed in Jonah's God, but because he was grasping for the last possible hope. Nothing else was working.

D. Discovery (vv. 7, 8)

7. And they said every one to his fellow, Come, and let us cast lots, that we may know for whose cause this evil is upon us. So they cast lots, and the lot fell upon Jonah.

There are instances in Scripture in which God's will was made known by some method of casting lots (see Joshua 7:13-18; 1 Samuel 10:17-24; Acts 1:21-26). It is apparent that these heathen seamen felt that divine guidance would be given by the casting of lots. Inasmuch as God's hand was involved in bringing on the storm, we presume that His oversight in the casting of lots led also to the storm's abatement.

8. Then said they unto him, Tell us, we pray thee, for whose cause this evil is upon us; What is thine occupation? and whence comest thou? what is thy country? and of what people art thou?

Since the lot fell upon Jonah, the seamen supposed that they had found the one responsible for the terrible danger they were in. But they did not immediately take action against him. Instead, amidst the roaring tempest, they bombarded him with questions, giving him the opportunity to declare his innocence or confess his guilt. Perhaps his occupation was offensive to the gods; or perhaps his country or family was guilty of something that had aroused the wrath of Heaven.

Not only had Jonah been trying to avoid God, but also he evidently had been avoiding the ship's crew. They seemed to know very little about him. What about us? Do the people we associate with every day know that we are Christians?

E. Confession (v. 9)

9. And he said unto them, I am a Hebrew; and I fear the Lord, the God of heaven, which hath made the sea and the dry land.

Verse 10 indicates that Jonah confessed that he was running away from the Lord. Here in verse 9 he made it clear that his God is the God that could indeed cause the storm, because He is the Lord of Heaven who created the sea and the earth. We must commend Jonah here. He did not make an excuse or try to rationalize his actions. He came clean. He confessed his disobedience to God, and thus took responsibility for placing the sailors in jeopardy.

In the verses omitted from our text, we see the perplexity of the sailors. They believed that Jonah was a prophet of Jehovah, and yet the life-threatening storm was sent as a result of Jonah's sin. They then appealed to him as to what they should do to him to appease Jehovah's wrath. Jonah responded by telling them to throw him into the sea, for he acknowledged, "I know that for my sake this great tempest is upon you" (v. 12).

There is a positive note here: Jonah was willing to die in order to save others who were pagans. Is it possible that he was softening up and being more compassionate for the heathen? Of course. But what was the difference between these sailors and the inhabitants of Nineveh? One difference was that he had come to know these men better. The more we know non-Christians on a one-to-one basis, the more we may care about them. The more we stay aloof and to ourselves, the less likely we are to put ourselves out for the salvation of others.

The sailors did not want to throw Jonah overboard. In fact, they rejected Jonah's suggestion at first and tried their best to bring the ship to land, but the storm grew only worse (v. 13). Finally, praying now to Jehovah, they recognized His hand in this whole affair and implored Him not to let them die for doing as the prophet said and taking his life (v. 14).

III. Man Overboard
(Jonah 1:15-17)

A. Result (v. 15)

15. So they took up Jonah, and cast him forth into the sea: and the sea ceased from her raging.

One can imagine that even yet with reluctance, and with a certain reverence, the sailors lifted Jonah and threw him into the sea. Suddenly the sea grew calm, and the men knew that the storm had been sent because of Jonah.

B. Reverence (v. 16)

16. Then the men feared the Lord exceedingly, and offered a sacrifice unto the Lord, and made vows.

The sudden quieting of the storm led the pagan sailors to affirm that Jonah's God was indeed the Lord. They offered a sacrifice and made a vow to Him. The vows they made may have been that from then on, Jehovah would be their God. Jonah had influence on those sailors, but he did not know of the change in their lives, because he was now in the sea and soon to be inside a fish.

C. Rescue (v. 17)

17. Now the Lord had prepared a great fish to swallow up Jonah. And Jonah was in the belly of the fish three days and three nights.

While the storm had ceased for the sailors, in a sense it was continuing for Jonah. God's purpose was not to destroy Jonah but to demonstrate grace so he could be a dispenser of grace to others. Jonah could have been lost by drowning, but God prepared a fish to swallow him for his preservation.

There is no use arguing whether a fish is big enough to swallow a man or whether such a fish could live in the Mediterranean Sea. We know that fish in that region are large enough and have done that. Some sharks have been known to swallow a man whole, and even a horse.

So the miracle is not that a fish could do this, but that God had prepared a fish to be at the right place at the right time, and that Jonah was kept alive in the fish's belly.

Jonah was in the belly of the fish for three days and three nights. He probably tried every way he could think of to get out by his own

strength. But nothing worked. God wanted Jonah to know that if he came out of that fish, it would be because of God's grace and not by Jonah's efforts. We will study the conclusion of the story of Jonah in next week's lesson.

ICTHUS

Several of Jesus' miracles had to do with fish. He fed a multitude by multiplying just two fish and five loaves of bread. He paid his taxes with a coin provided in the mouth of a fish. More than once, He miraculously filled the nets of Peter and his co-workers, and the last time, He fed them fish for breakfast. Is it any wonder that the fish symbol identified Christ's earliest disciples? Ichthus was the Greek word for it.

When His enemies pressed Him for a miraculous sign to prove His messiahship, however, Jesus promised only "the sign of the prophet Jonah. For as Jonah was three days and three nights in the belly of a huge fish, so the Son of Man will be three days and three nights in the heart of the earth" (Matthew 12:39, 40, *New International Version*).

Jesus did not regard the record of "Jonah and the whale" as a fish story. He cited it as an illustration of the miraculous providence of God, a divine act of redemption. The great fish was not provided to destroy Jonah, but to save him, and through him to save the Ninevites as well.

Likewise, "God sent not his Son into the world to condemn the world; but that the world through him might be saved" (John 3:17)

—R. W. B.

Conclusion

A. Nothing Is Impossible With God

Early on in the Bible the question is asked, "Is any thing too hard for the Lord?" (Genesis 18:14). And the Biblical answer is a consistent no! The prophets said no (Jeremiah 32:17), Jesus said no (Matthew 19:26), an angel from Heaven said no (Luke 1:37), an apostle said no (Ephesians 3:20). Should we think any differently?

B. Prayer

O Heavenly Father, help us to see the futility of trying to escape from You. If we are walking contrary to Your revealed will, we ask that by Your grace You will do what needs to be done to get our attention, so that we will turn around and walk with You. In Jesus' name we ask it. Amen.

C. Thought to Remember

"Our God is in heaven; he does whatever pleases him" (Psalm 115:3, *New International Version*).

Home Daily Bible Readings

Monday, June 8—Running From the Call (Jonah 1:1-9)

Tuesday, June 9—Jonah Cast Into the Sea (Jonah 1:10-17)

Wednesday, June 10—Jonah's Prayer (Jonah 2:1-10)

Thursday, June 11—God Reigns (Psalm 65:1-8)

Friday, June 12—God Knows All (Psalm 139:1-6)

Saturday, June 13—No Escape From God (Psalm 139:7-12)

Sunday, June 14—Flee to God (Psalm 143:7-12)

Learning by Doing

This page contains an alternate lesson plan emphasizing learning activities. Classes desiring such student involvement will find these suggestions helpful.

Learning Goals

As a result of studying this lesson, the students will be able to:

1. Explain why Jonah chose to avoid doing what God wanted him to do.

2. Identify responsibilities for God they may have evaded.

3. State a willingness to obey God.

Into the Lesson

Before the class session begins, make a scrambled message puzzle for every two or three students. Use the words from the "Thought to Remember" on page 358: "Our God is in heaven; he does whatever pleases him" (Psalm 115:3, *New International Version*). Put each word on a separate slip of paper. Scramble the pieces and place them in an envelope. In each envelope include also a slip of paper with the Scripture reference on it.

As the class members arrive, give each two or three people a puzzle and ask them to work together to solve it. Ask them to use their Bibles only if they cannot otherwise solve the puzzle. When they have finished the puzzle, they can check their work in the Bible. Take no more than seven or eight minutes for this opening activity.

Make the transition into the Bible lesson by suggesting that the message just discovered is one of the principal truths demonstrated in the Bible text for this lesson.

Into the Word

Read Jonah 1 aloud to the class, or have a pupil whom you have asked earlier do it. Observe that this is a familiar Bible story.

Divide the class members into groups of three or four. Assign each group one of the following tasks. Provide each group with the resources necessary for their research.

Task One. Use the Bible dictionary, atlas, and other information provided for your group to discover what Nineveh was like. Describe the city, the culture, the population, and the nature of the people. Be prepared to share this with the rest of the class.

Task Two. Use the Bible dictionary, atlas, and other information provided for your group to discover why Jonah may not have wanted to see Nineveh spared from God's wrath. Be prepared to share this with the rest of the class.

Task Three. Using information from Scripture and the Bible dictionary provided for your group, prepare a monologue that God may have spoken as He determined to send Jonah to Nineveh to call the people to repentence. Why didn't He destroy Nineveh outright?

Task Four. Using information from Scripture and the Bible dictionary provided for your group, prepare a monologue that Jonah may have spoken as he determined his response to God's directive to go to Nineveh.

Allot ten to twelve minutes for the groups to do their work. Then call the class back together and let each group make its report in the order listed above.

Lead a brief discussion using the following questions:

1. Was Jonah justified in his attempt to avoid doing what God asked? Why?

2. What seems to have been Jonah's chief objection to going to Nineveh?

3. Why would God want these people saved since they were so evil?

Summarize the factual data discovered in this Bible passage before you go to the application. The discussion and summary should take four to six minutes.

Into Life

Develop the application of the Bible lesson by using the following questions:

1. What does this passage teach us about God and His regard for the peoples of the world?

2. Name some of the occasions when we try to avoid doing what God bids us to do. How do we try to carry out that evasion of responsibility?

3. How do we convince (or attempt to convince) ourselves that we are getting by with our evasion of responsibility?

4. God probably won't have a fish swallow us because we disobey. How, then, will we be reminded that we are evading or ignoring doing God's will?

5. How does Psalm 115:3 relate to this section of Jonah?

Distribute a small index card to each person in the class. Ask the class members to write a prayer expressing their response to the teaching of this lesson. Then ask the class to form pairs and pray together to close the session.

Let's Talk It Over

The questions on this page are designed to encourage review of the lesson Scriptures and to promote discussion of the lesson by the class. The answers provided are only discussion starters. Let your class talk it over from there.

1. Why is it important that we accept the events recorded in Jonah as historical facts?

If we regard the book of Jonah as an allegory, and thereby explain away the miracle of the prophet's being swallowed and expelled by the great fish, we embark on an approach to Biblical interpretation that can lead to a denial of basic Biblical truths. Jesus compared His resurrection to Jonah's stay in the fish's belly (Matthew 12:40). Shall we say that that also is so much symbolic language? Some religious teachers have treated the resurrection in just that way. On the surface, the book of Jonah reads like a historical narrative, and Jesus spoke of the events described in it as historical events. On what basis, therefore, can anyone conclude that it is an allegory? This is a critical battleground between those who accept the Bible as it is and those who choose to dissect it with high-sounding theories.

2. As Christians we are to warn people about God's coming judgment. How can we do this without appearing to be hopeless pessimists?

The world sometimes sees Christians as purveyors of gloom and doom. They devise clever caricatures and jokes to minimize the impact our messages of judgment could have on them. The threats of judgment delivered by the Old Testament prophets were interspersed with promises of blessing for the penitent. We should aim to maintain that kind of balance. Their messages of doom did not win them many friends, but they would have been unfaithful to God and man had they not delivered them. Even so, we dare not shirk our duty of announcing the bad news of God's wrath against sin. Like those prophets, however, we should delight in proclaiming the good news that God's forgiveness and favor are available to all who turn to Him.

3. It is impossible to get away from God. How may that truth both comfort and disturb us?

We could say that Jonah experienced both aspects of this truth. He found it disturbing when the storm engulfed the ship in which he was escaping, but in the belly of the great fish he must have been comforted to know that God was with him. David asked, "Whither shall I go from thy Spirit? Or whither shall I flee from thy pres-

ence?" (Psalm 139:7). Then, in the following verses, he showed the impossibility of escaping God. For David also, that was a truth with positive and negative implications. When we trust God, obey Him, love Him, and serve Him, it is reassuring to know that we are never out of His sight. But how terrible it must be for the disobedient, the rebellious, the wicked, to awaken to the fact that there is no place to hide from God (see Revelation 6:15-17).

4. How can knowing non-Christians on a one-to-one basis aid us in witnessing to them?

We are irritated when we hear sweeping generalizations made about Christians: "Christians are hypocrites" or "Christians talk a lot about love, but they don't practice it." Similarly some Christians may thoughtlessly state that all non-Christians are preoccupied with material things or that they are all afflicted with pride and pleasure-seeking. When we come to know them personally, however, we find that the generalizations do not always fit. We may better understand their hopes and goals, as well as their fears and frustrations. We can identify with them in cherishing some of the same hopes and struggling with some of the same fears. And this can provide the setting for introducing them to Jesus Christ, who has strengthened our hopes and calmed our fears.

5. Why does it often take a crisis to turn one back to faith in God and obedience to Him?

How many Christians can testify that a serious health problem, a family tragedy, a financial reversal, or some other such crisis was instrumental in bringing them to Christ or drawing them back to Christ after a period of backsliding? We are creatures of habit, and we tend to follow a certain pattern of behavior unless it is disrupted by an emergency. There is a kind of law of spiritual momentum that helps us stay faithful in worship, service, and holiness of life, if we will work with it. But the same law operates in terms of indifference and inconsistency in holiness if we allow ourselves to drift away from Christ. At such times, a personal crisis can be God's gift to us to draw our attention back to Him and to provide us with an opportunity to make a fresh start in faithful living.

God Saves, and Jonah Sulks

LESSON SCRIPTURE: **Jonah 3, 4.**

PRINTED TEXT: **Jonah 3:1-5, 10; 4:1-4, 10, 11.**

Jonah 3:1-5, 10

1 And the word of the LORD came unto Jonah the second time, saying,

2 Arise, go unto Nineveh, that great city, and preach unto it the preaching that I bid thee.

3 So Jonah arose, and went unto Nineveh, according to the word of the LORD. Now Nineveh was an exceeding great city of three days' journey.

4 And Jonah began to enter into the city a day's journey, and he cried, and said, Yet forty days, and Nineveh shall be overthrown.

5 So the people of Nineveh believed God, and proclaimed a fast, and put on sackcloth, from the greatest of them even to the least of them.

. . . .

10 And God saw their works, that they turned from their evil way; and God repented of the evil, that he had said that he would do unto them; and he did it not.

Jonah 4:1-4, 10, 11

1 But it displeased Jonah exceedingly, and he was very angry.

2 And he prayed unto the LORD, and said, I pray thee, O LORD, was not this my saying, when I was yet in my country? Therefore I fled before unto Tarshish: for I knew that thou art a gracious God, and merciful, slow to anger, and of great kindness, and repentest thee of the evil.

3 Therefore now, O LORD, take, I beseech thee, my life from me; for it is better for me to die than to live.

4 Then said the LORD, Doest thou well to be angry?

. . . .

10 Then said the LORD, Thou hast had pity on the gourd, for the which thou hast not labored, neither madest it grow; which came up in a night, and perished in a night:

11 And should not I spare Nineveh, that great city, wherein are more than sixscore thousand persons that cannot discern between their right hand and their left hand; and also much cattle?

GOLDEN TEXT: Should not I spare Nineveh, that great city, wherein are more than sixscore thousand persons that cannot discern between their right hand and their left hand; and also much cattle?—Jonah 4:11.

Lesson Aims

This lesson is designed to help the students be able to:

1. See how the question in the last verse of the book of Jonah speaks to them.

2. Reaffirm the Biblical truth that people are to be valued above things.

3. Commit themselves to sharing the gospel of salvation with people of all nationalities and races.

Lesson Outline

INTRODUCTION
    A. On the Jericho Road
    B. Lesson Background
I. NINEVEH'S REPENTANCE (Jonah 3:1-5)
    A. Repeated Command (vv. 1, 2)
    B. Reluctant Obedience (vv. 3, 4)
    C. Revival (v.5)
II. GOD'S RESPONSE (Jonah 3:10)
III. JONAH'S RESENTMENT (Jonah 4:1-4)
    A. Remonstrance (vv. 1, 2)
        Call Reluctance
    B. Request (v. 3)
    C. Rebuke (v. 4)
IV. DIVINE REASONING (Jonah 4:10, 11)
    A. Relative Value (v. 10)
    B. Remaining Question (v. 11)
CONCLUSION
    A. Jonah Chapter Five
    B. Prayer
    C. Thought to Remember

Display visual 3 of the visuals packet throughout this class session. The visual is shown on page 365.

Introduction

A. On the Jericho Road

There's an old spiritual that I suspect that most of us enjoy hearing. The tune is catchy, and the rhythm is upbeat. Some of the words, however, may tend to restrict our thinking regarding fellowship with the Lord. They are "On the Jericho Road, there's room for just two . . . just Jesus and you."

But is there room only for two? Is it just "Jesus and you"? Of course not. On the Jericho road,

there is room for everyone. As we are on that road, we need to be saying to those off to the side, "Come on, join us."

John captured what our spirit should be when he wrote, "That which we have seen and heard declare we unto you, that ye also may have fellowship with us: and truly our fellowship is with the Father, and with his Son Jesus Christ. And these things write we unto you, that your joy may be full" (1 John 1:3, 4).

Jonah had a warped view of God's desire for fellowship with humankind. And the prophet certainly had little, if any, interest in being a party to bringing the joy of forgiveness to a wicked people. How much room is there on the road to Jericho with Jesus and us/you?

B. Lesson Background

God does not will that anyone should perish, so He commissioned Jonah to go to the great city of Nineveh. Of course, it was a godless city, a mean city, and a foe to God's people. However, Jonah refused to evangelize those people whom he did not like. Not only did he go the opposite direction from Nineveh, he also tried to run away from the presence of God. But God did not give up on Jonah, because God did not give up on Nineveh. In last week's lesson we saw the steps God took to bring Jonah around.

Jonah was in the fish for three days and three nights. How long was it before he uttered the prayer recorded in chapter two? We cannot tell. Realizing that he was hopelessly lost depending on his own strength and ingenuity, he cried out to God for deliverance. The entire second chapter is Jonah's prayer.

Prayer makes a difference; prayer affects God. It was after Jonah prayed that God intervened again with nature and commanded the fish to spit Jonah onto dry land. Our lesson begins with the Lord encountering Jonah on that beach.

I. Nineveh's Repentance
(Jonah 3:1-5)

A. Repeated Command (vv. 1, 2)

1, 2. And the word of the Lord came unto Jonah the second time, saying, Arise, go unto Nineveh, that great city, and preach unto it the preaching that I bid thee.

God's second command to Jonah was a repetition of His first command. He did not change His plan because Jonah didn't like it. The command had three parts: (a) get up, (b) get going, (c) start proclaiming what I tell you.

Those are three essentials for any of us in carrying out God's commands. Laziness is a threat to many persons. The cares of this life may weigh us down. These can lead to spiritual paralysis if we allow them to gain the upper hand. We need to "get up." Then we need to "get going." The first word of the Great Commission (Matthew 28:19, 20) is "Go." But we are to go with a purpose—with the message of God on our hearts and lips.

B. Reluctant Obedience (vv. 3, 4)

3. So Jonah arose, and went unto Nineveh, according to the word of the Lord. Now Nineveh was an exceeding great city of three days' journey.

It appears that Jonah did not delay in responding to the Lord's command this time. Jonah hardly had time to catch his breath when God said, "Get up and go." And Jonah obeyed. He went to Nineveh. His attitude, which was exhibited later, indicated, however, that he still was reluctant to have anything to do with the Ninevites. Perhaps he went thinking, "I'll go, but I won't like it."

While Jonah saw Nineveh as an exceedingly evil city, God saw it as an exceedingly great city. It was great in size, with perhaps more than one-half million residents. It was great in potential, for it was the capital of Assyria and thus had far-reaching influence. It was great in readiness for Jonah's preaching. Outwardly, there may not have been one fact about Nineveh to suggest that it was a ripe mission field. But God looks upon the heart, not only on what we can observe.

The text says that Nineveh was *an exceeding great city of three days' journey*. This does not mean that it was a three-days' journey from where Jonah was spit up on the beach by the great fish (presumably on the eastern shore of the Mediterranean Sea). Rather, it is a description of the size of the city itself. Three explanations of the phrase have been suggested, as follows:

1. It would take three days to walk around the circumference of the city limits.

2. It would take three days to walk around the city of Nineveh and the outlying territories that depended upon Nineveh.

3. It would take three days to walk through Nineveh, going in and out of the side streets and through the marketplaces preaching as he was walking.

4. And Jonah began to enter into the city a day's journey, and he cried, and said, Yet forty days, and Nineveh shall be overthrown.

The Hebrew word for *overthrown* is the same one that is used to describe the destruction of Sodom and Gomorrah (Genesis 19:25; Deuteronomy 29:23). The destruction would be total.

Nineveh was a proud and powerful city. Jonah was an outsider, a citizen of a nation that not too many years earlier had been forced to pay tribute to Assyria. Jonah's entrance into this city, therefore, was potentially dangerous to himself. To his credit, however, he disregarded the danger and made his way through the streets and marketplaces throughout the day.

Yet forty days, and Nineveh shall be overthrown. Some students think that Jonah simply repeated this phrase over and over as he made his way through the city. It seems more likely, though, that he would have specified Nineveh's sins that were bringing God's judgment and that he would have told them the destruction would not come if they would repent. Isaiah 36:11, 13 indicates that there were persons in Assyria and Israel who understood the languages of both nations. So Jonah's message would have been understood by at least some of the Ninevites, who, in turn, would have told others.

C. Revival (v. 5)

5. So the people of Nineveh believed God, and proclaimed a fast, and put on sackcloth, from the greatest of them even to the least of them.

As a result of Jonah's preaching, a city-wide revival took place. All elements of society responded to the warning that he delivered, from the greatest of them even to the least of them. Verses 6-9 indicate the king's involvement in this spiritual revival. How, it may be asked, could such a response come from the preaching of one man? First, it should be observed that Jonah preached to all. He did not just go to the poor or to the most influential. All had sinned, thus all were in danger of destruction. It is interesting to note in this regard that Jesus said that Jonah was "a sign" to the Ninevites (Luke 11:30). Perhaps word of Jonah's experience in the belly of the great fish had preceded his coming to Nineveh. Or, perhaps Jonah related the account himself as he spoke to the people. The citizens of this land were not unaware of the prophets of Israel, such as Elijah and Elisha, through whom God had done great things. Here now was one of these prophets standing in their midst, recounting to them his frightening experience, yet living proof that God may save the disobedient when

---

How to Say It

ELISHA.   Ee-*lye*-shuh.
JERICHO.   *Jair*-ih-ko.
NINEVEH.   *Nin*-uh-vuh.

they repent and turn to Him. Such a God as the God of Jonah was not to be trifled with. But since God had spared Jonah, perhaps He would yet spare Nineveh.

The people's response to Jonah's "cry" was such that they believed in the God of whom he spoke and they proclaimed a fast in one locality after another. The wearing of sackcloth, a coarse cloth usually made of goat's hair, was a means of indicating the distress of one's spirit. The spirit of repentance among the people grew, and soon the king himself lent his influence to it by example and proclamation.

The people of Nineveh turned to God in order to save themselves from terrible punishment, and this is legitimate. On the Day of Pentecost when the church began, Peter said, "Save yourselves from this corrupt generation" (Acts 2:40, *New International Version*). A time of judgment is coming that will result in either damnation or salvation. Everyone in this, and every, generation needs to hear both sides of that.

II. God's Response
(Jonah 3:10)

10. And God saw their works, that they turned from their evil way; and God repented of the evil, that he had said that he would do unto them; and he did it not.

"God is not a man, that he should lie; neither the son of man, that he should repent: hath he said, and shall he not do it? Or hath he spoken, and shall he not make it good?" So spoke an unwilling prophet, but a true one (Numbers 23:19). The thought of God's repenting, therefore, raises questions for us. Is He changing, undependable? Most assuredly not. He is changeless, eternally the same. James says of Him, "Every good gift and every perfect gift is from above, coming down from the Father of lights, with whom can be no variation, neither shadow that is cast by turning" (1:17, *American Standard Version*). His desire that all persons be saved remains unchanged. But changing circumstances and changing people call for different attitudes and actions on His part, all of which are a part of His unchanging nature.

God promises blessing or punishment according to the principle stated in Jeremiah 18:7-10. In each case, God's actions are conditional—they are called forth by the actions of people. Thus, God told Jeremiah to preach His word to Judah, "if so be they will hearken, and turn every man from his evil way, that I may repent me of the evil, which I purpose to do unto them because of the evil of their doings" (Jeremiah 26:3). That was an expression of God's unchanging grace and committed love. The principle stood that there was destruction for those who stayed outside of His will; but for those who would bring themselves near to Him, and would obey His will, the threatened destruction would be withheld.

This same principle is applied to individuals (see Ezekiel 33:13-16). The Biblical teaching that states, "Whosoever shall call on the name of the Lord shall be saved" (Acts 2:21; Joel 2:32) is consistent with that principle. God "is a rewarder of them that diligently seek him" (Hebrews 11:6). God's threat can be turned into a treat if met by the repentance of the people. God warns of the punishment for sin, not because He enjoys destroying people, but so that people may change and receive His blessing instead.

In Nineveh's case, notice what God saw that caused His response to be different from what Jonah had announced. He observed their works. From the highest of them to the lowest, they fasted and put on sackcloth. Their belief in God was expressed by what they did. Genuine faith always results in works. The devil and his demons believe (they know that God is God and that Jesus is His only Son), but they do not work for God (James 2:19). Faith unaccompanied by corresponding deeds is useless (James 2:24, 26).

III. Jonah's Resentment
(Jonah 4:1-4)
A. Remonstrance (vv. 1, 2)

1. But it displeased Jonah exceedingly, and he was very angry.

Jonah had repented of his disobedience, but it seems apparent that he had never repented of his prejudice against Nineveh. It displeased him that Nineveh had repented and that God had withheld destruction of the city. Jonah had received God's grace when he was spewed out of the fish's mouth, but he was not interested in allowing others to enjoy that same grace.

Some Bible students believe that Jonah's anger may have been due in part to the fact that he felt he had been made a fool of. Having prophesied a destruction that never came, he would be ridiculed as a false prophet. In any case, his prejudice against Nineveh had not lessened.

Jonah had desired the destruction of Nineveh and inwardly gloated about it. In so doing, he was going against the teaching of God's Word, which states, "Rejoice not when thine enemy falleth, and let not thine heart be glad when he stumbleth" (Proverbs 24:17; see also Proverbs 17:5). Jonah was harsh and judgmental in spirit. He was not loving what God loved—people.

2. And he prayed unto the Lord, and said, I pray thee, O Lord, was not this my saying, when I was yet in my country? Therefore I fled before unto Tarshish: for I knew that thou art a gracious God, and merciful, slow to anger, and of great kindness, and repentest thee of the evil.

Jonah felt that he had reason to be angry and did not hesitate to state his complaint before God. He said he disobeyed God because he knew that He was gracious, merciful, and kind and that He would forgive the Ninevites if they repented. He fled because he did not want the people of Nineveh to experience God's grace. He wanted them to get the punishment they deserved.

Are we sometimes like Jonah in this regard? Are there times when we don't want God's grace to be extended to people we don't like? It seems that there have always been people of God who have been reluctant to allow God's grace to slip out of their grip and control. To them Paul declares, "What shall we say then? Is there unrighteousness with God? God forbid. For he saith to Moses, I will have mercy on whom I will have mercy, and I will have compassion on whom I will have compassion" (Romans 9:14, 15).

We are all glad for the Scripture that says, God "is kind unto the unthankful and to the evil" (Luke 6:35). If that were not true, we could not be saved. But are we as comfortable with the command in the next verse, "Be ye therefore merciful, as your Father also is merciful"? (Luke 6:36). Jonah wasn't.

CALL RELUCTANCE

Direct-sales training usually includes strategies and disciplines to overcome "call reluctance"—the sometimes-overpowering inclination of salespersons to stay at home, piddle with paperwork, run errands, make phone calls, anything but make sales calls. The force of call reluctance varies according to temperament and self-esteem, but probably most salespersons at times have rung doorbells while hoping that no one was home. This neurosis is linked to a fear of failure.

Jonah was extremely reluctant to call on the Ninevites, but for a different reason. His was a fear of success. He suspected that his preaching would bring Nineveh to repentance, and he knew that God then would save them rather than destroy them. He wanted justice, and he had no mercy.

What makes us reluctant to call on big cities and big sinners? Is it the fear of failure, or the fear of success? Whatever the cause, we cannot ignore the mandate. We too must warn evildoers, but we have good news about grace.

visual 3

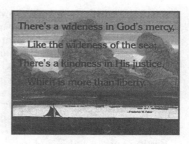

There's a wideness in God's mercy,
Like the wideness of the sea;
There's a kindness in His justice,
Which is more than liberty.
—Frederick W. Faber

Christ has commissioned us to disciple the whole world. There is no justification for discrimination in sharing the gospel.   —R. W. B.

B. Request (v. 3)

3. Therefore now, O Lord, take, I beseech thee, my life from me; for it is better for me to die than to live.

In spite of himself, Jonah had been the means of bringing repentance and deliverance to the people who were the enemies of his nation! He felt like a traitor. So great was Jonah's prejudice and hatred toward the Ninevites that he would rather die then live knowing that he had had a part in sparing them from destruction. Truly Jonah had much to learn about God and the kind of attitudes that He desires to find in the hearts of His people.

C. Rebuke (v. 4)

4. Then said the Lord, Doest thou well to be angry?

How gently God dealt with His ungrateful and unreasonable prophet! In asking this question, God was administering a mild rebuke. In effect, He was saying, "Jonah, you don't have any right to be angry." God might have said, "Think about it for a moment, Jonah. You are alive today because of my grace. It was I who saved you from drowning in the sea, and it was I who rescued you from the belly of the great fish. How, then, can you be angry if I choose to extend my grace to these penitent Ninevites?"

Verses 5-9 are omitted from the printed text of this lesson, but an understanding of them is necessary if we would grasp the significance of the final verses of the text.

Jonah saw that God was not going to permit him to die, so he went outside the city and constructed a booth in which to live while he waited to see "what would become of the city" (v. 5). We get the impression that the prophet still clung to the hope that destruction would come to Nineveh. The booth that he made was probably fashioned from scrub branches that would provide a little shade from the hot sun of the middle east.

At this point, God intervened by showing mercy to Jonah once again. He prepared a special plant that grew up over Jonah's arbor and provided shade for him, delivering him "from his grief." And Jonah was very glad for the relief it brought him! (v. 6). The next morning, however, God prepared a worm that attacked the plant, causing it to wither. The scorching east wind that God then sent upon Jonah caused the prophet to want to die (vv. 7, 8).

Having concluded His object lesson, God then spoke to Jonah about his feelings for the plant that had been destroyed. Jonah responded by expressing his sorrow and anger over the destruction of the plant that had been a source of blessing for him. God's reply is seen in verse 10.

IV. Divine Reasoning (Jonah 4:10, 11)

A. Relative Value (v. 10)

10. Then said the Lord, Thou hast had pity on the gourd, for the which thou hast not labored, neither madest it grow; which came up in a night, and perished in a night.

Jonah had not planted the gourd that provided shade for him, neither had he watered it or tended it in any way. And yet he had pity on it when it died. All the while, however, he had no pity on an entire city of human beings. He had more compassion for a temporary object than for eternal people. What a perversion of priorities! A plant is made after the image of its own seed. People are made after the image of God.

Before we get too critical of Jonah, we need to take a good look at ourselves. Does a scratch or a dent on our new car give us more discomfort than knowing that a friend or neighbor is outside of Christ? Would we spend as much time nurturing someone in Christ as we do in landscaping our lawns? Would we spend as much time with someone who is lonely as we do with our television sets? Upon what do we lavish our concern?

B. Remaining Question (v. 11)

11. And should not I spare Nineveh, that great city, wherein are more than sixscore thousand persons that cannot discern between their right hand and their left hand; and also much cattle?

The word translated *spare* is the Hebrew word for "pity." If Jonah could pity a plant that had grown up without any help from him, shouldn't God feel as strongly about a city full of people whom He had created and sustained, a city wherein were a hundred and twenty thousand innocent children?

We may be disappointed with the ending of this book, because we do not know how Jonah answered God's question. But we don't need to. What is important is, do we understand how wide God's mercy is and are we willing to be the means whereby other people may experience it? Our answer is seen in our actions and reactions to the people of every race and nationality around us.

Conclusion

A. Jonah Chapter Five

In His divine wisdom, God has planned that those who have received His mercy and grace should be the ones to share them with others. He says to us, therefore, "Arise, go to _____ (that individual, that section of town, that group of people) and share the gospel of salvation with them." How do we respond to that divine directive? Are we like Jonah who tried to flee from his responsibility? Do we harbor the notion that there are limits to God's mercy? The message of the book of Jonah is that God's love knows no ethnic or racial boundaries. It is inclusive. Let us rejoice that it is so and do what we can to share the knowledge of God's love with everyone. How does your Jonah chapter five read?

B. Prayer

Thank you, Father, that when we were citizens of our own Nineveh, You cared and sent someone to us. Now help us to go and do likewise as an ambassador of Jesus. In His name, amen.

C. Thought to Remember

"Be ye therefore merciful, as your Father also is merciful" (Luke 6:36).

Home Daily Bible Readings

Monday, June 15—Jonah's Second Call (Jonah 3:1-4)

Tuesday, June 16—Nineveh Repents (Jonah 3:5-10)

Wednesday, June 17—Jonah Is Not Pleased (Jonah 4:1-5)

Thursday, June 18—God Has Pity for Nineveh (Jonah 4:6-11)

Friday, June 19—Sign of Jonah (Luke 11:29-32)

Saturday, June 20—God's Mercy Is Endless (Lamentations 3:22-33)

Sunday, June 21—God Cares (Isaiah 44:21-28)

Learning by Doing

This page contains an alternate lesson plan emphasizing learning activities. Classes desiring such student involvement will find these suggestions helpful.

Learning Goals

After this lesson, students will be able to:

1. Identify Jonah's attitudes that displeased God.

2. Determine how they may share the gospel with those persons their congregation may have ignored in the past.

3. Apply the challenge in Jonah 4:11 to themselves.

Into the Lesson

Before the class members arrive, place the word *heathen* on the chalkboard or a sheet of newsprint. After the class has assembled, ask your students to think of words that they associate with the word displayed. Have the class members work together in groups of two or three. After three to five minutes, ask the class members to share their responses.

Lead into the Bible lesson by stating that God directed Jonah to go to a heathen nation to proclaim their destruction. Jonah refused to do this and tried to flee from God, because he didn't want the Ninevites to escape the destruction he felt they deserved. This lesson examines Jonah's further response to God's dealings with this heathen nation.

Into the Word

Review the events recorded in Jonah 1 to establish the background for this lesson. See last week's lesson for details.

Than have chapters 3 and 4 of Jonah read aloud in their entirety. Assign someone to be the voice of God and read Jonah 3:2; 4:4b, 9b, 10b, 11. Assign another to be the voice of Jonah and read 3:4b; 4:2b, 3, 8b, 9d. Assign a third student to be the voice of the king and read 3:7b-9. A fourth may be the narrator and read 3:1, 3, 4a, 5-7a; 4:1, 2a, 4a, 5-8a, 9a, c, 10a. It would help if you provided each with a photocopy of the complete text and highlighted each person's verses with a color marker.

Direct the attention of the students to the text and use the following questions to guide them through an examination of the Biblical material.

1. When God spoke to Jonah the second time and told him to go preach to Nineveh, what was Jonah's response? (He did what God told him to do—he went to Nineveh and proclaimed the word of the Lord.)

2. What seems to have been Jonah's attitude as he did this? Why? (Although he obeyed the letter of God's command and proclaimed His word, it seems apparent that he hoped his preaching would fall on deaf ears. His hatred for an enemy of his nation was stronger than the desire to see sinners turn to God.)

3. What was surprising about the response of the Ninevites to Jonah's warning? (The entire city repented, from the king to the lowest subject.)

4. How did Jonah respond to this repentance? (He was angry and went outside the city, apparently still hoping to see Nineveh destroyed.)

5. What object lesson did God provide for Jonah as he sat waiting to see what would become of Nineveh? (God caused a plant to grow up to shelter Jonah from the hot sun; He then sent a worm to wither the plant; finally, He sent a hot east wind to increase Jonah's discomfort.)

6. What was God trying to teach Jonah? (In evoking Jonah's pity for a plant that died suddenly, God hoped Jonah would better understand His pity for human beings who were in danger of dying.)

7. What should we learn from Jonah 3 and 4? (God wants everyone everywhere to repent of evil, and we should enthusiastically share that message with the whole world.)

Into Life

Apply this lesson to life by discussing the following questions:

1. What groups do we sometimes see as being so wicked or unapproachable that God will relieve us of our responsibility to call them to repentance?

2. How can our class and congregation take up God's challenge implied in 4:11? How can we reach those who seem unapproachable?

3. Some groups that we feel are unapproachable are so far from us geographically that we rarely, if ever, have personal contact with them. How can we be involved in reaching them?

4. How can you personally respond to the challenge implied in Jonah 4:11?

Ask your students to select one way they can become involved in sharing the good news with others in the week to come. Ask them to share their decision with one other person in the class. Close with a prayer of commitment.

Let's Talk It Over

The questions on this page are designed to encourage review of the lesson Scriptures and to promote discussion of the lesson by the class. The answers provided are only discussion starters. Let your class talk it over from there.

1. How does God's command to Jonah— "Arise, go unto Nineveh . . . and preach unto it"—fit in with the Great Commission Jesus has given the church?

Perhaps the command to "arise" can serve as a reminder that we dare not spend our time and energy simply talking about evangelism. We need to arise from our planning meetings and fulfill the Great Commission by going and preaching. The reference to Nineveh could call our attention to certain individuals or groups that we have avoided evangelizing because we are inclined to regard them as unworthy of our efforts, or we fear that they will reject us and mock us. The command to preach, in harmony with the Great Commission, reminds us that we must not "beat around the bush," but must boldly deliver God's message.

2. Should Christians feel a sense of anticipation regarding God's judgment on the wicked? Why or why not?

When we see wicked people arrogantly defying God by their words and their behavior, it is tempting to relish the thought of their facing fiery judgment from that One they defy. If we long for God's judgment because we want to see Him vindicated as a just and holy God, and do not merely desire to sooth our own wounded pride, then we are in harmony with the wishes David expressed in Psalm 9:19, 20. But the New Testament expresses more the fact of God's compassion toward the lost and His desire for their salvation. "The Lord is . . . long-suffering to usward, not willing that any should perish, but that all should come to repentance" (2 Peter 3:9). The salvation of the wicked, rather than their punishment, should be of principal concern to God's servants.

3. Why is it important that priority be given to winning great cities to Christ?

First of all, the cities contain a large concentration of people who need to hear and heed the gospel. While in Corinth, Paul, who made it his usual procedure to center his evangelistic efforts in large cities, was told by the Lord, "I have much people in this city" (Acts 18:10). And it is equally likely that in modern cities there are many persons who are potential converts to Christ, if we get His message to them. Also, the cities are the centers of influence in most nations. In them are found the prominent publishing enterprises, the television networks, the strongholds of political power, and the like. It is vital that the gospel be allowed to penetrate these institutions so that its effect can be brought to bear on those who direct them and on those who are influenced by them.

4. Can we think of some individuals or groups to whom we would be reluctant to see God's grace extended? How can we change this tendency to reluctance?

Murderers and other notorious criminals, international terrorists, movie stars with blatantly immoral life-styles, publishers of pornography, crooked politicians—these are some who may come to mind. It is interesting to note that from these general classifications of sinners one can think of several individuals who have responded to God's grace and received salvation. In New Testament times, Saul of Tarsus probably would have impressed many Christians as unfit for salvation. Many years after his conversion, Saul, now called Paul, still referred to himself as chief of sinners (1 Timothy 1:15). Perhaps if we would recall more often the sins that God forgave us through His grace, we would be less reluctant to see that grace extended to others.

5. How can we determine whether or not we value things more than people?

One way is to examine the expenditure of our time. It may be useful to keep a record of our activities for a period of time and note which are people-centered and which are things-centered. The earning of wages, the maintenance of possessions, the relaxation provided by a hobby are all necessary and worthwhile, but do we balance them out with quality time for our family, friends, neighbors, and others? The way we spend our money provides another test. An examination of our budget may reveal a preoccupation with the material. It is true that we must use a significant portion of our income on food, clothing, and other essentials, but we should be able to demonstrate by our spending that we set a high value on the temporal and eternal needs of other human beings.

Judgment and Salvation

LESSON SCRIPTURE: Nahum.

PRINTED TEXT: Nahum 1:2, 3, 6-9, 12, 13, 15.

Nahum 1:2, 3, 6-9, 12, 13, 15

2 God is jealous, and the LORD revengeth; the LORD revengeth, and is furious; the LORD will take vengeance on his adversaries, and he reserveth wrath for his enemies.

3 The LORD is slow to anger, and great in power, and will not at all acquit the wicked: the LORD hath his way in the whirlwind and in the storm, and the clouds are the dust of his feet.

. . . .

6 Who can stand before his indignation? and who can abide in the fierceness of his anger? his fury is poured out like fire, and the rocks are thrown down by him.

7 The LORD is good, a stronghold in the day of trouble; and he knoweth them that trust in him.

8 But with an overrunning flood he will make an utter end of the place thereof, and darkness shall pursue his enemies.

9 What do ye imagine against the LORD? he will make an utter end: affliction shall not rise up the second time.

. . . .

12 Thus saith the LORD; Though they be quiet, and likewise many, yet thus shall they be cut down, when he shall pass through. Though I have afflicted thee, I will afflict thee no more.

13 For now will I break his yoke from off thee, and will burst thy bonds in sunder.

. . . .

15 Behold upon the mountains the feet of him that bringeth good tidings, that publisheth peace! O Judah, keep thy solemn feasts, perform thy vows: for the wicked shall no more pass through thee; he is utterly cut off.

GOLDEN TEXT: The LORD is good, a stronghold in the day of trouble; and he knoweth them that trust in him.—Nahum 1:7.

God's Judgment and Mercy

Unit 1: Warnings and Promises
From God (Lessons 1-5)

Lesson Aims

This lesson should help the student:
1. List reasons why God is slow to express His anger toward sinners.
2. Understand that God's punishment of the wicked is certain.

Lesson Outline

INTRODUCTION
    A. God, Where Are You?
    B. Lesson Background
  I. THE NATURE OF GOD'S JUDGMENT (Nahum 1:2, 3, 6)
    A. With Jealousy and Vengeance (v. 2)
    B. With Powerful Patience (v. 3)
      Long Fuse
    C. With Devastation (v. 6)
 II. GOD'S DEFENSE OF HIS PEOPLE (Nahum 1:7-9)
    A. Refuge for the Troubled (v. 7)
      God of Refugees
    B. Revenge for the Troublers (vv. 8, 9)
III. REASSURANCE TO JUDAH (Nahum 1:12, 13)
    A. A People Destroyed (v. 12)
    B. A People Delivered (v. 13)
IV. REJOICING IN SALVATION (Nahum 1:15)
      Celebrating Peace
CONCLUSION
    A. God, Where Are You Today?
    B. Prayer
    C. Thought to Remember

Display visual 4 from the visual packet and let it remain before the class throughout the session. The visual is shown on page 373.

Introduction
A. God, Where Are You?

Some of us were around when Hitler began his cruel march to become the world conqueror and master of peoples. It is difficult to watch historical movies relating Hitler's atrocities inflicted on the Jewish people without asking from time to time, "God, where were You?"

Isn't it interesting, however, that during those years, most of those Jewish people refused to deny their belief in God or felt that God had given up on them? They were convinced that God had powerful patience and would eventually rain down vengeance upon their enemies.

Today, look around. Where are Hitler and the results of his efforts to achieve global conquest? He's gone, and his plans were destroyed with him. But the Jewish people? They are still here and giving another evidence that God's ways and thoughts are as high above ours as the heavens are above the earth. God is still almighty. No person, no government, no philosophy, no system has been able or will ever be able to oppose Him with lasting effectiveness.

B. Lesson Background

Last week we saw that the city of Nineveh responded to the preaching of Jonah, repented, and turned to God. This week it is a different story. In 721 B.C., approximately sixty years after Nineveh repented from Jonah's preaching, the Assyrians conquered the northern kingdom of Israel and carried most of its people into captivity.

The Assyrians increased in their wicked lifestyle and cruelty in warfare. They were drunk with greed and flaunted their power.

Today's message is the message of the prophet Nahum regarding the coming destruction of Nineveh. Nahum prophesied in the southern kingdom of Judah about 640 B.C. His message sounds like a rerun of Jonah's cry of destruction, but at least 135 years had passed since Nineveh repented.

What happened to Nineveh that caused her to be the target of God's destruction? A nation can change a great deal in 135 years. Just think how the United States has changed since 1857. Don't just trace the changes in our wealth, but think of the changes in our values and life-styles.

Surely most would agree that there has been a general decline in the moral and spiritual values in our society. How, we wonder, could such changes occur?

Is it possible that the revival in Nineveh had a short life partly due to the fact that Jonah evidently did not return to the city to nurture, to teach, and to build up the people in the faith? We don't know the answer to that, but we do know that somewhere along the line the torch of faith in the Creator-God was not passed on. Nineveh went back to her old ways, and eventually God had had enough.

Could that happen in this country? Of course it could, and it may—unless our citizens turn to God to live with Him and for Him.

The prophet's name, Nahum, literally means "consolation" or "consoler." While his message condemned the capital of the Assyrian Empire, it brought consolation to God's people who were the victims of the Assyrian atrocities.

I. The Nature of God's Judgment (Nahum 1: 2, 3, 6)

A. With Jealousy and Vengeance (v. 2)

2. God is jealous, and the Lord revengeth; the Lord revengeth, and is furious; the Lord will take vengeance on his adversaries, and he reserveth wrath for his enemies.

Galatians 5:19, 20 indicates that jealousy is a work of sinful flesh, but here we read that God is jealous. Is there a contradiction? Not at all. There are two kinds of jealousy—an evil kind and a good kind.

Jealousy literally means "zeal." There is a jealousy that is an expression of selfishness. It reflects one's resentment toward someone else because of that person's accomplishments or possessions. But there is a jealousy, a zeal, that has as its goal another person's good. For example, a teenage Christian boy might get jealous if someone else wants to date his special girl friend. The jealousy could be only selfish, if it arises because he does not want anyone else to date her. Or his jealousy could be godly, if he knows that the person who wants to date her is a non-Christian who sells and takes drugs. In this situation his jealousy would be for the good of his friend.

Whenever we do something to protect our children or our mates, it is done out of a jealousy, or zeal, for their good. So it is with God. He has zeal that people should let go of idols and worship Him only for their good. That is righteous jealousy.

By mentioning three times that God is vengeful, Nahum left no doubt that Nineveh would be severely punished for the atrocities they had committed against God's people. Implied is the fact that God's people are not to take vengeance into their own hands. Paul wrote that we should not repay anyone evil for evil, but leave room for God's wrath. Our responsibility is to overcome evil with good and leave vengeance to God (Romans 12:17-21).

B. With Powerful Patience (v. 3)

3. The Lord is slow to anger, and great in power, and will not at all acquit the wicked: the Lord hath his way in the whirlwind and in the storm, and the clouds are the dust of his feet.

God's vengeance is not like a "flash in the pan" temper tantrum. He is *slow to anger.* That doesn't mean that God is slow to get upset at evil, but He is slow to express that anger with destruction. He balances His anger with patience. Patience has two meanings: (a) to put up

with difficult people; (b) to remain under difficult situations.

God is not quick to destroy the rebellious, and aren't we glad for that! We would not survive were it not for His patience. God's patience allows us time to repent of evil and thus escape the destruction that will come on those who persist in their sins.

Is your anger fuse short or long? Do you keep your trigger cocked? Repeating quick anger can become a habit. When we become Christians, God's divine nature begins to live in us (2 Peter 1:4). James tells us to be slow to anger, for our anger does not bring about the kind of life God desires (James 1:19, 20).

God's slowness does not mean weakness. Power is inherent in His patience. In other words, He has himself under control. Nahum gives the assurance that God *will not at all acquit the wicked.* Although time passes, and it seems, as James Russell Lowell expressed it, that truth is "forever on the scaffold, wrong forever on the throne," the truth is that the punishment of the wicked is certain. The time of punishment will come when God wills it.

Regardless of how the situation may look to us, God will have His way, not only with people but with nature—*in the whirlwind and in the storm.* God has power over all things that He has created.

It is easy to believe that life on earth is totally under the control of natural laws. But there is no such thing as true "natural" laws, as if those laws belong to nature. They belong to God; He created them, and His power and majesty are displayed in the working of those forces.

Nahum seems to be depicting the Lord as a man of war (Exodus 15:3) who is advancing on His enemies. The clouds appear majestic as we view them from earth, but to God they are but as the dust raised by the feet in walking.

Verses 4 and 5, which are omitted from our text, continue the thought of God's power as seen at work in the world. Great physical changes and convulsions in the physical world are depicted, and these are symbols of God's wrath, which He will unleash on sinful nations.

How to Say It

ASSYRIA.   Uh-*sear*-ee-uh.
HEZEKIAH.   Hez-ih-*kye*-uh.
MANASSEH.   Muh-*nass*-uh.
NAHUM.   *Nay*-hum.
NINEVEH.   *Nin*-uh-vuh.
SENNACHERIB.   Sen-*nack*-er-ib.

LONG FUSE

Ralph Kramden, the TV character created by the late Jackie Gleason on *The Honeymooners*, is funny when he explodes in anger at the slightest frustration. So are Archie Bunker, George Jefferson, and Fred Flintstone. Several more of our favorite television characters could be named, all of whom have one trait in common—a short fuse!

We are amused and entertained by personalities with fiery temperaments. We laugh at their foibles, often because we personally identify with them.

A short temper is not considered an admirable personality trait. People of great strength and self-control, however, are respected and emulated. Nahum says God has a long fuse—He is "slow to anger." Though "great in power," God is patient and tolerant. He doesn't explode in wrath each time someone disobeys His commands, forgets His promises, or ignores His warnings. His anger is fierce because of the sinfulness of mankind, but He postpones vengeance. Peter gives one reason: He is longsuffering, "not wanting anyone to perish" (2 Peter 3:9, *New International Version*).

Something worth remembering: even long fuses eventually ignite the dynamite. Nineveh finally pushed God to His limits; they became vile enemies of the Almighty. We revere God for His perfect patience, but we must not presume upon His generous grace.   —R. W. B.

C. With Devastation (v. 6)

6. Who can stand before his indignation? and who can abide in the fierceness of his anger? his fury is poured out like fire, and the rocks are thrown down by him.

Nineveh, capital of Assyria, had planned and carried out one fierce military campaign after another. As their conquests mounted, their pride and arrogance increased. But they had encountered no foe like the Lord God. His *indignation* and *the fierceness of his anger* were to be felt by them. They would be overcome as one who stood in the path of molten lava, or who was in the epicenter of a great earthquake and had huge rocks thrown down upon him. There would be no escape; their destruction was certain.

We cannot read this verse without thinking of the end of the world, the great day of the Lord's wrath. Who, then, "shall be able to stand?" (Revelation 6:17). The wicked shall not escape God's condemnation, regardless of what may be their status, wealth, alliances, and memberships.

What can we humans do? We can repent and trust in the death, burial, and resurrection of Jesus now, before that day comes. All who do are the recipients of the promise penned by the apostle Paul: "There is therefore now no condemnation to them which are in Christ Jesus" (Romans 8:1).

II. God's Defense of His People (Nahum 1:7-9)

A. Refuge for the Troubled (v. 7)

7. The Lord is good, a stronghold in the day of trouble; and he knoweth them that trust in him.

The word *good* refers not only to God's moral righteousness, but also to His benevolent kindness and concern for the well-being of His people. *A stronghold in the day of trouble* harks back to the time, some sixty years earlier, when the Assyrians, under Sennacherib, threatened Jerusalem. On that occasion, God smote the Assyrian army, and in one night 185,000 warriors mysteriously died. Whereupon, the Assyrians immediately returned to their own land, and Jerusalem was spared (see Isaiah 37).

Likewise, the Lord knows the difficulties being experienced by all who *trust in him*. He loves and cares for them and gives them strength for the ordeal. The psalmist expressed it well: "My foes . . . confronted me in the day of my disaster, but the Lord was my support" (Psalm 18:17, 18, *New International Version*).

GOD OF REFUGEES

America has always been a racial and cultural "melting pot," and "huddled masses yearning to be free" have flocked to these shores in droves. In recent years alone, refugees from Viet Nam, Cambodia, Laos, and Cuba have found asylum, peace, and prosperity here.

God has blessed America abundantly, and those blessings have been shared with millions who are less fortunate. This land has been looked upon as a refuge for many persons in distress, because we are "one nation under God," guided by the divine absolutes of "liberty and justice for all."

While God prophesied through Nahum the destruction of Nineveh, at the same time He promised refuge for Judah, because "He cares for those who trust in Him" (1:7, *New International Version*). Will the motto on our currency remain true in the next century? The majority of United States citizens claim that they pray. People of prayer should petition God for continuing providence and protection. He will "hear from heaven" and will heal our land (2 Chronicles 7:14), for He alone "is our refuge and strength, a very present help in trouble" (Psalm 46:1).   —R. W. B.

B. Revenge for the Troublers (vv. 8, 9)

8. But with an overrunning flood he will make an utter end of the place thereof, and darkness shall pursue his enemies.

The *place* is the city of Nineveh, whose destruction is the subject of Nahum's prophecy (1:1). In metaphorical language he pictured God's judgment that was coming on the city. A flood is a common image that denotes calamity (see Psalm 32:6). It would be *overrunning*. No barrier would stand before it; all would be swept away. Just as frightful is the thought contained in the expression, *darkness shall pursue his enemies*. There would be no letup in the darkness, dawn would never come again to the Assyrian kingdom. The *New International Version* translates this as, "he will pursue his foes into darkness." The force is the same in either case. Their doom was absolutely certain and would be complete.

9. What do ye imagine against the Lord? he will make an utter end: affliction shall not rise up the second time.

The prophet here addressed the "enemies" mentioned in verse 8, the people of Nineveh. He asked what they were imagining, or plotting, in the way of resistance to the Lord. Did they dare think that they could fight against Him? Gravely, Nahum decreed that Nineveh's ruin was certain and would be complete. The Assyrians severely afflicted Judah when Sennacherib invaded the land some sixty years earlier, but they would never afflict Judah again.

It seems that there is no limit to the plottings of the wicked in packaging and executing evil. Our society is rife with influences that seek the moral and spiritual breakdown of people, especially the young.

Man's creativity in devising evil will not go forever unchecked. God will make an utter end to it. It may happen during our lifetime (such as the end to Hitler's violence), but it will assuredly occur at the end of the world.

III. Reassurance to Judah (Nahum 1:12, 13)

A. A People Destroyed (v. 12)

12. Thus saith the Lord; Though they be quiet, and likewise many, yet thus shall they be cut down, when he shall pass through. Though I have afflicted thee, I will afflict thee no more.

Though they be quiet literally means "though they have full strength." It refers to the fact that the Assyrians lacked nothing from a material standpoint that could give them security. Thus they felt that they had the ability to withstand

visual 4

The **Lord** is good, A stronghold in the day of trouble; and He knows those who trust in Him.

any potential enemy. The Assyrians had already nearly annihilated many peoples/nations. Her strength made her a seemingly unbeatable force.

Though they had complete strength and were many, yet they would be *cut down*. As grass falls before a scythe, so would the Assyrians fall when God moved upon them. *When he shall pass through* is better translated "and he shall pass away." The singular pronoun *he* may refer to the king of Assyria; or, by referring to the people as one man, Nahum may be emphasizing their insignificance before the mighty power of God.

The remaining part of this verse is addressed to the people of Judah. *Though I have afflicted thee, I will afflict thee no more.* The sufferings that He had permitted to come on Judah at the hands of the Assyrians would come to an end. Saying He would afflict them no more did not mean that the Jewish people would never see difficulty again; but this phrase is parallel to *the second time* in verse 9. He will not destroy Assyria the second time because the destruction will be total; the Assyrians would not afflict God's people "the second time" (*no more*), because the Assyrians would be no more.

B. A People Delivered (v. 13)

13. For now will I break his yoke from off thee, and will burst thy bonds in sunder.

These words also are addressed to Judah. God promised that He was going to *break his yoke from off thee*, that is, He was going to remove the evil mastery of the Assyrians over Judah. At one point, Hezekiah, king of Judah, had been forced to pay tribute to the king of Assyria (2 Kings 18:13, 14). Two Assyrian kings report receiving tribute from Manasseh, who succeeded his father, Hezekiah, as king of Judah. So, for many years the Assyrians had succeeded in reducing Judah to the status of a vassal nation. But as God had rescued His people from bondage in Egypt many centuries earlier, He was going to break their bonds once again in the final overthrow of Assyria.

IV. Rejoicing in Salvation
(Nahum 1:15)

15. Behold upon the mountains the feet of him that bringeth good tidings, that publisheth peace! O Judah, keep thy solemn feasts, perform thy vows: for the wicked shall no more pass through thee; he is utterly cut off.

The prophet has been speaking of the downfall of Assyria, which was yet to occur. He turns now to the reaction of Judah when word comes to them of it. The messengers come from the east and appear *upon the mountains* that encompass Jerusalem. From there they shout the *good tidings* that Assyria has been overthrown. It is a message of deliverance, of salvation, of freedom from an evil master. Peace once again will reign in the land.

While Judah suffered under the heavy hand of their oppressors, the observation of their *solemn feasts* was often interrupted. Now, with their freedom assured, they are to begin again the festivities associated with the worship of the Lord. Those who had made vows to Him during the time of distress are to see that they perform them. In safety they may do this, for the Assyrians will never again pass through the land. He has been *utterly cut off*.

The language employed here by Nahum is very like that of the prophet Isaiah when he proclaimed the coming Messiah (Isaiah 52:7; Romans 10:15). Thus, while this verse speaks of the timely release of Judah due to the destruction of Assyria, it points also to Christ's victory over Satan and our release from his mastery. That is good tidings for everyone. By the sacrifice of himself, Jesus Christ overcomes the effects of our sin, reconciles us to God, and brings peace to all who will receive Him. We no longer need fear our arch enemy, the devil.

CELEBRATING PEACE

On Saturday, Americans will fly flags, march in parades, and set off fireworks to celebrate their independence. The document signed on July 4, 1776, declared the colonies' freedom from British rule. Independence and freedom had to be hard fought for, however, and peace was not won until several years later. Even so, later wars and conflicts have disturbed the peace from time to time, though not on American soil since 1865 (with the exception of the Pearl Harbor attack in 1941, which was an invasion of American territory).

Judah was promised relief from Nineveh's invasions and harassment. That peace was a true blessing, even if only temporary. God's people could resume religious ceremonies without fear.

Though the peace didn't last forever, it was well worth celebrating while it continued.

The best national independence holidays are those that celebrate peace as well as freedom. The peace that the world gives, however, is tenuous at best. The only peace that lasts is the spiritual reconciliation and tranquility given by God through Christ and the Holy Spirit. "Peace I leave with you, my peace I give unto you" (John 14:27). Celebrate the Lord's peace!   —R. W. B.

Conclusion

A. God, Where Are You Today?

At times we still ask the question, "God, where are you?" Jesus answers this way: "Surely I will be with you always, to the very end of the age" (Matthew 28:20, *New International Version*). It has been said that 365 times in the Bible God says to His people in one situation or another, "I am with you." That is one per day.

As we have seen in this text from Nahum, God forgets neither the wicked nor the godly. In the time of His choosing, He will bring judgment on those who oppose Him, and He will save those who are His people.

B. Prayer

Our Father, we thank You, we honor You, we exalt You for being a God who gives good promises and carries them out. Thank You especially for the promise of eternal life through Your Son, Jesus. May we show our gratitude by our words and deeds. In Jesus' name, amen.

C. Thought to Remember

"The Lord is good, a stronghold in the day of trouble; he knows those who take refuge in him" (Nahum 1:7 *Revised Standard Version*).

Home Daily Bible Readings

Monday, June 22—God Judges (Nahum 1:1-5)

Tuesday, June 23—The Lord Is Good (Nahum 1:6-11)

Wednesday, June 24—The Lord Commands (Nahum 1:12-14)

Thursday, June 25—Nineveh Overthrown (Nahum 1:15—2:12)

Friday, June 26—Nineveh Ruined (Nahum 2:13—3:7)

Saturday, June 27—Nineveh Doomed (Nahum 3:8-19)

Sunday, June 28—God Is King (Psalm 66:1-12)

Learning by Doing

This page contains an alternate lesson plan emphasizing learning activities. Classes desiring such student involvement will find these suggestions helpful.

Learning Goals

After having studied selections from the prophecy of Nahum, the pupils will be able to:

1. Cite reasons why God is slow to execute condemnation, yet certain to do so when the guilty are not repentant.

2. Thank God for His patience.

3. Identify an area of repentance to make to God today.

Into the Lesson

Collect newspapers and news magazines that contain accounts of atrocities that have been committed in our society or in other places in the world. As the class members arrive, divide them into groups of three or four and have them search these news sources for these horrible events. Have them clip out what they find and make a montage on a piece of posterboard or newsprint. Allot five to seven minutes for the groups to complete their work. Then display the montages, commenting briefly about the events.

Into the Word

Make a transition into the Bible study section by pointing out that when we learn of atrocities, such as these on the montages, we wonder why God doesn't pronounce immediate judgment on the persons responsible for them. Yet God is patient, as we saw in the prophecy of Jonah. Even so, the day comes when God's patience ends, as we shall see in this lesson. Read Nahum 1:1 aloud and state that in this lesson we see another prophecy directed toward Nineveh.

Present the thoughts from the "Lesson Background" section, and tie them in with the events pictured on the montages.

Have a pupil who was chosen ahead of time read Nahum 1:2, 3, 6-9, 12, 13, 15. Emphasize Nahum 1:7, which is a key verse for this session.

Lead the class members in a discussion, using the following questions:

1. Jealousy, revenge, and wrath are usually evaluated as negative emotions. How, then, can we explain verse 2? (God's jealousy is holy and designed for our good. He cannot tolerate sin and will eventually pass judgment upon it.)

2. How does verse 3 help us to understand verse 2? (God doesn't act on a whim; He gives His people many opportunities to repent. But the time comes when His patience ends.)

3. How can we explain verse 7 in light of verses 2 and 6? How can we judge God as good when He is vengeful? (Because God *is* good, He cannot permit evil to reign forever. His goodness is directed to the wicked by allowing them time to repent. But that will not last forever. Justice will be done.)

4. What specific promises does God give His people through Nahum? (They will be free from the oppression of Nineveh, and peace will once again come to the land.)

5. What is the specific prophecy to the Ninevites? (They will be utterly cut off.)

6. What do we learn about God from this passage of Scripture? (God is great and powerful; God experiences emotion—wrath toward His enemies and compassion and concern for those who trust in Him. He longs for our worship and obedience. God is patient, but He will execute justice in His time. God is good.)

7. Why is God patient with the wicked? (He wants them to come to repentance.)

8. What truths concerning judgment and salvation can be seen in Nahum 1? (God expects us to obey Him. The salvation of His people, as well as the judgment of the wicked, will be accomplished in His time.)

Into Life

Divide the class members into groups of three or four. Give each group a copy of the situation described below and ask them to discuss it. Then let each group share their thoughts with the entire class.

Joe and Donna had three children. Their oldest son was killed in an automobile accident when he was eighteen: the driver of the other vehicle was drunk. Their third son, who just graduated from college, was shot at his work place by a crazed gunman and has been permanently paralyzed. The gunman has not been apprehended. Joe and Donna are crushed and are experiencing many questions: Why did God allow this to happen? Why doesn't God swiftly punish the guilty person? How can this section of Scripture help them?

Let the class work in the same groups to compose a prayer. Ask them to express their thanks to God for being patient with them, and also to express repentance for their sins. Close by having the groups share their responses.

Let's Talk It Over

The questions on this page are designed to encourage review of the lesson Scriptures and to promote discussion of the lesson by the class. The answers provided are only discussion starters. Let your class talk it over from there.

1. Some have suggested that the continuing existence of the Jewish race is an example of God's providence. How may this be so?

The Bible shows us some of what the Jewish people have endured in the way of destruction and persecution. Assyrian and Babylonian conquests, the extermination plotted by the Persian Haman (see the book of Esther), and the ravaging of God's people by Roman armies are all described or alluded to in the Scriptures. We do not need to know a great deal about history to be aware that the Jews have faced other occasions of destruction during the past two thousand years. The lesson writer reminds us of Hitler's diabolical efforts to exterminate them in this century. Christians may disagree on just how the Jews fit into God's plans for the present and future, but we all must be amazed at their preservation through centuries of ill treatment.

2. Why is it spiritually helpful to ponder God's jealousy toward us?

Paul told the Corinthians, "For I am jealous over you with godly jealousy: for I have espoused you to one husband, that I may present you as a chaste virgin to Christ" (2 Corinthians 11:2). This is a way of showing the importance of our being faithful to God. We who are married know how jealousy can affect us. If our mate were to give his or her attention to another person, it would trouble us not only through wounded pride, but also because our mate belongs to us in a unique way. So if we neglect God because of our devotion to material things or pleasures, we can appreciate His righteous jealousy. We belong to Him, not only because He has created us, but because He has redeemed us through Christ; therefore, we owe Him our undistracted attention, our undivided allegiance, and our undiminished affection.

3. Why is it spiritually helpful to ponder God's patience toward us?

It is difficult for us to comprehend God's infinite patience, because we tend to be very impatient beings. Parents snap at children who are slow to complete their household duties. Teachers grow weary with students who struggle to master basic facts pertaining to the subject at hand. Employers become irritable toward employees who have difficulty following instructions. When we are the persons who are the objects of someone else's impatient words and actions, we become upset, confused, and discouraged. Paul wrote of "the riches of [God's] goodness and forbearance and long-suffering" and noted that "the goodness of God leadeth thee to repentance" (Romans 2:4). Meditation upon this attribute of God strengthens our assurance that God loves us in spite of our flaws and that He guides us in eliminating those flaws.

4. What are some modern examples of human ingenuity in devising and disseminating evil?

One example is the various ways pornography is marketed. Not only are books and magazines utilized for this purpose, but movies, videos, and so-called "art exhibits" are used also. Pornographic messages available over the telephone illustrate how pervasive this poison is in our society. Another example is the way violence and bloodshed are graphically depicted in entertainment media. Producers of movies and videos have been very imaginative in devising scenes that will cater to their viewers' appetites for slaughter and destruction. One more example is the clever means by which the usage of drugs and alcohol are promoted. The lures of pleasure, relaxation, sophistication, and the like are employed to draw the undiscriminating into enslavement to these substances.

5. How can we fix more firmly in our minds the realization that God is with us?

Since the word of God is compared to seed, we can sow into our minds certain Biblical assurances of God's presence in our lives. Then they will take root and grow within us. We can accomplish this sowing by memorizing a verse such as Isaiah 41:10: "Fear thou not; for I am with thee: be not dismayed; for I am thy God: I will strengthen thee; yea, I will help thee; yea, I will uphold thee with the right hand of my righteousness." Repeating this promise when we need assurance of God's nearness can be a powerful help. Many of the hymns we sing also can help. "God Will Take Care of You," "Near to the Heart of God," "His Eye Is on the Sparrow," and "Shepherd of Love" are among such hymns.

A Question and an Answer

LESSON SCRIPTURE: Habakkuk.

PRINTED TEXT: Habakkuk 1:1-7; 2:1-4.

Habakkuk 1:1-7

1 The burden which Habakkuk the prophet did see.

2 O LORD, how long shall I cry, and thou wilt not hear! even cry out unto thee of violence, and thou wilt not save!

3 Why dost thou show me iniquity, and cause me to behold grievance? for spoiling and violence are before me: and there are that raise up strife and contention.

4 Therefore the law is slacked, and judgment doth never go forth: for the wicked doth compass about the righteous; therefore wrong judgment proceedeth.

5 Behold ye among the heathen, and regard, and wonder marvelously: for I will work a work in your days, which ye will not believe, though it be told you.

6 For, lo, I raise up the Chaldeans, that bit-

ter and hasty nation, which shall march through the breadth of the land, to possess the dwelling places that are not theirs.

7 They are terrible and dreadful: their judgment and their dignity shall proceed of themselves.

Habakkuk 2:1-4

1 I will stand upon my watch, and set me upon the tower, and will watch to see what he will say unto me, and what I shall answer when I am reproved.

2 And the LORD answered me, and said, Write the vision, and make it plain upon tables, that he may run that readeth it.

3 For the vision is yet for an appointed time, but at the end it shall speak, and not lie: though it tarry, wait for it; because it will surely come, it will not tarry.

4 Behold, his soul which is lifted up is not upright in him: but the just shall live by his faith.

GOLDEN TEXT: The just shall live by his faith.—Habakkuk 2:4.

God's Judgment and Mercy

Unit 1: Warnings and Promises From God (Lessons 1-5)

Lesson Aims

This lesson is designed to help the student:
1. Develop enlightened patience amid increasing wickedness.
2. Develop courage to speak about the wickedness and the results it will produce if it is continued.

Lesson Outline

INTRODUCTION
  A. It's Not the Same World
  B. Lesson Background
I. HABAKKUK'S QUESTION (Habakkuk 1:1-4)
  A. The Questioner (v. 1)
  B. The Apparent Slowness of God (v. 2)
    Sons-of-Thunder Syndrome
  C. The Speed-up of Wrong (v. 3)
  D. The Neglect of the Law (v. 4)
II. GOD'S FIRST ANSWER (Habakkuk 1:5-7)
  A. God Promises Action (v. 5)
  B. God Identifies His Instrument (v. 6)
    Incredible Providence
  C. God Describes His Instrument (v. 7)
III. GOD'S SECOND ANSWER (Habakkuk 2:1-4)
  A. Waiting for the Answer (v. 1)
  B. Write (v. 2)
  C. Wait (v. 3)
    Good Things for Those Who Wait
  D. Trust (v. 4)
CONCLUSION
  A. Faith and Faithfulness
  B. Prayer
  C. Thought to Remember

Refer to visual 5 of the visuals packet when discussing Habakkuk 2:4. The visual is shown on page 381.

Introduction

A. It's Not the Same World

I was born before frozen foods, plastic, credit cards, dishwashers, air conditioners, and ballpoint pens. I guess it makes me old-fashioned, but I remember when people got married first and *then* lived together. Being gay meant having a good time. Grass was something we mowed, coke was a cold drink, and pot was something we cooked in. Children could walk across town at night without fear. Going to a movie used to be a wholesome family activity. People had guns for hunting, not for self-defense. Teenage drunkenness was a rarity; today drunk driving is the number-one cause of teenage deaths. There are 148 divorces in the United States every minute. In a national survey, one out of every six female college students said she had been raped, and one out of every twelve male students had either committed rape or had tried to.

How long will this continue? How long before God pulls the plug on this "Christian" nation? That's what Habakkuk was asking about his nation. God's answer, however, dealt with how God's people should live in their world before the end came. Sometimes we get more concerned about when the world will end than about how we should live in it. Jesus never told us *when* He will return, but He did tell us what to do until then.

B. Lesson Background

Last week we read about Nahum's prophecy of destruction for Nineveh, the capital city of Assyria. Nineveh did not repent with Nahum's preaching as it had done with Jonah's, and Nineveh was destroyed.

Habakkuk probably was written a little before or after the destruction of Nineveh, but before uninspired people saw the Babylonians as a threat to Judah. God had given His people plenty of time to repent, but they refused. Now God was assuring Habakkuk that He would use the Babylonians as an instrument of punishment for the rising wickedness of Judah.

I. Habakkuk's Question (Habakkuk 1:1-4)

A. The Questioner (v. 1)

1. The burden which Habakkuk the prophet did see.

Burden is a name given to a prophetic utterance. Often such a burden is heavy with predictions of punishment, as this one is.

A *prophet* is a person inspired by God, either to predict the future or to give instruction for the present. *Did see* means Habakkuk received this message from God, whether in a vision that was literally seen or in some other way.

B. The Apparent Slowness of God (v. 2)

2. O Lord, how long shall I cry, and thou wilt not hear! even cry out unto thee of violence, and thou wilt not save!

When things seem to be going downhill, haven't we often asked, *How long?* We are impatient, aren't we? Impatience is seen in Psalm 10:1: "Why, O Lord, do you stand far off? Why do you hide yourself in times of trouble" (*New International Version*). Habakkuk felt like that. Evidently he had been calling to God for help for some time—*How long shall I cry.* To him it seemed that God was slow in responding—*and thou wilt not hear.* Habakkuk wanted God to rescue the people from the violence among them. The word *violence* sometimes means physical violence that hurts or kills, but sometimes it means wild, reckless wrongdoing such as is described in several places in this book—the law was paralyzed and justice was perverted (1:4); people were treacherous (1:13), full of pride, and greedy (2:5); they had drunken orgies and worshiped idols (2:15-19). Habakkuk was concerned because it seemed that God was doing nothing to stop such violence.

Today, people express that concern like this: "If God is all good, He must not be all powerful or He would stop the evil." Or "If God is all powerful, He must not be all good or He would stop the evil." However, God is all good and all powerful. He does things in the "fullness of time," not in the "fastness of temper."

SONS-OF-THUNDER SYNDROME

The nightly news tells us more than we want to know about murders, rapes, child abuse, and other violent crimes. Terrorist activity in the Middle East, uprisings in South Africa, religious war in Ireland, and violent political demonstrations in the Philippines are recurring topics. Why doesn't God just cinderize the whole planet and forget it?

Why does God tolerate man's inhumanity to man? Since He drowned Noah's civilization and consumed Sodom with fire, why isn't He bringing swift retribution on today's sinners?

These are the same frustrations that Habakkuk was feeling when he cried out, "How long, Lord? How long?" This impatience for justice could be called the "Sons-of-Thunder syndrome." Remember how James and John reacted to the

---

How to Say It

ASSYRIA. Uh-*sear*-re-uh.
BABYLONIANS. Bab-uh-*low*-nee-unz.
CHALDEANS. Hal-*dee*-unz.
HABAKKUK. Huh-*bak*-kuk.
JONAH. *Jo*-nuh.
JUDAH. *Joo*-duh.
NAHUM. *Nay*-hum.
NINEVEH. *Nin*-uh-vuh.

Samaritans who declined to receive Christ? "Lord, wilt thou that we command fire to come down from heaven, and consume them?" (Luke 9:54). Jesus condemned His disciples' vengeful spirit, and they "went to another village" (v. 56).

Isn't it fortunate that *we* aren't in control of the universe? We trigger-happy vigilantes soon would decimate God's creation. Eye-for-an-eye vengeance has been superseded by Christ's turn-the-other-cheek-and-pray-for-your-enemies precepts of grace. "For the Son of man is not come to destroy men's lives, but to save them" (Luke 9:56).
—R. W. B.

C. The Speed-up of Wrong (v. 3)

3. Why dost thou show me iniquity, and cause me to behold grievance? for spoiling and violence are before me: and there are that raise up strife and contention.

Habakkuk was tired of seeing so much iniquity—*Why dost thou show me iniquity*—with the resulting grief that surrounded him–*and cause me to behold grievance.* Can't we relate to that with all the violence, rapes, drug-related crimes, homosexuality, abortions, vile language, nudity in films, and other abominations that continue to bombard us? Aren't there times we wish we could just get away from it all?

Such iniquity brings *spoiling.* It spoils our relationships to God, to ourselves, to others. It damages our hopes, our dreams, our happiness, our peace. It brings *strife and contention* within families, between friends, and even among members of the same church.

Wouldn't it be nice if we didn't have to see iniquity around us? But we do. We see it unfolding before our eyes, and then we see it reported in the papers and on television. Seeing the acts is not all; we also see the results—broken homes, depression, child abuse, spouse abuse, and other evils.

D. The Neglect of the Law (v. 4)

4. Therefore the law is slacked, and judgment doth never go forth: for the wicked doth compass about the righteous; therefore wrong judgment proceedeth.

God's law, God's way, God's wishes, God's character—all were being ignored. The psalmist says he hides God's word in his heart so he may not sin against God (Psalm 119:11). But if we ignore God's Word, we lose one of the primary governors to keep us from iniquity. Before we point our fingers at all the wrong around us, perhaps we should ask, "How much do *I* read God's Word and apply it in *my* life?" God's Word is one means of equipping us "for every good work" (2 Timothy 3:16, 17).

God's people in that day belittled the significance of God's Word for their modern age. We do the same thing today. We may not admit it, but we show it by how we 1) don't read it, 2) don't study it, 3) don't challenge our traditions by it, 4) don't challenge our priorities by it, 5) don't change in accordance with it.

The influence of God's Word has been shrinking slowly but surely. Shrinkage begins when people think man is self sufficient, life on earth is wholly controlled by natural laws, and miracles have natural explanations. Then people begin to think the Bible is not directly inspired by God, but is merely the thoughts of men. Then it is supposed that the Bible contains errors. If it has errors in one place, how can we trust what it says in another? In this gradual way, the Bible becomes ignored and its effect is lost.

When that happens, justice in the community, in the nation, and even in the church is buried—*judgment doth never go forth.* The wicked are rewarded, and the righteous are belittled—*the wicked doth compass about the righteous.* When God's law is not taken seriously, right judgments are not made *therefore wrong judgment proceedeth.*

Doesn't that sound like our world today? God's people must take some of the responsibility for that, for we are called to be salt, light, and leaven. When we weaken the teaching and application of God's Word, we dim the light, we box up the salt, and we don't allow the leaven to get into the dough.

But how can we spend more time with God's Word when our schedules are so crowded? Here are some suggestions:

1. Listen to the Bible on cassette tape while driving in the car.

2. Listen to the Bible on cassette while walking, jogging, or doing other exercising.

3. Turn the television off half an hour or an hour earlier at night.

4. Get up half an hour earlier and/or stay up half an hour later.

Just one hour a day would give us seven hours a week. That's almost one work day. That's nearly fifty-two work days a year. We can have plenty of time to study the Word if we want to.

II. God's First Answer (Habakkuk 1:5-7)

A. God Promises Action (v. 5)

5. Behold ye among the heathen, and regard, and wonder marvelously: for I will work a work in your days, which ye will not believe, though it be told you.

Someone has said that love is blind, while marriage is the eye-opener. That is not true.

Love is not blind but kind. God, the world's lover, was not blind to the iniquity of Judah; but He was kind. We read elsewhere that God's kindness is meant to lead us to repentance (Romans 2:4, *New International Version*). God did not react with a temper tantrum, because God wanted Judah to repent.

Aren't we that way with our children? Do we punish them instantly? Or does that come after some counsel, some talk about expectations, some warnings?

When God said, *I will work a work in your days,* He was referring to the punishment of Judah. He gave a clue about it when He said, *Behold ye among the heathen* which means "Look at some of the pagans." God was going to use pagans to punish Judah. Telling Judah to look at them was like saying to a child, "Look at that paddle. If you don't change, I'm going to apply it." God was saying, "Unless you repent, the pagan nations will bring you down."

That would be hard for those people to accept—*which ye will not believe*—even though it would be foretold in Habakkuk—*though it be told you.* Aren't we like that? Isn't it hard to believe that God would allow our country to go down the tubes as a nation? We think we will be world leaders forever, don't we? Regardless of how immoral we may become? That's the thinking of irresponsible arrogance.

B. God Identifies His Instrument (v. 6)

6. For, lo, I raise up the Chaldeans, that bitter and hasty nation, which shall march through the breadth of the land, to possess the dwelling places that are not theirs.

The Chaldeans were the Babylonians, a terribly ungodly action. *Bitter and hasty* means they were fierce and hotheaded. God said, *I raise up.* The Chaldean victory would not be just the result of more military power. It would result from God's decision to use this nation. God was going to intervene in the affairs of man. Here He was foretelling the Babylonian captivity that would devastate Jerusalem and Palestine. The Babylonians would take the land and possess places that belonged to God's people—*possess the dwelling places that are not theirs.*

That happened, but it did not have to happen. When God says He will destroy a nation, that means He will destroy it if that nation will not repent as a result of His warnings (Jeremiah 18:7, 8). But the prideful and the arrogant would not repent.

Do we believe that God may bring our nation to become a no-nation, as twenty-two significant civilizations have done? If we don't believe it, we won't repent either.

Why would God change His sentence of destruction? He tells us why in Ezekiel 18:32: "For I take no pleasure in the death of anyone, declares the Sovereign Lord. Repent and live!" (*New International Version*).

INCREDIBLE PROVIDENCE

That's Incredible, a short-lived television series, seemed popular while it lasted. Maybe it just ran out of unbelievable phenomena. The public is generally fascinated with truth that is stranger than fiction. We are awed by whatever we cannot understand.

God promised His prophet an incredible demonstration of divine wisdom and power, an unbelievable event that would bring judgment and restore justice. Habakkuk would see it and he would be "utterly amazed" (*New International Version*).

God produces, on a daily basis, "special effects" of His providence that are astounding. If we are *underwhelmed* by His daily doings, it is simply because we take them for granted. The natural phenomena alone—the change of seasons, plant growth, animal instincts, gravity, rainbows, and sunsets—should prompt awe and wonder and praise from us. Add to those His activity in human affairs, His intervention in history for the cause of righteousness, His healing of broken bodies and broken relationships, His guidance for our decision making—it's just incredible!　　　　　　　　　　—R. W. B.

C. God Describes His Instrument (v. 7)

7. They are terrible and dreadful: their judgment and their dignity shall proceed of themselves.

The Babylonians were *terrible and dreadful.* God did not use them because they were better than Judah. *Their judgment and dignity* or exaltation were self-centered—*proceed of themselves.*

They believed in themselves, not in God. They thought they were above God and a law unto themselves.

It's tough to be brought down, but it hurts worse when you are brought down by somebody worse than you, more perverted than you. That's what God did to the people of Judah by using the Babylonians.

But good came out of this. In the Babylonian captivity, many of God's people repented and returned to God's way. God did not intend the Babylonian captivity to destroy Judah totally, but rather to preserve her—to bring her to her knees, to bring her to her senses, to bring her back to himself.

The Lord wants us all to see beyond the negative past and present, to see the new thing God

visual 5

can do. He can make a way in the desert times of our lives (Isaiah 43:18, 19). Even though we have all fallen, God can turn our scars into stars. Although we may be marred in His hands, He can reshape us as it seems fit to Him (see Jeremiah 18:1-6).

III. God's Second Answer (Habakkuk 2:1-4)

A. Waiting for the Answer (v. 1)

1. I will stand upon my watch, and set me upon the tower, and will watch to see what he will say unto me, and what I shall answer when I am reproved.

This is the last verse of Habakkuk's second question, which began in chapter 1 verse 12. The prophet was surprised that God would use someone more wicked than Judah to teach Judah a lesson. However, he finished the question by saying he would not be discouraged to the point of quitting, but would watch and wait for God's answer. *I will stand*— I will not be impetuous. *Upon my watch*—I will not be irresponsible. Habakkuk would not give in or give up. He would not take things into his own hands, but position himself to receive God's answer and pass it on.

B. Write (v. 2)

2. And the Lord answered me, and said, Write the vision, and make it plain upon tables, that he may run that readeth it.

Before God answered Habakkuk's question about using someone more wicked to destroy Judah, He told Habakkuk to *write the vision,* which means God's revelation. What Habakkuk wrote was exactly what God gave him to write. He was not to write it in such intellectual terms that the common person couldn't understand it. He was to *make it plain.* He was to give it so that any person who read it could *run* with it and could share it.

Today we too should speak God's truth in an understandable way. Jesus was a master in using plain words and illustrations that caused children to want to sit on His lap.

C. Wait (v. 3)

3. For the vision is yet for an appointed time, but at the end it shall speak, and not lie: though it tarry, wait for it; because it will surely come, it will not tarry.

The vision was for a later time—*an appointed time*—but its fulfillment was certain—*it shall speak, and not lie*. What God predicts, will happen. The bumper sticker says it well: "If God said it, that settles it, I believe it." To that we should add, "I will obey it and share it."

But we need not take the timing in our own hands. Some like not only to proclaim that the end of the world is coming with destruction for the wicked, but also to give the date for it. God's people must learn that God is not controlled by our calendars. We must wait for His time. Ever notice how hard it is for children to wait? Waiting is a grown-up activity.

GOOD THINGS FOR THOSE WHO WAIT

Someone has estimated that an average American uses six years of his life waiting for traffic lights to change; another five years is spent waiting in lines of one kind or another. Those statistics are significant only because most of us hate waiting so much. In this age of instant pudding and microwave meals, waiting is clearly not a favorite activity. Indeed it is the very *inactivity* of waiting that bores and frustrates us. It seems a total waste of time. Habakkuk became impatient waiting for justice. He was anxious for his prayers to be answered. God told him to wait—to wait believing that relief from violence and oppression would come.

Faith is essential for those who wait. We believe the traffic lights will eventually change, or waiting would be intolerable. We observe lines moving, or we would quit the queue and go home. We must believe that the wait will ultimately end, or we will not wait at all.

Patient waiting is a specialty of God's people. Because we live by faith, we can bide our time until Christ returns. "The day of the Lord will come. . . . Look forward to the day of God and speed its coming" (2 Peter 3:10-12, *New International Version*).
—R. W. B.

D. Trust (v. 4)

4. Behold, his soul which is lifted up is not upright in him: but the just shall live by his faith.

Anyone who is *lifted up* with arrogant pride is not likely to be *upright*. He is as crooked as he needs to be to get what he wants. This was true of the arrogant men of Judah who would not obey God, but verse 5 indicates that it here applies to the arrogant Babylonian who would be trying to gather all nations into their empire. They would destroy many of the proud in Judah, but the righteous one would *live by his faith*, because of his steadfast, unfailing trust in the Lord. That is how we Christians shall live when all the evil of the world is destroyed. We are just, not because we are faultless, but because we are forgiven and we trust in the Savior.

Faith sets us before God in dependence on His grace. Faith keeps us from the arrogance of trying to do everything on our own. Faith confesses we are not self-sufficient. Faith affirms that God has power beyond our abilities, and wisdom beyond our IQ.

Faith motivates us to keep proclaiming, waiting, watching, and growing even though the waiting seems to be long. We do not live up to His acceptance. We live by faith: we are sure of what we hope for, certain of what we do not yet see (Hebrews 11:1).

Conclusion

A. Faith and Faithfulness

Faith is not a passive word—just believe and sit. Faith is an active word. A boy with faith that his father will catch him will jump out of the tree into his father's arms. Our faith in God enables us to live God's way in man's world.

B. Prayer

Thank You, Father, for trusting us with Your Word and with Your plan for planet earth. Help us to recognize our unbelief and to change it to belief. Amen.

C. Thought to Remember

God's people shall live by faith.

Home Daily Bible Readings

Monday, June 29—Habakkuk Complains (Habakkuk 1:1-4)

Tuesday, June 30—The Lord Answers (Habakkuk 1:5-11)

Wednesday, July 1—Lord, How Long? (Habakkuk 1:12-17)

Thursday, July 2—Habakkuk Watches (Habakkuk 2:1-5)

Friday, July 3—The Woes (Habakkuk 2:6-20)

Saturday, July 4—Habakkuk Prays (Habakkuk 3)

Sunday, July 5—God Saves (Psalm 25:1-10)

Learning by Doing

This page contains an alternate lesson plan emphasizing learning activities. Classes desiring such student involvement will find these suggestions helpful.

Learning Goals

After studying Habakkuk's prophecy, the students will be able to:

1. Relate the events that led the prophet Habakkuk to ask God how long he must wait for help.

2. Tell what answer God gave to Habakkuk.

3. Explain how God's answer aids the believer to live in the midst of evil.

4. Thank God that He is in control of the world.

Into the Lesson

Before the pupils arrive in the classroom, write the following sentence on the chalkboard, a sheet of news-print, or an overhead transparency: "When I see the evil, suffering, and unrepentance in the world, I sometimes think . . ." As the pupils arrive, ask each one to work with two others to write several endings for the sentence. You may want to ask three or four people to share their responses before you proceed with the lesson.

Make the transition into the Bible study by stating that people of all ages have at times wondered if God is aware of the evil in the world. We will see that concern in the question of Habakkuk today.

Into the Word

Briefly present the "Lesson Background" material on page 378 to provide the setting for this prophecy.

Read the Scripture text, Habakkuk 1:1-7; 2:1-4. Do this by assigning one person to read 1:1, another to read Habakkuk's words in 1:2-4 and 2:1, and a third to read the words of the Lord in 1:5-7 and 2:2-4.

Divide the class into groups of four or five. Ask half of the groups to identify Habakkuk's chief concerns as stated in the text. The other half of the groups are to identify exactly what God will do. Allot five to seven minutes for this. Then let the groups report their findings. Add any information missed by the groups.

Then use the following questions to develop a brief discussion:

1. Why do you think Habakkuk, a prophet of God, asked the questions he did? (Be sure someone points out that though Habakkuk was a prophet of God, he did live in a world much like ours—and that world prompted the same kinds of questions we ask.)

2. Why would God wait so long to punish? (Be sure God's patience and mercy are mentioned.)

3. What principle did God give for those who await His action? (The just shall live by faith.)

Into Life

Continue the discussion by using the following questions:

1. How are we today like Habakkuk? (Explore our feelings that God doesn't know or care about our plight.)

2. What message do you think God would give us today?

Have class members work together again in the same groups formed during the Bible study. Have half of the groups write a modern paraphrase of Habakkuk's thoughts recorded in 1:2-4 and 2:1. The other half should write a paraphrase of God's thoughts recorded in 1:5-7 and 2:2-4. Allot six to eight minutes for this. Then let the groups share their paraphrases. What hope is seen for us in today's world?

Then ask the groups to think about the paraphrases and deal with the following problem: In May of 1988, a bus loaded with teenagers from a church were returning to their Kentucky home when their vehicle was struck by a drunken driver going the wrong way on the interstate highway. Many were killed; others injured severely. The driver was tried in December of 1989 and given less than twenty years imprisonment, even though he was found guilty on eighty or so counts, including the death of over twenty. What does Habakkuk's prophecy have to say to the survivors of the crash? Their families? The guilty driver? The family of the driver? Allow the groups four to six minutes to formulate a response. Then lead a brief discussion to show how the principles of the passage hold out hope for people today.

Conclude the session by asking each person to write down a way that he has received hope from this section of Scripture. Ask several individuals to share their responses. Then ask each group to spend the final minutes of the class session sharing responses and praying for God's strength to live by faith throughout the coming week.

Let's Talk It Over

The questions on this page are designed to encourage review of the lesson Scriptures and to promote discussion of the lesson by the class. The answers provided are only discussion starters. Let your class talk it over from there.

1. What are some sins in our society with which God seems to be slow in dealing?

When we read of the staggering numbers of abortions performed each year, we may be inclined to cry out, "How long, O Lord, will You allow this slaughter to continue?"Homosexuality is another sin widely practiced and increasingly defended in the media. Romans 1:26, 27 is one passage that shows how abominable that practice is in God's eyes. The Bible also testifies to God's hatred of occult practices, which have become popular in our society. If people persist in sins such as these, we can be certain that the time will come when God will deal decisively with them.

2. What are some signs in our society of an erosion of confidence in the Bible?

Biblical illiteracy is one sign. When people are remarkably knowledgeable concerning science, health, and entertainment, it is tragic to see how many are ignorant of the basic truths of the Scriptures. Another sign is the silence of some pulpits about "Thus saith the Lord," while they feature extensive quotes from poets, philosophers, theologians, and social commentators. The present-day debate over Biblical inerrancy is one more sign. If human beings have become so self-assured as to pass judgment on what is acceptable or unacceptable in the Bible, we have reached a stage in which we are in danger of losing a solid foundation for our faith.

3. How would it affect our lives if we were to spend more time reading and studying the Bible? How can we make more time for the Bible?

The more time we spend with the Bible, the stronger will be our faith (Romans 10:17), the more we will experience the power of God (Hebrews 4:12), and the better equipped we will be to overcome the devil (Ephesians 6:17; 1 John 2:14). The Word of God is often compared with food. Following through on this figure we can say that many Christians are probably malnourished. A more consistent diet of the Scriptures will make them healthier, stronger, and more productive in the Lord's work. This concept of Scripture as food also suggests one approach to a regular study of the Bible. Either during our meals or immediately before or after them would be some handy times for feeding our souls. Only twenty minutes per meal could give us an hour's worth of reading in a day.

4. It is terrible to contemplate the possibility of our nation collapsing. Why should we think of such a possibility?

The most disturbing reason is that the possibility is very real. Our materialism, our preoccupation with various forms of immorality, and our spiritual shallowness all show that we are vulnerable to collapse. What can we do about it? If our own personal habits and practices have contributed to our nation's weakness, we can change these. Also, we can pray earnestly for political leaders, religious leaders, and others whose influence can affect our nation for good or ill. Finally, we can use our influence in private conversation, in correspondence, in our business, and in our church to effect godly changes.

5. "Write the vision, and make it plain upon tables, that he may run that readeth it." How can we put this counsel into practice today?

The use of tracts and leaflets comes to mind here. Whether we produce our own literature of this kind or use the works of commercial publishers, we want these to be impressive enough to catch the attention of the reader and plain enough to enable him to understand. If a plain and readily understandable presentation of divine truth was necessary in Habakkuk's time, it is even more so today. Consider how we must compete with radio and television and a seemingly endless variety of literature in order to catch and hold people's attention today.

6. How does the Old Testament help in building our faith?

Hebrews 11 tells of some Old Testament people of faith. Abraham's consistent faith in God's promises, Joseph's determination to remain faithful in spite of a succession of setbacks, and Moses' unshaken faith amid the disbelief that characterized his people—all these are instructive for us. The Bible functions somewhat as a mirror (James 1:22-25), and in the experiences of Old Testament believers we may see reflected the strengths and weaknesses of our own faith.

Threatened Destruction of Humankind

LESSON SCRIPTURE: Zephaniah 1, 2.

PRINTED TEXT: Zephaniah 1:1-3, 7, 12; 2:1-3.

Zephaniah 1:1-3, 7, 12

1 The word of the LORD which came unto Zephaniah the son of Cushi, the son of Gedaliah, the son of Amariah, the son of Hizkiah, in the days of Josiah the son of Amon, king of Judah.

2 I will utterly consume all things from off the land, saith the LORD.

3 I will consume man and beast; I will consume the fowls of the heaven, and the fishes of the sea, and the stumblingblocks with the wicked; and I will cut off man from off the land, saith the LORD.

. . . .

7 Hold thy peace at the presence of the Lord GOD: for the day of the LORD is at hand:

for the LORD hath prepared a sacrifice, he hath bid his guests.

. . . .

12 And it shall come to pass at that time, that I will search Jerusalem with candles, and punish the men that are settled on their lees: that say in their heart, The LORD will not do good, neither will he do evil.

Zephaniah 2:1-3

1 Gather yourselves together, yea, gather together, O nation not desired;

2 Before the decree bring forth, before the day pass as the chaff, before the fierce anger of the LORD come upon you, before the day of the LORD's anger come upon you.

3 Seek ye the LORD, all ye meek of the earth, which have wrought his judgment; seek righteousness, seek meekness: it may be ye shall be hid in the day of the LORD's anger.

GOLDEN TEXT: Seek ye the LORD, all ye meek of the earth, which have wrought his judgment; seek righteousness, seek meekness.—Zephaniah 2:3.

God's Judgment and Mercy

Unit 2: A Remnant Is Saved
(Lessons 6, 7)

Lesson Aims

This lesson is designed to help the student to be able to:

1. Reaffirm the reality of hell—man's ultimate punishment.

2. Affirm the opportunity for repentance, and repent when necessary.

Lesson Outline

INTRODUCTION
  A. Whatever Happened to Hell?
  B. Lesson Background
  I. WARNING OF JUDGMENT (Zephaniah 1:1-3)
    A. The Messenger (v. 1)
    B. Devastating Judgment (v. 2)
      Noah II?
    C. Comprehensive Judgment (v. 3)
 II. RESULTS OF JUDGMENT (Zephaniah 1:7, 12)
    A. It Will Sacrifice Some People (v. 7)
    B. It Will Expose the Wicked (v. 12)
III. CALL TO REVIVAL (Zephaniah 2:1-3)
    A. For Whom (v. 1)
    B. When (v. 2)
    C. How (v. 3)
      Escaping Judgment
CONCLUSION
    A. Preaching Makes a Difference
    B. Prayer
    C. Thought to Remember

Visual 6 of the visual packet illustrates an important truth in the comments under verse 7. The visual is shown on page 389.

Introduction

A. Whatever Happened to Hell?

Whatever happened to the fear of Hell? It doesn't seem to be around much these days. In fact, some say we are planting paranoia in people's minds by talking about Hell. But Jesus, who is our model of compassion—so considerate that He would not snuff out a smoldering wick (Matthew 12:20)—said with clarity, "Do not be afraid of those who kill the body but cannot kill the soul. Rather, be afraid of the one who can destroy both soul and body in hell" (Matthew 10:28, *New International Version*).

To pretend there is no Hell or to neglect it in our teaching is as unkind as telling toddlers that fire will not burn. It is as unkind as stripping the poison warnings from bottles or removing the warning signs on a curving mountain road.

It seems likely that the deterioration of values, priorities, lifestyles, and morals in this country can be traced partially to a low view of the deity of Jesus, a low view concerning the integrity of the Bible, a low view concerning the continuing power of God, and a low view concerning the realities of life after death—Heaven and Hell.

There are two destinations for us after we die—where the devil is or where the Father is. One is called life, eternal life, Heaven; the other is called the second death, Hell, separation from God and God's people forever.

We will exist forever somewhere. That's why Jesus came, lived, died, and rose again. That's why He's coming back. He's coming back to accompany His disciples to Heaven.

B. Lesson Background

Zephaniah may have been born during one of the darkest periods in the history of God's people. King Manasseh was so ruthless that he shed innocent blood until it filled Jerusalem from one end to another (2 Kings 21:16). But Zephaniah was inspired with God's message during the reign of Manasseh's grandson, Josiah. It stressed two truths: 1) God would bring discipline upon unrepentant people; 2) there was still time to repent, to have a revival, to reform. This message may have helped King Josiah restore true worship and obedience to God (2 Chronicles 34, 35).

I. Warning of Judgment (Zephaniah 1:1-3)

A. The Messenger (v. 1)

1. The word of the Lord which came unto Zephaniah the son of Cushi, the son of Gedaliah, the son of Amariah, the son of Hizkiah, in the days of Josiah the son of Amon, king of Judah.

Hizkiah may be an abbreviated form of *Hezekiah,* king of Judah (2 Kings 18—20). If it is, *Zephaniah* was of the royal family. To him came *the word of the Lord.* This affirms the nature of Scripture as seen in 2 Peter 1:21, "For prophecy never had its origin in the will of man, but men spoke from God as they were carried along by the Holy Spirit" (*New International Version*).

Because the Bible is inspired by the Holy Spirit and the Holy Spirit is the Spirit of truth, original manuscripts of the Bible were without error or flaw. Such Scriptures are profitable or useful for teaching, rebuking, correcting, and training in righteousness, so that any of God's people may be completely equipped for every good work (2 Timothy 3:16, 17).

While we do not have the original manuscripts, the messages of those manuscripts are our present copies and versions. If we would not only read but heed what the apostles and prophets wrote, our lives would be built on a foundation that cannot be shaken (Ephesians 2:20). To build elsewhere is to build on the sand that is not firm in the storms and the floods.

Josiah was one of the best kings Judah had. He started to reign when he was eight years old, but when he was twenty years old he began a significant religious reform that was probably helped by Zephaniah's preaching (2 Chronicles 34, 35). Never belittle the power of preaching. For us it is the bridge that connects what God said long ago to what we are facing today.

B. Devastating Judgment (v. 2)

2. I will utterly consume all things from off the land, saith the Lord.

I will utterly consume all things does not mean every single person, every sheep, every tree must be destroyed. But the nation of Judah would totally cease to exist for a time. Most of the people would be driven to Babylon, and the rest would take refuge in Egypt (2 Kings 25). The good people in Judah would suffer along with the bad, for the wrong some people do has an effect on others.

We are living in a time when people want their "private rights" to do whatever they feel like doing. But the results of wrong are never private. It's like shaking a spider web on one end—the whole web feels the vibrations. Wrong living is never totally private, nor is it painless. Pain, sorrow, disappointment, depression, and devastation are the harvest of our wrongs, and they exceed the excitement and pleasure of sowing those wrongs.

There is a sense in which all of us will someday be taken *off the land*. When Christ comes, His people who have died will be raised and His people who are living will be lifted with them and transported *off the land* into Heaven (1 Thessalonians 4:16, 17). The rest of the people will be taken *off the land* as captives of the devil. Unlike the captivity in Babylon, that captivity will never end (Matthew 25:41).

NOAH II?

What would Hollywood do without sequels? As soon as a movie becomes a big box-office success, producers want another like it. *Psycho* spawned *Psycho II* and *Psycho III*. James Bond, Indiana Jones, and Rocky were all serialized.

How to Say It

AMARIAH.   *Am*-uh-*rye*-uh. (Stronger accent on *rye*).
AMON.   A-mun.
CUSHI.   *Koo*-shy.
GEDALIAH.   *Ged*-uh-*lye*-uh.
HIZKIAH.   Hiz-*kye*-uh.
JOSIAH.   Jo-*sye*-uh.
ZEPHANIAH.   Zef-uh-*nye*-uh.

Does history repeat itself as often as Hollywood? Zephaniah must have thought he was about to witness a sequel to the great flood. The wrath and words of God revealed in today's text are very similar to those of Noah's time: "And the Lord said, I will destroy man whom I have created from the face of the earth" (Genesis 6:7). God promised that He would never again destroy civilization by water, but He can use fire or other means. He might simply withdraw from human affairs long enough to let mankind self-destruct.

This generation is concerned about the possibility of a nuclear holocaust. It is a relief to know that the major powers have agreed to reduce their atomic arsenals. That seems to lessen the threat of annihilation. But God's wrath over wrongdoing still remains. The Scriptures warn of a final destruction, with "great noise" and "fervent heat" (2 Peter 3:10). Only the righteous will survive, even as "Noah found grace in the eyes of the Lord" (Genesis 6:8). The logical question, then, is in Peter's words: "What manner of persons ought ye to be?" (2 Peter 3:11).—R. W. B.

C. Comprehensive Judgment (v. 3)

3. I will consume man and beast; I will consume the fowls of the heaven, and the fishes of the sea, and the stumblingblocks with the wicked; and I will cut off man from off the land, saith the Lord.

The coming disaster would affect not only people, but also the animals, birds, and fish. That should not surprise us, for in our time we are learning that whatever man does affects his whole environment. When man first sinned in the Garden of Eden, all creation was affected. It had been working in harmony, but now came disharmonious relationships that are evident in thorns and thistles (Genesis 3:17-19). All creation still is suffering, waiting to be set free when the redemption of man is complete (Romans 8:19-23).

One obvious evidence of man's effect on the environment is seen in a devastating war. It hurts not only man, but everything in the environment. Anyone who has been in a war zone has seen it.

Sin never hurts one person only. It is like a double-barreled scattergun, not a well-aimed rifle. Our righteousness has comprehensive effects and so does our unrighteousness.

II. Results of Judgment (Zephaniah 1:7, 12)

A. It Will Sacrifice Some People (v. 7)

7. Hold thy peace at the presence of the Lord God: for the day of the Lord is at hand: for the Lord hath prepared a sacrifice, he hath bid his guests.

Put in English letters, the Hebrew word for *hold thy peace* is *hass*. Equivalent to the English *hush*, it means to be quiet, not to protest or argue or struggle against God. Some versions translate it, *Be silent.* Elsewhere God says "Be still and know that I am God" (Psalm 46:10)! Instead of trying to fight our way out or brag about who we are and what we have done, we are to be humble and silent in the presence of God. We ought to submit in humility because God will not be deceived or mocked or overpowered.

We are to decrease while allowing God to increase His influence in our lives. We are not to allow the self to be the center of our life and our universe. The ego, the individual human spirit we have, may be at war with God. The ego lives to get all it can for itself, while God lives to give all He can to others.

One way to understand ego is this: E - Easing, G - God, O - Out. When the ego is more dominant than God, we try to ease God out while we manipulate and control others and circumstances. The person who wants to control everything selfishly is a competitor against God, not a co-worker with God. Man's ego can express itself better by Elevating God Over self.

We need to hold our peace so that we can be at peace. We are at peace when we live with the confidence that God is still on the throne, that He knows what is best, that He is in control, and that we don't have to take the responsibility for Him. To hold our peace means that we submit to God. We must face His judgment if we do not so submit.

The day of the Lord is the day of His triumph and the defeat of His enemies. On that day men will admit that they have been wrong, will bow their knees and confess that He is indeed Lord, and will realize that they should have listened, learned, and lived in His way. This phrase, *the day of the Lord* can refer to the final Judgment Day, or it can refer to a time when God punished

some people by an event of history. Here it refers to the time when God would bring the Babylonians to punish Judah. For that day God had *prepared a sacrifice*—many of God's people would die during that siege and captivity. *His guests* were the Babylonians who participated in sacrificing God's people.

A *sacrifice* is costly, but it has benefits too. Some of God's people were sacrificed in the Babylonian attack and captivity, but that sacrifice caused God's people to come to their senses and return to Him. It was a sacrifice for salvation. It was like a sacrifice fly in a ballgame. The batter will sacrifice and make an out with a fly ball to advance a runner so he can get closer to home. The sacrifice God prepared was to stop the downward rush of God's people into total wickedness, to change their direction, to move them toward home.

We make a *sacrifice* when we cut out cancerous parts of a body to save the whole body. Men who went to battle in the World Wars, Korean War, and the Vietnam War were willing to sacrifice their lives to save the lives of their families and friends, and the freedom of their country. Jesus is the supreme example of the sacrifice of one to save many. To sacrifice some to save many is not an act of cruelty, but an act of love—and no one knows more about love than God.

When the people repented in the Babylonian captivity, God set them free. He would not have sent them into captivity if they had repented before. "If at any time I announce that a nation or kingdom is to be uprooted, torn down and destroyed, and if that nation I warned repents of its evil, then I will relent and not inflict on it the disaster I had planned" (Jeremiah 18:8, *New International Version*).

B. It Will Expose the Wicked (v. 12)

12. And it shall come to pass at that time, that I will search Jerusalem with candles, and punish the men that are settled on their lees: that say in their heart, the Lord will not do good, neither will he do evil.

At that time refers to the Babylonian attack on Jerusalem. God then *will search Jerusalem with candles*, search it so thoroughly that no person, regardless of his position or prestige, will be able to hide. All camouflaged wickedness will be exposed. We must learn that nothing today is hidden from God. Candles or lamps exposed dark corners in that day; today we might use the word "floodlights."

Whom God exposes in wickedness, He can and will punish if there is no repentance. Here He promised punishment to *men that are settled* on their lees. There are two truths here: 1) the people were living it up, 2) they thought God was asleep and would do nothing about it. The lees were the sediment deposited from the wine or liquor. To settle on one's lees meant to become self-satisfied with partying and drunkenness. Instead of worshiping God, they worshiped their entertainment; and they thought God's patience was merely unconcern—the Lord will not do good, neither will he do evil. What a misunderstanding of God. It is not just a misunderstanding of God; it is a misplacing of God—placing self in the center.

How is our understanding of God today? They felt secure because they continued to prosper in their wickedness. As our nation continues to grow richer and more wicked, is it possible that we believe we are such privileged people that God will wink at our wickedness and not eventually bring us to destruction as He has many other civilizations?

We must never forget that God is not mocked; He will allow us by our own free choice to go only so far into evil before He pulls the plug and brings us to devastation like that of many others—unless we repent. It is possible that this nation is presently at the crossroads. Should we not take more seriously the God who created us? Should we not put ourselves under His lordship? God surely does not take lightly the continual rise in homosexuality, abortions, divorces, use of drugs, pornography, child abuse, and other evils. At some point He will simply say, "I have had enough."

Instead of loving God with their whole hearts, the people of Judah ignored Him in their heart. Jesus said evil thoughts and deeds come out of the heart (Mark 7:21, 22). If a holy and active God is not in our hearts, then an unholy and active devil is. That was what was happening in the hearts of God's people in Judah. They should have learned from the flood, from Israel's disobedience at Mount Sinai, from God's people who balked at the border of the promised land, and from other times of disobedience and punishment. And shouldn't we learn as well? For the history of what happened was written "for our

admonition," to keep us from following their bad example (1 Corinthians 10:1-12).

The people said The Lord will not do good, neither will he do evil. To think God will do nothing, is to totally misunderstand the Lord God Almighty, Creator of this world.

III. Call to Revival (Zephaniah 2:1-3)

A. For Whom (v. 1)

1. Gather yourselves together, yea, gather together, O nation not desired.

No one will escape the punishment (1:2, 3), and every wickedness will be exposed (1:12). Therefore—gather yourselves together. The prophet is calling for the entire nation to come together, not for a party, but for piety; not for reveling, but for reforming; not for drunkenness, but for the deity; not to increase sensuality, but to restore sacrifices to God.

We must continually remind ourselves that when God promises to bring a nation down, He will save that nation if it repents (Jeremiah 18:7, 8). God wants to heal a country, not destroy it; and God calls for His people to be His instruments to bring that about (2 Chronicles 7:14). That's why Christ's people are called light, salt, and leaven. We are the representatives of God's character and truth.

B. When (v. 2)

2. Before the decree bring forth, before the day pass as the chaff, before the fierce anger of the Lord come upon you, before the day of the Lord's anger come upon you.

There is no time to delay in bringing reform. It must happen before the day of judgment comes. That means we as individuals and we as a nation should enter into it now, because God's day of judgment comes at an hour when we think not (Matthew 24:44). It has always been that way in historical times of punishment, and it will be that way at the end of the world.

Jesus made it clear that no one knows the day or the hour (Matthew 24:36-44). Since we do not know the day or the time and since it will be at a time when we expect not, our responsibility is to be alert, be watchful, be ready with our lives turned toward God. Today is the day to return to the Lord, for no one knows what tomorrow holds.

C. How (v. 3)

3. Seek ye the Lord, all ye meek of the earth, which have wrought his judgment; seek righteousness, seek meekness: it may be ye shall be hid in the day of the Lord's anger.

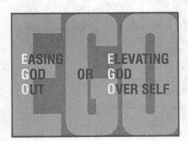

EASING GOD OUT   OR   ELEVATING GOD OVER SELF

visual 6

Repentance is described as seeking the Lord. To seek the Lord is paralleled with seeking righteousness. Seeking righteousness is paralleled with seeking meekness. To seek the Lord is to seek His way, His guidance, His control, His filling, His dominance. To seek righteousness is to seek right relationships with God, with self, and with others. Meekness means to have ourselves under control. We are not to be out of control in the way we think, act, or react.

If we repent, we *shall be hid in the day of the Lord's anger.* That is, our sins will be covered by His forgiveness. That happened when death passed over God's people in Egypt. That will happen when death passes over us on the Day of Judgment.

This prophecy was speaking about the destruction of Jerusalem by the Babylonians, but it also applies to the end of the world when Christ returns. Those who have not repented and are outside of Christ will call for the rocks and the hills to fall upon them (Revelation 6:5-17). Those who have had their sins covered by the grace of God in Christ will be confident and unashamed before Him at His coming (1 John 2:28).

The question is, Do you want to be exposed or covered? Do you want to be condemned or saved? Do you want to become your own sacrifice for your sins in Hell, or to let Christ be the sacrifice for them on the cross.

ESCAPING JUDGMENT

Plea bargaining in court is a common strategy these days. Criminals can escape judgment for felonies by pleading guilty to less-serious crimes. Judges cooperate with this maneuvering because court dockets are jammed and prisons are overflowing.

In Zephaniah 2:3 God told citizens of Judah how to escape judgment. They should humble themselves, seek God, and seek righteousness. A big problem with execution of justice is that guiltless folk suffer right along with wrongdoers. When God punished the sins of His people by allowing them to be defeated in combat, innocent citizens suffered the consequences of national sin.

Actually, of course, none of us is innocent except in Christ. "All have sinned, and come short of the glory of God" (Romans 3:23), and "the wages of sin is death" (Romans 6:23). Peter said of Jesus Christ, "Neither is there salvation in any other: for there is none other name . . . whereby we must be saved" (Acts 4:12). Those facts make the question of Hebrews 2:3 quite pertinent: "How shall we escape if we ignore such a great salvation?" (*New International Version*). —R. W. B.

Conclusion
A. Preaching Makes a Difference

While Zephaniah's preaching did not keep the Babylonian captivity from happening, probably it did help prevent a total destruction of the people because it brought a significant difference into the lives of many people in Judah who eventually repented. He preached in the time of King Josiah, and King Josiah prepared God's temple, declared God's anger against Judah because of its sins, called all the people together, and had God's law read before them all. He did away with pagan priests and places where Baal was worshiped. He restored the celebration of the Passover, and got rid of mediums and spiritualists.

Zephaniah's preaching made a difference. It helped this tremendous reformation. But the next king returned to evil ways, and the time clock for the destruction of Jerusalem began to run again. Have you stopped the clock of God's eternal punishment of you by accepting Christ, or is that clock still ticking? That clock is like the timer of a bomb, and you don't know when it will go off!

B. Prayer

Thank You, Father, for balancing Your promise of destruction with the offer of Your grace. Thank You for Your loving patience that has given each of us time to turn toward You. Help us to please You this day and forevermore. Amen.

C. Thought to Remember

Seek the Lord, seek righteousness, seek meekness; and be sheltered on the day of the Lord's anger.

Home Daily Bible Readings

Monday, July 6—Zephaniah Prophesies (Zephaniah 1:1-6)
Tuesday, July 7— The Lord's Sacrifice (Zephaniah 1:7-13)
Wednesday, July 8—The Day of the Lord (Zephaniah 1:14-18)
Thursday, July 9—Zephaniah's Plea (Zephaniah 2:1-4)
Friday, July 10—The Nations Warned (Zephaniah 2:5-11)
Saturday, July 11—The Nations Are Judged (Zephaniah 2:12-15)
Sunday, July 12—Righteousness Desired (Psalm 89:14-18)

Learning by Doing

This page contains an alternate lesson plan emphasizing learning activities. Classes desiring such student involvement will find these suggestions helpful.

Learning Goals

After examining selected portions of the prophecy of Zephaniah, students will be able to:

1. List the consequences of sin that were to come upon God's people if they refused to repent.

2. Define the word *repent*.

3. Explain how repentance is demonstrated.

4. Choose an area of life to commit to God in repentance.

Into the Lesson

Before class begins, place the words of the following message on 3" x 5" cards or small slips of paper, one word per card: "Seek the Lord—seek righteousness—seek meekness and be sheltered on the day of the Lord's anger." Scramble the cards and put them in an envelope. Make one set of cards for each four to six students.

As the class members arrive, have them form groups of four to six. Give each group a set of the cards. Ask them to unscramble the message. Allot five to seven minutes for this. Then have the groups share the message. Display the message on the chalkboard or a sheet of newsprint for the remainder of the session.

Make the transition into the Bible study by explaining that the unscrambled message is the gist of Zephaniah's message that forms the basis for today's lesson.

Into the Word

Briefly present the "Lesson Background" material to your class. Include also the commentary material for Zephaniah 1:1. Then read Zephaniah 1:1-12; 2:1-3 aloud (or have someone in the class do it).

Then have the class members work together in pairs to discover the answers to the following questions:

1. What will be the scope of the Lord's impending judgment? (1:2, 3). (It will cover the whole land of Judah with devastation; the devastation will be complete.)

2. Describe what will happen in the judgment (1:4-12). (Judah will be punished; Baal worship will be destroyed; Malcham worship will be destroyed; all idol worship will be destroyed; some people will be sacrificed.)

3. What invitation does God offer to the people of Judah? (2:1-3). (He invites them to repent,

to do what is right, to obey in order to escape judgment.)

4. Basing your thinking on this passage, define "repent." (It means to change behavior.)

5. What seems to be the overriding message of this passage? (God is in control, and He will punish those who do not repent and turn to Him.)

Allot five to seven minutes for the teams to work. Then develop a general discussion based on the five questions. As the discussion develops, you can add insights you have gleaned from your study.

Into Life

Continue the discussion you have begun by using the following questions:

1. If God were to issue a warning of impending doom directly to us today, what would He say? How would it be like Zephaniah 1:4-12? How would it be different? (Be sure the students think of the way people focus their hearts on things other than God, and therefore try to get things and enjoy life rather than to do right. The students may be tempted to spend all of their time talking about the "awful" crimes featured in the daily headlines. But Zephaniah directed His prophecy to the "average" person and talked about the wrongs that "everybody" was doing.)

2. Zephaniah's prophecy indicates that God's judgment would come as a surprise to people in the midst of their daily activities. What evidence would you cite to indicate that the same will be true for us?

3. What are some ways in which we might repent and do better than we are doing?

4. What message of hope would God hold out to us?

5. How can we live righteously in the midst of an unrighteous world? Give some tips.

Give each person a 3" x 5" card. Ask each one to write a diary entry telling some way in which he would like to repent and what difference that repentance will make in his way of living. Explain that this is for the person himself, not to be shared with the class. Allow three or four minutes for the students to do this.

Briefly review the message of today's lesson. Urge students to do what they have written on the cards. Close with a prayer seeking God's strength for the students to make any changes they have indicated.

Let's Talk It Over

The questions on this page are designed to encourage review of the lesson Scriptures and to promote discussion of the lesson by the class. The answers provided are only discussion starters. Let your class talk it over from there.

1. What are some objections people make to the doctrine of Hell, and how may we respond?

One of the most popular is the oft-repeated assertion that "God is too loving to send anyone to Hell." While the love of God is emphasized in the Bible, His holiness and justice are also emphasized. It is unwise to exalt one attribute of God above the rest.

Some object to teaching about Hell as a "scare tactic," a way of frightening people into the church. But sinful people need to be frightened, if it will motivate them to repentance.

To many critics the idea of Hell is an old-fashioned notion that should be discarded in this enlightened age. But since Jesus spoke plainly about Hell, we can only deny it by assuming Him to be either deceived or a deceiver.

2. Preaching by Zephaniah and others has a large place in the Bible. Why is preaching important today?

Never before has a generation been so pervaded by the spoken word as ours has. When we hear the polished voices of television actors and the upbeat chatter of radio disc jockeys, it may seem that the words spoken from the church pulpit are rather plain. However, the utterances of a preacher attuned to the Word of God are more significant than the speeches of the most prominent political leader, the phrases of the most skillful actor, or the pronouncements of the so-called experts we hear over our radio or television.

3. The destruction of our natural environment is one of today's most-discussed issues. What are some ways in which sin has contributed to such destruction?

The finger of accusation has often been pointed at modern industry as a major culprit in polluting land, water, and air. The sin of greed for greater and greater profits has been a factor. However, families and individuals also contribute to this problem. There is a streak of selfishness in us that leads us to throw out trash in public places or drive our car with a faulty exhaust system or persist in using products that are known to damage the environment. We who realize that "the earth is the Lord's, and the fulness thereof" (Psalm 24:1) should be protectors of the environment.

4. How can we tell if we are fighting against God, and how can we overcome such a practice?

We may fight against God by resisting His work within us or by standing in the way of His working in others. He may be urging us to repentance, while we are determined to go on with a certain attitude or habit. He may be calling us to commitment to some area of service, while we stubbornly seek our own will. If we perceive that we are fighting against God in any way, we need to come to our own "road to Damascus," as Saul did, and utter our own humble "What shall I do, Lord?" (Acts 22:10).

5. In what ways do people attempt to hide from God today?

Perhaps much of the extreme busyness in our society represents an unconscious effort to hide from God. In their frantic rush from one business meeting to another, one party or game or show to another, even one church activity to another, people leave themselves little time or opportunity to think about God, their souls, and eternity. Some people actually seem to be hiding from God by reading the Bible or theological works. They approach their reading on a purely intellectual basis, never allowing their wills to be affected. The intellectual approach to hiding from God is a popular one. By amassing information on science, history, philosophy, and various other topics, some individuals think they become too well educated or well informed to believe in God.

6. What does it mean to "seek the Lord"?

It does not mean that God is lost, but that we are lost from God and in need of finding Him. It implies an effort on our part (Deuteronomy 4:29), but not an effort in which we must rely only on our human strength or ingenuity (Job 11:7). God has revealed himself and the means of our having fellowship with Him through His Son and His Word. Jesus pointed out in Matthew 6:33 that we must give first priority to this task of seeking. If we are tempted to focus our efforts on seeking things or pleasures or earthly security, that counsel of Jesus offers us quite a challenge. Jesus also promised, "Seek, and ye shall find" (Matthew 7:7).

God Will Restore Israel

LESSON SCRIPTURE: Zephaniah 3.

PRINTED TEXT: Zephaniah 3:12, 14-20.

Zephaniah 3:12, 14-20

12 I will also leave in the midst of thee an afflicted and poor people, and they shall trust in the name of the LORD.

. . . .

14 Sing, O daughter of Zion; shout, O Israel; be glad and rejoice with all the heart, O daughter of Jerusalem.

15 The LORD hath taken away thy judgments, he hath cast out thine enemy: the King of Israel, even the LORD, is in the midst of thee: thou shalt not see evil any more.

16 In that day it shall be said to Jerusalem, Fear thou not: and to Zion, Let not thine hands be slack.

17 The LORD thy God in the midst of thee is mighty; he will save, he will rejoice over thee with joy; he will rest in his love, he will joy over thee with singing.

18 I will gather them that are sorrowful for the solemn assembly, who are of thee, to whom the reproach of it was a burden.

19 Behold, at that time I will undo all that afflict thee: and I will save her that halteth, and gather her that was driven out; and I will get them praise and fame in every land where they have been put to shame.

20 At that time will I bring you again, even in the time that I gather you: for I will make you a name and a praise among all people of the earth, when I turn back your captivity before your eyes, saith the LORD.

GOLDEN TEXT: The LORD thy God in the midst of thee is mighty; he will save, he will rejoice over thee with joy; he will rest in his love.—Zephaniah 3:17.

God's Judgment and Mercy

Unit 2: A Remnant Is Saved
(Lessons 6, 7)

Lesson Aims

This lesson is designed to help the student to be able to:

1. Commit himself to faithful Christian living, understanding that a faithful few can influence many to be faithful.

2. Trace the Biblical truth that God's grace is greater than man's disgrace.

Lesson Outline

INTRODUCTION
    A. Twice Mine
    B. Lesson Background
I. GOD'S FAITHFUL REMNANT (ZEPHANIAH 3:12)
II. GOD'S CALLING (ZEPHANIAH 3:14-17)
    A. Call to Joy (v. 14)
    B. Reason for Joy (v. 15)
       Will the Real King Please Stand Up?
    C. Call to Courage (v. 16)
    D. Reason for Courage (v. 17)
III. GOD'S PROMISES (ZEPHANIAH 3:18-20)
    A. Reunion (v. 18)
    B. Restoration (vv. 19, 20)
       From Shame to Fame
CONCLUSION
    A. God's Grace Is Great
    B. Prayer
    C. Thought to Remember

Refer to visual 7 of the visuals packet as you develop the thoughts carried under Zephaniah 3:17. The visual is shown on page 396.

Introduction

A. Twice Mine

The story has been around for decades; it beautifully expresses God's restoration. The little boy built a sailboat. He loved that boat, enjoyed it, and was proud of it. One day as he was sailing it on the stream, a puff of wind took it away from the shore—so far that the little boy could no longer reach it. With sadness he watched the boat disappear into the distance.

A few weeks later, as he was walking by a secondhand store, he noticed his little boat in the window. He went in to buy it, but did not have enough money. He worked for days at odd jobs

until he finally returned to the shop to buy the boat he had made. As he was walking out of the shop, he held the boat closely to his chest and was overheard to say, "Little boat, you're mine. You are twice mine: first, I made you; then when you slipped away, I bought you and restored you to me."

That's what God does for His people. As soon as man sinned, God announced that He would move to restore fallen humanity to himself (Genesis 3:15). He made us in His own image, then He bought us in His Son. "You are not your own; you were bought at a price. Therefore honor God with your body" (1 Corinthians 6:19, 20, *New International Version*). "Forasmuch as ye know that ye were not redeemed with corruptible things, as silver and gold, from your vain conversation received by tradition from your fathers; but with the precious blood of Christ, as of a lamb without blemish and without spot" (1 Peter 1:18, 19).

B. Lesson Background

Last week we studied the announcement that God would punish His people with devastating and comprehensive discipline. Many of the people would be sacrificed, and wickedness would be exposed—regardless of how well some people thought they had hidden it from God. In spite of that announcement, God through the prophet invited His people to a revival–to seek the Lord and return to Him.

That happened temporarily under King Josiah, who helped lead the people to significant reform. Probably the reform was helped also by the preaching of Zephaniah the prophet. However, the kings that followed Josiah put the spiritual life of the nation into a spiritual tailspin. So God carried out His announced remedial discipline. He brought the Babylonians to destroy Jerusalem and take its people into captivity. While that was painful, it turned out to be fruitful.

Zephaniah foretold the punishment, as we saw last week. Now we are to see that he looked beyond the punishment to foretell the restoration that would follow it. That prophecy of restoration was fulfilled in part when the Jews were liberated from captivity and resumed their national life. It will be fulfilled more completely when the kingdom of Christ becomes complete.

No remedial discipline is pleasant when we are receiving it, but God gives it to His children because of His love. God was looking beyond the now to their future needs. It was during the Babylonian captivity that the hearts of God's people returned to Him, for they realized that their captivity was the result of their greedy and crooked lifestyle. In this lesson we read about the promised restoration that was to result from their practical repentance.

There are several lessons to learn from this:

1. The spark of faith kept in the hearts of a few can spread to many.

2. God gives discipline and punishment out of His grace, care, and love for His people.

3. This illustrates the truth that God disciplines us for our good, that we may share in His holiness. No discipline seems pleasant at the time; it is painful. Later on, however, it can produce a harvest of righteousness and peace for those who are trained by it (Hebrews 12:10, 11, (*New International Version*).

I. God's Faithful Remnant
(Zephaniah 3:12)

12. I will also leave in the midst of thee an afflicted and poor people, and they shall trust in the name of the Lord.

The proud and haughty, the stiffnecked and godless, would die in captivity and gain no profit from the punishment (v. 11). But among the captives *afflicted* and poor in worldly goods would be some who would also be poor in spirit. They would be blessed by their affliction, for it would bring them to *trust in the name of the Lord.*

Jesus picks up this concept in the Beatitudes when He says, "Blessed are the poor in spirit: for theirs is the kingdom of heaven" (Matthew 5:3). The poor in spirit are those who admit that without God they are spiritually bankrupt and impotent. Brokenhearted because of their sins against God they long for God's presence and power, and they are submissive to His way.

While most of God's people were still rich–filled with pride of self even as captives–a few were saying what John the Baptist said, "He must increase, but I must decrease" (John 3:30). These few no doubt began to carry out the instructions of 2 Chronicles 7:14, which resulted in the future healing of the land. They became the seed that changed the entire nation (v. 13).

How to Say It

BABYLON. *Bab*-uh-lon.
BABYLONIAN. Bab-uh-*low*-nee-un.
CYRUS. *Sigh*-russ.
JERUSALEM. Jee-*roo*-suh-lem.
JOSIAH. Jo-*sye*-uh.
SODOM. *Sod*-um.
ZEPHANIAH. Zef-uh-*nye*-uh.
ZION. *Zi*-on.

What a lesson! The faith, repentance, fasting, and prayers of these few made an impact upon their brothers and sisters. Priorities began to change in the hearts of God's people in Babylon.

There is another lesson here. Christians today are often upset because they are not in the "majority" on certain issues in the world or community, but a minority standing with God makes a powerful majority.

God promised Abraham that if there were ten righteous people in Sodom and the surrounding villages He would not destroy them. Just ten could have saved the region, for ten righteous people can be like light in darkness, leaven in the dough, and salt on the food (Genesis 19).

Why was Sodom destroyed? Because of sin? Yes, but what can be said about God's people in Sodom, Lot and his family? Were they even trying to influence the community? There were four righteous people in that area of perhaps five hundred thousand–Lot, his wife, and their two daughters. All they needed were six more to save half a million people. But Lot and his family evidently kept their religion to themselves and did not influence any other people.

We shouldn't wring our hands waiting on someone else to stand up for the Lord; we can be a part of the minority that God uses to influence others.

II. God's Calling
(Zephaniah 3:14-17)
A. Call to Joy (v. 14)

14. Sing, O daughter of Zion; shout, O Israel; be glad and rejoice with all the heart, O daughter of Jerusalem.

It was certainly a sad time when Jerusalem was captured by the Babylonians. The sadness turned even deeper when the people were driven from their homes, cities, and land into a foreign place. They were deep in grief in Babylon (Psalm 137:1-6). But even before the captivity began, Zephaniah invited God's people to rejoice because their salvation was near. The faith of a few (vv. 12, 13) would result in the transformation of many, and joy would follow. See the words that say God's people again will celebrate: *sing, shout, be glad, rejoice.*

How can anyone claim there should be no emotionalism in our religion? Isn't there emotion when a doctor declares an ill person has been healed? Isn't there emotion when a lost child is found? Isn't there emotion when your favorite team is two points behind but wins at the sound of the buzzer? So why does anyone think our relationship with God should be devoid of emotion?

In the Old Testament it is clear that God commanded His people to enter into celebrations several times a year. Shouldn't we celebrate with the same joyous emotion? Isn't it a natural reaction to God's grace and love for us?

It was no shallow joy that Zephaniah predicted. He said, *Be glad and rejoice with all the heart.* We cannot experience God with just our heads; we must allow our hearts to become bigger than our heads. The majesty, the grace, the love of almighty God cannot be fully appreciated just by intellectualizing about them. Joy that fills *all the heart* cannot be confined to the heart. It overflows in the voice, in instruments of music, even in clapping the hands and getting excited. Read Psalm 150.

God does not want His people to live in the dumps, but in delight. Celebration was a big part of God's involvement with His people. He established several different festivals. One in spring lasted for a week; so did one in autumn. God created us to share His kind of joy. There may be sadness in the night, but that can be followed by joy in the morning (Psalm 30:5).

Jesus came that we might have life and have it more abundantly—now as well as later (John 10:10). The second taste of the fruit of the Spirit is joy (Galatians 5:22). It is rightly sandwiched between love and peace, for joy comes from knowing we are loved and joy leads to peace—the end of alienation.

B. Reason for Joy (v. 15)

15. The Lord hath taken away thy judgments, he hath cast out thine enemy: the King of Israel, even the Lord, is in the midst of thee: thou shalt not see evil any more.

The Lord hath taken away thy judgments reminds us of Psalm 18:28, "God turns my darkness into light," and Psalm 30:5, "his anger lasts only a moment, but his favor lasts a lifetime." God's anger is for our benefit, so we will not continue a lifestyle that is self-destructive. No one who really loves you will stay angry at you forever. God will not "harbor His anger forever" (Psalm 103:9, *New International Version*).

During the Babylonian captivity, God's people renewed their allegiance to God as their king. When they did that, God took away their punishment (*judgment*); He *cast out thine enemy* by raising up another king, Cyrus, who conquered Babylon, was a friend of the Jews, and released them from captivity. He helped the Jews rebuild Jerusalem and restore their religion in peace.

This verse sounds as if this had already happened when Zephaniah wrote, but really it was to happen years later. That is one of the ways the Hebrew prophets wrote to assure the people of something that would happen. When God promises something, it is as if it were already done—though the event may be many years in the future.

The *enemy*, Babylon, would be *cast out*, never to rise again as a world power. *Thou shalt not see evil any more* will be finally and completely fulfilled when Jesus comes and takes His people to be with Him forever (1 Thessalonians 4:16, 17). As applied to the Babylonian captivity, it means that God's people would not see that particular evil any more. They would find peace from their perplexities and tranquility from their disturbances. Whenever we are going through difficult times, we can say to ourselves and to others, "This too will pass."

WILL THE REAL KING PLEASE STAND UP?

Remember that old game show, "To Tell the Truth"? Three contestants would all claim to be the same person. A panel of celebrities would question them, trying to find out who was telling the truth. When time ran out, the celebrities cast votes for Mystery Guest 1, 2, or 3. Then the host would say, "Will the real John Doe please stand up?" After a dramatic pause, the truthful contestant would stand, and the game was over.

Judah had forgotten who was their real King. Hundreds of years before, when Israel first demanded an earthly ruler, God told Samuel, "They have rejected me, that I should not reign over them" (1 Samuel 8:7). Of the dozens of kings who sat on the thrones of Israel and Judah, only a few were righteous and faithful. God's people forsook their divine King, and thus were forsaken while their enemies took them into captivity.

Judah was reminded through Zephaniah that their real king was the Lord. God still reigns. He is King of the universe. All earthly rulers are imposters, if they usurp the throne of our spiritual allegiance. We should know Him—no questions asked!   —R. W. B.

visual 7

C. Call to Courage (v. 16)

16. In that day it shall be said to Jerusalem, Fear thou not: and to Zion, Let not thine hands be slack.

In that day pointed forward to the time when the Babylonian captivity would end. Joyous as the release would be, it would bring new problems. *That day* would be fifty years after Jerusalem was destroyed. The Jews who could remember the old home would be getting old themselves. At their age they might be afraid to undertake the task of rebuilding Jerusalem. Younger Jews then in Babylon would have been born there. They might shrink from becoming pioneers in a ruined homeland that they had never seen. In fifty years many of the Jews would be comfortably settled in Babylon. They would have jobs, businesses, homes. Some would be wealthy. Naturally they would be afraid to leave their comfortable situation and return to Jerusalem, or *Zion*, as it is also called. To all those persons who might be fearful, God's call would be clear: *Fear thou not*. With courage and fortitude they should rejoice in their liberation and the opportunity to rebuild their ancient homeland.

On the other hand, they should not think going back home would be easy. Jerusalem was a heap of rubble; the farm land of Judah was overgrown with brush. It would take hard work and lots of it to make that country what it had been before the captivity. So God's call would be *Let not thine hands be slack*. The people should be prepared to work energetically.

Are you ever afraid to do what you know you ought to do? Do you feel yourself paralyzed by anxiety, and sinking into depression? While you remain inactive, fear and depression will grow. *Fear thou not!* Get up and go to work with energy and determination.

D. Reason for Courage (v. 17)

17. The Lord thy God in the midst of thee is mighty; he will save, he will rejoice over thee with joy; he will rest in his love, he will joy over thee with singing.

Mighty reminded the people of the kind of God they had. No people can rise above their perception of the God they serve. What vision of God do we have? Do we often see Him as weak or indifferent or inactive? Zephaniah assured the people that God would not keep "hands off" when the time came for their liberation and the rebuilding of the homeland. He would be directly involved in their lives and through their lives. That was reason enough to cast off fear and work with confidence.

He will save—His activity will deliver His people from all their troubles. *He will rejoice over thee*—God does not delight in punishment. We are told elsewhere that Heaven breaks out in joy when people repent (Luke 15:7, 10). Remember the father's joy over the prodigal son?

He will rest in his love—what a beautiful description of a loving father after giving gracious discipline for the good of others! Real love disciplines and then embraces. Real love chides but cherishes. Real love punishes but provides. Real love gives correction but does it in charity.

He will joy over thee with singing—God does not keep His joy locked up inside; He bursts out in singing. Look again at the words that tell about God in the midst of His people—*mighty, save, rejoice, joy, rest, love, singing*. What a God and what an environment to enjoy here and forever!

III. God's Promises (Zephaniah 3:18-20)

A. Reunion (v. 18)

18. I will gather them that are sorrowful for the solemn assembly, who are of thee, to whom the reproach of it was a burden.

God's people would be separated. Some would be taken to Babylon; some would flee to Egypt (2 Kings 25). No doubt some would escape to other places that are not recorded. They would be *sorrowful* (Psalm 137). The *reproach* of their sin and captivity would be *a burden* to them. But all that would end. God would release them from the captivity and gather them together for a magnificent reunion. They would be given the freedom to return to their homeland.

This is also a pre-picture of the future coming of Jesus. When He comes back, He will bring with Him those of His people who have already died. We who remain will gather together with them in the air and be with our Lord (1 Thessalonians 4:16, 17).

That is why we read, "Blessed are the dead which die in the Lord" (Revelation 14:13). Separation of God's people is never permanent. It will be followed by eternal reunion where God will be in our midst. We all will rest in love, rejoicing, and singing. Every *reproach* and *burden* will be eliminated.

B. Restoration (vv. 19, 20)

19. Behold, at that time I will undo all that afflict thee: and I will save her that halteth, and gather her that was driven out; and I will get them praise and fame in every land where they have been put to shame.

This reaffirms what God was going to do *at that time*—the end of captivity. He would take away the enemies—*undo all that afflict thee*. There would be crippling setbacks, power and property would be lost; but He would reverse that—*save her that halteth*. There would be separation by deportation, but He would bring reunion—*gather her that was driven out*. God's people would be shamed in the eyes of others, but God would reverse that—*get them praise and fame in every land*.

What a message for us when we are going through setbacks in the church or in our individual lives! Let's remember that although storms come, no storm stays. Although God's discipline may come, no discipline stays if we allow the chastisement to minister to us, to enlighten our hearts, to humble our thoughts, and to change our ways.

20. At that time will I bring you again, even in the time that I gather you: for I will make you a name and a praise among all people of the earth, when I turn back your captivity before your eyes, saith the Lord.

For emphasis the prophet repeats what he has just said. The repetition does not mean that God will be more likely to keep His promise than He would be if He said it just once, but repetition reassures those who have it or read it. Repeating the promise emphasizes the fact that restoration was in God's mind before He began this discipline. God's people would be restored—*Will I bring you again*. They would be restored to their families—*I gather you*. They would be restored to their reputation and honor—*make you a name and a praise among all people*. They would be restored to peace—*I turn back your captivity*. The restoration would be plainly evident—*before your eyes*. It would come from the Lord—*saith the Lord*.

This book begins with "the word of the Lord" and ends with "saith the Lord." It is a reminder that God is the alpha and omega (the first and last letters in the Greek alphabet; Revelation 21:6). He has the first word to say, and He will have the last word to say. No people, no dictator, no country, no conqueror, no council can outthink, outdo, outpower, or outtalk God.

If we have a "thus saith the Lord," we should respond with "Your servant heareth and heedeth."

FROM SHAME TO FAME

The corruption of celebrities seems more common in recent years. This is partly an illusion created by the media that sensationalize the sins of famous folk. Add to that the permissiveness of our current culture, and we have nightly news that could shock the socks off a sailor. Just as "pride goes before destruction," so shame often follows fame. The wealth and power that accompany recognition and popularity can corrupt many.

Judah had fallen into disgrace in a similar fashion. Their wealth and power were once well-known among nations. Then they shamed themselves with sin, forsaking their God and King. Zephaniah's prophecy brought the bad news of imminent defeat and captivity. But he also brought good news of future deliverance and restoration. Their sin had degraded them from fame to shame; their Redeemer promised to lift them from shame to fame.

Our personal story is the same. Our pride and selfishness begat sin and shame. But our Redeemer lifts us from shame to fame, for in Him we are not only justified, but also glorified (Romans 8:30).

—R. W. B.

Conclusion

A. God's Grace Is Great

Over and over, these studies from some of the minor prophets have revealed disobedience and wickedness on the part of God's people. Jonah did the opposite of what God commanded, and so did the nation of Judah. Through it all, we have seen God's grace to forgive, to restore, and to reuse. That is the good news from God—we are saved through grace.

B. Prayer

Thank You, Father, for being perfect and for loving us who are not, for being right and waiting for us who are wrong, for correcting us by discipline that sometimes hurts, yet embracing us with your mercy. Amen.

C. Thought to Remember

God's grace is greater than man's disgrace.

Home Daily Bible Readings

Learning by Doing

This page contains an alternate lesson plan emphasizing learning activities. Classes desiring such student involvement will find these suggestions helpful.

Learning Goals

After examining Zephaniah 3:12-20, the student will be able to:

1. Define *grace*.
2. Tell how this passage demonstrates grace.
3. List examples of God's grace extended to him.
4. Express thanks for God's grace.

Into the Lesson

Put the following acrostic (without the filled-in words) on a chalkboard, a sheet of newsprint, or an overhead transparency.

Make an Acrostic

Use each letter of the word *grace* to form a word or phrase that comes to mind when you see or hear that word *grace*.

G–ift of God
R–edemption
A–doption
C–leansing
E–verlasting life

As the class members arrive, ask each one to complete the assignment, then share his response with at least one other person. Allot four to six minutes for this. After the assigned time, have class members help you fill in the acrostic you have put before them.

Make the transition into the Bible study by pointing out that the central thrust of the lesson is the grace of God.

Into the Word

Briefly present the "Lesson Background" to provide a setting for today's study. Also briefly mention the gist of the lesson for last week. Then read aloud Zephaniah 3:12-20.

Lead the students in an inductive study of the text by using the following questions to guide their understanding:

1. Who does Zephaniah say will be left once God's judgment is finished? (Afflicted and poor people.)
2. What will distinguish these people from those who had lived in Jerusalem before? (They will trust the Lord.)
3. Why should Jerusalem rejoice? (God has stopped punishing them and has sent their enemies away. Also God is with them, and He will save them.)

4. What else does God promise in verse 18? (A reunion.)
5. List the promises given to God's people in verses 19 and 20. (God will undo their enemies, end their captivity, save them, gather them, get praise and fame for them.)
6. Why or how would these promises be encouraging to a people facing persecution? (Be sure the students express their own thinking.)
7. How is God's grace shown in this passage? (In connection with this, you may lead your students to define grace. Probably they will say correctly that it is undeserved favor.)

As the discussion develops, of course you will add insights you have gained from your advance study.

Into Life

Continue the discussion by using the following questions:

1. We live in an era quite different from that of Zephaniah. We recognize the value of his warnings, but we need also to focus on the way God's grace is extended to us in spite of our sinfulness. Mention some of the ways in which God's grace is extended to you. (Let the students suggest ways in which they personally experience God's grace. Record the ways on the chalkboard, overhead transparency, or sheet of newsprint.)
2. What is an appropriate way to respond to God for the grace He has shown to you? (Record responses.)

Make the following statement: God's grace extends to us in many ways every day. Certainly we should demonstrate our gratitude for His mercy and grace to us.

Then divide the class into groups of four to six. Let each group choose a way to acknowledge God's grace and their gratitude for it. A group may write a poem or song or prayer, or simply make a list of gracious acts of God. Allot eight to ten minutes for the groups to complete their work. Then have each group share its work. This will almost certainly produce a sense of profound worship.

Depending upon the mood of the class after the presentations have been made, you may take a minute to summarize the thrust of this lesson. Close with a prayer of thanksgiving for God's grace so freely given every day.

Let's Talk It Over

The questions on this page are designed to encourage review of the lesson Scriptures and to promote discussion of the lesson by the class. The answers provided are only discussion starters. Let your class talk it over from there.

1. The Old Testament record of God's people is one of continual ups and downs. We see similar periods of growth and decline in many churches. How do we respond to this?

Some churches seem to move along at the same pace for years. But some go through very evident ups and downs. The departure of a popular preacher may bring a decline; the commencing of a new ministry may witness vigorous growth. A squabble in the church, the moving away of key leaders, the deaths of some long-standing "pillars"—these can all affect the church adversely. How the church needs steadfast members who will continue to serve and continue to tithe through all these vicissitudes! The church owes much to those who are "steadfast, unmovable, always abounding in the work of the Lord" (1 Corinthians 15:58).

2. God may work in those who are poor, but He surely works in those who are poor in spirit. Why must we make this distinction?

Being poor in material goods does not necessarily make one poor in spirit. Often there is a stubborn pride among the needy, and in our time the poor are frequently very aggressive in demanding their rights. On the other hand, affluence does not preclude being poor in spirit. We occasionally hear of wealthy people who are humble, kind, and generous in sharing their riches with the needy. Whether we take pride in our lack of material goods or take satisfaction in gaining wealth, we need to give priority to being poor in spirit. God can do mighty things in any person, rich or poor, who commits all he is and has to his Creator.

3. Spiritual renewal or revival in a church often results from the prayers and labors of a faithful few. Why is this?

Perhaps it is because the Lord delights in working wonders through small groups (see Judges 7). Or perhaps special power is generated "where two or three are gathered together in my name" (Matthew 18:20). A few embers can ignite a great fire, and a few members can start a great revival. If two or three in the church are "on fire" for the Lord, there is a good chance that they can pass on the flame to others until the entire church is ablaze.

4. How can we become emotionally involved with Christ and His church?

How do people become excited about sports or automobiles or clothes? Emotional involvement with something usually goes hand-in-hand with knowledge of it. One can hardly be caught up in football, for example, without knowing what goes on on the field. Knowledge of the Bible contributes to emotional involvement with it. Another aspect of our excitement with sports or the like is the companionship of other fans. A Bible class or prayer group can give us the setting for emotional involvement with Christ.

5. "If you are depressed, do something for someone else." Is this good counsel? If so, why?

Some individuals who suffer from severe depression need professional help. But the above advice is excellent for those who suffer from occasional "downs." Helping our neighbors with lawn work or household repairs, calling on shut-ins, providing a listening ear to the lonely, or other helpfulness can lift us out of our gloom. When we minister to other people's needs, we tend to forget about our own. Often we see how small our problems are in comparison with those of others. And when we serve others, we align ourselves more closely with the Lord Jesus "who came to earth" to minister, and to give his life a ransom for many" (Mark 10:45). There is tremendous joy in being fellow workers with our Master.

6. We think often of God's grace revealed in the New Testament, but the Old Testament also contains many instances of God's undeserved favor toward people and nations. What does this tell us about the God of the Bible?

"For the law was given by Moses, but grace and truth came by Jesus Christ" (John 1:17). The New Testament records for us the supreme act of God's grace in the atoning death and resurrection of Jesus Christ, but we are not to think this marked a change in God's attitude toward men. He has always been a God of love and mercy. His wrath and His judgment against sin are plain in the Old Testament. But the New Testament also tells of His wrath and judgment (Matthew 25:14-46; John 3:36; Romans 1:18), and the Old Testament also tells of His grace. God is always the same.

Understand What You Teach

LESSON SCRIPTURE: 1 Timothy 1.

PRINTED TEXT: 1 Timothy 1:3-11, 18-20.

1 Timothy 1:3-11, 18-20

3 As I besought thee to abide still at Ephesus, when I went into Macedonia, that thou mightest charge some that they teach no other doctrine,

4 Neither give heed to fables and endless genealogies, which minister questions, rather than godly edifying which is in faith: so do.

5 Now the end of the commandment is charity out of a pure heart, and of a good conscience, and of faith unfeigned:

6 From which some having swerved have turned aside unto vain jangling;

7 Desiring to be teachers of the law; understanding neither what they say, nor whereof they affirm.

8 But we know that the law is good, if a man use it lawfully;

9 Knowing this, that the law is not made for a righteous man, but for the lawless and disobedient, for the ungodly and for sinners, for unholy and profane, for murderers of fathers and murderers of mothers, for manslayers,

10 For whoremongers, for them that defile themselves with mankind, for menstealers, for liars, for perjured persons, and if there be any other thing that is contrary to sound doctrine;

11 According to the glorious gospel of the blessed God, which was committed to my trust.

. . . .

18 This charge I commit unto thee, son Timothy, according to the prophecies which went before on thee, that thou by them mightest war a good warfare;

19 Holding faith, and a good conscience; which some having put away, concerning faith have made shipwreck:

20 Of whom is Hymeneus and Alexander; whom I have delivered unto Satan, that they may learn not to blaspheme.

Jul 26

GOLDEN TEXT: The end of the commandment is charity out of a pure heart, and of a good conscience, and of faith unfeigned.—1 Timothy 1:5.

Lesson Aims

The study of this lesson should help the students:

1. State the goal of Christian teaching.
2. Exercise caution when listening to an eloquent teacher.
3. Commit themselves to study and evaluate teaching before accepting it and living by it.

Lesson Outline

INTRODUCTION
    A. Do Your Own Thing?
    B. Lesson Background
  I. PROBLEMS (1 Timothy 1:3, 4)
    A. Wrong Teaching (v. 3)
    B. Attention to Wrong Teaching (v. 4)
 II. THE GOAL OF TEACHING (1 Timothy 1:5-7)
    A. The Goal Is Love (v. 5)
    B. Missing the Goal (vv. 6, 7)
III. THOUGHTS ON THE LAW (1 Timothy 1:8-11)
    A. It Is Beneficial (v. 8)
    B. It Is Preventive (v. 9)
    C. It Is Revealing (vv. 10, 11)
      A Sacred Trust
IV. TIMOTHY'S CHARGE (1 Timothy 1:18-20)
    A. Fight the Good Fight (v. 18)
    B. Hold On to the Faith (vv. 19, 20)
      Scuttling Faith
CONCLUSION
    A. Garbage In, Garbage Out
    B. Prayer
    C. Thought to Remember

Visual 8 of the visuals packet illustrates a vital truth mentioned in the section entitled "Scuttling Faith" on page 406. The visual is shown on page 404.

Introduction

A. Do Your Own Thing?

A student in pharmacy school asked about a certain complex prescription. The instructor replied. "That prescription does not taste good. No one likes it. Do your own thing with it. Put together a combination that has a better taste."

The cardiologist was taking a special course on open-heart surgery. The expert said, "Once you get inside the heart, do your own thing. If you can take some short cuts to save time and money, do it; your patient will eventually die anyway."

While a commercial pilot was in flight school, learning the ins and outs of a 727, he was taught, "When you have a malfunction in the air, forget about the manual and don't take time to radio our central control for instructions. Just do your own thing."

Do your own thing? As a pharmacist? Do you want him filling your prescription? Do your own thing as a heart surgeon? Is that the doctor you want? Do your own thing as a pilot? Do you want to fly in his plane? The above paragraphs are fiction, of course. No one advises "your own thing" in such situations.

There's a book entitled, *When All Else Fails, Read the Directions*. We don't wait until all else fails, do we? Perhaps a better title would be *Before Anything Fails, Read the Directions*. We would veto "your own thing" in the above situations where temporary physical lives are in danger. Why do we give a green light to everybody's "own thing" in the field of Christian teaching, which affects our eternal and spiritual lives?

B. Lesson Background

Paul had been released from his Roman imprisonment referred to in Acts 28:30. In his later travels he came to the vicinity of Ephesus, where he had ministered for more than two years at an earlier time. Whether he stopped at Ephesus itself or not, he learned of some significant problems there. Eager to go on to Macedonia, he left Timothy to work with the Ephesians on these problems.

Paul then wrote back to Timothy, not because Timothy had forgotten his assignment, but to instruct and encourage him as he no doubt met some opposition when he tried to correct what was wrong in the church at Ephesus.

I. Problems
(1 Timothy 1:3, 4)

A. Wrong Teaching (v. 3)

3. As I besought thee to abide still at Ephesus, when I went into Macedonia, that thou mightest charge some that they teach no other doctrine.

The word *besought* is from a Greek word that can be translated "encouraged." When Paul left Timothy, he left him with the kind of encouragement that a father would give to a son who was facing a tough situation. This letter was to continue such encouragement. Timothy stayed at Ephesus to solve some problems. One problem had to do with false teaching. If the false teaching continued, the people would find themselves with a shipwrecked faith (v. 19).

Some, not all, were involved in the false teaching. Paul did not tell Timothy to denounce the teaching in front of the entire church, but to charge the ones who were doing it. What was he to charge them to do?

To *teach no other doctrine.* The word *other* means a doctrine of a different kind: that is, different from the Christian teaching of Paul and other apostles.

Paul had been preaching a gospel of grace—"By grace are ye saved through faith" (Ephesians 2:8). Christian Jews had a tough time with that concept. They wanted to teach that people are saved by obedience to the law, not that salvation is a gift of God's grace. It is easy to slip into that way of thinking, for doing right is very important to a Christian. But no one does right enough to earn his way to Heaven. The best of people have to depend on God's grace for forgiveness of their sins and the gift of life eternal.

B. Attention to Wrong Teaching (v. 4)

4. Neither give heed to fables and endless genealogies, which minister questions, rather than godly edifying which is in faith: so do.

The problem was not just that some were giving false teaching, but also that some were paying attention to it. To *give heed* is not just to hear. It is to accept something and hold to it. This is not just casual listening: it is becoming attached to what is heard. However, getting attached to false teaching begins by casual listening.

Isn't it easy to listen to different doctrines today? They are in religious literature, in television and radio programs, and in everyday talk. We need not close our minds to ideas that are new to us; but we need to examine them carefully. We need to be like the Christians in Berea who searched the Scriptures to see whether what they heard was so or not (Acts 17:10, 11).

The word *fables* probably refers to stories and teachings that were calculated to please the hearers rather than to speak the truth. Fables were untruths that came out of someone's imagination. They did not square with Scriptural teaching. For the sake of popularity or money, many people today will teach what people want to hear.

Endless genealogies probably referred to the Jewish interest in tracing their ancestry to prove that they were God's people. That interest is not common among Christians today, but there is a similar interest in proving that our teaching can be traced to some famous person of the past or present rather than to the Word of God. There

---

How to Say It

EPHESUS. *Ef*-eh-sus.
HYMENEUS. Hi-me-*nee*-us.
MACEDONIA. Mass-eh-*doe*-nee-uh.

---

are some among us who question the Christianity of anyone who does not hold the view of Augustine or Pelagius, Calvin or Arminius, or some twentieth-century leader.

Do we hold to the teachings of men more firmly than we hold to God's Word? Do we evaluate a person by his adherence to a human teacher or group rather than by his devotion to Christ? Such practices produce questioning and quarreling. Our care should be rather for *godly edifying,* for building each other up *in faith.*

II. The Goal of Teaching (1 Timothy 1:5-7)

A. The Goal Is Love (v. 5)

5. Now the end of the commandment is charity out of a pure heart, and of a good conscience, and of faith unfeigned:

End means goal or target. The goal of Christian teaching is not: a) that we know more than others, b) that we become superior to others, c) that we judge others. The goal of Christian teaching is *charity.* That word has changed its meaning so much that most versions use love instead, but they mean a special kind of love, an unselfish love that is active in doing good. The goal of Christian teaching is that right actions become the life-style of the right kind of person.

The right action is the right kind of helpfulness motivated by the right kind of love. The right kind of person is one who has the right motivation unmixed with wrong motives (a *pure heart*). He does not say one thing and mean something else. He has a good *conscience*—a conscience that leads according to God's Word. His *faith* is sincere: *unfeigned* means genuine. He is no fake.

We are taught elsewhere in Scripture that we fulfill the law and the prophets if we love God and others as we ought (Matthew 22:37-40). All that God said in the law and the prophets was to help us know how to love one another. God's commandments were given to keep us from hurting someone else or ourselves. Paul said, "The entire law is summed up in a single command: 'Love your neighbor as yourself'" (Galatians 5:14, *New International Version*).

The goal of Christian instruction is not just to be correct, but also to love correctly.

B. Missing the Goal (vv. 6, 7)

6. From which some having swerved have turned aside unto vain jangling.

If we don't keep our sights on love, it is easy to take detours and miss God's intention for us. Without intending to get off course, one loses sight of the goal and gradually beings to wander. One translator put it this way: "Such people have missed the whole idea."

It is easy to miss the idea that God wants us to live in unity with love for others in His family, in spite of differences of opinion. Notice that paying attention to false teaching is the first step toward wandering, straying, or sidestepping God's whole idea. We wander when we aim for something else rather than the love of people.

When we do that, we easily stray into *vain jangling*, empty, meaningless talking, speculation and disputation. One translator calls it "high-flown gobbledygook."

Sometimes we major in minors and minor in majors. Rather than teaching in order to build people up to love the way God loves, some teach to promote their own pet hobby—whether it is a theory about how or when Jesus is coming back, or about the gifts of the Spirit, or whether Christians should listen to rock music.

How many times in our Bible-school classes or Bible-study groups do we get off of the meaning and application of the text and engage in meaningless discussions that have nothing to do with God's Word? How often do we ask people for their opinions, and end up with many opinions but no truth? A hodgepodge of human ignorance is not Bible study.

7. Desiring to be teachers of the law; understanding neither what they say, nor whereof they affirm.

It is not wrong to desire to be teachers of God's Word if we also desire to keep God's goal for teaching. When one teaches with a selfish aim of gain in money or prestige or popularity, he goes astray. Focusing on one part of Christian teaching and ignoring other parts of it, one has misunderstandings and teaches them. The person who sticks with his or her opinions and re-

GOD'S WORD IS THE COMPASS

A GOOD CONSCIENCE IS THE WHEEL

visual 8

jects anything else becomes conceited and understands nothing (1 Timothy 6:3, 4).

God did not give us just one passage of theBible. He gave all of it, and He wants us to study all of it. Some people center their study on what they know best and ignore what they do not know. That causes problems. One who doesn't study with an open mind is one who should not teach God's Word.

III. Thoughts on the Law (1 Timothy 1:8-11)

A. It Is Beneficial (v. 8)

8. But we know that the law is good, if a man use it lawfully.

The *law* mentioned here is the Old Testament law with all its rituals, regulations, and commandments. In Paul's time, many Jewish Christians thought all Christians ought to be bound by that law as the non-Christian Jews were. Paul said the law was nailed to the cross with Jesus (Colossians 2:14). He said we are not under law, but under grace (Romans 6:14). He here affirms that the law is good: it is beneficial *if* a man use it *lawfully* or properly.

A man uses the law properly when he uses it to help him move closer to the goal of love. He is not using it properly if he uses it only as a checklist to condemn the sins of others.

The law is good for the purposes for which it was designed: a) it pointed out what sin is; b) it taught that sin is punished; c) it was a schoolmaster to bring us to Christ (Galatians 3:24-28). Once we come to Christ, we are to live "in Christ": that is, to be so guided by His will that we do not need the law.

B. It Is Preventive (v. 9)

9. Knowing this, that the law is not made for a righteous man, but for the lawless and disobedient, for the ungodly and for sinners, for unholy and profane, for murderers of fathers and murderers of mothers, for manslayers.

The law was good but limited. It could not make people righteous, but it could help them stay within boundaries until Jesus came. Christ is the one who makes us righteous. "God made him who had no sin to be sin for us, so that in him we might become the righteousness of God" (2 Corinthians 5:21, *New International Version*). A righteous person is not a perfect person, but someone who has been acquitted by forgiveness and equipped by the Holy Spirit.

Several kinds of the unrighteous are mentioned in this verse: The *lawless* are those who ignore God's way. The *disobedient* are rebels who will not submit to authority. The *ungodly* are those with no respect for God. *Sinners* are those without moral standards. The *unholy and profane* are those who are thoroughly secular. *Murderers of fathers and murderers of mothers* (literally tramplers) are all who abuse their parents. *Manslayers* are murderers.

The law was set up for those people—to point out their wrong and keep them from continually escalating their wrong. People who prefer to do right do not need such constraint. For instance, honest people in college do not need a rule against cheating. It is a rule for the dishonest.

C. It Is Revealing (vv. 10, 11)

10, 11. For whoremongers, for them that defile themselves with mankind, for menstealers, for liars, for perjured persons, and if there be any other thing that is contrary to sound doctrine; according to the glorious gospel of the blessed God, which was committed to my trust.

This continues the list of the kinds of people for whom the law was established. *Whoremongers* are adulterers. *Them that defile themselves with mankind* are homosexuals. *Menstealers* are kidnappers of people for slave trade; *liars* are people who lie. *Perjured persons* are those who lie under oath.

God's law lets us know that the above kinds of activities are wrong. History and experience show that they are destructive. But God's law revealed also the kinds of relationships that can help people live together with mutual respect and unselfish love.

These harmful activities and others are *contrary to sound doctrine*. *Doctrine* simply means teaching. *Sound* means wholesome, healthful. The Greek word is the word from which we get our English word "hygiene." Medical science now is finding it literally true that non-loving actions escalate disease. Stress, depression, guilt, hatred, anger, self-centeredness all affect our physical glands and cells.

God's way for us is not just to get us to Heaven, but also to enhance our lives in the here and now. Teaching that brings health is in accordance with God's good news that Paul masterfully preached. One medical doctor has observed that if people would love one another as the New Testament teaches, medical bills in nearly every church would be reduced by half.

A SACRED TRUST

In 1898, Cuban revolutionaries were trying to throw off Spanish domination. When the battleship *Maine* was "accidentally" destroyed in Havana's harbor, the United States decided to assist Cuba in the fight for freedom. President McKinley dispatched a communique to the

Cuban leader, Calixto Garcia, announcing that decision and pledging support.

Lieutenant Andrew S. Rowan was entrusted with the message to Garcia. Delivery of it in the war-torn country required the utmost care and daring. Elbert Hubbard's essay, "A Message to Garcia," tells how the lieutenant proved worthy of his commission.

The apostle Paul considered his commission of carrying the "glorious gospel of the blessed God," a sacred trust. He was right, and we too are entrusted with the same vital message. No more significant communication has ever been transmitted. God cares about our plight with sin, and He has pledged to free us from oppression, guilt, and fear. He has declared war on the forces of evil that threaten to destroy us. And that is the message we must deliver with dispatch to the lost world.   —R. W. B.

IV. Timothy's Charge (1 Timothy 1:18-20)

A. Fight the Good Fight (v. 18)

18. This charge I commit unto thee, son Timothy, according to the prophecies which went before on thee, that thou by them mightest war a good warfare.

Paul's charge was for Timothy to stick with the ministry he began *according to the prophecies which went before on thee*. This seems to indicate that God had inspired a prophet to announce that Timothy should be chosen for a special service, and the elders then had laid their hands on him and commissioned him to that ministry (1 Timothy 4:14). Paul now urged Timothy to battle valiantly in the task God had assigned to him through the prophet.

There is a bad fight and a good fight. The bad fight might involve following the wrong commander, fighting our own brothers and sisters, becoming deserters, or refusing to submit to others. The *good warfare* involves following the right commander, Jesus, loving our brothers and sisters, standing against Satan and his forces, and using the armor that God has provided for us (Ephesians 6:10-18).

B. Hold On to the Faith (vv. 19, 20)

19. Holding faith, and a good conscience; which some having put away, concerning faith have made shipwreck.

Good warfare involves fighting with *faith*, not fists; and doing it with *a good conscience*, not with bad conduct. In the good war, a *good conscience* is one guided by the commander's orders in the Bible. Without such a conscience some have destroyed their faith as a ship is destroyed when high seas smash it on a reef.

20. Of whom is Hymeneus and Alexander; whom I have delivered unto Satan, that they may learn not to blaspheme.

Not having a good conscience, these two did not fight the good fight. Probably they engaged in false teaching or evil living or both, and their faith was wrecked.

Delivered unto Satan does not mean they had died and gone to Hell; but Paul, with apostolic authority, had disfellowshipped them, put them out of the church. By their actions they made it plain that they belonged to Satan, not to God; so Paul handed them over to Satan. That is the proper way to deal with persistent, defiant sinners in the church (1 Corinthians 5:9-13). This is not done with hatred or ill will, but with the hope that the sinners will change their ways when they see that willful sin is not tolerated in the church. We are using the same principle when we tell a child to go to his room and be isolated from the family. We welcome him back when he is ready to behave properly. Likewise the banished sinner is welcomed back to the church when he gives up his sinning (2 Corinthians 2:6-8). In the case of Hymeneus and Alexander, Paul hoped they would *learn not to blaspheme*, not to speak falsely about God and His way.

SCUTTLING FAITH

Ships hardly ever are sunk intentionally by those on board. When an iceberg ripped great holes in the hull of the *Titanic*, the captain and crew were just as shocked as the passengers. The *Lusitania* was sunk by a German submarine, not by a suicidal pilot. More recently, two hundred lives were lost when an English Channel ferry sank shortly after leaving the port of Dover. The disaster was certainly unplanned, not designed by owners or passengers.

Sometimes we hear of ships sinking due to carelessness, drunkenness, or over-confidence. Some shipwrecks must be chalked up to "human error." Hymeneus and Alexander of ancient Ephesus, shipwrecked their faith. Perhaps their intentions were good, but the result was disastrous. Paul indicates in our lesson that they were guilty of blasphemy. Probably they had allowed themselves to be seduced by some false doctrine. Maybe they had fallen under the spell of a charismatic cult leader of their day. Whatever their sin and whatever its cause, the scuttling of their faith could have been avoided by holding fast to the instructions and prophecies of the glorious gospel and by maintaining a clear conscience.

Our ship of faith travels sea lanes that are often perilously mined with heresies, doubts, fears, and temptations. None of us *intend* to scuttle our Christianity, but unless we remain alert and sensitive, disciplined and obedient, we risk spiritual shipwreck. Paul's advice to Timothy and the example of the Ephesian heretics can help us keep our faith afloat.   —R. W. B.

Conclusion

A. Garbage In, Garbage Out

We are living in the midst of a battle for our minds. Whatever we take into our minds is likely to come out in what we say and do. That's why Paul was so concerned about what we teach and what we pay attention to.

This is not just a matter of what religious teaching we pay attention to. It involves what we pay attention to on TV, in newspapers and magazines, in books. There is a law of the landfill—"garbage in, garbage out." The fruit of the Spirit (Galatians 5:22, 23) is not easily produced in a mind full of garbage. Good living is born in a mind full of good (Philippians 4:8).

B. Prayer

Heavenly Father, we are continually bombarded by a multitude of words that claim to be the truth. Please help us, guide us, and give us Your Spirit of discernment. Motivate us to study Your truth and make it a part of our lives. Guard us against the world's lies. In the name of Jesus we pray. Amen.

C. Thought to Remember

The goal of Christian teaching is love out of a pure heart, a good conscience, and a sincere faith.

Home Daily Bible Readings

Monday, July 20—Don't Teach False Doctrines (1 Timothy 1:1-4)

Tuesday, July 21—Teaching and the Law (1 Timothy 1:5-11)

Wednesday, July 22—Paul, an Example (1 Timothy 1:12-17)

Thursday, July 23—Paul Teaches About Prayer (1 Timothy 2:1-7)

Friday, July 24—Qualifications for Bishop (1 Timothy 3:1-7)

Saturday, July 25—The Teacher Is Judged (James 3:1-5)

Sunday, July 26—Shun Strange Teachings (Hebrews 13:9-16)

Learning by Doing

This page contains an alternate lesson plan emphasizing learning activities. Classes desiring such student involvement will find these suggestions helpful.

Learning Goals

As a result of this lesson students should:

1. Realize that we all teach by word or by example.

2. Evaluate religious teaching they hear or read, comparing it with what the Bible says.

3. Build unity and love among Christians.

Into the Lesson

Begin by saying, "Whether we realize it or not, we are all teachers. What do we teach, and how well do we teach it?" Mention ways in which some of the class members teach. Examples are:

As Sunday-school teachers

As leaders of youth groups in the church

As members of civic groups

As helpers in public schools

As parents in the home.

Continue by asking, "What do you teach?" Ask students to consider what their attitudes, actions, and words teach about the following: prayer, church attendance, patience, forgiveness, giving, Bible study.

Close this part of the lesson by emphasizing again that all of us teach. It is important that our teaching be "sound doctrine."

Into the Word

Divide the class into groups of three to five students. Give each group one of the following questions written on a card, or put the questions on the chalkboard (without the answers printed in parentheses). If you have more than three groups, two or more groups can have the same question.

Group 1. What do these verses from 1 Timothy 1 tell about false teachers or false teachings?

v. 4 (They stir up questions and quarrels.)

v. 6 (They lead to meaningless discussion).

v. 7 (They don't know what they're talking about.)

v. 19 (They put away a good conscience.)

What additional information do you find in:

Ephesians 4:14-(They are crafty and deceitful.)

Colossians 2:8-(They teach human traditions.)

Colossians 2:20-23 (They have many prohibitions.)

1 Timothy 6:20 (They claim to be scientific.)

Hebrews 13:9 (They have various strange doctrines.)

Group 2. What elements of sound teaching are seen in these Scriptures?

Ephesians 2:8-10 (Saved by grace through faith.)

Colossians 2:12 (Buried and raised with Christ.)

Acts 2:38 (Repent and be baptized.)

1 Corinthians 15:3 (Christ died for our sins.)

2 Timothy 3:16 (Scripture is inspired of God.)

Group 3. The goal of Christian teaching is love (or charity). What clue do these verses of 1 Timothy tell us about love?

1:5 (It comes from a pure heart, a good conscience, and sincere faith.)

1:14 (It abounds along with grace and faith.)

4:12 (Timothy should set a good example of love along with other things.)

6:11 (A man of God should continue faithfully in love and other good things.)

Make a list of characteristics of love found in 1 Corinthian 13.

After ten or fifteen minutes, ask a spokesman from each group to summarize his group's findings. Write the summaries on the chalkboard.

Into Life

Let the whole class discuss these questions:

Question 1. How can we properly evaluate the truth of what we read in books, hear in sermons, or listen to in our Bible-school class?

(Try to steer the discussion to include these:

1. Be sure you understand what is being said before you form an opinion.

2. Compare what you hear with what you already know about Bible teaching.

3. Be alert for the characteristics of false teaching discovered by Group 1.)

Question 2. At what point does a teaching cross the line between "a matter of opinion" and "false teaching"?

(Probably no specific point can be defined, but the discussion can be helpful. Help the students to understand that we can have different opinions without denying the Scriptures. For instance, some students thought the world would end about 1972. Time proved them mistaken, but they were faithful believers.

However, some teachings of Scripture are so plain that they cannot be denied without contradicting God's Word. Some of them were indicated in the work of Group 2. These we want to hold firmly and teach powerfully.)

Let's Talk It Over

The questions on this page are designed to encourage review of the lesson Scriptures and to promote discussion of the lesson by the class. The answers provided are only discussion starters. Let your class talk it over from there.

1. Why is it important that a church's elders maintain a careful oversight of the teaching programs?

Young children are impressionable; new converts are eager to learn; and neither are in a position to separate truth from error. In any church there is a danger of doctrinal error. Those who teach are exposed to a good deal of popular but erroneous religious opinion, the vigorously-propagated doctrines of cults, and the frequently watered-down or twisted teachings set forth over radio or television. False doctrines regarding the person of Christ, the nature of salvation, the work of the Holy Spirit, and the reality of Heaven and Hell can influence any Christian who is undiscerning. Such influence can affect a teacher's classroom presentation. For the sake of both teachers and those who are taught, the elders need to practice vigilance.

2. How can we practice discernment when we are reading religious literature or viewing religious programming on radio or television?

One obvious way is to keep our Bible handy. When Bible passages are cited in support of a suspicious-sounding claim, we can look them up and see if they really mean what the writer or speaker says they do. It is a good practice to jot down notes and questions about anything that puzzles or disturbs us. Then we can take these to a minister or elder or other dependable Bible teacher for further explanation. Perhaps we can watch or listen to religious programs in company with Christian friends so we can discuss what we hear. We exercise caution in eating food from an unknown source, and we should be just as careful in tasting the religious fare in print or on the air.

3. How can we develop the kind of teaching that edifies or builds up us and others?

We fail to do this when our teaching is mostly negative. We can spend much of our time attacking false doctrines and erroneous interpretations of Scripture, and fail to supply something positive and helpful to our students. But even teaching that is positive and upbeat may be lacking in substance. Such teaching provides a bit of an emotional uplift, but it does not offer any intellectual stimulation, and it fails to affect the will.

The ideal lesson touches the mind, emotions, and will together. The teacher can contribute to that with a variety of approaches to the text. The students can also participate with personal experiences and anecdotes that tie in with the textual material. Both teacher and students must keep in mind the aim of a mutual building up in the faith.

4. What can we do to avoid pointless and unprofitable discussions in Bible-school classes?

First of all, let us postpone all discussion of sports, weather, our jobs, our hobbies, etc. Unless some of these have a direct bearing on the lesson at hand, they should be avoided. We have comparatively little time for group Bible study, and we should use it as efficiently as possible. Second, we must not linger long on personal opinions. Our job is to master what the Lord has said in regard to our thinking and behavior. We may have our opinions in regard to how the lesson text should be applied, but let us not lose sight of the text in the multitude of applications. Finally, let us not repeat old discussions over and over, when we should have taken action on them long ago. Discussion cannot be a substitute for action.

5. How can we develop the kind of teaching that prepares Christians to engage in spiritual warfare?

Perhaps we could introduce a stronger element of urgency and purpose into our teaching is we spoke of "battle planning sessions" instead of "Sunday-school classes." Or would that make people think we were going to fight with our brethren? We want to realize that the devil is living and active (1 Peter 5:8), and we need Biblical teaching for defensive armor against Satan's attacks and for offensive weapons to cast down Satan's strongholds (Ephesians 6:10-18; 2 Corinthians 10:4). Thinking back to question 3, we should note that sometimes it is necessary to expose the weaknesses and dangers of false doctrines, along with worldly philosophies and humanistic ethical standards. But when we do that, let us also stress the Christian alternatives and answers to these weapons of Satan. When we get rid of bad ideas we want to replace them with good ones.

Train Yourself in Godliness

LESSON SCRIPTURE: 1 Timothy 4.

PRINTED TEXT: 1 Timothy 4.

1 Timothy 4

1 Now the Spirit speaketh expressly, that in the latter times some shall depart from the faith, giving heed to seducing spirits, and doctrines of devils;

2 Speaking lies in hypocrisy; having their conscience seared with a hot iron;

3 Forbidding to marry, and commanding to abstain from meats, which God hath created to be received with thanksgiving of them which believe and know the truth.

4 For every creature of God is good, and nothing to be refused, if it be received with thanksgiving:

5 For it is sanctified by the word of God and prayer.

6 If thou put the brethren in remembrance of these things, thou shalt be a good minister of Jesus Christ, nourished up in the words of faith and of good doctrine, whereunto thou hast attained.

7 But refuse profane and old wives' fables, and exercise thyself rather unto godliness.

8 For bodily exercise profiteth little: but godliness is profitable unto all things, having promise of the life that now is, and of that which is to come.

9 This is a faithful saying, and worthy of all acceptation.

10 For therefore we both labor and suffer reproach, because we trust in the living God, who is the Saviour of all men, specially of those that believe.

11 These things command and teach.

12 Let no man despise thy youth; but be thou an example of the believers, in word, in conversation, in charity, in spirit, in faith, in purity.

13 Till I come, give attendance to reading, to exhortation, to doctrine.

14 Neglect not the gift that is in thee, which was given thee by prophecy, with the laying on of the hands of the presbytery.

15 Meditate upon these things; give thyself wholly to them; that thy profiting may appear to all.

16 Take heed unto thyself, and unto the doctrine; continue in them: for in doing this thou shalt both save thyself, and them that hear thee.

GOLDEN TEXT: Godliness is profitable unto all things, having promise of the life that now is, and of that which is to come.—1 Timothy 4:8b.

Guidelines for Ministry
Unit 1: Guidelines for Leading
(Lessons 8-10)

Lesson Aims

This lesson will help students:
1. Be alert to recognize false teaching.
2. Train themselves in godliness as well as physical fitness.
3. Recognize God's goal for them and evaluate their progress toward it.

Lesson Outline

INTRODUCTION
    A. From Being a "Mr." to Being an "Airman"
    B. Lesson Background
I. AVOID BAD TEACHING (1 Timothy 4:1-5)
    A. Source (v. 1)
    B. Result (v. 2)
    C. Samples (v. 3)
    D. Contradictions (vv. 4, 5)
II. BE A GOOD SERVANT (1 Timothy 4:6-10)
    A. What a Good Servant Does (v. 6)
       Good Ministers
    B. What a Good Servant Does Not Do (v. 7)
    C. A Good Servant's Training (v. 8)
       Soul Aerobics
    D. A Good Servant's Trust (vv. 9, 10)
III. BE A GOOD MODEL (1 Timothy 4:11-16)
    A. In Teaching (v. 11)
    B. In Life-style (v. 12)
       Age Discrimination
    C. In Leadership (v. 13)
    D. In Use of Gifts (v. 14)
    E. In Progress (v. 15)
    F. In Carefulness (v. 16)
CONCLUSION
    A. Our Mortality Rate
    B. Prayer
    C. Thought to Remember

Visual 9 of the visuals packet illustrates 1 Timothy 4:8. The visual is shown on page 412.

Introduction

A. From Being a "Mr." to Being an "Airman"

I raised my hand and made an oath; and suddenly I was transferred from a "Mr." (a civilian) to an "airman" (in the military). At first it did not seem to be much of a change, but soon I saw the difference. I received a uniform and went into training. First I trained to be an airman; then I trained for a specific task that fit my aptitudes. During the eight years I was in the service, I never ceased to be in some kind of upgrading, updating, progress.

When we become Christians, we make a similar transfer. The Christian has a new commander-in-chief, is on a different side, puts on a new uniform (is clothed with Christ, Galatians 3:27), carries God's armor (Ephesians 6:10-18), has a constant supply depot (the worship and educational program of the church), and has a hotline to headquarters (prayer).

The Christian is in God's army and is to be in constant training—first training to be a Christian, then training to use his gifts for God's purposes. We are never to quit upgrading, updating, and growing toward the "rank" that God has set as our goal.

B. Lesson Background

Some of us settle too easily into our Christianity, resting securely in knowing a few facts and being involved in church activities. We find it easier to stay put than to progress. Some of us rest on what someone else believes and teaches. We use that as a lazy-boy chair, and do not plan to grow and progress in our faith. We ought rather to advance constantly by avoiding bad teaching, being good servants, and being good models.

I. Avoid Bad Teaching
(1 Timothy 4:1-5)

A. Source (v. 1)

1. Now the Spirit speaketh expressly, that in the latter times some shall depart from the faith, giving heed to seducing spirits, and doctrines of devils.

The word *now* is from a Greek word that means "but." Chapter 3:15, 16 speaks of how one in the church ought to behave in harmony with God's plan (mystery) of godliness. Chapter 4 begins with a contrast: some will be detoured from that plan.

The Spirit speaketh emphasizes God's inspiration. Read Paul's statement in 1 Corinthians 2:12, 13.

Expressly, specifically, the Holy Spirit gave Paul the teaching recorded here.

The latter times refers to the Christian era, the time from Jesus' first coming to His return. That time provides the only opportunity man has for accepting or rejecting Christ. During that time some will *depart from the faith*. They will no longer believe the plain teaching of Christ and

His apostles. They will be led away from the faith when they listen to false teachings. Such teachings come from seducing spirits and devils. God's Spirit influences people to do things His way, and the devil's spirits influence people to do things his way. Satan can put ideas in people's minds that affect their actions: for example, "then entered Satan into Judas," and Judas betrayed Jesus (Luke 22:3-6).

There are teachings that come from the Spirit of truth, and teachings that come from the spirit of error. Christians have the responsibility to evaluate what they hear by the standard of God's Holy Word, which is inspired by the Spirit of truth.

B. Result (v. 2)

2. Speaking lies in hypocrisy; having their conscience seared with a hot iron.

A person who has degrees is called "Doctor" or "Reverend," is a fantastic speaker, and is backed by an organization may still be *speaking lies*. He may be "play acting," which is what the word *hypocrisy* means. He may speak superficial truth as a mask for deeper falsehood.

Jesus warned against "wolves" who come in "sheep's clothing" (Matthew 7:15). Paul said the devil disguises himself as a messenger of light, and so do his servants (2 Corinthians 11:14). A habit of lying sears the conscience, makes it insensitive to right and wrong.

C. Samples (v. 3)

3. Forbidding to marry, and commanding to abstain from meats, which God hath created to be received with thanksgiving of them which believe and know the truth.

Some false teachers forbade marriage, thinking that any sexual expression was sinful. Such teaching not only contradicted Paul's inspired word in 1 Corinthians 7:1-3; it also contradicted one of God's earliest pronouncements and one of His first beneficial acts for man (Genesis 2:18). What the false teachers said needed to be corrected by comparison with inspired Scripture.

False teachers also said people must abstain from certain foods. It is easy to turn to some passages in the Old Testament and see that many foods were forbidden. See Leviticus 11, for example. However, the law given to the Hebrew nation was not intended for the Church.

Some preachers now try to make us feel guilty by filling their sermons with things "a Christian is not supposed to do." Many of the specific "sins" preached against are not mentioned in the Bible. As I was growing up I used to hear a great deal of preaching against playing pool, playing

---

> **How to Say It**
>
> CHARISMA (Greek). *kah*-ris-mah.
> CHARIS (Greek). *kah*-ris.

---

cards, going to a skating rink, attending a movie, and other activities the Bible does not condemn. To those speakers, being a Christian did not mean acting and reacting with the kindness and the love of Jesus; it meant obeying the "do not's" the speakers believed in personally.

D. Contradictions (vv. 4, 5)

4. For every creature of God is good, and nothing to be refused, if it be received with thanksgiving.

The false teaching cited in verse 3 contradicted creation. God did not create anything that was evil in itself. God declared His creation and mankind to be "very good" (Genesis 1:31). It is our misuse of creation, not our use of it, that is wrong. Instead of being paranoid and running scared of strict prohibitions created by man, Paul tells us to receive God's gifts with thanksgiving.

5. For it is sanctified by the word of God and prayer.

The false teaching cited in verse 3 contradicts consecration. At one time God established dietary laws for His people. Perhaps one reason was that food often was not thoroughly cooked in those days. For example, people can get trichinosis from rare pork. But food that is set before us can be considered consecrated or set apart for our use (*sanctified by the word of God*). When did God sanctify it by His word? Jesus did it (Mark 7:18, 19), and God did it (Acts 10:9-16). The Holy Spirit inspired Paul to confirm it (Colossians 2:16).

Whenever we pray and thank God for the food in front of us, we are affirming that God has provided the food and has sanctified it (set it apart) for our benefit. To say that we must abstain from some wholesome foods is to contradict God's creation, God's Word, and the reason for prayer before eating.

II. Be a Good Servant (1 Timothy 4:6-10)

A. What a Good Servant Does (v. 6)

6. If thou put the brethren in remembrance of these things, thou shalt be a good minister of Jesus Christ, nourished up in the words of faith and of good doctrine, whereunto thou hast attained.

Paul said that Timothy would be a *good minister* if he pointed out to God's family the truths of the Christian faith. The word *minister* means "servant." A good minister is not necessarily one who preaches in the pulpit. All of us who are God's servants can be a good minister in their way.

Nourished up means growing as a Christian. Peter wrote, "As newborn babes, desire the sincere milk of the word, that ye may grow thereby" (1 Peter 2:2). The *words of faith* that nourish us are words of the Bible and of Christian teachers who believe the Bible and teach what it teaches. The Word of God nourishes us and equips us for every good work (2 Timothy 3:16, 17).

GOOD MINISTERS

Our ministerial association established an emergency chaplaincy program to assist police and firemen in serving the special needs of crime and crisis victims. We took training at the police academy, and frequently rode with officers to get acquainted and to counsel when we had opportunities. Some chaplains gave more time than others to this work. One preacher was fired by his congregation "for devoting too much of his time to non-members."

Whatever your opinion about that instance, you must acknowledge that many church members are confused about the role of professional ministers. Who is "boss" in the local church? What are the duties of located evangelists? How is the church best served and time best invested by today's minster?

Paul's advice to Timothy is instructive. Apparently the preacher is to concentrate on the preaching and teaching of sound doctrine, but his example also must train the flock in the pursuit of holiness. He may shape his own daily program, but he must be faithful in bringing people to salvation and mature discipleship.

—R. W. B.

B. What a Good Servant Does Not Do (v. 7)

7. But refuse profane and old wives' fables, and exercise thyself rather unto godliness.

A good servant does not get caught up in peoples' pet hobbies, pet peeves, pet imaginations— *old wives' fables*. The word *profane* means common, ordinary. It describes beliefs not derived from Scripture, but developed in the gossip of silly old women or men.

We are to be nourished on words of faith, not words of fables. Instead of being involved in trivial pursuits, we are to be involved in godliness training.

C. A Good Servant's Training (v. 8)

8. For bodily exercise profiteth little: but godliness is profitable unto all things, having promise of the life that now is, and of that which is to come.

Paul did not belittle physical exercise. The more sedate our daily activities are, the more we need *bodily exercise*. Medical science affirms its value in stress reduction, blood-pressure management, healthy hearts and lungs, and a strong immune system. For this earthly life it profits much, but it *profiteth little* in comparison with *godliness*. Some students take this to mean that *bodily exercise profiteth* for a little while. It helps only as long as we live on earth.

Over against that, godliness *is profitable unto all things*. It has value not only for our physical lives, but also for our mental lives, our social lives, and our eternal lives. To be godly is to be Christlike. We are now discovering that such characteristics as generosity, patience, and forgiveness, are good for our health here on earth, and we certainly know they are good for our immortality in the world to come: Godliness promises good for *the life that now is, and of that which is to come*.

SOUL AEROBICS

The fitness craze is a phenomenon of our time. The exercise industry is one of our fastest growing enterprises. Millions of dollars are invested in spas, and other millions in home-exercise machines.

Christians naturally have jumped on this fitness bandwagon, for we regard our bodies as temples of God. We want to protect and sustain good health for eternal reasons as well as temporal.

Paul writes that physical exercise is a little profitable, but godliness has both finite and infinite dimensions, with implications for life now and life hereafter.

Some workout programs combine the stimulation of muscles, mind, and spirit simultane-

visual 9

ously. Scriptures, prayers, and Christian music accompany the calisthenic routines. Such a holistic approach seems appropriate for believers. Spiritual fitness requires proper diet and exercise, and the disciplines of prayer, worship, and Christian service. Keep your muscles toned and your heart tuned—to God's will.   —R. W. B.

D. A Good Servant's Trust (vv. 9, 10)

9. This is a faithful saying, and worthy of all acceptation.

Believe it! God says godliness is good for us both here and hereafter. We can depend on that.

10. For therefore we both labor and suffer reproach, because we trust in the living God, who is the Saviour of all men, specially of those that believe.

Taking God at His word, we work hard to be godly. We accept whatever reproach or ridicule it brings us. False teachers put their trust in themselves and their rules, but *we trust in the living God*. God is the *Saviour of all men*: that is, He is ready, willing, and able to save all. *Specially* He is the Savior *of those that believe*, those who trust in Him. They are the ones who are actually saved. To *trust in the living God* is to adopt His way as our way. How do we know about His way? We know about it through Jesus. God is like Jesus. When we learn about Jesus' life and attitudes, imitate them, confess our sins and failures, and beg forgiveness, we become godly and enjoy the benefits of godliness now and forever.

III. Be a Good Model
(1 Timothy 4:11-16)

A. In Teaching (v. 11)

11. These things command and teach.

Read all of 1 Timothy to see what *things* he was to *command and teach*. The word *command* here represents the same Greek word that was translated "charge" in last week's lesson (1:3). Timothy was to charge certain people not to teach false doctrines: he was to teach about prayer and about women (chapter 2); he was to teach about bishops and deacons (chapter 3); he was to teach the matters seen in this text.

B. In Life-style (v. 12)

12. Let no man despise thy youth; but be thou an example of the believers, in word, in conversation, in charity, in spirit, in faith, in purity.

Timothy was younger than many of the people to whom he ministered. Sometimes we allow age to be a barrier. Either we think people who are much older do not have anything to share or people who are much younger do not have

enough experience. Instead of looking at age, we need to look at a person's Christlikeness.

The word *example* means a pattern for others to copy. Timothy was to set a good example in several ways, and so are we: 1) *in word*—in what we say and how we say it; 2) *in conversation*—in the antique English of our version, this means the way we act, our life-style; 3) *in charity*—in sincere, unselfish, active, helpful love; *in spirit*—having our human spirit influenced by the fullness of the Holy Spirit; 5) *in faith*—in what we believe and whom we trust; 6) *in purity*—in sincerity, having only good motives. We are to set an example in a variety of ways, from what we say to our inner motivations.

AGE DISCRIMINATION

In recent years, our society has become concerned about the rights and privileges of senior citizens. New laws forbid discriminating against them merely on account of age.

It seems that Timothy's culture had an opposite age-discrimination problem. Paul thought his young protege might be discriminated against because he was so young. Age was generally revered in that time and place. Young people, on the other hand, were suspect because they lacked experience.

Actually, there is still discrimination against both the elderly and the young. The optimum age bracket, as perceived by employers, voters, and consumers, seems to be the middle years. Both the young and the old sense a handicap in finding employment, winning elections, or simply generating confidence.

Christians must exercise care in selecting leaders. Age should not be the biggest consideration. Christian workers earn respect by providing a good example of holiness and faithfulness, perfectly practicing what they preach. —R. W. B.

C. In Leadership (v. 13)

13. Till I come, give attendance to reading, to exhortation, to doctrine.

Paul had gone to Macedonia (1:3), but apparently he meant to join Timothy in Ephesus later. In his absence, Timothy was to do what Paul would do if he were there. *Reading* probably means especially the reading of Scripture. *Exhortation* is urging or encouraging people to live by the Scripture. *Doctrine* is simply teaching.

D. In Use of Gifts (v. 14)

14. Neglect not the gift that is in thee, which was given thee by prophecy, with the laying on of the hands of the presbytery.

Apparently Paul or some other prophet had received from God an inspired prophetic message that Timothy was called to a special ministry and gifted with special ability for it. This happened *with the laying on of the hands of the presbytery*: that is, when the elders laid their hands on Timothy to ordain him to his ministry. Timothy knew of his gift, and Paul told him not to neglect it. The word *gift* is the Greek word *charisma*, which comes from *charis*, grace. By the grace of God every Christian has been gifted with some ability or talent that can benefit others (Romans 12:4-8; 1 Corinthians 12:4-11). We are to develop our gifts and not allow them to become stagnant.

If you don't know whether or not you are gifted in a certain area, try it. Don't make excuses for doing nothing by saying, "I'm not gifted in that area." A teenager learning to drive may not shift gears smoothly at first. Does he then give up, saying, "I'm not gifted to drive"? A child learning to walk may fall down. Does he say, "I won't try anymore. I'm not gifted in that area"? How much God has lost because his people excuse themselves from serving by saying, "I'm not gifted"! Perhaps we will all be shocked when we get to Heaven and learn how much God has gifted us and how little of His gifts we gave back to Him in service.

E. In Progress (v. 15)

15. Meditate upon these things; give thyself wholly to them; that thy profiting may appear to all.

We are a rush-aholic, go-aholic people, but the Bible suggests that we take time to meditate (Psalm 119:15, 97; Philippians 4:8). But meditating about good things is not the end. Paul says also, *give thyself wholly to them*. When we do that, we will both develop our inner selves and demonstrate our outer selves. People will see

our progress—*that thy profiting may appear to all*. Into what are we progressing? Into the image of God's Son (Romans 8:29; 2 Corinthians 3:18; Ephesians 4:11-15). Are we more like Christ today than yesterday? If we are born again, we are to grow up into the likeness of the one who begat us—we are to become godlike.

F. In Carefulness (v. 16)

16. Take heed unto thyself, and unto the doctrine; continue in them: for in doing this thou shalt both save thyself, and them that hear thee.

In order to progress toward Christlikeness, we must be careful about:

1. Ourselves. Don't do something just because it feels good. Do what really is good—for others as well as yourself.

2. Doctrine. Our teaching should square with Biblical truths.

3. Continuation. We must take care to progress, not just start.

4. Saving ourselves. We must take care not to be castaway as we are ministering to others. Paul talked about that in 1 Corinthians 9:27.

5. Saving others. It is possible to be so concerned about self that we neglect people around us.

This verse begins with concern for self, but ends with concern for others. We are to love others as we love ourselves.

Conclusion

A. Our Mortality Rate

Given enough time, the mortality rate for all mankind is a hundred percent. While we are in the process of dying, we are to be also in the process of advancing. Paul put it this way; "Though outwardly we are wasting away, yet inwardly we are being renewed day by day" (2 Corinthians 4:16, *New International Version*).

Our destiny is not determined by the outer self. It is determined by the inner self. Ask yourself, "Is my inner self staying in shape through continuous and effective training in godliness?"

B. Prayer

Thank you, Father, for knowing our weakness and touching it with strength, for knowing our fallen state and reaching out to us with your hand, for knowing our spirits and filling them with Your divine Spirit. In Jesus' name. Amen.

C. Thought to Remember

The outer person is decaying daily—we can't stop it. The inner person is to be renewed daily—let's not stop that.

Home Daily Bible Readings

Monday, July 27—Some Heed False Teaching (1 Timothy 4:1-5)

Tuesday, July 28—Godliness Is of Value (1 Timothy 4:6-10)

Wednesday, July 29—Set an Example (1 Timothy 4:11-16)

Thursday, July 30—Learn to Love (1 Timothy 5:1-8)

Friday, July 31—"All Things to All Men" (1 Corinthians 9:19-24)

Saturday, Aug. 1—Seek God's Guidance (Psalm 27:7-14)

Sunday, Aug. 2—"Walk in the Spirit" (Galatians 5:13-26)

Learning by Doing

This page contains an alternate lesson plan emphasizing learning activities. Classes desiring such student involvement will find these suggestions helpful.

Learning Goals

As a result of participation in today's lesson, students should:

1. Identify specific tasks of godliness.
2. Understand the training required to perform each task.
3. Plan and make some improvement in their own godly lives.

Into the Lesson

Early in the week before the class session, ask two or three members of the class (or outside guests) who have undergone training for a specific job or task to join you in a panel discussion and briefly share with the class a description of the task and the specific training that was required. Explain that the purpose is to emphasize the importance of preparation and training. (You may ask someone in the medical profession to describe his or her training, someone in the armed services to describe preparation for a mission, someone in sales to describe sales training, a secretary to tell of learning computer skills, or a teacher to tell about preparation in college and student teaching. You may ask your preacher to talk about his Bible-college training. A carpenter or bricklayer or machinist may tell how he learned his trade. You will want to note that skill is perfected by actually working at the job. Serve as a moderator, asking specific questions like, "Was the training more difficult than the task?" or "Did the training really prepare you for the task?" Conclude the panel discussion with a comment to the effect that if we want quality performance from a worker, we must expect to provide quality training.

Split the class into groups of three to five students each. Give each group these instructions: "Suppose you were given the task of training someone to be a Christian. As a group, decide what the task of a Christian is. Decide what training would prepare a person for that task." Allow the groups eight to twelve minutes to prepare their answers. Let them report their findings to the class.

Into the Word

Have the students turn to the fourth chapter of 1 Timothy. Ask someone to read the text aloud. As the text is read, have people hold up their hands when they hear something that indicates godly living. It may be either a positive encouragement or something ungodly to be avoided. For example, "Be thou an example" (v. 12) is a positive encouragement; "Some shall depart from the faith" (v. 1) indicates an ungodly act to be avoided.

The discussion should include the following negative and positive guides for godly living:

Verse 1. Do not follow deceiving spirits.
Verse 2. Do not be hypocritical.
Verse 2. Do not let your conscience be seared.
Verse 3. Receive God's gifts with thanks.
Verse 6. Follow good teaching.
Verse 7. Avoid godless myths and gossip.
Verse 10. Trust in the living God.
Verse 12. Set an example in every way.
Verse 13. Do much reading and teaching.
Verse 14. Do not neglect your gift.
Verse 15. Be diligent in these matters.
Verse 16. Watch what you do and what you teach.

Into Life

Give each student paper and pencil for the final part of today's lesson. You should also have several study Bibles or concordances for students to use. Have each student select an area of godliness that he or she would like to develop personally and write the phrase from 1 Timothy 4 that deals with that area. Using a concordance or study Bible with cross references, they then may find one or more other references in the Bible to support this encouragement to godliness. Finally, the students may write specific ways that they intend to put the encouragement into effect in their own lives. You may use the following example to help explain the assignment to your students.

Example of Godliness: Give attendance [attention] to reading, to exhortation, to doctrine (v. 13).

Cross References: 2 Timothy 3:16; Luke 4:16; Acts 13:14-16; Colossians 4:16

Application to My Life: I will read through the whole Bible in the coming year. I will read one book by a Christian writer each month. I will take notes on the sermons preached at my church each week.

If the students complete this before the class period ends, they may repeat the process with another area of godliness—and as many other areas as time allows.

Let's Talk It Over

The questions on this page are designed to encourage review of the lesson Scriptures and to promote discussion of the lesson by the class. The answers provided are only discussion starters. Let your class talk it over from there.

1. The term "doctrines of devils" may remind us of the growing popularity of Satanism in our time. What are some of today's "doctrines of devils"?

Some recent movies seem to suggest that Satan is all-powerful. Evil triumphs over good, and the demonic powers are able to prevail over Christian representatives and symbols in these films. The suggestion that Satan is irresistible and invincible is certainly a demonic doctrine. On the other hand, various occult practices are often viewed as harmless or mere fun. Some people are lightly participating in seances, exploring astrology, and dabbling in witchcraft. Satan must be pleased with the teaching that there can be no harm in these activities.

2. Paul was speaking about our diet when he asserted that "every creature of God is good, and nothing to be refused, if it be received with thanksgiving." How may we apply this to our dietary circumstances today?

We have been taught to look on our food with a measure of suspicion. It may contain too many calories, too much cholesterol, or an excessive amount of sodium. To be thankful for our food may be difficult when we perceive it as a threat to our health and well-being. Of course many of our dietary problems have resulted from man's creation of "junk food." We can express our unreserved gratitude for fresh fruits and vegetables, but we can also thank God for the meat, the canned goods, and the other processed foods we partake of in sensible amounts.

3. What other comparisons may we draw between physical exercise and spiritual exercise?

Regular exercise is what contributes to physical health. Spiritual exercise also requires a consistent effort in personal prayer and Bible study, in worship, fellowship, and service. Worthwhile physical exercise requires effort. The athlete gains by pushing himself or herself. The spiritual athlete must also push, toil, press on with a genuine effort. Christianity was not meant to be easy. Paul spoke in 1 Corinthians 9:24-27 of rigorously disciplining himself in order to run successfully the Christian race. We need to follow his example, "get tough with ourselves," and press on toward spiritual goals.

4. How would it affect the church if every member were to aim to be a living example of what a Christian should be?

Paul urged, "Follow my example, as I follow the example of Christ" (1 Corinthians 11:1, *New International Version*). If we were to pattern ourselves after Jesus Christ himself, a sense of compassion, caring, and love would pervade the congregation. Visitors would feel it and would be drawn to the Christ who inspired it. The work of the church would be accomplished promptly and enthusiastically. The worship offered to God would be irresistible in its heavenward pull. The witness of the church to its unsaved neighbors would be powerful. The church would become the dynamic force it is meant to be.

5. How can we lead members of the church to recognize and put to use their gifts for service?

We put emphasis on gifts of leadership, and this is good. However, we may neglect proper attention to less prominent gifts. Some individuals have a special ability for ministering to the needy; others are good at telephoning absentees; still others have a gift for writing or editorial work that could be utilized in connection with the Sunday bulletin and the church newsletter. It may be well to review Biblical teaching about the variety of gifts that can be used to enhance the church's worship, teaching, and outreach.

6. Why do we need to take time to meditate on spiritual truths?

Since meditation is associated with certain pagan religions, we may be inclined to be wary of it. But the Bible refers to it as desirable. In Psalm 119:97, for example, we find the psalmist exclaiming, "O how love I thy law! It is my meditation all the day." God is interested in our thoughts. If we meditate on money or pleasure or the bolstering of our ego, that displeases Him. Such meditation tends toward greed and selfishness. But thoughts of spiritual truths inspire words and actions that edify others and glorify God. Memorizing Scripture, praying over Biblical truths, and cherishing Scriptural promises are practical ways of meditating that result in lasting good.

Set Your Priorities

LESSON SCRIPTURE: 1 Timothy 6:2c-21.

PRINTED TEXT: 1 Timothy 6:6-14, 17-21.

1 Timothy 6:6-14, 17-21

6 But godliness with contentment is great gain.

7 For we brought nothing into this world, and it is certain we can carry nothing out.

8 And having food and raiment, let us be therewith content.

9 But they that will be rich fall into temptation and a snare, and into many foolish and hurtful lusts, which drown men in destruction and perdition.

10 For the love of money is the root of all evil: which while some coveted after, they have erred from the faith, and pierced themselves through with many sorrows.

11 But thou, O man of God, flee these things; and follow after righteousness, godliness, faith, love, patience, meekness.

12 Fight the good fight of faith, lay hold on eternal life, whereunto thou art also called, and hast professed a good profession before many witnesses.

13 I give thee charge in the sight of God, who quickeneth all things, and before Christ Jesus, who before Pontius Pilate witnessed a good confession;

14 That thou keep this commandment without spot, unrebukable, until the appearing of our Lord Jesus Christ.

· · · · · · · · · · · · ·

17 Charge them that are rich in this world, that they be not high-minded, nor trust in uncertain riches, but in the living God, who giveth us richly all things to enjoy;

18 That they do good, that they be rich in good works, ready to distribute, willing to communicate;

19 Laying up in store for themselves a good foundation against the time to come, that they may lay hold on eternal life.

20 O Timothy, keep that which is committed to thy trust, avoiding profane and vain babblings, and oppositions of science falsely so called:

21 Which some professing have erred concerning the faith. Grace be with thee. Amen.

Aug 9

GOLDEN TEXT: Follow after righteousness, godliness, faith, love, patience, meekness.
—1 Timothy 6:11b.

Guidelines for Ministry
Unit 1: Guidelines for Leading
(Lessons 8-10)

Lesson Aims

This lesson is designed to help students:
1. Assess their attitudes about their material assets.
2. Develop a plan for increasing their material investment in kingdom work.

Lesson Outline

INTRODUCTION
  A. The Glen Penrods
  B. Lesson Background
I. PRIORITY OF CONTENTMENT (1 Timothy 6:6-10)
  A. It Is Profitable (v. 6)
  B. It Is Realistic (v. 7)
  C. It Accepts (v. 8)
    The Discipline of Simplicity
  D. Its Enemy—Greed (vv. 9, 10)
II. PRIORITIES IN LIVING (1 Timothy 6:11-14)
  A. Fleeing and Following (v. 11)
  B. Fighting (v. 12)
  C. Keeping (vv. 13, 14)
III. PRIORITIES FOR THE RICH (1 Timothy 6:17-19)
  A. Trust in God (v. 17)
    Uncertain Riches
  B. Do Good (v. 18)
  C. Take Hold of Real Life (v. 19)
IV. SUMMARY OF PRIORITIES (1 Timothy 6:20, 21)
CONCLUSION
  A. Attitude and Altitude
  B. Prayer
  C. Thought to Remember

Display visual 10 of the visuals packet and let it remain before the class throughout this session. The visual is shown on page 420.

Introduction

A. The Glen Penrods

I was teaching a men's Sunday-school class when they came to church. Both had been married more than once. They had spent many years bar hopping. Glen, the husband, was unemployed. They certainly were unlikely people to become members of the church, but they came forward to become Christians.

Later the preacher told me a shattering bit of news—at least it was shattering to a guy who had been a Christian for a while and was teaching a Bible class. The news was that Glen began to tithe his unemployment check as soon as he became a Christian. He lined up his priorities immediately.

This prompted me to evaluate my own priorities. I began to tithe for the first time in my life, and what blessings I immediately began to discover!

B. Lesson Background

Christians at Ephesus soon straightened out their priorities with material assets. Many had been in pagan professions that were anti-Christian. They gave up those professions and even burned their tools (books). The assets they burned were worth fifty thousand days' wages (Acts 19:18, 19). They would not even have a garage sale, for they knew their anti-Christian tools (books) should not be used by anyone. Then we read an amazing report in the very next verse, "In this way the word of the Lord spread widely and grew in power" (Acts 19:20, *New International Version*).

The Christians in Ephesus would not let their assets support non-Christian practices. It is something else to use material possessions to directly support Christian causes, to help the needy, to spend as God would spend if He were here in person. Our lesson today deals with that issue.

I. Priority of Contentment (1 Timothy 6:6-10)

A. It Is Profitable (v. 6)

6. But godliness with contentment is great gain.

Godliness comes by being forgiven and becoming like Christ in attitudes and actions, thus imitating our Heavenly Father. Some people claim to be godly—"holier than thou"—but remain uneasy, unsettled, and always unsatisfied. There is little gain in that kind of godliness; in fact, there is no such thing as thorough godliness without contentment.

Contentment means being happy with the necessary things, not always struggling to accumulate more. We do not try to get ahead of others. We do not envy what others have. A person's happiness is not measured by what he has, but by what he shares.

What is the *great gain* the apostle Paul speaks of? Here are some dividends of godliness with contentment:
  1. We can love the way God loves.
  2. We can share as God shares.
  3. Our relationship with God is improved.

4. Our gratitude overflows.

5. Our relationships are free of envy.

6. We are not possessed by things.

7. We are not shackled by greed.

8. Our priorities are right.

9. We have peace, not the stress of anxiety and worry.

10. We give cheerfully when the church needs money for kingdom work.

11. Great gain includes treasures in Heaven with dividends continually building up (Matthew 6:19-24).

12. Contentment allows us to have life in its fullness; contentment allows us to be rich in good deeds.

B. It Is Realistic (v. 7)

7. For we brought nothing into this world, and it is certain we can carry nothing out.

Have you ever seen a U-Haul truck filled with a person's possessions following a hearse? No, and you probably never will either. We all know we can't take our possessions with us. We are eternal, but our material possessions are only temporary.

Someone may think, "I was born with plenty of wealth waiting for me." Yes, but you did not bring it; you did not produce it; you did not control it at that time. Someone else may think, "At death I will have accumulated a lot." Yes, but you will not be able to use any of it. If you keep it till you die you will miss the joy of sharing. Greed that hoards for self is unrealistic. Godliness with contentment is realistic. It sees that wealth is useless unless it is used. It allows us to share.

C. It Accepts (v. 8)

8. And having food and raiment, let us be therewith content.

Food is necessary for life, and raiment is necessary for life among other people. We accept these with gratitude realizing that they are gifts from God. Who can have food and clothing without sunshine and rain to make the raw materials grow? Who can manufacture sunshine and rain? If we make our clothes, we make them with abilities God has given us. If we buy our food, we buy it with money earned by muscle or mind that God has given us. So we accept these needed things with thanks; and if we do not have everything we want, we accept the lack and are contented still. Perhaps our lack is also a gift from God. It may keep us from being proud and arrogant. It may remind us that we are not self-sufficient. How happily we can be content with poverty if the kingdom of God is ours! (Luke 6:20).

THE DISCIPLINE OF SIMPLICITY

Doris Janzen Longacre's book, *Living More With Less*, reports "the experiences of people trying to live by standards of simplicity." She describes it as an old-fashioned testimony meeting. The "testimonies" share information about saving money, time, and natural resources. Ideas include inexpensive menus, preventive care maintenance, wedding rings made from paper clips, and homemade coffins. Some of the suggestions do seem a bit bizarre, but the contributors are godly folk making sincere efforts to conserve, to share, and to exercise conscientious stewardship. They take seriously Paul's advice to Timothy about the dangers of materialism and the blessings of simplicity.

By Longacre's own admission, living the simple life is not simple. It can be difficult and demanding, but God's Word promises (and experience bears out) that the discipline of simplicity is uniquely rewarding. One of Christ's requirements for discipleship is self-denial, and that is where simplicity begins.

Paul reduces the necessities of life to the basics of food and clothing. And Jesus said that we shouldn't be overly concerned even about those items (Matthew 6:25-33). Simple living is a formidable challenge, especially for affluent Americans. Most of us, to some extent, have conformed to the world's distorted perception of what we actually need. Isn't it time for Christians to begin practicing genuine self-denial?

—R. W. B.

D. Its Enemy—Greed (vv. 9, 10)

9. But they that will be rich fall into temptation and a snare, and into many foolish and hurtful lusts, which drown men in destruction and perdition.

Greed is a deadly *snare. They that will be rich* does not mean simply those who are going to be rich; it means those who desire to be rich, those whose will is set on riches, those who make wealth their goal in life, who organize their priorities and make their decisions in order to reach that goal. Their desire governs what they say and do. Notice what a collection of unpleasant words it takes to describe the results of that desire: *temptation, snare, foolish, hurtful, lusts, drown, destruction, perdition.* A lot of negative words in one verse. They add up to disaster.

How does our desire for riches cause us to fall into temptation? A person is tempted by his own desires (James 1:13, 14). The word *lust* means "desire." When we allow our desires to run wild, they become foolish and hurtful because: 1) we cannot afford them; 2) we put our desires above

God's will; 3) we become insensitive to the needs of others and live for self; 4) we use dishonest methods to get rich; 5) we mar our marriage and other relationships. Instead of floating in the satisfaction of riches, we drown. The desire to be rich propels us to destruction rather than to happiness.

10. For the love of money is the root of all evil: which while some coveted after, they have erred from the faith, and pierced themselves through with many sorrows.

Greed is a bad root. Money is not *the root of all evil*, but *the love of money* is. This does not mean the love of money is the only root of evil, but it is a root from which all kinds of evil grow. Robbery, fraud, embezzlement, injustice in the courts, pornography, the illegal drug traffic, the liquor traffic, abortion clinics, murder—can you think of anything bad that does not arise sometimes from the love of money?

Is love of money a problem in the church? Some people simply will not let go of their money to support the Master's work, because the object of their affection is not the Master. A miser may love money for itself; others love it for what it can get them—independence, luxury, services, recognition, power, status, prestige.

What are you working for? What do you want? The object of our affection determines our priorities, and our priorities determine our actions. Not all rich men love money more then the Master. Think of God's fine servants who were rich—Abraham, Job, David, and others. It is hard for a rich man to enter the kingdom of God, "but with God all things are possible" (Matthew 19:23-26). It is not important to be rich or to be poor; it is important to love the Master more than money. The desire to be rich focuses affection on riches. The desire to serve God focuses attention on His will. If one loves God most of all, he can use money for the benefit of others and his own eternal benefit (Luke 16:9).

People who have shifted their affection from the Master to money have *erred from the faith*.

THE PRICELESS PRIZE

visual 10

They have *pierced themselves through with many sorrows*. They have lost goodness and character. They have alienated themselves from family, friends, and God—and they have been disappointed to find that money cannot make them happy.

II. Priorities in Living
(1 Timothy 6:11-14)

A. Fleeing and Following (v. 11)

11. But thou, O man of God, flee these things; and follow after righteousness, godliness, faith, love, patience, meekness.

Do you know someone who might be called a man of money, or a man of gadgets, or a man of fun? Paul called Timothy a *man of God*. Timothy found his satisfaction in God. But a *man of God* must be self-disciplined, for the lure of the material is real and powerful. Paul told Timothy to flee and to follow.

To *flee these things* is to flee from the snare, the lust, the drowning environment (v. 9), and the love of money (v. 10). But we are not just to flee into nowhere; we are to follow things approved of God: *righteousness*—right relationships; *godliness*—right attitudes; *faith*—right trust; *love*—right sharing; *patience*—right contentment; *meekness*—right reactions.

B. Fighting (v. 12)

12. Fight the good fight of faith, lay hold on eternal life, whereunto thou art also called, and hast professed a good profession before many witnesses.

Paul's advice to Timothy has moved from "flee" to "follow," and now it moves to *fight*. The word for *fight* is the Greek word from which our word "agonize" comes. It calls for strenuous effort, mental or physical or both. In this highly competitive, materialistic world, we must give a lot of energy to this activity. We must battle against the enemy who wants to misplace our priorities. This is not a fight of fists, but of faith. We are not to fight others in this competitive world just to get ahead. That is a bad fight. We are to fight *the good fight*, making every effort to *lay hold on eternal life*, not trying to lay hold on the temporary things of this life.

The *good profession* is often called "the good confession." That confession is not, "I take my possessions to be my Lord and Savior." It is, "I take Jesus Christ to be my Lord and Savior."

This confession was made *before many witnesses*, and our confession is not to be private either. When was Timothy's confession made? Probably at many different times: 1) at his first statement of belief that Jesus is the risen Lord, 2) at his baptism, 3) at his ordination, 4) during his preaching and teaching activities, 5) in his reaction to persecution, 6) in his persistence even when material possessions were lacking. Like Timothy, we declare our faith in Jesus again and again, by what we do as well as by what we say.

C. Keeping (vv. 13, 14)

13, 14. I give thee charge in the sight of God, who quickeneth all things, and before Christ Jesus, who before Pontius Pilate witnessed a good confession; that thou keep this commandment without spot, unrebukable, until the appearing of our Lord Jesus Christ.

When Paul said *I give thee charge*, he was in a sense saying, "Obey your orders as a good soldier in God's army." *In the sight of God* reminded Timothy of who the commander-in-chief is. God *quickeneth all things*. This means He gives life—energy, inspiration, encouragement, strength. Much as we depend on material food, it is God who gives life to all. Consequently we should continue to put our trust in God—even though it may look as if our last meal or our last dollar is gone. Nowhere do we see that better portrayed than in the life of Jesus. *Before Pontius Pilate* Jesus testified that He was the Christ, the Messiah. Pilate's term was "King of the Jews," but Jesus made it plain that His kingdom was greater than that—"not of this world" (John 18:33-37). Timothy would need to remember that example when he faced deprivation, disillusionment, and disappointments. And so do we.

The charge that Paul gave to Timothy was to *keep this commandment without spot, unrebukable*. The commandment was to flee from wrong, to follow after right, and to fight the fight of faith without being trapped and drowned by materialism. A person may gain material possessions while serving God, but that is not his basic motive.

Material things are temporary. We are to be thinking of the future and continuing our service *until the appearing of our Lord Jesus Christ*. When Jesus returns we will be joint-heirs with Christ, walk on streets of gold, and possess far more than what all the money on earth can buy.

III. Priorities for the Rich (1 Timothy 6:17-19)

A. Trust in God (v. 17)

17. Charge them that are rich in this world, that they be not high-minded, nor trust in uncertain riches, but in the living God, who giveth us richly all things to enjoy.

In worldly possessions, people considered poor in the United States are among the top five

Home Daily Bible Readings

Monday, Aug. 3—Priorities for Widows (1 Timothy 5:9-16)

Tuesday, Aug. 4—Priorities for Elders (1 Timothy 5:17-24)

Wednesday, Aug. 5—Priorities of Teachers (1 Timothy 6:1-10)

Thursday, Aug. 6—Set an Aim (1 Timothy 6:11-16)

Friday, Aug. 7—Priorities for the Rich (1 Timothy 6:17-21)

Saturday, Aug. 8—Priorities of Servants (1 Corinthians 9:13-18)

Sunday, Aug. 9—Righteousness as a Priority (1 John 3:7-12)

percent of the world's population. Read that again! When we consider the material possessions of everybody who is now alive, the poorest people in the United States are among the richest five percent of the world's people. If we want to compare, perhaps we ought to compare ourselves with people on the other side of the globe. But such comparisons are not a part of fighting the good fight.

Who are the *rich in this world*? They are those who have more than the food, clothing, and shelter necessary for life. You and I are among the rich. Comparison is one of the snares of riches. We compare ourselves with others who have more, and we become discontented because we have less. If we equate having more with being better, we begin to put our trust in what we have. That is a mistake. We are to put our trust in *the living God*—Him who is certain—instead of material things that are transient and uncertain. God is not just passing by; He is alive always and forever. He *giveth us richly all things to enjoy*: things spiritual as well as material, things eternal as well as temporary.

UNCERTAIN RICHES

Has Donald Trump, one of the world's richest men, fallen on hard times? He owes the banks more than three billion dollars. He may be forced to sell his yacht and some other assets. Sadder than that is the break-up of his marriage. He won't be able to buy back the trust and love he has lost. And wealth cannot purchase real estate in Heaven.

Timothy learned from Paul, and Paul from Jesus, how difficult it is for the rich to enter God's kingdom. It is like a camel going through the eye of a needle, Jesus said (Mark 10:23-27). Though possible with God, salvation for the wealthy probably will be found by only a few. The odds are against it, because trusting money is an occupational hazard for the rich. Riches appear to be trustworthy, but moths and rust corrupt; thieves break through and steal. Stock markets crash, wives and other plaintiffs sue, and trusted employees may rob the till. "Easy come, easy go" is all too true.

Trump, and everybody else, must trust "in the living God" for guaranteed security. When we talk about "learning the value of a dollar," we usually mean learning how much it is worth. We need rather to learn just how little value a dollar represents, how little of true worth there is in wealth. "Lay up for yourselves treasures in heaven!"

—R. W. B.

B. Do Good (v. 18)

18. That they do good, that they be rich in good works, ready to distribute, willing to communicate.

Why does God let us have more things than are absolutely necessary? He does it so we will have something to give to those in need (Ephesians 4:28). It is great gain to *be rich in good works* rather than to be rich in possessions. Our riches will not follow us when we die, but good works will (Revelation 14:13).

C. Take Hold of Real Life (v. 19)

19. Laying up in store for themselves a good foundation against the time to come, that they may lay hold on eternal life.

How do we lay up for ourselves *a good foundation*? Jesus told us how in Luke 16:10: "Whoever can be trusted with very little can also be trusted with much" (*New International Version*). If you have been trustworthy in handling worldly wealth, God will trust you with true riches in Heaven.

"I tell you, use worldly wealth to gain friends for yourselves, so that when it is gone, you will be welcomed into eternal dwellings" (Luke 16:9, *New International Version*). God wants us to use our wealth in such a way that eternal friends will be gained. One way to do this is to support evangelism and the teaching of Christians. Then when our wealth is gone, we will discover that those whom we have helped to become Christians will be in Heaven to welcome us. What a wonderful kind of treasure to have laid up in Heaven!

Someone has said that a truly wise person invests in that which outlasts life. Giving some of our wealth for God's work is an investment that will outlast life. Simon Peter once asked Jesus what the apostles would receive because they had given up so much. Jesus said they would re-

ceive a hundredfold—that's interest at the rate of ten thousand percent—and eternal life besides (Mark 10:28-30).

God is storing up for us significant rewards in the future. Our receiving them is based on our willingness to share with Him in the here and now. Only a foolish man who doesn't understand reality will fail to share what he cannot keep—his earthly wealth. Only a foolish man will fail to keep what he should not lose—his treasure in Heaven.

IV. Summary of Priorities (1 Timothy 6:20, 21)

20, 21. O Timothy, keep that which is committed to thy trust, avoiding profane and vain babblings, and oppositions of science falsely so called: which some professing have erred concerning the faith. Grace be with thee. Amen.

Paul summarized here the priorities mentioned in the letter—stick to the Word of God and do not be fooled by godless chatter or the opposing ideas of what is falsely called knowledge or *science*. Some who have been misled have *erred* (wandered) from the faith.

Paul ended the letter with a word that all of us need—grace, God's active kindness to us who do not deserve it. We receive grace so that same kind of kindness can flow through us to others. That spotlights the major priority in our life and from our life—God's grace.

Conclusion

A. Attitude and Altitude

Some have observed that our attitude determines our altitude. There is no greater altitude than godliness. Which of the following attitudes is yours? 1) What is mine is mine, and I will keep it—hoarding; 2) What is yours is mine, and I will take it—stealing; 3) What is mine is mine, and I will spend it on me—selfishness; 4) What is mine is God's, and I will share it when there is need—godliness.

B. Prayer

Our Heavenly Father, we recognize that no one has ever had or will ever have greater resources and riches than You. With that recognition comes our gratitude for what you provide for us day by day. Thank You for putting us on Your generosity list. In Jesus' name we pray. Amen.

C. Thought to Remember

Christlikeness is not weighed by the bigness of the purse but by the bigness of the heart.

Learning by Doing

This page contains an alternate lesson plan emphasizing learning activities. Classes desiring such student involvement will find these suggestions helpful.

Learning Goals

As a result of today's lesson, students should:

1. Examine the priorities they have set in their own lives.

2. Understand the Biblical principles for godly contentment.

Into the Lesson

Before class, procure some "play money"—enough for each member of your class to have five or six bills. During the class session, distribute the money to students for "nice" things they do—participate in the lesson, give a correct answer, offer a prayer, etc. Do this throughout the session, with no explanation. Try to have everyone participate and receive some money. Explanation of this activity is in the final segment of the lesson.

Prepare for the lesson by making a week's time chart, listing the hours from 8 A.M. till 10 P.M., Sunday through Saturday. The chart should look something like this but be much larger and include the rest of the hours till 10 P.M.

SUN	MON	TUE	WED	THU	FRI	SAT
8						
9						
10						

Give each student a chart. Let them map out their previous week's activities, including work, church, leisure activities, and other events, then add up the number of hours spent on each kind of activity. Conclude by saying, "Can you see by last week's schedule what your priorities are? Were you surprised?" (Allow for discussion.) "We want our priorities to be right, but it is hard to put first things first."

Into the Word

Write on notecards the following statements from the *New International Version* of the Bible.

1. The love of money is a root of all kinds of evil (1 Timothy 6:10).

2. Godliness with contentment is great gain (1 Timothy 6:6).

3. Some people, eager for money, have wandered from the faith (1 Timothy 6:10).

4. Some people, eager for money, have . . . pierced themselves with many griefs (1 Timothy 6:10).

5. People who want to get rich fall into temptation (1 Timothy 6:9).

Divide the class into five groups of three to five people. If your class is too small, eliminate one or more of the statements. Give each group a notecard with a statement. Make available concordances and study Bibles with cross references. Have each group discuss the following questions with respect to their statement:

a. What present-day examples show this to be true?

b. Why is this statement true?

c. What does this teach you about money or material possessions?

d. What does this teach you about priorities?

e. Using concordances, cross references, and study Bibles, what other Scriptures can you find to confirm this teaching?

After about ten or twelve minutes of research and discussion, reassemble the students into one group. Let members share what they have learned. Be sure those who have found other Scriptures have a chance to share them. Use thoughts from the lesson commentary to conclude this discussion.

Into Life

Begin the final part of the lesson by saying, "The secret of a contented life is to have our priorities in proper order. It would be easy to be content if money were handed out as readily as it has been in today's session. But God does supply our needs in other ways, doesn't He?" Have students read Proverbs 15:16; Philippians 4:11; Hebrews 13:5; and 1 Timothy 6:6-8. Lead into a discussion on contentment by asking "How can we practice godly contentment when everybody else seems to be measuring success by possessions and achievements?" Lead to the conclusion that we can be content when we achieve things that are more important to us. If we give priority to happy family relationships, maturing in Christ, serving in His church, and reaching the lost with the gospel, then material possessions will not seem too important.

Give each student a sheet of paper. Ask them to evaluate the things that are important to them by listing them on the paper. They may wish to reorder the priorities revealed by their schedule. Let each one think of specific things he or she can do this week to put them in proper order.

Let's Talk It Over

The questions on this page are designed to encourage review of the lesson Scriptures and to promote discussion of the lesson by the class. The answers provided are only discussion starters. Let your class talk it over from there.

1. How can we help people to see the folly of making the acquisition of riches their primary goal?

Jesus said, "A man's life consisteth not in the abundance of the things which he possesseth" (Luke 12:15); but this may be one of His least-accepted statements. It is easy to think the lack of material wealth is a major hindrance to our happiness. Perhaps it will help us to clarify our thinking if we do an analysis of our present possessions. If we own our home, are we happier than we were before? We can view our furniture and appliances, our automobile, our recreational equipment, and other possessions similarly. If these have not brought perfect contentment, why should we imagine that more possessions would do so?

2. Aside from robberies, murders, and political corruption, what are some common evils that result from the love of money?

Families are torn apart and friendships are destroyed by conflicts over money. Many people are victims of "get-rich" schemes. The love of money can dull a person's judgment and cause him to invest in an unsound venture. Finally, how does the quest for money affect the church? How many miss the church's services to work at second jobs out of the love of money? How many churches are struggling with financial problems because members are failing to give sacrificially?

3. How can a person flee from the love of money?

If the love of money is a genuine temptation, it may be unwise for us to spend much time at shopping malls. We may do well to switch off television commercials, keep catalogs and advertisements out of our sight. These suggestions may be extreme, but they acknowledge the danger in the influence of a materialistic society. But fleeing from the love of money also has a positive side. By putting an emphasis on values that are non-material, we can cool our affection for money. Serving fellow human beings in and through the church is one way. Investing some of our time in community enterprises is another. Simply working to strengthen family relationships can be one of the best.

4. How can we confess our faith in Christ by the way in which we handle our money and possessions?

First of all, we can look at the negative side of our actions. When Christians praise the life to come and then grasp for material things just as avidly as their neighbors, unbelievers are likely to be suspicious. When church leaders proclaim the importance of spreading the gospel, but give only a tiny percentage of their income to missions, it may impress some observers as hypocrisy. On the positive side, however, Christians and churches can make a powerful confession by a consecrated usage of their money. It does impress unbelievers when they see sacrificial giving by Christians to minister to the needy and to send missionaries to foreign lands.

5. How is it encouraging to know that God "giveth us richly all things to enjoy"?

This statement helps us maintain a balance in the way we view material things. Sometimes it may seem that Christians in our nation should feel guilty about enjoying their homes, food, and clothing when millions of people are physically and spiritually malnourished. But we do those needy people no good by partaking of God's gifts in sadness or shame. Of course we should share sacrificially with those in need, but the part we keep for ourselves we should use with enjoyment and thanksgiving. The statement above indicates that God wants us to be generally happy and content. His kind of happiness is consistent with holiness, discipline, service toward others, and appropriate self-denial; but it is a genuine happiness.

6. How can we be "rich in good works"?

This expression may bring to mind the deep satisfaction that comes from doing something to benefit others. To see the smile on the face of a child we have cheered, to hear the tearful thanks of a needy family to whom we have taken food, to witness the baptism of a person whom we have taught, to know we have given comfort to a bereaved neighbor—these experiences bring a warmth to our hearts that is indeed a treasure. And later we will know the riches of Jesus' commendation: "Well done, good and faithful servant" (Matthew 25:23).

Handle God's Word Rightly

LESSON SCRIPTURE: 2 Timothy 2:1-19.

PRINTED TEXT: 2 Timothy 2:1-15.

2 Timothy 2:1-15

1 Thou therefore, my son, be strong in the grace that is in Christ Jesus.

2 And the things that thou hast heard of me among many witnesses, the same commit thou to faithful men, who shall be able to teach others also.

3 Thou therefore endure hardness, as a good soldier of Jesus Christ.

4 No man that warreth entangleth himself with the affairs of this life; that he may please him who hath chosen him to be a soldier.

5 And if a man also strive for masteries, yet is he not crowned, except he strive lawfully.

6 The husbandman that laboreth must be first partaker of the fruits.

7 Consider what I say; and the Lord give thee understanding in all things.

8 Remember that Jesus Christ of the seed of David was raised from the dead, according to my gospel:

9 Wherein I suffer trouble, as an evildoer, even unto bonds; but the word of God is not bound.

10 Therefore I endure all things for the elect's sake, that they may also obtain the salvation which is in Christ Jesus with eternal glory.

11 It is a faithful saying: For if we be dead with him, we shall also live with him:

12 If we suffer, we shall also reign with him: if we deny him, he also will deny us:

13 If we believe not, yet he abideth faithful: he cannot deny himself.

14 Of these things put them in remembrance, charging them before the Lord that they strive not about words to no profit, but to the subverting of the hearers.

15 Study to show thyself approved unto God, a workman that needeth not to be ashamed, rightly dividing the word of truth.

Aug 16

GOLDEN TEXT: Study to show thyself approved unto God, a workman that needeth not to be ashamed, rightly dividing the word of truth.—2 Timothy 2:15.

Lesson Aims

This lesson is designed to help the student:

1. Describe the strength of a committed Christian.

2. Describe the reward of Christian commitment.

3. Improve his use of "the word of truth."

Lesson Outline

INTRODUCTION
   A. Let the Character Match the Name
   B. Lesson Background
I. BE STRONG (2 Timothy 2:1-7)
   A. Strong in Grace (v. 1)
   B. Strong in Communication (v. 2)
     Each One Teach One
   C. Strong Like a Soldier (vv. 3, 4)
   D. Strong Like an Athlete (v. 5)
   E. Strong Like a Farmer (v. 6)
     Meaningful Metaphors
   F. Strong in Mind (v. 7)
II. TROUBLE AND TRIUMPH (2 Timothy 2:8-13)
   A. Our Leader (v. 8)
   B. Our Trouble (v. 9)
   C. Our Endurance (v. 10)
   D. Our Triumph (vv. 11-13)
III. WORK TO BE APPROVED (2 Timothy 2:14, 15)
   A. Remember and Remind Others (v. 14)
   B. Try Harder (v. 15)
     A Handy Handle
CONCLUSION
   A. The Next Generation
   B. Prayer
   C. Thought to Remember

When discussing 2 Timothy 2:2, refer to visual 11 of the visuals packet. The visual is shown on page 429.

Introduction

A. Let the Character Match the Name

A young soldier in the heat of battle turned and ran away, overcome with fear. He was arrested for his desertion, and brought before the commander, Alexander the Great.

"What is your name?" the commander demanded.

The soldier answered, "Alexander, sir."

"What?" stormed Alexander the Great. "Your name is Alexander, and you are a coward?! Young man, you either change your name or change your character."

The name *Christian* also calls for noble character. This lesson calls to mind some of the characteristics to be cultivated by everyone who wears the name.

B. Lesson Background

Sometime after writing his first letter to Timothy, Paul was arrested and taken to Rome. Nero's furious persecution of Christians was raging then, and the prisoner did not expect to be released (2 Timothy 4:6-8). He wrote to Timothy, his son in the faith, his close companion and fellow worker in the ministry, and one to whom he was passing the torch in this Christian relay race. It was now more dangerous to be a Christian leader, but Paul called on Timothy to be strong and brave, a good soldier in the army of the Lord. The same call is our call as we face the difficulty of being Christian today.

I. Be Strong
(2 Timothy 2:1-7)

A. Strong in Grace (v. 1)

1. Thou therefore, my son, be strong in the grace that is in Christ Jesus.

Grace is not weakness, but strength. God's grace brings His divine help to us. No one knew that better than Paul himself. He had asked the Lord to take away his physical weakness; but the Lord had replied, "My grace is sufficient for thee: for my strength is made perfect in weakness." Paul then was content to be weak in himself and rejoice in God's strength working through him (2 Corinthians 12:7-9). God's grace brought God's power. We can be *strong in the grace that is in Christ Jesus* if we admit that we are weak in ourselves and humbly open ourselves to God's power.

If we are strong in the Lord's grace, we depend on His ability, not ours.

If we are strong in the Lord's grace, we are gracious to others as He is to us. We give them what they need, not just what they deserve.

If we are strong in the Lord's grace, we are gracious in manner: not proud, not dictatorial, not bitter, not envious.

B. Strong in Communication (v. 2)

2. And the things that thou hast heard of me among many witnesses, the same commit thou to faithful men, who shall be able to teach others also.

Paul was saying to Timothy what Jesus had said to His apostles: "Freely ye have received, freely give" (Matthew 10:8). Timothy must be strong to tell the good news in a world that was used to bad news—and so must we.

Notice the partnership—Christ shared with Paul; Paul shared with Timothy; Timothy was to share with others; they were to pass it on to others. They did pass it on, and so it has come through the centuries to us.

Sharing the good news is not just something for ordained ministers to do; it is a job for all Christians. We are the "light," the "salt," the "leaven" (Matthew 5:13-16; 13:33). To pass on the good news God has not given us a spirit of fear, but a spirit of power, love, and a sound mind (2 Timothy 1:7).

Commit carries the idea of entrusting something to another person for safekeeping or use. The finest way to keep the gospel safe and alive is to pass it on to *faithful men* who will *teach others*. The gospel is preserved by our proclaiming it to others.

EACH ONE TEACH ONE

Frank Laubach is known for his world-literacy program, which is based simply on the principle of each reader teaching at least one more person to read. Non-readers still exist in the world because not all readers have shared their skills.

Paul outlined a program of evangelism that has wonderful potential for success. Paul told Timothy the good news; Timothy was to tell others, who in turn would tell others. Like compounding interest, the possible results of such evangelism are mind-boggling. If each New Testament Christian would win just one more in nine months, and each one who was won would win one more in nine months, the total world population would be converted by the turn of the century. But not more than ten percent of today's Christians are working at it.

It's important for everyone to know how to read; it is *vital* for everyone to know how to be saved. How many more generations will die illiterate?   —R. W. B.

C. Strong Like a Soldier (vv. 3, 4)

3. Thou therefore endure hardness, as a good soldier of Jesus Christ.

There is a spiritual battle going on, and Jesus calls for soldiers. We are not fighting against flesh and blood, but against principalities and powers in heavenly places (Ephesians 6:12). Soldiers expect hardship. In 1990, soldiers of many nations were guarding Saudi Arabia against attack from Iraq. Sympathizing with the men, a reporter mentioned the searing heat, the endless sand, the insects, the dirt, the danger. One of the men responded with a shrug. "We're soldiers," he said. A Christian soldier also takes his share of hard knocks, suffering, and ill-treatment from those who do not appreciate the Christian way. Enduring hardships is a part of soldiering.

A soldier has to change his habits, dress, and conduct. He is ready at a minute's notice. The Christian life likewise is a life of service. It is being on the front line with some heavy loads, long days, and lonely nights.

Soldiering involves taking risks, as does Christianity. Jesus said, "Follow me," and He went to the cross. Soldiering is not a soft job for the lazy, and neither is Christianity.

4. No man that warreth entangleth himself with the affairs of this life; that he may please him who hath chosen him to be a soldier.

Soldiering involves not only service, but also separation. In time of war a soldier cannot work at his civilian job or business or profession. A Christian is not to be tangled up in his former life-style, even if it is acceptable in the culture and popular among his peers.

A soldier forgets everything else to please his commander by carrying out orders promptly and well. A secret of Jesus' effectiveness was that He sought to please God in everything He did (John 8:29). Paul said the goal of the Christian is to please the Lord (2 Corinthians 5:9).

Do we please God by disobeying, by questioning His orders, by doing our own thing, by staying in "boot camp" all of our lives, by wounding our fellow soldiers? Would He be pleased with a deserter, or one who refused to get out of the barracks and go to the front line?

D. Strong Like an Athlete (v. 5)

5. And if a man also strive for masteries, yet is he not crowned, except he strive lawfully.

Paul pictures an athlete trying hard to win. This applies to the Christian life in several ways. The athlete must *strive for masteries*—he has goals and seeks to achieve them. He stays in good physical shape, avoiding food or drugs that would be detrimental, and exercises. Christians do the same—set goals, seek to achieve them, stay away from what is detrimental, and exercise their faith. The Christian life is not just something to know; it is something to live.

The athlete competes. We Christians do not compete with other Christians, but against our opponent—the devil—and we do it as a team.

The athlete will not be victorious unless he competes *lawfully*. He is disqualified if he breaks the rules. Christians are to stick to the rules in their relationships with God, themselves, the church, and the world. A good athlete follows the instructions of his coach; the Christian follows, imitates, and obeys his Lord.

If an athlete did all the above and won his contest, he was *crowned* with a wreath of leaves that soon withered, but the Christian who is faithful in his contest has a reward that lasts forever (1 Corinthians 9:25).

E. Strong Like a Farmer (v. 6)

6. The husbandman that laboreth must be first partaker of the fruits.

A *husbandman* is a farmer. He *laboreth*: he works hard. He prepares the soil, plants the seed, cultivates the field, repairs the machinery, and keeps abreast of new methods. He does not just pray for the harvest; he works for it. There is a balance between prayer and work in the Christian life. Jesus prayed much, but worked hard.

Jesus told His disciples to pray for laborers for the harvest, and as He told them that, He was sending them to be the answer to the prayer (Luke 10:1, 2). As we pray for workers in God's field, we should be workers ourselves.

The farmer has a lot of faith: he puts his seed in the ground and trusts God for the rain, germination, and growth. The farmer has patience: he doesn't put seed in the ground and expect a crop the next day. He knows how to wait. We too must work and wait, expecting a harvest.

MEANINGFUL METAPHORS

The only picture I have of myself as a soldier is a snapshot taken when I was six years old, wearing a tike-size army uniform. My athletic competition is limited to occasional horseshoe pitching, Ping-Pong, and carroms. Aside from vegetable gardening, my farming experience amounts to a few hay-baling episodes as a teenager, the most memorable of which is the summer when I managed to overturn two loaded wagons in a ditch.

Despite my own inexperience as soldier, athlete, and farmer, however, I can still grasp Paul's message. He told Timothy, "Consider these three illustrations of mine and the Lord will help you to understand all that I mean" (v. 7, J. B. Phillips translation).

I too can understand that Christians must be *loyal* like good soldiers, *disciplined* like winning athletes, and *hard-working* like productive farmers.
                                                          —R. W. B.

F. Strong in Mind (v. 7)

7. Consider what I say; and the Lord give thee understanding in all things.

Neither the soldier, the athlete, nor the farmer does his job without thinking. Paul says, *Consider what I say*. The Christian must put his mind

to his Christianity, not just his muscles and feelings. But when we think seriously about God's will and His way, we can expect Him to help us understand. In the *King James Version,* the last part of this verse is Paul's prayer: *And the Lord give thee understanding.* Following different ancient manuscripts, some versions make it a promise: The Lord will give you understanding.

The soldier or athlete or farmer who is effective understands what he is doing. The Christian also needs *understanding in all things*. So he needs to think about what Paul says. We are not to let someone else do our thinking for us. Many who have been Christians for years have no more understanding of their faith than they had when they were born again. They know little of the Bible, of the nature of God, of apostolic teaching, or of the church and how it works. We must think as well as act, ponder as well as practice.

II. Trouble and Triumph
(2 Timothy 2:8-13)

A. Our Leader (v. 8)

8. Remember that Jesus Christ of the seed of David was raised from the dead, according to my gospel.

A good soldier never ignores his commander; a good athlete never ignores his coach; a good farmer never ignores the signs of nature. It is easy for the Christian to get involved in church machinery and activities without keeping Jesus in mind.

One of the main things to keep in mind is that Jesus *was raised from the dead*. That was an outstanding fact in the gospel, the good news that Paul carried. It means Jesus is alive right now and is Lord of all. He is to be invited to direct all that we do.

B. Our Trouble (v. 9)

9. Wherein I suffer trouble, as an evildoer, even unto bonds; but the word of God is not bound.

Paul did not want Timothy to think only of the soldier's victory, the athlete's prize, and the farmer's crop. He wanted Timothy to know that we all go through suffering. Because he preached the gospel, Paul must *suffer trouble,* as an *evildoer*. That did not mean Paul did anything evil, but he was a prisoner in chains, treated *as an evildoer* was treated.

People misunderstand Christians, belittle Christians, hurl insults at Christians, seek to destroy Christians as if they were evil. All this may seem to restrict us as the prison restricted Paul, but God's Word is still free. His Word is not in chains, in paralysis, in early retirement, or wearing out; neither does it have a terminal disease. Opposition may cause discomfort and rob us of some of our audience, but still we are passing on God's Word, which is totally unrestricted in its power. That is why it is important to study His Word, understand it, and share it.

C. Our Endurance (v. 10)

10. Therefore I endure all things for the elect's sake, that they may also obtain the salvation which is in Christ Jesus with eternal glory.

We think of the apostolic teaching (v. 7), the nature of Jesus (v. 8), and the power of God's Word (v. 9). We think also of our fellow Christians and our commitment to them. We *endure all things*, not only for the Lord's sake and for our own sake, but also *for the elect's sake*.

The maturing Christian is not interested in his or her salvation alone, but also in the salvation of the whole family of God. We want to spend time fellowshipping with our brothers and sisters in Christ, praying for them (not preying upon them), loving them, forgiving them, enjoying them, helping them. *For the elect's sake*, we think of how our actions look to them; we consider whether they will be hurt or helped by what we do.

D. Our Triumph (vv. 11-13)

11. It is a faithful saying: For if we be dead with him, we shall also live with him.

In our troubles we can sink in grief and self-pity, or we can look beyond these troubles to the glorious triumph of those who endure (Romans 8:18). Paul now calls attention to what lies beyond our troubles—triumph for the faithful, disaster for the unfaithful. To be *dead* with Christ is to give up our former worldly and sinful lifestyle and be buried in baptism (Romans 6). For our new life with Jesus, He invites us to take up our cross daily (Luke 9:23), which involves self-denial for the sake of others. But if we follow faithfully after dying with Christ, *we shall also live with him* forever.

12. If we suffer, we shall also reign with him: if we deny him, he also will deny us.

We may suffer now, but we will certainly reign throughout eternity. How can all of us reign? Who will be left for us to reign over? All of us will be so attuned to the Master's will that we will want just what He wants—and so each of us will have his own way. Isn't that what reigning means?

Suffering of the Christian may include: 1) being misunderstood, 2) being shunned, 3) giving up weekend pleasures for worship and fellowship, 4) depriving ourselves to give for the

visual 11

PASS IT ON... OR IT MAY PASS AWAY

advancement of God's kingdom, 5) saying no when everyone else is saying yes, 6) being so tuned in to God's will that the evil around us gives us pain.

When suffering comes, there is a temptation to walk away from it and forget our Christianity. That leads to tragedy. *If we deny him, he also will deny us.* That does not mean we are lost for eternity if we just deny Him once. Peter denied Him on the night He was betrayed, but never again. Jesus forgave him and used him to start His church. But if we go back to our former unChristian life-style and continue to deny the Lord till we die, we will die without hope.

13. If we believe not, yet he abideth faithful: he cannot deny himself.

We may become unfaithful, but the Lord will not. He stands firm, calling us back from our faithlessness. If we respond and become faithful again, He brings us safely to the blessed eternity He has promised. But if we persist in being faithless, He can only let us go on to the eternal torment He has promised, for *he cannot deny himself.* Even if many become faithless, the church will continue to be victorious because the head of the church will not waver.

III. Work to Be Approved (2 Timothy 2:14, 15)

A. Remember and Remind Others (v. 14)

14. Of these things put them in remembrance, charging them before the Lord that they strive not about words to no profit, but to the subverting of the hearers.

In this letter Paul has been reminding Timothy of essential truths, and asking Timothy to keep reminding others of these truths (v. 2). That was the positive side of Timothy's work. On the negative side, he was to warn people to *strive not about words to no profit*. How many theological debates through the ages have been mere quibbles about words? How many modern church quarrels are in the same class? Our discussions should be profitable: they should edify ourselves and others (1 Timothy 1:4), build us up in our faith. In planning what to say we should ask ourselves, "Will this be helpful to the hearers?"

B. Try Harder (v. 15)

15. Study to show thyself approved unto God, a workman that needeth not to be ashamed, rightly dividing the word of truth.

We who have spent much time in school may have too narrow an idea of the word *study*. Here the *New International Version* translates it "do your best." This includes earnest Bible study and much more. It means we should try hard to control everything we do and say and think so it will be acceptable unto God.

There are two kinds of workmen in God's field—one is *approved* and one is *ashamed*. The difference between the two is in two areas: 1) *study*: that is, making an earnest effort; 2) *rightly dividing the word of truth*. The Greek word for *rightly dividing* literally means "cutting straight," but obviously it does not mean literal cutting. It means using God's Word properly.

How do we do that in studying the Bible? We can begin by knowing Jesus and His teaching. If any teaching violates His attitudes, activities, priorities, or practices, we can know it does not square with the intention of God's Word. Then we can remember to study any passage in its context, compare it with other passages, look for the intention of the writer, and apply it to our own life. We can let the New Testament shed light on the Old Testament and vice verse; let the clear passages shed light on the unclear passages; let the epistles give us the application of Christ's teaching.

Proper use of God's Word involves: 1) knowing to whom the text was written, 2) knowing who did the speaking or writing, 3) knowing how it was to be applied in that day, 4) knowing how it can be applied to situations today, 5)believing it, 6) obeying it, 7) teaching it.

A HANDY HANDLE

If I were an inventor, I think I would work on a portable handle, a handy gadget to use in those situations when you need to grip an object and there's nothing to hold onto. Just think how useful it would be on moving day! Everything from mattresses to major appliances could be moved with ease if a handle could be attached in the right places. We have invented a phrase for the more abstract need to understand principles or instructions. We say, "I can't seem to get a handle on it," meaning, "I don't grasp the full sense of it." Paul had given Timothy a "handle"

on the gospel. Understanding the good news is accomplished by faith in the resurrection of Christ (v. 8) and in the salvation obtainable through Him (v. 10).

Timothy also was instructed as to how to handle the "word of truth." He was to concentrate on his commission (v. 4), discipline himself by God's absolutes (v. 5), work hard to plant gospel seeds (v. 6), and avoid fruitless arguments over semantics (v. 14). He was to do his best to please God, remaining faithful to the Scriptures and the apostles' doctrine.

Have you got a handle on the truth? The handle of faith will help you understand and receive the gospel; it also will help you share it with others.   —R. W. B.

Conclusion

A. The Next Generation

No farmer continues to farm forever. No athlete continues to run forever. No soldier remains in uniform forever. Then how do we keep having crops raised, games played, and a military service ready? The farmer teaches others to work the farm when he is gone; the athlete coaches others; the soldier trains others to be soldiers.

The success of the next generation depends largely on the farmer, the athlete, and the soldier of today—and the Christian of today.

B. Prayer

Thank You, Father, for not being stingy with Your understanding, Your good news, and Your salvation. Now fill us with Your Spirit so we will continue to grow up to be like You.

C. Thought to Remember

Pass it on or it may pass away.

Home Daily Bible Readings

Monday, Aug. 10—A Family of Faith (2 Timothy 1:1-7)

Tuesday, Aug. 11—Be Not Ashamed (2 Timothy 1:8-18)

Wednesday, Aug. 12—Be Committed (2 Timothy 2:1-7)

Thursday, Aug. 13—The Word Is Not Bound (2 Timothy 2:8-13)

Friday, Aug. 14—Do Your Best (2 Timothy 2:14-19)

Saturday, Aug. 15—Be Disciplined (2 Timothy 2:20-26)

Sunday, Aug. 16—Suffering for the Gospel (Philippians 1:12-26)

Learning by Doing

*This page contains an alternate lesson plan emphasizing learning activities. Classes
desiring such student involvement will find these suggestions helpful.*

Learning Goals

As a result of participating in this lesson, students should:

1. Be able to list some marks of Christian commitment, some things committed Christians do.

2. Participate in organized, systematic study of a Biblical passage, "rightly dividing the word of truth."

Into the Lesson

As you prepare for today's lesson, make sure there are plenty of Bible-study helps for the students' use. The helps needed are listed under the four projects in "Into the Word."

Before students arrive, draw on the chalkboard three columns with the words SOLDIER, ATHLETE, and FARMER above them. As you begin the lesson, tell the students they are going to be thinking about commitment. Ask them to mention some things the soldier, athlete, and farmer do because they are committed to their jobs. (For example, a soldier goes where he is sent, giving up the privilege of choosing. An athlete spends many hours in vigorous training. A farmer works from daylight to dark.) When students have supplied a few items for the three columns, add a fourth column and label it CHRISTIAN. Ask for examples of what a Christian does because he is committed to following Christ.

Into the Word

From what a Christian does because he is committed to following Christ, go on to ask specifically how one shows commitment to God's Word. The answers may include daily Bible reading, study of the Sunday-school lesson at home and in class, other home Bible studies alone or with a group, teaching others about the Bible, living by Bible teachings. Have someone read 2 Timothy 2:15. Use thoughts from the lesson commentary to explain "rightly dividing the word." Announce that the class will now participate in some Bible study.

Divide the class into research teams of two to five members. Give each team one of the research projects listed below. You may wish to give also a card with written instructions.

1. *The background of 2 Timothy.* Who wrote this book, and to whom? What was going on in the writer's life, and in the life of the recipient? Why was the book written? Students may find answers in the book itself, in a Bible dictionary or handbook, in the introduction of a commentary on 2 Timothy.

2. *What did this book mean to Timothy?* What would he do because he was "strong in the grace that is in Christ Jesus"? (2 Timothy 2:1). Besides the book of 2 Timothy, this group may use commentaries, including the one in this lesson book.

3. *What other Bible passages can help us understand 2 Timothy 2:1?* The team may use a concordance, topical Bible, or cross-references Bible to find other New Testament Scriptures on *strength* and *grace.*

4. *What does "be strong in the grace that is in Christ Jesus" mean for us today?* What specific things will we do if we are strong? How can we build up our strength? Help may be found in the lesson text and in commentaries, but this group will need to do some keen thinking about Christians today.

Let each group report to the class, briefly giving the results of its research. Encourage students to take notes on what their classmates have discovered. If you have time and resources, you may want to prepare some stapled handouts. Provide four pages with the four areas of study typed at the tops of the pages. This will be a convenient form for the notes students will take as the four groups give their reports. If you can, you may wish to include a map of Paul's journeys and a map of the Roman world of that time. Perhaps you will include an extra page and suggest that each student use it to prepare his own outline of 2 Timothy. He can give his own title to each of the four chapters. These can be the main headings in the outline. The student can read the four chapters in his home study, and supply subheads under each of the main heads.

Into Life

Application of the lesson can begin with the report of the fourth team. Let students discuss it fully, giving special attention to items they think will be most helpful, and adding other items. Some may take note of circumstances in which they are weak in grace instead of strong. As closing time comes near, turn the thinking to how we can be more gracious toward fellow employees, toward supervisors, toward subordinates, toward fellow Christians, toward our families.

Let's Talk It Over

The questions on this page are designed to encourage review of the lesson Scriptures and to promote discussion of the lesson by the class. The answers provided are only discussion starters. Let your class talk it over from there.

1. We are to commit or entrust God's word to others in such a way that they also can teach it. What does this indicate about our teaching methods or approaches?

Students in Bible classes need to do more than listen. When they participate in discussion and ask questions, they master Scriptural truths and prepare to communicate them. Also, we need to put our Bible lessons into practice in daily living. When Bible lessons feature specific actions that students may take, the truths of Scripture are seen as practical, workable, and teachable. Another helpful approach is to enlist the students in the actual teaching of the class by assigning reports or by asking them to bring items from newspapers or magazines to illustrate a Bible lesson.

2. Why should we welcome hardships and risks in connection with our Christian faith?

A popular saying of our day is, "No pain, no gain." In many of our activities, progress comes only when we risk pain, embarrassment, failure, and the like. When we "stick our necks out" in witnessing to an unsaved neighbor, in tackling a difficult job in the church, in taking our stand against immorality or injustice, or in investing a significant portion of our time and money in the Lord's work, then we experience the real adventure of following Jesus.

3. How spiritual goals help us to become better Christians?

Goals tend to keep us from drifting. For example, if we set a goal of going to church every Sunday, we are less likely to be absent. Another benefit of goals is that they help us measure our progress as Christians. When we aim to read through the Bible, or overcome some questionable habit, or give so many hours per week to Christian service, we can look back after some time and see how we are progressing. Goals provide an element of excitement in the Christian life. As we move close to completing a project, we feel a keen sense of anticipation. And when the task is done, the joy of accomplishment is sweet. Every Christian should set goals, work toward them, and periodically review them to ascertain the progress that he or she is making in attaining those goals.

4. In what ways is the Word of God unbound?

It is not bound to any one translation. The *King James Version* is beautiful and reverent, but we can enrich our understanding by comparing other translations. The word of God is not bound to any man's or group's interpretation of it. No person or sect has an exclusive grasp of Biblical truth. The word of God is unbound in its power to work in human lives. People of all races and nations, rich and poor, male and female, even the worst sinners, can experience its might by believing and obeying it.

5. Why is it vital that we receive constant reminders regarding spiritual truths?

Paul told the Philippians, "To write the same things to you, to me indeed is not grievous, but for you it is safe" (Philippians 3:1). Those who listen to sermons and lessons may grow weary of hearing certain themes over and over again; those who preach and teach may tire of having to repeat them; but like the Philippians we are spiritually safest when we are reminded of vital doctrines and duties. Even though Biblical truths are the most important sounds we hear, it is easy to forget them in the wearisome volume of voices, and noises. Furthermore, in our remembering we frequently lack the sense of urgency we should feel toward obeying God's commands. Classroom and pulpit reminders can rekindle that urgency.

6. The idea of being a workman in our handling of the Bible is a stimulating one. How can we benefit from seeing ourselves as workmen?

Being a workman suggests knowing how to use the right tools in the right way. One of the goals of the church's teaching program is to acquaint every member with such tools as a Bible dictionary, concordance, commentaries, and similar study helps. Such tools should be available in the church library. Another aspect of being a workman is the organizing of the job, planning when and how to perform each step required. Examples of the organized approach to Bible study are topical studies of grace, faith, obedience, and others; character studies of Bible people; and a thorough examination of a specific book.

Fulfill Your Ministry Faithfully

LESSON SCRIPTURE: 2 Timothy 3:10—4:8.

PRINTED TEXT: 2 Timothy 3:10—4:5.

2 Timothy 3:10-17

10 But thou hast fully known my doctrine, manner of life, purpose, faith, longsuffering, charity, patience,

11 Persecutions, afflictions, which came unto me at Antioch, at Iconium, at Lystra; what persecutions I endured: but out of them all the Lord delivered me.

12 Yea, and all that will live godly in Christ Jesus shall suffer persecution.

13 But evil men and seducers shall wax worse and worse, deceiving, and being deceived.

14 But continue thou in the things which thou hast learned and hast been assured of, knowing of whom thou hast learned them;

15 And that from a child thou hast known the holy Scriptures, which are able to make thee wise unto salvation through faith which is in Christ Jesus.

16 All Scripture is given by inspiration of God, and is profitable for doctrine, for reproof, for correction, for instruction in righteousness:

17 That the man of God may be perfect, thoroughly furnished unto all good works.

2 Timothy 4:1-5

1 I charge thee therefore before God, and the Lord Jesus Christ, who shall judge the quick and the dead at his appearing and his kingdom;

2 Preach the word; be instant in season, out of season; reprove, rebuke, exhort with all longsuffering and doctrine.

3 For the time will come when they will not endure sound doctrine; but after their own lusts shall they heap to themselves teachers, having itching ears;

4 And they shall turn away their ears from the truth, and shall be turned unto fables.

5 But watch thou in all things, endure afflictions, do the work of an evangelist, make full proof of thy ministry.

Aug 23

GOLDEN TEXT: Preach the word; be instant in season, out of season; reprove, rebuke, exhort with all longsuffering and doctrine.—2 Timothy 4:2.

Lesson Aims

This lesson is designed to help the student to be able to:

1. Understand that a faithful Christian may face difficulties and problems.

2. Be faithful through every difficulty.

3. Understand and describe the nature of Scripture.

Lesson Outline

INTRODUCTION
    A. Bitter or Better
    B. Lesson Background
  I. A CHRISTIAN'S PERSECUTION (2 Timothy 3:10-13)
    A. Paul's Experience (vv. 10, 11)
    B. Continuing Persecution (v. 12)
    C. Growing Evil (v. 13)
 II. A CHRISTIAN'S GUIDEBOOK (2 Timothy 3:14-17)
    A. Be Faithful (v. 14)
    B. The Inspired Scriptures (vv. 15, 16)
      Breath of Life
    C. The Goal (v. 17)
III. A CHRISTIAN'S WORK (2 Timothy 4:1-5)
    A. His Task (vv. 1, 2)
    B. The Need (vv. 3, 4)
      Itching Ears
    C. Persistence (v. 5)
CONCLUSION
    A. Counterattack
    B. Prayer
    C. Thought to Remember

Visual 12 of the visuals packet illustrates the thoughts developed in the introduction of this lesson. The visual is shown on page 437.

Introduction

A. Bitter or Better

God never promised that following Him would be an easy street. Jesus is the model of the Christian life, and He was questioned, belittled, ridiculed, contradicted, ignored, slandered, schemed against, deserted, and executed as a criminal. Joseph went through devastating suffering, but was better on the other side of it.

David was schemed against, but was better on the other side of it.

Difficulties in life either make us bitter or make us better, depending on how we deal with them. Christians are like stained glass windows. When all is dark outside, they shine brilliantly if the light is turned on inside. Though we walk through the valley of the shadow of death, gloom, or disappointment, the Lord is with us. There can be no shadow unless a light is shining somewhere. When difficulties come, it is marvelous to have the perspective of David. He said, "It is good for me that I have been afflicted; that I might learn thy statutes" (Psalm 119:71).

B. Lesson Background

Paul was near the end of his last letter to Timothy. He hoped Timothy and Mark would come to him soon (2 Timothy 4:9-11), but there was no assurance that he would live till they arrived. His last letter to Timothy included a final charge that summarized what Paul wanted to leave in Timothy's heart as Timothy was facing people who would resist the truth and do evil (2 Timothy 3:1-9). Our text describes the appropriate response for Timothy to make as he faced those evildoers.

I. A Christian's Persecution
(2 Timothy 3:10-13)

A. Paul's Experience (vv. 10, 11)

10. But thou hast fully known my doctrine, manner of life, purpose, faith, longsuffering, charity, patience.

But announces a contrast. We turn away from the evildoers described in verses 1-9. Now we shall read of Paul's way of life.

The words *fully known* are from a Greek word that more literally means "followed closely" or "accompanied." Timothy not only knew how Paul had lived; he had committed himself to the same life-style. He was closely following Paul in essential ways that Paul listed:

1. *Doctrine* is another word for "teaching." Paul's teaching was always right, because he received it from Jesus and the Holy Spirit. Timothy was doing well when he taught what Paul taught.

2. *Manner of life.* Paul moved from teaching to conduct. That is appropriate, for behavior comes from beliefs. We teach not only by our lips, but by our lives.

3. *Purpose* refers to Paul's intentions, his motivations, his reasons for doing what he did. In another letter, Paul wrote that he proclaimed Jesus Christ, teaching everyone, so that he could present everyone mature in Christ (Colossians

1:28). In his first letter to Timothy he wrote that the goal or purpose of instruction is that love may come from changed people (1 Timothy 1:5).

4. *Faith* can mean either belief or trust or faithfulness. Paul believed in Jesus; He trusted in the eternal one and did not let temporary things deter him, and so he was faithful, loyal, in his teaching and life.

5. *Longsuffering* refers to Paul's reaction to difficult people and mistreatment. It means he put up with them.

6. *Charity* means love that is sincere, unselfish, and active. Paul could put up with difficult people because he loved them with an unselfish care that was translated into sacrificial compassion and service.

7. *Patience*. Longsuffering means putting up with difficult people or mistreatment without being angry, without striking back, without seeking revenge; patience means putting up with them without going in, without being stopped from doing right. Patience is endurance, steadfastness. It highlights stick-to-it-ive-ness rather than quitting when the going gets tough.

11. Persecutions, afflictions, which came unto me at Antioch, at Iconium, at Lystra; what persecutions I endured: but out of them all the Lord delivered me.

With the kind of life-style we see in verse 10, wouldn't it seem reasonable that the Christian would have no problems, sufferings, anxieties, or difficulties? But Paul said some stinging experiences come with the Christian life-style. Beware of those who preach a life of ease for Christians. With some, it has become a fad to promise Christians that all of their problems will be erased if they will get spiritual enough. But that did not happen with Jesus, and it did not happen with Paul. The Christian life is not spent in the "easy chair."

Some people teach that if Christians are having difficulties it is because they have done something against God. But the Bible shows that many of God's people faced difficulties because they were doing something for God that ungodly people did not like. Like God's people in former times, we Christians are aliens on this earth (Hebrews 11:13-16, *New International Version*). Our citizenship is in Heaven (Philippians 3:20, *New International Version*). The world usually is not very cordial to aliens. Purity in our lives can automatically bring persecution.

Persecution primarily means pursuits. Almost everywhere Paul went, people were after him, chasing, pursuing, for the purpose of hindering, hurting, or driving out. Do you ever feel like someone is after you because of your Christian stance? That is because the Christian life is so counter to the non-Christian way that the ungodly consider it a threat.

Afflictions are the results of persecutions or misfortunes. (See a partial list of Paul's afflictions in 2 Corinthians 11:24-27.) He accepted them all with patience (v. 10), which means steadfast endurance. He did not give up, give out, give way, or give in. That was not because Paul depended on his own strength, ingenuity, or power. The Lord was with Him (Philippians 4:13).

The Lord is our refuge, our protector, and our deliverer. Over against suffering is the Savior; over against the destroyer is the deliverer; over against our foe is our friend, Jesus. Among His last words to His disciples were "I am with you" (Matthew 28:20).

B. Continuing Persecution (v. 12)

12. Yea, and all that will live godly in Christ Jesus shall suffer persecution.

Not only did Paul have difficulties, but he also promised that those who live a godly life will suffer persecutions. That was not just a first-century phenomenon, for Christianity still challenges the culture around us.

We must consider whether or not our godly lives are *in Christ Jesus*. Sometimes we take a position that is more rooted in traditions or in our denomination or in our opinions. To live *in Christ Jesus* is to live by His example and His teaching, guided by His Word in the Bible and strengthened by His Spirit within us.

Persecution is not easy. It causes us to suffer, but we can choose to become either bitter or better as a result. Persecution comes when we are *in Christ Jesus* and in the world at the same time. Instead of giving in to the world, we bring the life-style of Christ to the world in which we live.

C. Growing Evil (v. 13)

13. But evil men and seducers shall wax worse and worse, deceiving, and being deceived.

Here we see the widening gap between the Christian and the non-Christian. While the Christian is to be progressing more and more toward Christlikeness, non-Christians regress more and more into devilishness. They proceed from bad to worse. They regress because they are deceived by the great deceiver—the devil—and they pass his deception on to those they associate with.

The world will never get better through non-Christians, who are seducers trying to hook others into their system. We must not be taken in. The word *seducers* in early Christianity meant swindlers or cheaters. They cheat people out of peace and joy and eternal life.

II. A Christian's Guidebook
(2 Timothy 3:14-17)

A. Be Faithful (v. 14)

14. But continue thou in the things which thou hast learned and hast been assured of, knowing of whom thou hast learned them;

Paul was telling Timothy to stick with what he had learned from Paul, because he knew where it came from. Paul was an inspired apostle of the Lord, and his teaching and life were in harmony with that position. We are not to believe everything we hear; but when we hear anything from God's Word, we had better continue in that.

Don't let any hotshot speaker lure you away from your Christian foundation. That does not mean we are not to grow beyond our present understanding, but we can't build a more mature spiritual life by destroying the foundation.

B. The Inspired Scriptures (vv. 15, 16)

15. And that from a child thou hast known the holy Scriptures, which are able to make thee wise unto salvation through faith which is in Christ Jesus.

Before Timothy learned from Paul, he had learned from the Holy Scriptures. His mother and grandmother had taught him *from a child* (2 Timothy 1:5). Every child should get acquainted with the Scriptures at home with his family. The Sunday school can help, but it cannot take the place of the family. Several important truths appear in this verse:

1. *Hast known*. Scriptures are to be known. Let's get better acquainted with them.

2. *From a child*. Scriptures are not for adults only. Let's teach them to the kids.

3. *Make thee wise*. Scriptures improve our understanding. Let's use them more.

4. *Unto salvation*. Scriptures show us the way to Heaven. Let's follow it.

5. *Through faith*. Scriptures will not bring us to Heaven unless we believe them, trust them, follow them faithfully. Let's do it.

6. *In Christ Jesus*. Faith that brings us to Heaven is faith in Jesus, not just in the Scriptures; but we learn that faith from the Scriptures.

7. Scriptures are *holy*, consecrated for sacred use. Scriptures are different from any other literature.

16. All Scripture is given by inspiration of God, and is profitable for doctrine, for reproof, for correction, for instruction in righteousness.

This is true of *all Scripture*: not just the Old Testament but also the New, even though it had not yet been completed. Paul was writing as an apostle—one sent from God to speak God's words (2 Timothy 1:1). Elsewhere he affirmed that he spoke and wrote the words of God (1 Corinthians 2:12, 13; 14:37; Galatians 1:11, 12; 1 Thessalonians 2:13). Peter also wrote of Paul's writings in connection with "the other Scriptures," thus indicating that Paul's writings also were Scriptures (2 Peter 3:16).

Scripture was not created by man, imagined by man, or copied from other writings. All Scripture is *given by inspiration of God*. It is Godufactured, not manufactured. Its inspiration is different from that of a poet or artist whom we loosely say is inspired. Literally the Greek calls the Scripture *God-breathed*. Holy men of God wrote as they were moved by the Holy Spirit (2 Peter 1:21).

This does not tell us exactly how the Spirit of God managed the writing of men. Perhaps He chose every single word that was written in the Scriptures. But whether He chose every word or not, He chose the message that was to be conveyed and made sure the inspired men wrote the message He chose.

Because it is from God, all Scripture is profitable or useful. What is it useful for?

1. *Doctrine* is teaching. Scripture is used in teaching what God is like and what man is like, what is right and what is wrong, what Heaven and Hell are like, how we may escape Hell and go to Heaven.

2. *Reproof*. Scripture is used in proving that Jesus is the Christ (Acts 18:28), and so convicting and rebuking any who would deny the truth.

3. *Correction*. Scripture is used to bring about changes in our lives by means of its teaching and rebuking.

4. *Instruction in righteousness*. When we are convinced that Jesus is Christ and Lord, when we are ready to follow Him and do right, Scripture is useful in teaching about righteousness. Righteousness has to do with right relationships with God, self, the world, and others. We are not to study Scriptures only in order to have full heads, but also to foster proper relationships. Paul wrote that knowledge puffs up, but love builds up (1 Corinthians 8:1). Love is basic in right relationships (Romans 13:10).

C. The Goal (v. 17)

17. That the man of God may be perfect, thoroughly furnished unto all good works.

The word *perfect* means fully mature. The goal of Scripture is the goal of God for our lives, and that is that we become mature. When are we fully mature? When we are Christlike (Romans 8:29; Ephesians 4:11-15). We are to be mature in order to be useful and beneficial—*thoroughly furnished unto all good works*. Scriptures are to furnish or equip us for doing the kind of works God would approve if He were here in person—and He is, for our bodies are the temples of His presence (1 Corinthians 6:19).

BREATH OF LIFE

Thousands of lives have been saved by mouth-to-mouth resuscitation. This technique involves forcing the breath of a rescuer into the lungs of someone who has stopped breathing. The victim literally receives the breath of life from the savior.

When God created Adam, He "formed man of the dust of the ground, and breathed into his nostrils the breath of life"(Genesis 2:7). His creation of written revelation is described in similar terms. The *New International Version* renders verse 16 of our text, "All Scripture is God-breathed."

Because the Scriptures are so inspired, they can make us "wise unto salvation" (v. 15). The Creator becomes our Savior as He administers spiritual resuscitation to our souls.

Mouth-to-mouth resuscitation might be called *inspiration*, because it forces the recipient to inhale, as it were. "To inhale" is Webster's first definition of *inspire*; his third definition is, "to motivate by divine influence." *God-breathed* is a literal and appropriate translation of the word that the *King James Version* renders *given by inspiration of God*. Paul, Timothy, and all of us can trust the Scriptures as the unique Word of God.

—R. W. B.

III. A Christian's Work
(2 Timothy 4:1-5)
A. His Task (vv. 1, 2)

1. I charge thee therefore before God, and the Lord Jesus Christ, who shall judge the quick and the dead at his appearing and his kingdom.

Paul's charge to Timothy was so serious that he called God and the Lord Jesus Christ as witnesses to it. Paul was not giving Timothy a choice, but a charge, an order. It was an order with eternal significance, and so it was given in the sight of the judge of the living and the dead. Timothy's obedience to this charge would determine whether some people would be judged with acquittal or with condemnation.

2. Preach the word; be instant in season, out of season; reprove, rebuke, exhort with all long-suffering and doctrine.

This charge with eternal significance has several important elements:

1. *Preach.* Christianity is a proclaiming religion, a communicating religion; it is not a "private act."

visual 12

2. *The word.* It is not enough just to be proclaiming. We are to proclaim God's Word—both the living Word (Jesus) and the written Word (Scriptures).

3. *Instant.* Probably this means to be urgent, though the word can mean to take a stand and stick to it. We must be ready to communicate at any time—*in season, out of season.* We are not to judge whether the time is right or not. We know God's Word is right. We are to make it relevant to the situation at hand. Thus we can be workmen approved by God (2 Timothy 2:15).

4. *Reprove.* Make the proclamation convincing. This is one meaning of reprove. Probably it is the meaning here, since the other meaning of reprove is given in the word that follows.

5. *Rebuke.* This is not to be done in an angry or insulting way. The Greek word primarily means to set a value on something. The way to rebuke anything that is wrong is simply to point out the worthless nature of it.

6. *Exhort.* This does not suggest an angry harangue. The Greek word may be translated "encourage." Not only do we show the way of salvation; we also help the hearers find courage to take that way.

7. *Longsuffering.* Patiently we put up with all the heckling, doubting, scoffing, contradicting, and insults we meet. Never do we fly off the handle and attack our attacker with furious words or fists. How could we cut a heckler down with anger when we are teaching God's Word of grace?

8. *Doctrine.* Again we note that this is another word for teaching. Whatever opposition we have to endure, we keep on teaching God's Word.

B. The Need (vv. 3, 4)

3. For the time will come when they will not endure sound doctrine; but after their own lusts shall they heap to themselves teachers, having itching ears.

It is important for us to be well prepared and take a firm stand with the proper attitude, because there are people ready and willing to lure us or frighten us away from our proper work. Some of them are described:

1. *They will not endure sound doctrine*—they will not listen to healthy teaching. If we are not careful, we may change our teaching in order to attract them.

2. They will follow their own desires. *Lusts* is another word for desires. Rather than please the deity above, they please the desire that is within themselves.

3. They will support their own kind of teachers—*heap to themselves teachers*. They want teachers who are for them and their ways, not for God. They would rather be stroked than saved. If we are not careful, we may change in order to win their support. We all want to be liked, accepted, popular.

4. *Having itching ears*. Those who can't stand sound doctrine have ears eager to hear what pleases them, not what is right. Our task is to give them what they need, not what they want.

ITCHING EARS

A mid-life patient complained to his doctor, "Doc, I think my ears are aging faster than the rest of me. They itch constantly!" Many of us mid-lifers share his problem.

We can tolerate such physical annoyances, but the spiritual affliction that Paul calls "itching ears" can be critical, even *terminal*, for one's soul. He is describing a chronic human desire to hear only what pleases and praises, never what convicts and condemns. Such people, both in and out of the church, prefer messages that soothe. They don't want to hear indictments of sinful life-styles and challenges for evangelism and Christian service. They reject the truth to follow myths and fables. They want conve-

nience and comfort that require neither courage nor commitment.

In times like these, as in Timothy's era, Christians must stand fast on divine doctrine, correcting, rebuking, and encouraging "with great patience and careful instruction" (2 Timothy 4:2, *New International Version*).   —R. W. B.

4. And they shall turn away their ears from the truth, and shall be turned unto fables.

Selfish attitudes result in self-centered listening. People like sensational teachings that make them feel good rather than motivating them to be good. *Turn away their ears* means to quit listening. They turn away from truth and turn to *fables*—imaginations of people's minds. Some of the fables may be labeled "positive thinking," but they are negative if they deny or weaken the truth. There is more power in truth than in positive thinking.

C. Persistence (v. 5)

5. But watch thou in all things, endure afflictions, do the work of an evangelist, make full proof of thy ministry.

Watch means to be wide awake, alert, to think carefully. We take note of the opposition, we try to understand it, we plan to meet it with reason and persistence.

Endure afflictions. We stand firm under every difficulty and go on with our work.

Do the work of an evangelist. This was Timothy's work, and it is ours. We have good news to share, and we keep on sharing it.

Make full proof of thy ministry means "'fully carry out your service." Timothy must never be a slacker or a loafer or a timid soul. He must give himself to his task wholeheartedly and courageously—and so must we.

Conclusion

A. Counterattack

The more determined people are to ignore, neglect, or detour God's teaching, the more determined we must be to observe it and share it by the way we live, talk, and act. When the devil's forces attack us we do not hide, we counterattack.

B. Prayer

Father, we thank You that Jesus did not give up, give out, or give in when He faced opposition. Help us to walk in His way as we continue what He began. Help us to rely on Your Word as our guide. In Jesus' name, amen.

C. Thought to Remember

Outthink, outlive, outtalk, and outlove those who tear down Christianity.

Home Daily Bible Readings

Monday, Aug. 17—Do Not Oppose the Truth (2 Timothy 3:1-9)

Tuesday, Aug. 18—Paul's Faithfulness (2 Timothy 3:10-17)

Wednesday, Aug. 19—"Preach the Word" (2 Timothy 4:1-8)

Thursday, Aug. 20—Though Deserted, God Rescues (2 Timothy 4:9-18)

Friday, Aug. 21—Confident in Christ (2 Corinthians 5:1-10)

Saturday, Aug. 22—Respond Faithfully (2 Corinthians 6:1-10)

Sunday, Aug. 23—Choose Wisely (2 Corinthians 6:11-18)

Learning by Doing

*This page contains an alternate lesson plan emphasizing learning activities. Classes
desiring such student involvement will find these suggestions helpful.*

Learning Goals

As a result of this lesson, students should:

1. Consider their gifts and abilities, find a work they can do in the church, and do it well.

2. Recognize that opposition to godliness is to be expected and may even come from those who have professed faith in Christ.

3. Rely on the Scriptures as the source for combating opposition.

Into the Lesson

Begin with this discussion starter: "A group of people over the age of ninety-five were asked, 'If you could live your life over again, what would you do differently?' Their answers fell into three categories: 1) They would reflect more on what they did. 2) They would take larger risks. 3) They would do more things that would have an impact after their death." Ask the students, "What do you see in your own life? Are there things you would do differently? What are you doing that will live on after your death?" Students may mention the effect they are having on their children, influence they have on others, or money and service given to charitable organizations. Say, "helping others is a great way to invest your life. It requires much thinking; it involves some risks; its effects will last beyond your life here on earth."

Into the Word

Divide the class into two groups. (If you have a large class, you may wish to have more groups and let two or more groups study the same topic.) Give each group a written copy of the discussion guides printed below.

Group One. Examine the opposition that Paul faced in his ministries. Begin with 2 Timothy 3:10-12. What sufferings does Paul mention here? Learn more about them from Acts 13:14—14:23. Read also 2 Corinthians 11:23-28. In what similar ways do Christians suffer today? Are there differences in the sufferings of today? What does Paul mean in 2 Timothy 3:12 when he says all who wish to live godly lives will be persecuted? Can you give specific examples? For additional thoughts, look up Matthew 10:22; Acts 14:22; Philippians 1:27-30; 1 Peter 4:12, 13.

Group Two. Study the work that Paul charged Timothy to do. Begin with 2 Timothy 4:1-5. What specific kinds of service should be a part of Timothy's work? Are these the works of a "paid evangelist" only, or are these instructions for all Christians? What does Paul mean when he says, "Preach the word"? Is that charge applicable to all Christians today? What services does your church perform? How do the members of this study group take part in this ministry? Look at 2 Timothy 3:16, 17. How do the Scriptures help the church or Christians in combating opposition from outside? How do they help in handling differences within the church? How does the church today use the Scriptures? Are there times when the church or its members rebuke or correct? How is this done? How do people respond? Does it do any good?

Gather the groups together to report on their findings. Make two columns on the chalkboard. Let the class give examples of ways the church is opposed from the outside today. List these in the left column. Try to get specific examples from your community—recent court decisions, criminal offenses, or direct persecution of a church or a Christian.

Then ask for ways the church is troubled from within. Though you want to be specific, try to avoid name-calling or griping about problems in your church. Conclude this section of the study by asking, "In what specific ways do you feel persecution? How do you react?" Allow time for responses. Ask, "How does Scripture help us meet our opposition?"

Into Life

Be sure all students have paper and pencils for the final part of the lesson. Return to the three ideas that were expressed in the beginning. On the papers (or in the adult student lesson book), let students write comments on their spiritual lives—their lives of service. Help them along with questions like these: What talents and gifts has God given you? Put the more useful ones at the top of the list. Does your service correspond to your gifts and talents? What other service are you fitted for?

Let students make a list of risks they have taken in ministry lately. Why did they take the risks? What were their fears? Has good come out of them? What have you learned from them? Finally, encourage students to do more things that will help in leading others to Christ—an activity with results in eternity.

Let's Talk It Over

The questions on this page are designed to encourage review of the lesson Scriptures and to promote discussion of the lesson by the class. The answers provided are only discussion starters. Let your class talk it over from there.

1. We are tempted to slip into an easy Christian life. How can we combat that temptation?

Perhaps a dose of the "woes" will help. Some preachers have applied to the church the outcry of Amos: "Woe to them that are at ease in Zion!" (Amos 6:1). Then there is Jesus' stern warning: "Woe unto you, when all men shall speak well of you!" (Luke 6:26). Luke 6:24, 25 contains similar warnings. An easy discipleship is not what the Lord wants. We do well to check and see if we are becoming spiritually careless and lazy. Then we need to ask the Lord to direct us into real service.

2. Do some Christians complain of being persecuted when really they are not?

What some Christians call persecution is not the result of "living godly in Christ Jesus," but is the consequence of meddling or misuse of an employer's time. In regard to the latter, we occasionally hear of a Christian losing his job or being reprimanded for trying to evangelize during work hours. Paul's instructions to slaves in Colossians 3:22-25 seem applicable to modern employees. A Christian witnesses by doing his job well and by saving his evangelistic efforts for other times. Similarly a Christian may feel he is being persecuted when his advice or help is rejected, when actually he is a "busybody" (2 Thessalonians 3:11).

3. Are "evil men and seducers" growing worse and worse in our time? If so, give examples.

Truth is increasingly twisted and distorted by people and groups seeking profit or advantage. Note the promises of salvation, wisdom, and success set forth by various cults. Another example is the promotion of sexual immorality. Even the threat of AIDS has not hindered many people from advocating their "anything-goes" doctrine. We see also an escalation of attacks against the Bible and the Christian faith in television programs that focus on negative and unscrupulous and hypocritical elements within the church, while ignoring what is noble and good.

4. Some young people discard their faith or embrace the doctrines of a cult. What can we do to prevent this?

It is important that they have a faith of their own before they leave home for college, the military, or a career. We can encourage them to investigate the Biblical foundations of their faith and to think through what it means to follow Jesus Christ. Thus they can become confident enough to speak out for Christ even among His enemies. We can also train them to be alert for the seduction of false prophets and their teachings.

5. The word of God enables us to be "thoroughly furnished unto all good works." What are some examples of how this divine furnishing works?

Let us consider the work of preaching and teaching. The Bible furnishes us not only with specific doctrines to explain, but with examples of how to do it from Jesus and the apostles, and with many excellent illustrations afforded by the Old and New Testaments. When we focus on the task of leading in worship, we are abundantly supplied by the psalms with calls to worship, while the New Testament describes the proper elements in our worship. We have a ministry of comfort and encouragement to fulfill, and again both Old and New Testaments equip us with a variety of effective texts. Psalm 23 is a reliable standby. Among other psalms that are especially encouraging are 34, 46, 91, and 103. Jesus' declarations in John 10:14, 15, 27-30; 11:25, 26; 14:1-6, 27 are among the best to comfort the dying and the bereaved.

6. Paul's charge to Timothy, "Make full proof of thy ministry," reminds us of the importance of completely fulfilling our responsibilities in the church. Why is this significant?

How often do we see jobs in the church only half done? How many times are a few workers in the congregation overloaded because they must finish someone else's job along with their own? Whatever our job in the church, great or small, we need not only to *fill* it, but to *fulfill* it. That means doing everything that is required and more. If we see fellow members shirking their duties, we still keep on. Even when we see no definite results from our efforts, we press on. Perhaps our persistence will encourage others to make full proof of their ministries.

Be a Model in Deed and Word

Titus 3:1-8

LESSON SCRIPTURE: Titus.

PRINTED TEXT: Titus 2:7, 8, 11-14; 3:1-8.

Titus 2:7, 8, 11-14

7 In all things showing thyself a pattern of good works: in doctrine showing uncorruptness, gravity, sincerity,

8 Sound speech, that cannot be condemned; that he that is of the contrary part may be ashamed, having no evil thing to say of you.

. . . .

11 For the grace of God that bringeth salvation hath appeared to all men,

12 Teaching us that, denying ungodliness and worldly lusts, we should live soberly, righteously, and godly, in this present world;

13 Looking for that blessed hope, and the glorious appearing of the great God and our Saviour Jesus Christ;

14 Who gave himself for us, that he might redeem us from all iniquity, and purify unto himself a peculiar people, zealous of good works.

1 Put them in mind to be subject to principalities and powers, to obey magistrates, to be ready to every good work,

2 To speak evil of no man, to be no brawlers, but gentle, showing all meekness unto all men.

3 For we ourselves also were sometime foolish, disobedient, deceived, serving divers lusts and pleasures, living in malice and envy, hateful, and hating one another.

4 But after that the kindness and love of God our Saviour toward man appeared,

5 Not by works of righteousness which we have done, but according to his mercy he saved us, by the washing of regeneration, and renewing of the Holy Ghost;

6 Which he shed on us abundantly through Jesus Christ our Saviour;

7 That being justified by his grace, we should be made heirs according to the hope of eternal life.

8 This is a faithful saying, and these things I will that thou affirm constantly, that they which have believed in God might be careful to maintain good works. These things are good and profitable unto men.

GOLDEN TEXT: In all things [show] thyself a pattern of good works.—Titus 2:7.

Lesson Aims

This lesson is designed to help the student to be able to:

1. Commit himself to specific ways of being a good example.

2. Evaluate his attitude toward government and toward authority in general.

3. Praise God for His grace.

Lesson Outline

INTRODUCTION
    A. A Bumper Sticker and Us
    B. Lesson Background
 I. BE AN EXAMPLE (Titus 2:7, 8)
    A. Do Right in All Things (v. 7)
    B. Be Above Criticism (v. 8)
II. WHAT GRACE TEACHES (Titus 2:11-14)
    A. What Grace Brings (v. 11)
    B. What to Do (v. 12)
      Just Say "No"
    C. What to Look For (v. 13)
    D. What the Savior Did (v. 14)
III. THE CHRISTIAN'S CHANGE (Titus 3:1-8)
    A. Relationship to Authority (v. 1)
    B. Relationship to People (v. 2)
    C. What We Were (v. 3)
    D. What Changed Us (v. 4)
    E. The Transition (vv. 5, 6)
    F. The New Position (v. 7)
    G. The New Practice (v. 8)
      Faith and Works
CONCLUSION
    A. Fishing Tackle
    B. Prayer
    C. Thought to Remember

Visual 13 of the visuals packet relates to the lesson writer's comments under Titus 2:7. The visual is shown on this page.

Introduction

A. A Bumper Sticker and Us

Bumper stickers come in many different sizes, colors, and messages. Many months ago I saw a bumper sticker in our neighborhood that caused me to think about our Christian lives. It said, "Caution, I drive the way you do." It made me

think about what driving would be like on the highways if everyone drove the way I do.

Then I transferred that thought into the Christian life. What if every Christian around me wore a T-shirt that had one of the following messages on it:

"Caution, I study the Bible the way you do."

"Caution, I pray the way you do."

"Caution, I talk about people the way you do."

"Caution, I love the way you do."

"Caution, I forgive the way you do."

"Caution, I give the way you do."

"Caution, I demonstrate the fruit of the Spirit the way you do."

In what they do and how they speak, more people are guided by our examples than we can even imagine. We are all imitators. We imitate someone all the time; some people are imitating us.

B. Lesson Background

Paul probably wrote his letter to Titus soon after he wrote his first letter to Timothy. The apostle had been released from his first imprisonment in Rome. He was traveling among the churches as he had done before he was put in prison. In an earlier lesson we saw that he asked Timothy to stay in Ephesus to help the Christians there (1 Timothy 1:8). Perhaps a little earlier he left Titus to minister in Crete.

Crete was one of the toughest places in Paul's travels. He left Titus there so he could "set in order" the things that were lacking in the church (1:5). The words *set in order* come from a Greek word meaning to straighten what is crooked or arrange what is out of order. As a medical term it meant to set a bone that was broken or out of joint. Titus was to be involved in a correcting and healing type of ministry.

Crete was known for its loose living, liars, evil brutes, and lazy gluttons. Titus was to bring correction to them so the people could be sound in the faith (1:12, 13). But the Cretans did not need just a mouth with words, but also a worthy model. They needed a "show and tell." They needed more than Christianity in a book or sermon; they needed it with skin wrapped around

visual 13

it. Paul encouraged Titus to be the kind of person that would please God and thus would be the right kind of model for others to follow and imitate.

I. Be an Example
(Titus 2:7, 8)

A. Do Right in All Things (v. 7)

7. In all things showing thyself a pattern of good works: in doctrine showing uncorruptness, gravity, sincerity.

In verses 1-6 we read that Titus was to tell the people of Crete how Christians ought to behave. Now in verse 7 we see that he was also to show them. Women who make their own clothes understand what a *pattern* is. It is a model or standard by which something else is shaped. Titus was to shape his own life just as the Cretans ought to shape theirs. As the *New International Version* has it, Paul wrote, "In everything set them an example by doing what is good."

While many people in the world cannot read, most of them see and hear. They may not be able to read letters, but they do read lives. Elsewhere Paul reminded Christian readers that they were letters "known and read of all men." They were "the epistle of Christ," he added (2 Corinthians 3:2, 3). In a sense, each Christian is a piece of God's correspondence. Are we first class mail or junk mail?

On another occasion Paul wrote "Be ye followers of me, even as I also am of Christ" (1 Corinthians 11:1). The Greek word for "followers" is the word from which our word *mimic* comes. Would you dare to say to another, "Mimic me just as I mimic Christ"? Paul said it, and he wanted Titus to be able to say it.

The church is the body of Christ (1 Corinthians 12:27). One thing that means is that Christians take seriously the responsibility of mimicking Christ so others will be drawn to Him. To be a mimic of Christ, to be a letter of Christ, to be a pattern of Christian living—all these mean the same.

In what are we to be a pattern? *In all things*, Paul said; but he mentioned three areas in this verse and the next: *good works, doctrine*, and *speech*.

It is interesting that *good works* are mentioned before *doctrine*. That doesn't mean good deeds come before doctrine; more often our good deeds come out of the doctrine we believe. But many people see our deeds before they hear our doctrine. They want to know how much we care before they care how much we know. When they see our good deeds, they want to pay more attention to our teaching.

The word *doctrine* literally means teaching. What kind of teaching shall Titus give, and what kind should we be giving? Paul describes it with three words:

1. *Uncorruptness*—Christian teaching should be that given by Christ and His apostles, not spoiled or decayed, not tainted with anything untrue. This stands in direct contrast to the "fables, and commandments of men" that were turning some people away from the truth (Titus 1:14). Sometimes teaching can sound correct but not go far enough. It may be filled with half truths. Or true teaching may be corrupted by going too far, by being mixed with fables and commandments of men. Some corrupt teaching is too permissive; some is too restrictive.

For instance, it seems that some in Corinth were teaching that since the stomach is made for the food it enjoys, then the body must be for the sex it enjoys, without any regard for marriage. That was too permissive, and Paul sharply contradicted it (1 Corinthians 6:13-15). On the other hand, some were teaching that it was not proper for Christians to marry (1 Timothy 4:3). That was too restrictive. Some were teaching just to please the itching ears of people with no regard for truth (2 Timothy 4:3, 4). Jesus encountered some people whose teaching was corrupted by putting so much stress on religious activities that they neglected to care for their aged parents (Matthew 15:1-9).

It is not easy to keep our teaching uncorrupted, but it is right. That calls for each of us to study the Word, considering the interpretations and applications of others, but not accepting any that do not square with the Word itself.

2. *Gravity* means being serious about what we teach. Seriousness is seen in our careful preparation, in practicing the application of our teaching, in believing the eternal significance of what we teach.

3. *Sincerity*. Some of the ancient manuscripts do not have that word, and so it is left out of some modern versions. But no one doubts that Christian teaching ought to be sincere, genuine, without hypocrisy.

One of the ways to show that our teaching is untainted, serious, and genuine is to live by the teaching ourselves.

B. Be Above Criticism (v. 8)

8. Sound speech, that cannot be condemned; that he that is of the contrary part may be ashamed, having no evil thing to say of you.

Sound represents the Greek word from which our English word "hygiene" comes. It means well and strong, healthy. The proper speech of a Christian not only is strong and true in itself, it also is good for those who hear it. Sound speech brings healing and help to the total well-being of other people. It benefits their minds, their relationships, their spirits, and even their physical lives. We are learning that our health is not due to physical causes only. Our minds affect our bodies; our attitudes affect our well-being. Sound speech encourages the attitudes of godliness that can bring healing to the physical body, to the inner self, and to relationships with others.

Paul said that kind of speech *cannot be condemned*. That is because it benefits people. Our speech ought to be so true, so uplifting, so helpful that no one can find fault with it even if he wants to.

II. What Grace Teaches
(Titus 2:11-14)

A. What Grace Brings (v. 11)

11. For the grace of God that bringeth salvation hath appeared to all men.

Verses 9 and 10 tell one way Titus could be helpful with his sound speech. He could teach slaves to do their work well, to be respectful and obedient. This would reflect credit on the Christian teaching as well as producing a healthy relationship between slave and master. The word *for* introduces the reason—*the grace of God* has appeared in Jesus and has been spread abroad by the gospel. It brings *salvation* for *all men* who will accept it. We have been touched by the grace of God, so our speech is to be seasoned by that grace: "Let your speech be always with grace" (Colossians 4:6). Saved by God's grace, we ought to be gracious. A slave should be gracious to his master, even an abusive master (1 Peter 2:18). How much more should free Christians be gracious!

B. What to Do (v. 12)

12. Teaching us that, denying ungodliness and worldly lusts, we should live soberly, righteously, and godly, in this present world.

Some people misunderstand God's grace. "God is gracious," they say. "He will forgive all our sins. So why not keep on sinning and make use of His abundant grace?" Paul says that thinking is wrong (Romans 6:1, 2). Grace does not teach that at all. God's forgiveness is not an act of blindness to let us keep sinning; it is an act of kindness to bring us to repentance (Romans 2:4). Rather than teaching us to increase our ungodliness, grace teaches us to be *denying ungodliness and worldly lusts*. It teaches us to *live soberly, righteously, and godly, in this present world*.

How does grace teach us that? In the same way our parents' grace teaches us to respect

them. They care for us, sustain our lives, give us food, clothing, and shelter that we do not earn. In response we respect them, love them, and try to please them. So God gives us eternal life that we do not earn, and we show respect by trying to please Him with the way we live.

JUST SAY "NO"

Historians will surely be kind to Nancy Reagan, if for no other reason than for her antidrug campaign and motto: *Just Say "No."* With the media blitz and celebrity endorsements, the word certainly got out. The result is hard to measure, but if even a handful of kids turn down dope, the effort is worthwhile.

It is ironic that children, whose first clearly-spoken word is often *"No,"* need to be taught to say "No" at the right times. They quite naturally say "No" to spinach, liver, naps, and all kinds of medication. Yet they (and all of us) must be taught to say "No" to alcohol, pot, heroin, vandalism, and premarital sex.

The *New International Version* translates verse 12 of our printed text, "It [the grace of God] teaches us to say 'No' to ungodliness and worldly passions." By the grace of God, Christians can "live self-controlled, upright and godly lives in this present age." We can say "No" to violent and sexually explicit movies. We can say "No" to unwholesome television programs that present immorality and deviant life-styles as acceptable. We can say "No" to humanism and materialism.

We *can* say "No"—and we *must* say "No."
—R. W. B.

C. What to Look For (v. 13)

13. Looking for that blessed hope, and the glorious appearing of the great God and our Saviour Jesus Christ.

Bringing forgiveness and salvation, God's grace teaches us to expect what we hope for, *the glorious appearing of the great God and our Saviour Jesus Christ*. Hope is tied to denying ungodliness in verse 12. We deny ungodliness because we are looking for Jesus to come back. When He comes, we shall be like Him. Everyone who has the hope of becoming like Christ starts that process here and now (1 John 3:2, 3). Peter says we have been born again to a living hope and to "an inheritance incorruptible, and undefiled, and that fadeth not away" (1 Peter 1:3, 4).

D. What the Savior Did (v. 14)

14. Who gave himself for us, that he might redeem us from all iniquity, and purify unto himself a peculiar people, zealous of good works.

Our Savior Jesus Christ (v. 13) *gave himself*, gave His life on the cross, to *redeem us from all iniquity*. By doing wrong we made ourselves slaves of sin (John 8:34). Jesus bought us back for himself. The price He paid was His own life (1 Peter 1:18, 19). That purchase was made to separate us from something—*iniquity*; but its purpose is also to unite us to something—*good works*. We are not just delivered from our wrongs; we are put in a position to make a difference in our world by what we do. Belonging to Jesus brings us to "pie in the sky by and by"; it also governs what we do here and now.

III. The Christian's Change (Titus 3:1-8)

A. Relationship to Authority (v. 1)

1. Put them in mind to be subject to principalities and powers, to obey magistrates, to be ready to every good work.

We are living in a time when people have learned to disrespect and disregard authority; but authority, particularly the authority of government, is God's means of bringing order to our lives, punishment to the evil, and reward for the good (Romans 13:1-7). *Principalities and powers* mean the officials of government. Other versions translate it "rulers and authorities." How are we doing in little things like our speed on the highway, paying our income taxes, saving water during water shortages, and other requirements that seem inconvenient?

To *be subject* does not mean blind obedience, but it does mean to give up our self-centered interests for the well-being of others. God wants us to be good citizens in the community in which we live. We are examples that others may be following. But notice that our submission to governmental authorities does not give us permission to follow them if they ask us to be involved in evil work. We are *to be ready* for *every good work*, not bad. If the government orders us to go against a clear command of God, of course "we ought to obey God rather than men (Acts 5:29). But normally and usually, "rulers are not a terror to good works, but to the evil" (Romans 13:3).

B. Relationship to People (v. 2)

2. To speak evil of no man, to be no brawlers, but gentle, showing all meekness unto all men.

Speak evil of no man. Obviously this does not forbid God's people to expose falsehood or rebuke wrong (Titus 1:13, 14). But when this is necessary we can speak against the falsehood or the wrong rather than against the person. And we should speak to the person himself before mentioning it to others (Matthew 18:15).

We must be good stewards of information we have about people, not scattering it recklessly, but keeping it to ourselves or using it prudently. The information we have is under our control as long as we don't tell anyone; but the moment we tell someone else, we lose control of it. It then can run wild. It is like dropping a match in the California brush country in summer. While we have the match, we are in control. But when we strike it and drop it, we lose control of it, and homes are destroyed along with the brush. Instead of being critical of others and quarrelsome brawlers, it is better to be *gentle, showing all meekness unto all men*.

C. What We Were (v. 3)

3. For we ourselves also were sometime foolish, disobedient, deceived, serving divers lusts and pleasures, living in malice and envy, hateful, and hating one another.

Here is another reason we should not speak evil about someone else. We too have been evil. Before becoming Christians we were *foolish* enough to be *disobedient* to God. *Deceived* by the lure of the godless world, we served our own *lusts* or desires; we sought our own *pleasures* instead of seeking to please God. Do you want someone to dig up all the garbage in your past? We have all sinned and come short of the glorious character of God (Romans 3:23). Be careful if you think you are an exception (1 Corinthian 10:12).

D. What Changed Us (v. 4)

4. But after that the kindness and love of God our Saviour toward man appeared.

"Why are we no longer the land of people we were, the land described in verse 3? What brought about a change in us? It was not our own merit, not our own goodness, not our own wisdom, not our own power! It was *the kindness and love of God our Saviour toward man*. In kindness and love He sent the Savior to die in our stead. Moved by such kindness and love we saw the truth and were no longer deceived. We began to deny our own lusts and seek God's will. Instead of showing malice and envy, we began to reflect God's kindness and love.

E. The Transition (vv. 5, 6)

5, 6. Not by works of righteousness which we have done, but according to his mercy he saved us, by the washing of regeneration, and renewing of the Holy Ghost; which he shed on us abundantly through Jesus Christ our Saviour.

It was not our goodness but His mercy that saved us. The transition came in the *washing of regeneration*, which means our re-birthing. Moved by God's kindness and love, we were baptized and washed away our sins (Acts 22:16). Thus we were born again, regenerated, renewed, by water and the Spirit (John 3:5). Being thus born again we received the gift of the Holy Spirit (Acts 2:38), *which he shed on us abundantly through Jesus Christ our Saviour*. Therefore we have God's own life and nature living in us (1 Corinthians 6:19).

F. The New Position (v. 7)

7. That being justified by his grace, we should be made heirs according to the hope of eternal life.

Paul stresses again that the change is not accomplished by us, but *by his grace*. That has changed us from outsiders to insiders, from non-heirs to *heirs*. We are God's reborn children who will inherit all He has in mind for us. We are joint-heirs with Christ (Romans 8:17), and He is heir of everything (Hebrews 1:2). The inheritance is reserved for us in Heaven (1 Peter 1:3-5).

G. The New Practice (v. 8)

8. This is a faithful saying, and these things I will that thou affirm constantly, that they which have believed in God might be careful to maintain good works. These things are good and profitable unto men.

We are not only in a changed position, "heirs" of God, but we are also to be manifesting a change in practice—*maintain good works*. Good works benefit or profit other people. That is the bottom line of what it means to be a Christian, a follower of Jesus. The goodness of God is seen in what we do.

FAITH AND WORKS

"Love and marriage go together like a horse and carriage . . . you can't have one without the other." So says the old song, though we know it's not exactly true. Some marriages do exist without much love, and sometimes a man and a woman fall in love but never marry.

Faith and works, on the other hand, go together without exception, like trust and obedience. Titus was to keep on teaching so believers would keep on believing, and keep on manifesting their faith by "good works." People who quit doing good have quit believing; when they quit obeying, they have quit trusting.

Paul is not teaching that we are saved by good deeds. Look at verse 5: "Not by works of righteousness . . . but according to his mercy he

Home Daily Bible Readings

Monday, Aug. 24—Select Good Leaders (Titus 1:1-9)
Tuesday, Aug. 25—Rebuke False Teachings (Titus 1:10-16)
Wednesday, Aug. 26—Teach Sound Doctrine (Titus 2:1-6)
Thursday, Aug. 27—A Model of Good Deeds (Titus 2:7-15)
Friday, Aug. 28—Be Ready for Any Honest Work (Titus 3:1-7)
Saturday, Aug. 29—Apply Yourself to Good Deeds (Titus 3:8-15)
Sunday, Aug. 30—"Be Doers of the Word" (James 1:19-27)

saved us." Elsewhere Paul wrote, "By grace are ye saved . . . not of works" (Ephesians 2: 8, 9). But the very next verse reminds us that we are "created in Christ Jesus to do good works" (*New International Version*).

James, too, insists that faith and works are inseparable, that faith without action is dead (James 2:14-17). Saving faith demonstrates itself by righteous deeds. James says, "I will show you my faith by what I do" (2:18, *New International Version*). "Trust and obey, for there's no other way to be happy in Jesus."   —R. W. B.

Conclusion

A. Fishing Tackle

Recently a husband and wife survived over sixty days of floating in the ocean after their sailboat went down. That may be a record. How did they survive so long? As their boat was sinking, they ignored their "valuables" and grabbed their fishing tackle and all the bottled water they could get into their tiny lifeboat. With fish to eat and water to drink, they had the essentials for survival.

Paul told Titus about some of the essentials that Titus needed while afloat on the sea of life. How about us? What are we hanging onto? What are we letting go of? How will that affect our survival when our ship goes down?

B. Prayer

Thank you, Father, for giving us spiritual food and water. Keep our appetites tuned to Your nourishment for our souls. Amen.

C. Thought to Remember

People are following you—where are you leading them?

Learning by Doing

This page contains an alternate lesson plan emphasizing learning activities. Classes desiring such student involvement will find these suggestions helpful.

Learning Goals

As a result of this lesson, students should:

1. Accept the responsibility of being a good example.

2. Find one way of improving their example.

3. Tell some practical benefits of our relationship with God.

Into the Lesson

Before class, find pictures of five to ten well-known people. Mount the pictures for display as the students come into the classroom. Let students discuss the image or example each person conveys. There may be some difference of opinion. For example, one student may think a heavyweight boxer is a good example of strength and skill, while another thinks he is a bad example of conceit and arrogance.

Have one last picture, that of Jesus Christ, prepared and hidden until discussion on the others is over. Then bring it out in the open and ask, "What kind of an example do you see in Jesus?" After a few answers, go on to ask, "What do you suppose a non-Christian might think of Him? Why are there different opinions?" Conclude the introduction by saying that each of us sets an example of some kind. What kind of example are you setting to those who know you?

Into the Word

Give students paper and pencils and have them draw three columns with these headings: HOME, COMMUNITY, CHURCH. (Students who have the adult student book may fill in the columns provided in the book.) Let someone slowly read Titus 2:7, 8, 11-14; 3:1-8. Ask the listeners to notice ways in which Titus was to be a good example, and to write each one in the appropriate column to show where that example might be noted and followed. Some examples may be listed in more than one column. A sample is given below.

HOME	COMMUNITY	CHURCH
uncorruptness	uncorruptness	uncorruptness
	gravity	gravity
sincerity	sincerity	sincerity

Go over the completed lists in class. Encourage students to fill in any answers they missed. Ask them to hold these lists for use later in the lesson.

Divide the class into three groups for a look at other Scriptures that tell about being a good example. Assign each group some Scriptures to examine.

Group One—The Example of Jesus. Examine the following Scriptures, which tell about the example that Christ sets for us: Matthew 11:29; 16:24; John 13:14, 15; Hebrews 3:1, 2; 12:2; 1 Peter 2:21-23. What characteristics of Jesus are set forth as an example to us? What are some ways that we can make these characteristics a part of our own lives?

Group Two—Turning From an Evil Example. Look at these Scriptures about bad examples: Leviticus 20:23; Proverbs 22:24, 25; Ezekiel 20:18; Hebrews 4:11; 2 Peter 3:17. What are the characteristics that we are to avoid? Why are these evil influences detrimental? How can we avoid them? Are there ways that we can help our children avoid them?

Group Three—Paul's Example. What do we learn of Paul's example in 1 Corinthians 4:16; 11:1; Philippians 3:17; 4:9; 2 Thessalonians 3:7-9; and 2 Timothy 1:13. What effect do you think Paul's life before his conversion had upon the example he set? How important is it for our example to be blameless? How can our past haunt or help us?

Allow ten minutes for the groups to discuss their Scriptures. Let each group present its findings to the class. Then write this on the chalkboard: "Being a good Christian example means . . ." Allow students to suggest endings while you record them on the board.

Into Life

Have each student look again at his list of godly examples at home, community, and church. For each item on the list, let him write a specific way of applying it during the coming week. For example, under COMMUNITY, the student may have listed "be subject to rulers and authorities" (3:1, *New International Version*). His specific application may be, "I will conform to speed laws on my drive to work each morning."

Conclude the lesson by asking students to list the benefits of living in a proper relationship with God and setting a good example. If they seem slow to start, suggest that they look again at Titus 2:11, 14; 3:5-7. Praise God for these benefits as you close the lesson with prayer.

Let's Talk It Over

The questions on this page are designed to encourage review of the lesson Scriptures and to promote discussion of the lesson by the class. The answers provided are only discussion starters. Let your class talk it over from there.

1. How can we make a favorable impression on others for the sake of Christ?

One way of making a favorable impression for Christ is a combination of strength with humility. One of Jesus' most beloved sayings demonstrates such a combination: "Come unto me, all ye that labor and are heavy laden, and I will give you rest. Take my yoke upon you, and learn of me; for I am meek and lowly in heart: and ye shall find rest unto your souls. For my yoke is easy, and my burden is light" (Matthew 11:28-30). We need to exhibit strength in faith, in commitment to Christ, and in our zeal for His cause. But we also must be approachable, willing to listen and to give of ourselves. Our prayer should be the familiar request: "Let them see Christ in me."

2. How can we achieve a proper balance between seriousness and humor?

Sometimes humor is overdone at the expense of reverent worship and serious Bible study. On the other hand, some Christians are so sober or intense that they make people think Christianity is gloomy. Perhaps we can get help from one another. If we fear that our humor is giving an impression of irreverence or of shallowness, we may want to ask Christian friends about it. If we are concerned that our lack of humor may give an impression of harshness or unfriendliness, here again the counsel of friends may help.

3. We are tempted to become cynical when Christians disappoint us. How can we replace cynicism with sincerity?

It is interesting to note that we see no cynicism in Jesus. Before the feeding of the five thousand, when He saw multitudes coming to interrupt His time alone with the apostles, He could have sneered at them. But He "was moved with compassion toward them, because they were as sheep not having a shepherd" (Mark 6:34). Certainly Jesus' example should stir the hearts of the most confirmed cynics.

4. How can we train ourselves to use our tongues for healing and strengthening others?

Consider how potent an instrument the tongue is and how little forethought we give to our use of it! Much of our speech is a matter of quick response. Sometimes the response is angry, bitter, cutting. What a project it would be to plan what we will say to the people we encounter! A word of praise for our husband or wife, some encouragement for our children, a compliment for a fellow employee, a cheery greeting to a harassed store clerk—how much good we could accomplish by using our tongues in such ways! And if we really think about it, pray about it, and work at it, we can also learn to answer abusive, angry speech with a gracious response.

5. How does our hope for Christ's return make us better people in this world?

Unbelievers like to belittle Christians as being so preoccupied with "pie in the sky" that they are of little earthly good. But the same God who is preparing Heaven for us is the Creator of earth, and so we want to honor Him here as we shall there. That means working for His will to be done on earth as it is in Heaven (Matthew 6:10). We begin the Heavenly life here. We want to practice now the holiness, peace, joy, and service that will characterize our life in Heaven. Also, if we remember that only two destinies are open to human beings and that only one of these offers eternal happiness, we will want to live in such a way as to attract our friends and neighbors to the way that leads to Heaven.

6. Why should Christians be exemplary in their respect for and obedience to civil authorities?

"Let every soul be subject unto the higher powers. For there is no power but of God: the powers that be are ordained of God" (Romans 13:1). Other citizens may treat authorities with contempt because of their personalities, their past records, or their political affiliations; but we are not free to do that, because they are serving under God's authority. Indeed, we recognize them as God's servants (Romans 13:4). They are responsible to maintain order and dispense justice. While we are not likely to agree with all they do, we continue our obedience to them because they are our shield against political tyranny, oppression, and bloodshed. It may well be we Christians by our conscientious citizenship keep our society from falling into such horrors.